# The Handbook of Technology and Second Language Teaching and Learning

# Blackwell Handbooks in Linguistics

This outstanding multi-volume series covers all the major subdisciplines within linguistics today and, when complete, will offer a comprehensive survey of linguistics as a whole.

The most recent publications in the series can be found below. To see the full list of titles available in the series, please visit www.wiley.com/go/linguistics-handbooks

# The Handbook of Technology and Second Language Teaching and Learning

Edited by

*Carol A. Chapelle
and Shannon Sauro*

**WILEY** Blackwell

*Registered Office*
John Wiley & Sons, Inc., 111 River Street, Hoboken, NJ 07030, USA

*Editorial Office*
The Atrium, Southern Gate, Chichester, West Sussex, PO19 8SQ, UK

For details of our global editorial offices, customer services, and more information about Wiley products visit us at www.wiley.com.

Wiley also publishes its books in a variety of electronic formats and by print-on-demand. Some content that appears in standard print versions of this book may not be available in other formats.

*Library of Congress Cataloging-in-Publication Data*

Names: Chapelle, Carol A., editor. | Sauro, Shannon, 1973– editor.
Title: The handbook of technology and second language teaching and learning / edited by Carol A. Chapelle and Shannon Sauro.
Description: First edition. | Hoboken, NJ : John Wiley & Sons, Inc., [2017] | Series: Blackwell handbooks in linguistics | Includes bibliographical references and index. |
Identifiers: LCCN 2017017176 (print) | LCCN 2017050852 (ebook) | ISBN 9781118914052 (pdf) | ISBN 9781118914069 (epub) | ISBN 9781118914038 (cloth) | ISBN 9781119108474 (paper)
Subjects: LCSH: Language and languages–Study and teaching–Technological innovations. | Second language acquisition.
Classification: LCC P53.855 (ebook) | LCC P53.855 .H375 2017 (print) | DDC 418.0078/5–dc23
LC record available at https://lccn.loc.gov/2017017176

Cover Design: Wiley
Cover Image: © OttoKrause/GettyImages

Set in 9.5/11.5pt Palatino by SPi Global, Pondicherry, India
Printed and bound in Singapore by Markono Print Media Pte Ltd

10 9 8 7 6 5 4 3 2 1

*In memory of Teresa Pica*

# Contents

# Notes on Contributors

**Robert J. Blake** (PhD University of Texas) is Distinguished Professor of Spanish linguistics and director of the Spanish Language Program at the University of California, Davis. He has developed online Spanish courses for the first and second years, authored *Brave New Digital Classroom* (2013, GUP), and co-authored *El español y la lingüística aplicada* (2016, GUP). He was inducted as a member of the North American Academic of the Spanish Language in 2004.

**Thierry Chanier** is Professor of Applied Linguistics at Université Blaise Pascal, Clermont-Ferrand, France. His main research interest over the past 25 years has been CALL and, since 1999, online learning in telecollaborative situations. He coordinated the Mulce project which developed an open-access repository of Learning and Teaching Corpora

**Carol A. Chapelle** is Distinguished Professor of Liberal Arts and Sciences at Iowa State University. She is Editor of the *Encyclopedia of Applied Linguistics* (Wiley-Blackwell, 2013), Co-editor of the Cambridge Series in Applied Linguistics, as well as a past Editor of *TESOL Quarterly and Language Testing*.

**Dorothy M. Chun** is Professor of Applied Linguistics at the University of California, Santa Barbara. Her research areas include: L2 phonology and intonation, L2 reading and vocabulary acquisition, computer-assisted language learning (CALL) and telecollaboration for intercultural learning. She has conducted studies on cognitive process in learning with multimedia, has authored courseware for language and culture acquisition, and recently edited a volume on intercultural learning via telecollaboration. She edits the journal *Language Learning & Technology*.

**Yoo-Ree Chung** is a Postdoctoral Research Associate at the Center for Communication Excellence at Iowa State University. She coordinates the International Teaching Assistants (ITA) program, which includes the administration and management of the Oral English Certification Testing for ITAs enrolled in the university. Her research interests include validity/validation, computer-assisted language testing, assessment of productive grammatical writing ability, speaking assessment, learning-oriented language testing, and interfaces between language testing and second language acquisition research.

**Elena Cotos** is Assistant Professor in the English Department and the Director of the Center for Communication Excellence of the Graduate College, Iowa State University. Her research interests include EAP/ESP genre analysis, automated writing evaluation, CALL, learner corpora and language assessment. Her work was published in a number of professional journals, edited volumes, and a book-length monograph.

**Melinda Dooly** holds a Serra Húnter fellowship as teacher and researcher at the Education Faculty of the Universitat Autònoma de Barcelona (Spain) where she teaches English as a Foreign Language Methodology (TEFL) and research methods courses. Her principal research addresses technology enhanced project-based language learning in teacher preparation. Her current research interest is in project-based telecollaborative language learning and very young learners.

**Ahmet Dursun** is the Assessment Coordinator at the University of Chicago Language Center's Office of Language Assessment, where he is responsible for developing and managing the University's language assessment programs. His research interests include language assessment, language assessment through technology, test design, test development and validation, and CALL. He has presented his work at a number of professional conferences, including TESOL, CALICO, AAAL, EALTA, and MwALT.

**Kathryn English** is a *Maître de conférences* at the Université Panthéon Assas (Paris II) and the École Polytechnique. She holds a PhD in *Sciences du Langage* and has designed, co-authored and participated in cross-cultural, computer-mediated language teaching projects based in the United States, France, Finland and Taiwan. She also worked as a conference interpreter for the European Union, German Television and Radio, the French National Assembly.

**Maja Grgurović** is Clinical Assistant Professor and Clinical Director of the MA TESOL Program at the University of Illinois at Chicago. She holds a PhD in Applied Linguistics and Technology from Iowa State University. Maja has worked in the field of blended language learning as a researcher and teacher trainer for a number of years. Her other professional interests include CALL, language assessment, and language teacher education.

**Volker Hegelheimer** is Professor of English at Iowa State University. He researches applications of emerging technologies in language learning and language testing. His publications have appeared in journals such as *Language Learning & Technology*, *Language Testing*, *System*, *Computer-Assisted Language Learning*, *ReCALL*, *CALICO Journal*, and he contributed to several edited volumes on CALL. He co-edited the *CALICO Journal* special issue on automated writing evaluation and has presented at numerous national and international conferences.

**Trude Heift** is Professor of Linguistics in the Department of Linguistics at Simon Fraser University, Canada. Her research focuses on the design as well as the evaluation of CALL systems with a particular interest in learner-computer interactions and learner language. Her work has appeared in leading CALL/SLA journals and she is co-author, with Mathias Schulze, of *Errors and Intelligence in Computer-Assisted Language Learning: Parsers and Pedagogues* (Routledge). She is co-editor of *Language Learning & Technology*.

**Philip Hubbard** is Senior Lecturer in Linguistics and Director of English for Foreign Students in the Stanford University Language Center. He has published articles on CALL theory, research, methodology, courseware evaluation, teacher education, learner training, mobile learning, and listening. He is associate editor of *Computer Assisted Language Learning* and *Language Learning & Technology*. His current work focuses on content curation and learner training for technology environments with an emphasis on online listening.

**Joan Jamieson**, Professor of English at Northern Arizona University, teaches in the MA-TESL and PhD in Applied Linguistics programs. Her areas of specialty include second language testing, research design and statistics, and CALL.

**Agnes Kukulska-Hulme** is Professor of Learning Technology and Communication in the Institute of Educational Technology at the Open University and past-president of the International Association for Mobile Learning. She is on the editorial boards of the *International Journal of Mobile and Blended Learning*, *ReCALL*, and *SYSTEM*, and co-editor of *Mobile Learning: The Next Generation*. Her current research focuses on technology-supported learning for migrants, intelligent personal assistants, and language learning in smart cities.

**Robert Godwin-Jones** is Professor of World Languages and International Studies at Virginia Commonwealth University. His research is principally in applied linguistics, in the areas of language learning and technology, and intercultural communication. He has published four books, multiple articles and book chapters, and writes a regular column for *Language Learning & Technology* on emerging technologies for language learning.

**Greg Kessler** is the Director of the Language Resource Center and Associate Professor of Computer-Assisted Language Learning in the Department of Linguistics at Ohio University. He is also an affiliated faculty member in Instructional Technology in the Patton College of Education. His research addresses instructional technology, teacher preparation, language teaching, and associated human behavior. He has published widely and delivered featured talks around the world.

**Marie-Noëlle Lamy** is Emeritus Professor of Distance Language Learning at the Open University. She has more than 20 years' experience of designing and implementing courses involving synchronous voice-enabled e-tutorials. Her research focuses on methodologies for the description of online learning conversations, the co-construction of group cultures by language learners in social networking environments, and cultural hegemonies in global CALL.

**Helen Lee** has worked as a business language trainer for global organizations. She holds a Masters degree in TESOL and ICT from the University of Brighton and has presented at the University of Oxford, the British (BAAL), and the American Association for Applied Linguistics (AAAL). Helen is a member of the BAAL Special Interest Group in Language and New Media. Her doctoral research at the Open University focuses on language learning with mobiles.

**Zhi Li** is Language Assessment Specialist at Paragon Testing Enterprises, British Columbia, Canada. He holds a PhD in applied linguistics and technology from Iowa State University. His research interests include language assessment, CALL, corpus linguistics, and systemic functional linguistics. He has presented his work at a number of professional conferences such as AAAL, LTRC, and TESOL. His research papers have been published in *System* and *Language Learning &Technology*.

**Meei-Ling Liaw** is Professor of English at National Taichung University of Education. Her research focuses on intercultural learning, teacher education, and using computer technology to facilitate EFL teaching and learning. Her publications have appeared in professional journals including *System*, *Foreign Language Annals*, *Computer-Assisted Language Learning*, *ReCALL*, and *Language Learning & Technology*. She is the chief editor of *Taiwan International ESP Journal*.

**Hui-Fen Lin** is Professor of Foreign Languages and Literature, National TsingHua University in Hsinchu, Taiwan. She has published three meta-analyses on CALL. Her research interests include computer-mediated communication, automated writing assessment, and animated instruction.

**Hsien-Chin Liou**, is Professor of Foreign Languages and Literature, Feng Chia University, Taichung, Taiwan. He specializes in CALL and related topics such as corpus use, academic writing, and vocabulary learning. She has published quite a few articles in various CALL or language learning journals as well as book volumes.

**Marta González-Lloret** is Professor of Spanish at the University of Hawai'i. She investigates CALL and its intersections with task-based language teaching (TBLT), second language pragmatics, and conversation analysis for SLA. She is currently one of the associate editors of the Wiley Encyclopedia of Applied Linguistics, co-editor of the Pragmatics and Language Learning series. She co-edited a volume with Lourdes Ortega (2014) entitled *Technology-mediated TBLT: Researching Technology and Tasks* (John Benjamins), and recently published *A Practical Guide to Integrating Technology into Task-Based Language Teaching* with Georgetown University Press (2015).

**Qing Ma** is Assistant Professor of Linguistics and Modern Language Studies at the Hong Kong Institute of Education. Her main research interests include second language vocabulary acquisition, corpus linguistics, and CALL. More recently, she moved on to mobile assisted language learning (MALL) and is particularly interested in how students self-regulate their MALL when they are left on their own to explore online learning resources.

**Matteo Musumeci**, Senior Instructional Specialist, at Northern Arizona University, has focused his research on oral languaging on writing feedback in the foreign language classroom (with emphasis in Italian language teaching), and on the effects of video-subtitles for English language learners.

**Lucy Norris** is an independent international education consultant in the field of language teacher development and training, formerly Research Associate at the Institute of Educational Technology of the Open University, and author of English language course book materials for adults and younger learners. Her research and professional interests include teacher development and digital literacies, and the role of technologies in supporting learning and teaching. She tweets as http://twitter.com/@MobilePedagogy

**Sue E. K. Otto** is Adjunct Associate Professor Emerita of Spanish, former co-Director of the FLARE Second Language Acquisition doctoral program and former Director of the Language Media Center at the University of Iowa. For nearly four decades, she devoted her research and development efforts to CALL authoring tools and to the use of authentic video materials for language learning. Her email address is: sue-otto@uiowa.edu

**Donald E. Powers** is Principal Managing Research Scientist in the Educational Testing Service's Research and Development Center for English Language Learning and Assessment. Powers has directed a wide variety of research projects in support of numerous ETS-sponsored testing programs, and he has served as the research coordinator for several of these programs, including the TOEIC, TOEFL, and GRE testing programs.

**Jonathon Reinhardt** is Associate Professor at the University of Arizona. His research interests lie in the relationship between technology and the epistemologies of CALL theory and practice, and focus on technology enhanced second and foreign language pedagogy and learning, especially with emergent technologies like digital gaming and social media.

**Julio C. Rodríguez** directs the Center for Language & Technology and the National Foreign Language Resource Center and co-directs the Language Flagship Technology Innovation Center at the University of Hawai'i at Mānoa. Within the broad area of instructional technology, he is primarily focused on faculty development, project-based learning, materials development, online course design, and design-based research. Julio leads several design-based research projects and has published and presented extensively in this area.

**Randall W. Sadler** is Associate Professor of Linguistics at the University of Illinois at Urbana-Champaign, where he teaches courses on Computer-Mediated Communication and Language Learning (CMCLL), Virtual Worlds and Language Learning (VWLL), and the Teaching of L2 Reading and Writing. His main research area is on the role of technology in language learning, with a particular focus on how CMC and Virtual Worlds may be used to enhance that process.

**Shannon Sauro** is Associate Professor in the Department of Culture, Languages and Media in the Faculty of Education and Society at Malmö University, Sweden. She is the past president of the Computer-Assisted Language Instruction Consortium (CALICO).

**Jonathan E. Schmidgall** is Associate Research Scientist in the Educational Testing Service's Research and Development Center for English Language Learning and Assessment. Jonathan's research has focused on the assessment of oral proficiency, the affordances of new technology for learning-oriented assessment, and designing comprehensive research programs to support large-scale international language assessment.

**Bryan Smith** is Associate Professor of Applied Linguistics in the Department of English at Arizona State University in Tempe, Arizona. His research focuses on the nexus of CALL and SLA. He is the co-editor of the *CALICO Journal* (along with Mat Schulze) and has published widely in the areas of computer-mediated communication, research methods, and learner interaction in instructed second language learning contexts.

**Julie M. Sykes** is the Director of the Center for Applied Second Language Studies and Associate Professor in Linguistics at the University of Oregon. Her research focuses on the development of interlanguage pragmatics and the use of digital technologies for language acquisition. She has published on CALL-related topics, including synchronous computer-mediated communication and pragmatic development, gaming and CALL, and lexical acquisition in digitally mediated environments.

**Nina Vyatkina** is Associate Professor of German and Applied Linguistics at the University of Kansas. She is the 2009 co-recipient of the ACTFL/MLJ Paul Pimsleur Award for Research in Foreign Language Education. Her research interests include instructed SLA, applied corpus research, computer-mediated communication, and interlanguage pragmatics. Her articles have appeared in leading Applied Linguistics journals and she serves on the editorial boards of *Language Learning & Technology* and *International Journal of Learner Corpus Research*.

**Paige Ware** is Professor in the Department of Teaching and Learning at Southern Methodist University. She earned her PhD at the University of California at Berkeley and taught English as a second/foreign language for many years. Her research focuses on intercultural communication, second language writing, and adolescent literacy practices. She has received a National Academy of Education/Spencer Postdoctoral Grant, a TIRF English Language Teaching grant, and an OELA professional development grant.

**Cynthia J. White** is Professor of Applied Linguistics, Massey University, New Zealand. She has published widely on distance and online learning, learner autonomy, learning strategies, and teacher identity and agency in online language teaching. She is a member of Editorial Boards of seven international journals, and has been plenary speaker at international conferences in Germany, Thailand, Singapore, China, the United Kingdom, Hawai'I, and Malaysia.

# Acknowledgments

A large handbook project such as this one is the result of diligent work on the part of many. We would like to gratefully acknowledge in particular the perseverance of the authors as they worked through multiple drafts of their papers to achieve the right length, content, and accessibility for the *The Handbook of Technology and Second Language Teaching and Learning*. Their efforts have resulted in a collection that we expect will serve as an authoritative reference work for years to come. We would also like to acknowledge with gratitude the foresight of Danielle Descoteaux, who recognized the need for *The Handbook of Technology and Second Language Teaching and Learning* and encouraged us to pursue it years ago. As the project moved forward, we have been consistently supported by the editorial team at Wiley Blackwell. We most graciously appreciate their steady presence throughout the project. We would also like to thank Yundeok Choi for her careful editorial assistance in the final phases of the project.

# 1 Introduction to the *Handbook of Technology and Second Language Teaching and Learning*

## CAROL A. CHAPELLE
## AND SHANNON SAURO

The *Handbook of Technology and Second Language Teaching and Learning* was conceived in response to the fact that technology has become integral to the ways that most language learners in the world today access materials in their second and foreign language, interact with others, learn in and out of the classroom, and take many language tests. In the title for this volume, we have used the expression "second language" as shorthand for all of the many language teaching and learning situations that include both children and adults learning additional languages beyond their mother tongue (which may be third, fourth, or more languages for them) in settings where the language being studied is the medium of daily life, education, business, or only a subject in the language classroom. We include both learning and teaching in the title to make explicit our concern with the two related but distinct areas—the pedagogy that teachers and materials designers are preoccupied with and the processes that students engage in both in an out of the classroom.

For the many diverse learners, the use of computer technology for all facets of second language learning has dramatically increased as the reach of the internet continues to spread, providing access to social media, reference materials, online instruction, and more. The implications for language teachers, learners, materials developers, and researchers are extensive. Our goal in creating the *Handbook of Technology and Second Language Teaching and Learning* was to communicate to a broad range of readers, within the field and beyond, the shape and texture of the technology-rich environments that language learners inhabit today as well as the relevance of these environments for second language teaching and learning. The chapters in the *Handbook* demonstrate that technology has added multifaceted new dimensions to teaching and learning, which include new ways of teaching every aspect of language, new pedagogical and assessment approaches, as well as new ways of conceiving and conducting research and development.

Reference works are needed to gather and synthesize the scholarly treatment of these dynamic practices and research that are so central to the profession. In view of the central role it plays, technology and language learning needs to be represented among the other areas of study in applied linguistics through its appearance in major reference works such as the Wiley-Blackwell Handbooks in Applied Linguistics. In fact another such handbook, *The Routledge Handbook of Language Learning and Technology* (Farr and Murray 2016) was recently published in the Routledge Handbooks in Applied Linguistics. Technology and language learning is also well-represented in the *Encyclopedia of Applied Linguistics* (Chapelle 2013) with its own section (edited by Thomas Cobb) as well as entries that include technology-related issues across the entire *Encyclopedia*. With these major reference works now available, our goal was to provide another, different point of entry into this area of applied linguistics for the broad range of learners, teachers, materials developers, and researchers who want to learn more about this as an area of research and practice. Anyone with an interest in languages and cultures today has recognized that technology has affected their potential for access to more and more of their language interests. This recognition can evolve into professional knowledge and action when personal interests meet the history, practices, theory and research of the profession.

The *Handbook* was designed to create the opportunity for such meetings to take place. Its organization reflects the goal of inviting in and engaging readers with little professional knowledge of how technologies are transforming practices. The first section contains chapters that explain the ways that technology is integrated in the teaching and learning of specific aspects of language knowledge and skills, most or all of which are familiar to all readers. Each of these chapters includes how technology-based tutors, tools, and pedagogy contribute to language development. The second section builds on discussion of methodology for teaching and learning to identify new pedagogies that have been developed by exploring the language and communication affordances of various technologies. Integral to but distinct from pedagogy, the third part contains chapters pertaining to issues of language assessment that are important in teaching and learning practice. Broadly speaking, the fourth section addresses the areas that converge in research and development of technology-mediated pedagogy for language learning. The final chapter provides an analysis of the contribution these chapters make to the profession and a looks toward their implications for the future.

The remainder of this chapter provides a more detailed introduction of the chapters in the *Handbook* to situate each one within one of these four areas of language abilities, pedagogies, assessment, and research and development. As background to the four areas, the first chapter provides a historical account of the development of language learning and technology as an area of practice and research in applied linguistics. One of the pioneers, Sue E. K. Otto, who worked in research and development in computer-assisted language learning (CALL) at the University of Iowa for over 40 years, provides a chronological view of how technologies have intersected with and served in the evolution of practices in language teaching and learning. Her broad view begins with the printed text, drawings, photos, audio, and video technologies that teachers and learners have taken for granted for years. Otto describes the gradual evolution of recording and delivery formats, for example, that have given way to today's digital, computer-based formats that are contributing to evolving language pedagogies. From photos passed around the classroom, to those broadcast on Twitter, this chronology sets the stage for the many technologies that come into play in the rest of the volume. New technologies seldom replace the old; instead, they create more options for technology users. The past practices therefore hold their place with the present technologies, inviting language learners and teachers to explore how to select, mix, and create new practices using them all. The new practices that appear to be most influential are included in this *Handbook*.

# Part I: Language teaching and learning through technology

Most learners studying another language hope to be able to use the language to communicate with other speakers. Their end goals are communication, but most teachers and learners approach language teaching and learning through a multi-strand process targeting particular areas of language knowledge and skills. The first section is divided according to these areas of language abilities that readers will recognize as forming the basis of most instructional programs: grammar, vocabulary, reading, writing, listening, speaking, and pragmatics and intercultural competence. Each of these chapters reviews practices for use of technologies as well as the theoretical and research bases for these practices.

In Chapter 3, Trude Heift and Nina Vyatkina provide an overview of technologies for teaching and learning L2 grammar by focusing on four distinct CALL environments: tutorial CALL, intelligent CALL (ICALL), data-driven learning (DDL), and computer-mediated communication (CMC). They situate these approaches to grammar teaching and learning within discussion of pedagogical approaches to teaching and learning L2 grammar more broadly and with theoretical perspectives from second language acquisition. They provide examples of each of the four types of technologies and describe the research studies that have focused on learner feedback in Tutorial CALL, ICALL and CMC, and on learner autonomy in DDL. Throughout their examples, it is clear that grammar cannot be seen as a separate or isolated activity. In particular, readers will see the integration between grammar and vocabulary learning in this chapter and in the next one, which covers vocabulary learning.

In Chapter 4, Qing Ma describes how new technologies have expanded pedagogical options for teaching and learning second language vocabulary. She describes the affordances technology provides in view of a memory-based model of L2 vocabulary learning. She introduces software tools for desktop and mobile learning technologies, explaining their rationales in view of the vocabulary learning model. She draws upon the theory and research of self-regulated learning to describe how teachers can offer strategy training that helps students make the most of technology-mediated vocabulary learning.

In Chapter 5, Meei-Ling Liaw and Kathryn English introduce second language reading technologies that support second language reading development. The description of technologies is based on their theoretical conception technology-assisted second language reading as a process that engages particular cognitive processes and strategies involved in second language reading. An important characteristic of second language reading is that is must extend beyond the classroom; students need to read materials that are interesting to them outside the classroom to get sufficient exposure and practice. Thus, the primary challenge for current language teachers that the authors identify is how language educators can leverage students' intense use of social media and consumption of a vast and diverse quality of reading materials on the Web for learning second language reading. The chapter ends with suggestions for applying technologies to help second language learners to engage in independent, autonomous reading that may help promote their active global participation in the digital age.

Continuing to examine pedagogical practices for teaching the written language, Chapter 6, by Zhi Li, Ahmet Dursun, and Volker Hegelheimer explores the implications for second language teaching and learning that are based upon the reality that all writing practices today are shaped by new technologies. Li, Dursun, and Hegelheimer introduce three types of technologies for teaching and learning second language writing: Web 2.0 applications, automated writing evaluation systems, and corpus-based tools. The authors explain that the effects of these tools have begun to be explored in research on writing, and they provide an overview of the research results for each of the three types of tools. The chapter concludes with a description of promising but not yet widely incorporated technologies for second language writing research and a discussion of the directions for future research and development of technologies and pedagogies for writing.

Chapter 7 shifts from the written to the spoken with Philip Hubbard's discussion of CALL for L2 listening. Hubbard traces the development of technology and technology-enhanced listening activities for second language learning, paying particular attention to the affordances and mediating characteristics of different tools as well as the potential they hold for facilitating comprehension and learning. His overview of approximately 20 years of research on technology for L2 listening draws upon a typology of four help options found in different learning and communication technologies that have been examined for affecting listening in a second language. Looking forward, Hubbard concludes with a call for the development of curated collections of listening material assembled from freely available online materials that could be organized by L2 listening experts in a manner that reflects the language proficiency needs, interests and digital skills of L2 learners.

Moving from language comprehension to production in Chapter 8, Robert J. Blake discusses CALL for support of students' learning to speak a second language. Blake describes two types of technology-assisted activities: tutorial exercises and CMC. Blake's analysis of the principles for designing good CALL activities are consonant with best practices for teaching oral language in the classroom; they include providing opportunities for the negotiation of meaning, focus on form, and a heightened sense of learner autonomy and agency. CALL activities can be used to foster all aspects of second language speaking proficiency including the dimensions of accuracy, complexity, and/or fluency, depending on the type of assigned task. Blake notes that students no longer need to rely on classroom activities to engage in these speaking activities because they can use CMC tools to exchange text, sound, and video in a variety of formats, each with its own set of affordances.

In Chapter 9, Julie Sykes describes how technology has changed and expanded the teaching of pragmatics, which refers to the expression and understanding of meaning in the contexts of language use. Pragmatic abilities are important for meeting the goals of intercultural competence because they govern the selection of how and what to communicate to a particular person in specific contexts. Many contexts where interlocutors use their second languages are created and mediated by the very technologies that may help learners to develop their second language pragmatic abilities. Sykes explores ways in which technology can facilitate the multilingual online and face-to-face interactions, provide opportunities for meaningful teaching and learning of interlanguage pragmatics, and extend professional knowledge of pragmatic behaviors from a transnational perspective.

Together these chapters introduce the technologies that are being used to address specific areas of the big project of learning to communicate in a second language. The following section builds upon these pieces to describe pedagogical tools, configurations, and approaches that draw upon combinations of affordances of one or more of these technologies for teaching language.

## Part II: Innovation at the Technology-Pedagogy Interface

This section develops the new issues, concepts and practices that have emerged at the interface of technology and language pedagogy. Each chapter takes a particular vantage point on pedagogy that assumes a new character and significance in view of the options provided by technology. Accordingly, each chapter provides an extended definition of pedagogy issues with examples showing how the technology creates new practices or transforms existing ones for second language teaching. Summaries of research in each area present findings to-date about the effects on learning and directions for future research and development.

In Chapter 10, Cynthia J. White situates technology within a history of distance learning which originated years before the digital technologies that are widely used in distance education today. She identifies distinctive features of distance learning as well as practices and forms of enquiry into distance language teaching with technology. The technologies she sees as important for shaping and expanding distance education today are CMC, audiographic- and video-conferencing, learning management systems, and telecollaboration. She argues that the development of quality distance language education relies on increasing professional knowledge in many of the areas covered in the *Handbook*, including task design, assessment of student learning, teacher education, and evaluation of distance learning programs.

Blended learning, defined as a combination of face-to-face classroom meetings and computer-mediated learning, is commonplace in many language classes today. Such configurations arise out of teachers' desire for innovation, by mandate, or because of circumstances that have made blended learning normal practice. In Chapter 11, Maja Grgurović demonstrates why some researchers are looking at blended learning as anything but ordinary. Grgurović's summary of the recent research investigating blended language learning from 2006 through 2014 uncovers studies examining comparisons with other forms of learning, teacher perceptions, learner perceptions, specific technology tools, and course implementation. Grgurović argues that the research results warrant developing a better understanding of blended language learning through theoretical grounding of studies, better approaches to assessing effectiveness, and engagement with the teachers' and students' needs.

Potentially instrumental in both distance and blended language learning, telecollaboration has become an important component of many second language classes, particularly for intercultural learning. In Chapter 12, Melinda Dooly defines telecollaboration in education as the use of the computer and/or other digital tools to promote learning through social interaction and collaboration. Dooly outlines pedagogical approaches used in telecollaboration for language learning including task-based language teaching, project-based language learning, and communication-oriented language teaching. She emphasizes the value of telecollborative exchanges for developing learners' autonomy and providing opportunities for cross-cultural interactions. She outlines the considerable opportunities for future research and practice in telecollaboration.

Virtual environments and gaming are two other areas that have been the focus of research in many subject areas, but authors in the *Handbook* describe how these two domains have been explored for language learning. In Chapter 13, Randall W. Sadler introduces Virtual Worlds (VWs) in language education, illustrating the VWs language learners are using today. He describes what researchers have found in their studies of language learners' use of VWs and the ongoing developments that may impact the future of language teaching and learning. There can be and often is an element of play when learners participate in VWs. In this sense, some overlap exists between VWs and language learning games. As Jonathon Reinhardt points out in Chapter 14, however, digital gaming can be undertaken in many different forms. Reinhardt lays the groundwork for understanding gaming in language education by reviewing the history and theory of games in CALL. He describes examples of games used by language learners and findings from research into language learners' use of games. He points to the need for collaboration among the stakeholders in the field—CALL researchers, second language instructors, and the language education gaming industry.

Implementation of all of the above configurations for learning may rely on mobile technologies including cell phones and tablets. Use of these commonplace mobile technologies for learning is referred to as "mobile pedagogy." Agnes Kukulska-Hulme, Helen Lee, and Lucy Norris introduce the mobile learning "revolution" as a response to learners' natural attachment to their interactive mobile devices. The idea is that their social media devices can be used for learning if they know how to do so. The know-how required to repurpose mobile devices into learning devices requires new conceptualizations of what is to be learned and reconceived activities for learning. The authors explain that because learners may act with more self-determination beyond the classroom walls, where online interactions and mobile encounters typically take place, learning tasks need to address students' interests and needs. Never has needs analysis been as important as when learners are outside class, on their own devices, and left to their own discretion as to how to engage with learning materials and activities. The authors provide a number of ideas for out-of-class mobile language learning that offer the learner the opportunity to promote communication and outline some of the implications for mobile language learning.

Pedagogical configurations such as distance, hybrid, or mobile learning are shared with all subjects in education. In contrast, the following three chapters describe technology-enhanced pedagogical approaches and issues that focus specifically on language education. In Chapter 16, Marta González-Lloret describes how task-based language teaching (TBLT) is implemented through the use of technology. TBLT is informed by second language acquisition theory and research, which hypothesizes how the learning of both language form and function can occur. González-Lloret presents key principles of TBLT stemming from these hypotheses and defines the concept of technology-mediated tasks. In Chapter 17, Elena Cotos introduces corpus-based pedagogies used for teaching language for specific purposes (LSP). By drawing upon corpus linguistics methods, she describes how individualized CALL materials can be developed to allow students to engage in hands-on explorations of texts relevant to their needs. In Chapter 18, Paige Ware examines the new literacies that have evolved through CMC and the language learning contexts and practices where these new literacies develop. Ware situates new literacies conceptually and historically and describes new literacy research focusing on texts, learners, classrooms, and connected sites for learning. Research on new literacies has raised issues of differential access to technology and linguistic and cultural hegemony, which are particularly relevant to second language learners. All three of these chapters identify directions for future research to better understand pedagogical practices.

The chapters in this section present a wealth of material to form the basis for pedagogical innovation in language teaching and learning. In order to bring these ideas to life, however, teachers play the central role, and therefore teacher education has been a critical topic in any discussion of new pedagogical practices. In Chapter 19, Greg Kessler and Phil Hubbard argue that, as technology has become integrated into language teaching, its integration in language teacher education remains an ongoing challenge. They provide a historical overview of developments and technology content in teacher education programs as well as current and future challenges facing CALL teacher preparation. The latter point should be evident from the contents of this *Handbook*, which could by itself form the basis for an entire graduate program or more. The challenges for teacher education are therefore significant, requiring collaboration across the curriculum in higher education.

# Part III: Technology for L2 assessment

The third section of the *Handbook* contains three chapters introducing issues in the use of technology for second language assessment. In Chapter 20, Joan Jamieson and Matteo Musumeci's analysis of classroom assessments that accompany foreign language learning materials shows how technology has expanded the options for assessing students' learning in a manner that connects to their learning materials. Jamieson and Musumeci's evaluation suggests that the assessments they investigated had a sufficient match with the instructional materials, but that they could be improved by better addressing learning goals, and by providing more thorough explanatory feedback and detailed score reporting to learners. Improvements might be possible through better communication between researchers studying second language acquisition, teachers, materials developers and assessment specialists.

In Chapter 21, Jonathan E. Schmidgall and Donald E. Powers describe the important role that technology has played in all stages of high-stakes testing development and use. Schmidgall and Powers introduce high-stakes testing in language education. They describe the critical role of technology in developing, administering, and scoring high-stakes tests as well as in supporting security in the testing process. They also identify future research on the use of technology in high-stakes language testing. Their discussion is grounded in the idea that technology is of interest to the extent that it can be shown to work toward the validity of test score interpretations and uses. Chapter 22, expands on the meaning of validity. Yoo Ree Chung describes multiple layers of considerations that the use of technology brings to the validity of language tests when it is used for delivery and scoring. Specifically, she outlines a framework for an argument-based approach for validation that provides a means for understanding the technology considerations in language assessment.

These three chapters only scratch the surface of the work being done with technology in language assessment. Much of the professional research and development in this area remains on the innovator's workbench, at the prototype stage, and in research projects because of the impact that tests have on learners. Unlike instruction, where teachers feel it is appropriate to innovate in the classroom, it is more difficult to try out a new test without extensive research prior to roll-out. Moreover, the need for teacher education in technology and assessment is even greater than it is in technology and pedagogy.

# Part IV: Research and development of technology for language learning

All of the previous chapters in the *Handbook* show how technology has been central to innovative practice in language teaching and learning. A renowned investigator of innovation, in social practice, Rogers, defined innovation as "an idea, practice, or object that is perceived as new by an individual or other unit of adoption" (Rogers 2003, 12). In language education, technology is regularly included in conceptualizations of innovation such as this one from the *Encyclopedia of Applied Linguistics*: "Examples of innovation in language education over the past few decades include new pedagogic approaches, such as TBLT; changes to teaching materials; technological developments, such as CALL; and alternative assessment methods, such as the use of portfolios" (Carless 2013, 2689). In Markee's study of the diffusion of innovation in language teaching, he paints a broader picture by including the people, their skills, and their values when he defines curricular innovation as "a managed process of development whose principal products are teaching (and/or testing) materials, methodological skills, and pedagogical values that are perceived as new by potential adopters" (Markee 1997).

In this section, the chapters address the practices that are instrumental in creating innovations with technology in language learning and disseminating them to classrooms and the profession. These are the basic practices of research and development, which have developed an identity of their own in the area of technology and language learning. The identity has evolved to fulfill the pragmatic goal of creating practices and knowledge that allow for the best use of technologies for language learning, as described in the previous chapters. Many areas of applied linguistics work toward improving language instruction, but the unique identity of language learning and technology arises from the significant, multifaceted contributions that technology can make in the learning process. The complex affordances of the technologies are a critical part of the context of language learning.

The chapters in the first three sections reveal some of the complex interactions of technology with multiple avenues for language learning. In Chapter 23, Robert Godwin-Jones takes a closer look at the development of the affordances that appear in CALL materials. He describes how authoring tools and templates allow language teachers to construct their own materials, and how larger teams working on research projects or for publishers create extensive packages of materials. In such development work, authors are faced with numerous design questions including everything from how big the font should be in the instruction lines to how much control the student should have over help options. Many such design questions are at the same time pedagogical questions for which the field has no clear response. In this context, developers have borrowed from research and development in learning sciences to engage in design-based research. Julio C. Rodríguez starts Chapter 24 with a brief introduction to the evolution of design-based research, an activity in which researchers and practitioners attempt to create new knowledge about educational software design through progressive testing and revision. Many developers have used some form of design-based research in practice for years, but Rodríguez presents a clearer conception of what it is and how important it is for technology and language learning.

The current research literature on technology and language learning consists of a range of types of evaluations of technology uses in, for example, learning vocabulary, improving field-specific writing, or experimenting with tellecollaboration with a combination of desktop and mobile devices. In some cases these evaluations are designed as comparisons between a technology intervention and a "no technology" control, but in the majority of cases such designs would be either not feasible, uninformative, or both. In Chapter 25, Carol Chapelle reviews alternative approaches taken by professionals to conduct evaluations of technology and language learning. She exemplifies five types of arguments that are found in the published research on technology and language learning and describes how each one has been supported using a variety of research methods. In the following chapter, Dorothy M. Chun provides an overview of the research methods used in the technology and language learning literature. Basing the analysis on studies that are the most highly-cited or considered seminal or influential, she describes various qualitative, quantitative, and mixed-methods approaches that appear frequently in technology and language learning research, which she clarifies as referring to "Computer-Assisted Languaculture Learning," to denote the fact that second language learning also entails learning about the cultures and developing intercultural competence.

Each of the following three chapters addresses a line of inquiry intended to improve the quality and utility of research on technology and language learning. In Chapter 27, Hsien-Chin Liou and Hui-Fen Lin examine how the methodology of meta-analysis can advance the profession's understanding of the effects of technology-based pedagogies for second language learning. Considering the multiple meta-analyses that have been conducted in this area, they look at the rigor with which the meta-analyses are reported. The criteria they provide for rigor as well as their analysis of existing studies should help to prompt progress in future meta-analyses. Bryan Smith takes a different approach to improving research on technology and language learning in Chapter 29. He shows that many of the research questions posed about technology and second language learning can best be conceptualized by drawing upon theory and research on instructed second language acquisition. Moreover, research conceived in this way can benefit from and contribute to this line of research in the field. In Chapter 28, Thierry Chanier and Marie-Noëlle Lamy add methodological considerations unique to the study of multimodal environments. Their definition of multimodal environments captures much of the research and practice described in this volume. The discussion, which is grounded in their experience gathering and analyzing multimodal data in the Open Educational Resources movement, is widely relevant.

The final chapter identifies themes from the chapters included in the *Handbook* and looks to the future of technology and second language learning and teaching. From the first section of chapters, it is evident from the integral role that technology plays in teaching aspects of language knowledge and skills that the conception of those knowledge and skills needs to be updated to include the technology-mediated contexts in which language learners communicate and learn. The second and third sections introducing pedagogical innovations that have been developed as a result of the affordances provided by technology indicates the need for a dynamic professional agenda of innovation in teaching and assessment, teacher education, and research. The final section reveals some of the key concepts and practices that should help to move such an agenda forward. The chapters show research and development going hand-in-hand as well as how the identity of this area of applied linguistics has developed by integrating ideas and practices from other areas of applied linguistics, predominately second language acquisition, as well as other fields. The chapters in this *Handbook* suggest the need to strengthen the research base for language learning and technology in part by engaging more fully with each of the areas that has contributed to the significant developments in technology and language learning. We hope that this *Handbook* will contribute to this engagement with other areas by presenting a clear statement about the nature and scope of technology and language learning.

# REFERENCES

Carless, David. 2013. "Innovation in Language Teaching and Learning." In *Encyclopedia of Applied Linguistics*, edited by Carol A. Chapelle, 2689–2692. Oxford: Wiley-Blackwell.

Chapelle, Carol A., ed., 2013. *Encyclopedia of Applied Linguistics*. Oxford: Wiley-Blackwell.

Farr, Fiona, and Liam Murray, eds., 2016. *The Routledge Handbook of Technology and Language Learning*. London: Routledge.

Markee, Numa. 1997. *Managing Curricular Innovation*. Cambridge: Cambridge University Press.

Rogers, Everett. 2003. *Diffusion of Innovations*, 5th ed. New York: Free Press.

# 2 From Past to Present: A Hundred Years of Technology for L2 Learning

## SUE E. K. OTTO

The history of the use of technology for language learning in the early decades of the 20th century is sparsely documented. However, a number of excellent retrospective publications have documented the history of computer-assisted language learning (CALL), including Sanders (1995), Levy (1997), Davies (2008), Delcloque (2000), Jung (2005), Butler-Pascoe (2011), Davies, Otto and Rüschoff (2012) and Fischer (2013). These publications have different emphases and different time frames, but together serve to document in depth the evolution of CALL in the United States, Canada, and Europe. This chapter is informed by their work, but expands the scope to include influential language learning methods from the early 20th century as well as non-computer technologies; and it focuses primarily on language education in the United States

The basic media used in language instruction—written texts, drawings, photos, audio, and video—have remained constant over time, although the technologies that delivered them have not. Technologies of the distant past seem quaint to us now, but issues and caveats voiced 100 years ago regarding technology and language learning still apply, even after decades of technological "advances" and changing perspectives on how best to approach language instruction. In 1918, Charles Clarke began his article on "The Phonograph in Modern Language Teaching" by observing that "[t]he use of the talking machine in teaching foreign languages is by no means new" (116). Having previously used cylinder recordings (a technology rejected by most language professionals), Clarke discussed the advantages and limitations of new and improved phonograph discs as an ancillary to French language teaching. His recommendations for effective use of this audio technology included: selecting high quality recordings of native speakers; enthusiastic teacher involvement in the delivery of the materials to students (with caveats about extra time and expertise needed to learn and deploy the technology); adhering to an effective method (reading the text when the audio is first played and later listening without the written text); and curbing expectations of the technology—in Clarke's case, restricting the use of recordings to building pronunciation skills.

As each new technology materializes, we repeat the process of evaluating and refining our rationale and methods for implementing it. At the core of this process are the same key issues that Clarke addressed: quality of materials, teacher engagement and training, suitability of technology to specific instructional goals, and sound pedagogical principles.

*The Handbook of Technology and Second Language Teaching and Learning,* First Edition.
Edited by Carol A. Chapelle and Shannon Sauro.
© 2017 John Wiley & Sons, Inc. Published 2020 by John Wiley & Sons, Inc.

Just as essential language learning media types and issues have persisted over time, so have our aspirations for language classroom outcomes. In 1919 a university president articulated a charge to language teachers that still resonates with us today:

> What I want modern language teachers to do is to teach American boys and girls how to read, write, speak and understand the particular foreign language in which they are giving instruction, and through that attainment to have some comprehension of the people and the civilization which the foreign language reflects, and to leave off trying to make specialists or linguistic experts out of the great body of school and college students who would like to learn one or more of the modern European languages. (Hills 1919, 1–2)

Since then we have made repeated attempts to find new and better ways to guide our students to become proficient readers, writers, speakers and listeners of the languages they study as well as to understand the culture; and technologies have played a role in these attempts every step of the way. During the first three decades of the 20th century, technology played a decidedly ancillary role to teacher talk and print materials. Yet over time, technology has come to play a crucial role in language learning.

## Early 20th century: Progressive eclecticism

In the first half of the 20th century, the technologies of choice delivered audio and visual materials to accompany written texts; and, as has been always the case, use of the technology was driven by language teaching methods of the time. The Grammar-Translation Method, the traditional approach used to teach Latin and Greek, played a dominant role in modern language instruction during this period and technology had no part in supporting it. However, Grammar-Translation was far from the only method that influenced language learning in the early years of the 20th century. Alternatives included the Berlitz Method, which originated in 1878 in Rhode Island (Stieglitz 1955), the Natural Method (an adaptation of the 1902 German *Reform-Methode*), and the Direct Method (Skidmore 1917). Like the term *communicative language teaching*, *Direct Method* became the catch-all term for the "progressive eclecticism of modern language teaching" (Skidmore 1917, 218) for the first half of the century. All these methods emphasized the ability to speak and advocated extensive oral practice, while deemphasizing the teaching of grammar (Purin 1916; Skidmore 1917). In addition, the Direct Method prescribed frequent phonetics/pronunciation exercises, free composition (instead of translation), and use of authentic ("national") texts (Purin 1916, 46). As a consequence, teachers of Romance Languages and German who espoused these methods embraced audiovisual technologies that brought the language as spoken by native speakers to the classroom, providing oral and aural practice.

Audio formats used in classrooms evolved from cylinder recordings to phonograph records (Clarke 1918; Stocker 1921), for practice in pronunciation and intonation, as well as listening comprehension. Later, radio was a conduit for distance language learning for students in school and for the general public (BBC 1943; Koon 1933; Meiden 1937). Photographs and slides, which were commonly used for language instruction, were joined by films as media to bring culture and language to life in the classroom (Bernard 1937).

## Mid-century: Repetition as the mother of learning

Starting in the 1950s, the influence of B. F. Skinner's behaviorist learning theory (Mitchell, Myles, and Marsden 2013) and of the Audio Lingual Method (ALM) (Richards and Rodgers, 2001), both of which emphasized repetition, prompted a surge in language laboratories.

From the 1950s through the 1970s most schools and universities had a reel-to-reel audiotape language laboratory classroom, which provided students access to native-speaker voices and drills to internalize sentence patterns and promote automaticity (Otto 1989). As the popularity of ALM declined, so did the use of language labs in the foreign language curriculum.

During the late 1950s, mainframe computers, whose computing power was accessed primarily via paper punch cards, began to appear widely on campuses. However, it was not until the late 1960s and early 1970s that computers had evolved enough to support multiple terminals that allowed interaction with the computer via keyboard, which opened the pathway to CALL. Early CALL developers recognized the benefits of using computers to practice the forms of language, particularly grammar and vocabulary: self-pacing and self-selection of exercises; immediate performance feedback; assessment of mastery, based on cumulative performance; liberating the teacher from correcting endless workbook assignments; and freeing up class time so that the teacher could focus on communicative activities (Ahmad et al. 1985).

CALL began in the United States with several high-profile projects that pioneered the use of mainframe computers for language learning in the 1960s and early 1970s: (1) the Programmed Logic for Automated Teaching Operations (PLATO) project at the University of Illinois at Urbana-Champaign; (2) the Tutorial Russian project at Stanford University; and (3) the Time-shared Interactive Computer Controlled Information Television (TICCIT) project at the University of Texas and Brigham Young University (BYU). These projects were distinguished by their groundbreaking advances in delivering automated media-enriched interactive practice to students, providing immediate feedback and comprehensive recordkeeping of exercise scores and progress through lessons.

The PLATO system featured a number of services that foreshadowed contemporary use of computers: tutorials and practice exercises, testing, email, forums, message boards, instant messaging, and multiplayer games. The custom-designed plasma terminals that were used to interact with the PLATO mainframe produced smooth graphics, allowed touch-screen input and audio playback (via a computer-controlled audio device), and could display complex language characters, including Chinese, Russian, Hindi and Hebrew. The capacity to display international characters was particularly advanced, because most teletype and CRT computer terminals commonly connected to mainframes did not have this capability. Consequently, CALL developers resorted to special conventions to render accents and diacritics, such as *a'* for *á*, or *u:* for *ü*, and CALL was not generally available for languages with non-Roman character sets until the advent of the microcomputer.

Instructors used TUTOR, PLATO's programming language, to develop lessons. PLATO delivered thousands of hours of online language instruction (over 50,000 hours per semester on campus at its peak in the mid-1970s) for Chinese, ESL, French, German, Hebrew, Hindi, Latin, Russian, Spanish, Swahili, and Swedish (Hart 1995). These programs could be accessed by any PLATO terminal either on the Illinois campus or off campus via a telephone modem. In concept, PLATO represents an early form of cloud computing. Centralized services and storage were sold to other institutions for a subscription fee and registered users could remotely access the power of PLATO from anywhere. Unfortunately, costs and content issues combined to limit the realization of PLATO developers' vision to create a nation-wide network of users.

Much smaller in scope than PLATO, Stanford's computer-assisted language instruction initiative focused on tutorials and drills for first-year Russian (Suppes 1968). Stanford's Russian courses were taught in five 50-minute class periods per week, with required written homework and language lab sessions to practice pronunciation and speaking. The aim of the Russian project was to eliminate the in-class component, while retaining the lab and homework components. Their post-semester tests revealed that the computer-based section fared significantly better than the in-class sections and had a much lower dropout rate. This experiment was probably the first technology-delivered course that completely replaced face-to-face instruction.

TICCIT began in 1972 as a collaborative grant project between BYU, the University of Texas and the Mitre Corporation to develop computer-assisted instruction materials for English that combined both computer and television technologies (Anderson 1976). In 1977 the TICCIT project moved to Brigham Young University (Jones 1995), where it expanded to include French, German and Spanish. The courseware featured detailed recordkeeping and an advisor function, but students controlled how they completed the exercises and what help features they accessed.

Although some CALL materials were available for adoption, the *Not Invented Here* mind-set drove some language teachers to develop CALL courseware tailored to their specific needs, resulting in the unfortunate reinvention of the wheel. A number of authoring languages and systems were available for mainframe users, including IBM's (1966) *Coursewriter.* Among the first CALL lessons to be developed in *Coursewriter* were German grammar, vocabulary, translation and phonology exercises created by Adams, Morrison, and Reddy (1968). The program utilized a computer-controlled audiotape machine and introduced an answer-judging algorithm that used dashes to indicate error locations in students' typed answers, an algorithm that inspired another developer, James Pusack, to recreate it for the authoring tool *Dasher.*

One of the most widely distributed *Coursewriter* projects for languages was the *Deutscher Computerunterricht/Tutorial Computer (DECU/TUCO)* tutorial and drill package, developed by Taylor and Haas at Ohio State University (Taylor 1979). The exercises provided targeted feedback through extensive programming of anticipated errors. Generic programing languages common during the 1970s, including multiple versions of *BASIC*, were used to create CALL materials during this period. A few authoring tools created specifically for CALL, such as *CALIS* (Phelps, Hossein, and Bessent 1980) and *Dasher* (Pusack and Otto 1983–2010), were also available as easier-to-learn alternatives.

During mainframe days, it was faculty who programmed or authored computer-based lessons. This practice was frequently detrimental to their careers, since it required an enormous investment in time to build expertise and to create the lessons; and CALL work was not recognized as a legitimate academic pursuit. At the time, given many failed tenure cases, CALL faculty developers were advised to wait until after tenure to get involved with computers.

The vast majority of CALL exercises were vocabulary flashcards, text-based grammar drill-and-practice of uncontextualized forms and sentences, and translations. We lapsed back into grammar-translation and ALM approaches for the computer, because these types of interactions matched the capabilities of the technology and development tools of the time and because these were the formats usually found in standard paper workbooks. However, communicative language learning, which mirrored the tenets of the old Direct Method that called for an emphasis on speaking and reading proficiency and a de-emphasis of overt grammar instruction, was gaining widespread acceptance among language professionals in the 1970s. Thus, CALL was a hard sell for many language teachers, who remained unconvinced of its value.

Olsen (1980) conducted a survey in 1978–179 on the use of computer-assisted instruction (CAI) in foreign language departments in the United States Out of 602 responses only 62 language departments reported using CAI for language learning, primarily in commonly taught language—Spanish, French, German and Latin. Frequently reported barriers to CALL were general suspicion of computers by humanities faculty, lack of recognition of CAI development for tenure and promotion, and the lack diacritical marks and fonts for non-roman scripts. These barriers, together with growing movement toward communicative language methodologies, impeded broad acceptance of CALL well into the 1990s.

# The 1960s to early 1980s: Interactivity and authenticity

During this period, a plethora of new methods and Second Language Acquisition (SLA) theories that emphasized communication through interaction gained the attention of language educators: Curran's Community Language Learning, Terrell and Krashen's Natural Approach, Asher's Total Physical Response, Long's Interaction Hypothesis, and Omaggio's Proficiency-Based Instruction (Richards and Rodgers 2001). Nevertheless, CALL continued to fulfill its established role as drillmaster and tutor, not only because of the persistent belief in the efficacy of individual practice on vocabulary, grammar, and reading skills, but also because computer technology had not evolved enough to handle sophisticated communicative interactions.

On the technology front, the face of computing changed radically with the introduction of microcomputers, among them the Apple II in 1977 and the IBM PC in 1981. Whereas mainframe ownership was the province of governments, corporations, and institutions of higher education, microcomputers ushered in the consumerization of computing. Individuals and schools gained direct personal access to the power of computers and CALL software projects began to proliferate in the United States, Canada, and Europe.

At first, early microcomputers were viewed as little more than toys for hobbyist geeks who liked to program and play games. Film, audiotape, and videotape continued as the principal instructional technologies for languages. However, language faculty who had begun CALL development on mainframes were immediately drawn to microcomputers because of their graphics capabilities, which enabled display of images, animations, and, at last, foreign characters. Language-specific peripheral devices also appeared, including computer-controlled audiocassettes, for example, the Tandberg Computer-Controlled Cassette Recorder (Wagers 1984), the Instavox Random-Access Audio system (Henry, Hartman, and Henry 1987), and random-access VHS videotape with the BCD board for the Apple II (Jensen and Lyman 1989). These peripherals allowed language software developers to integrate interactive audio and video in a controlled way for listening comprehension exercises. Although this hardware was soon superseded by newer and better technologies, language teachers were able to begin to explore new computer-based strategies for building listening comprehension.

By the late 1980s and early 1990s numerous free or inexpensive instructional software authoring tools that required no programming skills, such as *HyperCard* (Atkinson and Winkler 1987), were being marketed. New tools specifically for language software development also became available, including *WinCALIS* (Borchardt and Kunst 1985), *MacLang* (Frommer 1986), *Storyboard* (Higgins 1982), *Dasher* (Pusack and Otto 1983) and *Libra* (Fischer and Farris 1990). Microcomputers and their authoring tools hastened the demise of mainframe-based CALL.

The abundance of authoring tools kept much of language courseware development in the hands of teachers, working as individuals or collaboratively. An increasing number of faculty developers produced their custom materials with the intention of distributing them commercially. For example, *Spanish MicroTutor*, developed by Domínguez (1989), comprised grammar tutorials, exercises, and texts for first-year Spanish students and was distributed by a book publisher. The *CLEF* (Computer-assisted Learning Exercises for French) project, an initiative realized by a consortium of language faculty from the Universities of Western Ontario, Guelph, and Calgary, produced a comprehensive suite of French language lessons covering basic grammar and vocabulary (Paramskas 1989). *CLEF* was distributed commercially by software publishers in Canada, the United States, and Europe. Similarly, the *Apfeldeutsch* (Williams, Davies, and Williams 1981) package, a large collection of exercises for beginning German, was distributed commercially in Europe and North America. Most commercial software targeted Spanish, French, and German, because the market for materials for less commonly taught languages was not lucrative.

# The 1980s: Compelling new contexts

In an attempt to break out of the drill-and-practice mold that typified CALL in the 1980s, some developers experimented with games and simulations. The beginnings of intelligent CALL (ICALL) could be seen in the work of Bassein and Underwood's (1985) *Juegos Communicativos,* a Spanish game for communicative practice, and in Sanders and Sanders' (1995) *Spion,* a German spy game. These programs utilized semantic and syntactic parsers that allowed users to enter a limited amount of natural language input and be "understood" by the programs. Games constituted the antithesis of drill-and-practice, offering instead a fun context for communicative language use.

Given the pedagogical emphasis on communication skills, interest in exploiting authentic media—that is, media that were produced by and for native speakers of the language—increased dramatically. Students who were exposed only to teacher talk and to instructionally-adapted text, audio, and video materials found themselves clueless and speechless when confronted with authentic language. Response to the demand for authentic video materials by publishers and non-profit distributors of language media programming was immediate. Altman (1989) listed 32 companies distributing international videotape materials for language learning: feature films, documentaries, news, drama and comedy shows, short features, commercials, weather reports, music performances, talk shows, game shows, and children's programs.

As recognition of the importance of authentic language grew, data-driven language learning on microcomputers—using authentic language corpora (large bodies of text) and concordancers (programs use to search corpora)—began to take hold, particularly in Europe (Ahmad et al. 1985; Johns 1986). Language corpora and concordancers had been available on mainframes. However, the transition to microcomputers made them more accessible to students and teachers. Early microcomputer concordancing programs, like Johns' (1986) *Micro-concord,* were designed to search corpora to find keywords in context and teachers could use them to provide authentic language examples of specific words and forms in their context. For students, use of concordancers represented an active learning environment, in which they could read numerous examples and inductively figure out grammar rules, discover new meanings, and observe how words are positioned in sentences. Later, some researchers and teachers explored the use of learner corpora (collections of student-produced language) to analyze learner interlanguage development and to identify common student lexical and grammar problems that could be addressed by the instructor (Grainger, Hung, and Petch-Tyson 2002).

In the 1980s a number of projects using satellite technology for language learning were begun. In 1982 Father Lee Lubbers, an art teacher at Creighton University, founded SCOLA (Satellite Communications for Learning), an initiative that pioneered satellite communications for language learning by broadcasting authentic foreign language television news programming from many countries. Satellite TV was also used as a medium connecting language teachers and learners. One groundbreaking satellite telecourse was developed at Oklahoma State University in 1985 by Wohlert (1989), who taught German I and II to rural high school students in Oklahoma and surrounding states. In addition to participating in the broadcasts twice a week, students were required to do three hours of CALL work per week. This program provided German instruction to many schools that had not been able to offer languages before.

Among the most promising technologies of the 1980s was interactive videodisc, which featured rapid precise playback of video clips. While software programs for the commonly taught languages still dominated the language market, videodisc-based courseware for less commonly taught languages had begun to appear, including Arabic, Chinese, Hebrew, Japanese, Korean, Quechua, and Russian (Rubin et al. 1990). BYU pioneered interactive videodisc in the early 1980s with interactive videodisc programs for Spanish, most notably the innovative Spanish conversation simulation, *Montevidisco* (Gale, 1983; Schneider and Bennion 1984). In *Montevidisco*, the learner played the role of a visitor to a fictitious Mexican town and interacted with people they encountered while there. *Montevidisco* featured 1,100 different situations and branching opportunities, so each a student could interact with *Montevidisco* multiple times and have a different experience every time (Gale 1989).

Other noteworthy videodisc projects included Coffin and Shitai's, *The Safe Affair* (1988), a courtroom drama simulation for Hebrew, Nippon Television's (1984) *Understanding Spoken Japanese*, and *ELLIS* (Otto 1990), a multilevel course in ESL. Several hundred videodiscs for foreign language instruction were produced, but the consumer market for videodiscs never flourished, so the format was relatively short lived, replaced by CDs and DVDs in the 1990s.

Computerized adaptive testing (CAT) for languages attracted the attention of the second language community in the mid-1980s. The major benefits of CAT were decreased testing times, decreased student frustration, and increased test security, since items were drawn at random and were adapted during the test session to the individual's performance. In 1985, Larson (1989) developed at BYU the first S-CAPE, a Spanish computerized adaptive placement exam that drew on a large bank of grammar, vocabulary, and reading items. S-CAPE was followed by exams for English, French, German, and Russian. Others computerized adaptive tests for language were Yao's (1995) Computer-Adaptive Test for Reading Chinese (CATRC), Kenyon and Malabonga's (2001) Computerized Oral Proficiency Instrument (COPI), Ke and Zhang's (2002, 2005) *Chinese Computerized Adaptive Listening Comprehension Test* (CCALT), and ETS's *CBT TOEFL* (Chalhoub-Deville and Deville 1999). However, because of the challenges in calibrating and determining the reliability and validity of test items, relatively few computerized adaptive language tests have been developed and marketed.

# The 1990s: Toward new competencies

In the 1990s, language methods were very much anchored in communicative competence—with the emphasis on effective and appropriate use of the target language and meaningful engagement with the culture. In 1996 ACTFL published the *Standards for Foreign Language Learning: Preparing for the 21st century* (1996), which reflected current trends in the language profession and focused on building proficiency in five spheres: Communication, Cultures, Connections, Comparisons, and Communities. In Europe, they produced the *Common European Framework of Reference for Languages,* which was released in 2001(Council of Europe 2001). Like the U.S. *National Standards*, the *Common European Framework* focused on building successful communication and intercultural skills and well as the social and political dimension of language learning. The media and CALL software that were used by world languages educators—authentic television materials, hypermedia, simulations, games, social media, and online virtual communities—resonated with these standards of communication.

A new generation of networkable multimedia microcomputers emerged in the 1990s. Although multimedia CALL had been possible in the past, what distinguished this genera-tion of computer was the integration of CD/DVD players, making it possible to deliver media in digital form without cumbersome external audio and video peripherals. Microphones became a standard input device, allowing audio recording and voice input for software that featured speech recognition as a form of interaction. Moreover, the Unicode Consortium, formed in 1991, established an internationally recognized set of standard codes for characters of all languages, thereby solving persistent problems in displaying characters across platforms.

Networking of microcomputers to both local and remote servers became the norm during this period. Microcomputers became intelligent workstations, supporting not only localized activities, for example, with word processing, graphics/paint programs, and software development tools, but also centralized internet services, such as email and the World Wide Web.

The Web (the brainchild of British computer scientist Tim Berners-Lee) was first tested in 1990 and expanded quickly across the globe to host a vast digital multilingual repository of authentic media—text, images, video, and audio. This unified multimedia environment could deliver in-depth learning through presentation of content of different types linked together in meaningful ways (Pusack and Otto 1997). Search engines served as research tools for students to find, analyze, and synthesize information from foreign sites, constructing their own knowledge about their target language and culture. Thus, the Web began to profoundly revolutionize the world of information and communication, opening up compelling new horizons in technology-based language learning and teaching.

Not all media were immediately replaced by digital forms, however. As always, the old technologies overlapped with the new and persisted as long as their formats could be played by readily available equipment. VHS videocassettes and audiocassettes were widespread inexpensive formats for AV materials starting in the 1970s. Different world video standards (NTSC, PAL, and SECAM) constituted a special challenge for language instruction, prompting the need for multistandard video players, which were more expensive than regular consumer models. The standards issue has continued into the era of DVDs, which, in addition to being recorded in NTSC or PAL, have a regional code that prevents their playback on consumer video players in different countries. For many years cassettes coexisted with CDs and DVDs to deliver audio and video material, formats that persisted long after the introduction of streaming digital media servers.

The Annenberg/CPB project funded many video-based learning projects in the late 1980s and early 1990s. A number of major foreign language video and videodisc projects were launched with their funding: *French in Action*, a 52-episode video story (Capretz and Lydgate 1987); *Destinos*, a 52-episode Spanish telenovela (soap opera) (VanPatten 1992); MIT's Athena Project that focused on artificial intelligence and videodisc-based simulations, including *À la rencontre de Philippe*, an interactive fiction set in Paris (Murray, Morgenstern, and Furstenberg 1989); and Project for International Communication Studies (PICS) (Pusack, Altman, and Otto 1986–2004), which sold authentic television programming on videocassette and videodisc.

During this time a great many multimedia CALL programs were produced and distributed by commercial foreign language software publishers with names like Hyperglot, Transparent Language, and Rosetta Stone. Conventional multimedia tutorial/drill products were complemented by more innovative offerings, such as Syracuse Language Systems' *TriplePlay Plus!* (1994) game software, which featured voice recognition, and *PuebloLindo* (1998), among the first online virtual communities for learning Spanish, developed in partnership with Heinle & Heinle. Heinle also published a series of writing assistants: *Système D* (Noblitt, Pet, and, Solá 1989–2005) for French, *Atajo* (Domínguez, Noblitt, and Pet 1994–2005) for Spanish, and *Quelle* (Noblitt, Kossuth, and Pet 1997) for German. These programs provided a writing environment that gave learners immediate access to language reference materials and a framework for tracking revisions. Unfortunately, the shelf life of this software was relatively short because of rapidly evolving computer operating systems and hardware.

Game software attracted moderate attention during this time, particularly in for K-12 learners. In addition to *TriplePlay Plus!*, a number of commercial single-player games, including *Where in the World is Carmen Sandiego?* (Elliott and Swanson 1985) and *Who Is Oscar Lake?* (1995), were used as ancillaries to language instruction. Although not targeted to the

CALL market, *Carmen Sandiego* was useful for ESL learners because of the extensive reading necessary to play the game and the practice in using an alphabetically arranged reference work, *The World Almanac*, which accompanied the software. *Oscar Lake*, while engaging and multilingual, proved less beneficial for language learning, since the ratio of time spent using the language to time spent playing the game was very poor.

In the late 1990s two web-based role play mystery games were published by Heinle & Heinle: *Meurtre à Cinet* and *Un Misterio en Toluca* (Nelson and Oliver 1997) and targeted post-secondary learners. These multiplayer murder mysteries for French and Spanish were text-based and required players to take on the role of a citizen from the towns of Cinet or Toluca. Learners had to read and write extensively to investigate and eventually solve a murder. *Cinet* and *Toluca* were played synchronously in a computer lab by the whole class and over multiple periods, which meant redesigning the curriculum to accommodate playing the game. Moreover, assessment of participation was difficult, just as it is today with language learning activities that take place in online apps and games.

Web-based development tools for languages were still in demand. One of the best-known authoring tools was *Hot Potatoes* (Arneil and Holmes 1998–2009), a suite of templates that enabled easy and rapid development of CALL multilingual exercises in a variety of formats, including multiple choice, matching, short answer, scrambled sentences, crosswords and cloze. *Hot Potatoes* provided the first experience for countless language professionals in developing CALL materials, online or otherwise.

A great many free web-based CALL materials in many languages began to appear on the web. For example, the BBC, which has a long record of offering free language materials to the public, offered *Learning English* and *Languages* for foreign languages at no cost. Many enterprising teachers also created learning websites like *Randall's ESL Cyber Listening Lab* (Davis 1998–2014) and the *Chinese Reading World* (Shen 2008). Thousands of language learning websites have been produced by language educators and aficionados, but the scope and quality of the materials varies enormously.

For commercial publishers, the textbook continued to be the centerpiece of language series products. Besides the typical student workbook, test bank, set of overhead transparencies, and audio series with lab manual, the set of ancillaries expanded to include a video and a computer software package. Much of the software was still oriented toward grammar and vocabulary practice, though some listening and reading comprehension exercises were also included.

As the Web developed, so too did a number of Learning Management Systems (LMCs) or Course Management Systems (CMSs), such as WebCT, Blackboard, and Moodle, for management of e-learning. These systems combined tools to distribute course materials, administer quizzes, manage grades, and host asynchronous threaded discussion and synchronous chats. At first, the only CMS to provide adequate support for foreign languages was Moodle. This serious deficit put a damper on the early adoption of CMS-embedded activities, such as chat, for language learning.

Work on intelligent CALL still constituted a minor strand of CALL in the 1990s. Natural language processing (NLP) for foreign languages remained an underdeveloped field, and yet NLP was viewed as necessary for true human-computer communication for language learning. Therefore, a number of determined researchers developed parsers, for processing natural language input in CALL contexts. The Athena Project included development of a multilingual NLP system (Felshin 1995; Murray, Morgenstern, and Furstenberg 1989) designed for conversation in English, French, German, Russian, and Spanish under the rubric of Language Instruction through Communication-based Software (LINCS). Nagata's (2009) ICALL program *Robo-Sensei* grew out of her research in the early 1990s with her parser for providing intelligent feedback in Japanese grammar exercises. Heift (2010) developed a German parser to drive an intelligent tutor for German language learning, which was used to provide intelligent feedback in her web-based *E-Tutor* system that went online in 1999. Despite slow progress in ICALL, intelligent language and speech processing became much more developed during the next decade, thanks to corporate investments in "smart" consumer technologies.

Other web-based experiments with virtual learning environments exploited Multi-user-domain Object Oriented (MOO), network systems that allowed multiple users to communicate and collaborate in building their own virtual community. *MOOssigang*, a very successful German MOO, involved an exchange between American university students of German and advanced learners of English at a German university. This student-centered environment supported peer teaching, autonomous learning, content-based instruction, and play (Von Der Emde, Schneider, and Kötter 2001).

With publishers taking over the production of CALL software, the role of faculty as CALL developers changed. Although language teachers were usually involved in the creation of CALL content, fewer were engaged in the actual authoring or programming of CALL packages. Technology had reached a point at which software production required development teams consisting of subject matter experts, instructional designers, and professional programmers. Once initial development was completed, major resources were required to maintain, provide technical support for, and upgrade the software and content on an ongoing basis. Usually those resources came from publishers with deep pockets and a stake in the success and longevity of the product.

# Early 21st century: The social turn

With the turn of the 21st century came a social turn in CALL and the Web. Sociocultural theoretical influences became more apparent in language instruction, with the view of the learner as a social being, whose cognitive and linguistic development occurs through social interaction mediated by language.

Multimedia and the Web continue to figure prominently in all aspects of language learning. Educational models have largely shifted away from exclusively teacher-centered classrooms toward student-oriented, active and collaborative learning environments, with the student as creator of digital texts and media and (co-)constructor of knowledge, both in and out of the classroom. No longer tied exclusively to desktop computer workstations, language students routinely use wireless mobile devices—laptops, tablets, and smart phones—to access lessons, to engage in development projects, and interact with other learners.

Levy (1997) described a dichotomy between *tutorial* CALL (programs that substitute for the teacher in delivering language instruction, practice, and evaluation) and *tool* CALL (the use of generic productivity, e-learning, and digital media creation applications for teaching). In general, tutorial CALL has lost ground to tool applications for CALL and the term *authoring* has broadened to include design of tool-based instructional experiences (Otto and Pusack 2009). These tools include programs like Microsoft Office, course management systems, Web teleconferencing tools, streaming media resources, animation and digital storytelling apps, and social apps. Such applications have become platforms for many communicative, collaborative, and creative language learning experiences.

In the late 1990s and early 2000s CMC technologies spawned numerous telecollaborative exchange partnerships conducted via CMC tools (Belz 2002; Furstenberg et al. 2001; Guth and Helm 2010; Kessler 2013; Kinginger, Gouvès-Hayward, and Simpson,1999; Thomas 2009; Thorne 2003; Ware and Kramsch, 2005; Warschauer 1996, 1997). One of the longest-running and successful telecollaborative projects is MIT's *Cultura* (Furstenberg et al. 2001).

*Cultura* is based on a model of a web-based intercultural exchange that enables students from different cultures to co-construct a deep understanding of each other's cultural attitudes, beliefs and values. Indeed, all these telecollaborative CMC projects aimed to build students' intercultural awareness and intercultural communication skills.

Technology plays a pivotal role in the delivery of hybrid language courses, courses that supplement face-to-face meetings with online components, and online courses, where every aspect of the course is conducted online. Due to economic and practical pressures in higher education, hybrid language courses, which meet fewer times per week face-to-face, have been launched as a means to save money. Fewer people can be responsible for more students and the computer offers an effective way to deliver the tutorial and practice aspects of the curriculum, making it possible to use in-class time exclusively for communicative activities. Completely online courses, such as *Arabic Without Walls* (UC Consortium for Language Learning & Teaching et al., 2004) and *eChineseLearning* (eChineseLearning.com, 2006–2016) represent a means of offering languages to people who otherwise would not have access to them—either because enrollments would not justify hiring a language teacher for just one institution, or because learners do not have the flexibility to enroll in regular classes because of work, location, or schedule conflicts. Both hybrid and online models require significant CALL courseware that combines both tutorial and tool software to sustain acceptable language instruction.

Tutorial CALL production has largely become the domain of publishers of language textbooks and of instructional language software for business, education, and home use. All language textbook publishers offer multimedia components for their books, some more elaborate than others. For example, Pearson developed a series of online course management systems, *MyLanguageLabs* (e.g., *MySpanishLab, MyEnglishLab*), to accompany their printed textbooks and that integrated an online interactive version of the textbook plus all the ancillaries, including audio and video components as well as vocabulary and grammar tutorials and exercises. The language software publisher *Rosetta Stone, Inc.*, sells courseware for many languages and is a dominant player in the market for business and home language learning solutions. With massive resources at their disposal these companies are able to develop and sustain their products, whereas major projects funded locally by educational institutions or by federal grants are hard-pressed to do so over time.

Games specifically designed for language learners still account for a relatively small percentage of CALL materials, despite a growing national interest in educational gaming. One of the most convincing examples of instructional gaming for language learning is *Mentira* (Sykes and Holden 2009), a place-based murder mystery game set in Albuquerque's Spanish old town and played with mobile devices. Another example is *Trace Effects* (U.S. Department of State 2012), an American English language video game with a time-travel theme. The game allows ESL students to explore American language and culture in an online 3D environment. In addition, games such as memory matching puzzles, hang-man, crosswords, and word-search puzzles, are often found within larger language software programs, particularly those for children.

A number of unstructured online activities, including public forums, fan fiction, social media sites and massively multiplayer games, have been found to be valuable language learning opportunities or what Thorne (2010) calls "intercultural communication in the wild" (144). Mobile devices play a prominent role in facilitating these unstructured activities as well. Researchers have begun to explore how students interact in such environments, construct new identities, and learn language and culture through these experiences (Hanna and DeNooey 2009; Klimanova and Dembovskaya 2013; Lomicka and Lord 2009; McBride 2009; Thorne 2008).

# Conclusion

While the fundamental media used in language instruction—text, audio, video, images—have remained constant over time, their technological formats and their role in language learning have changed dramatically. Language learning technologies and CALL have evolved from delivery via localized technological resources to any-time, any-place provision through networked digital means. Moreover, technology has advanced from its ancillary role in the curriculum to become a core source of content and a conduit for authentic language learning experiences. CALL scholars have described this evolution of CALL using different terms and approaches, for example, Warschauer and Healey's (1998) three proposed stages of CALL development based in technologies and pedagogical approaches—*Behaviorist > Communicative > Integrative* —and Bax's (2003, 2011) multidimensional analysis presented as *Restricted > Open > Integrative*. The end point is a state of *normalization*, that is, "technology becomes invisible, embedded in everyday practice" (Bax 2003 23). Regardless of how one describes the history of CALL, it is indisputable that technology has in fact become more integrated into language learning and is well on the way to becoming a normal part of everyday practice.

Before computers came along, we never referred to our tools as language learning "assistants" (early CALL as Chalk-Assisted Language Learning?), concentrating instead on language learning pedagogies and language acquisition theories (Chapelle 2009). Doubtless, in the future, our focus will return to our methods and goals, with less prominence given to the technologies that help us realize them.

# REFERENCES

Adams, E. N., H. W. Morrison, and J. M. Reddy. 1968. "Conversation with a Computer as a Technique of Language Instruction." *The Modern Language Journal*, 52, no. 1: 3–16. DOI:10.1111/j.1540-4781.1968.tb01857.x

Ahmad, Kurshid, Grenville Corbett, Margaret Rogers, and Roland Sussex. 1985. *Computers, Language Learning and Language Teaching*. Cambridge: Cambridge University Press.

Altman, Rick. 1989. *The Video Connection: Integrating Video into Language Teaching*. Boston: Houghton Mifflin Company.

Anderson, Steven J. 1976. "TICCIT Project." Report presented at the National Association of Educational Broadcasters, Chicago, Illinois, October 24–27, 1976. Accessed June 16, 2016. http://www.eric.ed.gov/, document number ED134226.

Arneil, Stewart, and Martin Holmes. 1998–2009. *Hot Potatoes*. Victoria, British Columbia: University of Victoria and Half-Baked Software, Inc.

Atkinson, Bill, and Dan Winkler *HyperCard*. 1987. Apple II, Macintosh. Apple Computer, Inc. 1987.

Bassein, Richard, and John Underwood. 1985. *Juegos Comunicativos: Games for Communicative Practice in Spanish*. Apple II. New York: Random House, Inc.

Bax, Steven. 2003. "CALL—Past, Present and Future." *System*, 31, no. 1: 13–28. DOI:10.1016/S0346-251X(02)00071-4

Bax, Steven. 2011. "Normalisation Revisited: The Effective Use of Technology in Language Education." *International Journal of Computer-Assisted Language Learning and Teaching*, 1, no. 2: 1–15. DOI:10.4018/ijcallt.2011040101

BBC. "1943-present. Learning English and BBC Languages." Accessed June 16, 2016. http://www.bbc.co.uk/learningenglish., http://www.bbc.co.uk/languages/

Belz, Julie. 2002. "Social dimensions of telecollaborative foreign language study." *Language Learning & Technology*, 6, no. 1: 60–81.

Bernard, Edward G. 1937. "Films and Other Visual Aids." *The Modern Language Journal*, 22, no. 8: 132–143. DOI:10.1111/j.1540-4781.1937.tb00573.x

Borchardt, Frank, and Rick Kunst. 1985, 2002. *WinCALIS*. Windows. Durham, NC: Duke University.

Butler-Pascoe, Mary E. 2011. "The History of CALL: The Intertwining Paths of Technology and Second/Foreign Language Teaching." *International Journal of Computer-Assisted Language Learning and Teaching*, 1, no. 2: 16–32. DOI:10.4018/ijcallt.2011010102

Capretz, Pierre, and Barry Lydgate. 1987. *French in Action*. Yale University, WGBH Boston with Wellesley College.

Chalhoub-Deville, Micheline, and Craig Deville. 1999. "Computer Adaptive Testing in Second Language Contexts." *Annual Review of Applied Linguistics*, 19: 273–299. DOI:10.1017/S0267190599190147

Chapelle, Carol. 2009. "The Relationship between Second Language Acquisition Theory and Computer-Assisted Language Learning." *The Modern Language Journal*, 93, Focus Issue, 741–753. DOI:10.1111/j.1540-4781.2009.00970.x

eChineseLearning.com. 2006–2016. *eChineseLearning*. Accessed June 16, 2016. http://www.echeselearning.com/.

Clarke, Charles C. 1918. "The Phonograph in Modern Language Teaching." *The Modern Language Journal*, 3, no. 3: 116–122. DOI:10.1111/j.1540-4781.1918.tb03384.x

Coffin, Edna, and Amit Shitai. 1988. *The Safe Affair: An Interactive Hebrew Video Lesson*. Windows. University of Michigan.

Council of Europe. 2001. *Common European Framework of Reverence for Languages: Learning, Teaching, Assessment*. Cambridge: Press Syndicate of the University of Cambridge.

Davies, Graham, ed. 2008. *Information and Communications Technology for Language Teachers (ICT4LT)*. Slough, Thames Valley University [Online]. Accessed June 16, 2016. http://www.ict4lt.org

Davies, Graham, Sue Otto, and Berndt Rüschoff. 2012. "Historical Perspectives on CALL." In *Contemporary Computer-Assisted Language Learning*, edited by Michael Thomas, Hayo Reinders and Mark Warschauer, 19–38. London: Bloomsbury.

Davis, Randall. 1998–2014. *Randall's ESL Cyber Listening Lab*. Accessed June 16, 2016. http://www.esl-lab.com/

Delcloque, Philippe. 2000. *The History of Computer-Assisted Language Learning Web Exhibition*. Accessed June 16, 2016. http://www.ict4lt.org/en/History_of_CALL.pdf

Domínguez, Frank. 1989. "Spanish MicroTutor." In *Modern Technology in Foreign Language Education: Applications and Projects*, edited by William Flint Smith, 327–339. Lincolnwood, IL: National Textbook Company.

Domínguez, Frank, James Noblitt, and Willem Pet. 1994–2005 *Atajo Writing Assistant for Spanish*. Macintosh/Windows. Heinle & Heinle Publishers, Inc.

Elliott, Lauren, and Janese Swanson. 1985. *Where in the World is Carmen San Diego?* Apple II. MS DOS, Commodore 64, TRS-80. Brøderbund Software.

Felshin, Sue. 1995. "The Athena Language Learning Project NLP system: A Multilingual System for Conversation-based Learning." In *Intelligent Language Tutors: Theory Shaping Technology*, edited by V. Melissa Holland, Jonathan D. Kaplan and Michelle R. Sams, 257–272. Mahwah, NJ: Lawrence Erlbaum Associates.

Fischer, Robert. 2013. "A Conceptual Overview of the History of the *CALICO Journal*: The phases of CALL." *CALICO Journal*, 30, no. 1: 1–9. DOI:10.11139/cj.30.1.1-9.

Fischer, Robert, and Michael Farris. 1990. *Libra Multimedia Authoring Environment*. Macintosh. Southwest Texas State University.

Furstenberg, Gilberte, Sabine Levet, Kathryn English, and Katherine Maillet. 2001. "Giving a Virtual Voice to the Silent Language of Culture: The *Cultura* Project." *Language Learning & Technology*, 5, no. 1: 55–192. Cultura Exchanges website, Accessed June 16, 2016. http://cultura.mit.edu/

Gale, Larrie E. 1983. "Montevidisco: An Anecdotal History of an Interactive Videodisc." *CALICO Journal*, 1, no 1: 42–46.

Gale, Larrie E. 1989. "Macario, Montevidisco, and Interactive Dígame: Developing Interactive Video for Language Instruction." In *Modern Technology in Foreign Language Education: Applications and Projects*, edited by William Flint Smith, 235–248. Lincolnwood, IL: National Textbook Company.

Grainger, Sylviane, Joseph Hung, and Stephanie Petch-Tyson, eds. 2002. *Computer Learner Corpora, Second Language Acquisition and Foreign Language Teaching*. Philadelphia: John Benjamins.

Guth, Sarah, and Francesca Helm, eds. 2010. *Telecollaboration 2.0: Language, Literacies and Intercultural Learning in the 21st Century*. Berne: Peter Lang.

Hanna, Barbara E., and Juliana de Nooy. 2009. *Learning Language and Culture via Public Internet Discussion Forums*. New York: Palgrave Macmillan

Hart, Robert S. 1995. "The Illinois PLATO Foreign Languages Project." *CALICO Journal*, 12, no. 4: 15–37.

Heift, Trude. 2010. "Developing an Intelligent Language tutor." *CALICO Journal*, 27, no. 3: 443–459. DOI:10.11139/cj.27.3.443-459.

Henry, George M., John F. Hartmann, and Patricia B. Henry. 1987. "Computer-Controlled Random Access Audio in the Comprehension Approach to Second Language Learning." *Foreign Language Annals*, 20, no. 3: 255–261. DOI:10.1111/j.1944-9720.1987.tb02953.x

Hills, Elijah C. 1919. "Has War Proved that our Methods of Teaching Modern Languages in the Colleges are Wrong? A Symposium." *The Modern Language Journal*, 4, no.1: 1–13. DOI:10.1111/j.1540-4781.1919.tb04937.x

Higgins, John. 1982. *Storyboard*. Apple II and PC. Wida Software.

IBM. *Coursewriter*. 1966, 1969. (Versions II and III). IBM 1500 and 360 mainframes.

Jensen, Alfred W., and Mary Ann Lyman. (1989). "SSI: Survival Spanish Interactive." In *Modern Technology in Foreign Language Education: Applications and Projects*, edited by William Flint Smith, 263–268. Lincolnwood, IL: National Textbook Company.

Johns, Tim. 1986. "Micro-Concord: A Language Learner's Research Tool." *System*, 14, no. 2: 151–162. DOI:10.1016/0346-251X(86)90004-7 DOI:10.1016/0346-251X%2886%2990004-7

Jones, Randall L. 1995. "TICCIT and CLIPS: The Early Years." *CALICO Journal*, 12, no. 4: 84–96.

Jung, Udo. 2005. "CALL: Past, Present and Future—a Bibliometric Approach." *ReCALL*, 17, no. 1: 4–17. DOI:10.1017/S0958344005000212

Ke, Chuanren, and Zizi Zhang. 2002, 2005. *Chinese Computerized Adaptive Listening Comprehension Test*. The Ohio State University Foreign Language Publications. Accessed June 16, 2016. http://ccalt.osu.edu/

Kenyon, Dorry M., and Valerie Malabonga. 2001. "Comparing Examinee Attitudes toward Computer-Assisted and Other Oral Proficiency Assessments." *Language Learning & Technology*, 5, no. 2: 60–83.

Kessler, Greg. 2013. "Collaborative Language Learning in Co-Constructed Participatory Culture." *CALICO Journal*, 30, no. 3: 307–322. DOI:10.11139/cj.30.3.307-322

Kinginger, Celeste, Alison Gouvès-Hayward, and Vanessa Simpson. 1999. "A Tele-Collaborative Course on French-American Intercultural Communication." *The French Review*, 72, no. 5: 853–866.

Klimanova, Liudmila, and Svetlana Dembovskaya. 2013. "L2 Identity, Discourse and Social Networking in Russian." *Language Learning & Technology*, 17, no. 1: 69–88.

Koon, Cline M. 1933. "Modern Language Instruction by Radio." *The Modern Language Journal*, 17, no. 7: 503–505. DOI:10.1111/j.1540-4781.1933.tb05781.x

Larson, Jerry. 1989. "S-CAPE: A Spanish Computerized Adaptive Placement Exam." In *Modern Technology in Foreign Language Education: Applications and Projects*, edited by William Flint Smith, 277–289. Lincolnwood, IL: National Textbook Company.

Levy, Michael. 1997. *CALL: Context and Conceptualisation*. Oxford: Oxford University Press.

Lomicka, Lara, and Gillian Lord. 2009. "Introduction to Social Networking, Collaboration, and Web 2.0 Tools." In *The Next Generation: Social Networking and Online Collaboration in FL Learning*, edited by Lara Lomicka and Gillian Lord, 1–11. San Marcos, TX: CALICO Consortium.

Frommer, Judith. 1986. *MacLang*. Macintosh. Kinko's Academic Courseware Exchange.

McBride, Kara. 2009. "Social-Networking Sites in Foreign Language Classes: Opportunities for Re-Creation." In *The Next Generation: Social Networking and Online Collaboration in FL Learning*, edited by Lara Lomicka and Gillian Lord, 35–58. San Marcos, TX: CALICO Consortium

Meiden, Walter E. 1937. "A Technique of Radio French Instruction." *The Modern Language Journal*, 22, no. 2: 115–125. DOI:10.1111/j.1540-4781.1937.tb00568.x

Mitchell, Rosamond, Florences Myles, and Emma Marsden. 2013. *Second Language Learning Theories*, 3rd edition. New York: Routledge.

Murray, Janet H., Douglas Morgenstern, and Gilberte Furstenberg. 1989. "The Athena Language Learning Project: Design Issues for the Next Generation of Computer-Based Language Learning Tools." In *Modern Technology in Foreign Language Education: Applications and Projects*, edited by William Flint Smith, 97–118. Lincolnwood, IL: National Textbook Company.

Nagata, Noriko. 2009. "Robo-Sensei's NLP-Based Error Detection and Feedback Generation." *CALICO Journal*, 26, no. 3: 562–579.

Nelson, Terri, and Walter Oliver. 1997. *Meurtre à Cinet and Un Misterio en Toluca*. Browser-based Role-playing Games. Heinle & Heinle Publishers, Inc.

Noblitt, James, Karen Kossuth, and Willem Pet. 1997. *Quelle: German Writing Assistant*. Macintosh/Windows. Heinle & Heinle Publishers, Inc. 1997.

Noblitt, James, Willem Pet, and Donald Solá, D. 1989–2005. *Système D Writing Assistant for French*. Macintosh/Windows. Heinle & Heinle Publishers, Inc.

Olsen, Solveig. 1980. "Foreign Language Departments and Computer-Assisted Instruction: A Survey." *The Modern Language Journal*, 64, no. 3: 341–349. DOI:10.1111/j.1540-4781.1980.tb05203.x

Otto, Frank. 1990. *ELLIS: A Digital Learning ELL Curriculum*. English Language Learning and Instruction System Inc: Salt Lake City; currently published by Pearson.

Otto, Sue E. K. 1989. "The Language Lab in the Computer Age." In *Modern Technology in Foreign Language Education: Applications and Projects*, edited by Williamm Flint Smith, 13–41. Lincolnwood, IL: National Textbook Company.

Otto, Sue E. K., and James P. Pusack. 2009. "Computer-Assisted Language Learning Authoring Issues." *The Modern Language Journal*, 93, Focus Issue, 784–801. 10.1111/j.1540-4781.2009.00973.x

Paramskas, Dana. 1989. "CLEF: Computer-Assisted Learning Exercises for French." In *Modern Technology in Foreign Language Education: Applications and Projects*, edited by William Flint Smith, 333–339. Lincolnwood, IL: National Textbook Company.

Phelps, Leland, Omar F. Hossein, and Helga Bessent. 1980. *CALIS (Computer-Assisted Language Instruction System)*. Windows. Duke University. 1980.

*PuebloLindo*. Browser-based MOO. 1998. Heinle & Heinle and Syracuse Language Systems.

Purin, Charles M. 1916. "The Direct Teaching of Modern Foreign Languages in American High Schools." *The Modern Language Journal*, 1, no. 2: 43–51. DOI:10.1111/j.1540-4781.1916.tb03240.x

Pusack, James, Rick Altman, and Sue Otto. 1986–2004. *PICS* (Project for International Communication Studies). University of Iowa.

Pusack, James, and Sue K. Otto. 1983, 1992, 1996, 2000. *Dasher* Authoring System. Windows and Macintosh. University of Iowa: CONDUIT/PICS.

Pusack, James P., and Sue K. Otto. 1997. "Taking Control of Multimedia." In *Technology-Enhanced Language Learning*, edited by Michael Bush and Robert Terry, 1–46. Lincolnwood, IL: National Textbook Company.

Richards, Jack C., and Theodore S. Rodgers. 2001. *Approaches and Methods in Language Teaching*. New York: Cambridge University Press.

*Rosetta Stone*. Windows and browser-based software. Rosetta Stone, Inc. 1996–2016. Accessed June 16, 2016. http://www.rosettastone.com/

Rubin, Joan, Anne Ediger, Edna Coffin, Donna Van Handle and Ann Whiskeyman. 1990. "Survey of Interactive Videodiscs." *CALICO Journal*, 7, no. 3: 31–56.

Sanders, Ruth H., ed. 1995. *Thirty Years of Computer-Assisted Language Instruction. Festschrift for John R. Russell*. *CALICO Journal*, 12, no. 4 (special issue).

Sanders, Ruth, and Alton Sanders. 1995. "History of an AI Spy Game: Spion." *CALICO Journal*, 12, no. 4: 114–127.

Schneider, Edward W., and Junius L. Bennion. 1984. "Veni, Vidi, Vici, via Videodisc: A Simulator for Instructional Courseware." In *Computer-Assisted Language Instruction*, edited by David H. Wyatt, 41–46. Oxford: Pergamon.

Shen, Helen. 2008. *Chinese Reading World*. The University of Iowa. Accessed June 16, 2016. http://collections.uiowa.edu/chinese/

Skidmore, Mark. 1917. "The Direct Method." *The Modern Language Journal*, 1, no. 6: 215–225. DOI:10.1111/j.1540-4781.1917.tb03267.x

*Standards for Foreign Language Learning: Preparing for the 21st Century*. 1996. Yonkers, NY: National Standards in Foreign Language Education Project.

Stieglitz, Gerhard J. 1955. "The Berlitz Method." *The Modern Language Journal*, 39, no. 6: 300–310. DOI:10.1111/j.1540-4781.1955.tb03457.x

Stocker, Clara. 1921. "French Speech-Tunes and the Phonograph." *The Modern Language Journal*, 5, no. 5: 267–270. DOI:10.1111/j.1540-4781.1921.tb06674.x

Suppes, Patrick. 1968. "Computer-Assisted Instruction: An Overview of Operations and Problems." In *Proceedings of the IFIP Congress, Edinburgh*, edited by Arthur John Havart Morrell, 1103–1113. Amsterdam: North Holland. Accessed June 16, 2016. http://suppescorpus.stanford.edu/articles/comped/102.pdf

Sykes, Julie, and Chris Holden. 2009. *Mentira*. Accessed June 16, 2016. http://www.mentira.org/

Taylor, Heimy F. 1979. "Students' Reactions to Computer Assisted Instruction in German." *Foreign Language Annals*, 12, no. 4: 289–291. DOI:10.1111/j.1944-9720.1979.tb00186.x

Thomas, Michael, ed. 2009. *Handbook of Research on Web 2.0 and Second Language Learning*. Hershey, PA: IGI Global.

Thorne, Steven. L. 2003. "Artifacts and Cultures-of-Use in Intercultural Communication." *Language Learning & Technology*, 7, no. 2: 38–67.

Thorne, Steven L. 2008. "Transcultural Communication in Open Internet Environments and Massively Multiplayer Online Games." In *Mediating Discourse Online*, edited by Sally Magnan, 305–327. Amsterdam: John Benjamins.

Thorne, Steven L. 2010. "The 'Intercultural Turn' and Language Learning in the Crucible of New Media." In *Telecollaboration 2.0: Language, Literacies and Intercultural Learning in the 21st Century*, edited by Sarah Guth and Francesca Helm, 139–164. Bern: Peter Lang.

*TriplePlay Plus!* Windows 95/98/3.1. 1994. Syracuse Language Systems,

UC Consortium for Language Learning & Teaching, National Middle East Language Resource Center at Brigham Young University, and Near Eastern Studies Department at UC Berkeley. 2004. *Arabic Without Walls*. Accessed June 16, 2016. http://arabicwithoutwalls.ucdavis.edu/aww/

U.S. Department of State, *Trace Effects*. 2012. Accessed June 16, 2016. http://traceeffects.state.gov/

VanPatten, Bill. 1992. *Destinos*. Annenberg/CPB, Geraldine R. Dodge Foundation, and WGBH Boston.

Von Der Emde, Silke, Jeffrey Schneider, and Markus Kötter. 2001. "Technically Speaking: Transforming Language Learning through Virtual Learning Environments (MOOs)." *The Modern Language Journal*, 85, no. 2: 210–225. DOI:10.1111/0026-7902.00105

Wagers, William D. 1984. "Voice-Based Learning." *CALICO Journal*, 1, no. 5: 35–38.

Ware, Paige, and Claire Kramsch. 2005. "Toward an Intercultural Stance: Teaching German and English through Telecollaboration." *The Modern Language Journal*, 89, no. 2: 190–205. DOI:10.1111/j.1540-4781.2005.00274.x

Warschauer, Mark, ed. 1996. *Telecollaboration in Foreign Language Learning*. Honolulu, HI: University of Hawaii Second Language Teaching & Curriculum Center.

Warschauer, Mark. 1997. "Computer-Mediated Collaborative Learning: Theory and Practice." *The Modern Language Journal*, 81, no. 4: 470–481. DOI:10.1111/j.1540-4781.1997.tb05514.x

Warschauer, Mark, and Deborah Healey. 1998. "Computers and Language Learning: An Overview," *Language Teaching*, 31: 57–71. DOI:10.1017/S0261444800012970

*Who Is Oscar Lake?* 1995. Windows. Language Publications Interactive, Inc.

Williams, Anthony, Graham Davies, and Ingrid Williams. 1981. *Apfeldeutsch*. Apple II. London: Wida Software.

Wohlert, Harry. S. 1989. "German by Satellite: Technology-Enhanced Distance Learning." In *Modern Technology in Foreign Language Education: Applications and Projects*, edited by William Flint Smith, 202–210. Lincolnwood, IL: National Textbook Company.

Yao, Tao-Chung. 1995. "A Computer-Adaptive Test for Reading Chinese (CATRC): A Preliminary Report." *Journal of the Chinese Language Teachers Association*, 30, no. 1: 75–85.

# 3 Technologies for Teaching and Learning L2 Grammar

## TRUDE HEIFT AND NINA VYATKINA

## Introduction

Technologies take their respective places in the ongoing dispute over grammar teaching, which has been appropriately described as a "linguistic and political battlefield" (Metcalfe 1992) due to the ever-changing levels of acceptance of focusing on grammar in second language (L2) teaching approaches over the past decades. There have been periods during which grammatical accuracy was the prime goal, but there also have been times where the teaching of grammar was abolished altogether. These debates, however, not only focused on the central question of *if* and *when* grammar should be taught but also *how* it should be taught.

In a history with many apparent recommendations about grammar teaching, the debate has focused on two main approaches to grammar teaching: explicit and implicit. Explicit grammar teaching emphasizes rules as a form of metalinguistic knowledge and is equated with the deductive teaching of discrete points of grammar. An emphasis is placed on systematically teaching isolated linguistic forms by following a structural syllabus. In contrast, implicit approaches to grammar teaching are exemplar based and derive from the assumption that there are similarities between L2 learning and L1 acquisition and that comprehensible language input arising from natural interaction is central (see Krashen 1988). The overall focus of this inductive teaching approach is on meaning and/or communication rather than linguistic form. These two main approaches to grammar teaching are also reflected in the ways in which L2 grammar is taught and learned with technology. Yet, newer technologies are not limited to the traditional dichotomy of implicit and explicit teaching approaches. Instead, they emphasize both learner-computer and interpersonal interactions by promoting independent discovery and learner autonomy through the exploration of authentic language.

This chapter discusses four technology-based pedagogies for L2 grammar: tutorial CALL, intelligent CALL (ICALL), data-driven Learning (DDL), and computer-mediated communication (CMC). We first describe their respective goals and SLA frameworks and then provide examples of the tools developed for the L2 grammar classroom by situating each learning environment within its teaching approach to L2 grammar instruction. Finally, we present an overview of research studies that have been conducted within these learning environments by focusing on learner feedback in ICALL and CMC, and learner autonomy in DDL.

*The Handbook of Technology and Second Language Teaching and Learning*, First Edition.
Edited by Carol A. Chapelle and Shannon Sauro.
© 2017 John Wiley & Sons, Inc. Published 2020 by John Wiley & Sons, Inc.

# Four technology-based pedagogies for L2 grammar

The origins of CALL in general as well as CALL-based L2 grammar teaching and learning in particular can be traced back to the 1960s. Influenced by the structural view of language dominant at the time, these CALL applications, commonly referred to as tutorial CALL, focused exclusively on explicit grammar teaching. Yet, due to technological advances and influenced by mainly the interactionist (Long 1996; Gass 1997) and sociocultural schools (Lantolf and Thorne 2006; Thorne 2003) of Second Language Acquisition (SLA), the teaching and learning of L2 grammar with technology shifted to emphasize the ways in which learners interact with the technology and their peers when they perform tasks and process language. Examples of such technologies are ICALL, DDL, and CMC which we discuss along with tutorial CALL in the following.

## *Tutorial CALL*

In tutorial CALL, the computer takes on the role of a *tutor* (Levy 1997) by evaluating learner responses and presenting new material in one-to-one interactions. In early tutorial CALL applications, learners were provided with mechanical practice of selected and graded grammatical phenomena, such as the use of personal pronouns or verb tense, in the form of drills, similar to those commonly found in the face-to-face classroom during the prevalence of the Audio-Lingual Method up to the 1970s. The focus of tutorial CALL applications was on repetition and immediate feedback, which were provided while allowing students to work at their own pace and time. Later applications placed an increased focus on record keeping and the individualization of the learning experience by paying particular attention to branching, that is, the individualization of practice sequences based on prior student performance (Burston 1989).

Tutorial CALL follows a deductive teaching approach to grammar by presenting explicit explanations of grammatical concepts and by focusing language practice on graded and discrete grammatical points. The grammar learning activities mainly consist of short sentence-based practice and cover isolated grammatical forms which are presented as multiple choice, fill-in-the-blank, match or rank, and reassemble or translate small chunks of text items (Hubbard and Siskin 2004; Schulze and Heift 2013). These activities are nowadays integrated in authoring programs that allow teachers to generate grammar exercises without programming expertise (see e.g., Arneil and Holmes 1999).

One of the main differences among tutorial CALL programs lies in the ways in which learner responses are processed and evaluated. These underlying algorithms determine the distinct ways in which the CALL application responds to learner errors. The three most commonly used algorithms are string matching, pattern mark-up, and error anticipation.

Tutorial CALL applications which are based on string-matching algorithms and binary knowledge of answer processing compare the learner input with a pre-stored, correct answer (e.g., Williams, Davis, and Williams 1981). For instance, the grammar activity given in example (1) illustrates a typical tutorial CALL exercise which asks the learner to complete the sentence with the correct word form.

(1) Prompt:             Are you afraid of _____ (to fly, fly, flying)?

   Learner response: *to fly*
   System response: *Wrong, try again!*

If the student answers with the infinitive "to fly," the system will identify that an error has occurred and respond with a generic error message (e.g., *Wrong, try again!*). However, even if the student chooses the correct answer "flying" but misspells it, the CALL program will provide the same error message and thus not make a distinction between different error types. Accordingly, and due to the underlying algorithm of processing learner input, simple string matching cannot channel learners toward the correct answer or focus their attention on the error. The algorithm is limited to a yes/no response.

Pattern mark-up is an example of a more sophisticated error processing algorithm also employed in tutorial CALL applications. Here, the computer makes a non-syntactic comparison of the student answer with the string stored as the correct answer, and also searches for variations on the correct response such as patterns consisting of inversions of characters, extra characters, missing words, extra words, and the like. Pattern mark-up was, for instance, implemented in the foreign language authoring package DASHER developed in the early 1980s (Pusack 1983). In a typical DASHER exercise, the program may instruct the student to change, for instance, the verb tense in a sentence by rewriting the entire sentence. The program then would scan the sentence left to right by performing a simple character-by-character match and informing the student of any character mismatch with a special symbol. While this answer-processing technique allows for less controlled and thus more challenging learning activities, a similar shortcoming as found with simple string-matching algorithms lies in its diagnostic capabilities in that it cannot explain an unanticipated error.

Finally, error anticipation, another popular answer-processing technique of tutorial CALL, is based on a collection of likely errors which commonly is established by means of a contrastive analysis between the L1 and L2 that the system targets in the learner response (see e.g., Liou, Wang, and Hung-Yeh 1992). Each error is associated with a pre-defined error message but the CALL program cannot provide informative feedback for errors which are not anticipated. For instance, if the student answers *to fly* for the activity in example (1) and the error has been anticipated, the system will be able to identify the error and inform the student that the infinitive is wrong because "afraid of" requires a gerund. In contrast, if the error has not been anticipated, the system response will result in a generic feedback message.

Despite relatively high levels of sophistication of the answer processing techniques in some tutorial CALL applications, the main challenges and limitations remain: the underlying algorithms are not scalable because the number of ill-formed responses that students might make to a prompt is infinite and thus cannot be anticipated. For this reason, the computer needs to be capable of a more sophisticated linguistic analysis of student input to detect errors and provide instructional guidance. Broadly speaking, this approach is taken in ICALL, which enriches the L2 grammar learning experience by providing contextual learner feedback and instructional guidance based on the complex linguistic processing of students' textual input.

## ICALL

ICALL relies on natural language processing (NLP), student modeling, and expert systems. NLP techniques model "understanding" of human language by a computer by producing a formal linguistic representation of learner input with the goal to provide informative and error-specific corrective feedback, instructional guidance and scaffolding, and information about the learner's current interlanguage state. The record of this information over time, which is maintained in student profiles, provides the basis for the construction of a student model. Expert systems provide the knowledge base of the facts and rules about the language. They represent a rich source of linguistic knowledge that can guide and scaffold learning processes, enable learners to query this knowledge base during task completion, and serve as a comprehensive reference tool in learner-computer interactions. Most ICALL applications for L2 grammar teaching and learning can broadly be categorized into two main categories: Intelligent Language Tutoring Systems (ILTSs) and language tools.

The article by Weischedel, Voge, and James (1978) is commonly cited as the first publication that reports on an ILTS which the authors developed for L2 German. The main advantage of ILTSs over tutorial CALL applications lies in its contextual corrective feedback in response to learner output. ILTSs place a strong focus on learner-computer interactions (Schulze and Heift 2013). However, these ICALL applications illustrate a different type of interaction and noticing process in the face-to-face interactions and classroom learning, where interactionist SLA originated. ICALL creates opportunities for learner-computer interactions with computer reactions and responses to learner output, error detection, and error-specific feedback, and they draw the learners' attention to a gap between their interlanguage and the target language through salient modified language input. Accordingly, and based on sophisticated NLP technologies, an ILTS identifies and interprets errors as well as correct constructions in learner input and then generates pedagogically appropriate, informative learner feedback by instructing the learner as to the exact location and source of an error. Example (2) illustrates such error-specific, metalinguistic feedback with a sentence-building activity which requires the learner to form a German sentence by providing missing articles and inflections.

(2)  Prompt: Kind/noch/klein/sein
     *child/still/young/to be*

Learner response: *<u>Der</u> Kind ist noch klein.

Correct answer: <u>Das</u> Kind ist noch klein.
*The child is still young.*

If the student incorrectly provides the article *Der* for the noun *Kind*, the ICALL system informs the learner that an error has occurred with the article of the neuter noun. In addition, an ILTS is capable of distinguishing among different types of errors. For instance, if the student misspells a word (e.g., "Kint" instead of "Kind"), the system also instructs the learner accordingly. Unlike tutorial CALL, ICALL is able to provide appropriate feedback to a large range of unanticipated errors that the student may make.

Examples of ILTSs that are used in regular L2 curricula are *E-Tutor* (Heift 2010) for L2 German, *Robo-Sensei* (Nagata 2009) for L2 Japanese, and *Tagarela* (Amaral and Meurers 2011) for L2 Portuguese. These three ICALL systems present materials to students in the form of an electronic textbook. As the students complete the exercises, the system provides feedback on spelling, morphological, syntactic, and semantic errors for L2 grammar practice. Due to the more sophisticated NLP analysis of ILTSs, their learning environments and activity types are also less restricted than those found in textbooks and especially than those found in tutorial CALL. An ILTS may also reflect an inductive approach to teaching and learning L2 grammar and emphasize peer collaboration and interaction during a goal-oriented CALL activity (see Thorne 2003). For instance, Dickinson et al. (2008) designed an ICALL system for teaching particle usage for first-year L2 Korean learners embedded in a CMC environment in which dyads engage in an information-gap activity. Learners are presented with a spot-the-differences task of two different cross-sections of a house and must identify similarities and differences in the actions and locations of family members shown in the two versions. The dyads construct Korean sentences by dragging words from a word bank and can obtain corrective feedback from the ICALL application on the grammaticality of their sentences before submitting them to their peer in a chat box. In contrast to explicit grammar teaching, however, the emphasis and goal of the activity is to provide an authentic, communicative task and the decision to check the grammaticality of their message with the ICALL application is left up to the learner.

In addition to ILTSs, a variety of ICALL language tools have also been developed to assist learners with their L2 grammar. In these environments, the computer takes on the role of a *tool* (Levy 1997) by empowering the learner to use or understand language and by enhancing L2 grammar awareness with strategies that highlight the salience of language categories and forms (Sharwood Smith 1993). Schmidt's (1990) Noticing Hypothesis underpins some of this ICALL work by recognizing the role of consciousness in L2 learning and drawing the learners' attention to salient grammatical forms. For instance, Meurers et al. (2010) designed WERTi, an NLP architecture which provides visually enhanced versions of web pages. Language input enhancement is achieved by highlighting and annotating certain grammatical forms (e.g., determiners, prepositions) that generally pose difficulties for ESL learners. These grammatical forms appear in texts that learners freely select from the internet. Similarly, *The Microsoft Research ESL Assistant* developed by Gamon et al. (2009) is a web-based proof-reading tool designed primarily for L1 speakers of East-Asian languages studying ESL. The system targets a variety of syntactic, morphological, and lexical selection errors. With the goal to stimulate language awareness, *The ESL Assistant* displays correction suggestions by allowing users to explore and compare their language production with real-world examples it found on the internet.

In addition to these more comprehensive ICALL tools, students may also have contingent access to online dictionaries (e.g., Hamel 2010), grammar, and spell checkers (e.g., Burston 2001; Cowan et al. 2014), and morphological analyzers (e.g., ten Hacken and Tschichold 2001; Wood 2011) which generate context-sensitive inflectional paradigms (e.g., Heift 2010) that assist learners with their language learning activities.

## Corpora and Data-driven Learning

Corpora, or large electronic collections of texts, have been applied for the purposes of language learning and teaching since their emergence in the late 1960s (Chambers 2005). Such applications can be of both indirect and direct nature. In indirect applications, corpus-based research studies have informed the development of new teaching materials: reference grammars and textbooks that accurately reflect actual language usage and that use attested and not invented examples. Over 25 years ago, however, priorities in the use of corpus research for language teaching expanded to include direct applications, although the origins of such applications are in the 1980s (Higgins and Johns 1984; Johns 1986). Johns (1991) singled out direct corpus-based applications as a distinct language teaching and research direction and called it DDL, adopting a term from computer science. Since then, the pedagogical variations that can be developed based on DDL have been expanding continuously (see Boulton and Pérez-Paredes 2014; Römer 2011 for overviews).

Theoretically, DDL is consistent with Usage-Based Grammar theory (e.g., Robinson and Ellis 2008) as we know it today, namely with its four principles. According to the first principle, languages are learned from exposure to specific linguistic exemplars in the environment that leads learners to gradually make generalizations and create linguistic rules. The second principle is that grammar and the lexicon are inextricably intertwined. Accordingly, in most DDL interventions, the teaching of grammar is integrated with the teaching of the lexicon and the main object of study is referred to as "lexico-grammar" (Chambers 2005; Conrad 2000). The third principle is what Conrad (2000) described as "a new view of grammar" (558) that takes into account choices that learners make among possible grammatical alternatives rather than purely formal accuracy. The fourth principle is the primacy of rich and salient target language input for language learning. Corpora are potential sources of rich language input as they allow teachers and learners to obtain large numbers of examples of target constructions (if the selected corpus is representative of these constructions). Furthermore, using concordancer tools for retrieving corpus search results makes the language input salient. This visual salience, or input enhancement, is realized through concordance lines, or stacked text excerpts with the search words highlighted and centered. For example, the search string *depend\** entered in the Michigan Corpus of Academic Spoken English (MICASE) (Simpson et al. 2002) concordancer interface yields 598 matches, an excerpt from which is presented in Figure 3.1. The visual highlighting of the words containing the stem *depend* facilitate analysis of usage patterns. Among other things, the learners may infer from this analysis that *depend* may function as the stem of verbs, participles, nouns, and adjectives; that the forms of the verb *to depend* are most frequently followed by the preposition *on* and sometimes *upon*, and that the noun *dependency* can be followed by the preposition *between*. Furthermore, by clicking on marginal links provided in each concordance line (not shown in Figure 3.1), the learners can see the whole transcript containing the line as well as contextual information (speaker ethnographic information, academic event type, etc.).

Owing to these characteristics, corpora lend themselves to an inductive approach to language teaching and learning, in which learners more or less independently engage in "pattern-hunting" and "pattern-defining" (Kennedy and Miceli 2010, 31) with the teacher assisting them as a facilitator. Furthermore, DDL has also been associated with learner autonomy: "the learner's psychological relation to the process and content of learning—a capacity for detachment, critical reflection, decision-making, and independent action" (Little 1991, 45). This emphasis on independent discovery, serendipitous learning, and learner autonomy has been reflected in metaphors like "researcher" and "observer" that have been used to describe a learner engaged in DDL. The number of resources providing guides and models for specific DDL activities for teachers and learners (e.g., Reppen 2010) has been recently growing, although still is insufficient (Römer 2011).

Although corpora have sometimes been referred to as research and teaching "tools," they are rather repositories of texts, which need to be distinguished from software tools that are required for their exploration (Anthony 2013). The corpora most frequently used for DDL purposes are large English native speaker corpora such as the British National Corpus (BNC) and the Corpus of Contemporary American English (COCA). However, increasingly more DDL studies have been reporting on the utilization of specialized corpora (Bloch 2009), learner language corpora (Cotos, 2014; Granger 2003), and corpora in languages other than English (Kennedy and Miceli 2010; Vyatkina 2013, 2016a, 2016b).

As far as corpus search and analysis tools are concerned, large online corpora are typically equipped with a number of built-in software tools that can be used either with free access or with the publisher's permission; in contrast, for utilizing locally designed corpora, researchers and teachers have to rely on external software or design their own tools (Anthony 2013). Tools beyond concordancers (see Figure 3.1) include annotation programs that allow for tagging raw corpus data for abstract grammatical categories and are thus especially valuable for DDL of L2 grammar (e.g., lemmatizers, part-of-speech (POS) taggers, syntactic parsers) and statistical analysis and visualization programs (e.g., key word lists, ranked word frequency lists, word association strength measures, distribution plots). For example, the search string *prep.ALL* in the "Chart" interface of COCA (Davies 2008), yields a chart showing how all prepositions are distributed among different genres/registers (Figure 3.2). It is revealing to see that prepositions are used with the highest frequency in academic texts and with the lowest frequency in spoken texts. This finding confirms that academic texts are characterized by a "nominal" style (with a high frequency of prepositional phrases) as opposed to spoken texts (see Biber 1988). An encouraging development is that several recent DDL publications have presented new online corpus-based grammar resources (concordancers and other tools), some of which are available to other teachers and researchers (e.g., Bloch 2009; Hegelheimer 2006).

| | depends | upon what you're trying to predict, and how you're gonna use the information. but no th |
| endent and this one is also dependent this one is also | dependent | right? oh. so i mean th- th- |
| better to take a bunch of samples from the lab rather than to do a pump test. so it | depends | on the retirement benefits that i get in each of those years... okay so notice that there's |
| LAUGH um... and, what's assumed is that my utility in those years | depends | on the aphasia. um, if in my uncle's case yes he actually was educated in a school for t |
| cate with like sign language. | depends | on how well integrated your thoughts and feelings are over time. the more psychologica |
| , there's no, hard and fast yes or no fact about you who you are, it's, who you are | depending | on where students fall and what your G-S-Is tell me, about um, about how you guys per |
| whether ninety-two or ninety-three percent ends up being an A just | depending | on what other news breaks. okay? so take a, just very quickly read through some of the |
| e top story on the online edition, when they start the day but of course it'll change | depends | on, the env- cell environment |
| because, you can't just tell it | dependency | between the two so you have to find to see if every path between two nodes is indepen |
| re. so, if this is independent but this is still_ then there is a | depends | on whether you're, already a very motivated individual, or whether you need, like exten |
| that i don't need and i think it detracts from learning sometimes, so i think it really | dependence | network. now these circles throughout the network represent the tasks or the resources |
| and we have to form a supply chain. um, so let me explain the portions of the task | dependent | effects. PAUSE WHILE ERASING BOARD |
| s an experiment that i think is pretty cool to introduce you to a concept of dosage- | | |

Figure 3.1

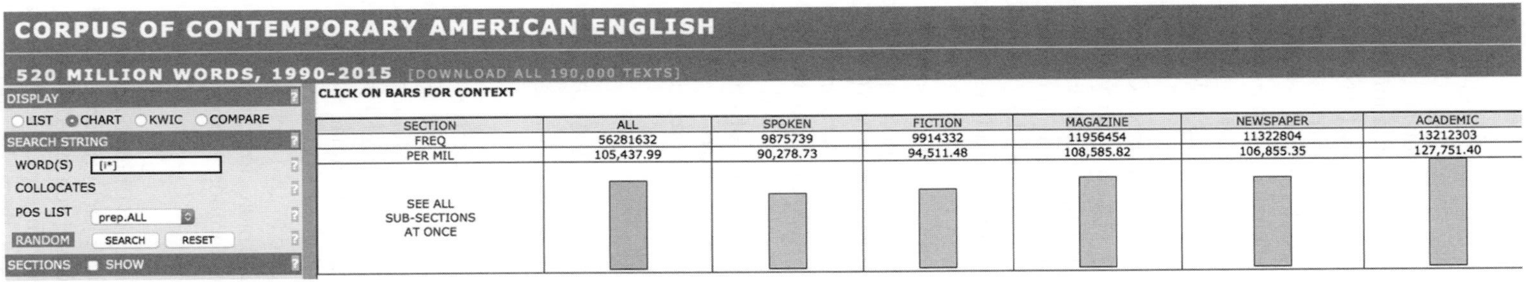
CORPUS OF CONTEMPORARY AMERICAN ENGLISH
520 MILLION WORDS, 1990-2015 [DOWNLOAD ALL 190,000 TEXTS]
DISPLAY
LIST CHART KWIC COMPARE
SEARCH STRING
WORD(S) [i*]
COLLOCATES
POS LIST prep.ALL
RANDOM SEARCH RESET
SECTIONS SHOW
CLICK ON BARS FOR CONTEXT
SECTION ALL SPOKEN FICTION MAGAZINE NEWSPAPER ACADEMIC
FREQ 56281632 9875739 9914332 11956454 11322804 13212303
PER MIL 105,437.99 90,278.73 94,511.48 108,585.82 106,855.35 127,751.40
SEE ALL SUB-SECTIONS AT ONCE

Figure 3.2

## Computer-mediated communication

The first attempts to use CMC technologies for language teaching purposes, primarily the asynchronous (ACMC) email and the synchronous (SCMC) chat, were made in the 1990s, and the field has been rapidly expanding ever since. Such pedagogical applications are grounded in theories that consider interpersonal communication a crucial driving force in L2 development: the interactionist theory (Chapelle 1998) and the sociocultural theory (Thorne 2003). Furthermore, CMC has been shown to have many features similar to face-to-face language classroom interactions such as clarification requests and feedback, but also some added benefits such as increased participation and improved learner attitudes (Chun 1994; Kern 1995). Additionally, due to its text-based nature, CMC provides more planning time and more monitoring and revision opportunities to learners as compared with face-to-face communication.

The first studies that reported on the potential of CMC for teaching of L2 grammar were informed by the interactionist theory (e.g., Salaberry 2000). They showed that L2 learners incidentally focused on language form during meaning-oriented CMC exchanges with their peers when communication broke down due to grammatical errors. Such incidents were manifested in so-called Language-Related Episodes (LREs), defined in face-to-face communication as "any part of a dialogue where the students talk about the language they are producing, question their language use, or correct themselves or others" (Swain and Lapkin 1998, 326). LREs could include corrective feedback provided by peers which can be explicit (if it includes an overt signal that an error has occurred) or implicit (without such a signal). Both explicit and implicit feedback can lead to uptake (error correction) by learners if noticed, understood, and accepted by them. Although such episodes occur virtually in any peer-to-peer L2 exchanges (both SCMC and ACMC), many teachers-researchers choose to pair up lower and higher proficiency learners or learners and native speakers as such configurations have been shown to trigger more negotiation of both meaning and form. The following excerpt from an SCMC exchange between two Persian learners of English—one with a higher L2 proficiency (H) and one with a lower proficiency (L)—exemplifies such an interaction (Shekary and Tahririan 2006, 562):

Far (L):      I mean I can at least be <u>familiar to this extensive major</u>.
Fatem (H):  <u>isn't it better to say</u> <u>familiar with</u>?
Far (L):      all right, familiar with

In this excerpt, Fatem (H) suggests an explicit correction of Far's error, and Far (L) accepts this correction in the next move, showing an example of uptake.

Despite this frequent occurrence of LREs in CMC, most of them revolve around lexical rather than grammatical targets (Blake 2000; Shekary and Tahririan 2006). This fact prompted many educators wishing to use these tasks for grammar teaching to add some planned focus on grammar to primarily meaning-based interactional CMC tasks. In peer-to-peer exchanges with such added focus, learners are instructed to give each other feedback on grammar in general or on specific grammatical forms. Furthermore, instructors can themselves participate in CMC interventions, acting as expert communication partners and providing corrective feedback to learners, as in the following SCMC example from Samburskiy and Quah (2014, 166):

**Learner:**  As i [sic] understand your stay in China has affected you. I have never tasted Chines [sic] cuisine but I know that it [sic] very specific and exotic. They cook fried worms, beetles, rats … Is it true? Do [sic] you tasted this?
**Teacher:**  Well, they do eat some exotic things in China. **Have** I tasted this? No, but I knew people who ate grubs, dragonflies, and things like that.

In this example, the teacher corrects the learner's grammatical error (verb tense) using a recast, a type of implicit corrective feedback, by repeating the learner's utterance with target-like grammar. To make the recast more salient to the learner, the teacher highlights the corrected form. From the interactionist perspective, a recast is less intrusive than explicit correction because it does not disrupt the communication flow while still drawing the learner's attention to form.

Pedagogical approaches informed by the sociocultural theory (SCT) framework have also capitalized on the benefits of interpersonal collaboration for language learning, yet from a different angle. In these approaches, language learning is conceived of as a socially-situated and goal-directed activity mediated by culturally embedded tools such as technology (see Lantolf and Thorne 2006; Thorne 2003). One such social tool that "leads learners to work collaboratively towards the achievement of a common goal" (Elola and Oskoz 2011, 180) is wikis, a web-based environment in which several authors jointly construct a text. The tool allows all authors to add, change, and delete text as well as documents all previous drafts and tracks all made changes (see Elola and Oskoz 2011, 205–206 for a list of available wiki tools). Wikis have been shown to promote attention to both global and local language aspects (including grammar) and to encourage revisions and error correction. Furthermore, educators who work within the SCT paradigm have been especially interested not only in inter*personal* but also inter*cultural* (also called telecollaborative) exchanges and have organized CMC (email, chat, audio, and video conferencing) between language learners from different countries. L2 grammar in SCT-informed pedagogical interventions has predominantly been targeted not as an end goal but as a means for conveying specific social actions and as a focus of peer-to-peer mediation in the zone of proximal development (Belz and Vyatkina 2008; Darhower 2014; Oskoz 2009; Thorne 2003; Zeng and Takatsuka 2009).

# Research on the use of technologies for L2 grammar teaching and learning

The research that has been conducted in the L2 grammar teaching and learning environments described in the previous sections is fairly diverse not only due to the different technologies involved but also due to the distinct theoretical and pedagogical approaches that underlie them. Two topics that have received particular attention, however, are corrective feedback in ICALL and CMC, and learner autonomy in DDL. Studies of corrective feedback in ICALL and CMC investigate both explicit and implicit grammar teaching approaches by exploring ways in which learners not only engage with the computer but also with their peers. DDL research examines the degrees of learner autonomy that are conducive to the learning of different linguistic features and skills by also considering distinct levels of L2 proficiency. The following sections examine the respective research carried out with a variety of learners in distinct learning conditions.

## *Feedback for L2 grammar*

The provision of feedback on grammar is a central topic in L2 grammar teaching and learning, and accordingly, an area of research that has been pursued in both ICALL and CMC. Research on these two distinct, yet complementary environments focuses on learner-computer and interpersonal interactions, respectively, by exploiting the strengths of different technology-mediated pedagogical approaches in providing explicit and implicit feedback for both form and meaning-based learning activities.

## Feedback in ICALL

In view of the powerful capacity of ICALL systems for generating error-specific feedback to learners, researchers examine the effectiveness of different types of corrective feedback on learners' L2 grammar performance to determine its impact on learning outcomes and/or learner-computer interactions. One of the early ICALL studies, for instance, investigated different feedback types for learning Japanese particles and found that error-specific metalinguistic feedback (see (2)) that explained the functions and semantic relations of nominal relations in a sentence was more effective than generic, traditional feedback (e.g., *wrong, try again!*) (Nagata 1993). A number of studies followed (e.g., Bowles 2005; Heift 2004; Heift and Rimrott 2008; Lado et al. 2014; Murphy 2007; Nagata 1996; Petersen 2010; Pujolà 2002; Rosa and Leow 2004) that generally supported the benefits of error-specific feedback in a CALL environment. However, a few studies also showed little or no advantage of metalinguistic feedback. For instance, Moreno (2007) investigated the effects of metalinguistic feedback compared to feedback that only signaled whether the student input was right or wrong. While both types led to an increase in scores on the immediate posttest, feedback without metalinguistic information was superior on the delayed posttest (see also Sanz and Morgan-Short 2004). Similarly, Kregar (2011) examined the effects of text enhancement and metalinguistic feedback on the acquisition of L2 Spanish verbal aspect and found that metalinguistic feedback was less effective than text enhancement.

In addition to these studies which investigated a *reactive* focus on form, that is, feedback that the ICALL system provides in response to learner input, a few studies have also examined *preemptive* focus on form which provides learners with relevant metalinguistic information before difficulties arise. The goal here is to reduce potential frustration by marking critical features in the language task to assist learners in task completion (Ellis, Basturkmen, and Loewen 2001). According to Ellis (1993), preemptive focus on form also assists in providing learners with explicit knowledge which helps improve performance through monitoring and facilitates acquisition through noticing. Heift (2013), for instance, investigated the impact of preemptive focus on form which consisted of exercise-specific grammar and vocabulary hints that the CALL system provided when students started an exercise. She showed that for different proficiency levels (beginner and early intermediate) of adult learners of German, preemptive focus on form was significantly more effective than not providing any assistance before students attempted to complete a task. Furthermore, according to retrospective interviews with some of the study participants, preemptive focus on form helped them avoid some errors thus also leading to a more positive learning experience.

While the research above focused on learning outcomes by studying the effectiveness of different feedback types, some studies have also considered learner strategies with respect to corrective feedback in CALL. For instance, Brandl (1995), studying L2 learners of German, found that lower-achieving learners, as determined by an initial placement test of reading comprehension, had a more limited set of strategies for processing feedback than learners of higher-achievement levels. Similarly, a study by Vinther (2005) investigated the difference in learner strategies employed by low- and high-achieving Danish university students of English as a foreign language. Her study confirmed Brandl's (1995) results by showing that high-performing students were more likely to make use of cognitive strategies throughout program use while lower-performing students employed only a few cognitive strategies, favoring affective strategies more, at least at the beginning of program use.

Some studies also examined learner error correction behavior in response to distinct feedback types thus focusing on the learning process as opposed to learning outcomes. The range of possible reactions and/or responses to corrective feedback is generally referred to as learner uptake. Research from face-to-face instruction (e.g., Lyster 2007) proposes that successful learner uptake is a good predictor of learning. Even in instances where no learning takes place at a particular moment, the research suggests that learners notice the feedback and process it, thereby increasing the likelihood of learning. As a result, researchers tend to view learner uptake as facilitative of L2 acquisition and examine its role when teaching L2 grammar with technology. For instance, Heift's (2002) study revealed that, when students were provided with error-specific feedback, the majority of them (85%) sought to correct errors on their own for most of the time instead of looking up a correct answer made available to them in her ICALL system (see also Hegelheimer and Chapelle 2000).

Overall, this line of research has shown that students generally benefit from explicit, metalinguistic feedback because they subsequently perform better on particular target language structures and/or because students' grammatical awareness is subsequently raised. Nevertheless, there are conflating factors such as feedback amount and timing, or more generally, the long-term impact of CALL feedback on L2 learning that make the research results less conclusive than one might hope and require further investigation.

## Feedback in computer-mediated communication

In CMC tasks for grammar learning, the feedback on learners' errors comes not from the computer but from other interlocutors and is manifested in LREs. To investigate the effectiveness of this feedback for L2 grammar learning from the interactionist perspective, researchers study (1) what specific CMC formats and pedagogical tasks are more conducive to grammar-focused LREs; (2) whether grammar-focused LREs lead to L2 grammar gains and whether these gains are higher in CMC than in face-to-face learning environments; and (3) what CMC feedback types lead to higher L2 grammar gains.

In the first research strand, most studies converge in their finding that vocabulary triggers more LREs than grammar in CMC interactions (e.g., Blake 2000). However, this finding holds true primarily for unmoderated interactions between peers. In contrast, both teachers and those learners who are instructed to provide corrective feedback in CMC, tend to focus on grammar either on a par with vocabulary (Bower and Kawaguchi 2011; Sotillo 2005) or even more (Smith 2009; Ware and O'Dowd 2008). Furthermore, ACMC has been found to trigger more LREs, including grammar LREs, than SCMC and within ACMC, wikis appear to be superior to forums for both peer and self-corrections (Bower and Kawaguchi 2011; Elola and Oskoz 2010). As far as specific feedback types are concerned, novice and native speakers have been found to provide more implicit and indirect feedback, whereas experts, especially non-native speakers, more explicit and direct feedback (Bower and Kawaguchi 2011; Oskoz 2009; Sotillo 2005).

The second strand has explored the CMC effectiveness for L2 grammar learning by measuring learning outcomes. Several studies have found higher accuracy gains following SCMC rather than face-to-face instructor-provided feedback focused on specific grammatical forms, such as Spanish tense and aspect morphology (Salaberry 2000) and Turkish noun morphology (Yilmaz 2012). In the context of peer-to-peer CMC, Stockwell and Harrington (2003) showed overall syntactic improvement in L2 Japanese learners' writing after a five-week-long ACMC exchange with native speakers. Hirotani (2009) also investigated L2 Japanese learners' development and showed that the SCMC group outperformed the ACMC group in accuracy but underperformed in syntactic complexity. Other studies focused on immediate learner uptake following LREs in CMC and found it to be fairly successful at up to 70% (Bower and Kawaguchi 2011; Zeng and Takatsuka 2009). Notably, Smith (2012) extended this line of research by correlating learner production outcomes with noticing. The learners noticed approximately the same amount of intensive SCMC recasts for all linguistic categories (measured with an eye-tracking methodology), whereas lexical and syntactic recasts triggered more learner recall than did morphological recasts. Smith also showed that the amount of both online and offline noticing predicted improvement on posttest performance, which lends support to using CMC feedback for L2 teaching purposes.

In the third strand, researchers have compared the effects of different feedback types on grammar learning. Vinagre and Muñoz (2011) showed that metalinguistic feedback led to more successful uptake than direct corrections in new pieces of writing in intercultural peer-to-peer ACMC exchanges. Results from studies that measured learner gains after receiving explicit and implicit expert SCMC feedback on specific grammar features vary across target features and learner populations. Yilmaz (2012) found that explicit feedback provided on noun morphology to learners with no knowledge of Turkish was more effective than implicit feedback (recasts). Similarly, Sauro (2009) found that only metalinguistic feedback but not recasts on English articles provided to advanced learners was significantly better than no feedback. On the contrary, Loewen and Erlam (2006) found no feedback effect and no difference between the feedback types for beginning L2 English learners' acquisition of past tense morphology. The discrepancies in findings can be explained by variation in the target features and research designs. Furthermore, socioculturally-informed studies have provided insight into the versatility of peer-to-peer scaffolding patterns as well as learner preferences regarding self-corrections and peer-corrections (Darhower 2014; Oskoz 2009; Ware and O'Dowd 2008; Zeng and Takatsuka 2009).

To summarize, CMC has been shown to be effective for L2 grammar learning in both expert-to-learner and peer-to-peer intercultural and intracultural exchanges due to the frequent occurrence of LREs, enhanced visibility of feedback, and extended time for feedback processing. In a rare meta-analysis study, Ziegler (2013) confirmed that SCMC had a small yet significant advantage over face-to-face interaction for L2 grammar gains. Although results regarding feedback types that work best in CMC exchanges are less conclusive, all researchers concur that for CMC feedback to be beneficial, it needs to be based on well-structured tasks that are tailored to specific CMC formats, learner populations, and grammar features.

## *Learner autonomy in DDL of L2 grammar*

Language learning with technology has long been associated with higher degrees of autonomy, which is considered beneficial for learners as it prepares them for life-long learning beyond the classroom (Warschauer 2002). Given that DDL, by definition, is "a language-learning environment focusing on learner autonomy and discovery learning" (Chambers 2005, 120), it is not surprising that most DDL research has addressed the construct of learner autonomy. Specifically, this research has explored what degrees of autonomy are conducive to the learning of what specific linguistic features and skills, at what levels of L2 proficiency, and under what conditions. Furthermore, whereas the benefits of corpora for lexical learning were recognized long ago, some scholars have recently argued that DDL can be equally conducive to grammar learning and even especially facilitative at lower-proficiency levels as it requires less metalinguistic knowledge than explicit grammar teaching (Boulton 2010; Estling Vannestål and Lindquist 2007). In regard to pedagogical designs, DDL studies can be subdivided into hands-on (more autonomous, direct, computer-based) and hands-off (less autonomous, indirect, paper-based) applications (see Boulton 2010 for an overview).

Much L2 grammar research on hands-on DDL has been exploratory and demonstrated by way of case studies the potential of learner use of corpora for grammar consultation (Chambers 2005; Estling Vannestål and Lindquist 2007; Kennedy and Miceli 2010). The number of quantitative studies has been small but recently growing. Such studies have explored whether learning outcomes improve after DDL activities or have compared the outcomes of DDL as a mostly inductive teaching method with those of more traditional deductive teaching methods. All L2 grammar studies had university students as participants and most of them focused on teaching English. One of the first studies was Gaskell and Cobb (2004) who found that concordance searches helped intermediate English learners significantly reduce the number of writing errors in some categories (e.g., word order, pronoun use) but not others. This result is in line with a recent study by Tono, Satake, and Miura (2014), who found that guided corpus consultations helped high-proficiency, but not low-proficiency, learners to successfully self-correct omission and addition but not misformation errors in their revised essays. In contrast to the findings from hands-on DDL studies, research on hands-off DDL with printed concordance lines reported positive learning outcomes for both high- and low-proficiency learners. Moreover, whereas Tian's (2005) higher- and lower-proficiency groups equally improved after hands-off DDL instruction, Vyatkina (2016a) found that it was especially beneficial to lower-proficiency L2 German learners and was more effective for them than traditional deductive instruction. In contrast, most studies have failed to detect a significant advantage over traditional deductive methods for teaching L2 grammar to intermediate learners (Boulton 2010; Tian 2005; Vyatkina 2016a). Finally, studies that compared hands-on and hands-off DDL found them equally effective for teaching selected grammatical targets to intermediate learners of English (Boulton 2012) and German (Vyatkina, 2016b).

Finally, a number of recent studies have pinpointed specific principles of DDL that facilitate L2 grammar learning. Frankenberg-García (2014) confirmed that richness of language input (multiple concordance lines) is a crucial factor for the effectiveness of paper-based DDL; Cotos (2014) showed that DDL tasks based on comparison of native and learner corpora (consisting of texts similar to the native texts the learners used as models) are superior to DDL work on native corpora only; whereas Smart (2014) demonstrated that guided inductive instruction is better than three other conditions: non-guided induction, deductive instruction with corpus examples, and non-DDL deductive instruction.

To summarize, DDL has been shown to be effective (leading to significant learning gains) and efficient (more effective than deductive teaching methods), including for L2 grammar learning, as demonstrated by a substantial effect size in Cobb and Boulton's (2015) meta-analysis of available quantitative studies. However, the research has also convincingly demonstrated that for reaching positive outcomes, the principle of learner autonomy needs to be applied judiciously progressing from less to more autonomous tasks depending on the learner population and instructional context. Furthermore, any L2 grammar DDL needs to be *guided* by a teacher or tutorial program. Additionally, research has demonstrated advantages of problem-solving DDL tasks and the potential of using learner and parallel corpora for DDL grammar instruction. Last but not least, most researchers who have explored learner DDL perceptions, found those to be generally favorable, which provides yet another argument in support of this CALL method for teaching and learning L2 grammar.

# Conclusion

This chapter outlined the variety of technologies teachers and researchers have explored for the teaching and learning of L2 grammar each of which reflects and promotes distinct affordances including language input, interaction, feedback, access to extensive language data, and opportunities for collaboration in different learning environments. Unlike traditional L2 grammar learning and teaching, newer technologies are not limited to the traditional dichotomy of implicit and explicit teaching approaches. They also place a strong focus on both learner-computer and person-to-person interactions by allowing learners to explore authentic language and promoting independent discovery and learner autonomy. Clearly, these technological changes have also had a direct impact on how L2 grammar learning and teaching is viewed by many language teachers. At the same time, and as supported by the studies cited above, language instructors are central to the successful realization of these new opportunities and affordances of L2 grammar learning and teaching independent of the particular technologies used. The involvement of instructors is crucial as they can trigger, stimulate, monitor, and guide online as well as offline activities conducive to L2 grammar teaching and learning. As a result of the pervasive use of technology, the way we teach grammar in the L2 classroom has been changing and therefore teachers need to be able to use technology-based approaches and materials with the goal to assist their learners.

# REFERENCES

Amaral, Luiz, and Detmar Meurers. 2011. "On Using Intelligent Computer-Assisted Language Learning in Real-Life Foreign Language Teaching and Learning." *ReCALL*, 23, no. 1: 4–24.

Anthony, Laurence. 2013. "A Critical Look at Software Tools in Corpus Linguistics." *Linguistic Research*, 30, no. 2: 141–161.

Arneil, Steward, and Martin Holmes. 1999. "Juggling Hot Potatoes: Decisions and Compromises in Creating Authoring Tools for the Web." *ReCALL*, 11, no. 2: 12–19.

Belz, Julie A., and Nina Vyatkina. 2008. "The Pedagogical Mediation of a Developmental Learner Corpus for Classroom-Based Language Instruction," *Language Learning & Technology*, 12, no. 3: 33–52.

Biber, Doug. 1988. *Variation Across Speech and Writing*. Cambridge: Cambridge University Press.

Blake, Robert. 2000. "Computer Mediated Communication: A Window on L2 Spanish Interlanguage." *Language Learning & Technology*, 4, no. 1: 120–136.

Bloch, Joel. 2009. "The Design of an Online Concordancing Program for Teaching about Reporting Verbs." *Language Learning & Technology*, 13, no. 1: 59–78.

Boulton, Alex. 2010. "Data-Driven Learning: Taking the Computer Out of the Equation." *Language Learning*, 60, no. 3: 534–572.

Boulton, Alex. 2012. "Hands-on/hands-off: Alternative Approaches to Data-driven Learning." In *Input, Process and Product: Developments in Teaching and Language Corpora*, edited by James Thomas and Alex Boulton, 152–168. Brno: Masaryk University Press.

Boulton, Alex, and Pascual Pérez-Paredes. 2014. "Editorial: Researching New Uses of Corpora for Language Teaching and Learning." *ReCALL*, 26, no. 2: 121–127.

Bower, Jack, and Satomi Kawaguchi. 2011. "Negotiation of Meaning and Corrective Feedback in Japanese/English eTandem." *Language Learning & Technology*, 15, no. 1: 41–71.

Bowles, Melissa. 2005. Effects of Verbalization Condition and Type of Feedback on L2 Development in a CALL Task. PhD dissertation, Georgetown University.

Brandl, Klaus. 1995. "Strong and Weak Students' Preferences for Error Feedback Options and Responses." *Modern Language Journal*, 79, no. 2: 194–211.

Burston, Jack. 1989. "Towards Better Tutorial CALL: A Matter of Intelligent Control." *CALICO Journal*, 6, no. 4: 75–89.

Burston, Jack. 2001. "Exploiting the Potential of a Computer-Based Grammar Checker in Conjunction with Self-Monitoring Strategies with Advanced Level Students of French." *CALICO Journal*, 18, no. 3: 499–515.

Chambers, Angela. 2005. "Integrating Corpus Consultation in Language Studies." *Language Learning & Technology*, 9, no. 2: 111–125.

Chapelle, Carol. 1998. "Multimedia CALL: Lessons to be Learned from Research on Instructed SLA." *Language Learning & Technology*, 2, no. 1: 21–39.

Chun, Dorothy. 1994. "Using Computer Networking to Facilitate the Acquisition of Interactive Competence." *System*, 22, no. 1: 17–31.

Cobb, Thomas, and Alex Boulton. 2015. "Classroom Applications of Corpus Analysis." In *The Cambridge Handbook of English Corpus Linguistics*, edited by Douglas Biber and Randy Reppen, 478–497. Cambridge: Cambridge University Press.

Conrad, Susan. 2000. "Will Corpus Linguistics Revolutionize Grammar Teaching in the 21st Century?" *TESOL Quarterly*, 34, no. 3: 548–559.

Cotos, Elena. 2014. "Enhancing Writing Pedagogy with Learner Corpus Data." *ReCALL*, 26, no. 2: 202–224.

Cowan, Ron, Jinhee Choo, and Gabseon Sunny Lee. 2014. "ICALL for Improving Korean L2 Writers' Ability to Edit Grammatical Errors." *Language Learning & Technology*, 18, no. 3: 193–207.

Darhower, Mark. 2014. "Synchronous Computer-Mediated Dynamic Assessment: A Case Study of L2 Spanish Past Narration." *CALICO Journal*, 31, no. 2: 221–243.

Davies, Mark. 2008. *The Corpus of Contemporary American English: 450 Million Words, 1990–Present*. Accessed February 15, 2016. http://corpus.byu.edu/coca/

Dickinson, Markus, Soojeong Eom, Yunkyoung Kang, Chong Min Lee, and Rebecca Sachs. 2008. "A Balancing Act: How Can Intelligent Computer-generated Feedback Be Provided in Learner-to-Learner Interactions?" *Computer Assisted Language Learning*, 21, no. 4: 369–382.

Ellis, Rod. 1993. "The Structural Syllabus and Second Language Acquisition." *TESOL Quarterly*, 27, no. 1: 91–113.

Ellis, Rod, Helen Basturkmen, and Shawn Loewen. 2001. "Preemptive Focus on Form in the ESL Classroom." *TESOL Quarterly*, 35, no. 3: 407–432.

Elola, Idoia, and Ana Oskoz. 2010. "Collaborative Writing: Fostering Foreign Language and Writing Conventions Development." *Language Learning & Technology*, 14, no. 3: 30–49.

Elola, Idoia, and Ana Oskoz. 2011. "Writing Between the Lines: Acquiring the Presentational Mode through Social Tools." In *Present and Future Promises of CALL: From Theory and Research to New Directions in Language Teaching*, edited by Nike Arnold and Lara Ducate, 171–210. San Marcos, TX: CALICO.

Estling Vannestål, Maria, and Hans Lindquist. 2007. "Learning English Grammar with a Corpus: Experimenting with Concordancing in a University Grammar Course." *ReCALL*, 19, no. 3: 329–350.

Frankenberg-García, Ana. 2014. "The Use of Corpus Examples for Language Comprehension and Production." *ReCALL*, 26, no. 2: 128–146.

Gamon, Michael, Claudia Leacock, Chris Brockett, William Dolan, Jianfeng Gao, Dmitriy Belenko, and Alexandre Klementiev. 2009. "Using Statistical Techniques and Web Search to Correct ESL Errors." *CALICO Journal*, 26, no. 3: 491–511.

Gaskell, Delian, and Thomas Cobb. 2004. "Can Learners Use Concordance Feedback for Writing Errors?" *System*, 32, no. 3: 301–319.

Gass, Susan. 1997. *Input, Interaction and the Second Language Learner*. Mahwah, NJ: Lawrence Erlbaum.

Granger, Sylviane. 2003. "Error-tagged Learner Corpora and CALL: A Promising Synergy." *CALICO Journal*, 20, no. 3: 465–480.

Hamel, Marie-Josée. 2010. "Prototype d'un Dictionnaire Électronique de Reformulation pour Apprenants Avancés de Français Langue Seconde." *Cahiers de l'APLIUT XXIX*, 1: 73–82.

Hegelheimer, Volker. 2006. "Helping ESL Writers through a Multimodal, Corpus-based, Online Grammar Resource." *CALICO Journal*, 24, no. 1: 5–31.

Hegelheimer, Volker, and Carol Chapelle. 2000. "Methodological Issues in Research on Learner–Computer Interactions in CALL." *Language Learning & Technology*, 4, no. 1: 41–59.

Heift, Trude. 2002. "Learner Control and Error Correction in ICALL: Browsers, Peekers and Adamants." *CALICO Journal*, 19, no. 3: 295–313.

Heift, Trude. 2004. "Corrective Feedback and Learner Uptake in CALL." *ReCALL*, 16, no. 2: 416–431.

Heift, Trude. 2010. "Developing an Intelligent Tutor." *CALICO Journal*, 27, no. 3: 443–459.

Heift, Trude. 2013. "Preemptive Feedback in CALL." In *Interaction in Diverse Educational Settings*, edited by Alison Mackey and Kim McDonough, 189–207. Philadelphia: John Benjamins.

Heift, Trude, and Anne Rimrott. 2008. "Learner Responses to Corrective Feedback for Spelling Errors in CALL." *System*, 36, no. 2: 196–213.

Higgins, John, and Tim Johns. 1984. *Computers in Language Learning*. London: Collins.

Hirotani, Maki. 2009. "Synchronous versus Asynchronous CMC and Transfer to Japanese Oral Performance." *CALICO Journal*, 26, no. 2: 413–438.

Hubbard, Phil, and Claire B. Siskin. 2004. "Another Look at Tutorial CALL." *ReCALL*, 16, no. 2: 448–461.

Johns, Tim. 1986. "Micro-Concord: a Language Learner's Research Tool." *System*, 14, no. 2: 151–162.

Johns, Tim. 1991. "Should You Be Persuaded: Two Examples of Data-driven Learning Materials." *English Language Research Journal*, 4: 1–16.

Kennedy, Claire, and Tiziana Miceli. 2010. "Corpus-Assisted Creative Writing: Introducing Intermediate Italian Learners to a Corpus as a Reference Resource." *Language Learning & Technology*, 14, no. 1: 28–44.

Kern, Richard G. 1995. "Restructuring Classroom Interaction with Networked Computers: Effects on Quantity and Characteristics of Language Production." *The Modern Language Journal*, 79, no. 4: 457–476.

Krashen, Stephen. 1988. *Second Language Acquisition and Second Language Learning.* Englewood Cliffs, NJ: Prentice-Hall International.

Kregar, Sandra. 2011. Relative Effectiveness of Corrective Feedback Types in Computer-Assisted Language Learning. PhD dissertation, Florida State University.

Lado, Beatriz, Harriet Wood Bowden, Catherine Stafford, and Cristina Sanz. 2014. "A Fine-grained Analysis of the Effects of Negative Evidence with and without Metalinguistic Information in Language Development." *Language Teaching Research*, 18, no. 3: 320–244.

Lantolf, Jim, and Steven Thorne. 2006. *Sociocultural Theory and the Genesis of L2 Development.* Oxford: Oxford University Press.

Levy, Michael.1997. *Computer-Assisted Language Learning: Context and Conceptualisation.* Oxford: Oxford University Press.

Liou, Hsien-Chin, Samuel Wang, and Yuli Hung-Yeh. 1992. "Can Grammatical CALL Help EFL Writing Instruction?" *CALICO Journal*, 10, no. 1: 23–44.

Little, David. 1991. *Learner Autonomy 1: Definitions, Issues, and Problems.* Dublin: Authentik.

Loewen, Shawn, and Rosemary Erlam. 2006. "Corrective Feedback in the Chatroom: An Experimental Study." *Computer Assisted Language Learning*, 19, no. 1: 1–14.

Long, Michael. 1996. "The Role of the Linguistic Environment in Second Language Acquisition." In *Handbook of Second Language Acquisition*, edited by William Ritchie and Tey K. Bhatia, 413–468. San Diego, CA: Academic Press.

Lyster, Roy. 2007. *Learning and Teaching Languages through Content: A Counterbalanced Approach.* Amsterdam: John Benjamins.

Metcalfe, Peter. 1992. "CALL, the Foreign-Language Undergraduate and the Teaching of Grammar: A Linguistic and Political Battlefield." *ReCALL*, 4, no. 7: 3–5.

Meurers, Detmar, Ramon Ziai, Luiz Amaral, Adriane Boyd, Aleksandar Dimitrov, Vanessa Metcalf, and Niels Ott. 2010. "Enhancing Authentic Web Pages for Language Learners." In Proceedings of the NAACL HLT 2010 Fifth Workshop on Innovative Use of NLP for Building Educational Applications, 10–18. Association for Computational Linguistics, 2010.

Moreno, Nina. 2007. The Effects of Type of Task and Type of Feedback on L2 Development in CALL. PhD dissertation, Georgetown University.

Murphy, Philip. 2007. "Reading Comprehension Exercises Online: The Effects of Feedback, Proficiency and Interaction." *Language Learning & Technology*, 11, no. 3: 107–129.

Nagata, Noriko. 1993. "Intelligent Computer Feedback for Second Language Instruction." *Modern Language Journal*, 77, no. 3: 330–338.

Nagata, Noriko. 1996. "Computer vs. Workbook Instruction in Second Language Acquisition." *CALICO Journal*, 14, no. 1: 53–75.

Nagata, Noriko. 2009. "Robo-Sensei's NLP-Based Error Detection and Feedback Generation." *CALICO Journal*, 26, no. 3: 562–579.

Oskoz, Ana. 2009. "Learners' Feedback in Online Chats: What Does it Reveal about Students' Learning." *CALICO Journal*, 27, no. 1: 48–68.

Petersen, Ken. 2010. Implicit Corrective Feedback in Computer-Guided Interaction. Does Mode Matter? PhD dissertation, Georgetown University.

Pujolà, Joan-Tomàs. 2002. "CALLing for Help: Researching Language Learning Strategies Using Help Facilities in a Web-Based Multimedia Program." *ReCALL*, 14, no. 2: 253–262.

Pusack, Jim. 1983. "Answer-Processing and Error Correction in Foreign Language CAI." *System*, 11, no. 1: 53–64.

Reppen, Randy. 2010. *Using Corpora in the Language Classroom.* Cambridge: Cambridge University Press.

Robinson, Peter, and Nick C. Ellis, eds. 2008. *Handbook of Cognitive Linguistics and Second Language Acquisition.* London: Routledge.

Römer, Ute. 2011. "Corpus Research Applications in Second Language Teaching." *Annual Review of Applied Linguistics*, 31, no. 1: 205–225.

Rosa, Elena, and Ronald Leow. 2004. "Computerized Task-Based Exposure, Explicitness and Type of Feedback on Spanish L2 Development." *Modern Language Journal*, 88, no. 2: 192–217.

Salaberry, M. Rafael 2000. "L2 Morphosyntactic Development in Text-based Computer-mediated Communication." *Computer Assisted Language Learning*, 13, no. 1: 5–27.

Samburskiy, Denis, and Joy Quah. 2014. "Corrective Feedback in Asynchronous Online Interaction: Developing Novice Online Language Instructors." *CALICO Journal*, 31, no. 2: 158–178.

Sanz, Cristina, and Kara Morgan-Short. 2004. "Positive Evidence Versus Explicit Rule Presentation and Explicit Negative Feedback: A Computer-Assisted Study." *Language Learning*, 54, no. 1: 35–78.

Sauro, Shannon. 2009. "Computer-mediated Corrective Feedback and the Development of L2 Grammar." *Language Learning & Technology*, 13, no. 1: 96–120.

Schmidt, Richard. 1990. "The Role of Consciousness in Second Language Learning." *Applied Linguistics*, 11, no. 2: 129–158.

Schulze, Mathias, and Trude Heift. 2013. "Intelligent CALL." In *Contemporary Computer-Assisted Language Learning*, edited by Michael Thomas, Hayo Reinders, and Mark Warschauer, 249–265. London and New York: Continuum.

Sharwood Smith, Michael. 1993. "Input Enhancement in Instructed SLA." *Studies in Second Language Acquisition*, 15, no. 2: 165–179.

Shekary, Moozeh, and Mohammad Hassan Tahririan. 2006. "Negotiation of meaning and noticing in text-based online chat." *Modern Language Journal*, 90, no. 4: 557–573.

Simpson, Rita C., Sarah L. Briggs, Janine Ovens, and John M. Swales. 2002. *The Michigan Corpus of Academic Spoken English*. Ann Arbor, MI: The Regents of the University of Michigan. Accessed February 15, 2016. http://quod.lib.umich.edu/cgi/c/corpus/corpus?page=home;c=micase;cc=micase

Smart, Jonathan. 2014. "The Role of Guided Induction in Paper-based Data-driven Learning." *ReCALL*, 26, no. 2: 184–201.

Smith, Bryan. 2009. "The Relationship between Scrolling, Negotiation, and Self-initiated Self- repair in a SCMC Environment." *CALICO Journal*, 26, no. 2: 231–345.

Smith, Bryan. 2012. "Eye Tracking as a Measure of Noticing: A Study of Explicit Recasts in SCMC." *Language Learning & Technology*, 16, no. 3: 53–81.

Sotillo, Susana. 2005. "Corrective Feedback via Instant Messenger Learning Activities in NS-NNS and NNS-NNS Dyads." *CALICO Journal*, 22, no. 3: 467–496.

Stockwell, Glenn, and Michael Harrington. 2003. "The Incidental Development of L2 Proficiency in NS-NNS Email Interactions." *CALICO Journal*, 20, no. 2: 337–359.

Swain, Merrill, and Sharon Lapkin. 1998. "Interaction and Second Language Learning: Two Adolescent French Immersion Students Working Together." *Modern Language Journal*, 82, no. 3: 320–338.

ten Hacken, Pius, and Cornelia Tschichold. 2001. "Word Manager and CALL: Structured Access to the Lexicon as a Tool for Enriching Learners' Vocabulary." *ReCALL* 13, no. 1: 121–131.

Thorne, Steven L. 2003. "Artifacts and Cultures-of-Use in Intercultural Communication." *Language Learning and Technology*, 7, no. 2: 38–67.

Tian, Shiauping. 2005. "The Impact of Learning Tasks and Learner Proficiency on the Effectiveness of Data-driven Learning." *Journal of Pan-Pacific Association of Applied Linguistics*, 9, no. 2: 263–275.

Tono, Yukio, Yoshiho Satake, and Aika Miura. 2014. "The Effects of Using Corpora on Revision Tasks in L2 Writing with Coded Error Feedback." *ReCALL*, 26, no. 2: 147–162.

Vinagre, Margarita, and Beatriz Muñoz. 2011. "Computer-Mediated Corrective Feedback and Language Accuracy in Telecollaborative Exchanges." *Language Learning & Technology*, 15, no. 1: 72–103.

Vinther, Jane. 2005. "Cognitive Processes at Work in CALL." *Computer Assisted Language Learning*, 18, no. 4: 251–271.

Vyatkina, Nina. 2013. "Discovery Learning and Teaching with Electronic Corpora in an Advanced German Grammar Course." *Die Unterrichtspraxis/Teaching German*, 46, no. 1: 44–61.

Vyatkina, Nina. 2016a. "Data-driven Learning for Beginners: The Case of German Verb-Preposition Collocations." *ReCALL*, 28, no. 2: 207–226.

Vyatkina, Nina. 2016b. "Data-driven Learning of Collocations: Learner Performance, Proficiency, and Perceptions." *Language Learning & Technology*, 20, no. 3: 159–179.

Ware, Paige, and Robert O'Dowd. 2008. "Peer Feedback on Language Form in Telecollaboration." *Language Learning & Technology*, 12, no. 1: 43–63.

Warschauer, Mark. 2002. "A Developmental Perspective on Technology in Language

Education." *TESOL Quarterly*, 36, no. 3: 453–475.

Weischedel, Ralph, Wilfried Voge, and Mark James. 1978. "An Artificial Intelligence Approach to Language Instruction." *Artificial Intelligence*, 10, no. 3: 225–240.

Williams, Anthony, Graham Davies, and Inrid Williams. 1981. *Apfeldeutsch*. London: Wida Software.

Wood, Peter. 2011. "Computer Assisted Reading in German as a Foreign Language. Developing and Testing an NLP-Based Application." *CALICO Journal*, 28, no. 3: 662–676.

Yilmaz, Yusel. 2012. "The Relative Effects of Explicit Correction and Recasts on Two Target Structures via Two Communication Modes." *Language Learning*, 62, no. 4: 1134–1169.

Zeng, Gang, and Shigenobu Takatsuka. 2009. "Text-based Peer–peer Collaborative Dialogue in a Computer-mediated Learning Environment in the EFL Context." *System*, 37, no. 3: 434–446.

Ziegler, Nicole. 2013. Synchronous Computer-Mediated Communication and Interaction: A Research Synthesis and Meta-Analysis. PhD dissertation, Georgetown University.

# 4 Technologies for Teaching and Learning L2 Vocabulary

## QING MA

## Introduction

The fast advances in language technologies in the era of information technology have brought considerable opportunities for L2 vocabulary learning and teaching. They provide inexhaustible language resources and a huge range of language learning software/applications which greatly facilitate how L2 vocabulary can be acquired. Nevertheless, the affordances and opportunities have also posed big challenges to learners and teachers (Chapelle 2007). How to select language resources and technologies as well as turn them into effective tasks for vocabulary learning for L2 learners with different needs is a critical challenge faced by teachers, learners, and computer-assisted language learning (CALL) researchers. How to raise the awareness and level of self-regulated learning in the learner-controlled environment is another area that merits great attention on the part of all parties involved: teachers, learners and software/app developers.

In this context rich in resources, it is important for language teachers and learners to understand what is involved in L2 vocabulary learning; such knowledge constitutes an important part of the metacognition of vocabulary learning/teaching and guides teachers and students to select online learning resources, attune their attention and make sustained efforts in each essential step. With the dominance of computer technologies and the fast-developing mobile technologies in recent decades, technologies have become a new form of social and cultural artifact that mediates and assists human beings' language learning experience. Against this background, a historical and theoretical framework, based on the work by Ma (2009, 2013), is presented to categorize applications/tools intended for vocabulary learning from the past till the present, covering both implicit and explicit approaches in terms of technology evolution and pedagogical development. Emphasis is placed on how each type of application/tool is geared to vocabulary learning and from what perspective(s). A section is devoted to how mobile technologies mediate or assist vocabulary learning, which impacts more and more the informal outside classroom learning. Finally, the critical issue of providing learner training and how to develop learners' self-regulated strategies is discussed as a response to the call from a number of researchers (Chapelle 2007; Hubbard 2013; Levy 2009).

*The Handbook of Technology and Second Language Teaching and Learning*, First Edition.
Edited by Carol A. Chapelle and Shannon Sauro.
© 2017 John Wiley & Sons, Inc. Published 2020 by John Wiley & Sons, Inc.

# A memory-based strategic model for vocabulary learning: How many essential stages?

Like any type of cognitive activity, learning new vocabulary requires mental processing including all essential memory systems. The new information needs to be first perceived by the visual or sensory store, then part of it will go through the short-term memory store (or working memory) before finally lodging in the long-term memory store (Baddeley, Eysenck and Anderson 2009). This theoretical perspective suggests that vocabulary learning is a staged process (Gu 2003; Nation 2001; Schmitt 1997), and researchers have also provided empirical evidence in support of this perspective (Brown and Payne 1994, as cited in Hatch and Brown 1995; Ma 2014a).

Ma (2014a) proposed a specific memory-based strategic model for vocabulary learning, and tested the model using data collected from a large-scale questionnaire study involving more than 300 participants. The model, which is shown in Figure 4.1, proposes two four-stage parallel vocabulary learning processes. At each stage, a cognitive process takes place in the internal memory system, which is unobservable, and a corresponding external, strategic behavior and internal thought takes place as well. The externally accessible reflection of the stage is either conscious to the learner or observable by an outsider, or both. The internal memory-based four stages is most relevant here. First, the new word form in visual or auditory input needs to be noticed by the brain, which could take place when the learner meets the new word either in reading or listening. Second, the meaning of the new word needs to be accessed from the mental lexicon; this could be made possible by looking up the word in a dictionary (paper or electronic) or guessing. Third, the new word needs to be established as a new L2 lexical entry in the mental lexicon by connecting the existing meaning (initially in L1 translation and later in L2 meaning) with the new word form via repetition,

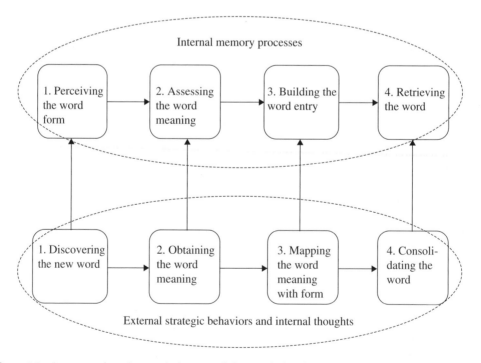

**Figure 4.1**   A memory-based strategic framework for vocabulary learning. Source: Ma (2014a, 43)

imagery, or rhyme, and so on. Lastly, each time the newly learned word is retrieved from the mental lexicon for receptive or productive use, the memory trace for this item will be strengthened.

This four-stage vocabulary learning process framework has two implications for technology- mediated L2 vocabulary acquisition. First, language teachers should take into account these essential mental stages when designing vocabulary learning/teaching tasks. Attention should not only be given to providing resources for learners to meet new words but also be attuned to creating opportunities for subsequent encounters with these items so that many partially learned items can be consolidated or processed to a deep level so as to ensure well-developed L2 lexical entries. Second, this knowledge should also be made explicit to learners when they are provided with strategies to cope with vocabulary learning in a technology-enhanced learning environment. Currently, many learners largely rely on incidental learning associated with online learning: they use an online dictionary or dictionary app to find out the meaning of unknown items encountered, this being restricted to stages 1 and 2: *discovering the word* and *obtaining the word meaning*, but rarely proceed to stage 3 or 4 (*mapping the word meaning with form* and *consolidating the word*). Encouraging learners to record the looked-up words by using the recording function embedded in e-dictionaries and spending some time reviewing these items makes their learning a lot more efficient and effective. These mental stages involved in vocabulary learning have implications for conceptualizing technologies for vocabulary.

# A framework for categorizing technology-mediated L2 vocabulary learning/teaching

Based on the work by Ma (2009, 2013), a framework is proposed to understand the mediation role of technologies on language learning. This framework is built with input from three perspectives: (1) the role of computer technologies; (2) the incidental/intentional approaches to vocabulary acquisition; and (3) actual technology-mediated lexical applications or tools and their impact on people's social life. First, a classic conceptualization of the role of computer technologies is provided by Levy (1997): the computer as a *tutor* or *tool*. The tutor-like role of technology, similar to that of a teacher, can guide and evaluate language learners' learning; technology may also serve as a tool to facilitate learners' learning and performance. The tutor-like lexical applications include intelligent lexical learning systems such as those described by Stockwell (2007, 2013) and by Chen and Chung (2008). These systems evaluate learners' performance and automatically generate vocabulary activities for L2 learners. In contrast, lexical tools comprise e-dictionaries (hand-held electronic dictionaries, online dictionaries or dictionary apps), and e-flashcards. Their primary role is to help learners obtain meanings for unknown items.

Second language researchers recognize two types of learning that are differentiated in L2 vocabulary acquisition: incidental learning and intentional learning (Hulstijn 2005; Ma 2009; Schmitt 2000). The former assumes that vocabulary can be acquired through repeated language exposure (e.g., reading) and the latter by making a deliberate learning effort to learn word forms. This incidental (implicit) and intentional (explicit) distinction influences how a particular lexical application is selected or implemented in learning/teaching contexts. When learning is incidental, the computer or mobile device mostly serves as an e-reader and the technology is mainly used as a tool to scroll down pages. On the other hand, the lexical applications are primarily tutors when the learner makes use of websites or mobile apps that are specifically designed for learning vocabulary items intentionally, for example, e-flashcards or interactive/intelligent applications which can evaluate the learner input to a certain degree.

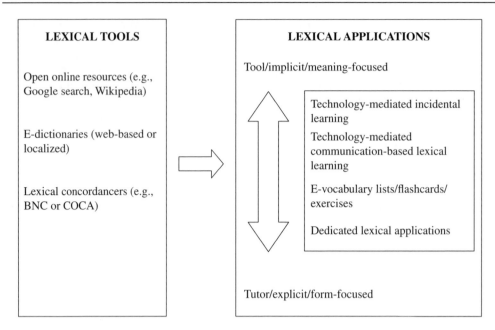

**Figure 4.2**   A framework for technology-mediated L2 lexical applications. Source: updated from Ma (2013, 232).

Third, many new forms of technology-mediated vocabulary learning combine the possibility of incidental and intentional learning: using dictionary apps or lexical concordancers during the class or doing homework, watching YouTube videos while commuting or listening to songs while walking, and so on, thus greatly enriching learners' in-classroom and outside classroom learning.

Lexical tools and lexical applications can be seen as two types of vocabulary learning technologies, as illustrated in Figure 4.2. The component *lexical tools* mainly comprises various e-dictionaries, dictionary apps, or lexical concordancers, which can be used on their own or facilitate the use of lexical applications (checking e-dictionaries/apps while engaging in online reading or doing vocabulary exercises). Thus the arrow from left to right shows that lexical tools can facilitate or support applications that may have multiple functions. Inside the component *lexical applications*, there is a tool and tutor continuum. The tool end of the continuum is mostly associated with incidental learning, for example, reading or listening to materials online or stored locally, which is largely meaning-focused. By contrast, the tutor function is more associated with intentional learning, that is, memorizing e-vocabulary cards or using dedicated lexical applications, which is essentially form-focused. In this sense, the double-barred arrow depicts a continuum where vocabulary learning mediated by technologies moves gradually from tool/implicit/meaning-focused to tutor/explicit/form-focused. To understand the utility of these applications and tools, they need to be examined in view of the four stages of vocabulary learning outlined in Figure 4.1.

## Lexical tools

*E-dictionary.* The first and second stages in L2 vocabulary acquisition are to *encounter* new vocabulary items and *access* their meaning. Lexical tools refer to the various meaning technologies (Hubbard 2001) used by learners to obtain the meaning of the new vocabulary items to complete these two learning stages. Apart from meanings, learners can also view other relevant lexical information, such as pronunciation, varied or derived forms, synonyms, collocations or example sentences. The most common ones are e-dictionaries, namely, web-based online dictionaries, those installed locally on desktops, and the dictionary apps installed on mobile devices; they are facilitative in nature and largely considered to be tools. Popular e-dictionaries include *Merriam Webster* (http://www.merriam-webster.com/), Dictionary.com (http://dictionary.reference.com/), and *Oxford Learner's Dictionary* (http://www.oxfordlearnersdictionaries.com/). These dictionaries are monolingual and are suitable for more advanced learners. Research generally shows that most learners prefer a bilingual dictionary (Koren 1997; Schmitt 1997). For example, it is found that e-dictionaries favored most by Chinese university students are two bilingual ones: *English EC Dictionary* (https://play.google.com/store/apps/details?id=com.csst.ecdict&hl=en) and *Youdao Dictionary* (http://www.youdao.com) (Ma 2014b). Most online dictionaries also have app versions to be installed on mobile devices (smartphone or tablet PC) due to the ubiquitous nature of current mobile technologies. Apart from providing various lexical information (meaning, word class, pronunciation, example sentences), these e-dictionaries are equipped with other functions: videos (e.g., *Merriam Webster*), translation (e.g., *EC dictionary* and *Youdao*), daily pushed messages containing words, phrases or sentences (e.g., *Youdao*), recording and testing vocabulary items looked up. *Google translate*, featuring multiple languages, is gaining increasing popularity and become an important meaning tool by many L2 learners.

*Open-online resources.* In addition, open-online resources, for example, search functions offered by Google, Wikipedia, various thesauruses, or other search engines (Yahoo! or IASK), become supplementary tools for searching for meanings of unknown items. For example, entering the word *lexicon* in Google resulted in a list of entries some of which contain the definition of the word. This means, as long as the learner is connected to the Internet, they can easily find out the meaning or definition of an unknown item on their desktop or mobile device, which shortens considerably the time that is usually required to look up a word in an online dictionary/app.

*Lexical concordancer.* As corpus research is becoming a mainstream branch in applied linguistics and L2 acquisition, it provides authentic and valuable language data for L2 learners and benefits their lexical learning in particular. The *BYU Corpora* website (http://corpus.byu.edu/) is one that accommodates two huge-sized corpora: a 100-million-word British National Corpus (BNC) and a 450-million-word Corpus of Contemporary American English (COCA). *Word Neighbors* (http://wordneighbors.ust.hk/), developed by the Hong Kong University of Science and Technology, has collected corpus data of up to 141 million words, divided into seven genres (articles and reports, newspapers, miscellaneous, correspondence, fiction, adventure, and spoken language). In addition, the keyword search is equipped with a part of speech (POS) function, that is, a word can be searched in different word classes as noun, verb, or adjective respectively. This concordancer is also linked to the Cambridge online dictionary so that learners can check definitions of the keyword. Tom Cobb's *Lexical Tutor* http://www.lextutor.ca/concordancers/) contains multilingual corpora: English, French, German, and Spanish. The main purpose of using lexical concordancers is to discover how words are used in text by observing the pattern of use (e.g., collocations) from the surrounding contextual clues. It should be noted that several factors need to be taken into consideration in order to make lexical concordancers effective tools for lexical learning: learner perception, learner proficiency, teacher help, instructional guidance and related vocabulary exercises (Ma 2009). A number of researchers (Horst, Cobb, and Nicolae 2005; John 2001; Pérez-Paredes et al. 2011) have showcased how to make use of lexical concordancers to enhance vocabulary learning for L2 learners at different proficiency levels.

## *Lexical applications*

Different from lexical tools whose role is to provide the meaning or use pattern of the target item, lexical applications provide the major platform whereby learners' attention is attuned to the combination of the meaning, form and use of the item, which completes the last two stages of L2 vocabulary learning (see Figure 4.1). They can be broadly divided into four categories: *technology-mediated incidental learning* with textual, aural, or visual input, *technology-mediated communication-based lexical learning, e-vocabulary lists/flashcards/exercises*, and *dedicated lexical applications*. Such a distinction is made based on the prominence each gives to vocabulary learning in terms of tool/tutor, implicit/explicit learning, and meaning/form focusing.

*Technology-mediated incidental learning.* When learners read online texts (e.g., Al-Seghayer 2001, 2007; Chun and Plass 1996; Laufer and Hill 2000, and Yoshii 2006), their primary concern is to understand the language input they receive. They may check unknown lexical items via e-glosses, hyperlinks, or e-dictionaries. As a result of doing so, some new items may be acquired, but these are usually limited to recognition only. This type of learning is largely implicit as there is little explicit attention to the forms of the lexical items. Similarly, incidental learning may take place when learners deal with listening (Jones and Plass 2002) or video-based input (Pérez et al. 2014; Winke, Gass, and Sydorenko 2010). Incidental learning may occur if learners pay attention to the new items encountered and access the meanings via lexical tools. In engaging in this type of learning, that is, reading, listening, or watching, learners only need to scroll up and down pages or click on some buttons (play, pause, or go back); the main function of this type of application is to execute the learner's command. These applications are primarily tools, which can be integrated into other lexical tools, as can be seen later. Most of the applications for incidental learning cited above are research-based.

*Technology-mediated communication-based lexical learning.* Researchers who draw upon theory from interactionist SLA, particularly Long's (1996) interaction hypothesis and Swain's (1995) output hypothesis, have investigated how technology-mediated communication technologies benefit learners' L2 learning. Only a few such studies (e.g., Blake 2000; Fuente 2003; Smith 2004) focused on lexical acquisition. Usually it is the negotiation of meaning: noticing input features, modified input, positive or negative feedback, and modified output (or pushed output) that are under study in the communication process. With carefully designed tasks, learners can practice using the previously learned lexical items. Recently, language teachers have begun to make use of some popular social communication tools such as WhatsApp or WeChat, available on mobile devices, to interact with learners or have learners interact among themselves with written or spoken language, as reported by *The Mobile Learning Community* (http://corpus.ied.edu.hk/mlc/). For example, the teacher may require the students to record their messages using WhatsApp and share them with the teacher and/or other peers. Such innovative use of mobile communication technologies to facilitate L2 learning, especially lexical learning, is gaining popularity among teachers and practitioners, but it is rarely reported in research and little is known about its effectiveness. Nevertheless, this type of meaning-focused communication-oriented lexical tasks should enable learners to pay more attention to the vocabulary forms (e.g., spelling or pronunciation) than the previous incidental type of learning.

*E-vocabulary lists/flashcards/exercises.* E-vocabulary lists/flashcards/exercises pay deliberate attention to vocabulary forms; they are e-vocabulary lists/flashcards/exercises. The purpose of utilizing an e-vocabulary list or flashcards is to consolidate the mapping of the word form and meaning in stage 3 of vocabulary learning (see Figure 4.1). The use of such paired-associate vocabulary learning has long been valued by researchers (e.g., Elgort 2011 and Nation 2001). Words can be arranged alphabetically, semantically, or by topic. One that is worthy of attention is *SuperMemo* (http://www.supermemo.com/index.htm), whose design rationale is based on spaced repetition and retrieval. The learner can create their own flashcards by inputting two types of lexical information: a question as a retrieval clue and the target word as the answer, for example, *What do you call the sister of your husband or wife? Sister-in-law.* The learner should rate the familiarity of the item when attempting to retrieve the target item. This intelligent system will store the rating information and schedule automatically the review path for this item. This learning system accommodates up to 25 different languages. A similar e-flashcard system, *Anki* (http://ankisrs.net/index.html), makes use of similar principles but adopts a much more user-friendly interface. Apart from creating flashcards by learners themselves, the web version of *Anki* has been preloaded with different sets of vocabulary lists for learners' convenience. McLean, Hogg, and Rush (2013) tested empirically the effectiveness of one intelligent web-based flashcard learning system, *Word Engine* (http://www.wordengine.jp/), with 182 Japanese university students; the results show that the focused use of Word Engine outperformed the other two groups who either combined reading with Word Engine or solely did extensive reading. Nakata (2011) compared a wide range of flashcard learning systems and claimed that *iKnow!* (http://iknow.jp/) is the best in that it "offers the most comprehensive support for data entry, automatically generates distractors for multiple-choice exercises and increases retrieval effort by systematically introducing various types of exercises" (17). Such e-vocabulary flash cards/lists/exercises should be useful in consolidating the learning of vocabulary items since such systematic rehearsal is necessary for keeping the words in long-term memory. The technologies used in these systems can evaluate the learner input and design the learning paths for the learner to a certain degree; this clearly bears some tutor features. This type of learning is mainly explicit as deliberate attention is paid to both the word form and the word meaning.

*Dedicated lexical applications.* As we can see, the three types of lexical applications reviewed above offer some opportunities to address only two or three of the four stages involved in vocabulary learning, but dedicated lexical applications are the all-in-one where all four stages involved in learning are addressed: from *meeting new items* in context, *accessing the meaning* via lexical tools, *mapping the word meaning and form*, to *receptive or productive use* of the items. In this sense, dedicated lexical applications are particularly geared to vocabulary learning in a more holistic and systematic way. In this type of application, vocabulary learning is both contextualized and itemized; attention is paid to both meaning (implicit learning) and form (explicit learning). The dedicated lexical applications often combine tutor functions with tool functions, providing the initial learning contexts as well as subsequent rehearsals or consolidated use. The learning benefits of such dedicated applications may encompass cultural knowledge and strategy learning. Good examples of dedicated lexical applications include Wordchip developed by Decoo et al. (1996), Lexica developed by Goodfellow (1999), Computer Assisted VOCabulary Acquisition (CAVOCA) developed by Groot (2000) and the WUFUN software described in Ma and Kelly (2006) and Ma (2007, 2008).

The WUFUN software provides learners with meaningful contexts where target items are embedded in short sentences and presented in multiple language input: visual, pictorial, and textual. Then the learner can look up target vocabulary items in a built-in e-dictionary. This follows the reading of the full context in the form of a story in which the target items occur again. This is followed by the introduction of a number of memory strategies (e.g., verbal association, imagery, rhyming, and alliteration) which are meant to help learners consolidate the meaning-form mapping of these target items. Afterwards, learners are required to practice using the target items both receptively and productively in a number of contextualized exercises. Finally, some idioms and culturally-related humor are presented to learners in order to arouse their awareness and appreciation of cultural elements in L2 acquisition. Recently, Stockwell (2013) presented an intelligent vocabulary learning system that is composed of two parts. In one, students read passages and look up words via hyperlinked glosses, which are followed by reading comprehension questions. In the other, the system generates automatically vocabulary exercises based on the words each student looked up. This system clearly combines incidental learning with deliberate vocabulary learning, echoing the concerns that incidental learning alone only results in limited learning and it is ideal to combine the reading with follow-up word-focused activities (Laufer and Rozovski-Roitblat 2011; Wesche and Paribakht 2000).

# Emerging mobile assisted vocabulary learning

The rise of mobile assisted language learning (MALL) includes a large number of vocabulary apps developed for mobile platforms (Android or Safari). Early research on mobile learning focused on the mobile devices; it is now generally agreed that more emphasis should be placed on the learner who constantly moves from one learning context to another (Kukulska-Hulme and Shield 2008). MAVL could thus be defined as learning vocabulary via *mobile devices* and with *mobility*. In the following sections, MAVL applications will be introduced with reference to their relevance to both the essential learning stages involved in vocabulary learning and the framework for categorizing lexical applications discussed earlier. Finally, it is pointed out that the newly emerging MAVL should be combined with the classic CAVL to truly make more effective use of technologies for vocabulary learning.

## *Primary MAVL applications*

Vocabulary learning is one of the earliest foci among app developers (Godwin-Jones 2010); it is also one of the most investigated areas among MALL researchers. Vocabulary lessons sent via mobile phones, via SMS or email are predominant in early MALL studies (Levy and Kennedy 2005; Thornton and Houser 2005). The textual information sent to students can be item-based or contextualized. For example, in Thornton and Houser's (2005) study, three contextualized messages which contain a highlighted target word were sent to Japanese university students at different times of the day (morning, noon, and late afternoon). The target word is glossed in the L1 when it is received for the first time. Each time the short message containing the word is a different one so that the students can see how it is used in different contexts. Referring to Figure 4.1, this repeated exposure (or spaced repetition) of the target item with changing contexts is to consolidate the learning as well as elaborate the meaning and use (mainly receptive), thus addressing the first three learning stages of *discovering the word, obtaining the meaning,* and *meaning and form mapping*; the final stage, *consolidating the word use,* is partially achieved as the use is only receptive. Usually such pushed textual information sent to learners via mobile devices leads to better learning than PC-based or paper-based learning. One disadvantage of such SMS-based learning is that learners mainly serve as passive recipients of all lexical information (meaning, form, and use). With reference to the framework presented in Figure 4.2, this type of MAVL activity is seen as largely the technology-mediated incidental learning type.

Intelligent or personalized vocabulary learning systems are another area of research. The design of such systems often makes use of a user-action-tracking system (e.g., Stockwell 2007) or is integrated with complicated arithmetic algorithms to analyze learner information (Chen and Hsu 2008) in order for the learning system to design suitable learning paths for the learner. Stockwell (2007) described an intelligent vocabulary tutor system where advanced English Japanese learners engaged in vocabulary-based exercises (stage 3: *meaning and form mapping*) for a whole semester. A built-in tracking system records various access and performance information of the learner: results for each exercise attempted, words with which the learner experienced learning difficulties and an overall lexical profile of the learner (vocabulary level, number of trials, study time, exercise types, etc.). The system generates automatically exercises for the vocabulary items that are more likely to cause learning difficulty to the learner. Such an intelligent mobile-based vocabulary learning system may make e-vocabulary lists/exercises more effective as compared with traditional CAVL applications. Working with a similar design rationale, Chen and Hsu (2008) presented another intelligent vocabulary system which also takes into account learners' personalization: English news reading (stage 1: *meeting the word*) is combined with focused study of vocabulary items (stages 3 and 4: *mapping* and *using the word*) that are deemed new or difficult for learners. The intelligent design enables the system to conduct a thorough analysis of the user input in terms of self-diagnosis of their comprehension level of the news article. Then this information will be used to identify the user's unfamiliar or personalized vocabulary items in the news reading. This personalized learning system bears many features pertinent to those dedicated lexical applications discussed earlier.

## *Diverse MAVL applications in mobile learning/teaching environments*

Naismith et al. (2004) forecasted innovative learning and teaching concepts that are suitable for mobile learning/teaching environments, including *situated learning, collaborative learning, constructivist learning*, and *informal and lifelong learning*. Their prediction gradually became a reality in vocabulary learning activities. Regarding *situated learning*, Beaudin et al. (2007) described a mobile learning activity which makes use of the built-in ubiquitous sensors of mobile devices in a home learning environment to detect real objects and generate audio files of these items in both English and Spanish. Chen and Li (2010) designed a context-aware vocabulary learning system that can automatically detect the learner's location, time (morning, noon; spring or winter; festival period or not), proficiency level, and affordable leisure time, based on which a set of context-specific vocabulary items will be recommended to the learner. These are largely varied forms of e-vocabulary lists/exercises. As for *collaborative learning*, Lin et al. (2014) examined how students learn vocabulary collaboratively in the classroom by adopting whiteboard technologies and all-in-one desktop screens. Wong et al. (2010) investigated how learners could construct knowledge and create a contextualized learning context for acquiring Chinese idioms via mobile phones to realize *constructivist learning*. As communication among group members is required in both lexical applications, they involve essentially mobile technology-mediated communication-based lexical learning.

In a recent review, Burston (2014) found that almost 90% of the MALL studies take place outside of the classroom. This suggests that most types of MAVL activities belong to the *informal and lifelong* categories. Informal learning takes place all the time: after school or at work. It is regarded as a "precursor of formal learning" and should be seen as "fundamental, necessary and valuable in its own right" (Coffield 2000, 8). In addition, informal outside classroom learning impacts directly the in-classroom learning/teaching in both language content and technology use (Chapelle 2007). Drawing on the typology used by Eraut (2000), informal learning activities for MAVL may include *deliberate learning*, for example, using a vocabulary app to increase vocabulary size on a daily basis in order to prepare for a high-stake language test (IELTS or TOFEL), *reactive learning*, for example, asking for the meaning of unknown word(s) encountered in a SMS exchange or WhatsApp communication via mobile phones, and *incidental learning*, for example, acquiring some L2 words through repeated exposure to online videos, news, or songs. As can be seen, referring to the framework, deliberate learning is similar to e-vocabulary lists/exercises; reactive learning is more or less the same as technology-mediated communication-based lexical learning and incidental learning is close to technology-mediated incidental learning.

Nowadays, the prevalence of mobile technologies in many parts of the world provides ample opportunities for learners to record, reflect on, exchange and share informal L2 vocabulary learning. For example, Song and Fox (2008) reported how some highly motivated Hong Kong university students acquire English vocabulary incidentally, collaboratively, and deliberately while studying academic courses delivered in English. Ma's (forthcoming) recent study on how mobile technologies mediate Hong Kong university students' language learning shows that the majority of the participants are active builders of vocabulary and this largely takes place outside the classroom. Their way of tackling vocabulary learning ranges from making use of lexical concordancers deliberately and building academic lexis, to incidental learning taking place in social networking (reading and responding to friends' online blogs). This study also shows that almost two-fifths of all MALL resources (e.g., e-news, videos, tools or tutors) belong to the category lexical tools, that is, dictionary apps, online dictionaries, translation websites/apps, or lexical concordancers for university L2 learners.

## Developing lexical tools to cater for MAVL

The prevalence of incidental and informal lexical learning indicates the importance for app developers to develop user-friendly and multifunction dictionary apps to help L2 learners learn vocabulary items independently, incidentally, and informally in a mobile learning environment. Learners often access online information, read news, listen to songs, or watch videos via mobile devices while they commute or when traveling. It is of great help if they can use a dictionary app equipped with a mouse-click-display function or desktop hanging function to speed up the dictionary look-up speed. A free bilingual dictionary app, Powerword (available on both Google Play and Apple's store), developed for Chinese learners of English is equipped with a desktop hanging function; a small icon for vocabulary search will stay in any webpage and can be clicked open for inputting the word with minimum disturbance to the continuous reading of the webpage. As shown earlier, vocabulary learning goes through four sequential stages. Meeting and looking up new words in a dictionary app only completes the first and second stages, so a well-designed dictionary app should include the functions for storing and testing words looked up. Ideally, not only simple meaning recognition test items should be provided, but also items for users to use the words productively. The dictionary app could also be linked with some lexical concordancers so that learners can be offered opportunities to view real-life examples of how the word(s) should be used. Similarly, a powerful lexical tool, *Collocator*, described by Wible, Liu, and Tsao (2011) turns any webpage into corpus data and extract collocations automatically. To make the Collocator more useful, a testing function for evaluating learners' learning of the extracted collocations could be built in or developed separately to consolidate learners' learning of these items.

## Combining MAVL with CAVL

While the growing mobile technologies portend great potential for language teachers and learners to teaching/learning L2 vocabulary, research (Stockwell 2007, 2010, 2013) tends to show that learners prefer to work on PCs if deliberate learning for a relatively long study time is required to work on mobile phones with small screens. This might be due to the learner perceived limitations on screen size and input method associated with mobile phones. However, mobile phones are only one of the mobile devices that learners may use; both tablet PCs and netbooks are large-screen-sized and easy to carry. Second, it is the mobility of the learner rather than the mobile devices that should receive more focus when teachers design MAVL activities/tasks. It is certain that the classic desktop technologies will continue to play an important role in L2 vocabulary learning/teaching whereas the access to online information brought by mobile technologies inspire many innovative practices; mobile technologies are readily connected to desktop technologies to form what is now often called *seamless learning* and which shall fundamentally impact language learners' informal learning (Wong and Looi 2011).

# Training and self-regulating the learner for CAVL and MAVL

Seamless learning assumes that learners are prepared to take responsibility. However, there is generally a lack of research evidence about how to train learners to do so (Castellano, Mynard, and Rubesch 2011; Hubbard 2013). Learner training is a term closely related to strategy training, learner development and learner autonomy or other similar terms, but it has never been clearly defined in the L2 field (Hubbard 2013; Ma 2007). Research has long documented that how learners interact with CALL learning systems directly influences the learning results (Chapelle and Mizuno 1989; Fischer 2007, 2012). However, learners do not inherently possess good knowledge and skills to tackle CALL tasks effectively and necessary training should be provided for them by teachers (Chapelle 2007; Hubbard 2004, 2013; Ma 2007). In the following sections, learner training, more familiar to CALL researchers, will be discussed, followed by self-regulated learning which has been rarely discussed in L2 learning but has direct relevance to L2 vocabulary learners in today's MAVL environment.

## *Learner training*

A few research studies attempted to address learner training in CAVL or MAVL. Ma and Kelly (2006) presented a CAVL application, *WUFUN*, integrating vocabulary strategy training into contextualized vocabulary learning. A number of memory strategies were introduced to learners such as verbal association, imagery, rhyming, and alliteration to which help to strengthen the meaning-form mapping in stage 3 of vocabulary learning (see Figure 4.1). The results show that this application helped the majority of participants acquire only one or two memory strategies; it is suggested that such embedded vocabulary strategy training should be made more explicit to learners in order to obtain more effective results. Ranalli (2009) developed a *Virtual Vocabulary Trainer* (VVT) website for training university ESL students. The training system comprises three components: an overview of important knowledge about vocabulary learning (e.g., multiple meanings, connotation, word families, spoken and written forms, collocation, register, and frequency); experiencing how monolingual or bilingual dictionaries can be used to facilitate lexical learning; different types of collocations and how to learn these items. These training components were used together with spoken and written L2 input. The results show that the learners were overall positive towards such vocabulary strategy training and found the training system useful, helpful, and interesting. In a more recent study, Ranalli (2013) utilized the VVT website and provided students with dictionary-focused word learning strategy instruction; the study showed that such explicit training helped university ESL learners learn to explore dictionaries more effectively and achieve better results in learning word collocations than those without such explicit strategy instruction.

Apart from strategy training, Reinders and Hubbard (2013) suggest that the focus of providing learner training should also be placed on better guidance of technology use, pedagogical training, and community building. In other words, learners and teachers should be equipped with increasing degrees of technological autonomy, pedagogical training should go with learner training in order to promote learner autonomy, and learner training programs should be developed to focus on raising not only cognitive but also metacognitive awareness of language learning. Creating more opportunities for learner-learner collaborative learning could also facilitate self-regulated learning.

## Self-regulating the learner

A small number of empirical studies that provide learner training aim at developing learner autonomy in CALL research (e.g., Raby 2007; Smith and Craig 2013). However, the term *learner autonomy*, similar to learner training, suffers from not having a clear definition (Thanasoulas 2000). What is agreed about learner autonomy is the ability to take charge of one's learning effectively (Little 1991). Perhaps this rather broadly and vaguely defined term is not sufficient to guide CALL or MALL researchers in effectively conceptualizing and conducting research in learner training. A similar term, *self-regulation*, has been long studied in the field of educational psychology and but rarely caught the attention of L2 researchers (Dörnyei 2005). It can be defined as "self-generated thoughts, feelings, and actions that are planned and cyclically adapted to the attainment of personal goals" (Zimmerman 2000, 14). Zimmerman (2000, 2011) proposed a three-phase framework for capturing the dynamic and stage-like process of self-regulation. Phase I is the forethought phase, where learners set up goals and make strategic planning, powered by their self-motivational beliefs. Phase II is where they execute and self-regulate the learning process by controlling or monitoring various aspects such as task strategies, time management, environmental structuring, and help-seeking, and so on. Phase III is the reflection phase, where they self-evaluate their learning performance and come up with possible adaptive actions for future tasks. The three self-regulated phases are cyclic because "the feedback from prior performance is used to make adjustments during current efforts" (Zimmerman 2000, 14).

Ma (in press) shows that in the MALL environment students often combine vocabulary learning with entertainment or personal interests (e.g., listening to songs while studying; watching videos on YouTube or Facebook); some reported that they were easily distracted by games or advertisements on the mobile devices while engaging in MAVL. With little evidence about learners' use of self-regulated learning in MAVL, it remains largely unknown how learners achieve effective and efficient learning when they engage in lexical learning on their own. A review of the literature shows that self-regulation only features in a small proportion of CALL or MALL studies (e.g., Chang 2007; Chen and Huang 2014; Lai, Shum, and Tian 2016; Kondo et al. 2012) in major CALL-related journals. In addition, the studies that aim for self-regulation training (e.g., Lai et al. 2016 and Kondo et al. 2012) do not necessarily yield evidence of substantial changes in learner behaviors after the training. This is possibly due to the fact that these studies are largely teacher- or researcher-driven and related more to classroom learning; learners may lack the motivation to fully engage or persist unremittingly in the training process.

As a way forward, future studies investigating how self-regulated training could be provided for students to facilitate their CAVL or MAVL should focus more on their out-of-class, informal learning. The cyclic three-phase for self-regulated learning proposed by Zimmerman (2000, 2011) may serve as a useful guide for CALL or MALL researchers in designing and implementing self-regulated research/training for L2 vocabulary learners. A good example of offering such out-of-class self-regulated vocabulary learning strategy (VLS) training is provided by Lan (2013). In this study, a lexical learning and training system, *Mywordtools*, contains 320 vocabulary items for Taiwan primary school pupils together with 12 embedded VLSs such as note-taking, key word, contextualization, grouping, imagery, analysis, physical response, and so on. This system comprises three modules: (1) a learning map module which helps L2 learners plan, monitor, and follow the learning path recommended by the system; (2) a strategy construct module which introduces the 12 VLSs to learners; and (3) a strategy co-sharing module which enables learners to look up strategies that are used by all the other users of the learning system. The results show that such self-regulation-based VLSs training embedded in *Mywordtools*, run on PCs, helped students gain more vocabulary as well as construct more VLSs. It is hoped that a similar lexical learning system could be developed on mobile learning platforms, thus benefiting more and more MAVL learners.

## Conclusion

Technologies-mediated vocabulary learning applications, used in the CAVL or MAVL environments, will continue to play a key role in teachers' classroom teaching and planning and, more importantly, learners' informal outside classroom learning. Conceptualizing the essential learning stages involved in vocabulary learning is useful for selecting and implementing learning resources as well as choosing the right technologies. Ideally, the selection and implementation process should balance implicit and explicit learning opportunities, combining lexical tools with lexical applications consisting of both tools and tutors, which address different vocabulary learning stages and are beneficial to learners' lexical development. As mobile technologies are making incidental and informal learning more and more prominent in the life of learners, it is of paramount importance to help/train their self-regulated strategies in order to make the CAVL or MAVL learning more efficient and effective. Mobile communication is naturally integrated into many learners' lives and has become a daily commodity; they constantly switch from desktop technologies to mobile technologies based on their needs and environment. CAVL or MAVL developers should develop more and more applications, particularly, lexical tools and concordancers, which are compatible with mobile learning.

## Acknowledgment

I am grateful to the Education University of Hong Kong who funded this article as part of an IRG project (R3559).

## REFERENCES

Al-Seghayer, Khalid. 2001. "The Effect of Multimedia Annotation Modes on L2 VocabularyAcquisition: A Comparative Study." *Language Learning & Technology*, 5, no. 1: 202–232.

Al-Seghayer, Khalid. 2007. "The Role of Organizational Devices in ESL Readers' Construction of Mental Representations of Hypertext Content." *CALICO Journal*, 24, no. 3: 531–559. DOI:10.11139/cj.24.3.531–559

Baddeley, Alan, Michael W. Eysenck, and Michael C. Anderson. 2009. *Memory*. Hove: Psychology Press.

Beaudin, Jennifer S., Stephen S. Intille, Emmanuel Munguia Tapia, Randy Rockinson, and Margaret E. Morris. 2007. "Context-sensitive Microlearning of Foreign Language Vocabulary on a Mobile Device." In *Ambient Intelligence, Vol 4794: Springer Lecture Notes in Computer Science*, edited by Bernt Schiele, Anind K. Dey, Hans Gellersen, Boris de Ruyter, Manfred Tscheligi, Reiner Wichert, Emile Aarts, and Alejandro Buchmann, 55–72. Berlin: Springer.

Blake, Robert. 2000. "Computer Mediated Communications: A Window on L2 Spanish

Interlanguage." *Language Learning &*
*Technology*, 4, no. 1: 120–136.

Brown, Cheryl, and Melinda E. Payne. 1994.
"Five Essential Steps of Processes in
Vocabulary Learning." Paper presented at the
TESOL convention, Baltimore, MD, March
8–12.

Burston, Jack. 2014. "The Reality of MALL: Still
on the Fringes." *CALICO Journal*, 31, no. 1:
103–125. DOI:10.11139/cj.31.1

Castellano, Joachim, Jo Mynard, and Troy
Rubesch. 2011. "Action Research Student
Technology Use in a Self-access Center."
*Language Learning & Technology*, 15, no. 3:
12–27.

Chang, Mei-Mei. 2007. "Applying Self-regulated
Learning Strategies in a Web-based
Instruction – an Investigation of Motivation
Perception." *Computer Assisted Language
Learning*, 18, no. 3: 217–230.
DOI:10.1080/09588220500178939

Chapelle, Carol A. 2007. "Computer Assisted
Language Learning." In *The Handbook of
Educational Linguistics*, edited by Bernard
Spolsky and Francis M. Hult, 585–595. Malden,
MA: Blackwell.

Chapelle, Carol, and Suesue Mizuno. 1989.
"Student's Strategies with Learner-
controlled CALL." *CALICO Journal*, 7,
no. 2: 25–47.

Chen, Chih-Ming, and Ching-Ju Chung. 2008.
"Personalized Mobile English Vocabulary
Learning System Based on Item Response
Theory and Learning Memory Cycle."
*Computers & Education*, 51, no. 2: 624–645.
DOI:10.1016/j.compedu.2007.06.011

Chen, Chih-Ming, and Sheng-Hui Huang. 2014.
"Web-based Reading Annotation system with
an Attention-based Self-regulated Learning
Mechanism for Promoting." *British Journal of
Educational Technology*, 45, no. 5: 959–980.
DOI:10.1111/bjet.12119

Chen, Chih-Ming, and Shih-Hsun Hsu. 2008.
"Personalized Intelligent M-learning System
for Supporting Effective English Learning."
*Educational Technology & Society*, 11, no. 3:
153–180.

Chen, Chih-Ming, and Yi-Lun Li. 2010.
"Personalised Context-aware Ubiquitous
Learning System for Supporting Effective
English Vocabulary Learning." *Interactive
Learning Environments*, 18, no. 4: 341–364.
DOI:10.1080/10494820802602329

Chun, Dorothy M., and Jan L. Plass. 1996.
"Effects of Multimedia Annotations on
Vocabulary Acquisition." *The Modern Language*

*Journal*, 80, no. 2: 183–198.
DOI:10.1111/j.1540-4781.1996.tb01159.x

Coffield, Frank. 2000. *The Necessity of Informal
Learning*. Bristol: The Policy Press.

Decoo, Wilfried, Els Heughebaert, Nancy
Schonenbert, and Dewig Van Elsen. 1996. "The
Standard Vocabulary Programs of Didascalia:
In Search of External Versatility and Didactic
Optimisation." *Computer Assisted Language
Learning*, 9, no. 4: 319–338.
DOI:10.1080/0958822960090404

Dörnyei, Zoltán. 2005. *The Psychology of the
Language Learner: Individual Differences in
Second Language Acquisition*. Mahwah, NJ:
Lawrence Erlbaum.

Elgort, Irina. 2011. "Deliberate Learning and
Vocabulary Acquisition in a Second
Language." *Language Learning*, 61, no. 2:
367–413. DOI:10.1111/j.1467-9922.2010.00613.x

Eraut, Michael. 2000. "Non-formal Learning and
Tacit Knowledge in Professional Work." *British
Journal of Educational Psychology*, 70, no. 1:
113–136. DOI:10.1348/000709900158001

Fischer, Robert. 2007. "How Do We Know What
Students are Actually Doing? Monitoring
Students' behavior in CALL." *Computer
Assisted Language Learning*, 20, no. 5: 409–442.
DOI:10.1080/09588220701746013

Fischer, Robert. 2012. "Diversity in Learner
Usage Patterns." In *Computer-assisted Language
Learning Diversity in Research and Practice*,
edited by Glenn Stockwell, 14–32. Cambridge:
Cambridge University Press.

Fuente, María J. 2003. "Is SLA Interactionist
Theory Relevant to CALL? A Study on the
Effects of Computer-mediated Interaction in
L2 Vocabulary Acquisition." *Computer Assisted
Language Learning*, 16, no. 1: 47–81.
DOI:10.1076/call.16.1.47.15526

Godwin-Jones, Robert. 2010. "Emerging
Technologies from Memory Palaces to Spacing
Algorithms: Approaches to Second-language
Vocabulary Learning." *Language Learning &
Technology*, 14, no. 2: 4–11.

Goodfellow, Robin. 1999. "Evaluating
Performance, Approach and Outcome." In
*CALL: Media, Design, and Applications*, edited
by Keith Cameron, 109–140. Lisse: Swets and
Zeitlinger.

Groot, Peter J. M. 2000. "Computer Assisted
Second Language Vocabulary Acquisition."
*Language Learning & Technology*, 4, no. 1: 60–81.

Gu, Peter Y. 2003. "Fine Brush and Freehand: The
Vocabulary-learning Art of Two Successful
Chinese EFL Learners." *TESOL Quarterly*, 37,
no. 1: 73–104. DOI:10.2307/3588466

Hatch, Evelyn, and Cheryl Brown. 1995. *Vocabulary, Semantics, and Language Education.* Cambridge: Cambridge University Press.

Horst, Marlise, Tom Cobb, and Ioana Nicolae. 2005. "Expanding Academic Vocabulary with an Interactive Online Database." *Language Learning & Technology,* 9, no. 2: 90–110.

Hubbard, Philip. 2001. "The Use and Abuse of Meaning Technologies." *Contact,* 27, no. 1: 82–86. Accessed March 5, 2015. http://www. teslontario.net/uploads/publications/ researchsymposium/ ResearchSymposium2001.pdf#page=82

Hubbard, Philip. 2004. "Learner Training for Effective Use of CALL." In *New perspectives on CALL for Second Language Classrooms,* edited by Sandra Fotos and Charles M. Browne, 45–68. Mahwah, NJ: Lawrence Erlbaum.

Hubbard, Philip. 2013. "Making a Case for Learner Training in Technology Enhanced Language Learning Environments." *CALICO Journal,* 30, no. 2: 163–178. DOI:10.11139/ cj.30.2.163-178

Hulstijn, Jan H. 2005. "Incidental Learning and Intentional Learning." In *The Handbook of Second Language Acquisition,* edited by Catherine J. Doughty and Michael H. Long, 349–381. Oxford: Blackwell.

John, Elke St. 2001. A Case for Using a Parallel Corpus and Concordancer for Beginners of a Foreign Language. *Language Learning & Technology,* 5, no. 3: 185–203.

Jones, Linda C., and Jan L. Plass. 2002. "Supporting Listening Comprehension and Vocabulary Acquisition in French with Multimedia Annotations." *The Modern Language Journal,* 86, no. 4: 546–61. DOI:10.1111/1540-4781.00160

Kondo, Mutsumi, Yasushige Ishikawa, Craig Smith, Kishio Sakamoto, Hidenori Shimomura, and Norihisa Wada. 2012. "Mobile Assisted Language Learning in University EFL Courses in Japan: Developing Attitudes and Skills for Self-regulated Learning." *ReCALL,* 24, no. 2: 169–187. DOI:10.1017/S0958344012000055

Koren, Shira. 1997. "Quality versus Convenience: Comparison of Modern Dictionaries from the Researcher's, Teacher's and Learner's Points of View." *TESL-EJ,* 2, no. 3. Accessed March 5, 2015. http://tesl-ej.org/ej07/a2.html

Kukulska-Hulme, Agnes, and Lesley Shield. 2008. "An Overview of Mobile Assisted Language Learning: From Content Delivery to Supported Collaboration and Interaction." *ReCALL,* 20, no. 3: 271–89. DOI:10.1017/ S0958344008000335

Lai, Chun, Mark Shum, and Yan Tian. 2016 "Enhancing Learners' Self-directed Use of Technology for Language Learning: The Effectiveness of an Online Training Platform." *Computer Assisted Language Learning,* 29, no. 1: 1–21. DOI:10.1080/09588221.2014.889714

Lan, Yu-Ju. 2013. "The Effect of Technology-supported Co-sharing on L2 Vocabulary Strategy Development." *Educational Technology & Society,* 16, no. 4: 1–16.

Laufer, Batia, and Monica Hill. 2000. "What Lexical Information do L2 Learners Select in a CALL Dictionary and How Does it Affect Word Retention?" *Language Learning & Technology,* 3, no. 2: 58–76.

Laufer, Batia, and Bella Rozovski-Roitblat. 2011. "Incidental Vocabulary Acquisition: The Effects of Task Type, Word Occurrence and their Combination." *Language Teaching Research,* 15, no. 4: 391–411. DOI:10.1177/1362168811412019

Levy, Michael. 1997. *Computer-assisted Language Learning: Context and Conceptualization.* New York: Oxford University Press.

Levy, Mike. 2009. "Technologies in Use for Second Language Learning." *The Modern Language Journal,* 93, no. 1: 769–82. DOI:10.1111/j.1540-4781.2009.00972.x

Levy, Mike, and Claire Kennedy. 2005. "Learning Italian via Mobile SMS." In *Mobile learning: A Handbook for Educators and Trainers,* edited by Agnes Kukulska-Hulme and John Traxler, 76–83. Abingdon: Routledge.

Lin, Chih-Cheng, Hsien-Sheng Hsiao, Sheng-ping Tseng, and Hsin-jung Chan. 2014. "Learning English Vocabulary Collaboratively in a Technology-supported Classroom." *The Turkish Online Journal of Educational Technology,* 13, no. 1: 162–173.

Little, David. 1991. *Learner Autonomy: Definitions, Issues, and Problems.* Dublin: Authentik.

Long, Michael. 1996. "The Role of the Linguistic Environment in Second Language Acquisition." In *Handbook of Second Language Acquisition,* edited by William C. Ritchie and Tej K. Bhatia, 413–468. Rowley, MA: Newbury House.

Ma, Qing. 2007. "From Monitoring Users to Controlling User Actions: A New Perspective on the User-centred Approach to CALL." *Computer Assisted Language Learning,* 20, no. 4: 297–321. DOI:10.1080/09588220701745783

Ma, Qing. 2008. "Empirical CALL Evaluation: The Relationship between Learning Process and Learning Outcome." *CALICO Journal,* 26, no. 1: 108–122. DOI:10.11139/cj.26.1.108–122.

Ma, Qing. 2009. *Second Language Vocabulary Acquisition*. Bern: Peter Lang.

Ma, Qing. 2013. "Computer Assisted Vocabulary Learning: Framework and Tracking User Data." In *Learner-computer Interaction in Language Education*, edited by Philip Hubbard, Mathias Schulze, and Bryan Smith, 230–243. San Marcos, TX: Computer Assisted Language Instruction Consortium (CALICO) Monograph.

Ma, Qing. 2014a. "A Contextualised Study of EFL Learners' Vocabulary Learning Approaches: Framework, Learner Type and Degree of Success." *Asia TEFL*, 11, no. 3: 33–71.

Ma, Qing. 2014b. "How Do University L2 Learners Make Use of E-dictionaries/apps in Mobile-Assisted Language Learning (MALL)?" Paper presented at the CALICO Conference, Athens, GA, May 6–10.

Ma, Qing. (In press). A Mutl-case Study of University Students' Language Learning Experience Mediated by Mobile Technologies: A socio-cultural perspective. Computer Assisted Language Learning.

Ma, Qing and Peter Kelly. 2006. "Computer Assisted Vocabulary Learning: Design and Evaluation." *Computer Assisted Language Learning*, 19, no. 1: 15–45. DOI:10.1080/09588220600803998

McLean, Stuart, Nicolas Hogg, and Thomas W. Rush. 2013. "Vocabulary Learning Through an Online Computerized Flashcard Site." *The JALT CALL Journal*, 9, no. 1: 79–89.

Naismith, Laura, Peter Lonsdale, Giasemi Vavoula, and Mike Sharples. 2004. *Literature Review in Mobile Technologies and Learning*. FutureLab Report 11. Accessed March 5, 2015. http://archive.futurelab.org.uk/resources/documents/lit_reviews/Mobile_Review.pdf

Nakata, Tatsuya. 2011. "Computer-assisted Language Vocabulary Learning in a Paired-associate Paradigm: A Critical Investigation of Flashcard Software." *Computer Assisted Language Learning*, 24, no. 1: 17–38. DOI:10.1080/09588221.2010.520675

Nation, Ian S. P. 2001. *Learning Vocabulary in Another Language*. Cambridge: Cambridge University Press.

Perez, Maribel Montero, Elke Peters, Geraldine Clarebout, and Piet Desmet. 2014. "Effects of Captioning on Video Comprehension and Incidental Vocabulary Learning." *Language Learning & Technology*, 18, no. 1: 118–141.

Pérez-Paredes, Pascual, María Sánchez-Tornel, José María Álcaraz Calero, and Pilar Aguado Jiménez. 2011. "Tracking Learners' Actual Uses of Corpora: Guided vs Non-guided Corpus Consultation." *Computer Assisted Language Learning*, 24, no. 3: 233–253. DOI:10.1080/09588221.2010.539978

Raby, Françoise. 2007. "A Triangular Approach to Motivation in Computer Assisted Autonomous Language Learning (CAALL)." *ReCALL*, 19, no. 2: 181–201. DOI:10.1017/S0958344007000626

Ranalli, Jim. 2009. "Developing Students' Effective Use of Vocabulary-learning Strategies." *CALICO Journal*, 27, no. 1: 161–186. DOI:10.11139/cj.27.1.161-186

Ranalli, Jim. 2013. "Online Strategy Instruction for Integrating Dictionary Skills and Language Awareness." *Language Learning & Technology*, 17, no. 2: 75–99.

Reinders, Hayo, and Philip Hubbard. 2013. "CALL and Learner Autonomy: Affordances and Constraints." In *Contemporary Computer Assisted Language Learning*, edited by Michael Thomas, Hayo Reinders, and Mark Warschauer, 359–376. London: Bloomsbury.

Schmitt, Norbert. 1997. "Vocabulary Learning Strategies." In *Vocabulary: Description, Acquisition and Pedagogy*, edited by Norbert Schmitt and Michael McCarthy, 199–227. Cambridge: Cambridge University Press.

Schmitt, Norbert. 2000. *Vocabulary in Language Teaching*. Cambridge: Cambridge University Press.

Smith, Bryan. 2004. "Computer-mediated Negotiated Interaction and Lexical Acquisition." *Studies in Second Language Acquisition*, 26, no. 3: 365–398. DOI:10.1017/S027226310426301X

Smith, Karen, and Hana Craig. 2013. "Enhancing Learner Autonomy through CALL: A New Model in EFL Curriculum Design." *CALICO Journal*, 30, no. 2: 252–278. DOI:10.11139/cj.30.2.252-278

Song, Yanjie, and Robert Fox. 2008. "Using PDA for Undergraduate Student Incidental Vocabulary Testing." *ReCALL*, 20, no. 3: 290–314. DOI:10.1017/S0958344008000438

Stockwell, Glenn. 2007. "Vocabulary on the Move: Investigating an Intelligent Mobile Phone-based Vocabulary Tutor." *Computer Assisted Language Learning*, 20, no. 4: 365–383. DOI:10.1080/09588220701745817

Stockwell, Glenn. 2010. "Using Mobile Phones for Vocabulary Activities: Examining the Effect of the Platform." *Language Learning & Technology*, 14, no. 2: 95–110.

Stockwell, Glenn. 2013. "Investigating an Intelligent System for Vocabulary Learning through Reading." *The JALT CALL Journal*, 9, no. 3: 259–274.

Swain, Merrill. 1995. "Three Functions of Output in Second Language learning." In *Principle and Practice in Applied linguistics: Studies in Honour of H. G. Widdowson*, edited by Guy Cook and Barbara Seidlhofer, 125–144. Oxford: Oxford University Press.

Thanasoulas, Dimitrios. 2000. "What is Learner Autonomy and How can it be Fostered?" *The Internet TESL Journal*, 6, no. 11. Accessed March 5 2015. http://iteslj.org/Articles/Thanasoulas-Autonomy.html

Thornton, Patricia, and Chris Houser. 2005. "Using Mobile Phones in English Education in Japan." *Journal of Computer Assisted Learning*, 21, no. 3: 217–228. DOI:10.1111/j.1365-2729.2005.00129.x

Wesche, Marjorie Bingham, and T. Sima Paribakht. 2000. "Reading-based Exercises in Second Language Vocabulary Learning: An Introspective Study." *The Modern Language Journal*, 84, no. 2: 196–213. DOI:10.1111/0026-7902.00062

Wible, David, A. L-E. Liu, and N-L. Tsao. 2011. "A Browser-based Approach to Incidental Individualization of Vocabulary Learning." *Journal of Computer Assisted Learning*, 27, no. 6: 530–543. DOI:10.1111/j.1365-2729.2011.00413.x

Winke, Paula, Susan Gass, and Tetyana Sydorenko. 2010. "The Effects of Captioning Videos Used for Foreign Language Listening Activities." *Language Learning & Technology*, 14, no. 1: 65–86.

Wong, Lung-Hsiang, and Chee-Kit Looi. 2011. "What Seams Do We Remove in Mobile-assisted Seamless Learning? A Critical Review of the Literature." *Computers & Education*, 57, no. 4: 2364–81. DOI:10.1016/j. compedu.2011.06.007

Wong, Lung-Hsiang, Chee-Kuen Chin, Chee-Lay Tan, and May Liu. 2010. "Students' Personal and Social Meaning Making in a Chinese Idiom Mobile Learning Environment." *Educational Technology & Society*, 13, no. 4: 15–26.

Yoshii, Makoto. 2006. "L1 and L2 Glosses: Their Effects on Incidental Vocabulary Learning." *Language Learning & Technology*, 10, no. 3: 85–101.

Zimmerman, Barry J. 2000. "Attaining Self-regulation: A Social Cognitive Perspective." In *Handbook of Self-regulation, Research, and Applications*, edited by Monique Boekaerts, Paul R. Pintrich, and Moshe Zeidner, 13–39. Orlando, FL: Academic Press.

Zimmerman, Barry J. 2011. "Motivational Sources and Outcomes of Self-regulated Learning and Performance." In *Handbook of Self-regulation of Learning and Performance*, edited by Barry J. Zimmerman and Dale H. Schunk, 49–64. New York: Routledge.

# 5 Technologies for Teaching and Learning L2 Reading

MEEI-LING LIAW
AND KATHRYN ENGLISH

## Introduction

With widespread access to reading resources and various forms of reading, the concept of reading nowadays may be different from what it once was. Online reading allows readers to interact in compelling ways with text and with others, but readers are at the same time being exposed to the danger of distractions or are overloaded by the volume of materials (Godwin-Jones 2010). This can be especially true for L2 learners reading in a language that they are not proficient in because they need support to overcome linguistic and processing practice limitations (Cobb, in press; Grabe 2014). Due to increased globalization and the spread of technology, many countries are making education policies to prepare students for emerging literacies that involve digital literacies (Leu et al. 2004) and abilities in collaborative inquiries and co-construction of knowledge (Chun 2007). Simultaneously, many Web 2.0 tools and technologies are being designed and used for all levels of L2 learners to build certain skills for effective L2 reading. L2 educators play vital roles in helping students acquire the skills necessary to take advantage of new technological tools so they can actively participate in global communities (Gonglewski and Dubravac 2006). The objectives of this chapter are (1) to inform L2 teachers, researchers, and software designers of the theoretical grounding of applying technological innovations to the teaching of L2 reading, (2) to introduce the variety of technology applications to foster successful L2 reading, (3) to discuss the pitfalls and challenges of reading in the technology age, and (4) to provide thoughts on future directions for applying technology to L2 reading development and the possibilities of cultivating ubiquitous, learner-centered, autonomous learning.

## Theoretical bases for technological applications to L2 reading

As Chun (2011b) points out, an understanding of technology use for learning and teaching a particular language skill, requires knowledge of research about how that language skill is learned. Thus, in this session, L2 reading theories are first briefly reviewed. Then the interconnectivity between second language acquisition (SLA) theories and technological application to language learning, especially in L2 reading, is discussed. These theoretical bases underlie the discussion of various types of technological tools that have been applied to teaching and learning of abilities required for successful L2 reading.

*The Handbook of Technology and Second Language Teaching and Learning*, First Edition.
Edited by Carol A. Chapelle and Shannon Sauro.
© 2017 John Wiley & Sons, Inc. Published 2020 by John Wiley & Sons, Inc.

## L2 reading theories

Reading theories for both L1 and L2 have attempted to explain reading processes from three perspectives: structural, cognitive, and metacognitive. Structural perspectives are also referred to by researchers as the "bottom-up" (Chun and Plass 1997; Nunan 1991) or the "outside-in" (McCarthy 1999) views. They focus on the printed form of a text and postulate that meaning exists in the text and readers are passive recipients of information. According to this view, reading is primarily a matter of decoding a series of written symbols into their aural equivalents in the quest to make sense of the text. For successful decoding, readers need to acquire a set of hierarchically ordered sub-skills that sequentially help improve comprehension ability (LaBerge and Samuels 1985). This view however, has been criticized as being inadequate due to overemphasis on the formal features of language, mainly words and structure, and downplaying the significance of contextual comprehension factors.

The cognitive view brings the role of background knowledge into play and highlights the interactive nature of reading and the constructive aspects of comprehension. It is also referred to as the "top-down" model and was introduced to counteract the over-reliance on linguistic forms in the structural perspective of reading (Chun and Plass 1997; Nunan 1991). From the cognitive view, reading is regarded as a psycholinguistic guessing game, a process in which readers sample the text, make hypotheses, confirm or reject them, make new hypotheses, and so forth (Goodman 1967). Background knowledge and schema development are seen as crucial in cognitive inferencing through contextual cues and hypothesis testing (Smith 2004). Without complete background knowledge or appropriate schemata, readers encounter difficulties processing and understanding the text because such knowledge is needed to interpret sensory data, retrieve information from memory, organize reading goals and sub-goals, allocate resources, and guide the flow of the processing system.

Contemporary models of metacognitive reading were proposed due to the tenuous affirmation of the roles for structural and cognitive language processing in reading development (Askildson 2011; Carrell and Grabe 2002). Although the structural view over-relied on language forms, a reader must know them to comprehend the text. The influence of background knowledge on reading comprehension also cannot be denied (Block 1992). Supporters of the metacognitive view regard reading as a process of active meaning construction during which readers make use of both linguistic information from the external printed text (Langer et al. 1990) as well as their own internal background knowledge (Brantmeier 2003). In addition, skillful readers often use a set of flexible, adaptable metacognitive strategies to make sense of a text and monitor their ongoing understanding of text (Dole 2002). Metacognition involves being aware of what one is doing while reading (Block 1992). Strategic readers are capable of reflecting on their level of understanding and know what to do when reading difficulties occur. By using metacognitive strategies, readers are better at activating background knowledge, identifying and planning reading tasks, and monitoring their own reading (Boulware-Gooden et al. 2007).

Taking together the research findings from both L1 and L2 reading, Grabe (2014) succinctly summarizes reading abilities as lower- and higher-level processes. It is postulated that lower-level processes include automatic word recognition skills, lexico-syntactic processing, and semantic processing of the immediate clause into relevant meaning units; higher-level processing involves using strategies to understand more difficult texts, such as identifying main ideas, recognizing related and thematic information, forming a text model of comprehension, and creating a situation model of reading by using inferencing, background knowledge, strategic processing, context constraints, and so on.

## *SLA theories and applications of technology to L2 reading*

When reading is seen as a means for second language acquisition and technology is added, the L2 reading process becomes even more complex to conceptualize. Digital environments add visual and auditory features to a text and require the reader to integrate the information afforded by these modes into the processes of comprehension. Furthermore, with the interactivity provided by Web technologies, reading is supplemented by a social dimension of instantaneous connectedness not just with text but also with other people for exchanges and co-construction of understanding. To create and evaluate technology for language learning, computer-assisted language learning (CALL) developers and researchers have looked to second language acquisition (SLA) theories for support and guiding principles (see Chapelle 2009 for a succinct summary). Similar to reading theories, SLA theories have also gone through stages of transition. Although SLA approaches of the different stages provide distinct implications for CALL, cognitive linguistic and psycholinguistic approaches have been most commonly adopted for the study of applications of technology to L2 reading (Chapelle 2009; Chun 2011a). More recently, as the Internet provides far-reaching and instantaneous interactivity, researchers and educators increasingly rely on sociocultural approaches.

The focus of cognitive theory on noticing, working memory, automatization of word recognition, and activating prior knowledge has provided theoretical bases for many studies examining how online or multimedia reading scaffolds, such as dictionaries, glosses, and annotation affect vocabulary learning and reading comprehension. For example, Schmidt's (1990) "noticing hypothesis" which maintains that attention is critical in the acquisition process of an L2 has provided the theoretical framework for exploring the effects of different types of multimedia glosses on text comprehension and vocabulary learning of computerized text (Hegelheimer and Chapelle 2000). Based on the noticing hypothesis, efforts have been made to compare reader performance in computerized and traditional paper-pencil glosses on vocabulary development, certain linguistic features, and comprehension (Bowles 2004).

Mayer's (2005) cognitive theory of multimedia learning (CTML) has also been applied to L2 reading studies and to developing multimedia text for L2 reading. Based on three general cognitive science principles (i.e., the dual-channel assumption, the limited capacity assumption, and the active processing assumption), CTML postulates that meaningful learning occurs when students select suitable words and pictures, organize them into coherent pictorial and verbal models, and integrate them with each other and appropriate prior knowledge. When information presented is similar to the learner's cognitive processes, the learner would have better information retention by storing it in long-term memory. An example of applying CTML to the design of multimedia materials for L2 reading is the study by Alkhasawneh et al. (2012), in which the researchers developed a multimedia text to increase students' abilities to comprehend the reading. In another study, Garrett-Rucks, Howles, and Lake (2015) examined the combined use of audiovisual features by 70 French language learners for the reading comprehension of L2 hypermedia text.

Metacognitive approaches also provide theoretical frameworks for understanding how new technologies might be changing L2 reading behaviors (Leu 2002). Research has compared reading strategies used in text-based contexts and online environments (Genc 2011), the strategies used by EFL learners (Omar 2014), as well as by L1 and L2 learners during online reading (Taki 2015). Studies are also exploring strategies and decision-making processes used as L2 learners engage in online reading (Park, Yang, and Hsieh 2014). As mobile devices become increasingly accessible, strategies used in mobile contexts are not left unexplored. Auer (2015) looks into the strategies employed by readers when using the functions afforded by tablets to support reading comprehension. The study by Fu et al. (2014) focused on the effects of reading strategy via e-book reading.

More recently sociocultural theories that posit mediation of understanding through cultural tools have been adopted by researchers to study technologies and L2 development. Different from the cognitive approaches that theorize language learning as processes of acquiring grammatical forms in a specific predetermined order, sociocultural theories maintain that learning occurs in a sociocultural milieu in which learners are active constructors (Lantolf 2010; Rémi and Lawrence 2012). From the sociocultural point of view, reading is not a series of individualistic skills to be mastered. Rather, it is a social skill requiring active participation and interaction of learners involved. Implications of sociocultural perspectives for investigating technology use for L2 reading have not been sufficiently explored (Chun 2011a). However the use of Web technology for social-networking-based learning has led to an increased interest among researchers and CALL material developers to draw on these perspectives as the theoretical framework for their work. Studies have been conducted to understand how sociocultural backgrounds influence L2 learners' use of web-based tools for vocabulary learning, collaborative reading, reading comprehension, and so on (Gao 2013; Juffs and Friedline 2014; Parisa, Mansoor, and Saeed 2014).

A review of the theoretical bases of technological applications to L2 reading demonstrates that SLA perspectives have provided theory-based development and evaluation of both commercial and academic CALL materials for language teaching and learning, including L2 reading. In the areas of vocabulary learning, reading comprehension, reading strategies, activation of background knowledge, motivation, and collaborative reading, they have fulfilled what Chapelle (2009, 742) describes as the "pragmatic goal of marshalling professional knowledge in a manner that is useful for creating learning opportunities and demonstrating successful learning." In turn, technologies are contributing to creating innovative approaches to teaching and learning as well as a means for developing materials for L2 reading.

# Technologies in use for teaching and learning of L2 reading

The range and quantity of applications of new technologies for reading have grown rapidly. Selecting the appropriate one from an ever-expanding pool can be an overwhelming task for teachers. The processes of making decisions about which technology to use to teach targeted language skills and for specific pedagogical objectives can also be complicated. To shed light on the matter, Stockwell (2007) reviewed the empirical research articles published in four major English-language journals in the field of CALL (*CALICO Journal, CALL, Language Learning & Technology,* and *ReCALL*) from 2001 to 2005 and identified four broad categories of technology: self-developed courseware, online activities, commercial/freeware, and computer-mediated communications (CMC). Levy (2009) also described the technologies in use for major L2 learning skills, including L2 reading. Golonka et al. (2014) reviewed over 350 studies and summarized the effectiveness of technology used in foreign language (FL) learning and teaching. Among the identified six major types of technologies, individual study tools and mobile and portable devices were found to have been applied to FL reading with various degrees of success. Cobb (in press), viewing reading itself as an interaction with a technology, highlights the technologies that expand this interaction particularly in L2 reading. In this section, the technologies most relevant to L2 reading are described using the categorization synthesized from listings provided by aforementioned researchers. They include (1) self-developed course and commercial courseware,

(2) online activities with individual tools and mobile devices, and (3) CMC. Empirical studies and their findings on the effectiveness on L2 reading are also provided.

## Self-developed and commercial courseware

### Self-developed courseware

Self-developed courseware is usually designed by collaborative teams to create language learning tools to suit a specific group of learners. It may involve several stages, components, or systems that are available online. Different modes of vocabulary annotation and multimedia glosses are often built-in to help learners increase vocabulary size and improve comprehension of text. The utilization of intelligent tutoring systems (ITSs) to provide immediate, customized instruction or feedback to learners is also increasing.

A fair amount of self-developed courseware for teaching L2 reading has been used and its effectiveness documented. Studies have explored users' preferences for different types of annotations. Chun (2001) designed a web-based learning environment, netLearn, for German learners who were preparing to study abroad. netLearn includes a program-internal glossary, an external online bilingual dictionary, and an audio narration of the text. Ercetin (2003) also explored users' preferences for different types of annotations but with the added element of language proficiency level. The study was based on a hypermedia learning environment in which word definitions, pronunciation of words, graphics, and videos were incorporated to assist EFL adult learners to read online. Yeh and Wang (2003) investigated EFL learners' preferences for different types of vocabulary annotations and whether learner perceptual learning style would impact the effectiveness of vocabulary annotations. Shalmani and Sabet (2010) explored the effects of three types of multimedia glosses on the reading comprehension of learners in an EFL context. Yamat, Ismail, and Shah (2012) developed a reading program on sulphuric acid with integrated hypermedia features, for learning the subject of English for Science and Technology.

A growing incorporation of intelligent tutoring systems (ITS) into self-developed courseware has been due to technological breakthroughs from the fields of computational linguistics, information retrieval, cognitive science, artificial intelligence, and discourse processing. ITSs are designed to simulate a human tutor's behavior and guidance. A well-designed ITS system provides users with convenient access to individualized practice, models good problem-solving approaches, and helps learners based on their learning rates and specific needs. Salomon, Globerson, and Guterman (1989) studied the effectiveness of their computerized reading tool, Reading Partner, and found students improved in metacognitive reconstruction, reading comprehension, and the quality of written essays. The technologies for creating an ITS have improved a great deal since then. A research team at Pennsylvania State University has developed a web-based ITS for improving learners' reading comprehension by presenting and training them to use the structure strategy to read (Wijekumar and Meyer, 2006). REAP, developed by researchers at Carnegie Mellon University, provides reader-specific lexical practice for reading comprehension (Brown and Eskenazi 2004).

Some systems have been created specifically with L2 learners in mind. For example, in Taiwan, Tsai (2011) created multimedia courseware for EFL learners to improve English language proficiency through readings on world heritage sites. Wang (2014) uses an adaptive Business English self-learning system for EFL vocabulary study. Given the rapid growth of wireless and mobile technologies, it is inevitable for intelligent tutoring systems to go mobile. The personalized mobile learning system created by Chen and Hsu (2008) uses Fuzzy Item Response Theory to evaluate learners' reading ability to recommend English news articles to learners via personal digital assistant (PDA) devices. Vocabulary unknown or unfamiliar to the individual learner can be automatically detected and retrieved for vocabulary enriching learning.

## Commercial courseware

Commercial courseware is ready-made, licensed, and sold by companies. It usually consists of a combination of lessons, activities, tests, and other relevant materials. It has been widely available and researchers have provided guidelines, principles, checklists for evaluations (for example, Borges 2014; Chapelle 2001; Hubbard 2006); however empirical studies evaluating their effectiveness specifically on reading are limited.

One popular commercial courseware that was studied for its effectiveness for L2 learning of listening and reading is Longman English Online. Jamieson, Chapelle, and Preiss (2004) evaluated its design and showed that it met most of their criteria. A newer version, Longman English Interactive (LEI), was again examined and compared to another commercially available online courseware, Quartet Online (Quartet Scholar) by Dinçer and Parmaksız (2013). Rosetta Stone and Auralog's TELL ME MORE are also popular, commercially available, technology-mediated self-study packages. Nielson (2011) conducted a study at the University of Maryland on how adult learners use Rosetta Stone and Auralog's TELL ME MORE. The study found that technological problems and insufficient support for autonomous learning could severely affect the effectiveness of the courseware.

While some educators are able to develop their own courseware to meet the specific needs of their students, most of them have neither the time nor the technical support. The market for commercial language learning courseware is vast and expanding. More studies on evaluating commercial courseware would help teachers to choose those most appropriate so institutional investment is not wasted.

# Online activities with individual study tools and portable devices

In Stockwell's (2007) view, online activities are different from "courseware," in that the former refers to smaller-scale independent activities that are not part of a larger package. Many of these activities incorporate digital scaffolding tools, such as dictionaries, annotations, glosses, concordances, reading-level classification tools, speech synthesis/recognition technology, and mobile devices.

## Dictionaries, glosses, and annotations

The increasing availability of electronic corpora and online technology has facilitated the creation of tools that aim to support L2 reading by accelerating and automatizing word recognition. Today one can easily access millions of word definitions, spellings, audio pronunciations, example sentences, and word origins free from publishers like Cambridge, Oxford, Macmillan, and Dictonary.com who have teams of experienced lexicographers to compile and continuously update the content of their dictionaries. There are also dictionaries created by individual enthusiasts, such as WordReference.com. Free web-based document annotation tools are also available, for example, Annotate.com allows users to add notes and tags to their text and images. Similar Web annotation tools that allow users to modify data from a Web resource without modifying the original Web page include Diigo, Bounce, Corcodoc, Markup.i0, and so on.

A great majority of studies dealing with technology or CALL for L2 reading have focused on teaching and learning L2 vocabulary. This is no surprise since knowing vocabulary is key to learning to read and comprehend just as exposure to texts containing key vocabulary is necessary for learning vocabulary. The use of electronic dictionaries, text-based glosses, as well as annotations and multimedia glosses has been extensively researched since they appeared in late 1990s (see Chun 2011a for a comprehensive review).

In recent years, as NLP tools and resources have become more versatile, vocabulary learning tools are increasingly adaptive to learner control and needs. The SmartReader designed by Oflazer, Kemal, and Mitamura (2013) allows users to either choose a text from the system's library or upload a document of their own to create intelligent e-books. The vocabulary learning tool MyVLS-Reader was specifically designed by Hsu and Ou Yang (2013) for university students majoring in science and technology and also provides multiple learning choices for its users.

## Concordancing tools

A concordancer is a corpus analysis tool that extracts instances of a given word from a corpus, database, or the Internet and then presents to the user a list of the occurrences of the word, part of the word, or combinations of words, together with their contexts, from a corpus of texts. The development of corpus analysis software and computer networking makes it easier for learners to access free online concordances. Tom Cobb's (2015) *LEXTUTOR* and William Fletcher's (2015) *Phrases in English* are two sophisticated websites with concordancing tools freely available to users. More concordancing tools and other text analysis software can be found on the website made by David Lee (2010) (http://www.uow.edu.au/~dlee/software.htm#Concordancers).

Since the 1990s much research has described how language learners could benefit from using concordancing tools (Aston, 2001; Johns and King 1991; O'Keeffe, McCarthy, and Carter 2007) or searching for innovative ways to effectively utilize them for L2 learning (Sorell and Shin 2007). In L2 reading, research has shown that using concordance can enhance the effects of online textual glosses and help learners seek productive vocabulary knowledge (Poole 2012), increase awareness of collocations of lexis (Binkai 2012), and increase vocabulary recall (Jalilifara, Mehrabib, and Mousavinia 2014). L2 users in general hold positive perceptions of and attitudes toward the use of concordance and concordancing related tasks (Aliponga 2013; Jalilifara, Mehrabib, and Mousavinia 2014; Poole 2012). Nevertheless, how to integrate corpora into English language teaching and learning can be a challenge (Binkai 2012). There is a need to provide students with enough practice to know how to use the concordancer. In addition, the contexts or corpora in the concordances need to be carefully chosen to meet students' proficiency levels so as not to frustrate them.

## Reading-level classification tools

Though based on the same belief that vocabulary knowledge is the foundation to reading comprehension, reading-level classification tools work from a different angle. They take the approach of modifying texts so readers understand them better. Supporters of text simplification uphold that linguistic modifications increase text comprehensibility and subsequently facilitate readers' abilities to interact with and comprehend a text (Allen and Widdowson 1979; Goodman and Freeman 1993; Long and Ross 1993).

Progress in computational linguistics, corpus linguistics, information extraction and retrieval enables the investigation of text using language variables related to text comprehension, cognitive processes, and other factors to go beyond the surface level features of language measured by traditional readability formulas (Crossley, Allen, and McNamara 2011; Loucky 2010). Cobb (2007) introduced frequency profiling software, VocabProfile, and a text comparison program, TexLexCompare. VocabProfile can find, adapt, or create texts to a pre-specified lexical profile and coverage. TexLexCompare can establish degree of lexical recycling over a series of texts. Ghadirian (2002) developed a computer program, TextLadder, which can sort through teacher-selected articles and find texts with a high proportion of target words ensuring multiple encounters with these words, and then sequence them for optimal presentation of vocabulary. Empirical findings suggest that using the procedures of language preparation and automatic text simplification tools is beneficial for L2 learners (Alhawiti 2015).

Cultural elements have also been considered by researchers when designing text classification tools. Huang and Liou (2007) incorporate authentic materials related to home culture to design a self-developed text selection system, Textgrader. Another interesting direction for text analysis and classification is in webpage analysis. Miltsakaki and Troutt (2008) have developed a system, Read-X, to perform keyword searches, thematic classifications, and analyses of Web text reading difficulty. The possibility of using NLP technologies to turn the vast variety of text resources, ranging from personal blogs to academic papers, into reading materials for users of different reading abilities is exciting. At the same time, empirical studies looking into the effectiveness of this futuristic system are needed.

## Speech synthesis and speech recognition

Text-to-Speech (TTS) is the process of synthesizing natural sounding speech from text via computer programs. Speech synthesis technology has been around since the 1960s and the tools applying the technology are now quite accessible. Many of them are freely available (e.g., Speak Selection, Screen Reader, Natural Reader) but some are commercial (e.g., Text Reader, Voice Dream Reader). Google Chrome also provides free TTS tools to support teaching and learning of reading (e.g., Select and Speak, SpeakIt!, Reading & Write for Google). Some TTS applications are created specifically for L2 learning. Voki, created by Oddcast, allows users to create their own talking avatar, speaking different accents. They can even be emailed, embedded on websites, or shared on social media. Teachers can use its classroom management system to assign students classwork.

TTS tools have been applied to assist struggling readers in L1 (Schmitt et al. 2011). They also receive attention from researchers for their potential to enhance L2 reading. Volodina and Pijetlovic (2015) report on the development and the initial evaluation of a dictation and spelling prototype exercise for L2 learners of Swedish based on TTS technology. Proctor, Dalton, and Grisham (2007) tested it on struggling readers, including Spanish-speaking English as L2 learners.

Speech recognition (SR), in essence, is the process of allowing computer software to interpret the meaning of a speaker's utterances. SR also has been increasingly incorporated in L2 learning. There are many providers of commercially available CALL systems that use technology, including Rosetta Stone (*Tell Me More*), Pearson (*MyLab*), Scientific Learning (*Soliloquy Reading Assistant*), eLanguage (*Learn to Speak*), Carnegie Speech (*NativeAccent*), L Labs (*MyET*), Livemocha, English Central, Duolingo, Babbel, Aleo, and Berlitz. Studies have examined some SR software (e.g., IBM *Reading Companion* and *Watch-me!-Read*, Carnegie Mellon's Project LISTEN, Colorado *Literacy Tutor*, University of Birmingham STAR Project), and findings suggest that their uses bring not only motivation and encouragement but also improve reading ability in children (Mostow et al. 2008). Reading Companion has been applied to help children in Taiwan improve reading in EFL (Liaw 2013). Meihami and Varmaghani (2013) reported how Tell Me More Software was used to help students improve EFL reading comprehension.

## Mobile devices

Mobile devices have many advantages as learning tools, which include learning written language. They are portable and provide access to an ever-expanding amount of information and resources, which can be shared through apps and/or social networking sites. The three-year observation made by Stockwell (2010) of EFL students in Japan suggests an increase in the use of mobile phones over time for vocabulary learning. In the study by

Motallebzadeh and Ganjali (2011) vocabulary was taught by sending short messages (SMS) via mobile phones and positive results were found. Gheytasi, Azizifara, and Gowhary (2015) conducted a similar study and found students receiving instructions via mobile phones achieved higher reading comprehension scores than the other group who were taught using a conventional approach. Alemi and Lari (2012) compared effects of using SMS and dictionaries for vocabulary learning and found SMS more effective and welcomed by the participants. Kim's study (2014) showed that students who discussed reading topics through their mobile device outside of class significantly outperformed the other group who did not in reading comprehension.

## CMC technologies (Chat, Moo, email)

Reading instruction is increasingly informed by sociocultural and learner-centered constructive perspectives, with one consequence that cooperative reading and co-construction of meaning from text are now making their way into L2 learning. Furthermore, in today's information age, CMC technologies, ranging from email, free browser extension tools, to innovative systems designed by researchers can be accessed to facilitate cooperative reading among learners of different cultural and linguistic backgrounds. Shang (2005) developed an electronic-based peer collaborative environment to explore students' attitudes toward email applications in reading classes. Lan (2013) designed a co-sharing-based strategy learning system for L2 vocabulary learning known as "Mywordtools." Lan, Sung, and Chang (2007) developed a mobile-device-supported peer-assisted learning (MPAL) system for collaborative EFL reading activities and found the system improved elementary school EFL learners' collaboration and reading skills. eComma, an open source Web application for textual annotation developed by the Center for Open Education Resources and Language Learning, was developed to turn reading into a group activity during which learners help each other understand a text (Blyth 2013).

# Challenges

Reading in the technological age is making a tremendous impact on how we see and interact with the world. For L2 learners, the abundant access to authentic information resources and technological tools to facilitate learning L2 reading are creating unprecedented opportunities for potential success. Nonetheless, the affordance of interactivity also leads to distracted minds, information overload, and fragmentation (Cobb, in press; Godwin-Jones 2010). Students nowadays constantly engage in reading and interacting often by using short, de-contextualized informal language that may distract them from focused thinking. One important challenge today for educators is then to find creative and effective ways to lead distracted readers back to productive language learning.

Another challenge faced by educators is keeping up with the ever-evolving technologies and selecting the most appropriate ones to design instruction with sound principles of reading. Technologies can support successful L2 reading; at the same time, they are increasingly complex and hard to follow. Often, factors for using technologies in the classroom are social and economically driven instead of pedagogically-oriented. Instructors frequently adapt tools on an ad hoc basis. New technologies emerge more rapidly than educators can connect them with theoretical or pedagogical grounding. The needs of this rapidly evolving environment do not fit well with predefined curricula, annualized budgets, and programmed institutional investments. Resources would need to be as reactive and the teaching environment then prioritized, and this is contingent on L2 teaching conditions which vary widely.

Traditionally, teachers are educated about the nature of reading and are ready to teach based on their education. However, as reading and required strategies change due to new technologies, many teachers find their knowledge obsolete and inapplicable to meet the needs of their students. Teacher education thus also faces challenges of cultivating teachers' abilities to continuously learn the changing technologies and develop new visions for literacy.

# Future directions

It is foreseeable that technology developers and educational researchers will continue to build products and learning environments for a wide range of student abilities and preferences. They can indeed be useful for the teaching and learning of L2 reading but should not be used simply because they are available (Chun 2007). Sound support of reading and SLA theories, as well as pedagogical considerations are essential. It is also important to envision how the notions of reading, writing, and literacy are changing in the global context. Reading in the digital age is not just about decoding text; it is also critically evaluating and co-constructing on the globally-connected information super highway. Goodwin-Jones (2010) points out that as we use available tools, we in turn are shaped by them. Therefore, by choosing the tools, we also select how and what we are becoming. In this context, L2 reading may be shaped by three trends in technology of learning.

First, ubiquitous learning may be possible because reading materials are widely available via mobile devices, which offer portability and instant forms of communication on the go. In mobile learning, computers are not limited by being embedded in the learner's surroundings. In a ubiquitous learning environment the learning is supported by embedded and invisible computers as well as networks in everyday life. While learners are moving with mobile devices, the system dynamically supports learning by communicating with embedded computers in the environment and mapping real objects and the information into a virtual world. Ubiquitous learning systems have been developed for L2 vocabulary learning and reading comprehension, and their future is encouraging as the technologies are fast-evolving to provide greater adaptability for diverse L2 reading needs in real-life contexts.

Second, adaptive learning and personalization may continue to be developed for learning L2 reading. As mentioned earlier, continuous efforts have been made on building flexible and adaptable scaffolding tools to address diverse learner needs. Learner-centeredness will continue to be the force leading design and selection of technological tools. More learner preferred features will be incorporated for students who need them, invisible to those who do not, and adjustable and removable to accommodate the learner's reading progress. As for learner preferences and needs, in addition to teachers' professional judgement, Big Data technology can be applied to turn information overload into useful knowledge for designing learner-fit L2 reading materials and learning systems. Additionally, alternative formats, such as visual-syntactic text formatting (VSTF) which replaces the block-shaped text of the standard format with a cascading pattern, have been suggested by researchers to help readers identify grammatical structure and increase reading comprehension (Yu and Miller 2010; Warschauer, Park, and Walker 2011).

Third, these technologies may continue to work toward autonomous learning. The ultimate goal of scaffolding and learner-centered technologies is to automate identification of appropriate learning tools for students. Researchers have taken up social-interactive approaches to foster learner autonomy with technology, including incorporating learner choices, learner productions, and project-based tasks (Collentine 2011). Researchers emphasize raising learner metalinguistic awareness and motivation for L2 learning by using technological innovations, but psychological differences in how language learners conceptualize and relate to particular technologies also need to be taken into account. The range of new technologies being applied to the evolving process of reading indicates that this is an area of continuing innovation.

# REFERENCES

Abdolrezapour, Parisa, Mansoor Tavakoli, and Saeed Ketabi. 2014, "Qualitative Analysis of Mediational Strategies in Emotionalized Dynamic Assessment of L2 Reading Comprehension," *International Journal of Research Studies in Language Learning*, 3, no. 1: 1–16.

Alemi, Minoo and Zahra Lari. 2012. "SMS Vocabulary Learning: A Tool to Promote Reading Comprehension in L2." *International Journal of Linguistics*, 4, no. 4: 275–287.

Alhawiti, Khaled M. 2015. "Innovative Processes in Computer Assisted Language Learning." *International Journal of Advanced Research in Artificial Intelligence*, 4, no. 2: 7–13.

Alkhasawneh, Sani Sami, F. Abd Rahman1, A. F. bin M. Ayub, and S. bin M. Daud. 2012. "Developing Multimedia Text for Reading Comprehension Based on Cognitive Theory of Multimedia Teaching." *International Journal of Innovative Ideas*, 12, no. 4: 11–19.

Allen, J. P. B., and Henry G. Widdowson. 1979. "Teaching the Communicative Use of English." In *The communicative Approach to Language Teaching*, edited by C. Brumfit & K. Johnson, 124–142. Oxford: Oxford University Press.

Aliponga, Jonathan. 2013. "What do EFL Students Think and Feel about Concordancing?" *Academic Journal of Interdisciplinary Studies*, 2, no. 1: 11–20.

Askildson, Lance R. 2011. "A Review of CALL and L2 Reading: Glossing for Comprehension and Acquisition." *International Journal of Computer-Assisted Language Learning and Teaching (IJCALLT)*, 1, no. 4: 49–58.

Aston, Guy, ed. 2001. *Learning with Corpora*. Houston, TX: Athelstan.

Auer, Natalia. 2015. "Promoting Strategic Reading Using the iBooks Author Application." In *Advancing Higher Education with Mobile Learning Technologies: Cases, Trends, and Inquiry-based Methods*, edited by J. Keengwe and M. B. Maxfield, 179. Hersey, PA: IGI Global.

Binkai, Jiao. 2012. "An Empirical Study on Corpus-driven English Vocabulary Learning in China." *English Language Teaching*, 5, no. 4: 131–137.

Block, Ellen L. 1992. "See How They Read: Comprehension Monitoring of L1 and L2 Readers." *TESOL Quarterly*, 26, no. 2: 319–343.

Blyth, Carl. 2013. "eComma: An Open Source Tool for Collaborative L2 Reading." In *Case Studies of Openness in the Language Classroom*, edited by A. Beaven, A. Comas Quinn, and B. Sawhill, 32–42. Research-publishing.net. https://research-publishing.net/publication/chapters/978-1-908416-10-0/Blyth_108.pdf

Borges, Vládia M. C. 2014. "Are ESL/EFL Software Programs Effective for Language Learning?" *Ilha Desterro*, 66. Accessed June 8, 2916. http://dx.doi.org/10.5007/2175-8026.2014n66p19

Boulware-Gooden, Regina, Suzanne Carreker, Ann Thornhill, and R. Malatesha Joshi. 2007. "Instruction of Metacognitive Strategies Enhances Reading Comprehension and Vocabulary Achievement of Third-Grade Students." *The Reading Teacher*, 61, no. 1: 70–77.

Bowles, Melissa A. 2004. "L2 Glossing: To CALL or Not to CALL," *Hispania*, 87, no. 3: 541–552.

Brantmeier, Cindy. 2003. "Technology and Second Language Reading at the University Level: Informed Instructors' Perceptions," *The Reading Matrix*, 3, no. 3: 50–74.

Brown, Jonathan, and Maxine Eskenazi. 2004. "Retrieval of Authentic Documents for Reader-specific Lexical Practice." In *Proceedings of InSTIL/ICALL Symposium 2004*. Venice, Italy. Accessed June 8, 2016. http://www.philippe-fournier-viger.com/ill-defined/ITS06_illdefinedworkshop_HeilmanEskenazi.pdf

Carrell, Patricia L., and William Grabe. 2002. "Reading." In *An Introduction to Applied Linguistics*, edited by N. Schmitt, 233–250. London: Arnold.

Chapelle, Carol A. 2001. *Computer Applications in Second Language Acquisition: Foundations for Teaching, Testing, and Research*. Cambridge: Cambridge University Press.

Chapelle, Carol A. 2009. "The Relationship between Second Language Acquisition Theory and Computer-assisted Language Learning." *The Modern Language Journal*, 93: 741–753.

Chen, Chih-Ming, and Shih-Hsun Hsu. 2008. "Personalized Intelligent Mobile Learning System for Supporting Effective English Learning." *Educational Technology & Society*, 11, no. 3: 153–180.

Chun, Dorothy M. 2001. "L2 Reading on the Web: Strategies for Accessing Information in Hypermedia." *Computer-Assisted Language Learning*, 14, no, 5: 367–403.

Chun, Dorothy M. 2007. "Come Ride the Wave: But Where is it Taking Us?" *CALICO Journal*, 24, no. 2: 239–252.

Chun, Dorothy M. 2011a. "CALL Technologies for L2 Reading Post Web 2.0." In *Present and Future Promises of CALL: From Theory a Research to New Directions in Language Teaching*, edited by N. Arnold & L. Ducate, 131–170. San Marcos, TX: The Computer Assisted Language Instruction Consortium.

Chun, Dorothy M. 2011b. "Computer-assisted Language Learning." In *Handbook of Research in Second Language Teaching and Learning*, vol. 2, edited by E. Hinkel, 663–680. New York: Routledge.

Chun, Dorothy M., and Jan L. Plass. 1997. "Research on Text Comprehension in Multimedia Environments." *Language Learning and Technology*, 1, no. 1: 60–81.

Cobb, Tom. 2007. "Computing the Vocabulary Demands of L2 Reading." *Language Learning & Technology*, 11, no. 3: 38–64.

Cobb, Tom. 2015. "The Compleat Lexical Tutor."Accessed June 8. 2016. http://www.lextutor.ca/

Cobb, Tom. (in press). "Technology for Teaching Reading" In *TESOL Encyclopedia of English Language Teaching*, Editor-in Chief John I. Liontas Wiley.

Collentine, Karina. 2011. "Learner Autonomy in a Task-based 3D World and Production." *Language Learning & Technology*, 15, no. 3: 50–67.

Crossley, Scott A., David B. Allen, Danielle S. McNamara. 2011. "Text Readability and Intuitive Simplification: A Comparison of Readability Formulas." *Reading in a Foreign Language*, 23, no. 1: 84–101.

Dinçer, Biçer, and Ramazan Şükrü Parmaksız. 2013. "Comparison of Computer Assisted Language Learning Software before Investment." *The Online Journal of Distance Education and e-Learning*, 1, no. 4: 1–9.

Dole, Janice A. 2002. "Comprehension Strategies." In *Literacy in America: An Encyclopedia of History, Theory and Practice*, edited by I. B. Guzzetti, 85–88. New York: ABC-CLIO.

Ercetin, Gulcan. 2003. "Exploring ESL Learners' Use of Hypermedia Reading Glosses." *CALICO Journal*, 20, no. 2: 261–283.

Fletcher, William H. 2015. "Phrases in English."Accessed June 8, 2016. http://phrasesinenglish.org/

Fu, Yu-Ju, Shu-Hui Chen, Shyh-Chyi Wey, and Shu-Chu Chen. 2014. "The Effects of Reading Strategy Instruction via Electronic Storybooks on EFL Young Readers' Reading Performance." *International Journal of Contemporary Educational Research*, 1, no. 1: 9–20.

Gao, Fei. 2013. "A Case Study of Using a Social Annotation Tool to Support Collaborative Learning." *The Internet and Higher Education*, 17: 76–83.

Garrett-Rucks, Paula, Les Howles, and William M. Lake. 2015. "Enhancing L2 Reading Comprehension with Hypermedia Texts: Student Perceptions." *CALICO Journal*, 32, no. 1: 26–51.

Genc, Humeyra. 2011. "Paper and Screen: Reading Strategies Used by Low-proficient EFL Learners." *Sino-US English Teaching*, 8, no. 10: 648–658.

Ghadirian, Sina. 2002. "Providing Controlled Exposure to Target Vocabulary through the Screening and Arranging of texts." *Language Learning and Technology*, 6, no. 1: 147–164.

Gheytasi, Maryam, Akbar Azizifar, and Habib Gowhary. 2015. "The Effect of Smartphone on the Reading Comprehension Proficiency of Iranian EFL Learners." *Procedia – Social and Behavioral Sciences*, 199: 225–230.

Godwin-Jones, Robert. 2010. "Emerging Technologies Literacies and Technologies Revisited." *Language Learning and Technology*, 14, no. 3: 2–9.

Golonka, Ewa M., Anita R. Bowles, Victor M. Frank, Dorna L. Richardson, and Suzanne Freynik. 2014. "Technologies for Foreign Language Learning: A Review of Technology Types and their Effectiveness," *Computer Assisted Language Learning*, 27, no. 1: 70–105.

Gonglewski, Margaret, and Stayc DuBravac. 2006. "Multiliteracy: Second Language Literacy in the Multimedia Environment," In *Present and Future Promises of CALL: From Theory a Research to New Directions in Language Teaching*, edited by N. Arnold & L. Ducate, 43–68. San Marcos, TX: The Computer Assisted Language Instruction Consortium.

Goodman, Kenneth S. 1967. "Reading: A Psycholinguistic Guessing Game." *Journal of the Reading Specialist*, 6, no. 4: 126–135.

Goodman, Kenneth S., and David Freeman. 1993. "What's Simple in Simplified Language." In *Simplification: Theory and Application*, edited by M.L. Tickoo, 69–76. Singapore: SEAMEO Regional Language Center.

Grabe, William. 2014. "Key Issues in L2 Reading Development." In *4th CELC Symposium Proceedings*, edited by Xudong Deng and Richard Seow, 8–18. National University of Singapore.

Hegelheimer, Volker and Carol A. Chapelle. 2000. "Methodological Issues in Research on Learner-computer Interactions in CALL." *Language Learning and Technology*, 4, no. 1: 41–59.

Hsu, Chihcheng, and Fang-Chuan Ou Yang. 2013. "A Vocabulary Learning Tool for L2 Undergraduates Reading Science and Technology Textbooks." *International Journal of Science Education*, 35, no. 7: 1110–1138.

Huang, Hung-Tzu, and Hsien-Chin Liou. 2007. "Vocabulary Learning in an Automated Graded Reading Program." *Language Learning & Technology*, 11, no. 3: 64–82.

Hubbard, Philip. 2006. "Evaluating CALL Software" In *Calling on CALL: From Theory and Research to New Directions in Foreign Language Teaching*, edited by Lara Ducate and Nike Arnold, 313–338. San Marcos, TX: CALICO.

Jalilifara, Alireza, Khodayar Mehrabi, and Seyyed Reza Mousavinia. 2014. "The Effect of Concordance Enriched Instruction on the Vocabulary Learning and Retention of Iranian EFL Learners." *Procedia – Social and Behavioral Sciences*, 98: 742–746.

Jamieson, Joan, Carol Chapelle, and Sherry Preiss. 2004. "Putting Principles into Practice." *ReCALL*, 16, no. 2: 396–415.

Johns, Tim, and Philip King, eds. 1991. *Classroom Concordancing*. Birmingham: The University of Birmingham Centre for English Language Studies.

Juffs, Alan, and Benjamin E. Friedline. 2014. "Sociocultural Influences on the Use of a Web-based Tool for Learning English vocabulary." *System*, 42:48–59.

Kim, Hea-Suk. 2014. "Effects of Using Mobile Devices in Blended Learning for English Reading Comprehension." *Multimedia-Assisted Language Learning*, 17, no. 2: 64–85.

LaBerge, David, and S. Jay Samuels. 1974. "Toward a Theory of Automatic Information Processing in Reading." *Cognitive Psychology*, 6: 293–323.

Lan, Yu-Ju. 2013. "The Effect of Technology-Supported Co-Sharing on L2 Vocabulary Strategy Development." *Educational Technology & Society*, 16, no. 4: 1–16.

Lan, Yu-Ju, Yao-Ting Sung, and Kuo-En Chang. 2007. "A Mobile-device-supported Peer-assisted Learning System for Collaborative Early EFL Reading." *Language Learning and Technology*, 11, no. 3: 130–151.

Langer, Judith A., Lilia Bartolome, Olga Vasquez, and Tamara Lucas. 1990. "Meaning Construction in School Literacy Tasks: A Study of Bilingual Students." *American Educational Research Journal*, 27: 427–471.

Lantolf, James P. 2010. "Sociocultural Theory and the Pedagogical Imperative." In *The Oxford Handbook of Applied Linguistics*, 2nd ed., edited by Robert B. Kaplan, 163–177. New York: Oxford University Press.

Lee, David. 2010. "Bookmarks for Corpus-based Linguists." Accessed June 8, 2016. http://tiny.cc/corpora

Leu, Donald J., Jr. 2002. "The New Literacies: Research on Reading Instruction with the Internet and other Digital Technologies." In *What Research Has to Say about Reading Instruction*, 3rd ed., edited by A. E. Farstrup and S. J. Samuels, 310–336. Newark, DE: International Reading Association.

Leu, Donald J., Jr., Charles K. Kinzer, Julie L. Coiro, and Dana W. Cammack. 2004. "Toward a Theory of New Literacies Emerging from the Internet and Other ICT." In *Theoretical Models and Processes of Reading*, 5th ed., edited by R. B. Ruddell and N. Unrau, 1568–1611. Newark, DE: International Reading Association.

Levy, Mike. 2009. "Technologies in Use for Second Language Learning," *The Modern Language Journal*, 93: 769–782.

Liaw, Meei-Ling. 2013. "The Affordance of Speech Recognition Technology for EFL Learning in an Elementary School Setting." *Innovation in Language Learning and Teaching*, 8, no. 1: 79–93.

Long, Michael H., and Steven Ross. 1993. "Modifications that Preserve Language and Content." In *Simplification: Theory and Application*, edited by M. L. Tickoo, 29–52. Singapore: SEAMEO Regional Language Center.

Loucky, John Paul. 2010. "Constructing a Roadmap to More Systematic and Successful Online Reading and Vocabulary Acquisition," *Literary Linguist Computing*, 25, no. 2: 225–241.

Mayer, Richard E. 2005. "Cognitive Theory of Multimedia Learning." In *The Cambridge Handbook of Multimedia Learning*, edited by Richard E. Mayer, 31–48. Cambridge: Cambridge University Press.

McCarthy, Ciaran P. 1999. "Reading Theory as a Microcosm of the Four Skills," *The Internet TESL Journal*, 5, no. 5.

Meihami, Hussein, and Zeinab Varmaghani. 2013. "The Effect of Integrating Computer-assisted Language Learning Materials in L2 Reading

Comprehension Classroom." *International Letters of Social and Humanistic Sciences*, 9: 49–58.

Miltsakaki, Eleni, and Audrey Troutt. 2008. "Real-Time Web Text Classification and Analysis of Reading Difficulty." In *Proceedings of the Third ACL Workshop on Innovative Use of NLP for Building Educational Applications* edited by Joel Tetreault, Jill Burstein, and Rachele De Felice, 89–97, Columbus, OH, June 2008. Published by Association for Computational Linguistics.

Mostow, Jack, Gregory Aist, Cathy Huang, Brian Junker, Rebecca Kennedy, Hua Lan, DeWitt Talmadge Latimer, R. O'Connor, R. Tassone, Brian Tobin, and A. Wierman. 2008. "4-Month Evaluation of a Learner-controlled Reading Tutor that Listens." In *The Path of Speech Technologies in Computer Assisted Language Learning: From Research Toward Practice*, edited by V. M. Holland and F. P. Fisher, 201–219. New York: Routledge.

Motallebzadeh, Khalil and Razyeh Ganjali. 2011. "SMS: Tool for L2 Vocabulary Retention and Reading Comprehension Ability." *Journal of Language Teaching and Research*, 2, no. 5: 1111–1115.

Nielson, Katharine B. 2011. "Self-study with Language Learning Software in the Workplace: What Happens?" *Language Learning and Technology*, 15, no. 3: 110–129.

Nunan, David. 1991. *Language Teaching Methodology*. Harlow: Prentice Hall International.

Oflazer, Mahmoud Azab, Ahmed Salama Kemal, and Hideki Shima Jun Araki Teruko Mitamura. 2013. "An English Reading Tool as a NLP Showcase," In *Proceedings of Recent Advances in Natural Language Processing*, edited by Galia Angelova, Kalina Bontcheva, and Ruslan Mitkov, 41–48, Hissar, Bulgaria, 7–13 September, 2013.

O'Keeffe, Anne, Michael J. McCarthy, and Ronald A. Carter. 2007. *From Corpus to Classroom: Language Use and Language Teaching*. Cambridge: Cambridge University Press.

Omar, Najwa Alsayed. 2014. "Online Metacognitive Reading Strategies Use by Postgraduate Libyan EFL Students." *International Journal of Social, Behavioral, Educational, Economic and Management Engineering*, 8, no. 7: 2259–2262.

Park, Jaehan, Jae-Seok Yang, and Yi Chin Hsieh. 2014. "University Level Second Language Readers' Online Reading and Comprehension Strategies." *Language Learning and Technology*, 18, no. 3: 148–172.

Poole, Robert. 2012. "Concordance-based Glosses for Academic Vocabulary Acquisition," *CALICO Journal*, 29, no. 4: 679–693.

Proctor, C. Patrick, Bridget Dalton, and Dana L. Grisham. 2007. "Scaffolding English Language Learners and Struggling Readers in a Universal Literacy Environment with Embedded Strategy Instruction and Vocabulary Support." *Journal of Literacy Research*, 39, no. 1: 71–93.

Salomon, Gavriel, Tamar Globerson, and Eva Guterman. 1989. "The Computer as a Zone of Proximal Development: Internalizing Reading-related Metacognitions from a Reading Partner." *Journal of Educational Psychology*, 81, no. 4: 620–627.

Schmidt, Richard W. 1990. "The Role of Consciousness in Second Language Learning." *Applied Linguistics*,11: 129–158.

Schmitt, Ara J., Andrea D. Hale, Elizabeth McCallum, and Brittany Mauck. 2011. "Accommodating Remedial Readers in the General Education Setting: Is Listening-While-Reading Sufficient To Improve Factual and Inferential Comprehension?" *Psychology in the Schools*, 48, no. 1: 37–45.

Shalmani, Hamed Babaie, and Masoud Khalili Sabet. 2010. "Pictorial, Textual, and Picto-Textual Glosses in E-Reading: A Comparative Study." *English Language Teaching*, 3, no. 4: 195–203.

Shang, Hui-Fang. 2005. "Email Dialogue Journaling: Attitudes and Impact on L2 Reading Performance." *Educational Studies*, 31, no. 2: 197–212.

Smith, Frank. 2004. *Understanding Reading*, 6th ed. Hillsdale, NJ: Erlbaum.

Stockwell, Glenn. 2007. "A Review of Technology Choice for Teaching Language Skills and Areas in the CALL Literature," *ReCALL*, 19, no. 2: 105–120.

Stockwell, Glenn. 2010. "Using Mobile Phones for Vocabulary Activities: Examining the Effect of Platform." *Language Learning and Technology*, 14, no. 2: 95–110.

Sorell, Joseph, and Dongkwang Shin. 2007. "The Next Step in Concordance-based Language Learning Constructing an Online Language Learning Resource for High-frequency Vocabulary and Collocations." *International Journal of Learning*, 13: 217–222.

Taki, Saeed. 2015, "Metacognitive Online Reading Strategy Use: Readers' Perceptions in L1 and L2." *Journal of Research in Reading*. DOI:10.1111/1467-9817.12048.

Tsai, Shu-Chiao. 2011. "Multimedia Courseware Development for World Heritage Sites and its Trial Integration into Instruction in Higher Technical Education." *Australasian Journal of Educational Technology*, 27, no. 7: 1171–1189.

Van Compernolle, Rémi A., and Lawrence Williams. 2012. "Promoting Sociolinguistic Competence in the Classroom Zone of Proximal Development." *Language Teaching Research*, 16, no. 1: 39–60.

Volodina, Elena, and Dijana Pijetlovic. 2015. "Lark Trills for Language Drills: Text-to-Speech Technology for Language Learners," In *Proceedings of the Tenth Workshop on Innovative Use of NLP for Building Educational Applications*, 2015, 107–117, Denver, CO, June 4, 2015. Accessed June 8, 2016. http://aclweb.org/anthology/W15-0613

Wang, Yen-Hui. 2014. "Developing and Evaluating an Adaptive Business English Self-Learning System for EFL Vocabulary Learning," *Mathematical Problems in Engineering*,Article ID 972184. Assessed June 8, 2016. http://dx.doi.org/10.1155/2014/972184

Warschauer, Mark, Youngmin Park, and Randall Walker. 2011. "Transforming Digital Reading with Visual Syntactic Text Formatting." *The JALT CALL Journal*, 7, no. 3: 255–270.

Wijekumar, Kay, and Bonnie J. F. Meyer. 2006. "Design and Pilot of a Web-based Intelligent Tutoring System to Improve Reading Comprehension in Middle School Students." *International Journal of Technology in Teaching and Learning*, 2, no. 1: 36–49.

Yamat, Hamidah, Ahmad Ismail, and Azlinawaty Azman Shah. 2012. "Developing Hypermedia Reading Courseware for English for Specific Purposes." *Procedia – Social and Behavioral Sciences*, 46: 4874–4879.

Yeh, Yuli, and Chai-wei Wang. 2003. "Effects of Multimedia Vocabulary Annotations and Learning Styles on Vocabulary Learning." *CALICO Journal*, 21, no. 1: 131–144.

Yu, Chen-Hsiang, and Robert C. Miller. 2010. "Enhancing Web Page Readability for Non-native Readers." CHI 2010, April 10–15, 2010, Atlanta, GA, USA. Accessed June 8, 2016. https://groups.csail.mit.edu/uid/projects/froggy/chi10-froggy.pdf

# 6 Technology and L2 Writing

## ZHI LI, AHMET DURSUN, AND VOLKER HEGELHEIMER

## Introduction

New information and communication technologies are altering writing practices in important ways. As Relles and Tierney (2013) put it, "the integration of communication technologies with academic culture suggests that the writing habits of tomorrow's students will be navigational across myriad discourse situations that do and will yet exist" (501). Students in fourth grade, for example, while still working on writing sentences, may be routinely asked to go beyond traditional writing tasks to put together PowerPoint slides, collages, or contribute text to blogs. High school students, while drafting persuasive essays, may be tasked with writing Facebook or Twitter posts. College students continue to write lab reports but also need to construct multimodal compositions that include both text and visuals. Successful business people must be able to write communications to be disseminated through a variety of social media.

In this context, all teachers, schools, and colleges are challenged to respond to the changing nature of writing (Herrington and Moran 2009). Fortunately, the same wave of technologies affecting writing practices provides a wealth of tools for the teaching of second or foreign language writing. Such tools have been adopted by business and education to improve the teaching and learning of writing. In this chapter, we describe technologies developed to aid in the writing process, which are also used for teaching. Following the description, we provide a critical analysis of the empirical research on the effectiveness of software and web-based technologies in teaching L2 writing. We conclude the chapter with a look at future research and development of technologies and pedagogies for L2 writing.

## Technologies for L2 writing

The wide variety of technologies for L2 writing can be divided into three general categories. The most general purpose of the three is the Web 2.0 application, which allows for authorship of multiple users who contribute content to a common repository online. The second category is automated writing evaluation systems developed specifically for analysis and feedback to writers during the writing process. The third category is the corpus-based tools, which serve as a reference to writers as they strategically examine the language used in

*The Handbook of Technology and Second Language Teaching and Learning,* First Edition.
Edited by Carol A. Chapelle and Shannon Sauro.
© 2017 John Wiley & Sons, Inc. Published 2020 by John Wiley & Sons, Inc.

collections of existing electronic texts. Many software tools exemplify each of these categories, but we have chosen a few to illustrate the affordances offered writers by tools of each of the three types.

## *Web 2.0 applications*

Web 2.0 tools include the variety of social media sites, such as Facebook and Twitter, as well as blogs. For L2 learners, these sites provide unprecedented opportunities to experiment with their language in settings where their language appears before and communicates with real audiences rather than being confined to communication for practice within the language classroom. The use of language for communication, rather than for practice alone, is a core goal of most language instruction. Beyond opportunities for communication, Web 2.0 applications like Google Docs provide the tools for collaborative writing.

   *Lang-8* (http://lang-8.com/) is a good example of a social networking site designed to encourage L2 communication by creating a community where language learners are matched with native speakers of target languages. Each member can contribute to the virtual language learning community by writing posts in the language they are learning and giving feedback or making corrections to other members' written posts in his or her native or stronger language. With a few buttons for editing, such as color changing and crossing out, users can easily correct or edit others' posts on Lang-8. Lang-8 rewards active users with "L" points, which help make their posts more visible to proficient users, thus increasing the probability that they will receive feedback or corrections. In other words, the more a member of the community contributes to the process of language correction, the more his or her own writing or posts are corrected. In addition to written corrections, Lang-8 has integrated Skype, an online tool allowing for international, live video communication. Lang-8 allows learners to practice writing on their own. Language instructors can also create groups on Lang-8 and design collaborative writing activities for their students and others in the larger community.

   *Google Docs*, another important example, is a free online word processor within Google Drive, an office suite developed by Google Inc. Users need a Google account to create, edit, and share Google Docs files. Google Docs features a full-fledged word processor with an easy-to-use text-editing interface. Compared to traditional word processing software, Google Docs is unique in its capability for real-time collaboration, including editing, commenting, and chatting by and among multiple users on a shared file. Additionally, the composing and revision history on Google Docs is automatically saved and a record of the entire composing process is available for review. A completed piece of writing can be published online or downloaded in different file formats, including Microsoft Word, pdf, plain text, html page, and so on. As a collaborative writing platform, Google Docs has gained popularity in language teaching classrooms at all levels.

## *Automated writing evaluation*

Automated writing evaluation (AWE) systems have been developed to assist both native speakers and L2 learners to write more accurately by providing them with automated corrective feedback. AWE systems utilize sophisticated natural language processing (NLP) techniques and machine learning to create tools that are more powerful than traditional spelling and grammar checkers (Shermis, Burstein, and Bursky 2013). NLP technologies have become sufficiently widespread that a number of these systems have been developed, although because of the substantial resources required to develop them, they are typically not freely available on the Internet. *Criterion*, *Turnitin*, and *Writing Pal* are among the widely used AWE systems.

*Criterion* (http://www.ets.org/criterion/) is a web-based commercial writing evaluation and feedback tool developed by Educational Testing Service (ETS, 2015). *Criterion* targets the writing instruction both in K-12 programs and higher education and provides a holistic score and feedback based on level-specific models considering both the age and proficiency levels of the learners. Building on *e-rater*, an automated scoring engine, *Criterion* is capable of providing holistic scores (1–4 or 1–6 points) to the essays written to its own prompts. In addition, detailed diagnostic trait feedback, in a mixture of both direct and indirect feedback formats, is available in five categories: grammar, usage, mechanics, style, and organization, and development. Beside the holistic score and individualized feedback, it provides resources such as an essay planning tool and the Writer's Handbook at different levels for students to understand and evaluate the feedback provided. The handbook is available in different languages for ESL learners speaking Chinese, Spanish, Korean, and Japanese. Teachers can assign writing tasks from the built-in pool of writing prompts or create their own essay topic. Moreover, it allows for teacher and peer feedback. This web-based tool can be used at different stages of writing instruction for various purposes. Language instructors can use it in-class for an essay planning or a peer-feedback activity, or out-of-class for students to submit and revise based on the feedback.

*Turnitin* (http://turnitin.com/) was initially launched as an online plagiarism prevention service by iParadigms, LLC, in 1997. Recently, through partnering with or acquiring other companies, iParadigms added more functions to *Turnitin* and transformed it from an originality-checking tool to a comprehensive platform of online automated grading and peer review (Turnitin, 2015). For example, *Turnitin* has integrated *e-rater*, the automated scoring engine developed by ETS as well as LightSide Labs' *LightSide Revision Assistant* to enhance its grammar checking and assessment function. In addition, *Turnitin* facilitates teacher feedback by providing frequently used comments and rubrics as well as a voice commenting tool. *Turnitin* can be integrated with mainstream learning management systems (LMS), such as Blackboard Learn, Moodle, Canvas, and so on. Turnitin targets customers in the field of education, including educators and students in middle and high schools, colleges and universities. *Turnitin* also provides online tutorials and training to teachers, students, and school administrators. Currently, *Turnitin* has found its place in a number of institutions as a plagiarism detection tool and several empirical studies have been conducted to investigate its utility and user perceptions (Rolfe 2011; Stapleton 2012). *Turnitin*'s recent expansion of grading and peer reviewing functions invite empirical investigations into its effects on writing pedagogy as well.

*Writing Pal* or *W-Pal* is an automated intelligent tutoring system (ITS) developed by the Science of Learning and Educational Technology (SoLET) Lab at Arizona State University. *W-Pal*'s intended users are native English-speaking students in high schools. However, English language learners in high school and college freshmen have also been included in some empirical studies of *W-Pal* in the United States. Unlike other AWE tools, *W-Pal* is designed as a writing strategy instruction tool based on four principles for teaching writing, namely, strategy instruction, modularity, extended practice, and formative feedback (Roscoe and McNamara 2013). Accordingly, *W-Pal* provides eight animated learning modules covering the typical writing process, including writing strategies used in the pre-writing phase, drafting phase, and the revision phase. The learning modules are coupled with two types of interactive practices to improve student engagement and learning motivation: game-based practices as well as essay-based practices. Student essays produced on *W-Pal* can be scored automatically with automated formative feedback, using *Coh-Metrix* –a system developed for computing cohesion in the written and spoken texts by the Institute for Intelligent Systems at the University of Memphis–and other text analysis tools.

## Corpus-based tools

Like AWE systems, a number of corpus-based tools have been developed as resources for L2 writers to gain access to examples of authentic language use in collections of electronic texts. Corpus-based pedagogies, data-driven learning, are based on the idea that students need to have access to examples of language (i.e., data) as they write, and that such examples need to meet specific writing needs at the time of writing (Flowerdew 2009). Corpus tools, therefore, consist of corpora of texts as well as the software tools required for searching and displaying the examples. The Corpus of Contemporary American English (henceforth COCA, Davies 2008) serves as a good example of a widely used corpus.

COCA (http://corpus.byu.edu/coca/) is a freely available online corpus of English, created by Mark Davies at Brigham Young University. The corpus has over 450 million words of text that covers spoken, fiction, popular magazines, newspapers, and academic text genres. Users can search for exact words and phrases, parts of speech, and collocations through the COCA interface. In addition, users can take advantage of semantically-based queries to differentiate usages of synonyms (e.g., little vs. small) or related words (e.g., men vs. women).

The COCA interface "Word and phrase" (http://www.wordandphrase.info/) permits users to interact with the tool differently. For example, users can submit a whole text for analysis and see a detailed frequency report on the words that they produced. Learners can also compare their use of phrases to the phrases in the corpus. The words and phrases can be limited to academic texts so that users can analyze an academic text as well as search for academic word lists and collocations. COCA can be used for different purposes in second language writing instruction. For example, language instructors can use it to expose learners to the authentic use of language and thus the form and functions of different language uses, which in turn might encourage learners to implement these features in their own writing.

## Summary of L2 writing tools

The pedagogical writing tools described above and summarized in Table 6.1 serve as an illustration of the technological support available to learners and teachers. In view of the energy and expertise being applied to the development of writing software today, it is likely that the future improvements on these tools as well as additional tools will continue to appear. In this environment, the pressing needs of writers and advances in technology are likely to result in tool development ahead of research on how people write and learn through the use of the tools.

# Empirical research on L2 writing technologies

Empirical investigations into the usefulness of writing technologies for L2 writing have been undertaken for each of the three categories of writing tools introduced above. Research encompasses a range of methodologies to address questions about learners' writing strategies, their language use, their writing practices, attitudes, and writing outcomes. Table 6.2 provides an overview of published research on various software tools, the context of the study as well as the methodology the authors employed and key findings.

## L2 writing with Web 2.0 applications

Social networking sites (SNS) and wiki-type tools as representative Web 2.0 platforms have allowed the researchers to investigate L2 writers' engagement in meaningful social interaction as well as collaborative writing (Lee 2010). Recent research has shown that collaborative writing

**Table 6.1** Example technologies for L2 writing.

| Category | Example technology | Type | Context/Target users | Key functions | Potential application |
|---|---|---|---|---|---|
| Web 2.0 applications | Google Docs | Free | Writers in general | Online collaborative writing | Collaborative writing practices (i.e., peer review, group projects) |
| | Lang-8 | Free | Language learning community with language learners and native speakers in multiple languages | Offer corrections on written posts in one's native language and receive corrections on written posts in a target language | Journal writing; grammar checking; collaborative writing with native speakers |
| Automated writing evaluation | Criterion | Commercial | K-12 and College level English language writers | Essay evaluation (holistic scores) and individualized feedback on grammar, usage, mechanics, style, and organization and development | Grammar checking Formative assessment tool |
| | Turnitin | Commercial | Teachers and students in middle and high schools, colleges and universities | Originality checking, grading, peer reviewing | Feedback on possible plagiarism Grammar checking |
| | W-Pal | Not publicly available | Native and non-native English speaking high school students | Strategy instruction, modularity, extended practice, and formative feedback | Teaching writing strategies used in the pre-writing, drafting, and revising phases |
| Corpus-based Tools | COCA | Free | Writers in general | Access to large corpus | Editing and revisions of words and phrases Evaluation of word choice |

**Table 6.2** Empirical research on L2 writing technologies.

| Category | Technologies or software | Example study | Context and focus | Research methods | Major findings |
|---|---|---|---|---|---|
| Web 2.0 applications | Wikis | Aydin and Yildiz (2014) | Effects of task type on Turkish English language learners' collaborative writing on three types of writing topics | Mixed-methods approach | Collaborative writing on different topics yielded differential writing behaviors. |
| | Google Docs | Strobl (2014) | Effects of collaborative writing on the writing performance of advanced Dutch learners of German | Mixed-methods approach | Collaborative texts appeared to have better content and text organization, but not different in terms of accuracy, fluency, and complexity, compared with individually written texts. |
| | Web 2.0 applications in general | Chen (2014) | Benefits of using Web 2.0 applications for peer review | Interpretive synthesis of 20 empirical studies (1990 to 2010) | Overall, positive impacts of technology-supported peer feedback were identified. |
| | Facebook | Shih (2010) | Peer assessment on Facebook for first-year English majors in Taiwan | Mixed-methods approach; pre- and post-test design | Better writing performance with peer assessment on Facebook and positive perceptions by the students were found. |

| | | | | |
|---|---|---|---|---|
| *MY Access!* | Chen and Cheng (2008) | The use of *MY Access!* in three EFL writing courses in Taiwan | Qualitative approach | The AWE tool was not perceived very positively. EFL instructor's approach to integrating the AWE tool affected students' perceptions. |
| *Writing Roadmap 2.0* | Rich (2012) | Effects of using AWE tool in a 7–10 week period in a middle school in China | Mixed-methods approach, quasi-experimental design | Students using the AWE tool had a higher automated score. The majority of the students showed positive views on the tool and became more confident in writing after the treatment. |
| *CorrectEnglish* | Wang et al. (2013) | The impacts of using AWE tools on EFL freshmen's writing in a Taiwanese university | Mixed-methods approach, quasi-experimental design | More accurate texts and better learner autonomy awareness were achieved by the students who used the AWE tool. |
| *Criterion* | Link et al. (2014) | Five ESL instructors' perception and use of *Criterion* at an American university | Qualitative approach with longitudinal data | A best practice model involving the use of AWE was proposed based on the qualitative analysis of five ESL instructors in seven ESL writing classes. |

Automated writing evaluation

*(Continued)*

**Table 6.2** (Continued)

| Category | Technologies or software | Example study | Context and focus | Research methods | Major findings |
|---|---|---|---|---|---|
| Corpus-based Tools | Concordance tools on COCA and MICUSP | Garner (2013) | Effects of data-driven learning (DDL) on ESL students' use of linking adverbials in English writing at an American university | Quantitative approach; quasi-experimental design | Students benefited from the DDL instructions and showed a better use of linking adverbials than the control group. |
| | AntConc 3.2.1; three learner corpora and one professional corpus of reports | Friginal (2013) | Effects of using corpora on students in forestry in developing reporting writing skills, specifically in four linguistic characteristics | Quantitative approach; quasi-experimental design | The two-week period of corpus-based training helped the experimental group in writing reports, which became more similar in the selected linguistic characteristics to those in the professional corpus. |
| | The Collins COBUILD Corpus | Yoon (2008) | Impacts of corpus technology on L2 students' writing development in a graduate-level ESL writing class | Qualitative approach; case studies | Use of general corpus helped L2 writers solve language problems in writing and promoted learner autonomy. |
| | PREFabricated Expression Recognizer (PREFER), corpus-based e-paraphrase tool | Chen et al. (2015) | Effects of PREFER on EFL freshmen's paraphrasing performance in an Asian university | Quantitative and qualitative; single group pre- and post-test design | PREFER was helpful for EFL students to improve their paraphrasing. The majority of the students were satisfied with paraphrase examples and functionality of the tool. |

on web-based word processing tools, such as Google Docs, benefit learners' writing development through peer editing and meaning-related revising. For example, Kessler, Bikowski, and Boggs (2012) investigated the use of Google Docs in a team-based project-oriented writing activity in an English for academic purposes training program with 38 L2 writers. The study found that the L2 writers focused more on meaning than form and the grammatical changes they made collaboratively were mainly accurate, which in general contributed positively to the quality of their writing. Overall, wiki-based collaborative writing tends to yield written pieces with higher accuracy (Storch 2011, 2012; Wigglesworth and Storch 2012).

Research has found that success of using wiki-based approaches to teaching L2 writing depends on factors including task type, writing topics, grouping methods, group dynamism, learner's L2 proficiency level, and so on. For example, Aydin and Yildiz (2014) studied the collaborative writing processes of 34 Turkish learners of English on three writing prompts, namely argumentative, informative, and decision-making topics. They found that the argumentative topic appeared to trigger more peer corrections while the informative topic elicited more self-correction. In terms of the effect of learner proficiency level, Strobl (2014) studied a group of 48 advanced university-level Dutch learners of German on Google Docs-based synthesis tasks and found that collaborative texts tended to have more appropriate content selection and text organization, possibly due to group members' engagement in their planning stage. However, Strobl (2014) also noticed that for this group of advanced L2 writers there were no significant differences in collaborative texts and individual texts in terms of accuracy, fluency, and complexity.

The benefits of using Web 2.0 applications for peer review in particular are well documented by Chen (2014), who carried out an interpretive synthesis of 20 empirical studies on technology-mediated peer feedback published from 1990 to 2010. The technologies involved in these studies include synchronous and asynchronous tools, such as email, course management systems, blog websites, online forums, real-time communication software, and Microsoft Word. In general, technology-supported peer feedback is characterized by motivating interaction, flexible discourse patterns and language usages, and effective shifts in teachers' and students' roles in the process of providing peer feedback.

Educational uses of social media websites, such as Facebook and Twitter, have begun to be investigated by researchers (Manca and Ranieri 2013). For example, Shih (2010) implemented a Facebook-integrated blended learning model in an English writing class for first-year students majoring in English at a Taiwanese university. Peer assessment was included on the Facebook page designed for English writing. Using a pre- and posttest design, Shih (2010) found that the students made significant improvement in English writing in terms of content, organization, structure, vocabulary and spelling, and genre awareness. The use of Facebook as a platform for peer assessment was positively perceived by the students as Facebook-based activities promoted collaborative learning and enhanced students' interest and motivation. However, as Manca and Ranieri (2013) note, the educational value of Facebook has not yet been fully explored and the assumption that using Facebook could meet the expectations of younger generations of learners, known as digital natives, is not well supported by empirical studies. Manca and Ranieri (2013) reviewed 23 research articles on using Facebook as an instructional platform and noticed that the digital natives or millennial learners did not necessarily have enthusiasm for educational technology and some of them were not willing to use Facebook for formal learning because it seemed to them in conflict with the purpose of Facebook.

## L2 writing and AWE

In the past decade, research has examined the use of AWE tools for helping learners with their writing, that in some cases these promising tools can be challenging to implement with the intended effects. For example, in a critical analysis, Stevenson and Phakiti (2014) evaluated outcomes from research encompassing AWE systems specifically designed as tools for providing corrective feedback in the writing classroom. Overall, they found "only modest evidence that AWE feedback has a positive effect on the quality of the texts that students produce using AWE" with the exception of few cases where the researcher reported error correction improvement in students' texts (Stevenson and Phakiti, 2014, 62). They also noted from their critical analysis of the research on the effects of AWE feedback on the quality of writing that "there is little clarity about whether AWE is associated with more general improvements in writing proficiency" (62). One problem that they noted with the research is the lack of clarity as to whether or not the feedback provided by AWE tools in their English class helps with writing students do in their content courses because "AWE programs generally offer only a limited number of genres, such as persuasive, narrative and informative genres" (Stevenson and Phakiti 2014, 13). Such a limitation might be avoided by having students work with more genres (see Burstein, Elliot, and Molloy 2016 for a detailed discussion of this issue) as well as by enabling teachers to use their own prompts such as in *Criterion* and *My Access!*.

Another issue identified in research on AWE is that the automated corrective feedback in the AWE systems need to be implemented in view of the target audience and learning context. For instance, Chen and Cheng (2008), in a qualitative study investigating the use of AWE in the EFL classroom context in Taiwan, found that AWE feedback can be more effective when it is combined with teachers' feedback. However, this study did not investigate the effects of the use of different feedback approaches on written production. Link et al. (2014) note that there are numerous possible ways of integrating AWE with teacher feedback. To illustrate, students can use AWE to help them improve the quality of initial drafts before submitting to the teacher for feedback or teachers can use AWE as a diagnostic tool to identify the problems that students have with their writing and provide feedback based on the automated analysis. Research needs to investigate the effects of these various options. Chen and Cheng's (2008) study also showed that "the teachers' attitudes towards AWE scores and feedback, their views on the role of human feedback, their conceptions of teaching and learning of writing, and their technology-use skills in working with the AWE program" (103) all affected the ways they used AWE in their classes.

In addition to the empirical studies on *Criterion* and *MyAccess!*, Rich (2012) conducted a quasi-experimental study using a pre- and post-test design to examine the effects of *Writing Roadmap* 2.0, an AWE tool developed by CTB/McGraw-Hill, on Chinese learners of English at a middle school in Dalian, China. In Rich's study, *Writing Roadmap 2.0* was used by the experimental group in two writing prompts during a period of 7–10 weeks and the AWE-generated scores were used to gauge students' improvement. The experimental group had a higher average gain score than the control group with an effect size of 0.30. In a post-test survey, Rich (2012) found that 94% of the respondents liked the AWE tool and 75% of them reported that they became more confident in English writing. Middle-school student participants in Rich (2012) were more active users of AWE and 61% of the respondents revised their essays three or more times. Wang, Shang, and Briody (2013) represent a research effort on a different AWE tool, *CorrectEnglish*, used in an EFL context in Taiwan. Through a comparison of the writing scores in a pre-test and a post-test of students in an experimental group and a control group, Wang et al. (2013) found that the experimental group had a positive perception of the AWE tool and they identified positive effects of the AWE tool on the experimental group students regarding error reduction and awareness of learner autonomy.

The previously mentioned studies approached the effects of AWE mainly from learner perspectives and paid limited attention to the instructors in AWE-supported classrooms. Grimes and Warschauer (2010), by contrast, investigated the perceptions of middle-school teachers' use of *MY Access!* in the United States. The middle-school teachers showed a high level of trust in the AWE tool and they expressed interest in balancing their use of the AWE tool and conventional feedback. However, Grimes and Warschauer (2010) did not address how these teachers actually used the AWE tool to complement their teaching. Addressing this question, Link et al. (2014) investigated university-level ESL instructors' perceptions and understanding of the use of *Criterion*. More specifically, their study looked at the ways that teachers used the tool in the ESL writing classroom, investigated teachers' experiences with the AWE tool, and outlined areas of concern and suggestions the teachers expressed. Overall, they found that AWE tools can be implemented to achieve a variety of purposes, ranging from fostering student autonomy and motivation, to enhancing students' metalinguistic knowledge. Also, some instructors used the AWE tool as a grammar checker to help them to spend "less time on students' language issues and more time on organization and meaning, which fits the nature of a process-based approach to writing" (338). Link et al. (2014) found that the teachers had a positive perception of the effectiveness of the AWE tool especially with the grammar feedback it provided. Moreover, they found the tool to be a motivational factor for their students to write better. Based on the teachers' reflections, Link et al. (2014) noted some key practices for an effective integration of AWE into the university-level ESL writing classrooms. Specifically, the lack of familiarity with the AWE tool had a direct impact on teachers' ability to integrate it into their classroom. Further, discussion and collaboration with the other teachers was a key to using the affordances of the tool creatively and effectively. Even when AWE tools exhibit flaws—as all tools will—knowing what these are can help teachers to identify potential learning opportunities for their students. For example, inconsistent and inaccurate feedback from an AWE tool can be pointed out to draw their attention to grammatical issues and show them how to overcome difficulties with less than perfect feedback.

## *L2 writing and corpus-based technologies*

Empirical studies of corpus use for data-driven learning have yielded positive findings (Flowerdew 2012). For example, Garner (2013) examined the effects of a data-driven learning approach on ESL undergraduate students' use of linking adverbials. Two data-driven learning activities were designed as treatments: (1) indirect corpus use by showing a concordance line and short context reading, and (2) direct corpus consultation using the COCA and the Michigan Corpus of Upper-level Student Papers (MICUSP). Through an analysis of pre- and post-treatment essays produced by the students in a control and a treatment group, Garner (2013) found that the students in the treatment groups used more academic linking adverbials with a higher accuracy in their post-treatment essay, compared with the students in the control group, who received traditional instruction on linking adverbials. Similarly, Friginal (2013) compared the development of report writing skills of two groups of students (N=28), one with corpus-based instruction and one with traditional instruction within a two-week period at an American university. A corpus of professional writing and learner corpora was used in the treatment group with special attention to four linguistic features: linking adverbials, verb tense, reporting verbs, and passive sentence structure. This study found that the post-treatment writing by the students in corpus-based instruction group was closer to the professional writing in terms of frequency and distribution of the targeted linguistic features.

Investigation of English language learners' interaction with corpus-based materials through micro-level analysis of learners' behaviors has revealed positive learning outcomes associated with intensive interactions with corpus tools. For example, Park (2012) followed three Chinese undergraduates in an academic English writing class at a U.S. university and analyzed their use of Google's Custom Search on a corpus of academic texts, based on screen recordings, oral and written reflections, and student essays. Analysis revealed that the students were active in solving language issues through "retrieving, evaluating, and appropriating search results from the corpus" (Park 2012, 380), Park highlighted the importance of evaluating and analyzing query results on the students' part, which calls for careful learner training in L2 writing classes. With a focus on the use of a corpus as a source to inform students' revision in a short essay-writing assignment, Tono, Sataka, and Miura (2014) studied 93 EFL undergraduates' revision behavior with the aid of IntelliText, an online corpus query system. The findings indicated that interacting with the corpus tool helped students correct grammatical errors. However, the accuracy of correction was significantly different among three types of errors, namely omission, mis-formation, and addition, which highlights the need for research to have a closer look at the learner-corpus interaction for different purposes.

Besides the use of corpus tools for lexico-grammatical learning, there are relatively fewer studies on the use of a corpus for discourse level learning and writing, especially for academic writing (Birch-Becaas and Cooke 2012; Chang 2012; Charles 2007; Tribble and Wingate 2013). Tribble and Wingate (2013) reported on their design and ongoing construction of the Apprentice Writing Corpus (AWC) at King's College, United Kingdom, which is unique in that it is a corpus in which genre features (move structure) are analyzed. The authors hosted seven workshops for the students in Applied Linguistics and Pharmacy separately and evaluated the materials based on a discipline-specific corpus using questionnaires and audio recordings of participants' discussion. It was found that the workshop participants positively perceived this top-down processing of corpus data with discipline-specific move structure.

Another major area of corpus-based research on L2 writing results is the development of new tools. For instance, Chen et al. (2015) built a paraphrasing tool called PREFabricated Expression Recognizer (PREFER) based on an English-Chinese parallel corpus using natural language processing technique and machine translation. According to Chen et al. (2015), PREFER features a multiword search and multiple types of output, including a list of paraphrases in English and Chinese, usage pattern, and example sentences. The utility of PREFER was investigated with 55 Chinese-speaking learners of English in a pre- and post-test design. Results suggest that students' paraphrasing performance improved and that students preferred this tool over online dictionaries and a thesaurus for paraphrasing purposes. Following the principles of accessibility, simplicity, and functionality, Bloch (2009) reported a design of a web-based concordancing program which is specialized for learning and choosing reporting verbs in academic writing. This online tool is designed to enable users to customize their queries regarding the functional features or rhetorical impact of reporting verbs. The output includes suggested reporting verbs, as well as sample sentences based on a search in an academic writing corpus. These two tools exemplify the advantages of combining corpus analysis and online technology for teaching writing and hint at technologies to come.

# Future research and development

Findings from empirical research on L2 writing technologies are promising. The availability of a wide range of technologies has the potential to facilitate the L2 writing, teaching, and learning process. At the same time, it also challenges L2 writing practitioners and researchers to investigate the best techniques and strategies to utilize these technologies to best answer the specific needs of their learning contexts. More emerging technologies are yet to be incorporated into L2 writing activities, L2 writing pedagogy, and L2 writing research. Some of the new technologies currently under investigation are learning analytics (i.e., data for recording learners' responses and choices) embedded in course management systems, keystroke logging, as well as eye tracking.

Learning analytics is defined as the educational instruments designed to collect, measure, and analyze students' learning data with a goal of better understanding learning processes and predicting learning outcomes in educational contexts (Long et al. 2011,). In many fields of study, efforts are being invested in analytic approaches to learn from large datasets. In education, such data mining research may inform approaches to L2 writing data collection and analysis. Writing-based learning analytics, such as Mi-Writer developed at Athabasca University, Canada, is one of the learning analytics designed to capture data throughout a writing process, including planning, composing, reviewing, editing, and feedback-giving. For example, students' writing behavior and interaction with peers and teachers can be recorded in real-time. Mi-Writer is also capable of generating writing-related metrics for both L2 writers and L2 writing instructors (Clemens, Kumar, and Mitchnick 2013). Such data collection mechanisms open the possibility of facilitating automated real-time feedback that is tailored to individual learners.

Learning analytics can be treated as a comprehensive technology which will also benefit from integrating other techniques such as keystroke logging and eye-tracking technologies. New unobtrusive data gathering techniques such as keystroke logging and economically more feasible techniques involving eye tracking can help practitioners and researchers better understand students' writing behavior, multimodal composition processes, as well as strategies employed for resource use and self-regulation (Anson and Schwegler 2012; Johansson et al. 2009; Leijten and van Waes 2013). For example, Johansson et al. (2009) employed keystroke logging software and eye tracking to explore the writing processes of two types of computer-based writers: monitor gazers and keyboard gazers. Their findings indicated different patterns of reading and writing behaviors from these two types of writers, as well as the impact of these behaviors on writing production. Miller, Lindgren, and Sullivan (2008) utilized keystroke logging software to record the bursts and pauses in 17 learners' typing as a way to monitor their writing process. Miller et al. (2008) argued that keystroke logging as an unobtrusive instrument can reveal learners' planning, formulation, and revising processes. They also suggested several applications of a keystroke logging instrument in teaching L2 writing. Replaying the keystroke logging data, for instance, may provide diagnostic information to teachers and valuable opportunities for learners to reflect on their writing process. Therefore, the analysis of keystroke logs shows potential in L2 writing research, even though aligning such data with L2 writers' cognitive process is not incorporated into CALL practices yet (Baaijen, Galbraith, and de Glopper 2012).

# Conclusion

This chapter reviewed the three major categories of technologies, namely Web 2.0 applications, AWE, and corpus-based tools. These new technologies are shaping how L2 writing is practiced and taught. Therefore, language teachers should be open to the development of new technologies that have the potential to assist L2 writing. Openness in this domain means that L2 writing teachers are expected to experience these technologies themselves and then to make critical evaluation of the technologies for their utility in L2 writing contexts. In using these technologies, language teachers should not underestimate the importance of learner training. Even when using technologies that L2 learners are already familiar with, teachers need to teach the desired practices through carefully designed learner training (Hubbard 2004; O'Bryan 2008; Pritchard 2013). Likewise, Reinders and Hubbard (2013) remind us of a potential mismatch between learners' "natural" use of technology and suggested "ideal" use of technology for learning (372). Consequently, learner training is even more critical with the technologies designed especially for writing pedagogy, such as corpus-based tools (Breyer 2009) and AWE tools (Link et al. 2014). While independent access remains possible, the relative success of many of these tools will continue to rely on classroom teachers as teachers play a pivotal role in technology-enhanced classrooms (Chen and Cheng 2008; Hubbard and Levy 2006; Kim 2007).

## REFERENCES

Anson, Chris M., and Robert A. Schwegler. 2012. "Tracking the Mind's Eye: A New Technology for Researching Twenty-first-century Writing and Reading Processes." *College Composition and Communication*, 64, no. 1: 151–177.

Aydin, Zelilha, and Senem Yildiz. (2014). "Using Wikis to Promote Collaborative EFL Writing." *Language Learning & Technology*, 18, no. 1: 160–180.

Baaijen, Veerle. M., Galbraith, David, and Kees de Glopper. 2012. "Keystroke Analysis: Reflections on Procedures and Measures." *Written Communication*, 29, no. 3: 246–277.

Birch-Becaas, Susan, and Ray Cooke. 2012. "Raising Collective Awareness of Rhetorical Strategies: Using an Online Writing Tool to Demonstrate Discourse Moves in the ESP Classroom." In *Corpus-Informed Research and Learning in ESP: Issues and Applications*, edited by Alex Boulton, Shirley Carter-Thomas, and Elizabeth Rowley-Jolivet, 239–260. Stillwater, OK: John Benjamins.

Bloch, Joel. 2009. "The Design of an Online Concordancing Program for Teaching Reporting Verbs." *Language Learning & Technology*, 13, no. 1: 59–78.

Breyer, Yvonne. 2009. "Learning and Teaching with Corpora: Reflections by Student Teachers." *Computer Assisted Language Learning*, 22, no. 2: 153–172.

Burstein, Jill, Elliot, Norbert, and Hillary Molloy. 2016. "Informing Automated Writing Evaluation Using the Lens of Genre: Two Studies." *CALICO Journal*, 33, no. 1: 117–141.

Chang, Ching-Fen. (2012). "Peer Review via Three Modes in an EFL Writing Course." *Computers and Composition*, 29, no. 1, 63–78. doi:10.1016/j.compcom.2012.01.001

Charles, Maggie. 2007. "Reconciling Top-down and Bottom-up Approaches to Graduate Writing: Using a Corpus to Teach Rhetorical Functions." *Journal of English for Academic Purposes*, 6, no. 4: 289–302.

Chen, Chi-Fen E., and E. Cheng Wei-Yuan. 2008. "Beyond the Design of Automated Writing Evaluation: Pedagogical Practices and Perceived Learning Effectiveness in EFL Writing Classes." *Language Learning & Technology*, 12, no. 2: 94–112.

Chen, Meihua, Shih-Ting Huang, Jason Chang, and Liou Hisen-Chin. 2015. "Developing a Corpus-based Paraphrase Tool to Improve EFL Learners' Writing Skills." *Computer Assisted Language Learning*, 28, no. 1: 1–19.

Chen, Tsuiping. 2014. "Technology-supported Peer Feedback in ESL/EFL Writing Classes: A Research Synthesis." *Computer Assisted Language Learning*, 29, no. 2: 365–397.

Clemens, Clayton, Vive Kumar, and Diane Mitchnick. 2013. "Writing-based Learning Analytics for Education." Paper presented at the 2013 IEEE 13th International Conference on Advanced Learning Technologies. Beijing, China, July 15–18.

Davies, Mark. 2008. *The Corpus of Contemporary American English: 520 Million Words, 1990–Present*. Accessed June 8, 2016. http://corpus.byu.edu/coca/

Educational Testing Service (ETS). 2015. "Criterion." Accessed June 8, 2016. https://criterion.ets.org/criterion/

Flowerdew, Lynne. 2009. "Applying Corpus Linguistics to Pedagogy: A Critical Evaluation." *International Journal of Corpus Linguistics*, 14, no. 3: 393–417.

Flowerdew, Lynne. 2012. "Corpora in the Classroom: An Applied Linguistic Perspective." In *Corpus Applications in Applied Linguistics*, edited by Ken Hyland, Chua Meng Huat, and Michael Handford, 208–224. New York: Continuum.

Friginal, Eric. 2013. "Developing Research Report Writing Skills Using Corpora." *English for Specific Purposes*, 32, no. 4: 208–220.

Garner, James R. 2013. "The Use of Linking Adverbials in Academic Essays by Non-native Writers: How Data-driven Learning Can Help?" *CALICO Journal*, 30, no. 3: 410–222.

Google, Inc. 2015. "Google Docs." Accessed June 8, 2016.

Grimes, Douglas, and Mark Warschauer. 2010. "Utility in a Fallible Tool: A Multi-Site Case

Study of Automated Writing Evaluation." *Journal of Technology, Learning, and Assessment*, 8, no. 6. Accessed June 8, 2016. http://www.jtla.org

Herrington, Anne, and Charles Moran. 2009. "Writing, Assessment, and New Technologies." In *Assessment in Writing (Assessment in the Disciplines, Vol. 4)*, edited by Marie. C. Paretti and Katrina Powell, 159–177. Tallahassee, FL: Association of Institutional Researchers.

Hubbard, Philip. 2004. "Learner Training for Effective Use of CALL." In *New Perspectives on CALL for Second Language Classrooms*, edited by Sandra Fotos and Charles. Browne, 45–67. Mahwah, NJ: Lawrence Erlbaum Associates.

Hubbard, Philip, and Mike Levy 2006. *Teacher Education in CALL*. Philadelphia: John Benjamins.

Johansson, Roger, Åsa Wengelin, Victoria Johansson, and Kenneth Holmqvist. 2009. "Looking at the Keyboard or the Monitor: relationship with Text Production Processes." *Reading and Writing*, 23, no. 7: 835–851.

Kessler, Greg, Dawn Bikowski, and Jordan Boggs. 2012. "Collaborative Writing among Second Language Learners in Academic Web-based Projects." *Language Learning & Technology*, 16, no. 1: 91–109.

Kim, Hoe Kyeung. 2007. "Beyond Motivation: ESL/EFL Teachers' Perceptions of the Role of Computers." *CALICO Journal*, 25, no. 2: 241–259.

Lee, Lina. 2010. "Exploring Wiki-mediated Collaborative Writing: A Case Study in an Elementary Spanish Course." *CALICO Journal*, 27, no. 2: 260–276.

Leijten, Mariëlle, and Luuk Van Waes. 2013. "Keystroke Logging in Writing research: Using Inputlog to Analyze and Visualize Writing Processes." *Written Communication*, 30, no. 3: 358–392.

Link, Stephanie, Ahmet Dursun, Kadir Karakaya, and Volker Hegelheimer. 2014. "Towards Best ESL Practices for Implementing Automated Writing Evaluation." *CALICO Journal*, 31, no. 3: 323–344.

Long, Philips., George Siemens, Gráinne Conole, and Dragan Gašević. 2011. "Message from the LAK 2011 General and Program Chairs." Paper presented at the 1st International Conference on Learning and Analytics & Knowledge, Banff, Alberta, Canada. February 27–March 1.

Manca, Stefania, and Maria Ranieri. 2013. "Is It a Tool Suitable for Learning? A Critical Review of the Literature on Facebook as a Technology-enhanced Learning Environment." *Journal of Computer Assisted Learning*, 29, no. 6: 487–504.

Miller, Kristyan. S., Eva Lindgren, and Kirk P. H. Sullivan. 2008. "The Psycholinguistic Dimension in Second Language Writing: Opportunities for Research and Pedagogy Using Computer Keystroke Logging." *TESOL Quarterly*, 42, no. 3: 433–454.

O'Bryan, Anne. 2008. "Providing Pedagogical Learner Training in CALL: Impact on Student Use of Language-learning Strategies and Glosses." *CALICO Journal*, 26, no. 1: 142–159.

Park, Kwanghyun. 2012. "Learner-corpus Interaction: A Locus of Microgenesis in Corpus-assisted L2 Writing." *Applied Linguistics*, 33, no. 4: 361–385.

Pritchard, Caleb. 2013. "Training L2 Learners to use Facebook Appropriately and Effectively." *CALICO Journal*, 30, no. 2: 204–225.

Relles, Stefani. R., and William G. Tierney. 2013. "Understanding the Writing Habits of Tomorrow's Students: Technology and College Readiness." *Journal of Higher Education*, 84, no. 4: 477–505.

Reinders, Hayo, and Philip Hubbard. 2013. "CALL and Learner Autonomy: Affordance and Constraints." In *Contemporary Computer-Assisted Language Learning*, edited by Michael Thomas, Hayo Reinders, and Mark Warschauer, 359–376. London: Bloomsbury Academic.

Rich, Changhua S. 2012. "The Impact of Online Automated Writing Evaluation: A Case Study from Dalian." *Chinese Journal of Applied Linguistics*, 35, no. 1: 36–79.

Rolfe, Vivien. 2011. "Can Turnitin be Used to Provide Instant Formative Feedback?" *British Journal of Educational Technology*, 42, no. 4: 701–710.

Roscoe, Rod. D., and Danielle S. McNamara. 2013. "Writing Pal: Feasibility of an Intelligent Writing Strategy Tutor in the High-school Classroom." *Journal of Educational Psychology*, 105, no. 4: 1010–1025.

Shermis, Mark D., Jill Burstein, and Sharon A. Bursky. 2013. "Introduction to Automated Essay Evaluation." In *Handbook of Automated Essay Evaluation: Current Applications and New Directions*, edited by Mark D. Shermis and Jill C. Burstein, 1–15. New York: Routledge.

Shih, Ru-Chu. 2010. "Can Web 2.0 Technology Assist College Students in Learning English Writing? Integrating 'Facebook' and Peer Assessment with Blended Learning." *Australasian Journal of Educational Technology*, 27, no. 5: 829–845.

Stapleton, Paul. 2012. "Gauging the Effectiveness of Anti-plagiarism Software: An Empirical Study of Second Language Graduate Writers." *Journal of English for Academic Purposes*, 11, no. 2: 125–133.

Stevenson, Marie, and Aek Phakiti. 2014. "The Effects of Computer-generated Feedback on the Quality of Writing." *Assessing Writing*, 19: 51–65. DOI:10.1016/j.asw.2013.11.007

Storch, Neomy. 2011. "Collaborative Writing in L2 Contexts: Processes, Outcomes, and Future Directions." *Annual Review of Applied Linguistics*, 31, no. 1: 275–288.

Storch, Neomy. 2012. "Collaborative Writing as a Site for L2 Learning in Face-to-face and Online Modes." In *Technology Across Writing Contexts and Tasks*, edited by Greg Kessler, Ana Oskoz, and Idoia Elola, 113–130. San Marcos, TX. CALICO.

Strobl, Carola. 2014. "Affordances of Web 2.0 Technologies for Collaborative Advanced Writing in a Foreign Language." *CALICO Journal*, 31, no. 1: 1–18.

Tono, Yukio, Yoshiho Satake, and Aika Miura. 2014. "The Effects of Using Corpora on Revision Tasks in L2 Writing with Coded Error Feedback." *ReCALL*, 26, no. 2: 147–162.

Tribble, Christopher, and Ursula Wingate. 2013. "From Text to Corpus—A Genre-based Approach to Academic Literacy Instruction." *System*, 41, no. 2: 307–321.

Turnitin. 2015. "Turnitin." Accessed June 8, 2016. http://turnitin.com/

Wang, Ying-Jian, Hui-Fang Shang, and Paul Briody. 2013. "Exploring the Impact of Using Automated Writing Evaluation in English as a Foreign Language University Students' Qriting." *Computer Assisted Language Learning*, 26, no. 3: 234–257.

Wigglesworth, Gillan, and Neomy Storch. 2012. "Feedback and Writing Development through Collaboration: A Socio-cultural Approach." In *L2 Writing Development: Multiple Perspectives*, edited by Rosa Manchón, 69–102. Boston: De Gruyter, Water Inc.

Yoon, Hyunsook. 2008. "More than a Linguistic Reference: The Influence of Corpus Technology on L2 Academic Writing." *Language Learning & Technology*, 12, no. 2: 31–48.

# 7 Technologies for Teaching and Learning L2 Listening

## PHILIP HUBBARD

## Background

Listening as a second language skill area is taught in many language programs, sometimes as a separate course and sometimes in a form integrated with speaking or even reading and writing. Listening activities and tasks typically have two purposes: (1) to help students improve aural processing and comprehension and (2) through that comprehension, to support acquisition of new language forms or to aid in the development of sociocultural and pragmatic understanding of how those forms are used. Technology can play an important role in both. As noted in Otto (this volume), throughout the 20th century there were technological developments that allowed the human voice to be captured and then replayed across time or broadcast through the airwaves. Vinyl records, film, and audio and video tapes brought native speaker voices, visages, and culture into the foreign language classroom. Radio and television also played a role, often in conjunction with recording tools. For second language listening, a qualitative shift can be traced back to two technologies from the 1980s: the laser videodisc and the appearance of digitized sound on PCs and early Macintosh computers. In both cases, the key transformation was the enhanced control these technologies allowed. No longer were teachers and learners forced to rely on time-consuming search, fast forwarding, and rewinding through unwanted material to get to what was desired. The computer programs allowed teachers, for example, to jump to any desired portion of an audio or video recording instantly to support their teaching activities or to toggle L1 and L2 subtitles off and on at will. Similarly, learners could get an immediate repetition of a segment that was not fully understood. Beginning in the 1990s, CD-ROMs and the World Wide Web made such controllable digital video and multimedia mainstream. Podcasts, YouTube, and other streaming media, and the mobility of mp3 players, smartphones, and tablets have placed listening materials within the reach of language learners across a large and growing portion of the globe. Modern digital tools have permanently changed the ways in which we interact with recorded media.

The following section looks in more detail at how these tools can impact the way students engage in listening for language learning. Later sections touch on their connection to second language acquisition (SLA) theory, research exploring both their advantages and limitations, and developing practices.

*The Handbook of Technology and Second Language Teaching and Learning*, First Edition.
Edited by Carol A. Chapelle and Shannon Sauro.
© 2017 John Wiley & Sons, Inc. Published 2020 by John Wiley & Sons, Inc.

# Digital affordances and new listening contexts

In recent years, it has become increasingly common to speak about technology tools and applications in terms of their *affordances*. According to Norman (1988), affordances are the perceived possibilities that a user has for such tools and applications. The term is used here in a broad sense where that "perception" is not necessarily universal but rather mediated through theory and practice toward the goals and objectives of second language learning. In this context Hampel (2006), referring to the online language learning environment *Lyceum*, defines affordances as "possibilities as well as limitations" having "an impact on its [*Lyceum's*] use" (107). For example, the affordance of a button for turning on and off captioning in videos may differ depending on whether a teacher or learner perceives it as (1) a shortcut to comprehension that can privilege reading over listening (Vandergrift and Goh 2012), (2) an enrichment of the audio channel to support noticing (Schmidt 1993) during dual coding (see Plass and Jones' (2005) multimedia model described below), or (3) a means to identify and capture new vocabulary items (Danan 2004) in combination with the additional function of pausing.

A framework introduced in Hubbard (2010) outlines in broad terms the characteristics of the digital devices and networks that make them potentially useful for computer-mediated listening for language learning, characteristics akin to underlying affordances. The goal of the framework is to lay out categories and subcategories of the operations digital devices and networks are capable of in a way that is relatively neutral to the specific device. The underlying rationale is that (1) computer mediation changes the way that humans interact with one another and with language content in particular ways that are different from face-to-face or one-to-many encounters, (2) those changes can impact the second language use and acquisition process in non-obvious ways, and (3) pursuing research and development with a goal of understanding the nature of that impact can be more fruitful than just considering a particular technology at a particular time and place with a particular group.

The primary categories in that framework are shown in Table 7.1: archiving and indexing, transferring, linking, controlling and shifting time, and transforming. *Archiving and indexing* make it possible to maintain digital copies and more importantly locate desired ones through search routines. Archiving can occur locally or on web servers, and in the latter case it can be

**Table 7.1**   Mediating characteristics of digital devices and networks.

| Characteristic | Definition | Examples |
|---|---|---|
| Archiving and indexing | Making copies and providing location information for searches | Copying and indexing through tagging, titles, or content |
| Transferring | Moving digital information from one place to another | Webcasting, streaming, and downloading audio and video, as with YouTube |
| Linking | Associated one item with another | Clicking on words for associated definitions |
| Controlling time and time shifting | Controlling time; moving non-linearly through materials | Tracking or limiting time; anytime listening; jumping to desired portions of a listening text |
| Transforming | Changing the form of a listening text | Text to speech; speech to graphic form |

open to the world if desired (e.g., through YouTube). Indexing through titles, keyword tagging or even the text of audio or video make it possible to locate desired material through search functions. *Transferring* is a basic digital media affordance. Audio and video can be broadcast live (webcast), streamed on demand from archived copies, or downloaded for local archiving and use. It is the latter two of these on contemporary wireless and mobile networks that allow for "anytime, anywhere" listening. *Linking* is a particularly powerful affordance allowing the association of one item to another. Linking can be automatically controlled by the program or triggered by a deliberate user action, such as clicking on a button. Examples of linking relevant to listening include connecting video to text captions or transcripts, audio to photos or other graphics, and both audio and video materials to meaning supports—definitions, translations, and explanations—or to other content. *Time* may be tracked by recording time on task or response time for an individual item. It may also be controlled by setting time limits on responses to individual items or on a whole activity. An important and understudied related affordance is *time shifting*. This includes the potential availability of recorded materials at any time (true of all recorded material, but a defining characteristic of online listening, especially in this era of mobile learning), standard and enhanced audiovisual controls (such as sliders, pause, rewind, and hot keys for jumping back a set number of seconds), and play speed controls for digitally increasing or decreasing speech rate (Zhao 1997) without the distortion in pitch associated with phonograph records and tape recordings. The final affordance category in this framework is *transforming*. Using text to speech programs, any machine-readable text can be used for listening practice. Programs transforming speech to graphic representations, although most commonly used in teaching pronunciation, can also allow learners to visualize stress, pitch, and length for improved perception (Chun 1998). Affordances also exist for enhancing quality, such as digital graphic equalizers found on media players that can be set to boost certain frequencies (mid-ranges) to optimize speech perception.

## Technologies for listening

The preceding categories broadly represent the potential characteristics of digital devices and networks for mediating listening both for aiding comprehension and for facilitating language learning (with an emphasis on *potential*). This section reviews a range of relevant technologies, describing them and discussing in general terms what their value to listening and language learning might be, singly or in combination. One major area, help options, is discussed through a framework developed by Cardenas-Claros and Gruba (2013).

*Digital Devices and Networks.* Listening is currently supported by a range of digital devices. Desktop and laptop computers remain widely used, but these have been supplemented by tablets and smartphones (which in reality are just small mobile computers). In addition to these general-purpose devices there are more narrowly dedicated ones such as DVD players, mp3 players, feature phones (the "traditional" mobile phone with some additions like an mp3 player but without the smartphone's web connectivity), and streaming media players like Apple TV and Google Chromecast that work with a digital TV or monitor. All can have a role in connecting language learners to listening experiences. The networks that connect these devices to servers and other devices are also critical as it is increasingly less common to load programs and content from a physical disk, CD, or DVD. Networks—wired, wireless, and mobile (e.g., 3G, 4G, and LTE)—can be used to download material for listening or to stream it. Increased bandwidth in both developed and developing countries is putting Internet audio and video readily into the hands of hundreds of millions of subscribers. By the end of 2014, the global average connection speed was 4.5 Mbps (megabits per second) (Akamai 2015). According to the U.S. Federal Communications Commission (FCC), 4 Mbps is sufficient for streaming HD video. Although mobile data connections are typically slower, ranging from 16 Mbps average in the United Kingdom to 1 Mbps in New Caledonia (Akamai 2015), even that 1 Mbps rate can support basic video at 640 Kbps. The primary issue for many remains the cost rather than the base technology; however, the cost continues to drop and many mobile users are able to rely on free or inexpensive Wi-Fi rather than mobile data plans, especially for listening with video.

*Content.* Content here refers to audio or video recorded spoken language texts of all types, from dialogues and short clips to academic lectures and movies. Content designed for and dedicated to enhancing listening skills is readily available online, especially for English language learners (e.g., http://www.esl-lab.com, http://www.elllo.com). Many multiskill programs have a substantial listening component, and online listening files accompany a number of foreign language textbooks. However, the most significant change for listening is that access to native speaker content has exploded in the last decade or so. In the space of those few years, language teachers and learners have gone from relying on limited personal and institutional physical collections of audio and video recordings to tapping into the enormous and continually expanding archives of free, authentic material available on institutional and commercial media websites and through YouTube (launched in 2005) and other streaming services. The problem for many teachers and independent learners now is not locating material but sorting the bountiful options for content that is likely to be effective for supporting the development of listening skills and target language proficiency. As noted below, one direction for addressing this issue is an expansion of authentic content curation by language learning experts (Hubbard 2011).

*Controls and Help Options.* There are a number of ways that technology can improve the listening experience for language learners so that comprehension, processing, and acquisition are potentially supported. Cardenas-Claros and Gruba (2013) have captured these in a relatively comprehensive framework, called CoDe, for conceptualizing (Co) and designing (De) help options to support second language listening. Although their focus is on help options for listening resources and environments dedicated to second language teaching and learning, elements of the framework are also relevant for supporting learner use of authentic audio and video content not targeted at that objective. Drawing on the work of Chapelle (2003) among others, they divide help options into four categories: operational, regulatory, compensatory, and explanatory.

*Operational* help fits into the category of technical support and training (Romeo and Hubbard 2010). These include user manuals, help menus, training modules, and introductory-level tutorials aimed at making learners aware of how to use the hardware and software, how the program functions, what help options are available and how to invoke them, and potential frustrations.

*Regulatory* help options are those that aim to prepare the learner for a particular task and understand and reflect on that task after its completion. In the former category they place listening tips, directions for specific strategy use and development, and guidance on which of the available help options to use for that task. For post-listening guidance, they list explanatory feedback; another example would be directions to reflect or comment on "lessons learned" in line with metacognitive approaches aimed at promoting autonomy (Vandergrift and Goh 2012).

The provision of *compensatory* help options taps into the affordances of digital technologies to provide modified input or to make input more salient in ways that can support both comprehension and subsequent acquisition (Chapelle 2003). For modified input, Cardenas-Claros and Gruba note various combinations linking text (subtitles and transcripts) to audio and video, audio to still images, and L1 to L2 transcripts. For increased saliency, they identify the various audio control buttons (volume, rewind, pause), the media controller bar or slider, and for some media players, the variable speed control for slowed playback of audio and video.

Their final category of *explanatory* help options similarly includes operations targeted at making input more salient through visible links to explanatory hints or links to definitions and glosses from subtitles or transcripts (de Ridder 2002; Cardenas-Claros 2005 cited in Cardenas-Claros and Gruba 2009). Explanatory help can also appear in the form of input elaboration, namely, the content found in cultural notes, grammar explanations, electronic dictionaries, and tools such as concordancing programs.

This framework is useful not only for developers. Looking beyond dedicated language learning software with a listening component, language teachers can exploit some of these concepts to help their students have a more productive learning experience with authentic materials. For compensatory help, they can identify specific media players (e.g., the VLC player—see http://www.videolan.org) with a rich set of options as well as sources of appropriate online audio or video materials that include captions and/or transcripts. They can offer some regulatory support themselves by suggesting effective procedures for using these materials and media tools. For explanatory help, teachers can also evaluate and recommend electronic dictionaries and sources of grammatical and cultural explanations, as well as train students in their use. Such recommendations have been prompted in some cases by connections made between technology, listening, and theories and models of second language acquisition.

## Technology, listening, and SLA theory

Many research studies on listening and related topics, such as vocabulary acquisition in audio and video contexts, draw on an SLA theory for their framing. However, these theories are often simply borrowed without taking into account the impact of the mediating role of the technology on the listening or learning process at the theoretical level. There have been few overt attempts similar to those by Cardenas-Claros and Gruba to bring technology and SLA theory explicitly together in a way that is relevant for listening. In this section, we review three of them: Chapelle's (2003) interpretation of SLA theory and technology, Plass and Jones' (2005) multimedia learning model, and Vandergrift and Goh's (2012) application of their metacognitive model of listening to technological environments.

Chapelle (2003) links technology to SLA theories by showing how several theories can be adapted to explore the role of the computer as a stand-in for a human interlocutor. Although she touches on sociocultural approaches as well as depth of processing theory, she draws most heavily on the interactionist perspective in this work. While not specific to listening, much of her proposal is relevant here.

Using concepts from the interaction hypothesis (Long 1996), Chapelle describes ways in which the computer can aid the learner by making input more comprehensible. As she explains, "The concern for developing good CALL tasks is how to design materials that can direct learners' attention to particular linguistic forms within the input" (Chapelle 2003, 41). Thus one important function of the computer for listening within this theoretical perspective is to provide *enhanced input* through increasing salience, input modification, or input simplification or elaboration. As we will see below, this provision can also be relevant for training learners to be autonomous so that they will direct their attention to these enhancements and use them appropriately when listening to authentic materials (Vandergrift and Goh 2012).

For salience, targeted language forms in text support for listening material (e.g., transcripts or captions) can be underlined, boldfaced, or colored differently, or a word or phrase could be stressed. In fact, following Cardenas-Claros and Gruba (2013) the presence of text in any form (captions or transcripts) can serve to make recorded input more salient (assuming learners have sufficient reading proficiency in the target language script; see Winke, Gass, and Sydorenko (2010)) by providing full versions of reduced forms and making word boundaries obvious. Audio material may also be repeated to increase saliency, and specific task elements can direct learners to such repetitions. Besides discussing strategies for increasing salience, Chapelle covers a range of options for input modification to make that input more understandable. Still images accompanying an audio clip or a video where the visual information supports the meaning of the spoken language is one form of modification, although it is worth noting that the visual dimension can interfere with rather than support comprehension if it is not congruent with the audio content (see Mayer 2001). Text supports in the form of either translations or target language definitions of words or phrases can also provide another form of input enhancement relevant to listening comprehension. Finally, input enhancement in computer-mediated listening can occur through a programmed feature providing simplification or elaboration.

Plass and Jones (2005) build on concepts from Chapelle's (1998) version of the interactionist perspective (adapted from Gass 1997) and combine them with Mayer's cognitive theory of multimedia (Mayer 2001) to synthesize an integrated model of multimedia language learning applicable to both listening and reading. Mayer's theory links verbal and pictorial input through parallel processing, or dual coding, reinforcing one another when conditions are right. A set of empirically supported principles in the theory describes those conditions. For example, Mayer's Contiguity Principle states that complementary text and pictorial material that are close to one another are processed better than when they are further apart. This would imply that presenting a video with captions on the screen should yield better comprehension than presenting a video with a transcript in a window to the side. Plass and Jones propose that this dual coding can strengthen each stage in Chapelle's model of the second language acquisition process: apperception (including noticing aspects of the input), comprehension, intake, and finally integration into the learner's linguistic system.

They use their model to interpret the multimedia research existing up to that time and offer three principles for using multimedia in support of language learning (Plass and Jones 480–481):

- Multimedia Principle: "Students acquire language better from input enhanced by text and pictures than by text alone."
- Individual Differences Principle: "Students acquire language better when they have the choice of visual versus verbal annotations…"
- Advance Organizer Principle: Advance organizers in reading and listening activities aid language acquisition and those "presented in visual and verbal modes are more effective than those presented only in the verbal mode."

The authors caution that these are not prescriptions but that they can provide guidance to researchers and designers of multimedia materials for language learning. Teachers and learners operating in multimedia environments can similarly invoke these principles, regardless of whether those environments and the content for them have been specifically designed for language learning. In addition to the three principles, Plass and Jones offer three recommendations, weaker claims that they distinguish from principles because the empirical support for them is more limited. These include allowing learner control over order, pace, and choice of materials, opportunities for producing comprehensible output, and vocabulary testing in the same mode as the annotations that are provided.

Vandergrift and Goh (2012) build their theoretical second language listening model on comprehension, using as its foundation Levelt's cognitive comprehension and production model. The authors identify a number of cognitive and affective factors that affect listening success (e.g., vocabulary size and motivation). However, the defining feature of the model is its emphasis on metacognition, along with their claim that metacognitive instruction can help learners become more effective and efficient especially in listening tasks and activities conducted outside of class. This instruction begins with a knowledge foundation for the learner:

- person knowledge (beliefs about listening and identification of individual listening problems),
- task knowledge (listening processes, different listening skills based on objectives, factors affecting performance, etc.),
- strategy knowledge (understanding of the roles of cognitive, metacognitive and affective strategies as well as identification of appropriate types for particular tasks and problems).

That foundation is then integrated into the metacognitive processes of planning, monitoring, and evaluation for learners. In each of these areas, Vandergrift and Goh address not just listening comprehension goals but also procedures for overall listening development.

The authors devote a full chapter to listening in multimedia environments, reviewing research in areas such as use of visual media, support options, and captions. Although they acknowledge the potential of these, they emphasize that the evidence for incorporating them is mixed and provide a set of useful guidelines to teachers to harness them appropriately. Returning to the metacognitive theme of the book, several of their points focus on the importance of helping learners develop what they refer to as *metatechnical skills*, for example include "instruction in media literacy …," "Provide learners with initial guidance on the use of help options …," and "For lower proficiency learners, provide more guidance…" (234).

## Technology-mediated listening: Research and practice

This section begins with an overview of research in four areas relevant to technology and listening that have been studied over the past 20 years or so, much of which overlaps with Cardenas-Claro and Gruba's (2013) typology of help options: (1) use of captions and transcripts, (2) multimedia, (3) electronic glossaries and dictionaries, (4) play speed control for slowing the speech rate. It then discusses some examples of techniques and strategies in practice as well as exploring the role of learner autonomy.

*Captions and transcripts.* The use of both L1 and L2 captions for enhancing listening comprehension and ensuing vocabulary development has been studied since the days of VHS video players (note that here captions and subtitles are not distinguished; see Danan (2004) for a more nuanced view). Although results of some of that early research was mixed, a number of more recent studies support the notion that captions are a valuable comprehension tool, especially for listening-based vocabulary development. Among the first studies using random access technology (a videodisc) was Borras and Lafayette (1994). They found that for their subjects (fifth-semester college French students) the presence of captions under learner control led not only to better comprehension than that of a control group without captions but also better subsequent performance on a related speaking task.

Winke, Gass, and Sydorenko (2010) noted that the use of captions involves a combination of factors including what learners are attending to when they read captions as well as how they process them. In addition to confirming prior research showing that captioned videos were better than non-captioned for both comprehension and for recognizing new vocabulary, they suggested that processing differences are likely to be influenced by the learner's familiarity with the writing system. Native English learners of Spanish and Russian in their study were most successful having captions on the first of two listenings while learners of Chinese and Arabic, whose orthography is more distant from that of English, did better on the second listening after context was established. Although they found no significant difference in benefits for second vs. fourth year students (in Spanish at least), other studies suggest caption use can indeed be influenced by language level. For instance, Leveridge and Yang (2013) tested learner reliance on captions with high school EFL students in Taiwan. They found that there was considerable individual difference but that overall, lower level learners were much more reliant on captions than their higher level counterparts.

There have been other issues related to captions that have been studied as well. Though most research has focused on target language captioning, some researchers have looked at differential effects of L1 vs. L2 captions. For example, Guichon and McLornan (2008) found that providing L1 captions led to more lexical interference than using L2 captions. On the other hand, Markham and Peter (2003) showed that listening with L1 captions first provided an advantage relative to L2 captions on a subsequent related uncaptioned assessment. A possible explanation for this result is that listening with L1 captions can provide a sort of advance organizer for subsequent listening with L2 or no captions, especially for more challenging material. There has also been research on distinguishing full captions from those that just provide keywords. Pérez, Peters, and Desmet (2014) review the literature in this area and follow up with their own study. They found that students provided with full captions outperformed the keyword caption group on global comprehension and that the students showed a strong preference for having full captions available. It may be that learners capable of reading full captions rapidly do better with those, while less proficient students or those reading in an unfamiliar script find keyword captioning more useful.

While some scholars such as Danan (2004) focus on the positive affordances of captions, Vandergrift and Goh (2012) among others acknowledge the value of captions for vocabulary development and overall comprehension, but caution that it is not possible in most cases to distinguish whether they enhance listening comprehension or simply replace it with comprehension by reading. A study that supports their position is Sydorenko (2010), who found that learners given captioned audio and video scored higher on written word recognition of presented vocabulary while those presented the same material without captions scored higher on aural recognition.

It is worth noting that Vandergrift and Goh's concerns are based on the assumption that language learners are not able to use captions in normal, real-time face-to-face encounters. Yet it could be argued that for many language learners, the great majority of their listening now and in the future will be one-way—listening to recorded media—rather than interactive, and that the online audio and video material they encounter will often be accompanied by captions. Thus, an environment of captioned listening may increasingly be considered as "authentic" as a traditional face-to-face one. Computer-mediated listening is simply a more complicated and varied phenomenon than is commonly acknowledged.

A less studied but related area of text support is the use of transcripts. The issues involving the impact of reading on the listening process discussed above are relevant here as well, coupled with the additional problem of transcripts and video not being as contiguous as captions and video (Mayer 2001). Although transcripts can aid in identifying word boundaries and new vocabulary, Grgurović and Hegelheimer (2007) found that the literature on the value for comprehension was mixed, with various studies showing an advantage, a disadvantage, and no effect. In testing learner preference of captions versus transcripts for support in video listening with a system that provided the two options under student control, they first found that learners used both less than expected. However, there was a clear preference for captions. They nevertheless concluded that it would be helpful to provide both if possible, along with training in their use, because a small group of students still showed a preference for transcripts.

*Multimedia.* Turning now from text support to multimedia in general, the area is a diverse one due to the options involved in selecting which media to combine, how to combine them, and who controls the result. For listening purposes, video is already multimedia when compared to audio (Yang 2014), and video or audio plus captions or transcripts are multi-media compared to written text alone. Captioned video as discussed above is an example of multimedia, as is video presented with a transcript available on the same screen.

Multimedia materials can provide for a richer and deeper processing of the material. For example, Jones and Plass (2002) found that students listening to aural texts in French that included written and pictorial annotations scored higher on recall protocol comprehension tests than those who listened to the aural text alone. However, much of the research for multimedia language learning has focused on vocabulary acquisition, possibly because vocabulary knowledge is easier to test for. Jones and Plass also found that learners with written and pictorial annotations performed better on a subsequent test of new vocabulary from the listening material. Al-Seghayer (2001) concluded that words glossed with text and video were more readily recalled than those with text plus a static picture. In a review of multimedia research for listening, Jones (2006) noted examples of listening studies showing (1) a stronger effect for visual annotations alone for high relative to low verbal ability students, (2) a text recall advantage for students working collaboratively with multimedia annotations in pairs rather than independently, (3) student attitudes toward multimedia improving with familiarity, and (4) value in providing ongoing comprehension feedback during multimedia listening tasks. Although the research is generally positive regarding multimedia as an aid to richer processing during listening activities, the number of studies is limited. In recent years, the term *multimedia* in CALL research seems largely to refer to just captioned video (Leveridge and Yang 2013; Li 2014) or even video as opposed to audio (Yang 2014).

*Electronic glossaries and dictionaries.* Cardenas-Claros and Gruba (2013) categorize both electronic glossaries and electronic dictionaries as explanatory help options. Functionally, though, they can be quite different. Glossed words and phrases typically provide an in-context explanation of their meaning, requiring intervention by materials writers at the development stage. In contrast, electronic dictionaries are independent of the text in which the links to their entries occur, so learners must interpret the results relative to the context in which an item occurs. Besides dictionary definitions, some electronic dictionaries will automatically link to Wikipedia entries (e.g., http://wordweb.info) to allow for elaboration. The previous research on mixing pictorial and written annotations of items in an audio text is relevant here, but there is little else covering electronic dictionaries and listening. Jin and Deifell (2013) report results of a survey study where of 211 respondents to a question regarding use of online dictionaries, only 21.3% employed them for listening in the target language as opposed to 73.9% for reading. As noted in Levy and Steel (2015), *usability* is one of the primary issues for electronic dictionaries in this context. A functionality missing from virtually all listening material is the ability to click on a word or phrase in a caption (automatically pausing the video) and get an instant popup definition in a desired dictionary. However, this is possible within transcripts for videos at the Clilstore site (http://multidict.net/clilstore/), a multilingual project funded by the European Union.

*Play speed controls.* As noted previously, one of the more remarkable affordances of digital technology is the potential to speed up or slow down speech rate. This is done through programs and media players that compress or stretch the time domain of the digital signal without shifting the frequencies of the sound waves. This means that language learners can slow the speech rate down to allow for more processing time, but that the pitch of the voice still sounds relatively natural. So, unlike analog systems where slowing speed also means lowering pitch, the original pitch can be maintained at the changed speed. Results of early research with slowed speech were somewhat mixed, but Zhao (1997) demonstrated clear advantages for comprehension when learners were allowed to control the speed rather than teachers or researchers.

Matsuura, Chiba, Mahoney, and Rilling (2014) specifically looked at effects of speech rate adjustments on accented speech. They found that neither low nor high proficiency Japanese students found a 20% slower speech rate helpful in listening to moderate accents, but that both groups found 20% slower speech more comprehensible when the accent was considered heavy. As with most previous studies, the subjects did not have any control over speed. Although much more research is needed in this area, a tentative claim can be made that there is some value in manipulating speech rate to allow more processing time. Besides making words more comprehensible, this potentially makes certain elements of connected speech such as linking and reduced forms more salient as well as providing additional time to identify familiar words, phrases, and grammatical markers embedded in an unfamiliar accent. However, variables such as learner level, learner control, task, and rate and clarity of the spoken text all may have an impact, and these remain understudied.

Shifting from research to practice, an important work in this area is Rost and Wilson (2013). Most previous books that focused on the teaching of second language listening, like Field (2008) and Flowerdew and Miller (2005), have limited references to computer-based technology. As noted above, Vandergrift and Goh (2012) devote a full chapter to it, emphasizing the role of metacognition in the selection of tools and techniques for listening. In contrast, in Rost and Wilson the use of digital technology is interspersed throughout as a natural part of language instruction.

The book is organized around the concept of *active listening*, which they paraphrase as "engaged processing." Building on prior theory, research, and practice, they conceptualize listening across five frames: affective, top-down, bottom-up, interactive, and autonomous. For the affective frame, for example, student motivation is a key element. With respect to technology integration, the authors suggest how activities involving personal interests like hobbies can be supported through learner selection and presentation of YouTube videos. In another suggested activity, Wrong Words, they direct the teacher to select songs and play mp3 recordings or online music videos. The lyrics to the songs are downloaded from one of several suggested websites, and the teacher changes the text to include words that sound similar to but are different from the actual lyrics. The learners' task is to locate the mistakes in the transcript when they hear the music played. There are similar examples provided for the next three frames.

It is in the autonomous frame, however, that technology moves into playing the most central role. Rost and Wilson note that new technologies allow for out-of-class listening, individualization of goals and tasks, and strategic use of comprehension and learning supports of the types described in Cardenas-Claros and Gruba's (2013) help option typology. The majority of the ten activities described in their chapter on the autonomous frame require listening mediated by technology, and several others include an optional technology component. Examples include using transcripts with online listening materials, listening to news sites, listening-based Webquests (http://webquest.org), creating a listening library of online materials, interacting through web-based discussion boards, using online listening games, and learning something new through narrow listening (Krashen, 1996) using multiple short audio or video clips on the same topic.

A key concept in developing autonomy for continuing a student's progress in listening outside of class and once the course is over is learner training. Romeo and Hubbard (2010) report on a pervasive learner training model employed in an advanced ESL listening course that incorporated a three-hour independent listening project each week. The model integrated technical training (*how* to use the controls and help options in media players and dedicated listening sites), strategic training (*what* to do to enhance comprehension and learning, especially of new vocabulary), and pedagogical training (*why* to utilize certain techniques and procedures, such as pre-listening and dictation, for specific objectives). Through pre- and post-testing, they found substantial gains on a listening proficiency test. Evidence from weekly reflective reports, bi-weekly individual tutorials, and exit interviews showed qualitative changes in the way students approached their independent listening, greater reflectivity over time, and a more positive attitude toward listening. A subsequent paper (Hubbard and Romeo, 2012) examined diversity among students in a number of areas including selection of material and development of different sets of preferred strategies. The conclusion was that although all students benefited to some degree from learner training, some incorporated it more rapidly and successfully into their work than others. The study underscores the fact that response to training is highly individual and may be affected by factors outside the control of instructors.

Vandergrift and Goh's (2012) metacognitive model also targets the development of autonomy. To be successful at independent listening tasks, it is helpful for learners to be able to *plan* by identifying learning goals and objectives, selecting appropriate materials and incorporating effective strategies that are attuned to the technologies and environments they will operate in. They need to be able to *monitor* themselves during the listening and make adjustments as necessary. Finally, they need to *evaluate* the effectiveness of their experience and make adjustments for future listening tasks. Vandergrift and Goh recommend activities such as listening diaries, self-report checklists, and peer discussions to trigger the metacognitive processes that facilitate learning.

## Current trends and future directions

A growing trend in multiple areas of language learning is the use of mobile devices, and listening is no exception. Demouy and Kukulska-Hulme (2010) report that the majority of students in an online French course were initially not using the mp3 players they had to practice listening, but after a course project employing these players, "They quickly saw the benefits of using their device to maximise exposure to the language in spaces and at times that suited their lifestyle" (12). Kukulska-Hulme (2012) notes that a number of interviewees in a study on mobile language learning, "…appreciated the experience of learning a language while not being fully focused on it, for example, by simultaneously engaging in another task, and they noted the unobtrusiveness of mobile learning. There was a sense of wanting to immerse oneself in the target language by listening to it often and getting used to its sounds and intonation" (5–6). This suggests a role for mobile devices in incidental rather than intentional language learning through listening (Hulstijn 2003b). Hoven and Palalas (2013) report on a design-based research study for creating a system to enhance ESP (English for specific purposes) learners' listening skills using mobile devices. The project employed podcasts, many of which were produced by students themselves either individually or collaboratively. Though highlighting listening, it integrated other language skills into tasks as well, in particular speaking and vocabulary development.

Another trend in development of content for listening involves the collection of enriched media for the learner in terms of topic, language level, and other features, a process known as content curation (Hubbard 2011). Curation offers both teachers and learners access to freely available online material, providing them with additional information relevant to making informed choices. Lying somewhere between unordered collections and fully articulated listening lessons, curated collections for listening ideally involve the input from a language learning expert. Analogous to a curator in a museum, a curator for listening materials locates and collects them, organizes them into logical groups and sequences, provides language level information of various sorts (vocabulary level, speech rate, speaker accent, etc.), and adds pedagogical support (pre-listening information, key vocabulary, etc.). Ideal content characteristics for a curated set of materials include being freely and legally available, likely to be interesting to the targeted audience, good technical quality, stable, accompanied by captions and/or transcripts, and linked to complementary material. A prototypical source meeting these requirements is www.ted.com: an example of curated TED Talks by the author is available at http://web.stanford.edu/~efs/TED1. As noted previously, the Clilstore site (http://multidict.net/clilstore/) also includes curated material for listening. In this case, audio and video content from over 50 languages is available, indexed by Common European Framework levels and accompanied by transcripts linked to a variety of bilingual dictionaries.

Little has been said here about the interactive listening typical of face-to-face encounters. The role of technology for that in the past has been primarily in (1) demonstrating interactive listening through recorded examples of it and (2) enabling audio and video computer-mediated communication (CMC). An understudied and underdeveloped area is the digital recording and subsequent analysis by learners (alone, with peers, or with an instructor) of the language that appears in those contexts. Applications such as Evaer (http://www.evaer.com) allow both audio and video recording of Skype interactions, for example. For both online social interactions and online language course work, such technologies can be an important new source of feedback to learners, allowing them to replay what they heard. As Robin (2007) points out, "The notion that L2 learners must grab a flow of speech on the first try or lose the meaning is valid only for those events where the audio is not repeatable" (110). Perhaps as important, recording technology allows us to capture not just the meaning but the *form* for future reflection and learning.

Looking to the future, one could produce a wish-list of resources and technologies, some of which have already been mentioned. Larger and more sophisticated curated collections can assist both teachers and learners in selecting materials that provide a close match to their needs. Media players optimized for instant repetition, adjustment of play speed and capable of streaming any online video would be helpful, as would a technology to automatically double or triple the pauses between thought groups to increase available processing time (see Hulstijn 2003a). The affordance of *time shifting* as embodied in instant repetition, play speed controls, and automatic pause insertion has the potential to influence perceptual accuracy and potentially the process and quality of connected speech processing. Along with these technologies, it will be important to adapt existing strategies and procedures and create new ones more targeted at capturing the power of such mediation.

Yet we can only go so far in predicting what future technologies will bring to second language listening. At the time of this writing, smart watches are bringing wearable computers into our everyday lives, and 3D immersive environments are on the rise. How will these and other innovations impact the field? Moving forward, the rapid pace of technological change means that it will be even more important to consider the affordances digital technology offers in general rather than in device or environment-specific terms so that research and practice from today can transfer and still have relevance in the future. Simple binary questions like "Are L2 video captions helpful or not for language learning?" are no longer appropriate if they ever were. Rather, using frameworks such as those described here and others yet to be developed, we need to continue to expand our research base to understand the conditions under which such features are more and less helpful, passing those findings on to developers, teachers, and learners who will in turn help us to refine them.

## REFERENCES

Akamai. 2015. State of the Internet: Executive Summary. Accessed April 11, 2015. http://www.akamai.com/dl/soti/q4-2014-executive-summary.pdf

Al-Seghayer, Khalid. 2001. "The Effect of Multimedia Annotation Modes on L2 Vocabulary Acquisition: A Comparative Study." *Language Learning & Technology*, 5, no. 1: 202–232.

Borras, Isabel, and Robert C. Lafayette. 1994. "Effects of Multimedia Subtitling on the Speaking Performance of College Students of French." *Modern Language Journal*, 78, no. 1: 61–75.

Cardenas-Claros, Monica S. 2005. *Field Dependence/Field Independence: How do Students Perform in CALL-based Listening Activities.* Unpublished M.A. Thesis, Iowa State University.

Cardenas-Claros, Monica S., and Paul A. Gruba. 2009. "Help Options in CALL: A Systematic Review." *CALICO Journal*, 27(1): 69–90.

Cardenas-Claros, Monica S., and Paul A. Gruba. 2013. "Decoding the "CoDe": A Framework for Conceptualizing and Designing help Options in Computer-based Second Language Listening." *ReCALL*, 25, no. 2: 250–271.

Chapelle, Carol A. 1998. "Multimedia CALL: Lessons to be Learned from Research on Instructed SLA." *Language Learning & Technology*, 2, no. 1: 22–34.

Chapelle, Carol A. 2003. *English Language Learning and Technology: Lectures on Applied Linguistics in the Age of Information and Communication Technology.* Amsterdam: John Benjamins.

Chun, Dorothy. 1998. "Signal Analysis Software for Teaching Discourse Intonation." *Language Learning & Technology*, 2, no. 1: 61–77.

Danan, Martine. 2004. "Captioning and Subtitling: Undervalued Language Learning Strategies." *Meta: Translators Journal*, 49, no. 1: 67–77.

Demouy, Valérie, and Agnes Kukulska-Hulme. 2010. "On the Spot: Using Mobile Devices for Listening and Speaking Practice on a French Language Programme." *Open Learning: The Journal of Open and Distance Learning*, 25, no. 3: 217–232.

De Ridder, Isabelle. 2002. "Visible or Invisible Links: Does the Highlighting of Hyperlinks Affect Incidental Vocabulary Learning, Text Comprehension, and the Reading Process?" *Language Learning & Technology*, 6, no. 1: 123–146.

Federal Communication Commission. n.d. "Broadband speed guide." Accessed April 11, 2015. http://www.fcc.gov/guides/broadband-speed-guide

Field, John. 2008. *Listening in the Language Classroom.* Cambridge: Cambridge University Press.

Flowerdew, John, and Lindsay Miller. 2005. *Second Language Listening: Theory and Practice.* Cambridge: Cambridge University Press.

Gass, Susan M. 1997. *Input, Interaction, and the Second Language Learner.* Mahwah, NJ: Lawrence Erlbaum.

Grgurović, Maja, and Volker Hegelheimer. 2007. "Help Options and Multimedia Listening: Students' Use of Subtitles and the Transcript." *Language Learning & Technology*, 11, no, 1: 45–56.

Guichon, Nicholas, and Sinead McLornan. 2008. "The Effects of Multimodality on L2 Learners: Implications for CALL Resource Design." *System*, 36: 85–93.

Hampel, Regine. 2006. "Rethinking Task Design for the Digital Age: A Framework for Language Teaching and Learning in a Synchronous Online Environment." *ReCALL* 18, no, 1: 105–121.

Hoven, Debra, and Agnieszka Palalas. 2013. "The Design of Effective Mobile-enabled Tasks for ESP Students: A Longitudinal Study." In *Learner Computer Interaction in Language Education: A Festschrift for Robert Fischer*, edited by Philip Hubbard, Mathias Schulze, and Bryan Smith, 137–165. San Marcos, TX: CALICO.

Hubbard, Philip. 2010. "Listening to Learn: New Opportunities in an Online World." In *RELC Anthology #51. The Impact of Technology on Language Learning and Teaching: What, How and Why*, edited by C. Ward. Singapore: RELC Publications.

Hubbard, Philip. 2011. "Some Practical Issues in Systemization and Autonomy." In *Peer Perspectives on Systemization. A Book Review of Wilfried Decoo's Systemization in Foreign Language Teaching*, edited by Mathea Simons and Jozef Colpaert. Antwerp: Universiteit Antwerpen.

Hubbard, Philip, and Kenneth Romeo. 2012. "Diversity in Learner Training." In *Computer-Assisted Language Learning: Diversity in Research and Practice*, edited by Glenn Stockwell, 33–50. Cambridge: Cambridge University Press

Hulstijn, Jan H. 2003a. "Connectionist Models of Language Processing and the Training of Listening Skills with the Aid of Multimedia Software." *Computer Assisted Language Learning*, 16, 5, 413–425.

Hulstijn, Jan H. (2003b). "Incidental and Intentional Learning." In *Handbook of Second Language Acquisition*, edited by Catherine. J. Doughty and Michael H. Long, 349–381. Oxford: Blackwell.

Jin, Li, and Elizabeth Deifell. 2013. "Foreign Language Learners' Use and Perception of Online Dictionaries: A Survey Study." *Journal of Online Learning and Teaching*, 9: 515–533.

Jones, Linda C. 2006. "Listening Comprehension in Multimedia Environments." In *Calling on CALL: From Theory and Research to New Directions in Foreign Language Education*, edited by Lara Ducate and Nike Arnold, 99–125. San Marcos, Texas: CALICO Publications.

Jones, Linda C., and Jan L. Plass. 2002. "Supporting Listening Comprehension and Vocabulary Acquisition in French with Multimedia Annotations." *The Modern Language Journal*, 86, no. 4: 546–561.

Krashen, Stephen. D. 1996. "The Case for Narrow Listening." *System*, 24: 97–100.

Kukulska-Hulme, Agnes. 2012. "Language Learning Defined by Time and Place: A Framework for Next Generation Designs." In *Left to My Own Devices: Learner Autonomy and Mobile Assisted Language Learning*, edited by Javier E. Díaz-Vera, 1–13. Bingley, UK: Emerald Group Publishing Limited.

Leveridge, Aubrey N., and Jie Chi Yang. 2013. "Testing Learner Reliance on Caption Supports in Second Language Listening Multimedia Environments." *ReCALL*, 25, no. 2: 199–214.

Levy, Mike, and Caroline Steel. 2015. "Language Learner Perspectives on the Functionality and Use of Electronic Language Dictionaries." *ReCALL*, 27: 177–196.

Li, Chen-Hong. 2014. "An Alternative to Language Learner Dependence on L2 Caption-Reading Input for Comprehension of Sitcoms in a Multimedia Learning Environment." *Journal of Computer Assisted Learning*, 30: 17–29.

Long, Michael. H. 1996. "The Role of Linguistic Environment in Second Language Acquisition." In *Handbook of Second Language Acquisition*, edited by William C. Ritchie, and Tej K. Bhatia, 413–468. San Diego, CA: Academic Press.

Markham, Paul, and Lizette Peter. 2003. "The Influence of English Language and Spanish Language Captions on Foreign Language Listening/reading Comprehension." *Journal of Educational Technology Systems*, 31: 331–341.

Matsuura, Hiroko, Reiko Chiba, Sean Mahoney, and Sarah Rilling. 2014. "Accent and Speech Rate Effects in English as a Lingua Franca." *System*, 46: 143–150.

Mayer, Richard E. 2001. *Multimedia Learning*. New York: Cambridge University Press.

Norman, Don. A. (1988). *The Psychology of Everyday Things*. New York: Basic Books.

Pérez, Maribel. M., Elke Peters, and Piet Desmet. 2014. "Is Less more? Effectiveness and Perceived Usefulness of Keyword and Full Captioned Video for L2 Listening Comprehension." *ReCALL*, 26: 21–43.

Plass, Jan. L., and Linda C. Jones. 2005. "Multimedia Learning in Second Language Acquisition." In *The Cambridge Handbook of Multimedia Learning*, edited by Richard E. Mayer, 467–488. Cambridge: Cambridge University Press.

Robin, Richard. 2007. "Learner-based Listening and Technological Authenticity." *Language Learning & Technology*, 11, no. 1: 109–115.

Romeo, Kenneth, and Philip Hubbard. 2010. "Pervasive CALL Learner Training for Improving Listening Proficiency." In *WorldCALL: International Perspectives on Computer-assisted Language Learning*, edited by Mike Levy, Françoise Blin, Claire Bradin Siskin, and Osamu Takeuchi, 215–229. New York: Routledge.

Rost, Michael, and J. J. Wilson. 2013. *Active Listening*. New York: Routledge.

Schmidt, Richard. 1993. "Awareness and Second Language Acquisition." *Annual Review of Applied Linguistics*, 13: 206–226.

Sydorenko, Tetyana. 2010. "Modality of Input and Vocabulary Acquisition." *Language Learning & Technology*, 14, no. 2: 50–73.

Vandergrift, Larry, and Christine C. M. Goh. 2012. *Teaching and Learning Second Language Listening: Metacognition in Action*. New York: Routledge.

Winke, Paula, Susan Gass, and Tetyana Sydorenko. 2010. "The Effects of Captioning Videos Used for Foreign Language Learning Activities." *Language Learning & Technology*, 14, no. 1): 65–86.

Yang, Hui-Yu. 2014. "Does Multimedia Support Individual Differences? – EFL Learners' Listening *Comprehension and Cognitive Load*." *Australasian Journal of Educational Technology*, 30, no. 6: 699–713.

Zhao, Yong. 1997. "The Effects of Listeners' Control of Speech Rate on Second Language Comprehension." *Applied Linguistics*, 18: 49–68.

# 8 Technologies for Teaching and Learning L2 Speaking[1]

## ROBERT J. BLAKE

## Introduction

One of the primary worries that language teachers voice with respect to using technology to teach a second language (L2) has to do with speaking. How can the use of the computer replace the face-to-face oral production that occurs in the classroom, along with all of the live interactions with the instructor, who represents the students' best model for correct usage?[2] In the context of a fully virtual language course, this issue often becomes an impediment to having the faculty grant online class credit. On the one hand, these doubts often arise because of lack of knowledge about the many speaking options offered by computer-assisted language learning (CALL). On the other hand, many teachers simply refuse to relinquish their traditional role *as the sage on the stage* in favor of a more up-to-date function as *the guide on the side*. The language teaching profession is resistant in recognizing that speaking practice that does not directly involve the instructor is no less valuable to the student's long-term L2 development. Clearly, the curricular activities for any given language course will depend not only on the degree of agency that teachers permit their students to exercise, but also on the instructor's appropriate choices of CALL activities that are performed outside of the classroom. In any event, we will grapple with some of these topics in this chapter with an eye to providing a clearer idea of the rich array of contexts, tasks, and CALL tools that can be used to promote L2 speaking.

## Theoretical frameworks

In theoretical terms, the use of CALL to promote L2 speaking is framed by some of the same fundamental ideas normally aired in the L2 literature. Each of the theories described here has a different way of conceptualizing how L2 learners develop their ability to speak, and therefore each provides a useful perspective on how instruction can help.

## Sociocultural theory

Fundamental to all modern language instruction—face-to-face in the classroom or virtually through CALL—is Vygotsky's (1962) notion of the *Zone of Proximal Development* (ZPD) in sociocultural theory (Lantolf and Thorne 2007). The idea that two or more individuals

*The Handbook of Technology and Second Language Teaching and Learning*, First Edition.
Edited by Carol A. Chapelle and Shannon Sauro.
© 2017 John Wiley & Sons, Inc. Published 2020 by John Wiley & Sons, Inc.

working together can produce more accurate, or at least more elaborate, L2 utterances underlies all L2 group activities. In essence, Vygotsky asserted that language, first or second, is always learned and used in a social setting. Accordingly, any CALL pedagogy for speaking must necessarily be situated within this broad framework of providing students with ample opportunities to collaborate with other speakers, native or non-native, with the resulting benefits of participating in language interactions with others. Vygotsky's seminal ideas also underlie the approach of other L2 researchers, known as *interactionists*, who sought to reinterpret the role of input in more complex ways than what Krashen (1985) had espoused.

## *The Interactionist Hypothesis*

Schmidt (1990) observed that all L2 learning requires learners to first notice their own deficiencies or gaps between their present L2 capacity and where they still need to go, as loosely defined by what a native speaker might be able to do with the target language. Long (1991), Long and Robinson (1998), Varonis and Gass (1985), Gass (1997)—to cite only a handful of the many studies carried out in this area—have showed that small groups of learners interacting with other learners or native speakers tend to engage in the *negotiation the meaning* of unfamiliar structures—whether words, grammar, or pragmatic situations—especially, when breakdowns in communication occur. Gass (1997) described this process of negotiating meaning as an important mechanism for priming the pump of second language acquisition (SLA). A pedagogical approach developed to create opportunities for noticing during meaning-oriented learning activities is *Focus on Form* (FonF, Long and Robinson 1998) where the breakdowns, once again, give rise to an examination of new linguistic structures that remain to be learned and controlled by the L2 learner.

Still other researchers, such as Ellis and Sheen (2006), have focused more specifically on the feedback learners received when breakdowns occur, which includes linguistic recasts or reformulations that more proficient partners provide L2 learners in response to the ongoing conversational exchanges. As part of this feedback routine, Swain (2000) also included the L2 speaker's own feedback loop that arises when pressed to produce output during a conversation; in other words, at the moment of speaking, the L2 learner must try out specific grammatical forms and lexical items, which in turn, results in felicitous or infelicitous utterances. The process of trying something out can be a point of learning, particularly if the speaker notices his or her lack of knowledge and then discovers how to modify and improve the original utterance.

## *Autonomy and student agency*

In general, current constructionist educational approaches endorse a more *student-centered* learning environment over a traditional *teacher-centered* model. Accordingly, many researchers have focused attention on creating an atmosphere where the principles of student autonomy and self-agency are heightened (Little 2007), which is especially relevant for the CALL context (Blin 2004; Guillén 2014; O'Dowd 2007; Schwienhorst, 2008). Briefly, autonomous learning means that students take responsibility for their own learning process, which should not be confused with self-instruction. This approach emphasizes learner empowerment, language reflection, and, finally, appropriate L2 usage. The teacher is involved at all stages as a guide, whereas with self-instruction there is no instructor presence at any point. In the CALL context, increased student agency not only guides how students use technology, but also implies that they become creators of L2 texts through their active creation of blogs, wiki entries, chat exchanges, audio and video postings (Blake 2013).

## Cognitive perspectives on speaking proficiency: Accuracy, complexity, and fluency

A cognitive perspective on speaking proficiency is useful for understanding the intended outcomes of speaking pedagogy. Cognitivists see it as consisting of three separate but inter-related constructs (Housen and Kuiken 2009): (1) accuracy (i.e., the lack of phonological, lexical, or grammatical errors), (2) complexity (i.e., the number of words or clauses per T-units or sentences; see Bardovi-Harlig 2012), and (3) fluency. Unfortunately, none of these factors is easy to define or measure (Kormos and Dénes 2004). For instance, the concept of L2 fluency depends on a series of relative time measures such as the delivery speed and length of the utterances, the number of pauses, repetitions, lexical lapses, or discontinuities/interruptions in spontaneous speech. Clearly, not all native speakers would score well with respect to these factors, let alone L2 learners, making these constructs difficult to pin down in absolute terms when assessing L2 speaking proficiency.

Hulstijn (2011) considers speaking accuracy to be part of what he calls the *basic linguistic proficiency* that all native speakers have acquired, but complexity and, to some extent, fluency, belongs to the realm of *extended linguistic proficiency* that is attained only by advanced study of the L1 or the L2. In Hulstijn's framework, an evaluation of speaking should not confound the characteristics of basic vs. extended linguistic proficiency. Nevertheless, in practice both researchers and instructors look to L2 students to perform well on both scales at the same time when they are speaking. In other words, instructors expect learners to improve globally in terms of accuracy, complexity, and fluency, while also commanding a good pronunciation or accent, the latter being something that is extremely difficult for any adult L2 learner to obtain.

To further complicate matters, speaking proficiency also depends on the type of task the L2 student is asked to carry out, which is the focus of the next section. Not all tasks contribute equally to the goal of increased accuracy, complexity, and/or fluency, as Bachman and Savignon (1986) observed long ago with regard to the ACTFL Oral Proficiency Interview, a widely recognized measure of speaking proficiency, and has since been an area of extensive research and theorizing. Likewise, all CALL speaking activities take place in response to specific task requirements. Accordingly, task type must always be part of the pedagogical considerations for using CALL to promote speaking.

# CALL pedagogical frameworks for speaking: Task-based instruction (TBI)

In the previous section, we briefly reviewed some of the important theoretical notions that underlie best practices in L2 teaching, whether in the classroom or in a CALL supported environment. A sound curricular implementation of some of these tenets is perhaps epitomized by task-based language teaching (TBLT), although this general label can refer to any number of realizations that underscore language production and analysis of meaning through real-world activities, collaborations, and problem-solving or information-gap activities (Robinson 2011; Skehan 2003; Willis and Willis 2009; see also González-Lloret, this volume for further discussion). Most of the time, a TBI approach also includes an analytic post-phase that carefully studies the linguistic structures needed to accomplish the assigned tasks (Willis 1996). Skehan (2003) suggests that the best tasks are those that (1) are carefully structured with both a pre-planning and a post-task phase, (2) are organized around familiar information, (3) require analysis or justification, and (4) are interactive or dialogic in nature by virtue of asking the participants to work together. Obviously, the role of the instructor in choosing appropriate tasks is indispensable, especially in CALL contexts where students are necessarily required to be more autonomous while actually completing the task.

# CALL learning environments

A common misconception about CALL is that it only refers to specific programs or mobile apps when, in fact, CALL activities not only consist of asking students to engage with the L2 by responding to prompts given by the computer, but also deal with students engaging in conversations with another person mediated through the use of the computer. The first case is called *tutorial CALL* and the second, *social CALL* (sCALL, see Guillén 2014), or *computer-mediated communication* (CMC). CMC activities themselves can be further divided into asynchronous communication events (ACMC) in deferred time or synchronous chat (SCMC) carried out in real-time. Each CALL context has its own unique set of affordances, as do the tasks themselves (Skehan 2003). Creating an online curriculum for L2 speaking, then, is not so much about choosing one type of CALL activity over another, but rather about combining the CALL tools and appropriate tasks in a variety of productive ways for L2 development (Chapelle 2001; Doughty and Long 2003; Hampel 2006). Both tutorial CALL and ACMC tend to allow students more pre-planning time, which should enhance speaking accuracy and complexity and lower individual frustration levels, while SCMC often stimulates students to produce more utterances (Abrams 2003) with a fluency that mirrors more closely the spontaneous turn-taking behavior found in real-world, face-to-face conversations. Skehan (2003) and Robinson (2011) have endeavored to untangle the complex relationships that exist among language tasks and the main components of speaking proficiency: namely, accuracy, complexity, and fluency. No single task and no single CALL activity can be expected to address all three aspects of speaking proficiency at the same time. Nevertheless, the language profession needs to cultivate better knowledge of the CALL options and their corresponding affordances, as we will outline below.

# Tutorial CALL and speaking

Tutorial CALL allows students to engage in different forms of self-directed speech practice in the absence of conversational partners or classroom instruction. While classroom instruction clearly provides opportunities for students to notice gaps in their L2 knowledge, individual language practice facilitates not only memory storage but also the retrieval of L2 words, collocations, and other details about appropriate usage (Loucky 2006; Teixeira 2015). Fortunately, computers are a good fit for this type of speak-aloud individual practice, especially for languages with a heavy morphological burden or unfamiliar sounds. Ideally, students should sub-vocalize or speak out loud when they are learning vocabulary lists (Arispe 2012). In the past, many tutorial CALL programs have been tagged with the unfavorable name of *drill and kill*, but Hubbard and Siskin (2004) have argued convincingly that tutorial CALL has a well-justified place in the language curriculum. Usually, the speaking tasks offered by tutorial CALL programs ask students to compare their own audio recordings with those of native speakers of diverse accents. Nevertheless, one obvious drawback of this type of exercise for improving L2 speech is the lack of any feedback. Here is where programs that offer some form of automatic speech recognition (ASR) can play an important role.

## Feedback with tutorial CALL

ASR systems work best when applied to clearly circumscribed linguistic sub-domains or micro-worlds: for example, words that only deal with the family or some other specific semantic domain, or important phrases used most often in public places such as banks, airports, pharmacies, and so on. Accordingly, the ASR system asks students to carry out specific tasks, such as individual sound practice, word recognition, or short sentence repetition (Ehsani and Knodt 1998, 56). Several commercially available programs provide ASR capabilities: for example, *Dragon Naturally Speaking* or *Dragon Anywhere* app from *Nuance.com*, and *TeLL Me More*, an algorithm that has been recently integrated into the *RosettaStone.com* online exercises.

The *Dragon* software offers a set of intriguing dictation tools that turn foreign language speech directly into text for American English, Australian English, Asian English, Indian English, UK English, Dutch, French, German, Italian and Spanish. This dictation tool is normally marketed to businesses, but there are obvious applications for the L2 curriculum. If the L2 pronunciation of a target word or phrase deviates too much from the statistical norms programmed into *Dragon*, the written dictation will come out corrupted and, therefore, oblige the user to analyze and restate the utterance in a more comprehensible way, thus providing an excellent feedback loop along the lines of forced output as described by Swain (2000). Plagwitz (2014, 2015) described how he used a similar tool from Windows, the *W7ASR* automatic speech recognition software (now available for Chinese, English, French, German, Japanese and Spanish), to carry out this type of pronunciation practice both in and outside of class by having students convert previously designed writing practice into speaking activities with the feedback loop being provided by the output of the text files. Dictation studies have a long and valued track record in foreign language instruction, as Swain and Lapkin (1998) have shown in their *dictogloss* implementations. Surprisingly, few CALL studies or practical applications have taken advantage of dictation software such as *Dragon*, despite its obvious affordances for enhancing L2 speaking—something that the CALL field needs to look at more closely in the future.

*Rosetta Stone* has also incorporated an ASR feature into its exercises, available in 25 languages, and based on the *TeLL me More* algorithm originally developed by *Auralog.com*. These exercises tend to focus on single word recognition, short collocations, or phrases. The ASR routines offer students a wave-analysis comparison of their recordings with those of a native speaker, but the visualizations are based on sound intensity and entail some trial-and-error experimentation on the part of the learner in order for them to be helpful as feedback. *Rosetta Stone* also offers online tutoring and its own version of a social network, but that service falls under the heading of CMC discussed below.

## Computer-assisted pronunciation training (CAPT)

Pronunciation and intonation, of course, are part and parcel of learning to speak an L2 well. Many researchers (Bley-Vroman 2009; Hulstijn 2011) have argued that learning native-like pronunciation and intonation is a difficult or even impossible goal for most adult L2 learners and, in the overall scheme of communication, may have less importance than gaining adequate control of the frequently used lexical and grammatical structures of the target language. However, O'Brien (2006) has argued that effective communication cannot take without comprehensible pronunciation and, therefore, it merits serious attention. Since class time is limited, the tutorial CALL context, again, becomes the ideal venue for computer-assisted pronunciation training (CAPT), which is designed to allow students to take control of their own learning in the risk free environment offered by working with a non-human helper. In other words, CAPT software provides more practice time, patience, flexibility, and no penalties for making errors. Eskenazi (1999) has stressed the importance to implementing CAPT software in a way that offers diverse speech sounds from different speakers and registers. Chun's research (1998, 2002) has focused on giving students clear feedback about L2 intonation through the use of CALL software. Both Chun (1998) and O'Brien (2006) have stressed the importance of linking instruction on L2 pronunciation with that of L2 intonation.

Gorjian, Hayati, and Pourkhoni (2013) have extolled the virtues of having students study L2 pronunciation and intonation using the PRAAT acoustic analysis software. However, as in the case of the *TeLL Me More* sound graphics, students need training on how to use these visualizations to improve their accent and prosody and only students who are committed to understanding and making use of visualization techniques may see their pronunciation improve. Once again, the issue of student autonomy raises its head here.

## Asynchronous CALL storytelling

Students can also become multimedia storytellers by using digital storyboard applications such as *StoryKit* to produce their own narratives complete with captions and audio recordings. With this program, students work either individually or in groups in order to bring their narratives to life with images, photos, text bubbles, and audio recordings. In the process, the participants receive feedback from the teachers and their peers on their L2 speaking while working on projects that are meaningful to them—their own multimedia creations.

*VoiceThread.com* provides another popular and easy-to-use online tool to combine images, photos, text and audio comments with the added advantage that individuals from different geographical sites can easily collaborate together on a *VoiceThread* project. When *VoiceThread* slides are shared online, the creators can allow anyone with an Internet address (URL) to add comments or answer questions posed by the creators, thereby enriching the entire project. The creator/instructor can always maintain control over which comments are posted by choosing the < *moderate comments* > option under the publishing menu. Because *VoiceThread* permits the formation of learning groups at a distance, it might also be considered a form of asynchronous CMC, but we have included it in tutorial CALL because individuals can always develop single-authored presentations on their own in a completely independent fashion. In practice, *VoiceThread* can be used to conduct both tutorial CALL for speaking or asynchronous CMC.

## Digital sound tools: Unleashing student creativity

In addition to the applications presented above, L2 students have at their fingertips many digital tools that can easily be used to embellish their own stories with images and sound so as to produce multimedia materials for the Web.[3] Blake and Shiri (2012) described how first-year Arabic students at UC Berkeley demonstrated their speaking progress at the end of the term by publishing their audio-enhanced finished products on *YouTube.com*. Several groups of students in this Arabic class opted for simple hand illustrations with hand-written Arabic captions, adding in later their audio narration (http://www.youtube.com/watch?v=Gc4gw6Ig564). These easy-to-use techniques result in an impressive finale to a language course to the great satisfaction to both students and instructors alike and can be viewed by the entire class with an eye to providing feedback on the students' L2 speaking.

## CMC

The other important CALL context deals with using the computer to mediate communication between people; what researchers in the field refer to as CMC. CMC actually has a long and established record starting with asynchronous textual exchanges. The main thrust of earlier CMC studies was to show that online text exchanges produced opportunities to nego-tiate meaning and generate feedback in ways similar to what had already been documented in face-to-face encounters (e.g., Abrams 2003; Blake 2000; Loewen and Erlam 2006; Meskill 2005; Pellettieri 2000; Peterson 2009; and Warschauer 1997; to name only a few). Early on in this line of research, Kern (1995) noticed that there existed many linguistic similarities bet-ween L2 oral speech patterns and asynchronous computer writing, which is why we include SCMC textual exchanges in this chapter on L2 speaking, although clearly other writing considerations are involved here as well (undoubtedly, some degree of sub-vocalization is occurring when people write via the computer keyboard, although this has not been sufficiently studied, as yet). Interesting enough, Kern found that the experimental group exchanging text messages via *Daedalus.com* writing software produced more utterances with more complexity than the control group speaking to each other in a face-to-face context.

Further evidence suggesting that SCMC writing helps L2 speaking emerged from Payne and Whitney's (2002) study where student keyboarding had a significant effect on improving L2 speaking proficiency. Nowadays, the linguistic congruities between texting and speech hardly would surprise anyone, especially given the way people generate tweets on *Twitter* or text on the mobile phone. Despite being a form of written communication, tweeting has been proven to be an effective tool for creating what sociocultural research calls a community of practice with geographically disperse speakers, native and non-native, who tend to respond back and forth as if they were chatting to each other in a cafe (Lomicka and Lord 2011).

Gradually, SCMC began to include the exchange of voice-over IP sound (VoIP), giving speakers two channels in which to communicate (Blake 2005). Many learners continued to prefer keyboarding perhaps because of its visual persistence (i.e., text stays on the screen) and extra processing time in comparison to the pressures of responding quickly to audio prompts. In the case of Sauro's (2009) study, the preference for keyboarding took on gender overtones. Two Japanese students of English, one male and one female, were assigned a col-laborative CALL task. The male participant started off by dominating the voice channel (VoIP) in order to take control of the task, which prompted the female participant to switch to using only the text chat modality in order to communicate. Eventually, her behavior forced the male partner to follow suit, tone down his aggressiveness, and respond to her textual directions and entries in order to finish the assigned task together.

VoIP sound soon gave way to true telephonic sound (i.e., synchronous audio) and now, synchronous video. Today´s CMC tools seamlessly combine asynchronous (text) and synchronous (sound and/or video) channels. Each application accents certain affordances, as Lafford and Lafford (2005) have analyzed in detail. Videoconferencing tools promise a communicative expe-rience most like face-to-face encounters, but this modality also demands lots of bandwidth, which puts great pressure on the user's local network. If the local network is not robust, instruc-tors need to make informed choices so as to use tools that are less greedy for bandwidth.

Adobe's *Connect* is perhaps the most complete videoconferencing program, but its cost is high and usually only institutions can afford it (*Connect* demands lots of bandwidth, too). *Skype* is free and ideal for working in pairs. For larger group chats up to ten individuals, *Google Hangout* is also free and provides a transparent interface that leverages many of *Google*'s other applications such as *YouTube*, *Google Drive*, and other third party *Google*-friendly applications.

In addition, many learning management systems (LMS) operate on platforms that allow users to record videos on the fly using *Flash* plugins in order to smoothly incorporate these clips into the LMS message system, posts, or discussion forums. The real question is how to design activities with these tools in order to enhance L2 speaking opportunities. Guillén and Blake (2015) have examined the speaking benefits from allowing students to post their *best video recording* through a LMS platform, with the added benefit of being able to rework and improve their video responses until they finally capture their best effort. These researchers found that the students' asynchronous video postings in Spanish exhibited more complex sentences and better accuracy than in their conversations from synchronous video sessions—as Robinson (2011) might have predicted given the increased planning time afforded by the asynchronous *best recording* format. Again, the choice of task is all-important (see Hampel 2006) and needs to be carefully thought through by the instructor because speaking proficiency, as we have previously discussed, involves accuracy, complexity, and fluency. Nevertheless, certain linguistic structures, such as intricacies of the Spanish subjunctive, in this particular case, will continue to cause difficulties for the students at the intermediate level no matter the instructor's interventions or assigned tasks. L2 acquisition takes a long time, which is another motivation for using CALL in the foreign language curriculum as a way of increasing the time on task (Muñoz 2006, 2008).

The availability of fully synchronous video has put SCMC activities at center stage with respect to fostering L2 speaking. Videoconferencing has become the norm for most telecollaborations (O'Dowd 2007), tandem learning (Guillén 2014), and social media exchanges (Lin, Warschauer, and Blake in press)—all topics that are addressed elsewhere in this volume. Synchronous speaking tasks now form part of most hybrid or fully online language courses (Blake 2011). Videoconferencing gives students an alternative to the speaking practice that is assumed to occur in the classroom. In actual fact, small group videoconferencing—for example, with one instructor working with two to three students—represents a far more intensive speaking experience than sitting in class and responding only two or three times in an hour. During the hour-long videoconference session, students are constantly taking turns speaking in the L2, which can be an extremely active and rigorous experience by the students' own admission (Blake 2015). Naturally, the instructor must prepare the conversational tasks ahead of time so that the students know exactly what to expect and are primed with the appropriate vocabulary and grammar constructions needed to bring the task successfully to completion. In this way, students can gradually build up greater fluency and smooth discourse transitions, which are important components of speaking proficiency.

Unfortunately, speaking progress via videoconference usage has not been well tracked or measured to date, partly because defining the construct of *speaking proficiency* remains a daunting, if not insurmountable, undertaking (Hultstijn 2011) whether in the face-to-face or CALL context. Hulstijn (2015) has recently challenged researchers in the L2 field to test out empirically whether or not speaking proficiency should be conceived as a continuum or, as he has suggested, a dichotomy (i.e., basic vs. extended linguistic proficiency). These same L2 theoretical issues are relevant to CALL research, as well, and deserve serious attention in future CALL research.

In the course of discussing SCMC, we do not wish to imply that videoconferences are exactly like face-to-face exchanges with all the same transparency, despite the existence of the computer screen mediating the experience between interlocutors. Ware and Kramsch's (2005) warnings, which were made concerning ACMC exchanges, should still be heeded: the interface changes the conversational dynamics. Students and instructors alike need training to help to avoid, or at least come to understand better, any intercultural miscommunications that might occur during these CALL contexts, especially during cross-cultural Internet collaborations. As always, well-designed tasks are needed to impact student outcomes significantly by promoting successful and satisfying online exchanges—videoconferencing being no exception.

## Conclusions

At present, SLA theory is a long way from providing precise definitions for even such basic concepts such as *speaking proficiency*, especially when the choice of the task impacts student outcomes so dramatically and varies so much from one instructor to the next. With respect to stimulating L2 speaking, the different CALL contexts described here equip the instructor with a rich array of options that can be used to stimulate more and better L2 production. Undoubtedly, one size does not fit all and teachers will have to adapt tasks and tools to each group of students they deal with. Likewise, new tools are being invented all the time, which is a good thing but it also creates the daunting task for the instructor of keeping up with these changes in the CALL field. Using technology can be intimidating because it keeps changing so rapidly. Continued training in the use of CALL applications to promote L2 speaking, or any other aspect of language proficiency, should be part of everyone's agenda.

## NOTES

1   We wish to thank our editors, Carol Chapelle and Shannon Sauro, for their helpful comments on earlier drafts.
2   Many language instructors have the impression that students talk a lot in class, but it goes unrecognized that in 50-minute period with a class size of 25 any given student will only have the chance to speak in the L2 at best from three to five times.
3   Here is a partial list of popular apps for recording digital sound: Recorder Plus, Capture, Voice Recorder, VoiceThread, SoundCloud, iProRecorder, iTalkRecorder, QuickVoice2Text Email Pro Recorder, Easy Voice Recorder, Hi-Q MP3 Voice Recorder, RecForge Pro, Voice Pro, ASR, Smart Voice Recorder.

## REFERENCES

Abrams, Zsuzsanna. 2003. "The Effects of Synchronous and Asynchronous CMC on Oral Performance." *Modern Language Journal*, 87, no. 2: 157–167.

Arispe, Kelly. 2012. Why Vocabulary Still Matters: L2 Lexical Development and Learner Autonomy as Mediated through an ICALL Took, *Langbot*. PhD dissertation, University of California Davis.

Bachman, Lyle F., and Sandra J. Savignon. 1986. "The Evaluation of Communicative Language Proficiency: A Critique of the ACTFL Oral Interview." *The Modern Language Journal*, 70, no. 4: 380–390.

Bardovi-Harlig, Kathleen. 2012. "A Second Look at T-units Analysis: Reconsidering the Sentence." *TESOL Quarterly*, 26, no. 2: 390–395.

Blake, Robert. 2000. "Computer-mediated Communication. A Window on L2 Spanish Interlanguage." *Language Learning & Technology*, 4, no. 1: 120–136.

Blake, Robert. 2005. "Bimodal Chatting: The Glue of a Distant Learning Course." *CALICO Journal*, 22, no. 3: 497–511.

Blake, Robert. 2011. "Current Trends in Online Language Learning." *Annual Review of Applied Linguistics*, 31: 1–17.

Blake, Robert. 2013. *Brave New Digital Classroom: Technology and Foreign Language Learning*. Georgetown, Washington, DC: Georgetown University Press.

Blake, Robert. 2015. "CALL Research and Practice: *Quo vadis?*" *International Journal of LASSO*, 32, no. 1: 1–7.

Blake, Robert, and Sonia Shiri. 2012. "Online Arabic Language Learning: What Happens After?" *L2 Journal*, 4, no. 2: 230–246. Accessed August 26, 2015. http://repositories.cdlib.org/uccllt/l2/vol4/iss2/art3/

Bley-Vroman, Robert. 2009. "The Evolving Context of the Fundamental Difference Hypothesis." *Studies in Second Language Acquisition*, 31, no. 2: 175–198.

Blin, Françoise. 2004. "CALL and the Development of Learner Autonomy: Towards an Activity-theoretical Perspective." *RECALL*, 16, no. 2: 377–395.

Chapelle, Carol. 2001. *Computer Applications in Second Language Acquisition: Foundations for*

*Teaching, Testing, and Research.* Cambridge: Cambridge University Press.

Chun, Dorothy M. 1998. "Signal Analysis Software for Teaching Discourse Intonation." *Language Learning & Technology*, 2, no. 1: 61–77.

Chun, Dorothy M. 2002. *Discourse Intonation in L2: From Theory to Practice.* Amsterdam: John Benjamins.

Doughty, Catherine J., and Michael H. Long. 2003. "Optimal Psycholinguistic Environments for Distance Foreign Language Learning." *Language Learning & Technology*, 7, no. 3: 50–80.

Ehsani, Farzad, and Eva Knodt. 1998. "Speech Technology in Computer-aided Language Learning: Strengths and Limitations of a New CALL Paradigm." *Language Learning & Technology*, 2, no. 1: 54–73.

Ellis, Rod, and Younghee Sheen. 2006. "Reexamining the Role of Recasts in Second Language Acquisition." *Studies in Second Language Acquisition*, 28: 575–600.

Eskenazi, Maxine. 1999. "Using a Computer in Foreign Language Pronunciation Training: What Advantages?" *CALICO Journal*, 16: 447–469.

Gass, Susan M. 1997. *Input, Interaction, and the Second Language Learner.* Mahwah, NJ: Lawrence Erlbaum Associates.

Gorjian, Bahman, Abdolmajid Hayati, and Parisa Pourkhoni. 2013. "Using *Praat* Software in Teaching Prosodic Features to EFL Learners." *Procedia – Social and Behavioral Sciences*, 84: 34–40.

Guillén, Gabriel. 2014. Expanding the Language Classroom: Linguistic Gains and Learning Opportunities through e-tandems and Social Networks. PhD dissertation, University of California Davis.

Guillén, Gabriel, and Robert Blake. (in press). "Can You Repeat, Please? L2 Complexity, Awareness, and Fluency Development in the Hybrid Classroom." In *Online Language Teaching Research: Pedagogic, Academic and Institutional Issues*, edited by Israel Sanz-Sánchez, Susana Rivera-Mills, and Regina Morin. Corvallis, OR: OSU Press.

Hampel, Regina. 2006. "Rethinking Task Design for the Digital Age: A Framework for Language Teaching and Learning in a Synchronous Online Environment." *ReCALL*, 18, no. 1: 105–121.

Housen, Alex, and Folkert Kuiken. 2009. "Complexity, Accuracy and Fluency in Second Language Acquisition." *Applied Linguistics*, 30, no. 4: 461–473.

Hubbard, Phil, and Claire Bradin Siskin. 2004. "Another Look at Tutorial CALL." *ReCALL*, 16, no. 2: 448–461.

Hulstijn, Jan. 2011. "Language Proficiency in Native and Nonnative Speakers: An Agenda for Research and Suggestions for Second-language Assessment." *Language Assessment Quarterly*, 8, no. 3: 229–249.

Hulstijn, Jan. 2015. *Language Proficiency in Native and Non-native Speakers: Theory and Research.* Amsterdam/Philadelphia: John Benjamins.

Kern, Rick. 1995. "Restructuring Classroom Interaction with Networked Computers: Effects on Quantity and Quality of Language Production." *Modern Language Journal*, 79, no. 4: 457–476.

Kormos, Judit, and Mariann Dénes. 2004, "Exploring Measures and Perceptions of Fluency in the Speech of Second Language Learners." *System*, 32, no. 2: 145–164.

Krashen, Stephen. 1985. *The Input Hypothesis: Issues and Implications.* London: Longman.

Lafford, Barbara, and Peter Lafford. 2005. "CMC Technologies for Teaching Foreign Languages: What's on the Horizon?" *CALICO Journal*, 22, no. 3: 679–710.

Lantolf, James, and Stephen L. Thorne. 2007. "Sociocultural Theory and Second Language Learning." In *Theories in Second Language Acquisition*, edited by Bill VanPatten and Jessica Williams, 201–224. Mahwah, NJ: Lawrence Erlbaum.

Lin, Chin-Hsi, Mark Warschauer, and Robert Blake. In press. "Language Learning through Social Networks: Perceptions and Reality." *Language Learning & Technology*, 20, no. 1.

Little, David. 2007. "Language Learner Autonomy: Some Fundamental Considerations Revisited." *Innovations in Language Learning and Teaching*, 1, no. 1: 14–29.

Loewen, Shawn, and Rosemary Erlam. 2006. "Corrective Feedback in the Chatroom: An Experimental Study." *Computer Assisted Language Learning*, 19, no. 1: 1–14.

Lomicka, Lara, and Gillian Lord. 2011. "A Tale of Tweets: Analyzing Microblogging among Language Learners." *System*, 40, no. 1: 48–63.

Long, Michael. 1991. "Focus on Form: A Design Feature in Language Teaching Methodology." In *Foreign Language Research in Cross-cultural Perspective*, edited by Kees De Bot, Claire Kramsch, and Ralph Ginsberg, 39–52. Amsterdam: John Benjamins.

Long, Michael, and Peter Robinson. 1998. "Focus on Form: Theory, Research, and Practice."

In *Focus on Form in Classroom Second Language acquisition*, edited by Catherine Doughty and Jessica Williams, 15–41. Cambridge: Cambridge University Press.

Loucky, John Paul. 2006. "Maximizing Vocabulary Development by Systemically Using a Depth of Lexical Processing Taxonomy, CALL Resources, and Effective Strategies." *CALICO Journal*, 23, no. 2: 363–399.

Meskill, Carla. 2005. "Triadic Scaffolds: Tools for Teaching English Language Learners with Computers." *Language Learning & Technology*, 9, no. 1: 46–59.

Muñoz, Carmen, ed. 2006. *Age and the Rate of Foreign Language Learning*. Clevedon: Multilingual Matters.

Muñoz, Carmen. 2008. "Symmetries and Asymmetries of Age Effects in Naturalistic and Instructed L2 Learning." *Applied Linguistics*, 29. no. 4: 578–596.

O'Brien, Mary Grantham. 2006. "Teaching Pronunciation and Intonation with Computer Technology." In *Calling on CALL: From Theory and Research to New Directions in Foreign Language Teaching*, edited by Lara Ducate and Niki Arnold, 127–148. San Marcos, TX: Computer Assisted Language Instruction Consortium.

O'Dowd, Robert. 2007. *Online Intercultural Exchange: An Introduction for Foreign Language Teachers*. Clevedon: Multilingual Matters.

Payne, Scott, and Paul J. Whitney. 2002. "Developing L2 Oral Proficiency through Synchronous CMC: Output, Working Memory, and Interlanguage Development." *CALICO Journal*, 20, no. 1: 7–32.

Pellettieri, Jill. 2000. "Negotiation in Cyberspace: The Role of Chatting in the Development of Grammatical Competence." In *Networked Based Language Teaching: Concepts and Practice*, edited by Mark Warschauer and Rick Kern, 59–86. New York: Cambridge University Press.

Peterson, Mark. 2009. "Learner Interaction in Synchronous CMC: A Sociocultural Perspective." *Computer Assisted Language Learning*, 22, no. 4: 303–321.

Plagwitz, Thomas. 2014. "'Mira, Mamá! Sin Manos!' Can Speech Recognition Tools be Soundly Applied for L2 Speaking Practice?" *ICT for Language Learning 2014. Conference Proceedings*. Firenze: libreriauniversitaria.it.

Plagwitz, Thomas. 2015. "Speech Recognition tools for Oral Proficiency." TheFLTMAG. Accessed May 27, 2016. http://fltmag.com/speech-recognition-tools/

Robinson, Peter. 2011. "Task-based Language Learning: A Review of Issues." *Language Learning*, 61: 1–36.

Sauro, Shannon. 2009. "Strategic Use of Modality during Synchronous CMC." *CALICO Journal*, 27, no. 1: 101–117.

Schmidt, Richard. 1990. "The Role of Consciousness in Second Language Learning." *Applied Linguistics*, 1:127–158.

Schwienhorst, Klaus. 2008. *Learner Autonomy and CALL Environments*. New York: Routledge.

Skehan, Peter. 2003. "Focus on Form, Tasks, and Technology." *Computer Assisted Language Learning*, 16: 391–411.

Swain, Merrill. 2000. "The Output Hypothesis and Beyond: Mediating Acquisition through Collaborative Dialogue." In *Sociocultural Theory and Second Language Learning*, edited by James P. Lantolf, 97–114. Oxford: Oxford University Press.

Swain, Merrill, and Sharon Lapkin. 1998. "Focus on Form through Conscious Reflection." In *Focus on Form in Classroom Second Language Acquisition*, edited by Catherine Doughty and Jessica Williams, 64–82. Cambridge: Cambridge University Press.

Teixeira, Annalisa. 2015. The Role of Keyboarding in the Development and Retention of L2 Spanish Vocabulary. PhD dissertation, University of California Davis.

Varonis, Evangeline, and Susan Gass. 1985. "Nonnative/nonnative Conversations: A Model for Negotiation of Meaning." *Applied Linguistics*, 6: 70–90.

Vygotsky, Lev.1962. *Language and Thought*. Cambridge, MA: MIT Press.

Ware, Page, and Claire Kramsch. 2005. "Toward an Intercultural Stance: Teaching German and English through Telecollaboration." *Modern Language Journal*, 89, no. 2: 190–205.

Warschauer, Mark. 1997. "Comparing Face-to-face and Electronic Discussion in the Second Language Classroom." *CALICO Journal*, 13: 7–26.

Willis, David, and Jane Willis. 2009. *Doing Task-based Teaching*. Oxford: Oxford University Press.

Willis, Jane. 1996. *A Framework for Task-based Learning*. London: Longman.

# 9 Technologies for Teaching and Learning Intercultural Competence and Interlanguage Pragmatics

## JULIE M. SYKES

## Introduction

A foundational component of human interaction is person-to-person understanding through pragmatic behaviors, that is, the expression and understanding of meaning. Human connections happen every day, all the time, and in numerous contexts. However, patterns for communicating and interpreting meaning are increasingly difficult to define, isolate, and teach. Meaning is not always linguistically encoded and is often understood through implicature, background knowledge, and cultural factors. Interlanguage pragmatics (ILP) is one approach to understanding and defining how meaning is expressed in interaction. ILP addresses the various ways (i.e., linguistic and nonlinguistic) in which this meaning is communicated and interpreted in interaction between interlocutors in multilingual interactions. In addition, pragmatics addresses the sociocultural factors (individual and collective), which influence the communicated and interpreted messages (Crystal 1997; LoCastro 2003; Yule 1996).

In recent years, digital technologies have expanded the possibilities for human interactions in ways that were never before imaginable, further complexifying the teaching and learning of interlanguage pragmatics. Thorne, Sauro, and Smith (2015) note, "the Internet has qualitatively transformed everyday communication…[and] constitutes a multiplicity of language contact zones that is unprecedented in human history" (215). Now, more than ever before, considerations around ILP necessitate a perspective that extends beyond traditional academic boundaries to include a wide variety of theoretical and practical approaches rooted in, but not limited to, linguistics, sociology, rhetoric and digital humanities, cultural studies, anthropology, and psychology. A comprehensive review is well beyond the scope of this chapter; however, two constructs are especially relevant to situating the role of technology in teaching and learning of interlanguage pragmatics—*intercultural competence* and *transnational languaculture*.

This chapter begins with a brief exploration of models of intercultural communicative competence (ICC) followed by an exploration of transnational languaculture as a meaningful perspective for considering pragmatic behaviors and instructional models beyond

*The Handbook of Technology and Second Language Teaching and Learning*, First Edition.
Edited by Carol A. Chapelle and Shannon Sauro.
© 2017 John Wiley & Sons, Inc. Published 2020 by John Wiley & Sons, Inc.

traditional national and language boundaries. The following two sections synthesize existing research to emphasize fundamental findings related to technology and the teaching and learning of pragmatics. The first highlights the many advantages and challenges of technology-based instructional interventions, tellecolaboration, and digital game-based approaches. This is followed by an exploration of the extended discursive contexts available as a result of digitally-mediated interactions, thereby significantly expanding the pragmatic repertoires needed for successful interaction. These expanded contexts increase instructional opportunities and, at the same time, extend the necessary contexts to be considered as part of one's pragmatic repertoire.

# A focus on meaning: Intercultural communicative competence, transnational languaculture, and interlanguage pragmatics

One of the complexities of teaching language, especially when considering pragmatic dimensions, is exploring the relationship of language and cultural behaviors. An often-cited difficulty in language and culture pedagogies is determining where language ends and where culture begins, or if they are separable at all (Byram 1997, 2009; Byram 1994; Raquel Díaz 2013). Interlanguage pragmatics is at the epicenter of this discussion. Historically, a theoretical distinction has been made between *pragmalinguisitic resources*, the linguistic forms that are used to carry out language functions, and *sociopragmatic resources*, the contextual and extralinguistic considerations relevant to the language function, including the knowledge of when, why, and with whom, to use the various pragmalinguistic forms. However, many insist it is impossible to make such a distinction because one is intimately tied to another (see, for example, Beebe and Waring 2001; Márquez Reiter and Placencia 2004). Pragmatics is inherently the place where language and culture meet and is encompassed in numerous approaches to operationalizing models of intercultural communication.

## *Intercultural communicative competence (ICC)*

Shaped by a robust literature, ICC is, perhaps, one of the best-known constructs used to describe where and how language and culture meet and, from the perspective of some, where they are inherently inseparable. Numerous paradigms defining ICC have been proposed in the literature with a series of comprehensive reviews and critiques available (e.g., Borghetti 2014; Kramsch 1999; Matsuo 2014; Moeller and Faltin Osborn 2014; Raquel Díaz 2013; Risager 2007, Spitzberg and Changnon 2009). The objective of the discussion here is not to revisit each of these models in-detail, nor reiterate proposed critiques, but rather highlight salient features most directly relevant to technology and the role of teaching and learning interlanguage pragmatics.

Most widely cited in language teaching and learning research is Byram's (1997) ICC model, re-visited in 2009, which outlines a set of competencies learners need to become proficient participants in intercultural interactions. Byram categorizes the model into six categories essential to preparing learners—(1) attitudes, (2) knowledge, (3) skills of interpreting and relating, (4) skills of discovery and interaction, (5) critical cultural awareness, and (6) critical cultural education/political education to enable learners to see the relationships among cultures different from their own. Pragmatic abilities are fundamental to realizing each of these competencies. Learners express a willingness to relate through appropriate pragmatic behaviors and meaningful interpretation of others' intentions. Byram notes, "… the efficacy of communication depends upon using language to demonstrate one's willingness to relate, which often involves the indirectness of politeness rather than the direct and 'efficient' choice of language full of information" (1997, 3). Most relevant to the discussion here are the elements of Byram's model which explicitly target analytic skills and linguistic knowledge necessary to carry out a task.

In a recent review, Moeller and Faltin Osborn (2014) isolate two additional models as being especially relevant to classroom instruction, and these also pertain to instruction mediated through technology. Deardorff (2006, 2008) offers a pyramid approach for reaching two sets of desired outcomes. Desired internal outcomes entail evidence that a learner has arrived at an "informed frame of reference" demonstrating adaptability, flexibility, an ethnorelative view, and empathy (Deardorff 2006, 254). The desired external outcome is "behaving and communicating effectively and appropriately (based on one's knowledge, skills, and attitudes), to achieve one's goals to some degree" (Deardoff 2008, 40). To achieve these outcomes, learners must have the requisite attitudes (i.e., respect, openness, curiosity and discovery), knowledge and comprehension (i.e., cultural self-awareness, deep understanding and knowledge of culture, culture-specific information, sociolinguistic awareness), and skills (i.e., analyze, evaluate, and relate). Most relevant to the teaching and learning of pragmatics is Deardorff's emphasis on cyclical work to arrive at desired outcomes as well as the critical role of the learner in making choices about interactions based on an informed set of assumptions. This leads to what Ishihara and Tarone (2009) refer to as *subjectivity* in the pragmatics literature. Promoting learners' informed choice making is essential to the teaching and learning of pragmatics.

Drawing on a thorough review of 12 existing ICC models, Borghetti (2011, 2014) proposes a methodological model for ICC in language instruction which includes four dimensions— (1) cognitive, (2) affective, (3) skill building, and (4) awareness. Each is designed to aid the learner in developing strong skills for intercultural interactions. Most relevant to the teaching and learning of pragmatics is the strong emphasis on attitudes and awareness coupled with knowledge and skill building, each serving as fundamental steps to the teaching of interlanguage pragmatics (Judd 1999; Ishihara and Cohen 2010).

While each ICC paradigm brings critical issues to the forefront, the sheer number of models available makes synthesis difficult, at best. In some instances, congruency between the models cannot be achieved, making it difficult to identify learning targets around ICC. Furthermore, the majority of ICC models emphasizes a unified national identity and lack the nimbleness needed to capture the ever-changing dimensions of human interaction which are not directly tied to a specific language or culture. As a result, ICC models are not an ideal theoretical approach for the analysis of technology's role in the teaching and learning of pragmatics. Alternatively, and more useful to the current discussion, is the paradigm of transnational languagaculture (Raquel Díaz 2013; Risager 2007, 2008).

## *Transnational languaculture*

*Transnational languaculture* moves beyond ICC models to propose a paradigm in which language and culture transcend national boundaries, are uniquely tied to individuals (not only particular languages or cultures), and develop across a lifetime as learners move between a variety of contexts, locations, and languages (Risager 2007, 2008). Most importantly, transnational languaculture emphasizes movement away from the native-speaker model and a national standard norm as representative of one culture or language, thereby addressing a noteworthy critique of the majority of ICC models (see Kramsch 1999). Instead, the transnational languaculture paradigm embraces a variety of possible options for successful, and unsuccessful, interactions and allows for multilingual speakers to consider varied patterns as related to local and transnational contexts. As one considers the multiplicity of pragmatic behaviors, especially in light of digitally-mediated discourse, a transnational approach is requisite.

Consider, for example, a Chinese Flagship student, trained in the United States, who decides to work for a British company in Taiwan and, as a hobby, is a prolific international food blogger. As an interlocutor, she brings multiple layers of cultural assumptions, understanding, and experience to each interaction. For this learner, the successful expression and interpretation of meaning will require cultural knowledge from four national spaces, but will ultimately be guided by the local norms of the people she encounters as well as the pragmatic expectations of the digital spaces in which she participates. By focusing on learners' abilities to traverse from place to place, interact with a variety of types of speakers, and make choices about pragmatic behaviors, which may or may not feel relevant to their particular context, instructors have the opportunity to prepare learners for multilingual interactions which may not even exist yet. From this perspective, interlaguage pragmatic teaching and learning moves away from the instruction of a set number of speech acts or semantic formulae, and becomes about skills and strategies for interactions through an intentioned pragmatic lens.

A transnational approach (Risager 2007, 2008) entails three aspects, each of which has implications for the technology and the teaching and learning of pragmatics—language and languaculture, topics and discourses, and contexts and contacts.

- *Language and languaculture.* This aspect emphasizes the fundamental role language instruction itself plays in the realization of meaningful interactions. Risager's paradigm recognizes the essential role of linguistic norms, but suggests an expansion of norms to be inclusive of a variety of patterns, including relevant local expertise. From a pragmatics perspective, this would entail the study of empirically-based native-speaker patterns as part of classroom practice, but not as the only model from which to draw. Instead, language study would include a variety of models in which successful outcomes and instances of miscommunication are carefully analyzed from a pragmatic perspective to help learners become more adept and maneuvering the multiple linguistic landscapes they encounter. Emerging modes of digitally-mediated communication such as digital forums, fan fiction sites, and digital games offer unique landscapes for this expanded linguistic view, as well as a tangible, salient space for pedagogical work to occur (Black 2009; Lam 2004; Sauro 2014; Thorne, Black, and Sykes 2009).
- *Topics and discourses.* This aspect focuses on an inclusive approach to topics, where national contextualization is avoided, unless it is a necessary condition of the discussion itself. Raquel Díaz (2013) further emphasizes that topics should be critical in nature, designed to improve learners' *criticality* (i.e., critical thinking, critical self-reflection, and critical action). In the teaching and learning of pragmatics, this would entail the inclusion of a variety of pragmatic practices, relevant to the learners themselves, and might include discursive practices traditionally out of the scope of instructional contexts (e.g., gaming forums, fandom sites, or *YouTube* commentaries). Each is readily available, and through instructional intervention, can be made accessible to the learner. Furthermore, topics would emphasize the power language plays in intercultural interaction and focus on ways pragmatic behaviors can be made more salient and relevant to critical action in the world. Regardless of the topics themselves, those chosen should focus on building the critical skills of the expression and interpretation of meaning in its individual context, and as related to surrounding linguistic landscapes.
- *Contexts and contacts.* This aspect emphasizes that teaching can take place anywhere in the world where there is significant contact with the target culture. For the purposes of this chapter, the teaching and learning of pragmatics, therefore, should take advantage of digitally-mediated interaction as an essential mechanism for learners to interact with one another and members of communities in which the target language is spoken. This can occur face-to-face, in fully-online environments, or, most likely as a complex compilation of online and offline interactions.

The transnational perspective frames the discussion in a way that is especially useful for an in-depth look at technology in the teaching and learning of pragmatics. As human interactions more and more frequently transcend national boundaries and mix and remix understood systems of language, a paradigm which recognizes local and transnational contexts is fundamental to exploring the interconnectedness of language and culture with pragmatics at the epicenter of that discussion. Furthermore, pedagogical models must also recognize the dynamic nature of co-constructed interaction and prepare learners to engage in a variety of international contexts through observation, analysis, and participation.

From a practical perspective, the teaching and learning of pragmatics presents a number of challenges in instructed language-learning contexts (Alcón Soler and Martínez Flor 2008; Bardovi-Harlig 2001; Félix-Brasdefer 2007; Kasper and Rose, 2001; LoCastro 2003; Martínez Flor and Usó Juan 2010; Rose 2005; Sykes 2009) and, is thus far, rather inconclusive in terms of ideal pedagogical models (for a comprehensive review see Taguchi 2015). A transnational approach further emphasizes these challenges through the consideration of an infinite set of possible interactions with dynamic pragmatic characteristics. Accordingly, it shifts the perspective away from idealized models to that of the local context, placing skill development at the forefront of instructional necessity and, in combination with emerging digital tools, offers a means to overcome barriers to instruction. For example, a key set of barriers focus on the difficulty in achieving communication through immense language variety, individual personality differences, and lack of instructor expertise in the pragmatic behaviors that need to be taught. A transnational perspective embraces this variety and accounts for the skills necessary to maneuver in and out of a number of interactional contexts. Instructor expertise then, instead of focusing on idealized models of pragmatic formulae, must focus on using their unique expertise to guide learners through the teaching and learning of skills to navigate the pragmatic aspects of such fluid contexts. Furthermore, as outlined in the section that follows, a variety of technological tools can enable instruction to simplify, enhance, and augment the teaching and learning of interlanguage pragmatics.

## Technology, instructed contexts, and interlanguage pragmatics

Concurrent with an expanding body of research addressing the teaching and learning of pragmatics (Taguchi 2015), the field has also witnessed an increase in studies with an explicit technological focus. Taguchi and Sykes (2013) provide a sampling of these advancements as related to both research and teaching, noting the increasing capacity for data analysis, research instrument development, instructional intervention, and expanded pragmatic behaviors. Much like other areas of computer-assisted language learning (CALL), the application of digital technologies in the service of the teaching and learning of interlanguage pragmatics is varied, ranging from pragmatically-focused content modules, delivered in a digital formats, to tellecollaboration and interactive digital simulations as pedagogical interventions. Each begins to bridge the gap between the theoretical necessity of pragmatic instruction and practical classroom application. In an intentional effort to avoid a focus on technological tools, and instead, highlight pedagogical innovation and challenges, this section categorizes existing work in three key areas:

1.  Digital curricular materials focused on the teaching and learning of pragmatics
2.  Digital tools as classroom interventions
3.  Digital tools to facilitate tellecollaboration

## Curricular materials

One key challenge in the teaching and learning of pragmatics is a lack of teacher training resources and curricular resources for the classroom (Bardovi-Harlig 2001; Bardovi-Harlig and Hartford 2005; Kasper and Rose 2003; Taguchi 2015). Emerging Internet technologies have facilitated the ability to create online materials and make those materials readily available to users internationally. Furthermore, shifts in practices around authorship, knowledge creation, review, and publication have added creditability and usability for digital content delivery. This enables the creation of accessible, dynamic content that can address the variability and complexity often associated with interlanguage pragmatics. In other words, the materials can be created to embrace a transnational perspective focused on the development of the pragmatics skills needed for success in a variety of contexts. Table 9.1 summarizes the currently available, open-access, online curricular resources for the teaching and learning of pragmatics.

While by no means complete or comprehensive, the available tools represent one end of the continuum in terms of potential for the use of digital technologies in the teaching and learning of pragmatics. Missing from this picture are a robust set of studies examining best practices for the use of online content for the teaching and learning of interlanguage pragmatics. However, a handful of studies suggest value in the use of digital materials for teaching pragmatic behaviors in Spanish (Cohen and Sykes 2012), Japanese (Utashiro and Kawai 2009) and Arabic (Ward et al. 2007). While by no means conclusive, this small set of studies indicates the usefulness of digital technologies to provide curricular content that is dynamic in nature and widely available across instructional contexts. As a side note, each of the sites maintains a strong native-speaker model focus and the sites are not yet reflective of a transnational approach to ILP development. Nevertheless, they create a strong foundation for the future creation, implementation, and evaluation of materials that consider a redefinition of what is possible in the creation of online materials. As technologies advance, it becomes more and more possible to take into account the robust set of global communities with an online presence, as well as the immense body of pragmatic behavior represented online.

## Classroom interventions

The second area, which has been addressed from a variety of perspectives, is the use of digital tools to facilitate classroom learning within the confines of the classroom itself. More specifically, synchronous computer-mediated communication (SCMC), asynchronous computer-mediated communication (ACMC), multiuser virtual environments (MUVEs), and mobile, augmented reality games have been implemented, and researched, as viable, and, in some cases, transformative tools.

Studies demonstrate a number of benefits of SCMC for pragmatic instruction in the classroom. CMC has been found to facilitate varied participant roles in interactions (Abrams 2001; Darhower 2002; Lee and Hoadley 2007), enabling the potential for pragmatic experimentation and reflection. Moreover, the use of written chat in the learning environment reduces the cognitive load (Payne and Ross 2005; Payne and Whitney 2002) and lessens the pragmatic pressure during development. Results indicate an increased use of quality and variety of pragmatic behaviors when grouping occurs using written chat, as compared to oral chat and face-to-face communication (Sykes 2005). Finally, the use of digital tools allows for the archiving of interaction for future analysis, feedback, and assessment with minimal effort on the part of the instructor (Belz 2003, 2004; Thorne and Reinhardt 2008) as well as the development of corpora, highly useful for analysis as a means of ILP development in the classroom (Belz 2007; Vyatkina and Belz 2005). Similarly, ACMC, more specifically, the use of

**Table 9.1** Online curricular materials for the teaching and learning of pragmatics.

| Title and Website | Description | Language | Author |
|---|---|---|---|
| Dancing with Words: Strategies for Learning Pragmatics in Spanish | A website focused on the learning of Spanish speech acts. The site includes 10 modules, each focused on a specific pragmatic function. Activities are designed to facilitate learning through observation, analysis, and reflection. The site is research-based and includes audio and video. | Spanish | Sykes and Cohen (2006) |
| American English: Teaching Pragmaticshttp://americanenglish.state.gov/resources/teaching-pragmatics | A collection of isolated modules for teaching and learning English pragmatics. The length, quality, and focus of each module varies based on the author. | English | U.S. State Department |
| Strategies for Learning Speech Acts in Japanesehttp://carla.acad.umn.edu/speechacts/japanese/introtospeechacts/index.htm | A website with seven modules focused on strategies for the learning of Japanese speech acts. Activities include analysis and reflection activities designed to facilitate the learning of Japanese pragmatics. | Japanese | Cohen and Ishihara (2005) |
| Multimedia interactive modules for education and assessment (MIMEA) http://mimea.clear.msu.edu/ | A set of video clips with exercises, language and culture descriptions centered on pragmatic functions. The site does not explicitly mention pragmatics, but addresses critical issues related to ILP development. | Arabic Chinese German Korean Russian Vietnamese | CLEAR (2007) |
| BrazilPodhttp://www.laits.utexas.edu/orkelm/ppe/intro.html | A series of video clips and resources to help learners focus on the analysis of communication tasks in Portuguese. The site does not explicitly mention pragmatics, but addresses critical issues related to ILP development. | Portuguese | Kelm (2015) |

blogs in the classroom has demonstrated usefulness for increasing awareness and documenting developmental patterns for pragmatic awareness and production (Li 2013; Takamiya and Ishihara 2013), in addition to ICC (Elola and Oskoz 2011).

Synthetic immersive environments and mobile, augmented reality games offer immense potential as tools for pragmatic instruction. Affordances include the opportunity for meaningful engagement with the potential for multilevel, environmental feedback (Bryant 2006; Holden and Sykes 2013; Sykes and Reinhardt 2012; Thorne, Black, and Sykes 2009) as well as the delivery of real-time resources as just-the-right-moment and at just-the-right-time (Gee 2014; Sykes and Reinhardt 2012). Simulations and augmented reality games are especially well suited to a transnational approach where scenarios can be created to assist learners in developing the necessary skills to express and interpret meaning across a variety of possible contexts and cultural expectations. Furthermore, learners can interact with speakers of varying interactional expectations and, in the case of place-based augmented reality, physical neighborhoods, and people they might not otherwise encounter. While empirical data remains limited, initial findings indicate sufficient positive results to continue the exploration of synthetic immersive environments, digital games, and mobile, place-based augmented reality experiences as transformative pedagogical tools.

While a great deal of theoretical support exists for the use of digital game spaces in ILP teaching and learning (see Sykes and Reinhardt 2012; Taguchi and Sykes 2013; Thorne 2008; Thorne, Black, and Sykes 2009), empirical data remains limited. In a series of studies investigating gameplay and ILP development, Sykes (2009, 2010, 2013, 2014) reports the findings of a large-scale development, implementation, and evaluation project explicitly on the use of synthetic immersive environments for learning to request and apologize in Spanish. *Croquelandia* is the first three-dimensional, immersive space built specifically for the teaching and learning of ILP. The player begins by learning he or she has won a study abroad trip and will need to successfully navigate a series of request and apology interactions with their host family, peers, and professors. Each scenario requires appropriately navigating the target language functions, with the ultimate success or failure dependent on the realization of appropriate pragmatic behaviors to the individual simulated characters in the space.

In order to investigate a variety of design constructs and learning outcomes, the research project(s) synthesized evidence from 120 hours of in-game behavior data and 30 hours of interview data from 53 advanced learners of Spanish who participated in *Croquelandia* as part of their advanced level language and culture course. For a full description of the data collection and analysis project see Sykes (2008). In terms of initial findings, results of the series of studies are mixed in terms of learning outcomes and target design elements and can be summarized as follows:

- In terms of the learning of requests, minimal improvement was made in the area of the production of pragmalinguistic forms from pre-test to post-test. However, evidence strongly indicates growth in the areas of interpretation, metapragamtic awareness, and analytical skills (Sykes 2009). This suggests future work should focus on the ways in which metapragmatic awareness, interpretation skills, and analysis can be made more salient.
- The learning of apologies demonstrated slightly more improvement in terms of the production of pragmalinguistic forms with similar results in the areas of metapragmatic awareness and interpretation skills (Sykes 2013). A possible design rationale for this difference is the extremely salient nature of the apologies scenarios, which learners commented on frequently throughout the interview data.
- Finally, a detailed look at isolated design features is absolutely critical for more thorough understanding of how design can best contribute to learning. Specifically, gameplay patterns were varied among the participants, with the majority approaching

*Croquelandia* as a homework assignment rather than a game-based experience (Sykes 2010). Furthermore, quest restart patterns (i.e., "the capability which allows payers during in-game tasks to voluntarily reset the task upon feedback" (Sykes 2014, 165), as a means to understanding task design should be automatic and in real time to encourage as much interaction and experimentation with the virtual scenarios as possible (Sykes 2014). Future research must continue to consider integrated design features with the most significant impact on the teaching and learning of ILP.

Most recently, place-based, augmented reality has been proposed as a feasible, productive technology for the inclusion of ILP teaching and learning in language classroom. *Mentira* (mentira.org) is the first mobile augmented reality game for the teaching and learning of Spanish pragmatic behaviors (Holden and Sykes 2011). The game leads learners through a series of interactions designed to make variation salient and noticeable, beyond varying pragmalinguistic structures. Learners begin by learning their family has been implicated in a murder and they must find clues in a physical neighborhood to clear their family name. The more pragmatically appropriate their choices, the better clues they get. *Mentira* plays out much like a historical novel in which a fictional story is overlaid on physical places and with critical issues related to the study of Spanish in the area (for a detailed description of the game itself see Holden and Sykes 2011). Preliminary results indicate a strong emphasis on place as a means for engaging learners in pragmatic analysis and reflection (Sykes and Holden 2011) as well as the necessity for pragmatic feedback that extends throughout the place-based experience, including game feedback, environmental feedback, peer-to-peer feedback, and expert-learner feedback (Holden and Sykes 2013). Much work remains to be done in this area and is a fundamental piece of our understanding of the role of technology in ILP teaching and learning.

## *Telecollaboration*

Telecollaboration, defined generally here as networked intercultural exchanges in which interlocutors of different linguistic and cultural backgrounds interact around a variety of tasks and topics (see Dooly, this volume), has been widely researched in comparison to other digital tools for the teaching and learning of ILP and, for many, is one of the most profound shifts in the ways pragmatic development can occur. Telecollaboration has a robust body of literature related to a variety of topics in language learning (for a thorough review see Belz and Thorne 2005 and Guth and Helm 2010). In an attempt to isolate findings across studies, Table 9.2 synthesizes current findings relevant to the teaching and learning of pragmatics in tellecollaborative partnerships. It should be noted that the majority of work addresses digitally-mediated collaboration through synchronous chat, asynchronous email, and asynchronous blogs, with a handful of studies examining collaboration via social networks and massively multiplayer games.

Overall, telecollaboration via digitally-mediated tools is highly advantageous for the teaching and learning of ILP. It affords opportunities for interaction, analysis, and reflection in ways that were not previously possible. Furthermore, it is an effective context for the learning of pragmatic behaviors as well as the application of patterns in authentic discourse. Critical to the successful realization of any telecollaboration project are strong partnerships, relevant tasks, and time for analysis and reflection around any especially positive or negative experiences learners might have. Future research should begin to address the varying potentials and outcomes afforded by the use of different technological tools for telecollaborative work. For example, how does ILP learning occur in intercultural interactions via written chat, email, video conference, social networking sites and/or a combination of a variety of platforms? While the general benefits for telecollabroation are clear, much remains to be seen about the ways emergent tools may or may not be useful for pragmatic development.

**Table 9.2**   Key findings from research on ILP in tellecollaboration.

| Key findings | Relevant studies |
| --- | --- |
| With explicit focus, tellecollaborative partnerships can foster the learning of target pragmalinguisitc features and are an effective means to elicit pragmatic functions (e.g., greetings, terms of address, leave taking). | Cunningham (2014), González-Lloret (2008), Vyatkina and Belz (2005) |
| Longitudinal interaction in an online community can be highly beneficial to the learner's developmental trajectory; however, reflection and mediation may be necessary for development to occur. | Gonzales (2013), Vyatkina and Belz (2005), Thorne (2008) |
| Tellecollaborative pedagogy, aligned with contrastive learner corpus analysis, is an effective approach to intercultural exchanges, but not the only possible approach. | Belz (2004), Urzúa (2013), Vyatkina and Belz (2005) |
| Asynchronous collaboration allows for reflection and careful analysis of pragmatic topics. | Takamiya and Ishihara (2013), Vyatkina and Belz (2005) |
| Careful attention should be paid to avoiding stereotype reinforcement or unanalyzed pragmatic missteps. Moreover, tellecollaboration is a promising and proven context for the development of pragmatic competence and intercultural reflection. | Belz and Kinginger (2002), Furstenberg et al. (2001), Reinhardt and Zander (2011), Vyatkina and Belz (2005) |
| Conversation analysis presents a promising approach for understanding pragmatic behaviors such as terms of address, turn sequencing, and multilingual interactions, allowing for a microlevel analysis to present an intentioned picture of discursive patterns. | Gonzales (2013), González-Lloret (2008, 2009), Thorne (2008) |
| In comparison to explicit instruction alone, an added telecollabroative approach is more effective for developing pragmatic comprehension skills. | Vahid Rafieyan et al. (2014) |
| Tellecolaboration is an effective means to provide consistent interaction with native speakers and to document the developmental stages of the learning of ILP. | Belz (2007), Gonzales (2013) |

# Emergent pragmatic behaviors

In addition to the consideration of digital technologies for instructional use, one discussion must also consider the critically important role of the pragmatics of digital contexts, termed by Yus (2010) as "ciberpragmatics." The qualitative transformation of everyday human interactions, resulting in shifts in both mediated and non-mediated contexts, necessitates critical reflection of the ways communication is occurring (Castells 1997). Furthermore, the dynamic, co-constructed behaviors of the infinite number of digital spaces must be considered as relevant, valid, and high-stakes contexts that impact both online and offline relationships (Brown and Adler 2008; Thorne, Black, and Sykes 2009; Thorne and Payne 2005). Thorne, Sauro, and Smith (2015) emphasize the fundamental role of the myriad of behaviors made salient in digital spaces:

> As settings for language contact, digital communication media juxtapose and often make publicly visible communication from individuals that represent great diversity in terms of special location, social positioning, and language-culture background. Emerging arrays of online environments now constitute primary settings through which routine constructions of identity are created, and curated. (2015, 215)

Pragmatic behaviors are a fundamental component of identity expression and must be considered from a transnational perspective that enables understanding dynamic, evolving, heterogeneous, communicative behavior. In light of the prolific nature of many of the digital spaces under consideration, it is no longer sufficient to merely contrast online behaviors with offline speaking or writing. Instead, learners must be equipped to participate in everyday interactions that occur in, through, and around digital discourse spaces (Belz and Thorne 2005; Jenkins 2006; Reinhardt and Thorne 2011; Yus 2010). Patterns for communicating and interpreting meaning are increasingly difficult to define, isolate, and teach; moreover, very little is known about the multilingual pragmatic practices of emergent spaces (see Sykes, forthcoming for a review of current work in this area).

In an updated analysis of the pragmatic behaviors of online spaces, Yus (2010) explores the pragmatic behaviors of six practices occurring in digitally-mediated environments—identity presentation (e.g., profile design), website design and development, social networks, online conversations, email, and politeness on the Internet. His analysis provides an initial step toward key understanding of behaviors in this area. However, future work should begin to extrapolate and define the discrete point differences and similarities as a result of fine grain analyses of pragmatic behaviors. While any number of examples could be drawn from the digital world, three practices are of particular interest to the teaching and learning of interlanguage pragmatics—social networks, hashtags, and social media contact zones.

Social networks have received noteworthy attention from researchers in the area of language learning (McBride 2009; Mitchell 2009; Reinhardt and Zander 2011), with one study in particular focused on Facebook groups for sociopragmatic competence (Blattner and Fiori 2009 2013). However, in light of dynamic behaviors, a thorough interdisciplinary analysis of the pragmatics of social networking behaviors, from a multilingual perspective, needs to be undertaken to discern patterns of pragmatic behaviors relevant to learners' participation in a variety of social networking sites with, undoubtedly varying participatory expectations. Take, for example, the recent emigration away from Facebook toward other social networking sites such as Instagram, SnapChat, and WhatsApp, which fundamentally move away from larger networks to smaller, more intimately connected groups of people. In this case, some patterns remain across each of the platforms, but, in all reality, are also quite varied and require intentioned analysis to assist learners in appropriate and meaningful interactions.

Another area of interest for the teaching and learning of pragmatics is a multilingual analysis of hashtags, a traditionally digital practice in which words or phrases follow a '#' symbol to indicate a topic, emotion, or context. Hashtags are an especially salient marker of sociopragmatic behavior and highly relevant to interlanguage pragmatic developments. Scott (2015) presents one of the first pragmatic analyses of Twitter hashtags through the lens of implicature and conversational style, noting hashtags in Twitter guide the hearer through explicit and implied meaning and are indicators of style, even in instances where the interaction is one-to-many. Language learners must not only know how to interpret hashtags, but if participating in online communities, must also know how to produce them to accurately express their own meaning.

Finally, research addressing the complex pragmatic behaviors in social media contact zones such as YouTube commentary threads or Flickr photo reviews present immense possibility for the realization of a transnational approach to ILP teaching and learning. In an analysis of *linguascpaing* behaviors of YouTube commentary threads around a Eurovision song contest, Thorne and Ivković (2015) demonstrate a "complex semiotic ecology which transcends national and physical borders" (188) to make salient the ways in which participants are their own agents in participating in an "open network catalyzed by shared interests" where "they also individually and collectively consume, display, contest, and negotiate discursive realities" (187). Fundamental to this discursive practice is the expression and interpretation of meaning from simultaneously local and transnational perspective. Future work must take into account the linguistic landscapes of digital contexts as both sources for curricular materials, as well as contexts for which learners must be prepared to participate.

Currently the field of technology-mediated teaching and learning of pragmatics is in its adolescence. It has a strong foundation, yet still carries a certain level of irreverence and unwieldiness in its approaches. Fundamental next steps will include isolating variables to determine the most useful approaches to classroom intervention which take advantage of the many affordances for teaching and learning. Ultimately, research and practice should target factors which yield the most meaningful, comprehensive results possible without sanitizing the variability at the core of the teaching and learning of pragmatics. For example, what design features lead to the development of pragmatic behaviors that enable learners to interact in a variety of multilingual interactions? Concurrently, a strong focus should be placed on describing pragmatic patterns of emergent digital contexts in order to expand the available instructional repertoires while simultaneously preparing learners for an extensive set of intercultural, transnational contexts.

# REFERENCES

Abrams, Zsuzsanna Ittzes. 2001. "Computer-Mediated Communication and Group Journals: Expanding the Repertoire of Participant Roles." *System* 29, no. 4: 489–503.

Alcón Soler, Eva, and Alicia Martínez Flor. 2008. *Investigating Pragmatics in Foreign Language Learning, Teaching and Testing*. Clevedon: Multilingual Matters.

Bardovi-Harlig, Kathleen. 2001. "Evaluating the Empirical Evidence: Grounds for Instruction in Pragmatics?" In *Pragmatics in Language Teaching*, edited by Kenneth R. Rose and Gabriele Kasper, 13–32. Cambridge: Cambridge University Press.

Bardovi-Harlig, Kathleen, and Beverly Hartford. 2005. "Institutional Discourse and Interlanguage Pragmatics Research." In *Interlanguage Pragmatics: Exploring Institutional Talk*, edited by Kathleen Bardovi-Harlig and Beverly Hartford, Chapter 1. Mahwah, NJ: Lawrence Erlbaum.

Beebe, Leslie, and Hansun Zhang Waring. 2001. "Sociopragmatic vs. Pragmalinguisitc Failure: How Useful is the Distinction?" Paper

Presented at the Annual Meeting of the NYSTESOL Applied Linguistics Winter Conference, New York, SUNY Graduate Center. November, 2001.

Blattner, Geraldine, and Melissa Fiori. 2009. "Facebook in the Language Classroom: Promises and Possibilities." *International Journal of Instructional Technology and Distance Learning*, 6: 17–28. Accessed April 15, 2015. http://www.itdl.org/Journal/Jan_09/Jan_09.pdf#page=21

Blattner, Geraldine, and Melissa Fiori. 2013. "Virtual Social Network Communities: An Investigation of Language Learners' Development of Sociopragmatic Awareness and Multiliteracy Skills." *CALICO Journal*, 29, no. 1: 24–43.

Belz, Julie A. 2003. "Linguistic Perspectives on the Development of Intercultural Competence in Telecollaboration." *Language Learning & Technology*, 7, no. 2: 68–117.

Belz, Julie A. 2004. "Telecollaborative Language Study: A Personal Overview of Praxis and Research." In the NFLRC Symposium,

Distance Education, Distributed Learning, and Language Instruction, Univerisity of Hawaii at Manoa, July 27–30. Accessed June 1, 2015. http://www.nflrc.hawaii.edu/networks/NW44/belz.htm

Belz, Julie A. 2007. "The Role of Computer Mediation in the Instruction and Development of L2 Pragmatic Competence." *Annual Review of Applied Linguistics*, 27: 45–75.

Belz, Julie A., and Celeste Kinginger. 2002 "The Cross-Linguistic Development of Address Form Use in Telecollaborative Language Learning: Two Case Studies." *Canadian Modern Language Review/La Revue Canadienne Des Langues Vivantes*, 59, no. 2: 189–214.

Belz, Julie A., and Steven L. Thorne. 2005. *Internet-Mediated Intercultural Foreign Language Education*. Florence, SC: Cengage Learning. Accessed February 1, 2017. http://www.alibris.com/search/books/isbn/9781413029925

Black, Rebecca W. 2009. "English-Language Learners, Fan Communities, and 21st-Century Skills." *Journal of Adolescent & Adult Literacy*, 52, no. 8: 688–697.

Borghetti, Claudia. 2011. "How to Teach It? Proposal for a Methodological Model of Intercultural Competence." In *Intercultural Studies and Foreign Language Learning*, edited by Arnd Witte and Theo Harden, 141–159. Oxford: Peter Lang.

Borghetti, Claudia. 2014. "Integrating Intercultural and Communicative Objectives in the Foreign Language Class: A Proposal for the Integration of Two Models." *Language Learning Journal*, 41, no. 3: 254–267.

Brown, John, and Richard Adler. 2008. "Minds On Fire." *EDUCAUSE Review*, 43, no. 1, 16–32.

Bryant, T. (2006). Using Word of Warcraft and other MMORPGs to foster a targeted, social, and cooperative approach toward language learning. *Academic Commons, The Library.* Accessed February 1, 2017. http://www.academiccommons.org/commons/essay/bryant-MMORPGs-for-SLA.

Byram, Michael. 1994. *Teaching and Learning Language and Culture*. Clevedon: Multilingual Matters.

Byram, Michael. 1997. *Teaching and Assessing Intercultural Communicative Competence*. Philadelphia: Multilingual Matters.

Byram, Michael. 2009. "Intercultural Competence in Foreign Languages: The Intercultural Speaker and the Pedagogy of Foreign Language Education." *The Handbook of Intercultural Competence*, edited by Darla K. Deardorff, 321–333. Los Angeles, CA: Sage.

Castells, Manuel. 1997. *The Power of Identity*. Malden, MA: Blackwell.

CLEAR. 2007. "Multimedia Interactive Modules for Education and Assessment (MIMEA)." Accessed June 15, 2015. http://mimea.clear.msu.edu/

Cohen, Andrew D., and Noriko Ishihara. 2005. "A Web-Based Approach to Strategic Learning of Speech Acts." Minneapolis, MN: University of Minnesota, Center for Advanced Research on Language Acquisition (CARLA).

Cohen, Andrew D., and Julie Sykes. 2012. "Strategy-based Learning of Pragmatics for Intercultural Education." In *Linguistics for Intercultural Education in Language Learning and Teaching*, edited by Frank Dervin and Anthony Liddicoat, 87–111. Amsterdam: John Benjamins.

Crystal, David, ed. 1997. *The Cambridge Encyclopedia of Language*. New York: Cambridge University Press.

Cunningham, Darren J. 2014. The Development of Pragmatic Competence through Tellecollaboration: An Analysis of Requesting Behavior. PhD dissertation, University of Kansas. Accessed May 15, 2015. https://kuscholarworks.ku.edu/bitstream/handle/1808/14529/Cunningham_ku_0099D_13406_DATA_1.pdf?sequence=1

Darhower, Mark. 2002. "Interactional Features of Synchronous Computer-Mediated Communication in the Intermediate L2 Class: A Sociocultural Case Study." *CALICO Journal*, 19, no. 2: 249–277.

Deardorff, Darla K. 2006. Identification and Assessment of Intercultural Competence as a Student Outcome of Internationalization. *Journal Studies in International Education*, 10, no. 3: 241–266.

Deardorff, Darla K. 2008. "Intercultural Competence: A Definition, Model and Implications for Education Abroad." *In Developing Intercultural Competence and Transformation: Theory, Research, and Application in International Education*, edited by Victor Savicki, 32–52. Sterling, VA: Stylus.

Elola, Idoia, and Ana Oskoz. 2011. "Writing Between the Lines: Acquiring the Presentational Mode through Social Tools." In *Present and Future Promises of CALL: From Theory and Research to New Directions in Language Teaching*, edited by Nike Arnold and Lara Ducate, 171–210. San Marcos, TX: CALICO.

Félix-Brasdefer, César J. 2007. "Pragmatic Development in the Spanish as a FL

Classroom: A Cross-sectional Study of Learner Requests." *Intercultural Pragmatics*, 4, no. 2: 253–286.

Furstenberg, Gilberte, Sabine Levet, Kathryn English, and Katherine Maillet. 2001. "Giving a Virtual Voice to the Silent Language of Culture: The Cultura Project." *Technology*, 5: 55–102.

Gee, James P. 2014. *What Video Games Have to Teach Us About Learning and Literacy*, 2nd ed. Basingstoke: Palgrave Macmillan.

Gonzales, Adrienne. 2013. "Development of Politeness Strategies in Participatory Online Environments: A Case Study." In *Technology in Interlanguage Pragmatics Research and Teaching*, edited by Naoko Taguchi and Julie M. Sykes, 101–120. Amsterdam: John Benjamins.

González-Lloret, Marta. 2008. "'No Me Llames de Usted, Trátame de Tú' : L2 Address Behavior Development through Synchronous Computer-Mediated Communication." PhD dissertation, University of Hawai'i at Manoa. Accessed November 3, 2011. http://scholarspace.manoa.hawaii.edu/handle/10125/20886

Guth, Sarah, and Francesca Helm. 2010. *Telecollaboration 2.0: Language, Literacies and Intercultural Learning in the 21st Century*. Bern: Peter Lang.

Holden, Christopher L., and Julie M. Sykes. 2011. "Leveraging Mobile Games for Place-Based Language Learning." *International Journal of Game-Based Learning*, 1, no. 2: 1–18.

Holden, Christopher L., and Julie M. Sykes. 2013. "Complex L2 Pragmatic Feedback via Place-Based Mobile Games." In *Technology and Interlanguage Pragmatics Research and Teaching*, edited by Naoko Taguchi and Julie Sykes,155–184. Amsterdam, the Netherlands: Benjamins.

Ishihara, Noriko, and Andrew D. Cohen. 2010. *Teaching and Learning Pragmatics: Where Language and Culture Meet*. New York: Pearson Longman.

Ishihara, Noriko, and Elaine Tarone. 2009. "Emulating and Resisting Pragmatic Norms: Learner Subjectivity and Pragmatic Choice in L2 Japanese." In *Pragmatic Competence*, edited by N. Taguchi, 101–128. New York: Mouton de Gruyter.

Jenkins, Henry. 2006. *Convergence Culture: Where Old and New Media Collide*. New York: New York University Press.

Judd, Elliott L. 1999. "Some Issues in the Teaching of Pragmatic Competence." In *Culture in Second Language Teaching and Learning*, edited by Eli Hinkel, 152–166. Cambridge: Cambridge University Press.

Kasper, Gabriele, and Kenneth R. Rose. 2001. *Pragmatics in Language Teaching*. Cambridge: Cambridge University Press.

Kasper, Gabriele, and Kenneth R. Rose.2003. *Pragmatic Development in a Second Language*. Hoboken, NJ: John Wiley & Sons, Inc.

Kelm, Orlando. 2015. "BrazilPod." *University of Texas – Austin*. Accessed June 1, 2015. http://www.laits.utexas.edu/orkelm/ppe/intro.html

Kramsch, Claire. 1999. Teaching language along the cultural fault line. In *Culture as the Core: Interdisciplinary Perspectives on Culture Teaching and Learning in the Second Language Curriculum. CARLA Working papers Series* no. 1, edited by Dale Lange, 15–32. Minneapolis, MN: University of Minnesota Center for Advanced Research on Language Acquisition.

Lam, Wan Shun Eva. 2004. "Second Language Socialization in a Bilingual Chat Room: Global and Local Considerations." *Language Learning & Technology*, 8, no. 3: 44–65.

Lee, J. and Hoadley, C. 2007. "Leveraging Identity to Make Learning Fun: Possible Selves and Experiential Learning in Massively Multiplayer Online Games (MMOGs)." *Innovate*, 3, no. 6. Accessed June 2008. http://nsuworks.nova.edu/cgi/viewcontent.cgi?article=1081&context=innovate

Li, Shuai. 2013. "Amount of Practice and Pragmatic Development of Request-Making in L2 Chinese." In *Technology and Interlanguage Pragmatics Research and Teaching*, edited by Naoko Taguchi and Julie M. Sykes, 43–70. Amsterdam, the Netherlands: John Benjamins.

LoCastro, Virginia. 2003. *An Introduction to Pragmatics: Social Action for Language Teachers*. Ann Arbor, MI: University of Michigan Press.

Márquez Reiter, Rosina, and María Elena Placencia. 2004. *Current Trends in the Pragmatics of Spanish*. Amsterdam, the Netherlands: John Benjamins.

Martínez Flor, Alicia, and Esther Usó Juan, eds. 2010. *Speech Act Performance: Theoretical, Empirical and Methodological Issues*. Amsterdam: John Benjamins.

Matsuo, Catherine. 2014. "A Dialogic Critique of Michael Byram's Intercultural Communicative Competence Model from the Perspective of Model Type and Conceptualization of Culture." Comprehensive Study of Sciences Grant Report, 347–380. Accessed September 1, 2016. http://www.tufs.ac.jp/common/fs/ilr/ASIA_kaken/_userdata/3-22_Matsuo.pdf

McBride, Kara. 2009. "Social Networking Sites in Foreign Language Classrooms: Opportunities for Recreation." In *The Next Generation: Social*

*Networking and Online Collaboration in Foreign Language Learning*, edited by Gillian Lord and Lara Lomika, 35–58. San Marcos, TX: CALICO.

Mitchell, Kathleen. 2009. "ESOL Students on Facebook." Master's Thesis, Portland State University.

Moeller, Aleidine J., and Sarah R. Faltin Osborn. 2014. "A Pragmatist Perspective on Building Intercultural Communicative Competency: From Theory to Classroom Practice." *Foreign Language Annals*, 47, no. 4: 669–683.

Payne, Scott J., and Brenda M. Ross. 2005. "Synchronous CMC, Working Memory, and L2 Oral Proficiency Development." *Language Learning & Technology*, 9, no. 3: 35–54.

Payne, Scott, and Paul J. Whitney. 2002. "Developing L2 Oral Proficiency through Synchronous CMC: Output, Working Memory, and Interlanguage Development." *CALICO*, 20: 7–32.

Raquel Díaz, Adriana. 2013. *Developing Critical Languaculture Pedagogies in Higher Education: Theory and Practice*. Clevedon: Multilingual Matters.

Reinhardt, Jonathon, and Steven Thorne. 2011. "Beyond Comparisons: Frameworks for Developing Digital L2 Literacies." In *Present and Future Promises of CALL: From Theory and Research to New Directions in Language Teaching*, edited by Nike Arnold and Lara Ducate, 257–280. San Marcos, TX: CALICO.

Reinhardt, Jonathon, and Victoria Zander. 2011. "Social Networking in an Intensive English Program Classroom: A Language Socialization Perspective." *CALICO Journal*, 28, no. 2: 326–344.

Risager, Karen. 2007. *Language and Culture Pedagogy: From a National to a Transnational Paradigm*. Towanda, NY: Multilingual Matters.

Risager, Karen. 2008. "Towards a Transnational Paradigm in Language and Culture Pedagogy." Paper presented at the annual meeting of the American Association of Applied Linguistics, Washington, DC, March 29–April 2.

Rose, Kenneth. 2005. "On the Effects of Instruction in Second Language Pragmatics." *System*, 33, no. 3: 385–399.

Sauro, Shannon. 2014. "Lessons from the Fandom: Task Models for technology-enhanced Language Learning." In *Technology-mediated TBLT: Researching Technology and Tasks*, edited by Marta González-Lloret and Lourdes Ortega, 239–262. Amsterdam,: John Benjamins.

Scott, Kate. 2015. "The Pragmatics of Hashtags: Inference and Conversational Style on Twitter." *Journal of Pragmatics*, 81: 8–20.

Spitzberg, Brian, and Gabrielle Changnon. 2009. "Conceptualizing Intercultural Competence." In *The SAGE Handbook of Intercultural Competence*, edited by Darla K. Deardorff, 2–52. Los Angeles, CA: Sage.

Sykes, Julie M. 2005. "Synchronous CMC and Pragmatic Development: Effects of Oral and Written Chat." *CALICO Journal*, 22, no. 3: 399–431.

Sykes, Julie M. 2008. "A Dynamic Approach to Social Interaction: Synthetic Immersive Environments and Spanish Pragmatics." PhD dissertation, University of Minnesota.

Sykes, Julie M. 2009. "Learner Requests in Spanish: Examining the Potential of Multiuser Virtual Environments for L2 Pragmatics Acquisition." In *The Next Generation: Social Networking and Online Collaboration*, edited by Lara Lomicka and Gillian Lord, 119–234. San Marcos, TX: CALICO.

Sykes, Julie M.2010. "Multi-User Virtual Environments: User-Driven Design and Implementation for Language Learning." In *Teaching Through Multi-User Virtual Environments: Applying Dynamic Elements to the Modern Classroom*, edited by Giovanni Vicenti and James Braman, 119–234. Hershey, PA: Information Science Reference.

Sykes, Julie M.2013. "Multiuser Virtual Environments: Learner Apologies in Spanish." In *Technology and Interlanguage Pragmatics Research and Teaching*, edited by Naoko Taguchi and Julie M. Sykes, 71–100. Amsterdam, the Netherlands: John Benjamins.

Sykes, Julie M. 2014. "TBLT and Synthetic Immersive Environments: What Can In-game Task Restarts Tell Us About Design and Implementation" In *Technology-mediated TBLT: Researching Technology and Tasks*, edited by Marta González-Lloret and Lourdes Ortega, 149–182. Amsterdam, the Netherlands: John Benjamins.

Sykes, Julie M., and Andrew Cohen. 2006. "Dancing with Words: Strategies for Learning Pragmatics in Spanish." *Regents of the University of Minnesota*. Accessed June 1, 2011. http://www.carla.umn.edu/speechacts/sp_pragmatics/home.html

Sykes, Julie M., and Christopher L. Holden. 2011. "Communities: Exploring Digital Games and Social Networking." In *Present and Future Promises of CALL: From Theory and Research to New Directions in Language Teaching*, edited by Nike Arnold and Lara Ducate, 311–336. San Marcos, TX: CALICO.

Sykes, Julie M., and Jonathon Reinhardt. 2012. *Language at Play: Digital Games in Second and*

*Foreign Language Teaching and Learning.* Boston, MA: Pearson Education, Inc.

Taguchi, Naoko. 2015. "Instructed Pragmatics at a Glance: Where Instructional Studies Were, Are, and Should be Going. State-of-the-art Article." *Language Teaching*, 48, no. 1: 1–50.

Taguchi, Naoko, and Julie M. Sykes. 2013. *Technology in Interlanguage Pragmatics Research and Teaching.* Amsterdam: John Benjamins.

Takamiya, Yumi, and Noriko Ishihara. 2013. "Blogging: Crosscultural Interaction for Pragmatic Development." In *Technology in Interlanguage Pragmatics Research and Teaching*, edited by Naoko Taguchi and Julie M. Sykes, 185–214. Philadelphia, PA: John Benjamins.

Thorne, Steven L. 2008. "Transcultural Communication in Open Internet Environments and Massively Multiplayer Online Games." In *Mediating Discourse Online*, edited by Sally Sieloff Magnan, 305–327. Amsterdam, the Netherlands: John Benjamins. http://search.proquest.com/llba/docview/822514037/3E251AB64B084894PQ/9?accountid=14698.

Thorne, Steven L., and Dejan Ivonkivić. 2015. "Multilingual *Eurovision* Meets Plurilingual *YouTube*: Languascaping Discursive Ontologies." In *Dialogue in Multilingual, Multimodal, and Multicompetent Communities of Practice*, edited by Dale Koike and Carl Blythe, 167–192. Amsterdam, the Netherlands: John Benjamins.

Thorne, Steven, and J. Scott Payne. 2005. "Evolutionary Trajectories, Internet-mediated Expression, and Language Education." *CALICO*, 22, 371–397.

Thorne, Steven, and Jonathon Reinhardt. 2008. "Bridging Activities, New Media Literacies, and Advanced Foreign Language Proficiency." *CALICO*, 25, 558–572.

Thorne, Steven L., Rebecca W. Black, and Julie M. Sykes. 2009. "Second Language Use, Socialization, and Learning in Internet Interest Communities and Online Gaming." *The Modern Language Journal*, 93, no. 1: 802–821.

Thorne, Steven L., Shannon Sauro, and Bryan Smith. 2015. "Technologies, Identities, and Expressive Activity." *Annual Review of Applied Linguistics*, 35: 215–233.

Urzúa, Alfredo. 2013. Attitudes Towards Computer-assisted Language Learning: Student and Teacher Perspectives. Annual Conference of the American Association of Applied Linguistics.

US State Department. "American English: Teaching Pragmatics." Accessed February 18, 2015. http://americanenglish.state.gov/resources/teaching-pragmatics

Utashiro, Takafumi, and Goh Kawai. 2009. "Blended Learning for Japanese Reactive Tokens: Effects of Computer-led, Instructor-led, and Peer-based Instruction." In *Pragmatic Competence*, edited by Naoko Taguchi, 275–300. New York: Mouton de Gruyter.

Vahid Rafieyan, Maryam Sharafi-Nejad, Zahra Khavari, Lin Siew Eng, and Abdul Rashid Mohamed. 2014. "Pragmatic Comprehension Development through Telecollaboration." *English Language Teaching*, 7, no.2. Accessed June 3, 2015. http://www.ccsenet.org/journal/index.php/elt/article/viewFile/33264/19213

Vyatkina, Nina, and Julie A. Belz. 2005. "Learner Corpus Analysis and the Development of L2 Pragmatic Competence in Networked Inter-Cultural Language Study: The Case of German Modal Particles." *Canadian Modern Language Review/La Revue Canadienne Des Langues Vivantes*, 62, no. 1: 17–48. DOI:10.3138/cmlr.62.1.17

Ward, Nigel, Rafael Escalante, Yaffa Al Bayyari, & Thamar Solorio. 2007. "Learning to Show You're Listening." *Computer Assisted Language Learning*, 20, no. 4: 385–407.

Yule, George. 1996. *Pragmatics.* Oxford: Oxford University Press.

Yus, Francisco. 2010. *Ciberpragmática 2.0*, 2nd ed. Barcelona: Editorial Planeta.

# 10 Distance Language Teaching with Technology

## CYNTHIA J. WHITE

## Introduction: Defining the field

The form and scale of technology-mediated distance language teaching has expanded markedly over the past two decades, with ongoing innovation providing access to increasingly rich language learning opportunities, for dispersed populations of learners. Language teaching at a distance is now geographically widespread around the world as a well-established means of extending access and opportunities to language learners in both public and private settings. While much of the research has been carried out by large-scale traditional providers such as the Open University in the United Kingdom, emphasis has also been given to the complexity and diversity of practices associated with technology-mediated distance language teaching, within particular institutional and sociocultural settings including for such languages as Chinese and Arabic. Importantly too there has been a shift in the positioning of distance language programs from being regarded by many as a somewhat marginal enterprise, to being recognized as sites for technological and pedagogical innovation that extend the theory and practices of language teaching. Central to these developments has been an abiding concern to identify the distinctive nature and effectiveness of technology-mediated distance language teaching, together with advancing theory, research and practice to inform what is a burgeoning domain of activity.

Defining features of all these forms of distance language teaching are that teachers and learners are physically separated, that "the bulk of the learning takes place in non-co-presence" (Lamy 2013a, 144), and that technology is used to mediate the teaching-learning processes within the presence of an educational organization (distinguishing it from private study). Distance language teaching has evolved largely in response to developments in technology, from early print-based courses, to educational radio and broadcast television, through to audio and videocassettes, and then to computer technologies, with further possibilities offered by interactive multimedia, Web 2.0 environments, and Second Life. Developments in technology-mediated distance language teaching mark a fundamental shift from early approaches concerned with the production and distribution of learning materials for independent study (including CD-ROMs, video-based courses, and broadcast education for example), to more contemporary approaches concerned with interaction, communication, collaboration and collective activity within virtual learning environments. Technology is no longer solely used for distribution purposes, as in broadcasting, and emphasis is now placed on opportunities for communication using both text and sound, as in the chat, and videoconferencing, meaning that it is possible for distance language education to focus on communication and learning as a social process.

*The Handbook of Technology and Second Language Teaching and Learning,* First Edition.
Edited by Carol A. Chapelle and Shannon Sauro.

A number of different generational models of distance language teaching have been identified from print-based courses, to broadcast education, multiple media courses, information and communication technology (ICT) courses including asynchronous learning opportunities, then synchronous virtual learning environments (for a review of these models, see White 2006). While generational models focus on technologies for distance language teaching, a useful distinction can also be drawn between traditional and emerging paradigms, shedding light on the associated affordances and practices of distance language teaching. For example, the development of course materials for independent study was at the core of traditional paradigms for distance language teaching, with an emphasis on learning the target language from carefully constructed print-based texts and tasks, and relying on one-way technologies to foster the acquisition of listening and, to a lesser extent, speaking skills. Ongoing advances in digital technologies were central to new, emerging paradigms for distance language teaching focusing on interaction initially via text and audio and then by graphics and video. Central to the new opportunities was the possibility of developing interactive competence (Kötter 2001) in the target language, and ways of managing individual learning within an interactive environment with more immediate opportunities for engagement and feedback from instructors and peers. Importantly, too, the new learning environments offered opportunities for peer support, and for reflection on learning experiences in both private (with teachers) and shared (with peers) conversations online. Thus, emerging paradigms for distance language teaching made possible different combinations of individual and collaborative language learning environments, and called for not only technological innovation but pedagogical innovation. Importantly, too, they introduced new expectations of what is required to work successfully in technology-mediated distance language learning environments for both learners and teachers, an issue which is revisited in section 3. Distance language programs around the world make use of both hi-tech and low-tech options, depending largely on infrastructure. Importantly, earlier research using older technologies such as the telephone (Graham 2000) can acquire new significance with the introduction of accessible tools such as Skype; the value of those earlier studies often lies in the rich accounts provided of pedagogical challenges, including for example attempts to make conversations more interactive.

## Technologies, tools, and learning environments

In distance language teaching while the terms technologies, tools, and learning environments are often used quite loosely, even interchangeably, technology is mostly used as a generic term (see for example Hampel and de los Arcos 2013) encompassing, for example, digital technologies and mobile technologies; tools is more specific and is often used to mark a distinction between synchronous and asynchronous tools for example or to refer to specific devices such as the videoconferencing tool NetMeeting (see e.g., Wang 2007). The term learning environment can refer to managed learning environments such as Moodle but more often refers to the complex, local ecology of a course including not only specific tools and content but also constellations of learners, teachers, tasks and interactions, including over time. Blake (2009), in his review of technological applications for second language distance learning, traces advances in the field, concluding that "the profession will need to rethink current best teaching practices and integrate CALL advances fully into the language curriculum including DL options" (832). While a wide range of technological developments have been trialed in pilot studies or introduced on a small scale, such as podcasting (Rosell-Aguilar 2007), mobile language learning (Comas-Quinn, Mardomingo, and Valentine 2009; Demouy and Kukulska-Hulme 2010; Kukulska-Hulme 2010; Kukulska-Hulme and Shield 2008), and Second Life (Deutschmann and Panichi 2009; Deutschmann, Panichi, and

Molka-Danielsen 2009), the most influential technologies, tools, and environments in distance learning have been computer-mediated communication, audiographic and videoconferencing, the use of learning management systems, telecollaboration, and Web 2.0 tools, all of which are discussed here.

## CMC-based environments

The advent of computer-mediated communication (CMC) opened up entirely new domains in distance language teaching, freeing students from the limitations of pre-determined curricula and materials, and introducing new options for learning through discussion and participation in collaborative environments. Importantly, for the first time distance language learners had the prospect of becoming more active agents in their learning: they could raise questions and participate in more open-ended, collaborative learning opportunities to complement the pre-determined course content. Crucially, isolation was no longer such a barrier, and students were able to connect with their peers, and, ideally develop a sense of affiliation and community. Blake (2005), for example, describes CMC as the essential "glue" that holds students together in distance language learning, arguing that it not only engages them, but allows them to put to use the language they learned during the week, and contributes to maintaining motivation.

White (2003) makes a distinction between static course content, and more fluid content which is most easily provided through the use of what are now multiple options for CMC, synchronous and asynchronous, in text, oral, and visual format. Chat, for example, has played a crucial role in providing interactive opportunities in distance language courses: Volle (2005), for example, details synchronous online oral tasks and online oral interviews incorporated into a course for distance learners of Spanish, which was then extended into desktop videoconferencing. A value of the study is the longitudinal tracing of the engagement with the learning environment and the kinds of oral skills that were developed.

Asynchronous forums were among the earliest forms of CMC used in distance language teaching (e.g., Lamy and Goodfellow 1999a, 1999b), with attention to ways in which reflection could be optimally combined with interaction in text-based conferencing. Subsequently both asynchronous and synchronous opportunities were used together as in the use of email and chat in an online distance writing course (Raskin 2001), at which point access to the opportunities needed to take account of time zones. A new issue was that of vicarious interaction, that is learners who preferred to read rather than contribute to online interactions. Importantly, this led to new understandings of the importance of social presence online, and the need to integrate computer-mediated communication into the course curriculum and assessment.

Blake and Shiri (2012) provide a valuable account of the place of CMC in their Arabic Without Walls distance language program, and of the practices of teachers and learners related to CMC. The US-based course, developed by the University of California, was designed to be available across the nation to provide two semesters of instruction in first-year Arabic. Bi-weekly chat sessions are integral to the course and provide opportunities for audio and textual exchanges and feedback through Wimba voice tools. Important design issues include the length of synchronous chat sessions (begins with 15 minutes twice a week and extending as proficiency develops), the focus of the sessions (including pre-prepared topics and more spontaneous ones thus opening up opportunities for contingent interaction), and feedback modes (the text format is used in bimodal CMC in order to maintain the audio exchanges). Importantly, the chat tool is used to connect the distance students with students in the face-to-face program: this opportunity was valued by the distance students as validating their levels of proficiency, and by classroom-based students as a new mode for learning Arabic. The quality and timeliness of exchanges is critical in developing the quality of CMC-based opportunities in distance language programs, a point emphasized by Blake and Shiri, as part of an effort to identify best practices for distance language teaching. Such best practices are informed by student reflections gathered from surveys at four points during the course (numbers of completed evaluations varied from 16 to 7).

CMC is important in distance language teaching not only as a learning tool but as a gateway to target language communities. An innovative step in this direction came from Tudini (2003). The use of CMC tools by intermediate distance learners of Italian was extended into participation in public native speaker chat rooms: the learners interacted in dyads with native speakers in open-ended tasks which were analyzed from an interactionist perspective on second language acquisition as promoting negotiation for meaning and attention to form. She analyzed a corpus of chat logs gathered over one year of 40 one-to-one chat sessions between 49 native speakers and nine university learners of Italian. The analysis of the open conversational tasks provided evidence that students did negotiate for meaning and modify their interlanguage when interacting on a web-based Italian native speaker chat program. Tudini concluded that the virtual chatting which was integral to the course, also provided "an authentic and purposeful cross-cultural experience" (2003, 157).

## *Audiographic and videoconferencing environments*

In terms of synchronous conferencing, both audiographic and video conferencing have become crucial components in many distance language courses, providing opportunities for interaction and collaboration, as both the means and the objective of language learning. Videoconferencing, as Guichon (2010) argues, was originally designed for social communication and has been "diverted for pedagogical purposes" (180), a comment that applies equally to the telephone, Skype, blogs and other technologies and tools. In providing face-to-face communication at a distance, videoconferencing has been seen as beneficial for the kinds of interactive opportunities it could provide distance language learners (see for example Goodfellow et al. 1996, Nicholson 1997, and Wang 2008). Importantly too videoconferencing has been recognized as complementing the more established interactive opportunities provided within written online environments (synchronous and asynchronous). A number of applications are available (including Adobe Connect, Blackboard Collaborate, Breeze, FlashMeeting, NetMeeting), and they combine different modes such as spoken and written language, and differing kinds of access to graphic and visual systems. While early studies identified benefits of videoconferencing, particularly relating to the affective factors of motivation and confidence (e.g., Goodfellow et al. 1996), there was an evident need to ensure that task design was well supported by the affordances of the technology. Drawing on Chapelle's (2001) criteria for CALL task appropriateness, Wang (2007) for example analyzed data from videoconferencing sessions, interviews' and surveys with distance learners of Chinese who had had the equivalent of the first year of university study of Chinese, and identified *practicality* as a key issue in task design for distance language teaching.

Both research and practice have focused not only on the affordances and constraints of task-based videoconferencing environments for distance language teaching, but also the new demands they placed on language learners and teachers. The challenge for participants has been seen as one of "making meaning in multimodal virtual learning spaces" (Hampel and Hauck 2006), and the complexity of that challenge has been identified as one of developing multimodal literacy, which involves not only becoming familiar with the technology but then learning to "represent meaning in more than one mode at a time, understand each mode and how to use different modes constructively, while remaining aware of. ... the affective demands of new media" (Hampel and de los Arcos 2013, 168).

Identifying the skills teachers need to work within synchronous distance language teaching environments, has also been a focus of much research (Hampel and Stickler 2005;

Lamy and Hampel 2007; Wang, Chen, and Levy 2010). Guichon (2009), for example, identifies the need for specific combinations of socioaffective skills (including to individualize the relationship with students), pedagogical skills that can be deployed in real time, and multimedia skills. He extends this analysis in a detailed case study of language teachers new to synchronous online teaching, and to videoconferencing in particular. The focus is on language teaching activity, the difficulties experienced by teachers, and the strategies they use to overcome them. A further aim is to identify specifications for a desktop videoconferencing system designed specifically for language teaching. On the basis of the findings Guichon refers to "the cognitive limitations met by teachers who had to manage several sub-tasks and deal with several channels almost simultaneously" (180). Key functionalities which would help teachers were identified as relating to planning the online session, communicating more successfully, and keeping track of some of the learner language for later feedback.

## Learning management systems

The expansion of technology-mediated distance language teaching also required course developers and language teachers to make decisions in relation to learning management systems (LMSs), also known as content management systems (CMSs) or virtual learning environments (VLEs). Doughty and Long (2003) were among the first to critique any prospect of the mass commercialization of distance language courses packaged into "ill-fitting courseware management programs" (55). The concern was that such systems were not created for language learning, with all the attendant limitations that implies. As they evolved, LMSs such as Moodle and Blackboard included a range of communication tools, both asynchronous and synchronous, thus potentially displacing some of the earlier concerns about a lack of opportunities for interaction or engagement with learner needs (Wang and Chen 2009). A significant study in this regard is Blake and Shiri's (2012) investigation of the Arabic Without Walls (AWW) distance language program, already referred to. In the AWW program, the course content for the first-year online Arabic course is delivered "in a Moodle wrapper" (230) with chat sessions, both voice and text, via Wimba voice tools. Blake and Shiri describe how Moodle connects and integrates the different elements of the course for learners (syllabus, content, interactive opportunities, feedback, in both synchronous and asynchronous modes). Their evaluation of student outcomes and reflections after the two-semester course, reveals that the Moodle-based course environment afforded students more personal attention than they thought would have been was possible in face-to-face classroom sessions. As a conclusion Blake and Shiri address enduring pockets of skepticism about distance environments for language learning, arguing that the profession should "increase all avenues of access to language instruction, especially for the LCTLs" (124).

## Telecollaboration

While technology-mediated distance language teaching has been concerned with providing opportunities for communication and interaction in the target language, access to those opportunities with native speakers has also remained an enduring ambition. Tudini (2013) argues that interactions which are moderated or mediated by a teacher "are likely to provide only limited preparation for naturalistic conversation outside of the classroom" (188). Tandem partnerships conducted by email were an early form of asynchronous bilingual exchanges incorporated into distance language courses providing access to authentic interactions with native speakers (see for example Kötter 2002; Stickler and Lewis, 2008). Subsequently, telecollaborative exchanges which aim "to bring together language learners in different countries in order to carry out collaborative projects or undertake intercultural exchanges" (O'Dowd and Ritter 2006, 623) were developed within distance language courses using increasingly rich environments (including Web 2.0 platforms such as blogs, wikis, YouTube, and Facebook). A number of detailed accounts are given of telecollaborative exchanges incorporated into distance language programs (see e.g., Hauck 2010; Stickler 2008; Stickler and Emke 2011; and vom Brocke et al. 2010). A recurrent finding is that participating in such exchanges places new and largely unpredictable demands on students to be able to learn about, meet, and adjust to the interactive requirements of participation in virtual communities in the target language; while this represents a rich learning experience, the role of the teacher is critical in supporting learners to productively manage those encounters. Similarly raising student awareness in relation to the tools and the intercultural nature of their experiences promotes individual agency and the ability to collaborate productively within telecollaborative projects.

## Web 2.0 tools

More recently, online distance language environments have included, and, in some cases incorporated Web 2.0 tools, such as blogs and wikis. Referring to a distance course for learning Chinese, Wang (2016) reports on the use of wikis for conducting and submitting collaborative writing tasks within an environment that includes Blackboard Collaborate (the synchronous classroom), a Journal (for individual tasks), online quizzes and voiceboard (used for recording and assessing character recognition and such features of spoken language as pronunciation and tones). While joint authoring is a key functionality of wikis, the critical dimension of learner support in distance language teaching also needs to be addressed: in the case of Wang's distance Chinese language course, scaffolding is provided through a series of suggested steps on how to proceed and complete the task with others. Organizational aspects are a further challenge related to collaborative work in distance learning, particularly the time it takes for learners to come together and get the work underway. Wang and Chen (2013) address this by staging the wiki group assessment: the process is divided into three stages beginning with an individual task and then progressing to the group work which involves more complex negotiation of workload and collaborative tasks.

The functionalities of blogs suggest that they could play an important role in distance language courses: they have an accessible interface and include opportunities to revisit, update, and comment on texts. However, the role of the teacher is critical in ensuring such tools are accepted and embedded within the way the course unfolds, as revealed by Comas-Quinn (2011), in her discussion of an upper-intermediate Spanish distance language course. While only 16 percent of the distance learners started a blog, for that small community of bloggers committed to posting and updating their blogs, it became an important tool for writing practice and a central element of their course. This finding aligns with White's (2003) argument that distance language learners can be seen as course producers, who actively construct their own version of the course from the sources available to them, and according to their own learning needs and agendas. In this case though there was teacher resistance to those tools which were not an integral part of the course, highlighting significant tensions that can arise in distance language teaching in relation to the degree of choice of learning sources and tools. Comas-Quinn (2011) noted that several teachers were reluctant to see "the pedagogic value of blogs and revision exercises that are not properly marked [by the teacher]" (228). Further to this, they expressed resistance to the distributed nature of the learning spaces, arguing that they would prefer to have fewer places to moderate, and that such a role could be assigned to an e-moderator as facilitator of learning opportunities online, separate from the tutor. In a subsequent article, Comas-Quinn, de los Arcos and Mardomingo (2012, 129) conclude that "our attempt to promote interaction through our VLE model has resulted in a contested space where traditional hierarchies and relationships between tutors and learners are in a state of flux and where new hierarchies and relationships are constantly being forged." The role(s) of teachers in distance language teaching has been an area of enduring debate, and of contestation, and the introduction of new technologically-mediated spaces tends to draw such debates to the surface once more.

# Enquiry into pedagogical issues

Technology-mediated distance language learning environments entail quite dramatic shifts in pedagogies developed for more traditional settings, requiring both learners and teachers to rethink their practices. While much emphasis has been placed on technological innovation, pedagogical innovation has tended to lag further behind, though arguably this gap has begun to close as the field matures. From a different perspective, Hampel and de los Arcos (2013) review the research and evaluation work carried out over more than one-and-a-half decades into technology-mediated distance language teaching in the context of one institution, the Open University in the United Kingdom. They chronicle the enquiry and evaluation into the use of technologies beginning with the telephone and email through to integrated VLEs using a range of tools. At each point they identify the kinds of emergent issues, the new forms of enquiry they provoked and ongoing technological and pedagogical innovation. The developments are framed in terms of the technologically-mediated means deployed by the institution to support learners in establishing an effective interface with distance-learning environments. To do this they draw on the learner-context interface theory (White 1999, 2005), based on the premise that a meaningful theory of distance language teaching and learning must view the contribution of the context (the learning environment, the task settings, assessment) and that of the learner (individual attributes, skills, needs, actions …) as integral, reciprocal, and dynamic constructs. In the longitudinal outline provided by Hampel and de los Arcos, the main features of enquiry into technology-mediated contexts were the following: task design, teacher roles in those environments, the skills required of teachers (including ways of developing that knowledge and expertise), functionalities of the environment (as in multimodality), and of the setting (as in telecollaboration). Features relating to learner contributions were diverse, and included a sustained focus on interaction, learning communities, metacognition, literacy, affect and learner support, and together they had a significant impact on how learning environments were configured, the design of tasks, and the kinds of training given to tutors within that institutional context. An analysis of the pedagogical issues highlighted by Hampel and de los Arcos, and within recent critical overviews of the field (Blake 2009, 2011, 2013; Lamy 2013a; Vorobel and Kim 2012; White 2006, 2014) reveals a prevailing concern with task design, assessment of learning, and teacher expertise.

## *Task design*

In the early forms of distance language teaching, there was a sustained interest in course design, and ongoing evaluation of materials. Approaches were informed by principles in the wider distance education literature such as tutorials-in-print and the need to ensure the presence of a "teaching voice" within the course content (Holmberg, Shelley, and White 2005). Course design tended to be a lengthy, detailed process involving trialing of materials during the developmental stage, with ongoing attention to such features as learning goals, assessment, the rate of progress that could be expected, and opportunities for feedback on course work. A useful account of this process is given by Hurd, Beaven, and Ortega (2001), outlining the stages involved in developing a linear course which also aimed to develop learner autonomy.

It is important to emphasize that the consequences for flawed design in distance language teaching can be quite significant, impacting on learner motivation and persistence for example, as noted by Lamy (2013a, 149): "remote, isolated learners whose learning is impeded or halted by design issues cannot obtain immediate help, nor can the designers intervene swiftly to recast pedagogical orientations that have been explicitly described for the learners in the self-study materials already released to them." While it is now possible to update or revise elements of a course through virtual learning environments, such mid-stream changes can result in confusion or negative impact on learner confidence and engagement. As knowledge of broader issues of course design has grown, the emphasis has shifted to task design, which remains an equally high-stakes activity. The prevailing focus has been on task design related to the affordances of particular online tools, the needs and preferences of learners, and the goals of specific learning events. And, as noted earlier, a central concern has been to provide optimal opportunities to develop interactive competence in the target language.

Technology-mediated environments provide the teacher and researcher with a view into the ways in which distance language tasks are interpreted, negotiated, and enacted by students, and by groups of students. This represents a quite dramatic departure from earlier forms of distance language teaching where the teacher was for the most part remote from the individual sites of student learning, and had to rely on inferences about students' interpretation of tasks drawn from submitted course work. The distinction between task-as-workplan and task-as-process was central to Hampel's (2006), now classic study of distance language online task design for a multimodal environment. The theoretical underpinnings of the analysis include interactionist SLA, sociocultural theory and theories of affordances, medium and mode, together with implicit awareness of the distinctive features of distance language teaching. Like Wang (2007), Hampel makes reference to Chapelle's (2003) features for CALL and CMC, with practicality a key consideration together with student interest (developing and maintaining motivation is a key challenge for distance language teaching). The particular technology central to the study was Lyceum, which allows students to interact synchronously via different modes (audio, writing, and graphics) through an environment consisting of a voicebox, whiteboard, text chat, a concept map, and documents. An overarching framework for the study concerns a tripartite model consisting of approach, design, and procedure stages: emphasis is placed on how the selected approach influences not only design and implementation stages, but how evaluation of task implementation then feeds back into the understanding of the approach stage in online settings (including theories of language and language learning as well as affordances of particular technologies).

Importantly, a sustained comparison is made between task design and implementation with not only different learners but also different tutors; the aim is to assist both teachers and course developers in enhancing task design in synchronous online settings. From this account we also have an expanded view of design which here includes syllabus, functions, and types of tasks as well as learner and teacher roles, and what each of these entails in distance language programmes. In subsequent studies, Hampel applies this model to other online activities, giving further insights into how it can usefully be applied to the recursive processes of planning, implementation, and evaluation which have long informed materials development in distance language teaching (Hampel 2010; Hampel and Pleines 2013).

## Assessment of learning

A prevailing concern has been how to assess the learning gains of distance language students in ways that are appropriate for the learning setting. Currently we do not have a well-developed philosophy of assessment in distance language teaching, and to date assessing the acquisition of the target language skills by distance language learners has been the focus of enquiry with two broad purposes: to investigate student gains in performance as a means of establishing the effectiveness of distance language teaching environments and processes (Blake et al. 2008; Volle 2005) and/or as a means of assessing particular skills and providing feedback to learners on their progress. In the first category, early studies focused on assessing and documenting the development of oral skills in online distance environments: Volle measured the oral skills of distance learners of Spanish in voice-email and online interviews based on scores for articulation (pronunciation, stress, intonation), accuracy and proficiency. An important contribution of this study is the careful account given of the course, the tools, the students, the assignment work, and the measures as well as sustained discussion of both issues with technology and limitations of the measures. The oral proficiency gains of learners of Spanish were also the subject of further research in a comparative study by Blake et al. (2008) of different cohorts of students in classroom, hybrid and distance-learning settings. They found that by the end of their first year of study, students across the three modes reached comparable levels of oral proficiency. In both these studies, and others, the rationale has been to dispel cynicism about the efficacy of technology-mediated distance language learning environments for the acquisition of oral skills.

An important development in technology-mediated assessment came with the increasing focus on tailoring assessment to match the kinds of interactive and collaborative opportunities integral to contemporary paradigms of distance language teaching. Hopkins (2010) reports on the use of FlashMeeting (which combines synchronous voice and text chat features, together with video, whiteboard, voting, file sharing, and other features) to develop and assess skills in real time, interactive speaking tasks for English as a foreign language students at the University of Catalonia. The main part of the learning in distance language courses is not directly mediated by a teacher, and a defining feature of Hopkins' study is that it incorporates the non-co-presence of the teacher into carefully scaffolded, assessed, small-group speaking tasks. Prior to the two assessed tasks, students were given opportunities to practice speaking skills in similar collaborative tasks with members of the class. This study extends the focus on task design and interaction in online distance language environments from speaking practice within optional course elements to compulsory assessed activities.

The focus of online assessment has also been extended in recent work by Wang and Chen (2013) addressing the fact that while multimodal tools increase the potential for including interaction, collaboration, and reflection, they introduce new complexities and specific constraints in relation to assessment. Referring to an online distance Chinese language course at Griffith University in Australia, using Blackboard (including Wimba voice tools, wikis, online quizzes, and blogs), the authors note that relatively few studies have investigated online assessment using dynamic tools such as videoconferencing or wikis. They align student assessments with the course design framework which encompasses a focus on interaction, collaboration, and reflection. Examples of online assessment tasks which require learners to interact with each other, to collaborate and work collectively, and to reflect on their learning (both individually and together) are presented and analyzed. An important feature of this work is the critical approach to the tools used (identifying the wiki and Wimba classrooms as the main sites for assessment at the beginner level), the evident theoretical underpinnings relating to the tripartite framework and its substantiation in assessment tasks within a broader course context.

## Teacher expertise

The knowledge, skills, and expertise required to participate in technology-mediated distance language learning (whether as a teacher, learner, moderator, assessor, course designer), has been explored from a number of perspectives. Here I focus on the large body of research that has been conducted into the roles of teachers (see the early studies of Hauck and Haezewindt 1999, and Shield, Hauck, and Hewer 2001), the training of tutors (Hampel and Stickler 2005), taxonomies of teacher expertise (Hampel and Stickler 2005), and areas for ongoing teacher development, including innovation (Ernest and Hopkins 2006). From such studies we have a picture of the kinds of knowledge required as an online distance language teacher, the nature of different domains of expertise and of different approaches to building the requisite skills and understandings within what is a very complex endeavor.

One of the earliest accounts of practices in virtual language classrooms comes from Lamy and Goodfellow (1999a) as they focus on asynchronous conferencing to encourage reflective interaction among distance language learners of French in a project termed Lexica Online. The project aimed to encourage student reflection on their vocabulary learning strategies through group discussions which were moderated by tutors over a period of six weeks. A significant feature of the study is that it analyzes the contributions of tutors and students in terms of message types and tutor styles, both of which are linked to student learning. Of the three text types, only "reflective conversations" (as opposed to monologues and social conversations) were identified as contributing significantly to language learning in that they were interactional "in both information processing-and social-interactional senses" (52). In terms of optimal tutor styles, Lamy and Goodfellow argue the need to attend to both cognitive and social dimensions of student participation and learning. Their work was part of a wider concern as to how to develop learner autonomy within collaborative online distance learning as a critical dimension of learner support.

Hampel (2009) identifies a key challenge in online distance synchronous settings as addressing the tendency for tutors to assume a more directive or teaching-centered approach than is congruent with the espoused benefits of learner-centered language teaching. It is evident that certain features of the setting may lead to this approach including student unfamiliarity with the online tools, technical problems, and the perceived need to direct students to the affordances of the environment. Importantly too Hampel notes that students often find it very difficult to collaborate, having been mostly used to the self-study aspects of distance language learning. Beyond these epistemological shifts in practices of distance language learning and teaching, Hampel identifies the critical importance of design in fostering interaction and collaboration online, referring to Mangenot and Nissen's (2006) framework: "A more learner-centred approach requires the ability on the part of the teacher to provide a setting in which learners can develop the socioaffective, sociocognitive and organisational skills that are prerequisites of collaboration. This can be facilitated by appropriate tasks, moderation and feedback" (47).

These findings underline the importance of affective and organizational dimensions of engagement across all aspects of the role: students for example argued that for them points of contact with tutors were generally high stakes, and that distance language teaching thus requires more attention to interpersonal aspects and relationships, better organization and focus than was often required in other settings, and a degree of sensitivity and empathy towards the learner's individual context. Much research has focused on understanding distance teacher skills in different virtual settings and in relation to specific task types (e.g., Comas-Quinn, de los Arcos and Mardomingo 2012 and Ernest, Heiser and Murphy 2013), with a sustained focus on how to encourage interaction and collaboration, to maintain motivation and to ensure student retention and course completion. Important operational practices include setting up online socialization in multimodal learning environments, providing access to support and timely feedback, ensuring congruence between coursework and course assessment, providing spaces where students can exchange ideas and get support in relation to assessment, and generating a feeling of "belonging" to the course and to a learning community

What has been less explored are the ways in which training impacts on actual practice, though this has been as aspect of some studies. For example, in a detailed case study of two participants, Levy, Wang, and Chen (2009) trace individual experience longitudinally in a four-week training course preparing them for technology-mediated distance language teaching, and then in their online teaching practice over eight weeks. The study provides rich descriptions of the design, structure, and sequencing of the workshop training materials, and of the participants' experiences as they developed their knowledge and skills, through sequences of action and reflection, including as they transitioned into actual teaching practice. An important next step identified in the conclusion of the study is to develop a means of checking and recording "the improvements made by trainee tutors on the previous cycles of development so that the new knowledge and skills may be pitched at the right level and communicated effectively and efficiently" (33).

## Research trajectories and a future agenda

Analysis of recent overviews of empirical studies of technology-mediated distance language teaching (Blake 2009, 2011, 2013; Lamy 2013a; Vorobel and Kim 2012; White 2006, 2014), reveal several major research trajectories: multimodality, learner characteristics and contributions, course design, task design, telecollaboration, teacher expertise and the evaluation of tools and learning environments. The studies themselves have been conducted almost exclusively in university or other higher education settings. This narrowing of research sites is disappointing given that earlier publications encompassed courses for adult migrants in Australia (Candlin and Byrnes 1995), access to interactive satellite-based classes at both elementary level and high school in Italian, Indonesian, Chinese, Japanese and French (Evans, Stacey, and Tregenza 2001), and workplace-based learning (Laouénan and Stacey 1999). As the field has matured, and we now have fewer reports of preliminary pilot studies in distance language teaching, it is important to ensure that research is carried out in as wide a range of settings as possible and with a wide range of target populations and target languages, including those with non-Roman scripts (White 2014). Looking ahead new areas for future inquiry include the need to identify best practices in technology-mediated distance language teaching at different stages of a language course including, for example, initial socialization, orienting learners towards assessments, addressing issues of motivation, and providing feedback. More fine-grained studies are also needed to identify the kinds of skills required to be able to learn and use the target language within particular multimodal environments, which could then be used as the basis for learner training. A third, and critical area, concerns the transfer of interactive competence in the target language from distance language settings to other settings (either face-to-face or mediated environments). While distance language teaching has been defined by ongoing processes of technological and pedagogical innovation, these processes themselves have received relatively little critical commentary (for one exception see White 2007 on innovation and identity in distance language teaching). Such critical approaches would be a valuable addition to the field, providing new perspectives on the complexities, challenges, and significant breakthroughs in forging new technology-mediated distance-learning opportunities.

Such an agenda also needs to be pursued in ways that extend the methodological and theoretical frameworks of technology-mediated distance language teaching and that contribute to an evidence base to inform practice. That agenda would then contribute to the wider field of applied linguistics through, for example, multimodal research tools aligned to the particular data sets available in those settings. Importantly, too, such an agenda needs to include enquiry into technology-mediated distance language teaching across several iterations of a course, in both small-scale and large-scale contexts of provision, thus enabling comparative analyses across those contexts and iterations.

# Conclusion

Warschauer (2000) depicted distance language teaching as a "site of struggle" (527) in which technology could either increase or lower the quality of learning opportunities: commenting at the turn of the millennium he noted that there was the potential for distance language learning to become more flexible and interactive, but whether that would be the case remained an open question. Some 15 years later, technology-mediated distance language teaching is a mature field, yet questions remain about the role of technology and quality of learning experiences, especially given the diversity of practices that come within the rubric of distance language teaching. While contemporary approaches to distance language teaching are based in social and collaborative virtual contexts, distance language pro-grammes around the world still vary considerably in terms of how they are designed, and then in terms of how they are used by instructors and learners, meaning again that the actual experience of distance language learning is highly varied.

While much work still remains to be undertaken to shed more light on the processes and best practices of distance language learning and teaching, the research enterprise has been aided enormously by access to archival data from within virtual learning environments. Such data provides us with a window into the actual sites of learning, from which points we can see how learners work with the affordances of the environments, moment by moment, and the ways in which those environments evolve as participants work together to construct the course and online events (see for example White, Direnzo, and Bortolotto, in press). To be of value, access to the situated practices of distance language learners and teachers in particular settings needs to be interpreted against a background of what we have long understood to be major challenges for the field: namely the need for ongoing attention to learner support that adds value to individual learning agendas, attention to community, and affiliations within that, feedback on individual and collective activity, and careful consideration of the affective aspects of distance language learning. In introducing new tools or opening up any new learning environments it is critical to consider questions relating to curricular articulation and assessed course components, given the constraints on distance language learners as they seek to adapt to particular learning environments and then learn to derive benefit from working within them. This latter point leads to an important question posed by Lamy (2013b) in relation to the value of informal social networking for distance learners of Chinese at the Open University: she identifies the central challenge as enabling students to identify and make use of the diverse affordances of social networking sites.Thus, looking ahead, there is a critical need not only for pedagogical innovation, but for sustained attention to how new tools and environments function from the point of view of learners, and through careful scaffolding to extend the value they can derive from technology-mediated distance language teaching.

## REFERENCES

Blake, Robert. J. 2005. "Bimodal CMC: The Glue of Language Learning at a Distance." *CALICO Journal*, 22, no. 3: 497–511.

Blake, Robert. J. 2009. "The Use of Technology for Second Language Distance Learning." *Modern Language Journal*, 93, no. 1: 822–835.

Blake, Robert. J. 2011. "Current Trends in Online Language Learning." *Annual Review of Applied Linguistics*, 31: 19–35.

Blake, Robert. J.2013. *Brave New Digital Classroom: Technology and Foreign Language Learning*: Washington, DC: Georgetown University Press.

Blake, Robert. J., and Sonia Shiri. 2012. "Online Arabic Language Learning: What Happens After?" *L2 Journal*, 4, no. 2: 230–246.

Blake, Robert J., Nicole L. Wilson, Maria Cetto, and Cristina Pardo-Ballester. 2008. "Measuring Oral Proficiency in Distance, Face-to-face, and Blended Classrooms." *Language Learning and Technology*, 12, no. 3: 114–127.

Candlin, Chris, and Fran Byrnes. 1995. "Designing for Open Language Learning: Teaching Roles and Learning Strategies." In *Language in Distance Education, How Far Can We Go?* Edited by Sue Gollin, 126–141. North Ryde, New South Wales, Australia: Macquarie University, National Centre for English Language Teaching and Research.

Chapelle, Carol. A. 2001. *Computer Applications in Second Language Acquisition*. Cambridge: Cambridge University Press.

Chapelle, Carol. A. 2003. *English Language Learning and Technology: Lectures on Applied Linguistics in the Age of Information and Communication Technology, Vol. 7.* Amsterdam: John Benjamins.

Comas-Quinn, Anna. 2011. "Learning to Teach Online or Learning to Become an Online Teacher: An Exploration of Teachers' Experiences in a Blended Learning Course." *ReCALL*, 23, no. 3: 218–232.

Comas-Quinn, Anna, Beatriz de los Arcos, and Raquel Mardomingo. 2012. "Virtual Learning Environments (VLEs) for Distance language Learning: Shifting Tutor Roles in a Contested Space for Interaction." *Computer Assisted Language Learning*, 25, no. 2: 129–143.

Comas-Quinn, Anna, Raquel Mardomingo, and Chris Valentine. 2009. "Mobile Blogs in Language Learning: Making the Most of Informal and Situated Learning Opportunities." *ReCALL*, 21, no. 1: 96–112.

Demouy, Valerie, and Agnes Kukulska-Hulme. 2010. "On the Spot: Using Mobile Devices for Listening and Speaking Practice on a French Language Programme." *Open Learning*, 25, no. 3: 217–232.

Deutschmann, Mats, and Luisa Panichi. 2009. "Talking into Empty Space? Signalling Involvement in a Virtual Language Classroom in Second Life." *Language Awareness*, 18, no. 3–4: 310–328.

Deutschmann, Mats, Luisa Panichi, and Judith Molka-Danielsen. 2009. "Designing Oral Participation in Second Life a Comparative Study of Two Language Proficiency Courses." *Recall*, 21, no. 2: 206–226.

Doughty, Catherine, and Mike Long. 2003. "Optimal Psycholinguistic Environments for Distance Foreign Language Learning." *Language Learning and Technology*, 7, no. 3: 50–80.

Ernest, Pauline, Sarah Heiser, and Linda Murphy. 2013. "Developing Teacher Skills to Support Collaborative Online Language Learning." *Language Learning Journal*, 41, no. 1: 37–54.

Ernest, Pauline, and Joseph Hopkins. 2006. "Coordination and Teacher Development in an Online Learning Environment." *CALICO Journal*, 23, no. 3: 551–568.

Evans, Terry, Elizabeth Stacey, and Karen Tregenza. 2001. "Interactive Television in Schools: An Australian Study of the Tensions of Educational Technology and Change." *The International Review of Research in Open and Distributed Learning* 2, no. 1: 1–16.

Goodfellow, Robin, Ingrid Jeffreys, Terry Miles, and Tim Shirra. 1996. "Face-to-face Language at a Distance? A Study of a Videoconferencing Try-out." *ReCALL*, 8, no. 2: 5–16.

Graham, Jane. 2000. "Casual Conversation at a Distance." In *Teachers' Voices 6. Teaching Casual Conversation*, edited by H. d. S. Joyce, 63–70. Sydney: NCELTR.

Guichon, Nicolas. 2009. "Training Future Language Teachers to Develop Online Tutors' Competence through Reflective Analysis." *ReCALL*, 21, no. 2: 166–185.

Guichon, Nicolas. 2010. "Preparatory Study for the Design of a Desktop Videoconferencing Platform for Synchronous Language Teaching." *Computer Assisted Language Learning*, 23, no. 2: 169–182.

Hampel, Regine. 2006. "Rethinking Task Design for the Digital Age: A Framework for Language Teaching and Learning in a Synchronous Online Environment." *ReCALL*, 18, no. 1: 105–121.

Hampel, Regine. 2009. "Training Teachers for the Multimedia Age: Developing Teacher Expertise to Enhance Online Learner Interaction and Collaboration." *Innovation in Language Learning and Teaching*, 3, no. 1: 35–50.

Hampel, Regine. 2010. "Task Design for a Virtual Learning Environment in a Distance Language Course." *Task-Based Language Learning and Teaching with Technology*, 131–153.

Hampel, Regine, and Beatriz de los Arcos. 2013. "Interacting at a Distance: A Critical Review of the Role of ICT in Developing the Learner-context Interface in a University Language Programme."*Innovation in Language Learning and Teaching*, 7, no. 2: 158–178.

Hampel, Regine, and Miriam Hauck. 2006. "Computer-mediated Language Learning:

Making Meaning in Multimodal Virtual Learning spaces." *The JALT CALL Journal*, 2, no. 2: 3–18.

Hampel, Regine, and Christine Pleines. 2013. "Fostering Student Interaction and Engagement in a Virtual Learning Environment: An Investigation into Activity Design and Implementation." *The CALICO Journal*, 30, no. 3: 342–370.

Hampel, Regine, and Ursula Stickler. 2005. "New Skills for New Classrooms: Training Tutors to Teach Languages Online." *Computer Assisted Language Learning*, 18, no. 4: 311–326.

Hauck, Miriam. (2010). "Telecollaboration: At the Interface between Multimodal and Intercultural Communicative." *Telecollaboration 2.0: Language, Literacies and Intercultural Learning in the 21st Century*, 1: 219.

Hauck, Miriam and Bernard Haezewindt. 1999. "Adding a New Perspective to Distance (Language) Learning and Teaching – The Tutor's Perspective." *ReCALL*, 11, no. 2: 46–54.

Holmberg, Borje, Monica Shelley, and Cynthia White, eds. 2005. *Distance Education and Languages: Evolution and Change*. Clevedon: Multilingual Matters.

Hopkins, Joseph E. 2010. "Distance Language Learners' Perceptions of Assessed, Student-led Speaking Tasks via a Synchronous Audiographic Conferencing Tool." *Innovation in Language Learning and Teaching*, 4, no. 3: 235–258.

Hurd, Stella, Tita Beaven, and Ane Ortega. 2001. "Developing Autonomy in a Distance Language Learning Context: Issues and Dilemmas for Course Writers." *System*, 29, no. 3: 341–355.

Kötter, Markus. 2001. "Developing Distance Learners' Interactive Competence – Can Synchronous Audio Do the Trick?" *International Journal of Educational Telecommunications*, 7, no. 4: 327–353.

Kötter, Markus. 2002. *Tandem Learning on the Internet*. Frankfurt: Peter Lang.

Kukulska-Hulme, Agnes. 2010. "Charting Unknown Territory: Models of Participation in Mobile Language Learning." *International Journal of Mobile Learning and Organisation*, 4, no. 2: 116–129.

Kukulska-Hulme, Agnes, and Lesley L. Shield. 2008. "An Overview of Mobile Assisted Language Learning: From Content Delivery to Supported Collaboration and Interaction." *ReCALL*, 20, no. 3: 271–289.

Lamy, Marie-Noelle. 2013a. "Distance CALL Online." In *Contemporary Computer-assisted*

*Language Learning*, edited by Michael Thomas, Hayo Reinders, and Mark Warschauer, 141–158. London: Continuum.

Lamy, Marie-Noelle. 2013b. "'We Don't Have to Always Post Stuff to Help us Learn': Informal Learning through Social Networking in a Beginners' Chinese Group." *Online Teaching and Learning: Sociocultural Perspectives*, 219–238. London: Bloomsbury Publishing.

Lamy, Marie-Noelle, and Robin Goodfellow. 1999a. "'Reflective Conversation' in the Virtual Language Classroom." *Language Learning and Technology*, 2, no. 2: 43–61.

Lamy, Marie-Noelle, and Robin Goodfellow. 1999b. "Supporting Language Students' Interactions in Web-based Conferencing." *Computer Assisted Language Learning*, 12, no. 5: 457–477.

Lamy, Marie-Noelle, and Regine Hampel. 2007. *Online Communication in Language Learning and Teaching*. Basingstoke: Palgrave Macmillan.

Laouénan, Michèle, and Sue Stacey. 1999. "A brief experiment in distance teaching and learning of French." *British Journal of Educational Technology*, 30, no. 2: 177–180.

Levy, Mark, Yuping Wang, and Nian-Shing Chen. 2009. "Developing the Skills and Techniques for Online Language Teaching: A Focus on the Process." *International Journal of Innovation in Language Learning and Teaching*, 3, no. 1: 17–34.

Mangenot, François, and Elke Nissen. 2006. "Collective Activity and Tutor Involvement in e-Learning Environments for Language Teachers and Learners." *CALICO Journal*, 23, no. 3: 601–622.

Nicholson, Ann. 1997. *Current Practice in the Use of Telematics to Support distance learners in the Adult Migrant English Program*. Sydney: National Centre for English Language Teaching and Research (NCELTR), Macquarie University.

O'Dowd, Robert, and Markus Ritter. 2006. "Understanding and Working with 'Failed Communication' in Telecollaborative Exchanges." *CALICO Journal*, 23, no. 3: 623–642.

Raskin, Jane. 2001. "Using the World Wide Web as a Resource for Models and Interaction in a Writing Course." In *Distance-learning programs*, edited by Lynn Henrichsen, 61–70. Alexandria, VA: TESOL.

Rosell-Aguilar, Fernando. 2007. "Top of the Pods—In Search of a Podcasting 'Podagogy' for Language Learning." *Computer Assisted Language Learning*, 20, no. 5: 471–492.

Shield, L., M. Hauk, and S. Hewer. 2001. "Talking to Strangers – The Role of the Tutor in

Developing Target Language Speaking Skills at a Distance." *Use of New Technologies in Foreign Language Teaching*, 11: 75–85.

Stickler, Uschi. 2008. "Chatting, Chatten or Chattare." *International Journal of Emerging Technologies in Learning*, 3: 69–76.

Stickler, Ursula., and Martina Emke. 2011. "LITERALIA: Towards Developing Intercultural Maturity Online." *Language Learning and Technology*, 15, no. 1: 147–168.

Stickler, Ursula, and Tim Lewis. 2008. "Collaborative Language Learning Strategies in an Email Tandem Exchange." In *Language Learning Strategies in Independent Settings*, edited by Stella Hurd and Tim Lewis, 237–261. Bristol: Multilingual Matters.

Tudini, Vincenza. 2003. "Using Native Speakers in Chat." *Language Learning and Technology*, 7, no. 3: 141–159.

Tudini, Vincenza. 2013. "Form-focused Social Repertoires in an Online Language Learning Partnership." *Journal of Pragmatics*, 50, no. 1: 187–202.

Volle, Lisa. M. 2005. "Analyzing Oral Skills in Voice E-mail and Online Interviews." *Language Learning and Technology*, 9, no. 3: 146–163.

Vom Brocke, Jan, Cynthia White, Ute Walker, and Christina vom Brocke. 2010. "Making User-generated Content Communities Work in Higher Education – The Importance of Setting Incentives." In *Changing Cultures in Higher Education*, edited by Ulf-Daniel Ehlers and Dirk Schneckenberg, 149–166. Berlin: Springer Verlag.

Vorobel, Oksana, and Deoksoon Kim. 2012. "Language Teaching at a Distance: An Overview of Research." *CALICO Journal*, 29, no. 3: 548–562.

Wang, Yuping. 2007. "Task Design in Videoconferencing-supported Distance Language Learning." *CALICO Journal*, 24, no. 3: 591–630.

Wang, Yuping. 2008. *Distance Language Learning and Desktop Videoconferencing: A Chinese Language Case Study*. Saarbrucken: Verlag.

Wang, Yuping. 2016. "Innovative Learning Design for Online Language Learning: A Systems Design Framework." In *Exploring Innovative Pedagogy in the Teaching and Learning of Chinese as a Foreign Language*, edited by Robyn Moloney and Hui Ling Xu, 253–271. Singapore: Springer.

Wang, Yuping, and Nian-Shing Chen. 2009. "Criteria for Evaluating Synchronous Learning Management Systems: Arguments from the Distance Language Classroom." *Computer Assisted Language Learning*, 22, no. 1: 1–18.

Wang, Yuping, and Nian-Shing Chen. 2013. Engendering Interaction, Collaboration, and Reflection in the Design of Online Learning Assessment in Language Learning: A Reflection from the Course Designers. In *Computer-assisted Foreign Language Teaching and Learning: Technological Advances*, edited by Bin Zou, Minjie Xing, Catherine Xiang, Yuping Wang, and Mingui Sun, 16–38. Hershey, PA: IGI Global.

Wang, Yuping, Nian-Shing Chen, and Mike Levy. 2010. "The Design and Implementation of a Holistic Training Model for Language Teacher Education in a Cyber Face-to-face Learning Environment." *Computers and Education*, 55, no. 2: 777–788.

Warschauer, Mark. 2000. "The Changing Global Economy and the Future of English Teaching." *TESOL Quarterly*, 34, no. 3: 511–535.

White, Cynthia J. 1999. "Expectations and Emergent Beliefs of Self-instructed Language Learners." *System: An International Journal of Educational Technology and Applied Linguistics*, 27: 443–457.

White, Cynthia J. 2003. *Language Learning in Distance Education*. Cambridge: Cambridge University Press.

White, Cynthia J. 2005. "Towards a Learner-based Theory of Distance Language Learning: The Concept of the Learner-context Interface." In *Languages in Distance Education: Evolution and Change*, edited by Borje Holmberg, Monica Shelley, and Cynthia White, 55–71. Clevedon: Multilingual Matters.

White, Cynthia J. 2006. "State of the Art Article: The Distance Learning of Foreign Languages." *Language Teaching*, 39, no. 4: 247–264.

White, Cynthia J. 2007. "Innovation and Identity in Distance Language Learning and Teaching." *Innovation in Language Learning and Teaching*, 1, no. 1: 97–110.

White, Cynthia J. 2013. "Emerging Opportunities in New Learning Spaces: Teacher, Learner and Researcher Perspectives." *TESOLANZ Journal*, 10: 8–21.

White, Cynthia J. 2014. "The Distance Learning of Foreign Languages: Defining the Research Agenda." *Language Teaching*, 47, no. 4: 538–553.

White, Cynthia, Raquel Direnzo, and Celina Bortolotto. in press. "The Learner-context Interface: Emergent Issues of Affect and Identity in Technology-mediated Language Learning spaces." *System: An International Journal of Educational Technology and Applied Linguistics*, 62: 3–14.

# 11 Blended Language Learning: Research and Practice

## MAJA GRGUROVIĆ

## Introduction

In the field of second language learning as well as general education, blended and hybrid learning is receiving a lot of attention. The results of the Babson 2012 study across disciplines in higher education show that more than 70% of faculty and 90% of administrators are excited about this type of instruction (Allen et al. 2012). According to the 2012 EDUCAUSE Center for Analysis and Research (ECAR) report of undergraduate students and information technology, "blended learning environments are the norm" and 70% of students say they learn most in them as opposed to face-to-face or fully online ones (Dahlstrom 2012, 5 and 7). Blended classes at the undergraduate level were already offered by 79% of public higher education institutions in the United States in 2004 (Allen, Seaman, and Garrett 2007) and the number is certainly higher now.

Researchers investigating blended learning tend to agree that "blended learning is a transformational force in education" (Dziuban, Hartman, and Mehaffy 2014, 328). According to Watson (2008), blended learning is "likely to emerge as the predominant model of the future and to become far more common than either [online or face-to-face instruction] alone" (3). This chapter provides an overview of the development of blended language learning research from the early 2000s to 2014. It focuses on the most recent state of research (2006–2014) through a research review of 26 blended learning studies. The review identifies the areas of inquiry and discusses important considerations for the present and future development of blended learning practices and research.

## Blended learning: Definition

A single definition for blended learning has proven difficult to identify. In the most general terms, blended learning is defined as a combination of face-to-face and computer-mediated instruction (Graham 2006). More specifically, Picciano (2009) describes blended classes as those where face-to-face and online activities are integrated in a planned, pedagogically valuable manner and where online activities replace a portion of face-to-face time. Both definitions include two main ingredients: online and face-to-face instructional modes. In addition, some definitions include the amount of instruction in each mode. For example, the website Blended Learning Toolkit 2014 quotes the definition from the Online Learning Consortium (formerly the Sloan Consortium) which "defines blended learning as a course

*The Handbook of Technology and Second Language Teaching and Learning*, First Edition.
Edited by Carol A. Chapelle and Shannon Sauro.
© 2017 John Wiley & Sons, Inc. Published 2020 by John Wiley & Sons, Inc.

where 30 percent to 70 percent of the instruction is delivered online." For others, this amount is a distinguishing factor between the terms blended and hybrid. According to the classification in Gruba and Hinkelman (2012, 4), blended language learning utilizes some significant online activities in otherwise face-to-face learning, but less than 45%, while online activities replace 45% to 80% of face-to-face class meetings in hybrid learning. For many other authors (e.g., Graham and Dziuban 2008) including this author, the terms blended and hybrid are synonymous and will be used as such in this chapter.

From the range of definitions currently in use, Picciano aptly concludes, "there is no generally accepted definition of blended learning" (2014, 3). While this may be problematic for designing and interpreting research on blended learning, it may be an inevitable result of current dynamic innovation in this area which "defies all attempts at universal definition" (Moskal, Dziuban, and Hartman 2013, 4). As shown by the range of instructional and curricular options reviewed in this chapter, the above definitions cover speaks to the versatility of blended learning.

## The beginnings of blended learning research: 2000–2005

The term blended learning started appearing in the literature across disciplines around 2000, according to Guzer and Caner (2014). Young and Pettigrew (2014), found no published research on blended foreign language learning on a large scale until Adair-Hauck, Willingham-McLain, and Youngs (2000) presented the findings on the effectiveness of redesigned French courses at Carnegie Mellon University in a *CALICO Journal* article. In the period from 2000 to 2005, additional studies followed. This time period roughly covers what Guzer and Caner (2014) label as *First attempts* (1999–2002) and *Definition period* (2003–2006) when the idea of supporting face-to-face and online instruction began to be explored.

A sample of language learning studies is summarized in Table 11.1 as a basis for examining trends at this early stage. The majority investigated the effectiveness of blended learning by comparing traditional (face-to-face without computer-assisted language learning (CALL) instruction) and blended classes (face-to-face with CALL instruction). Additionally, authors looked at blended program design and implementation as well as student and teacher attitudes. In these studies, the majority of participants are beginner French and Spanish students in foreign language programs at universities.

The overarching goal of most studies was to show that learning gains were not compromised due to moving some instruction online and reducing face-to-face contact time. Researchers were making a case for blended learning showing that technology can effectively enhance and replace face-to-face instruction while bringing cost savings for the institution. Indeed, no comparative study found a significant difference between the performance of blended and control classes although some groups did better on measures of some skills (e.g., better writing performance of blended groups in Adair-Hauck et al. (2000) while traditional groups did better in Sanders (2005)). Results also indicated student satisfaction with blended courses (Ushida 2005) and perceived self-improvements (Adair-Hauck et al. 2000; Green and Youngs 2001). Not all course redesigns went smoothly; technical difficulties were reported in many of them (Adair-Hauck et al. 2000; Barr, Leakey, and Ranchoux, 2005; Echavez-Solano 2003).

As can be expected in comparative research, course materials and assessments were kept as similar as possible and a lot of attention was devoted to describing activities students did in the CALL mode (for more information see Grgurović 2010), but not the face-to-face mode. Additionally, firm theoretical grounding of blended learning research was missing from all works except Barr et al. (2005) and Ushida (2005), a fact that Young and Pettigrew (2014) attributed to the interests of funders. To encourage and support the transition from traditional to

**Table 11.1**   A sample of early blended learning studies in foreign language programs.

| Study and publication source | Type of study: C: comparative, NC: non-comparative | Language taught | Proficiency level | Institution |
|---|---|---|---|---|
| Adair-Hauck et al., (2000), *CALICO Journal* | C | French | Beginner | Carnegie Mellon University, USA |
| Green and Youngs (2001), *CALICO Journal* | C | French and German | Beginner | Carnegie Mellon University, USA |
| Echavez-Solano (2003), Doctoral dissertation | C | Spanish | Beginner | University of Minnesota, USA |
| Chenoweth and Murday (2003), *CALICO Journal* | C | French | Beginner | Carnegie Mellon University, USA |
| Barr et al., (2005), *Language Learning and Technology* | C | French | Beginner | University of Ulster, UK |
| Sanders (2005), *Foreign Language Annals* | C | Spanish | Beginner and intermediate | Portland State University, USA |
| Ushida (2005), *CALICO Journal* | NC | French and Spanish | Beginner and intermediate | Carnegie Mellon University, USA |

blended classes, between 1999 and 2002, the Pew Charitable Trust gave the National Center for Academic Transformation substantial funding which was distributed to university foreign language programs to study cost-effectiveness and quality of teaching and learning. The resulting reports provided models of important elements in course redesign including delivery of blended instruction (number of meetings and length, reduction in class times), materials (in class and online activities), course delivery (teaching assistants, lecturers), and savings achieved (number of students taught with fewer teaching staff). Consequently, blended learning research was shaped by these elements (for an example, see Sanders 2005). Early non-language specific blended learning research also focused on definitions, models, and potential for blended instruction without a clear theoretical framework (Halverson et al. 2012).

# Review of blended learning research: 2006–2014

Blended learning research increased dramatically after the early period (see Guzer and Caner 2014). The review in this chapter is based on research reviews similar to those used in other CALL studies by Zhao (2003), Vorobel and Kim (2012), and Wang and Vásquez (2012).

## Methodology

The collection of studies used in this review was done in two phases: Spring 2012 and Spring 2014. The first phase began with searching a number of online research databases: LLBA, ERIC, EBSCOHost, Web of Science, and Google Scholar. *CALICO Journal's* online archive was also reviewed for studies relevant to the search. The studies were searched using keyword combinations of *CALL, blended, hybrid, multimodal, learning, e-learning, language, teacher training, implementation, integration, shift, and transition*. A combination of two or three of these terms was entered at a time so, for example, queries such as *hybrid transition, CALL implementation, blended learning transition*, and *hybrid language learning* were used. The publication date was limited from 2006 to Spring 2012. Altogether, around 70 studies and three dissertations were found. Studies retrieved were divided into two groups: approximately 50 language specific studies and 20 in content areas other than language learning. From the language specific group, we[1] reviewed 19 empirical studies that explicitly used the terms *blended* or *hybrid* in the title, abstract, or keywords and reported on the experiences of language learners taking and instructors teaching these courses. This group includes 17 journal articles and two doctoral dissertations.

The second search phase continued with the publication date between January 2012 to April 2014. The second phase was conducted to include additional research and thus make the pool of studies as up-to-date as possible as well as to include MLA and JSTOR databases which were not searched in the previous phase. The keyword combination for the searches used the same type of keywords as the previous inquiry; *CALL, blended, hybrid, learning, language, teacher training, integration, shift and transition*, in addition to *university, implementing*, and *computer*. Keywords not used included *e-learning* and *multimodal*. Altogether, 107 studies were located, all published as research articles. All studies were divided into two groups: 44 language specific and 63 in content areas other than language learning. From the language specific group, seven studies fit the inclusion criteria. The 26 studies included in the review are in Appendix 2. In the next step, studies were annotated according to the following categories: citation, keywords, setting, institution, number of participants, language studied, proficiency levels, research questions, technology used, variables, data collection instruments, and findings (see Table 11.9 in Appendix 1 for the list and explanations). Next, the studies were divided into several thematic categories based on the area of inquiry. Finally, the annotations guided the thematic analysis which resulted in summaries of findings.

## Results

A content analysis of the 26 studies was performed by analyzing annotations, in particular, research questions, variables, and findings. The studies were divided into the following five categories by the topic of investigation: (1) comparative studies of non-blended and blended classes; (2) teacher perceptions; (3) learner perceptions; (4) specific technology tools; and (5) course implementation. Works that covered multiple topics were included in more than one category.

### Category 1: Comparative studies

The comparative studies category (see Table 11.2) contains six studies (Blake et al. 2008; Chenoweth et al. 2006; Gleason 2013a; O' Leary 2008; Scida and Saury 2006, and Young 2008) divided into two groups based on whether they compared: (1) traditional vs. blended classes and (2) different types of blended classes and blended versus fully online ones.

In this first group, the following authors: Blake et al. (2008), Chenoweth et al. (2006), O'Leary (2008), Scida and Saury (2006), and Young (2008) investigated the performance of students in non-blended and blended classes. Non-blended classes (also called traditional, conventional, offline, or comparison classes) were described as those meeting more frequently than blended classes and employing a hard-copy textbook and/or workbook. Blended classes (also called hybrid or experimental) replaced some face-to-face meetings with online components in a Learning Management System LMS (see Table 11.3).

**Table 11.2** Comparative studies in foreign language programs.

| Study and publication source | Language taught | Proficiency level | Institution |
|---|---|---|---|
| Blake et al., (2008), *Language Learning and Technology* | Spanish | Beginner and intermediate | University of California-Davis, USA |
| Chenoweth et al., (2006), *CALICO Journal* | French and Spanish | Beginner and intermediate | Carnegie Mellon University, USA |
| Gleason (2013a), *Foreign Language Annals* | Spanish | Intermediate | Iowa State University, USA |
| O'Leary (2008), Doctoral dissertation | Spanish | Beginner | University of Alabama, USA |
| Scida and Saury (2006), *CALICO Journal* | Spanish | Beginner | University of Virginia, USA |
| Young (2008), *CALICO Journal* | Spanish | Beginner | University of Tennessee, USA |

**Table 11.3** Classes in comparative studies of blended and non-blended courses.

| | Non-blended class | Blended class | |
|---|---|---|---|
| Study | Time (per week) | Time (per week) | Online activities |
| Blake et al. (2008) | 2 times for 3 hours | 7 hours | Students did vocabulary and grammar activities, text and voice chat, and used CDs/DVD. |
| Chenoweth et al. (2006) | 1 hour in class, 20 min with instructor in groups or individually | 20 min | Students did text chat, sent e-mail messages, posted on the bulletin board, and did exercises in *Hot Potatoes*. |
| Gleason (2013a) | 4 times total for 3 hours and 20 min | 2 hours 5 min | Students did voice and text chat in Adobe Connect working on vocabulary and grammar exercises. |
| O'Leary (2008) | 4 times | 1 class period | Students did writing practice in cyber journals and completed web searches and practice quizzes. |
| Scida and Saury (2006) | 3 times | 2 hours | Students did structured vocabulary and grammar activities and practice in listening, reading, and writing. |
| Young (2008) | 2 times | Not reported | Students did online workbook activities and asynchronous writing assignments. |

The goals of first group were to determine: (1) if the mode of course delivery (blended vs. non-blended) significantly impacted student performance and (2) whether the reduction of face-to-face contact time disadvantaged blended learning students; the same research trend as in early blended research studies (2000–2005).

In the second subgroup, Gleason (2013a) and Young (2008) compared two blended formats while Blake et al. (2008) examined blended and distance learning classes. While Young (2008) and Blake et al. (2008) compared students' performance statistically, Gleason (2013a) analyzed students and teachers' discourse in different types of tasks (online and offline).

The results of the first group show that, overall, no statistically significant differences were found between learners in non-blended and blended classes (see a detailed explanation of findings in Table 11.4 above). Since most authors examined multiple classes, variables, and assessment measures, better performances of non-blended or blended groups were sometimes found but, on the whole, the students exhibited equal performance. A compelling support for blended learning was found in comparable gains in speaking skills which were sometimes cited as a cause of student concern in earlier research (see Adair-Hauck et al. 1999). Finally, it was found that blended courses do not put learners at a disadvantage but bring in advantages of logistical (e.g., cost reduction in O'Leary 2008) as well as pedagogical nature (e.g., better student preparation for in-class meetings in Young 2008). These findings are consistent with conclusions in many early blended learning research studies (2000–2005) and further confirm the trend of equal performance regardless of the delivery mode.

The results of the second group of studies are similar as no significant differences were found between two and three-day face-to-face blended classes (Young 2008) nor between fully online and blended ones (Blake et al. 2008). Gleason (2013a) found that some synchronous online tasks could be set up better to promote negotiation of meaning between students as well as with the instructor, involve all students, allow for focus on fluency, and promote real-life language use.

## Category 2: Teacher perceptions

Seven studies investigated teacher perceptions of and experience teaching blended courses (Chenoweth et al. 2006; Comas-Quinn 2011; Gleason 2013b; Murday et al. 2008; Scida and Saury 2006; Shelley et al. 2013, and Yang 2014) (Table 11.5). The themes that emerge are: (1) technological, curricular, and pedagogical changes necessary for blended instruction, and (2) importance of training for teaching blended classes and teacher development.

The first research interest in this category was identifying changes blended instruction brings when it comes to technology, materials, and pedagogy. Chenoweth et al. (2006), Murday et al. (2008), and Comas-Quinn (2011) reported that novice blended learning teachers quickly realized that online teaching is different from face-to-face teaching. Comas-Quinn echoes the views of other authors who all claim that online language teaching requires a set of skills different from face-to-face teaching but also from teaching in non-language specific disciplines. Face-to-face teaching techniques were modified and extended in blended environments (Shelley, Murphy, and White 2013). Teachers reported that the first semester of teaching blended courses was the most challenging, but that they grew more comfortable after second and third semesters (Chenoweth et al. 2006; Murday et al. 2008). Technical difficulties were some of the challenges faced (Chenoweth et al. 2006; Comas-Quinn 2011; Murday et al. 2008; Shelley et al. 2013; Yang, 2014) continuing the trend from the early research.

In a new course format, teachers had to adjust in terms of materials selected and covered. Some teachers decreased the amount of chat time especially at lower proficiency levels to allow students to stay on task (Murday et al. 2008). Blended course teachers (Gleason 2013b) reported insufficient time to cover the same amount of material as in the traditional class.

**Table 11.4** Findings of comparative studies of blended and non-blended courses.

| Study | Number of classes (non-blended+ blended) | Number of students (non-blended+ blended) | Variables | Findings |
|---|---|---|---|---|
| Blake et al. (2008) | Not reported | 233+65 | Oral proficiency | *No significant differences on oral proficiency measures.* |
| Chenoweth et al. (2006) | 21+ 13 | 191+80* | Listening and reading comprehension, grammar knowledge, vocabulary, and written and oral production | *No significant difference between groups on all outcomes measures listed on the left.* Exceptions: one non-blended group performed better in vocabulary outcome measures; two non-blended groups performed better in listening and reading comprehension outcome measures; three non-blended groups performed better in grammar knowledge outcome measures. One blended learning group performed better in oral production and one on written production measures. <br><br> * Number for grammar tests: other tests had different numbers of participants. |
| Gleason (2013a) | 1+1 | 28+20 | Language production | Not all tasks are equally comparable between non-blended and blended formats regarding the learning process, type of interaction, involvement of students, scaffolding, and language use. |
| O'Leary (2008) | 1+2 | 36+40 | Oral proficiency, written production, grammar, reading comprehension, and cultural knowledge | *No significant differences in the final exam* which comprised grammar, reading comprehension, writing, and cultural knowledge measures. *No significant differences* on written production measures (compositions) and *oral proficiency measures (midterm oral exam).* |
| Scida and Saury (2006) | 1+1 | 22+19 | Course grades | Median course grade higher for blended learning group. |
| Young (2008) | 5+5 (initial study) | 112 + 97 | Listening, reading, and speaking proficiency | *No significant differences between groups on listening and reading proficiency measures.* No significant difference in the final exam. More varied and enriched language use was demonstrated by students in the blended learning group in the speaking test. The non-blended group performed significantly better in the midterm exam. |

**Table 11.5**   Teacher perceptions studies in foreign language programs.

| Study and publication source | Type of study (C/NC) | Language taught | Proficiency level | Institution |
|---|---|---|---|---|
| Chenoweth et al. (2006), *CALICO Journal* | C | French and Spanish | Beginner and intermediate | Carnegie Mellon University, USA |
| Comas-Quinn (2011), *ReCALL Journal* | NC | Spanish | Not reported | Open University, UK |
| Gleason (2013b), *CALICO Journal* | NC | Spanish | Intermediate | Iowa State University, USA |
| Murday et al. (2008), *CALL Journal* | NC | French and Spanish | Intermediate | Carnegie Mellon University, USA |
| Scida and Saury (2006), *CALICO Journal* | C | Spanish | Beginner | University of Virginia, USA |
| Shelley et al. (2013), *System* | NC | French, German, Spanish, Italian, Dutch, and Mandarin | Not reported | Universities in UK and Australasia |
| Yang (2014), *CALL Journal* | NC | EFL | Not reported | A university in Taiwan |

Teachers in Comas-Quinn (2011) learned that online activities should be integrated into the course (for instance through assessments), so that students would perceive them as required and complete them.

Pedagogical changes identified involved (1) establishing a learning community and (2) a shift in teacher and student roles. Some teachers had difficulties forming relationships with learners due to reduced face-to-face time (Gleason 2013b; Shelley et al. 2013; Yang 2014). On the other hand, some instructors reported being able to get to know students better because of the shift in traditional roles of teachers and students (Shelley et al. 2013) and because blended classes improved teacher-student interaction and feedback exchange (Yang 2014). In the latter study teachers felt they were facilitating the learning process more than dominating it (also reported in Snodin 2013); a teacher-centered methodology was previously observed in these face-to-face university classrooms in Taiwan. Another pedagogical change involved paying increased attention to online communication with students which had to be very clear due to the absence of facial expressions, hand gestures, and body language present in face-to-face interactions (Gleason 2013b; Shelley et al. 2013). One last example of a pedagogical change was reported in Scida and Saury (2006) by teaching assistants (TAs) in blended classes who spent more class time on communicative activities and writing practice than in traditional courses. Moreover, all TAs did less in-class vocabulary presentations and 90% did fewer grammar presentations and practice.

The second theme shared by a number of studies was the importance of teacher preparation for blended instruction. A successful language teacher-training program, according to Comas-Quinn (2011), should be gradual, well-supported, and well-integrated and should require teachers' time, effort, and commitment. In this training, new skills and competencies (both both technical and pedagogical) need to be developed. A training program should go beyond familiarization with online tools to address methodological choices and explain how they are informed by SLA theory, CALL research, and communicative-language teaching practices. Teachers base opinions about language learning on their education and experience so advantages of the online environment may not be immediately visible to some. An excellent example is a comment from a teacher in Comas-Quinn (2011) who sees face-to-face instruction as superior to online instruction due to social interaction and communication it allows. In response, Comas-Quinn calls for support and guidance from teacher trainers and peers. One possible way is a creation of a teachers' community where instructors discuss students' difficulties with colleagues or a teacher trainer (see Yang 2014). In settings where teacher training is not readily available, significant individuals and peer collaboration helped teachers develop professionally (Shelley et al. 2013).

## Category 3: Learner perceptions

Learner perceptions, views, and attitudes of students presents the largest category with 16 studies (see Table 11.6). The following studies were included: Banados (2006), Chenoweth et al. (2006), Gleason (2013b), Goertler, Bollen, and Gaff (2012), Grgurović (2011), Jochum (2011), Kramer (2008a, 2008b), Murday et al. (2008), Sagarra and Zapata (2008), Scida and Saury (2006), Snodin (2013), Stracke (2007), Wichadee (2013), Winke and Goertler (2008), and Winke, Goertler, and Amuzie (2010). The studies were subdivided into those examining: (1) satisfaction with blended learning; (2) readiness for blended instruction, and (3) ways to improve students' experience. While not being their major focus, many of the 26 studies in this review investigated some aspects of learner perceptions indicating a continued trend from early blended learning research.

In the first thematic category, learner satisfaction, student surveys were the most frequently used data collection methods. Overall, the authors concluded that students were pleased with their blended courses. For example, 91% of students in Jochum (2011) and 94% in Scida and Saury (2006) reported satisfaction with Spanish blended instruction. This increase in student comfort level from the pre- to post-course survey was found to be statistically significant (Jochum 2011). Similarly, in Sagarra and Zapata (2008), two-thirds of learners showed the desire to take another blended Spanish course. In Murday et al. (2008), final course evaluation data indicated that students in blended classes increased their satisfaction in comparison to offline students over time.

Flexibility was cited as the main reason students choose blended courses (see Kraemer, 2008a). For example, in Goertler et al. (2012), 70% of students liked the decrease in face-to-face contact hours from five to three days a week, while the reduced class schedule was the main reasons students took the class (Murday et al. 2008). Similarly, in Scida and Saury (2006), blended courses were preferred not only to five-day non-blended courses but also to online courses.

In the second thematic category, readiness to take blended classes was investigated in several studies at Michigan State University (Goertler et al. 2012; Winke and Goertler 2008; Winke et al. 2010). These studies analyzed the data from a large sample of 2,149 general population students (Winke at el. 2010) or its 911-student subset (Goertler et al. 2012; Winke and Goertler 2008) not all of which were blended language learners and in addition 37 students in two Spanish blended classes (Goertler et al. 2012).

Overall results show that positive or negative previous technology experiences may have an impact on student preferences to take a blended class. Students explained the lack of interest with the fear online instruction will take away valuable face-to-face interaction which may impact oral skills development (Winke and Goertler 2008). In addition to quantitative evidence that oral skills do not suffer in blended environments (see the findings of comparative studies above), Gleason's qualitative data (2013b) show that online speaking practice "pushed" a shy student to increase participation in the face-to-face part of the class.

**Table 11.6** Learner perceptions studies

| Study and publication source | Type of study (C/NC) | Language taught | Proficiency level | Institution | Setting (foreign/second language program) |
|---|---|---|---|---|---|
| Banados (2006), CALICO Journal | NC | EFL | Not reported | Universidad de Concepción, Chile | Foreign |
| Chenoweth et al. (2006), CALICO Journal | C | French and Spanish | Beginner and intermediate | Carnegie Mellon University, USA | Foreign |
| Gleason (2013b), CALICO Journal | NC | Spanish | Intermediate | Iowa State University, USA | Foreign |
| Goertler et al. (2012), CALICO Journal | NC | French, German and Spanish | Beginner and intermediate | Michigan State University, USA | Foreign |
| Grgurović (2011), CALICO Journal | NC | ESL | Intermediate | Iowa State University, USA | Second |
| Jochum (2011), Journal of Instructional Psychology | NC | Spanish | Advanced | A university in the USA | Foreign |
| Kramer (2008a), Die Unterrichtspraxis | NC | German | Advanced | Michigan State University, USA | Foreign |
| Kramer (2008b), Doctoral dissertation | NC | German | Advanced | Michigan State University, USA | Foreign |
| Murday et al. (2008), CALL Journal | NC | French and Spanish | Intermediate | Carnegie Mellon University, USA | Foreign |
| Sagarra and Zapata (2008), ReCALL Journal | NC | Spanish | Beginner | A university in the USA | Foreign |
| Scida and Saury (2006), CALICO Journal | C | Spanish | Beginner | University of Virginia, USA | Foreign |
| Snodin (2013), Computers and Education | NC | EFL | Intermediate | Kasetsart University, Thailand | Foreign |

| Study | | Language | Level | Location | |
| --- | --- | --- | --- | --- | --- |
| Stracke (2007), *ReCALL Journal* | NC | French and Spanish | Not reported | University of Münster, Germany | Foreign |
| Wichadee (2013), *Electronic Journal of Research in Educational psychology* | NC | EFL | Not reported | A university in Taiwan | Foreign |
| Winke et al. (2010), *CALL Journal* | NC | Commonly and less commonly taught languages | All levels | Michigan State University, USA | Foreign |
| Winke and Goertler (2008), *CALICO Journal* | NC | French, German, and Spanish | Beginner and intermediate | Michigan State University, USA | Foreign |

The survey by Winke and Goertler (2008) also showed that the learners had good access to computers and the Internet, but lacked technological resources like digital cameras, microphones, web cameras, and headphones, necessary for "higher-tech" blended courses that could include podcasting, video-conferencing, and virtual realities. Moreover, both general population students and blended course participants in Goertler et al. (2012) reported having basic computer-literacy skills (e.g., using the Internet, emailing) but not so many advanced multimedia skills (e.g., developing websites, editing video). Through a further analysis, Winke et al. (2010) found that less commonly taught language students and students studying languages with non-Roman alphabets had lower technology literacy levels relative to other language students. As a result, Goertler et al. (2012) concluded that foreign language students may be ready for "low-tech" blended courses consisting of online workbook activities, Internet activities, and traditional CMC activities such as discussion boards, chats, and emails. Other than Wichadee's study (2013) which included video-conferencing, all studies in this review investigated "low-tech" courses indicating an appropriate fit between learner readiness and the state of blended course delivery. Winke and Goertler (2008), Goertler et al. (2012), and Winke et al. (2010) call for student training which would be both course-initial and ongoing.

In the third thematic group, improving learner experience, researchers paid attention to difficulties and challenges students had reported. The difficulties were found to be in relation to: course materials, course design, and learner skills. The lack of printed materials (Chenoweth et al. 2006; Murday et al. 2008; Stracke 2007) was cited as a main difficulty as students preferred to use a hard-copy textbook or workbook when the computer was not accessible. To some students, textbooks appeared to be more structured than online materials and thus easier to use (Chenoweth et al. 2006). In this case, a happy medium consists of both online and hard-copy materials; many publishers already offer this bundle usually at no additional cost.

The first course design issue included a lack of a clearly established course structure such as knowing types of online assignments and due dates and having a specific work plan (Chenoweth et al. 2006; Murday et al. 2008). The second challenge was a lack of integration between online and face-to-face components (Stracke 2007). In Stracke, students expressed a concern that face-to-face sessions did not directly tie to individual work with the CD-ROM which comprised their blended course. To address this issue, some blended learning instructors successfully established procedures to strengthen the connection. For instance, Kraemer (2008b) shared examples of students' online work in class and used them as a starting point for discussion. The instructor in Grgurović (2011) provided feedback on common pronunciation errors in class, always reminded students to check online feedback, and monitored students' progress in the LMS. When this group was surveyed, 94% of students reported seeing a clear connection between online and face-to-face work.

Problems with time management and learner persistence were connected to the lack of learner skills (Chenoweth et al. 2006; Murday et al. 2008; Stracke 2007). The authors stress that students needed to understand deadlines, study regularly, and not fall behind. Additionally, students needed an increased amount of self-discipline and self-regulation. Snodin (2013) gives a description of two autonomous learners who demonstrated the following skills in the online environment: setting their own goals, planning for practice to achieve the goals, and developing skills to monitor and evaluate learning.

## Category 4: Technology tools studies

The four studies in this category (Barragan 2009; Kraemer 2008b; Miyazoe and Anderson 2009; and Sagarra and Zapata 2008) investigated specific technology tools and how learners perceived and used them. Additionally, Sagarra and Zapata (2008) examined student performance gains (see Table 11.7).

**Table 11.7** Non-comparative technology tools studies in foreign language programs.

| Study and publication source | Language taught | Proficiency level | Institution |
| --- | --- | --- | --- |
| Barragan (2009), *Profile Issues in Teachers' Professional Development* | EFL | Not reported | Universidad Nacional de Colombia, Colombia |
| Kramer (2008b), Doctoral dissertation | German | Advanced | Michigan State University, USA |
| Miyazoe and Anderson (2009), *System* | EFL | Intermediate | A university in Japan |
| Sagarra and Zapata (2008), *ReCALL Journal* | Spanish | Beginner | A university in the USA |

Overall, discussion boards, blogs, wikis, electronic workbooks, and chats were the main tools used in blended contexts. On discussion boards, Barragan (2009) had students practice writing and argumentative skills, reflect on the learning process, and cooperate with peers on a cultural project. Discussion boards were found useful for the development of writing skills (Barragan 2009; Miyazoe and Anderson 2009), and autonomous learning (Barragan, 2009) while wikis were seen as useful for translation skills (Miyazoe and Anderson 2009). Kraemer's (2008b) students ranked chats, discussion boards, and blogs the highest due to peer collaboration they enabled.

Students in Sagarra and Zapata (2008) interacted with an electronic workbook which contained input and output grammar and vocabulary activities, a listening activity, and a content-based reading activity in each weekly homework set. The learners found multiple attempts, ability to work at one's own pace, and immediate feedback very beneficial. Their grammar scores increased from the second to the third semester of use; vocabulary and reading scores remained the same, and listening scores decreased (because of more difficult exams according to the authors).

These results show that a variety of online tools can be employed and that their perceived effectiveness may be context-dependent. The choice of tools should be made having specific linguistic outcomes in mind, while the outcome will partly depend on the task set up. For example, the highest rated wiki translation project from English to Japanese could not have so easily been done on paper and took the advantage of the online medium for easy access and collaboration (Miyazoe and Anderson 2009). Useful guidelines on how to set up online tasks, particularly synchronous audio or text chat, can be found in Gleason (2013a).

## Category 5: Course implementation

This is the smallest group with two studies (Grgurović 2011 and Hinkelman and Gruba 2012) (Table 11.8). They share the overall topic of blended course implementation with subtopics of blended course design, teaching materials, and facilities. The data were collected through class observations and interviews with instructors.

Both studies used commercially produced materials which were preferred to the teacher-created ones. A commercial LMS in Grgurović (2011) met the needs of teachers and students while in Hinkelman and Gruba (2012) teachers used open source LMS which they could design and customize without specialized software or skills. The ease of use should be a main consideration for a choice of an LMS. These studies also indicate important points for the design of blended classrooms (movable chairs and desks with computers against the walls), integration of face-to-face and online work, and choice of online materials; many of these were discussed previously.

**Table 11.8**   Non-comparative course implementation studies.

| Study and publication source | Language taught | Proficiency level | Institution | Setting (foreign/ second language program) |
|---|---|---|---|---|
| Grgurović (2011), *CALICO Journal* | ESL | Intermediate | Iowa State University, USA | Second |
| Hinkelman and Gruba (2012), *Language Learning and Technology* | EFL | Not reported | Two universities in Japan | Foreign |

# Blended learning: Important considerations

Based on the research reviewed, four main themes emerged as important considerations for the development and investigation of blended learning: (1) theoretical background, (2) effectiveness and value, (3) teachers, and (4) students.

## *Theoretical background in blended learning studies*

The analysis of a sample of early blended learning research studies (those published before/ in 2005) indicated that most were missing theoretical conceptualization, focusing instead on describing models and logistics of their implementation. The potential of blended learning was viewed through the lens of cost-effectiveness and quality of teaching and learning. In the more recent sample of 26 studies (2006 to 2014), theory begins to appear: Shelley et al. (2013) used a framework from Borg (2006) as a guide for studying teacher cognition; Grgurović (2011) employed Neumeier's framework (2005) to describe a blended learning class; Gleason (2013a) drew on an interpretive argument framework (Chapelle 2012) to guide the comparison of online and face-to-face tasks in blended classes; Gleason (2013b) applied a knowledge framework (Mohan 1986) to an analysis of student and teacher blended experiences; and Hinkelman and Gruba (2012) were guided by actor-network theory (Latour 2005) in the study of power within blended programs. These works provide a step in the right direction as they show that research can be grounded in frameworks used in other areas of applied linguistics (knowledge framework from systemic functional linguistics and validity argument from language assessment), frameworks from other disciplines (actor-network theory from education) as well as frameworks developed by blended learning researchers themselves (framework for blended teaching and learning of languages, Neumeier 2005). Researchers can also consider theoretical grounding of research in other disciplines; Online Learning Consortium quality framework (Online Learning Consortium website) and the Community of Inquiry (Akyol, Vaughan, and Garrison 2011) are just some examples.

## *Effectiveness and value of blended learning*

After examining the results of comparative studies, this review found no statistically significant differences between blended and non-blended groups across language skills and assessment measures, the same finding as in early research. These results are consistent with "no significant difference findings" in other works such as the meta-analysis by Grgurović, Chapelle, and Shelley (2013) who found that "second/foreign language instruction supported by computer technology was at least as effective as instruction without technology" (27). In another meta-analysis, Means et al. (2010) concluded that "instruction combining online and face-to-face elements had a larger advantage relative to purely face-to-face instruction than did purely online instruction" (xv) further showing the blended learning advantage in a number of content areas. This body of evidence indicates that blended learning does not disadvantage students. This appears to be the case even when it comes to the development of speaking skills (Blake et al. 2008; Chenoweth et al. 2006).

While blended language learning has strengthened its legitimacy through this line of research, a number of scholars believe that the time and effort that go into setting up comparative studies is better spent pursuing other lines of inquiry (Blake 2014; Goertler 2011). First, the authors point to the difficulties of conducting comparative research such as keeping all requirements parallel and minimizing extraneous variables. Second, most comparative studies put a strong focus on the description of the online environment unlike the face-to-face one. As a result, it is challenging to understand the set-up of different models and further compare them. Finally, at the beginning of the 21st century it will be difficult to find face-to-face, traditional courses that do not integrate any technology.

## *Participants in blended instruction: Teachers*

The review showed that teachers should be trained for technological, curricular, and pedagogical changes that blended learning environments bring. Teachers should understand that hardware, software, and network difficulties will likely be present and know how to assist their learners. They should also understand curricular choices regarding the selection of in-class and online materials, tasks, assessments, and online tools. Finally, pedagogical decisions about the use of face-to-face and online modes and ways to strengthen their integration should be clear to instructors. Best practices show that the online component must be seen as an essential part of the course and that connections between online and face-to-face work should be made in class (Kraemer 2008b; Grgurović 2011). According to research into online teacher preparation, teaching skills required for making such connections are unlikely to develop without training (Compton 2009). As opposed to a one-time training session, a number of opportunities to develop new expertise and skills should exist (for suggestions of teacher development techniques see Gallardo, Heiser, and Nicolson 2011).

## *Participants in blended instruction: Students*

Learners also need training because many lack advanced computer-literacy skills and technological resources necessary for high-tech blended classes that would employ, for example, video-conferencing and podcasting. This lack was particularly noticeable with less commonly taught and non-Roman alphabet language students. Learners also need help to develop the independent study skills, persistence, and motivation for work in the online environment where they operate without direct teacher control. Recognition of the need for learner training in CALL is not new (Hubbard 2013). One study found that the learners themselves were aware of this. In the 2012 ECAR study, 64% of undergraduate students believed that it is "very or extremely important to be better trained or skilled at using technologies to learn, study or complete coursework" (Dahlstrom 2012, 22). The blended learning literature suggests that learner training should share many of its attributes with teacher training: gradual, technological, and pedagogical in nature. Research in language learning strategies (see Macaro 2001 and Oxford 2011) shows that spreading out learner training works better than isolated interventions. The technological aspect of training should include both the hands-on (*how*) and the rationale (*why*) of using online tools while the pedagogical side should help students with strategies to use the online tools successfully.

# Conclusion

The 26 studies analyzed in the review reveal the major trends in blended language learning through 2014 even though it is possible that some additional studies not using the terms "blended" or "hybrid" exist. The positive findings suggest that blended learning is likely to continue as the preferred approach to language teaching and learning in the future. Future blended learning platforms will undoubtedly continue to evolve by using new technologies such as mobile technologies and learning analytics to create more customized learning opportunities for students. Mobile devices may become the primary access point for most of our students as their physical (e.g., small screen size of cell phones), psychological (e.g., students questioning whether cell phones can be a language learning tool) and pedagogical issues (e.g., activities suited for mobile delivery) are gradually overcome (for a detailed discussion see Stockwell 2012). Learner analytics are being explored as a way to personalize instruction and help predict learners' success and identify at-risk students based on their interaction and behavior within the LMS. As blended learning continues to evolve, it will continue to be important to develop the theory-pedagogy connections that are evident in recent research on blended language learning.

# Appendix 1

**Table 11.9**  Annotated categories used in the review.

| Category | Definition | Use of category |
|---|---|---|
| Citation | Full reference of the work | To check for inclusion criteria |
| Keywords | Keywords and primary author(s) used to describe the study | To check for inclusion criteria |
| Setting | Educational setting (primary, secondary, higher) and type of language program | To give more information about the context of the study |
| Institution | Name of the institution (if known) | To give more information about the context of the study |
| Number of participants | Number of students and teachers taking part in the study | To show the number of participants per study (e.g., see Table 11.4) |
| Language studied | Language(s) studied by student participants or taught by teachers | To provide info about individual studies (e.g., see Table 11.2) |
| Proficiency levels | Language proficiency level of student participants | To describe findings within thematic categories |
| Research questions | Research questions | To guide the organization of thematic categories; to check the type of study so categorization can be made |
| Technology used | List of technologies used in the study | To describe technologies in the specific technology tools section (see Category 4) and most common technologies within thematic categories (e.g., see Table 11.3) |

| Variables | Independent and dependent variables | To describe most common variables within thematic categories or variables in individual studies (e.g., see Table 11.4) |
|---|---|---|
| Data collection instruments | Measures used to collect data | To describe most common measures within thematic categories |
| Findings | Summary of results | To guide the organization of thematic categories; to describe findings within each thematic category or in individual studies (e.g., see Table 11.4) |

# Appendix 2

## *Studies included in the review*

Banados, Emerita. 2006. "A Blended-Learning Pedagogical Model for Teaching and Learning EFL Successfully through an Online Interactive Multimedia Environment." *CALICO Journal*, 23, no. 3: 533–550.

Barragan, Diana Isabel. 2009. "Discussion Boards as Tools in Blended EFL Learning Programs." *PROFILE*, 11, no. 1: 107–121.

Blake, Robert, Nicole L. Wilson, Maria Cetto, and Cristina Pardo-Ballester. 2008. "Measuring Oral Proficiency in Distance, Face-to-Face, and Blended Classrooms." *Language Learning & Technology*, 12, no. 3: 114–127.

Chenoweth, Ann N., Eiko Ushida, and Kimmaree Murday. 2006. "Student Learning in Hybrid French and Spanish Courses: An Overview of Language Online." *CALICO Journal*, 24 no. 1: 115–146.

Comas-Quinn, Anna. 2011. "Learning to Teach Online Or Learning to Become an Online Teacher: An Exploration of Teachers' Experiences in a Blended Learning Course." *ReCALL*, 23, no. 3: 218–232.

Gleason, Jesse. 2013a. "An Interpretive Argument for Blended Course Design." *Foreign Language Annals*, 46, no. 4: 588–609.

Gleason, Jesse. 2013b. "Dilemmas of Blended Language Learning: Learner and Teacher Experiences." *CALICO Journal*, 30 no. 3: 323–341.

Goertler, Senta, Magelone Bollen, and Joel Gaff Jr. 2012. "Students; Readiness for and Attitudes Toward Hybrid FL Instruction." *CALICO Journal*, 29, no. 2: 297–320.

Grgurović, Maja. 2011. "Blended Learning in an ESL Class: A Case Study." *CALICO Journal*, 29, no. 1: 100–117.

Hinkelman, Don, and Paul Gruba. 2012. "Power within Blended Language Learning Programs in Japan." *Language Learning & Technology*, 16, no. 2: 46–64.

Jochum, Chris J. 2011. "Blended Spanish Instruction: Perceptions and Design: A Case Study." *Journal of Instructional Psychology*, 38, no. 1: 40–46.

Kraemer, Angelika. 2008a. "Happily Ever After: Integrating Language and Literature through Technology." *Unterrichtspraxis/Teaching German*, 41, no. 1: 61–70.

Kraemer, Angelika. 2008b. "Engaging the Foreign Language Learner: Using Hybrid Instruction to Bridge the Language-Literature Gap." Unpublished PhD dissertation, Michigan State University.

Miyazoe, Terumi, and Terry Anderson. 2010. "Learning Outcomes and Students' Perceptions of Online Writing: Simultaneous Implementation of a Forum, Blog, and Wiki in an EFL Blended Learning Setting." *System*, 38, no. 2: 185–199.

Murday, Kimmaree, Eiko Ushida, and Ann N. Chenoweth. 2008. "Learners' and Teachers' Perspectives on Language Online." *Computer Assisted Language Learning*, 21, no. 2: 125–142.

O'Leary, Malinda Blair. 2008. A Case Study of Student Learning Outcomes Based on the Implementation of a Blended Course Format in Introductory Spanish. Unpublished PhD dissertation, University of Alabama, Birmingham.

Sagarra, Nuria, and Gabriela C. Zapata. 2008. "Blending Classroom Instruction with Online

Homework: A Study of Student Perceptions of Computer-Assisted L2 Learning." *ReCALL*, 20, no. 2: 208–224.

Scida, Emily E., and Rachel E. Saury. 2006. "Hybrid Courses and their Impact on Student and Classroom Performance: A Case Study at the University of Virginia." *CALICO Journal*, 23, no. 3: 517–531.

Shelley, Monica, Linda Murphy, and Cynthia J. White. 2013. "Language Teacher Development in a Narrative Frame: The Transition from Classroom to Distance and Blended Settings." *System*, 41, no. 3: 560–574.

Snodin, Navaporn. 2013. "The Effects of Blended Learning with a CMS on the Development of Autonomous Learning: A Case Study of Different Degrees of Autonomy Achieved by Individual Learners." *Computers & Education*, 61: 209–216.

Stracke, Elke. 2007. "A Road to Understanding: A Qualitative Study into Why Learners Drop Out of a Blended Language Learning (Bll) Environment." *ReCALL*, 19, no. 1: 57–78.

Wichadee, Saovapa. 2013. "Facilitating Students' Learning with Hybrid Instruction: A Comparison among Four Learning Styles." *Electronic Journal of Research in Educational Psychology*, 11, no. 1: 99–116.

Winke, Paula, and Senta Goertler. 2008. "Did we Forget Someone? Students' Computer Access and Literacy for CALL." *CALICO Journal*, 25, no. 3: 482–509.

Winke, Paula, Senta Goertler, and Grace L. Amuzie. 2010. "Commonly Taught and Less Commonly Taught Language Learners: Are they Equally Prepared for CALL and Online Language Learning?" *Computer Assisted Language Learning*, 23, no. 3: 199–219.

Yang, Yu-Fen. 2014. "Preparing Language Teachers for Blended Teaching of Summary Writing." *Computer Assisted Language Learning*, 27, no. 3: 185–206.

Young, Dolly. 2008. "An Empirical Investigation of the Effects of Blended Learning on Student Outcomes in a Redesigned Intensive Spanish Course." *CALICO Journal*, 26, no. 1: 160–181.

# NOTE

1   The author would like to thank Mark Augustine and Bianca Gavin for their help in this stage of the review.

# REFERENCES

Adair-Hauck, Bonie, Laurel Willingham-McLain, and Bonnie Youngs. 2000. "Evaluating the Integration of Technology and Second Language Learning." *CALICO Journal*, 17, no. 2: 296–306.

Akyol, Zehra, Norm Vaughan, and Randy Garrison. 2011. "The Impact of Course Duration on the Development of a Community of Inquiry." *Interactive Learning Environments*, 19, no. 3: 231–246.

Allen, Elaine, Jeff Seaman, and Richard Garrett. 2007. *Blending in: The Extent and Promise of Blended Education in the United States.* Needham, MA: Babson Research Group.

Allen, Elaine, Jeff Seaman, Doug Lederman, and Scott Jaschik. 2012. *Digital Faculty: Professors,*

*Teaching and Technology.* Needham, MA: Babson Research Group.

Barr, David, Jonathan Leakey, and Alexandre Ranchoux. 2005. "Told Like it is! An Evaluation of an Integrated Oral Development Pilot Project." *Language Learning & Technology*, 9 no. 3: 55–78.

Blake, Robert. 2014. "Best Practices in Online Learning: Is it for Everyone?" In *Hybrid language Teaching and Learning: Exploring Theoretical, Pedagogical and Curricular Issues*, edited by Fernando Rubio and Joshua Thoms, 10–26. Boston, MA: Heinle Cengage Learning.

Blended Learning Toolkit. 2015. "What is Blended Learning?" Accessed May 11, 2015.

https://blended.online.ucf.edu/about/what-is-blended-learning/

Borg, Simon. 2006. *Teacher Cognition and Language Education: Research and Practice*. London: Bloomsbury Publishing.

Chapelle, Carol. 2012. "Validity Argument for Language Assessment: The Framework is Simple. …" *Language Testing*, 29, no. 1: 19–27.

Chenoweth, Ann N., and Kimmaree Murday. 2003. "Measuring Student Learning in an Online French Course."*CALICO Journal*, 20, no. 2: 285–314.

Compton, Lily K. L. 2009. "Preparing Language Teachers to Teach Language Online: A Look at Skills, Roles, and Responsibilities." *Computer Assisted Language Learning* 22, no. 1: 73–99.

Dahlstrom, Eden. 2012. *ECAR Study of Undergraduate Students and Information Technology, 2012*. Louisville, CO: EDUCAUSE Center for Applied Research. Accessed May 30, 2013. http://www.educause.edu/ecar

Dziuban, Charles, Joel Hartman, and George Mehaffy. 2014. "Blending it All Together." In *Blended Learning: Research Perspective, Vol. 2*, edited by Anthony. G. Picciano, Charles. D. Dziuban, and Charles Graham, 325–337. New York: Routledge.

Echavez-Solano, Nelsy. 2003. A Comparison of Student Outcomes and Attitudes in Technology-Enhanced vs. Traditional Second-Semester Spanish Language Courses. Unpublished PhD dissertation, University of Minnesota.

Gallardo, Matilde, Sarah Heiser, and Margaret Nicolson. 2011. "Practical Approaches for Teacher Development." In *Language Teaching in Blended Contexts*, edited by Margaret Nicolson, Linda Murphy, and Margaret Southgate, 232–245. Edinburgh: Dunedin.

Goertler, Senta. 2011. "Blended and Open/online Learning: Adapting to a Changing World of Language Teaching." In *Present and Future Promises of CALL: From Theory and Research to New Directions in Language Teaching*, edited by Nike Arnolds and Lara Ducate, 471–501. San Marcos, TX: CALICO.

Graham, Charles. 2006. "Blended Learning Systems: Definitions, Current Trends, and Future Directions." In *The Handbook of Blended Learning: Global Perspectives, Local Designs*, edited by Curtis Bonk and Charles Graham, 3–21. San Francisco, CA: Pfeifer.

Graham, Charles, and Charles Dziuban. 2008. "Blended Learning Environments." In *Handbook of Research on Educational Communications and Technology*, edited by Michael Spector, David Merrill, and Jan Elen. 270–274. New York: Lawrence Erlbaum.

Green, Ann, and Bonnie E. Youngs. 2001. "Using the Web in Elementary French and German Courses: Quantitative and Qualitative Study Results." *CALICO Journal*, 19, no. 1: 89–123.

Grgurović, Maja. 2010. Technology-Enhanced Blended Language Learning in an ESL Class: A Description of a Model and an Application of the Diffusion of Innovations Theory. Unpublished PhD dissertation, Iowa State University.

Grgurović, Maja, Carol A. Chapelle, and Mack C. Shelley. 2013. "A Meta-Analysis of Effectiveness Studies on Computer Technology-Supported Language Learning." *ReCALL*, 25, no. 2: 165–198.

Gruba, Paul, and Don Hinkelman. 2012. *Blending Technologies in Second Language Classrooms*. New York: Palgrave Macmillan.

Guzer, Bayram, and Hamit Caner. 2014. The Past, Present and Future of Blended Learning: An in Depth Analysis of Literature. *Procedia-Social and Behavioral Sciences*, 116: 4596–4603.

Halverson, Lisa R., Charles R. Graham, Kristian J. Spring, and Jeffery S. Drysdale. 2012. "An Analysis of High Impact Scholarship and Publication Trends in Blended Learning." *Distance Education*, 33, no. 3: 381–413.

Hubbard, Philip. 2013. "Making a Case for Learner Training in Technology Enhanced Language Learning Environments." *CALICO Journal*, 30, no. 2: 163–178.

Latour, Bruno. 2005. *Reassembling the Social: An Introduction to Actor-network-theory*. New York: Oxford University Press.

Macaro, Ernesto. 2001. *Learning Strategies in Foreign and Second Language Classrooms: The Role of Learner Strategies*. New York: Continuum.

Means, Barbara, Yukie Toyama, Robert Murphy, Marianne Bakia, and Karla Jones. 2010. *Evaluation of Evidence-based Practices in Online Learning: A Meta-analysis and Review of Online Learning Studies*. Washington, DC: U.S. Department of Education.

Mohan, Bernard. 1986. *Language and Content*. Reading, MA: Addison Wesley.

Moskal, Patsy, Charles Dziuban, and Joel Hartman. 2013. "Blended Learning: A Dangerous Idea?" *Internet and Higher Education*, 18: 15–23.

Neumeier, Petra. 2005. "A Closer Look at Blended learning—parameters for Designing a Blended Learning Environment for Language Teaching and Learning." *Recall*, 17, no. 2: 163–178.

Online Learning Consortium. 2015. "Quality Framework: The 5 Pillars." Accessed May 11, 2015. http://onlinelearningconsortium.org/5pillars

Oxford, Rebecca. 2011. *Teaching and Researching Language Learning Strategies*. Harlow: Pearson Longman.

Picciano, Anthony. 2009. "Blending with Purpose: The Multimodal Model." *Journal of Asynchronous Learning Networks*, 13, no. 1: 7–18.

Picciano, Anthony. 2014. "Introduction to Blended Learning: Research Perspectives, Vol. 2." In *Blended Learning: Research Perspective, Vol. 2*, edited by Anthony G. Picciano, Charles D. Dziuban, and Charles Graham, 1–9. New York: Routledge.

Sanders, Robert F. 2005. "Redesigning Introductory Spanish: Increased Enrollment, Online Management, Cost Reduction, and Effects on Student Learning." *Foreign Language Annals*, 38, no. 4: 523–532.

Stockwell, Glenn. 2012. "Mobile-assisted Language Learning." In *Contemporary Computer-assisted Language Learning*, edited by Michael Thomas, Hayo Reinders and Mark Warschauer, 201–216. Huntingdon: Bloomsbury Publishing.

Ushida, Eiko. 2005. "The Role of Students' Attitudes and Motivation in Second Language Learning in Online Language Courses." *CALICO Journal*, 21, no. 1: 49–78.

Vorobel, Oksana and Deoksoon Kim. 2012. "Language Teaching at Distance: A Comprehensive Overview of Research." *CALICO Journal*, 29, no. 3: 548–562.

Wang, Shenggao, and Camilla Vásquez. 2012. "Web 2.0 and Second Language Learning: What does the Research Tell Us?" *CALICO Journal*, 29, no. 3: 412–430.

Watson, John. 2008. "*Blended Learning: The Convergence of Online and Face-to-Face Education. Promising Practices in Online Learning*." Vienna, VA: North American Council for Online Learning.

Young, Dolly, and Jason Lee Pettigrew. 2014. "Blended Learning in Large Multisection Foreign Language Programs: An Opportunity for Reflection on Course Content, Pedagogy, Learning Outcomes, and Assessment Issues." In *Hybrid Language Teaching and Learning: Exploring Theoretical, Pedagogical and Curricular issues*, edited by Fernando Rubio and Joshua Thoms, 92–136. Boston, MA: Heinle Cengage Learning.

Zhao, Yong. 2003. "Recent Developments in Technology and Language Learning: A Literature Review and Meta-Analysis." *CALICO Journal*, 21, no. 1: 7–27.

# 12 Telecollaboration

## MELINDA DOOLY

## Introduction

Collaboration in education—between peers, between classes, between schools, between educational institutions and other entities or communities—is not a new activity. Documentation of formal educational collaborative practices between geographically distanced classes can be traced back to the late 1800s and early 1900s. In language education, fomenting contact between language communities has always been a principal goal (as witnessed by international programs of exchange, e.g., Erasmus programs). Additionally, with the increase of Internet connections, the use of "telecollaboration" for promoting language learning has become more and more commonplace, providing teachers and students an economical and accessible means of contact and collaboration with speakers of other languages from around the world. As telecollaboration in language education moves to the mainstream, this educational practice is now often harked as "the beginning of a gradual shift towards new pedagogies, approaches and contexts" (Guth and Helm 2010, 17). This chapter begins by exploring definitions of telecollaboration before providing a brief historical overview of tellecollaborative learning in language education. Next, the chapter examines how telecollaborative activities have been categorized to identify tendencies in pedagogical design of such exchanges.

## Definition(s) of Telecollaboration

Etymologically speaking, telecollaboration can be defined simply as "collaboration" coupled with the Greek prefix "tele," which means "distance," as in telegraph, telephone, telescope, or telepathy. Thus, we have "collaboration at a distance." However, this definition is far too facile to encompass the complexities of the underlying learning principles and the activities involved in educational telecollaborative endeavors. Futhermore, such endeavors are not limited to language learning, nor even to education, as telecollaboration can also take place in the workplace, or in volunteer work or similarly oriented online communities. Thus, the definition of telecollaboration used in this chapter is the process of communicating and working together with other people or groups from different locations through online or digital communication tools (e.g., computers, tablets, cellphones) to co-produce a desired work output. Telecollaboration can be carried out in a variety of settings (classroom, home, workplace,

*The Handbook of Technology and Second Language Teaching and Learning*, First Edition.
Edited by Carol A. Chapelle and Shannon Sauro.
© 2017 John Wiley & Sons, Inc. Published 2020 by John Wiley & Sons, Inc.

laboratory) and can be synchronous or asynchronous. In education, telecollaboration combines all of these components with a focus on learning, social interaction, dialogue, intercultural exchange and communication all of which are especially important aspects of telecollaboration in *language* education.

The use of computer-mediated communication (CMC) to promote language learning or at least, to practice using a target language has become quite widely accepted among both language educators and the general public. As its popularity grows, so does related terminology. Evidence of this is the fact that telecollaboration was featured in *The Chronicle of Higher Education* (Pérez-Hernández 2014), wherein the author refers to the paired videoconferencing of students who practiced first the language of one of the partners and then the other partner's L1. This type of switch-off is commonly referred to as teletandem, which the article claimed to be synonymous with telecollaboration. In fact, teletandem conceivably fits into one type of configuration of telecollaboration (Telles 2009), but there are many other descriptions of telecollaboration that comprise different online partner configurations. As O'Dowd and Ware (2009, 175) point out, "acknowledging the wide variety of tasks and task designs that are used in foreign language telecollaboration can be difficult, as they are as varied as their counterparts in the traditional language classroom."

The multiplicity of applications of CMC in language teaching also highlights the difficulty of deciding upon a single definition of telecollaboration, especially as "the significant increase in the availability of user-friendly online technologies" has led to a sharp increase in the practice of "online interaction and exchange" in language teaching and learning (Dooly and O'Dowd 2012, 13). Moreover, as O'Dowd (2013, 124) points out, the use of the Internet to connect online language learners for different types of learning exchanges "has gone under many different names." These range from "virtual connections" (Warschauer 1995), "teletandem" (Telles 2009), "globally networked learning" (Starke-Meyerring and Wilson 2008) to the more generic term of "online interaction and exchange or OIE" (Dooly and O'Dowd 2012), to name just a few examples.

However, as seen in Dooly and O'Dowd's chapter, "online conversation," including asynchronous forums or emails and synchronous texting or audio/video chatting, is often seen as the definitive feature of telecollaboration in language education. The centrality of online conversation is due in large part to the easily accessible communication tools now often found in classrooms around the globe. As Davies, Otto, and Rüschoff (2013, 34) indicate, "digital tools for learning have become integrated elements in both the real world and also in foreign language syllabuses." Nonetheless, an important question for language educators soon emerges: can we consider any type of multilingual online communication (e.g., "chatting") as telecollaboration? Obviously the potential for language learning through online interaction is vast, but does this provide a suitable working definition of telecollaboration?

In October of 2014, the author of this text surveyed the published literature referenced in Education Resources Information Center (ERIC) on telecollaboration in both research and practice. ERIC is the Education Resources Information Center's online digital library of education research and information sponsored by the Institute of Education, U.S. Department of Education (until now the European Research Council does not offer a similar service). The survey indicated that telecollaboration is far more abundant within fields related to language teaching and learning (L1, L2, foreign, ESL, ESP, etc.) and intercultural education or intercultural competences than they are for teaching in other disciplines. Sixty-five percent of the articles in the ERIC bibliography on telecollaboration were published in journals specializing in language education and/or intercultural issues. The survey also revealed that the term has been most frequently defined within parameters of language teaching and learning, for instance O'Dowd describes it as the application of [synchronous and asynchronous] online communication tools to bring together classes of language learners in geographically distant locations to develop their foreign language skills and intercultural competence through collaborative tasks and project work. (O'Dowd 2012, 340)

One of the most widely referenced definitions of telecollaboration comes from Belz (2003), who explains the term as a partnership in which

internationally-dispersed learners in parallel language classes use Internet communication tools such as e-mail, synchronous chat, threaded discussion, and MOOs (as well as other forms of electronically mediated communication), in order to support social interaction, dialogue, debate, and intercultural exchange. (Belz 2003, 2)

Both Belz' and O'Dowd's definitions include key terms often used for defining telecollaboration: language(s), learners, (classes), electronically (or digitally) mediated communication, collaborative and social interaction, dialogue, and intercultural exchange.

Still, in their critical overview of research into telecollaboration, Lamy and Goodfellow (2010) point out how problematic defining telecollaboration can be given that the definition implicitly covers a wide range of pedagogical underpinnings of (mostly formal, institutional) online exchanges, ranging from loosely guided "language practice" of a target language to elaborately designed project-based collaborative problem-solving and shared knowledge construction. Along these lines, it should be noted that this chapter looks at telecollaboration principally within formal learning environments, including blended learning environments; it is not within its scope to consider individual, informally established language exchanges such as those that take place in specific platforms designed for informal language partnering (e.g. busuu or babble, both of which were still online at the publication of this chapter).

Within formal language learning settings, Helm (2013) also highlights the variegated pedagogical approaches that have evolved from and form part of telecollaboration, all of which have "diverse learning objectives, involv[e] different typologies and configurations of participants, and utiliz[e] a range of languages and modalities of language use" (28). She goes on to point out that "objectives of telecollaboration depend on the project and the participant groups" (31), which may range from the development of language (including professional repertoires), to online literacies and intercultural skills.

As Helm further indicates, apart from explicit (and implicit) reference to "language learning," telecollaboration has often been defined within parameters of "interculturality," to wit: intercultural awareness, intercultural development, intercultural competences, intercultural exchange, intercultural education (cf. Audras and Chanier 2008; Kinginger, Gourvès-hayward, and Simpson 1999; Jin 2013), to name just a few areas that are covered in the staple of research articles on intercultural issues and telecollaboration. *En bref*, "telecollaboration has come to be seen as one of the main pillars of the intercultural turn in foreign language education" (O'Dowd 2012, 340).

The definition of telecollaboration takes on a wider scope if one considers definitions coming from the considerable work beyond language education. A pioneer in the field, Harris wrote in 1999 that telecollaboration is "an educational endeavor that involves people in different locations using Internet tools and resources to work together" (55) without making an explicit reference to language learning. The following year, Feldman et al. (2000) edited the findings of a decade-long project begun in 1989 to promote telecollaboration in science classrooms. More recently, Narayan wrote that

> [W]eb-based collaboration tools [...] connect learners to other learners, teachers, educators, scholars and researchers, scientists and artists, industry leaders and politicians—in short, to any individual with access to the internet who can enrich the learning process. (Narayan 2013, 11)

Scholars and teachers from many areas of education have been engaging in telecollaborative exchanges for promotion of competences and knowledge gain for some time, for instance, in the area of art education (cf. Greh 2002; Prater 2001); in social studies (cf., Good et al. 2005; Mason and Berson 2000; Wellman, Creedman, and Flores 2000); in mathematics education (cf. Lynch et al. 2002; Staley, Moyer-Packenham, and Lynch, 2005; UNESCO 2006) as well as other more general competences such as self-regulated thinking skills (Lee 2001). Throughout this period of research and practice, key elements in the definitions of telecollaboration that have emerged are: the underlying basis of (collaborative) learning, dialogic and shared knowledge-building, reflection on learning processes, and communication among geographically-distanced learners in technologically-supported environments. In view of the common elements across different subject areas, Friedman (2006) sees the need for "the Great Synthesizers," people who specialize in interacting between disciplines and ideas—a notion that is inherent to any telecollaborative pursuit and in particular, educators involved in promoting communicative competences.

## Historical overview of telecollaboration in language education

Collaborative practices in formal education have been documented as early as the 1900s (Johnson, Johnson, and Holubec 1998), and even earlier in Jardine's pioneer work with collaborative writing at Glasgow University (1774–1826) as described in Lewis Gaillet's (1994) historical perspective on collaborative learning. Gouseti (2013) describes the historical idea of "twinning" as a legal or social agreement between locations such as towns or provinces to promote cultural and business ties. This concept has gradually developed into e-twinning aimed at "universal mutual understanding" (Vion, 2002, 623, quoted in Gouseti 2013, 377) and as a "means of breaking down pre-existing stereotypes and prejudices and bridging the cultural gap between nations" (Gouseti 2013, 377–378). Many of these initial "twinnings" included schools whose exchange efforts were supported, at least minimally, by some use of technology (at first, letter exchange, followed by emails, forums, and later on more advanced CMC technology). Many of these exchanges involved the use of more than one language.

As for telecollaboration, both O'Dowd (2013) and Kern (2013) trace the beginnings of online intercultural exchanges in FL education to the learning networks pioneered by Célestin Freinet in 1920s France and, according to O'Dowd, "later by Mario Lodi in 1960s Italy" (125). This coincides with an emergent general awareness of new horizons: in the 1960s the term "global village" was first used by McLuhan (1962 [2011]) to describe a shrinking planet linked by communications technology (for better or worse and, according to McLuhan, with an inherent risk of "tribalization"; see Corbett 2007). It was also during this decade that citizens of the world enjoyed their first views of the planet Earth from space (Gaudelli 2003), which in turn helped promote a vision of a single, united world system (Gooding Oran 2011).

Computer-mediated technology use in language learning did not really pick up speed until several decades later. Many scholars see Warschauer's (1996) collection of papers (in particular the three chapters by Kern 1996; Brammerts 1996; and Johnson 1996) as seminal work for laying down key pedagogical foundations for subsequent research and practice in telecollaboration in language teaching and learning. For a more in-depth overview of research and teaching paradigms in CMC and language learning, see Lamy and Hampel (2007). Around the same time as the appearance of Kern's publication, independent studies into the use of technology were beginning to emerge —many of them based on teacher-researcher case studies (e.g., Kinginger 1998; Kinginger, Gourvès-Hayward, and Simpson 1999; Kitchen and McDougall, 1998–1999; Marsh 1997), along with the advent of some websites, such as the Orillas Network in the early to mid-1990s which served as a clearinghouse for exchanges between classes in the American continents and Europe (O'Dowd 2007).

Following these initial studies, interest grew incrementally in telecollaboration in language education. This is evident in the breakdown of percentages of publications of articles and reports that have been written on the topic since 1995 (based on the ERIC survey mentioned in the above section). The main foci of these publications (in order of most recurrent to less frequent) can be loosely classified as: interculturality, design and/or socioinstitutional constraints, language learning, teacher education (both equally represented), followed to a much smaller degree by content-learning, multiliteracy, and state-of-the-question articles. Of the total number of articles that specifically discuss telecollaboration (research and/or practice), 25% were published between 1995 and 2005 and of the remaining 75%, 51% appeared from 2005–2010, 30% were written in the two-year span covering 2011–2013 and 19% were produced between 2013–2014, clearly indicating a growing focus of study and findings; especially considering that the number of publications in the most recent complete year in the database (2013) comprises more than half the total amount of works that were published during the ten-year span between 1995 and 2005.

Dooly and O'Dowd's (2012) analysis presents four principal reasons for the increased interest in and practice of telecollaboration in FL environments: the escalation of easily accessible communication technology in the classroom; a growing recognition of the importance of intercultural competence (IC) in foreign language learning and the way in which online exchanges can support IC development; the increasingly widespread acceptance of the "paradigm of language learning as a sociocultural process facilitated through carefully constructed purposeful, plausible communicative events" (14); and the melding of language competences and e-literacies "required in emerging labor markets" (15).

Just as interest has grown, so too has the complexity in telecollaborative configurations (use of multiple tools, inclusion of multiple partnerships, curriculum-embedded, long-term activities or projects, etc.). In his review of past studies into intercultural aspects of telecollaboration (O'Dowd 2012) remarks that "many of the initial publications in the literature involved rather superficial e-mail exchanges" (342) but now research in the field has become "more critical and in-depth" and practices have become "more complex," with "structured online projects and tasks" that require students to work together for common goals. Commonly, now, language education (and other disciplines) include "project" as part and parcel of what constitutes telecollaboration, implying that CMC-supported interaction between learners is fast becoming assimilated into social and cultural turns in pedagogy as project-based learning, along with competence-based learning, become more integrated into curriculum design (de Fur 2009; Dooly 2013a; Levin and Schrum 2013; Lingard and McGregor 2014; Maida 2011). Accordingly, telecollaborative global learning is perceived as

> connecting students in communities of learners around the world so that they can work together on projects that make a difference globally and locally. It is about building relationships and achieving authentic, meaningful learning. (Bickley and Carleton 2009, 20)

This evolution of how telecollaboration is conceived demonstrates that the use of online exchange in educational settings has gone from rather simple activities largely viewed as complementary (usually practice or drill) tasks to far more complex, embedded, and holistic components of language "learning ecologies" (Barron 2006, 195).[1]

# Paradigms of telecollaboration in language education

This section considers the ways in which education paradigms have influenced approaches and applications of telecollaboration in formal language learning settings. Paradigms refer to the underlying theory that informs a pedagogical approach including teaching design, instructional methods (including specific types of tasks), configurations of materials, and artefacts and so on used to achieve the educational goals. Many of the paradigms of tellecollaboration are associated with second language pedagogies, such as communicative language teaching (CLT), task-based language teaching (TBLT) or project-based language learning (PBLL). Furthermore, most of the prevalent paradigms associated with telecollaboration in education also include the promotion of learner autonomy.

## *Underlying theory*

The underlying theory that supports telecollaborative design of activities has undergone significant repositionings in the past decades (Bax 2003; Thomas, Reinders, and Warschauer 2013; Warschauer and Healey 1998). The most recent change is a "shift towards social technologies [...] constructivist principles promoting collaborative learning [...] now focused more on communicative ability" (Thomas, Reinders, and Warschauer 2013, 6–7). In other words, telecollaboration is now most often used to support a social learning frame designed to provide opportunities for the individual to construct his or her own abilities through collaboration with others. Given that telecollaboration is principally about communication, the move toward socioconstructivist underpinnings—which poses that learning takes place through social interaction—is quite comprehensible.

Beyond language education, socioconstructivism is a widely accepted paradigm in education (Doolittle and Hicks 2003; Fosnot 2005; Karpov 2003) wherein the role of the teacher is to set up an optimal environment where learners can construct knowledge through engagement with artefacts, all within their "zone of proximal development" (ZPD), so level-appropriate learning can take place. In such environments, learners are aided by expert and peer interaction during collaboration (Chaiklin 2004; Lantolf and Thorne 2006; Rieber and Carton 1987; Tharpe and Gallimore 1988; Vygotsky 1978; Wertsch 1988). Likewise, recent telecollaborative exchanges described for second language education tend to fall within socioconstructivist parameters (Dooly 2010; Lamy and Hampel 2007; Meskill 2013a; Meskill 2013b; Meskill and Anthony 2010), and some situate themselves within socioculturalism, which emphasizes the cultural context of learning as well.

## *Telecollaborative tasks*

Much of the research on telecollaboration for language learning is situated conceptually within task-based language teaching (TBLT), which theorizes 'task' as activities designed to foster second language acquisition. Early research into TBLT was based on task characteristics in face-to-face (f2f) learning environments (see Bygate 2001; Ellis 2003; Nunan 2004; Pica, Kanagy, and Falodun 1993; Robinson 2007; Samuda and Bygate 2008; Skehan 1998, 2003; Ur 1981; see also the chapter on task-based language teaching by González-Lloret in this volume). Shifting the focus from f2f to CMC, O'Dowd and Ware (2009) provide a synthesis of recurrent tasks in telecollaborative exchanges. The authors came up with 12 general task typologies, which they catalogued into three supracategories: information exchange, contrast and analysis, and collaborative, although the authors underscore the "heterogenic nature of the tasks" (178) and the difficulty of covering the wide variety of tasks that are designed and implemented in telecollaborative exchanges.

These three task categories closely coincide with two of three tasks in one of the first endeavors at writing a task taxonomy (Prabhu 1987): information gap, reasoning gap, and opinion gap. Arguably, from a communicative perspective, there is increased complexity in language demand between the first, second, and third task types. Information exchange, at first glance, seems more straightforward and easier to negotiate than collaboration, although there are studies that show that low-level language users can successfully negotiate collaborative situations with sufficient scaffolding and use of very simple language syntax and lexicon (Dooly and Sadler 2016; Gruson 2010; Gruson and Barnes 2012). These results highlight the need for research that advances effective design principles (Hauck and Warnecke, 2013) and that promotes full understanding of telecollaborative configurations in context.

Albeit not intended as a taxonomy *per se*, during her work to develop a telecollaborative task databank for language education in higher education[2], Kurek (2012) categorized tasks as "stand-alone," referring to relatively short and simple units of interaction that can be easily integrated into already existent study programmes; and "task sequences"—alluding to more long-term, structured exchanges aimed to help language students develop not only linguistically but also socially, cognitively, and interculturally. In the above-mentioned example of taxonomy (O'Dowd and Ware 2009), the focus appears to be more on the agent involved in the configuration (language learner) or the activity itself, whereas Kurek's example encompasses more of the pedagogical scope (understandably so as the database's target audience is teachers). These two approaches highlight the fact that there is no classifactory system that serves as a shared basis for studies by task-based language learning researchers. However, based on the systems that do exist, three broad categories emerge, namely *interactional* criteria, *cognitive* criteria, and *ability-determinant* criteria (Robinson 2007). The brunt of research into telecollaborative configurations and tasks appears to fall within the first category, with a focus on the interaction.

The emphasis on interactional criteria is consistent with the socioconstructivist theory underlying this work in addition to broadly-defined communicative language teaching (CLT), which aims to promote fluid, frequent, and authentic communication. At the same time, the difficulties of categorizing the types of configurations and tasks appear to corroborate Richards' and Rodgers' (2001) claim that the range of exercise types and activities compatible with CLT is unlimited. Still, a review of recent publications dealing with telecollaboration indicates a trend toward activities that fall within three of the five categories identified by Littlewood (2013) in the "communicative continuum": (1) communicative language practice; (2) structured communication; and (3) authentic communication; all of which tend toward "focus on meanings and messages" and "experiential strategies." These three contrast with Littlewood's other two categories on the continuum that are "non-communicative learning" and "pre-communicative language practice", both of which focus on meaning and form and analytical strategies. Studies into other CLT-based configurations (apart from task-based) indicate that telecollaboration appears to be advancing the CLT paradigm towards what Littlewood calls "communication-oriented language teaching" (COLT) (2004, 325; 2014, 355). COLT emphasizes the use of language in ways that are personally relevant to the learners while helping them develop communicatively, cognitively, and as a "global" person through collaborative learning.

These premises closely resemble those underlying project-based language learning (PBLL) in telecollaboration (Dooly 2010; Dooly 2013a; Dooly and Sadler 2013; Harris 2001; Redmond and Lock 2006; Wall et al. 2011). Online exchanges configured as PBLL have emerged with certain vigor in the past few years (cf. reports of recently funded UNESCO projects promoting telecollaborative project-based learning in Bangladesh and China). In her qualitative study of teachers' motivations for using telecollaboration for global education, Gooding Oran (2011) defined telecollaboration as "projects completed collaboratively by students and teachers through the use of online tools and/or ICT" (14), underscoring the importance teachers should give to the collaborative project-building. Dooly (2014) pushes this assumption forward in her argument that technology-enhanced project-based language learning (TEPBLL), in particular, a telecollaborative TEPBLL educational approach best suits our current interconnected society because it can promote non-linear, socially-distributed cognition which, in turn, foments the "capacity of 'thinking together' in what has been called 'participatory power'" (Dooly 2013b, 239).

## *Learner autonomy*

As the studies into task taxonomy and similar CLT-based educational approaches indicate, telecollaboration has been configured by practitioners and researchers in numerous ways, ranging from highly teacher-controlled, one-off language exchanges between learners to far more complex, student-oriented, longitudinal telecollaborative projects. The latter, student-focused configurations converge with another pillar of intercultural foreign language education: learner autonomy acquired (and required) in network-based language learning environments. Telecollaboration, with its focus on mutual support and reciprocity has been touted as an apt learning ecology for promoting student autonomy (Little 1996; Ushioda 2000; Warschauer and Kern 2000). This argument is based on studies of language learning that highlight the social dimension of autonomy, that is the interdependence, collaboration, and "shareability" of knowledge-building (Benson 1996, 2001; Carter 2006; Lewis 2014; Little 1996). For Schwienhorst (2007) learner autonomy is key for successful technology-pedagogy, which must support reflection, interaction, experimentation, and participation of learners.

Nonetheless, some caution must be applied. Several different factors can have an impact on the development of learner autonomy: just how much autonomy students begin with, how much teacher control is exerted during the execution of language activities and how much autonomy the interaction design promotes (Dooly 2008), to name just a few determinants. "Autonomy is not only given by the tools used for communication, but most and foremost by the nature of the tasks themselves" (Guarda 2013, 54). These observations point back to the interdependence among the factors involved in telecollaboration.

Additionally, a sole description of autonomy in telecollaboration can be elusive. Mangenot and Nissen see telecollaborative group autonomy as

> the capacity of a group to manage itself on three levels: a socio-affective level (getting along with others), a sociocognitive level (resolving problems together), and an organizational level (planning, monitoring, and evaluating work. (Mangenot and Nissen 2006, 604)

Furthermore, highlighting the intricate and complex configuration involved in telecollaboration, research into learner autonomy may focus on the use of tools, the use of language, or task interpretation and completion, just to name a few areas of recent studies. Fuchs, Hauck, and Mueller-Hartmann (2012) refer to "informed" (82) and proficient use of the myriad communication tools available to learners, while Hauck and Warnecke (2013) and Lewis (2014) focus on the social dimension of learner autonomy in online exchanges. In a similar vein, O'Rourke (2007) contemplates peer scaffolding as a significant part of telecollaborative learner autonomy. Along the lines of the work by Schwienhorst (2007) and Guarda (2013), Collentine (2009, 2011) spotlights the importance of task design for promoting learner autonomy in synchronous computer-mediated communication and according to Fisher, Evans, and Esch (2004) in contexts where teacher control is reduced (thereby creating optimal conditions for student initiative) there is increased learner autonomy.

Predictably, online learner autonomy has emerged as a point of interest for studies into informal language learning situations, although, as stated earlier, this is not within the scope of this chapter. (For recent studies, see Velghe 2012; Velghe and Blommaert 2014). Other studies (within formal educational settings) consider learner self-initiatives in activities directly related to language acquisition such as word search or self-correction (Pérez Cañado 2010). Noticeably, the term is often mentioned as a key emergent factor for language learners in telecollaboration without specific definition of how it is understood in the language-learning context, implying the need for further studies into emergent telecollaborative configurations that take into account the learner, goals, activities and design, and learner competencies, among a myriad of other factors that might come into play.

# Conclusion

Telecollaboration is becoming more and more elaborate as opportunities for engaging in online learning exchanges gain advocates in the world of language education. This is not only due to the growing number of participants, but also the boundless constituents that can entail its configuration. At the same time, it is also clear that telecollaboration implies a degree of social transformation that is often ignored in research—for instance, as language learners gain control of their own learning process and this same process moves outside the (physical) classroom, educational power structures inevitably shift (cf. Velghe and Blommaert 2014). This underscores the importance of further inquiry into related questions and issues concerning content, materials, assessment, and curriculum when dealing with telecollaboration as an integral part of the language learning process.

There is also a need for more research into political and social implications of telecollaboration. How can this type of learning ecology be optimized, not only in language education but in transdisciplinary projects in order to foment multiple competences that are key for the information society of today? For instance, do telecollaboration practices help prepare language learners and teachers for the 21st-century classroom and future work opportunities? Are curricula adapting to new literacies promoted through this type of learning configuration and if so, to what extent? Does telecollaboration ensure a more equitable distribution of social capital (e.g., digital knowledge; communicative competences) or exacerbate already existent inequalities? New domains of research are also emerging as telecollaboration becomes more mainstream. There is a growing call for more microanalytical approaches that take into consideration the participants' perspectives (e.g., through the application of Conversation Analysis) as well possibilities of exploiting research theories from other scientific areas (e.g., Complexity Theory, Chaos Theory). These are just a few of the numerous questions that will inevitably emerge as telecollaboration—that is, an embedded, dialogic process that supports geographically-distanced collaborative work, intercultural exchange, and social interaction of individuals or groups through synchronous and asynchronous communication technology (Internet, mobile services, etc.) so that they co-produce mutual objective(s) and shared knowledge-building—continues making prodigious strides in practice and research.

## NOTES

1   Barron (2006) refers to "learning ecology" to help conceptualize learning as bridged across the spaces of home, school, work, and community. According to Barron, the learning ecology is contextualized—but not limited to a singular context.

2   A component of the Erasmus Multilateral Project INTENT (Integrating Telecollaborative Networks into Foreign Language Higher Education; 517622-LLP-1-2011-1-ES-ERASMUS-ESMO; 2011-2014) which aimed to raise greater awareness among students, educators, and decision makers of telecollaboration as a tool for virtual mobility in FL education at the Higher Education level (www.intent-project.eu).

# REFERENCES

Audras, Isabelle, and Thierry Chanier. 2008. "Observation de la Construction d'une Compétence Interculturelle dans des Groupes Exolingues en Ligne." *Alsic*, 11, no. 1: Accessed July 16, 2014 http://alsic.revues.org/865. DOI: http://dx.doi.org/10.4000/alsic.865

Barron, Brigid. 2006. "Interest and Self-Sustained Learning as Catalysts of Development: A Learning Ecologies Perspective." *Human Development*, 49: 193–224. DOI:10.1159/000094368.

Bax, Stephen. 2003. "CALL -Past, Present and Future." *System*, 31, no. 1: 13–28. DOI:0.1016/S0346-251X(02)00071-4.

Belz, Julie A. 2003. "From the Special Issue Editor." *Language Learning & Technology*, 7 no. 2: 2–5. Accessed July 14, 2013. http://llt.msu.edu/vol7num2/speced.html

Belz, Julie A., and Andreas Müller-Hartmann. 2003. "Teachers as Intercultural Learners: Negotiating German-American Telecollaboration Along the Institutional Fault Line." *Modern Language Journal*, 87, no. 1: 71–89. DOI:10.1111/1540-4781.00179.

Benson, Phil. 1996."Concepts of Autonomy in Language Learning." In *Taking Control: Autonomy and Independence in Language Learning*, edited by Richard Pemberton, Edward S. L. Li, Winnie W. F. Or and Herbert D. Pierson, 27–34. Hong Kong: Hong Kong University Press.

Benson, Phil. 2001. *Teaching and Researching Autonomy in Language Learning*. Harlow: Longman.

Bickley, Mali, and Jim Carleton. 2009. "Students Without Borders." *Learning & Leading with Technology*, 37, no. 3: 20–23. Accessed October 15. http://www.learningandleading-digital.com/learningandleading

Brammerts, Helmut. 1996. "Language Learning in Tandem Using the Internet." In *Telecollaboration in Foreign Language Learning*, edited by Mark Warschauer, 121–130. Honolulu, HI: University of Hawai'i Press.

Bygate, Martin. 2001. *Speaking*. Oxford: Oxford University Press.

Carter, Beverly-Anne. 2006. *Teacher/Student Responsibility in Foreign Language Learning*. Bern/New York: Peter Lang.

Chaiklin, Seth. 2004. "The Zone of Proximal Development in Vygotsky's Analysis of Learning and Instruction." In *Vygotsky's Educational Theory in Cultural Context*, edited by Alex Kozulin, Boris Gindis, Vladimir S. Ageyev, and Suzanne M. Miller, 39–64. New York: Cambridge University Press.

Collentine, Karina. 2009. "Learner Use of Holistic Language Units in Multimodal, Task-Based Synchronous Computer-Mediated Communication." *Language Learning and Technology*, 13, no. 2: 68–87. Accessed November 16, 2014. http://llt.msu.edu/vol13num2/collentine.pdf

Collentine, Karina. 2011. "Learner Autonomy in a Task-Based 3D World and Production." *Language Learning and Technology*, 15, no. 3: 50–67. Accessed November 16, 2014. http://llt.msu.edu/issues/october2011/collentine.pdf

Corbett, John. 2007. "Foreword." In *Online Intercultural Exchange: An Introduction for Foreign Language Teachers*, edited by Robert O'Dowd, xv–xvii. Clevedon/New York: Multilingual Matters.

Davies, Graham, Sue E. K. Otto, and Bernd Rüschoff. 2013. "Historical Perspectives on CALL." In *Contemporary Computer-Assisted Language Learning*, edited by Michael Thomas, Hayo Reinders, and Mark Warschauer, 19–38. London/Sydney: Bloomsbury.

de Fur, Karen. 2009. "The Relationship Between the Fidelity of Project-Based Curriculum Implementation and Foreign Language Teachers' Beliefs in Teaching and Learning." Unpublished PhD dissertation, Southern Connecticut State University.

Doolittle, Peter E., and David Hicks. 2003. "Constructivism as a Theoretical Foundation for the Use of Technology in Social Studies." *Theory and Research in Social Education* 31, no. 1: 71–103. DOI:10.1080/00933104.2003.10473216

Dooly, Melinda. 2008. "Constructing Knowledge Together." In *Telecollaborative Language Learning. A Guidebook to Moderating Intercultural Collaboration Online*, edited by Melinda Dooly, 21–43. Bern: Peter Lang.

Dooly, Melinda. 2010. "The Teacher 2.0." In *Telecollaboration 2.0. Language, Literacies and Intercultural Learning in the 21st Century*, edited by Sarah Guth and Francesca Helm, 277–303. Bern/New York: Peter Lang.

Dooly, Melinda. 2013a. "Promoting Competency-Based Language Teaching Through Project-Based Language Learning." In *Competency-Based Language Teaching in*

*Higher Education*, edited by María Luisa Pérez Cañado, 77–91. Dordrecht/London: Springer.

Dooly, Melinda. 2013b. "Speaking like a 'Glocal': Using Computer-Mediated Communication in Language Teacher Education to Promote Network Learning." In *Language Teachers and Teaching: Global Perspectives, Local Initiatives*, edited by Selim Ben Said and Lawrence Jun Zhang, 237–255. New York: Taylor & Francis/ Routledge.

Dooly, Melinda. 2014. "Learning to e-Function in a Brave New World: Language Teachers' Roles in Educating for the Future." In *Insights into Technology Enhanced Language Pedagogy*, edited by Anna Turula and Beata Mikolajewska, 9–24. Bern/Vienna: Peter Lang.

Dooly, Melinda, and Randall Sadler. 2013. "Filling in the Gaps: Linking Theory and Practice Through Telecollaboration in Teacher Education." *ReCALL* 25: 4–29. DOI:10.1017/ S0958344012000237

Dooly, Melinda, and Randall Sadler. 2016. "Becoming Little Scientists: Technologically-Enhanced Project-Based Language Learning." *Language Learning & Technology*: 20, 1: 54–78. Retrieved 8 May 2016 from http://llt.msu. edu/issues/february2016/doolysadler.pdf

Dooly, Melinda, and Robert O'Dowd. 2012 "Researching Online Interaction and Exchange in Foreign Language Education: Introduction to the Volume." In *Researching Online Foreign Language Interaction and Exchange. Theories, Methods and Challenges*, edited by Melinda Dooly and Robert O'Dowd, 11–41. Bern/ Vienna: Peter Lang.

Ellis, Rod. 2003. *Task-Based Language Teaching and Learning*. Oxford: Oxford University Press.

Feldman, Alan, Cliff Konold, Bob Coulter, Brian Conroy, Charles Hutchinson, and Nancy London. 2000. *Network Science a Decade Later. The Internet and Classroom Learning*. Mahwah, NJ: Lawrence Erlbaum.

Fisher, Linda, Michael Evans, and Edith Esch. 2004. "Computer-Mediated Communication: Promoting Learner Autonomy and Intercultural Understanding at Secondary Level." *Language Learning Journal*, 30: 50–58. DOI:10.1080/09571730485200231

Fosnot, Catherine Twomey, ed. 2005. *Constructivism: Theory, Perspectives, and Practice*, 2nd ed. New York: Teachers College/ Columbia University Press.

Friedman, Thomas L. 2006. *The World is Flat: A Brief History of the Twenty-First Century*. New York: Farrar, Straus and Giroux.

Fuchs, Carolin, Mirjam Hauck, and Andreas Mueller-Hartmann. 2012. "Promoting Learner Autonomy Through Multiliteracy Skills Development in Cross-Institutional Exchanges." *Language Learning & Technology*, 16, no. 3: 82–102. Accessed May 18, 2014. http://llt.msu. edu/issues/october2012/index.html

Gaudelli, William. 2003. *World Class: Teaching and Learning in Global Times*. Mahwah, NJ: Laurence Erlbaum.

Good, Amy J., Katherine A. O'Connor, Carol H. Greene, and Eric F. Luce. 2005. "Collaborating Across the Miles: Telecollaboration in a Social Studies Methods Course." *Contemporary Issues in Technology and Teacher Education*, 5, no. 3/4: 300–317.

Gooding Oran, Holly. 2011. Teaching for Global Learning Through Telecollaboration: A Case Study of K-12 Educators' Conceptualizations and Practices About Global Education. Unpublished PhD dissertation, Kennesaw State University, Kennesaw, GA: DigitalCommons@KennesawStateUniversity.

Gouseti, Anastasia. 2013. "An Overview of Web-Based School Collaboration: A History of Success or Failure?" *Cambridge Journal of Education*, 43, no. 3: 377–390. DOI:10.1080/ 0305764X.2013.792785

Greh, Deborah. 2002. *New Technologies in the Artroom*. Worchester, MA: Davis Publications.

Gruson, Brigitte. 2010. "Analyse comparative d'une situation de communication orale en classe ordinaire et lors d'une séance en visioconférence." *Distances et Savoirs*, 8, no. 3: 395–423. DOI: http://dx.doi.org/10.3166/ ds.8.395-423

Gruson, Brigitte, and Françoise Barnes. 2012. "Case Study Investigation of CMC with Young Language Learners." *Journal of E-Learning and Knowledge Society*, 8, no. 3: 79–90.

Guarda, Marta. 2013. Negotiating a Transcultural Place in an English as a Lingua Franca Telecollaboration Exchange: A Mixed Methods Approach to the Analysis of Intercultural Communicative Competence and Third Space in an Online Community of Practice. Unpublished PhD dissertation, Dipartimento di Studi Linguistici e Letterari, Università degli Studi di Padova, Padova: Scuola Di Dottorato Di Ricerca In Scienze Linguistiche, Filologiche e Letteraie.

Guth, Sarah, and Francesca Helm. 2010. "Introduction." In *Telecollaboration 2.0. Language, Literacies and Intercultural Learning in the 21st Century*, edited by Sarah Guth and Francesca Helm, 13–35. Bern: Peter Lang.

Harris, Judi. 1999. "First Steps in Telecollaboration." *International Society for Technology in Education*, 27, no. 3: 54–57. Accessed October 18, 2014. http://virtual-architecture.wm.edu/Foundation/Articles/First-Steps.pdf

Harris, Judi. 2001. "Teachers as Telecollaborative Project Designers: A Curriculum-Based Approach." *Contemporary Issues in Technology and Teacher Education [Online serial]* 1, no. 3. Accessed October 15, 2014. http://www.citejournal.org/vol1/iss3/seminal/article1.htm

Hauck, Mirjam, and Sylvia Warnecke. 2013. "Materials Design in CALL: Social Presence in Online Environments." In *Contemporary Computer-Assisted Language Learning*, edited by Michael Thomas, Hayo Reinders, and Mark Warschauer, 95–115. London/Sydney: Bloomsbury.

Helm, Francesca. 2013. "A Dialogic Model for Telecollaboration." *Bellaterra Journal of Teaching & Learning Language & Literature*, 6, no. 2: 28–48. Accessed July 18, 2014. http://revistes.uab.cat/jtl3

Jin, Li. 2013. "Language Development and Scaffolding in a Sino-American Telecollaborative Project." *Language Learning & Technology*, 17, no. 2: 193–219. Accessed October 19, 2014. http://llt.msu.edu/issues/june2013/jin.html

Johnson, David W., Roger T. Johnson, and Edythe Johnson Holubec. 1998. *Cooperation in the Classroom*. Edina, MN: Interaction Book Company.

Johnson, Lewis C. 1996. "The Keypal Connection." In *Telecollaboration in Foreign Language Learning*, edited by Mark Warschauer, 131–142. Honolulu, HI: University of Hawai'i Press.

Lewis Gaillet, Lynée. 1994. "An Historical Perspective on Collaborative Learning." *Journal of Advanced Composition*, 14, no. 1, Special Issue: Collaboration and Change in the Academy (Winter): 93–110.

Karpov, Yuriy V. 2003. "Development Through the Lifespan." In *Vygotsky's Educational Theory in Cultural Context*, edited by Alex Kozulin, Boris Gindis, Vladimir S. Ageyev and Suzanne M. Miller, 138–155. New York: Cambridge University Press.

Kern, Richard. 1996. "Computer-Mediated Communication: Using E-mail Exchanges to Explore Personal Histories in Two Cultures." In *Telecollaboration in Foreign Language Learning*, edited by Mark Warschauer, 105–120. Honolulu, HI: University of Hawai'i Press.

Kern, Richard. 2013. "Technology and language learning." In *The Routledge Handbook of Applied Linguistics*, edited by J. Simpson and James Simpson, 200–214. London/New York: Routledge.

Kinginger, Celeste. 1998. "Videoconferencing as Access to Spoken French." *The Modern Language Journal*, 82, no. 4: 502–513. DOI:10.1111/j.1540-4781.1998.tb05537.x

Kinginger, Celeste, Alison Gourvès-Hayward, and Vanessa Simpson. 1999. "A Telecollaborative Course on French-American Intercultural Communication." *French Review*, 72, no. 5: 853–866. Accessed November 17, 2014. http://www.jstor.org/stable/398359

Kitchen, David, and Douglas E. McDougall. 1998–1999. "Collaborative Learning on the Internet." *Journal of Educational Technology Systems*, 27, no. 3: 245–258. Accessed October 19, 2014. http://www.editlib.org/p/87822/

Kurek, Malgorzata. 2012. "Developing a Databank of Telecollaborative Tasks—Challenges and Outcomes." Paper presented at CMC & Teacher Ed SIGs Joint Annual Seminar, Learning Through Sharing: Open Resources, Open Practices, Open Communication. Bologna: Università di Bologna, 29–30 March.

Lamy, Marie-Noëlle, and Regine Hampel. 2007. *Online Communication in Language Learning and Teaching*. Houndmills/New York: Palgrave Macmillan.

Lamy, Marie-Noëlle, and Robin Goodfellow. 2010. "Telecollaboration and learning 2.0." In *Telecollaboration 2.0. Language, Literacies and Intercultural Learning in the 21st Century*, edited by Sarah Guth and Francesca Helm, 107–138. Vienna/Bern: Peter Lang.

Lantolf, James P., and Steven L. Thorne. 2006. *Sociocultural Theory and the Genesis of Second Language Development*. Oxford: Oxford University Press.

Lee, Karen S. Y. 2001. "Using Telecollaboration for Self-Regulated Thinking Skills: Instruction with Regular and Gifted Students." *Higher Ability Studies*, 12, no. 2: 236–247. DOI:10.1080/13598130120084357

Levin, Barbara B., and Lynne Schrum. 2013. "Technology-Rich Schools Up Close." *Educational Leadership*, 70, no. 6: 51–55. Accessed July18, 2014. http://www.ascd.org/publications/educational_leadership/mar13/vol70/num06/Technology-Rich_Schools_Up_Close.aspx

Lewis Gaillet, Lynée. 1994. "An Historical Perspective on Collaborative Learning."

*Journal of Advanced Composition*, 14, no. 1: 93–110. Accessed April 16, 2014. https://xpv. uab.cat/stable/,DanaInfo=. awxyCnxzvzIy2s+20865949

Lewis, Tim. 2014. "Learner Autonomy and the Theory of Sociality." In *Social Dimensions of Autonomy in Language Learning*, edited by Garold Murray, 37–59. London: Palgrave Macmillan.

Lingard, Bob, and Glenda McGregor. 2014. "Two Contrasting Australian Curriculum Responses to Globalisation: What Students Should Learn or Become." *The Curriculum Journal*, 25, no. 1: 90–110. DOI:10.1080/09585176.2013.872048

Little, David. 1996. "Freedom to Learn and Compulsion to Interact. Promoting Learner Autonomy Through the Use of Information Systems and Information Technologies." In *Taking Control: Autonomy and Independence in Language Learning*, edited by Richard Pemberton, Edward S. L. Li, Winnie W. F. Or, and Herbert D. Pierson, 203–218. Hong Kong: Hong Kong University Press.

Littlewood, William. 2004. "The Task-Based Approach: Some Questions and Suggestions." *ELT Journal*, 58, no. 4: 319–326. DOI:10.1093/elt/58.4.319

Littlewood, William. 2013. "Developing a Context-Sensitive Pedagogy for Communication-Oriented Language Teaching." *English Language Teaching*, 68, no. 3: 3–25, Accessed October 19, 2014. http://connection. ebscohost.com/c/articles/90566960/ developing-context-sensitive-pedagogy-communication-oriented-language-teaching

Littlewood, William. 2014. "Communication-Oriented Language Teaching: Where Are We Now? Where Do We Go From Here?" *Language Teaching*, 47, no. 3: 349–362. DOI:10.1017/S0261444812000134

Lynch, Monique C., Patricia S. Moyer, Denise Frye, and Jennifer M. Suh. 2002. "Web-Based Learning: Telecollaboration Models to Enhance Mathematics Instruction." In *Proceedings of the International Conference on the Humanistic Renaissance in Mathematics Education*, edited by Alan Rogerson, 279–282. Palermo: Facoltà di Scienze della Formazione dell'Università di Palermo. Accessed October 20, 2014. http://works.bepress.com/patricia_moyerpackenham/54/

Maida, Carl A. 2011. "Project-Based Learning: A Critical Pedagogy for the Twenty-First Century." *Policy Futures in Education*, 9, no. 6: 759–768. DOI: http://dx.doi.org/10.2304/pfie.2011.9.6.759

Mangenot, François, and Elke Nissen. 2006. "Collective Activity and Tutor Involvement in e-Learning Environments for Language Teachers and Learners." *CALICO Journal*, 23, no. 3: 601–622. Accessed June 15, 2014. http://journals.sfu.ca.are.uab.cat/CALICO/index.php/calico/article/view/736

Marsh, Debra. 1997. "Computer Conferencing: Taking the Loneliness Out of Independent Learning." *Language Learning Journal*, 15, no. 1: 21–25. DOI:10.1080/09571739785200051

Mason, Cheryl L., and Michael J. Berson. 2000. "Computer Mediated Communication in Elementary Social Studies Methods: An Examination of Students' Perceptions and Perspectives." *Theory and Research in Social Education*, 28, no. 4: 527–545. DOI:10.1080/00933104.2000.10505922

McLuhan, Marshall. 1962 [2011]. *The Gutenberg Galaxy*, 15th ed. Toronto/London: University of Toronto Press.

Meskill, Carla. 2013a. "Introduction: Sociocultural Research Perspectives for Online Teaching and Learning." In *Online Teaching and Learning: Sociocultural Perspectives. Advances in Digital Language Learning and Teaching*, edited by Carla Meskill, 1–17. London/New York: Bloomsbury Academics.

Meskill, Carla, ed. 2013b. *Online Teaching and Learning: Sociocultural Perspectives. Advances in Digital Language Learning and Teaching*. London/New York: Bloomsbury Academic.

Meskill, Carla, and Natasha Anthony. 2010. *Teaching Languages Online*. Bristol/Toronto: Multilingual Matters.

Müller-Hartmann, Andreas. 2006. "Learning How to Teach Intercultural Communicative Competence Via Telecollaboration: A Model for EFL Teacher Education." In *Internet-Mediated Intercultural Foreign Language Education*, edited by Julie A. Belz and Steven L. Thorne, 63–84. Boston, MA: Heinle.

Narayan, Amarendra. 2013. "ICT: Change of Paradigm, Limitations and Possible Courses for Action for Future." In *Educational Technology in Teaching and Learning: Prospects and Challenges*, edited by Doris D'Souza, Upasana Singh, Durga Sharma, and Prabhas Ranjan, 9–14. Patna, Bihar: Patna's Women's College Publications.

Nunan, David. 2004. *Task-Based Language Teaching. A Comprehensively Revised Edition of Designing Tasks for the Communicative Classroom*. Cambridge: Cambridge University Press.

O'Dowd, Robert. 2007. "Introduction." In *Online Intercultural Exchange: An Introduction to Foreign Language Teachers*, edited by Robert O'Dowd, 3–16. Clevedon/New York: Multilingual Matters.

O'Dowd, Robert. 2012. "Intercultural Communicative Competence Through Telecollaboration." In *The Routledge Handbook of Language and Intercultural Communication*, edited by Jane Jackson, 340–356. Abingdon/New York: Routledge.

O'Dowd, Robert. 2013. "Telecollaboration and CALL." In *Contemporary Computer-Assisted Language Learning*, edited by Michael Thomas, Hayo Reinders, and Mark Warschauer, 123–139. London/Sydney: Bloomsbury.

O'Dowd, Robert, and Paige Ware. 2009. "Critical Issues in Telecollaborative Task Design." *Computer Assisted Language Learning*, 22, no. 2: 173–188. DOI:10.1080/09588220902778369

O'Rourke, Breffni. 2007. "Models of Telecollaboration (1): eTandem." In *Online Intercultural Exchange: An Introduction to Foreign Language Teachers*, edited by Robert O'Dowd, 41–61. Clevedon: Multilingual Matters.

Pérez Cañado, María Luisa. 2010. "Using Virtual Learning Environments and Computer-Mediated Communication to Enhance the Lexical Competence of Pre-Service English Teachers: A Quantitative and Qualitative Study." *Computer-Assisted Language Learning* 23, no. 2: 129–152. DOI:10.1080/09588221003666222

Pérez-Hernández, Danya. 2014. "Technology Provides Foreign-Language Immersion at a Distance." *The Chronicle of Higher Education*. Accessed July 14, 2014. http://chronicle.com/article/Technology-Provides/146369

Pica, Teresa, Ruth Kanagy, and Joseph Falodun. 1993. "Choosing and Using Communication Tasks for Second Language Research and Instruction." In *Tasks and Second Language Learning*, edited by Graham Crookes and Susan M. Gass, 9–34. Clevedon: Multilingual Matters.

Prabhu, Neiman Stern. 1987. *Second Language Pedagogy*. Oxford: Oxford University Press.

Prater, Michael. 2001. "Constructivism and Technology in Art Education." *Art Education*, 54, no. 6: 43–48. Accessed February 18 2015. http://www.jstor.org/stable/3193914?seq=4

Redmond, Petrea, and Jennifer V. Lock. 2006. "A Flexible Framework for Online Collaborative Learning." *The Internet and Higher Education*, 9, no. 4: 267–76.

DOI:https://dx.doi.org.are.uab.cat/10.1016/j.iheduc.2006.08.003

Richards, Jack C., and Theodore S. Rodgers. 2001. *Approaches and Methods in Language Teaching*, 2nd ed. New York: Cambridge University Press.

Rieber, Robert W. and Aaron S. Carton. 1987. *The Collected Works of L.S. Vygotsky Volume 1: Problems of General Psychology*. Translated by Norris Minick. New York: Plenum Press.

Robinson, Peter. 2007. "Aptitudes, Abilities and Contexts in Practice." In *Practice in Second Language Learning: Perspectives from Applied Linguistics and Cognitive Psychology*, edited by Robert M. DeKeyser, 256–286. New York: Cambridge University Press.

Samuda, Virginia, and Martin Bygate. 2008. *Tasks in Second Language Learning*. London: Palgrave Macmillan.

Schwienhorst, Klaus. 2007. *Learner Autonomy and CALL Environments*. New York: Routledge.

Skehan, Peter. 1998. *A Cognitive Approach to Language Learning*. Oxford: Oxford University Press.

Skehan, Peter. 2003. "Task-Based Instruction." *Language Teaching*, 36: 1–14. DOI:10.1017/S026144480200188X

Staley, John, Patricia Seray Moyer-Packenham, and Patricia Lynch. 2005. "Technology Supported Mathematics Environments: Telecollaboration in a Secondary Statistics Classroom." *The Australian Mathematics Teacher*, 61, no. 4: 28–32.

Starke-Meyerring, Doreen, and Melanie Wilson. 2008. *Designing Globally Networked Learning Environments: Visionary Partnerships, Policies, and Pedagogies*. Rotterdam: Sense Publishers.

Telles, João A., ed. 2009. *Teletandem: Um Contexto Virtual, Autônomo e Colaborativo Para Aprendizagem de Línguas Estrangeiras no Século XXI*. Campinas: Pontes Editores.

Tharpe, Roland G., and Ronald Gallimore. 1988. *Rousing Minds to Life. Teaching, Learning and Schooling in Social Context*. Cambridge: Cambridge University Press.

Thomas, Michael, Hayo Reinders, and Mark Warschauer. 2013. "Contemporary Computer-Assisted Language Learning: The Role of Media and Incremental Change." In *Contemporary Computer-Assisted Language Learning*, 1–12. London/Sydney: Bloomsbury.

UNESCO. 2006. *Directory of ICT Resources for Teaching and Learning of Science, Mathematics and Language*. Bangkok: UNESCO.

Ur, Penny. 1981. *Discussions that Work: Task-Centred Fluency Practice*. Cambridge: Cambridge University Press.

Ushioda, Ema. 2000. "Tandem Language Learning Via e-Mail: From Motivation to Autonomy." *ReCALL*, 12, no. 2: 121–128.

Velghe, Fie. 2012. "Deprivation, Distance and Connectivity: The Adaptation of Mobile Phone Use to Life in Wesbank, A Post-Apartheid Township in South Africa." *Discourse, Context & Media*, 1, no. 4: 2013–2216. DOI: http://dx.doi.org/10.1016/j.dcm.2012.09.004

Velghe, Fie, and Jan Blommaert. 2014. "Emergent New Literacies and the Mobile Phone: Informal Language Learning, Voice and Identity in a South African Township." In *Intercultural Contact, Language Learning and Migration*, edited by Barbara Geraghty and Jean E. Conacher, 89–111. London/New York: Bloomsbury Academic.

Vygotsky, Lev S. 1978. *Mind in Society: The Development of Higher Mental Processes*. Cambridge, MA: Harvard University Press.

Wall, A. E. Ted, Alain Breuleux, Gyeong Mi Heo, Karen Rye, Marie-Helen Goyetche, and Véronique Lemay. 2011. "Teacher-Based Inquiry in the BCT Project." *LEARNing Landscapes*, 4, no. 2: 325–344.

Warschauer, Mark, ed. 1995. *Virtual Connections: Online Activities and Projects for Networking Language Learners*. Honolulu, HI: University of Hawai'i Second Language Teaching and Curriculum Center.

Warschauer, Mark, ed. 1996. *Telecollaboration in Foreign Language Learning*. Honolulu, HI: University of Hawai'i Second Language Teaching and Curriculum Center.

Warschauer, Mark, and Deborah Healey. 1998. "Computers and Language Learning: An Overview." *Language Teaching*, 31: 57–71. DOI: http://dx.doi.org/10.1017/s0261444800012970

Warschauer, Mark, and Richard Kern. 2000. *Network-Based Language Teaching: Concepts and Practice*. Cambridge, MA: Cambridge University Press.

Wellman, Elizabeth, Maya Creedman, and Jana Flores. 2000. "Beyond Primary Sources: A Professional Development Collaboration Designing Technology Integrated Instruction for Supporting K-12 Historical Thinking and Understanding." In *Proceedings of Society for Information Technology & Teacher Education International Conference 2000*, edited by Dee Anna Willis, Jerry Price, and Jerry Willis, 1990–1996. Chesapeake, VA: AACE.

Wertsch, James V. 1988. *Vygotsky and the Social Formation of Mind*. Cambridge, MA: Harvard University Press.

## FURTHER READING

Guth, Sarah, and Francesca Helm. 2012. "Developing Multiliteracies in ELT Through Telecollaboration." *ELT Journal*, 66, no. 1: 42–51. DOI:10.1093/elt/ccr027

# 13 The Continuing Evolution of Virtual Worlds for Language Learning

## RANDALL W. SADLER

## Introduction

> He followed her up the passage that stretches straight and gently rising as far as the torchlight shone. They were walking a patch that could not be—or at least that no one in the Coven could have believed. The castle was basically a logical structure "fleshed" out with the sensory cues that allowed warlocks to move about it as one would a physical structure. Its moats and walls were part of that logical structure, and though they had no physical reality outside of the varying potentials in whatever processors were running the program, they were proof again the movement of the equally "unreal" perceptions of the inhabitants of the plane. (Vinge 2001, 269)

The quotation that begins this chapter comes from the novella *True Names*, written by Vernor Vinge and first published in 1981. It describes a computer hacker (referred to as "warlocks" in the story) interacting with a *virtual environment* (a "logic structure") that exists solely in a computer network. Although the term *cyberspace* was first used in the William Gibson short story *Burning Chrome* (1982) a year later, Vinge's novella is recognized as the first fully developed concept of the idea of a modern cyberspace. From this fictional foundation, programmers developed the VWs that we know today.

## What are virtual worlds?

While the basic concept of a virtual world has existed for some time (more on that in the next section), our modern concept of a VW is still a matter of some debate since their continuing evolution has led to refined definitions as well. While some might consider a massively multi-player online role-play game (MMORPG) like *World of Warcraft* to be entirely different from a VW like *Second Life*, others (including this author) see them as virtual cousins that share many of the same characteristics, with the key difference being that VWs are *primarily* considered as virtual environments that exist primarily for socializing or what Steinkuehler and Williams (2006) refer to as a "new third spaces" since they may provide virtual "spaces for social interactions and relationships beyond the workplace (or school) and home…" (889). For the purposes of this chapter, a VW will be defined as having the following characteristics:

*The Handbook of Technology and Second Language Teaching and Learning*, First Edition.
Edited by Carol A. Chapelle and Shannon Sauro.
© 2017 John Wiley & Sons, Inc. Published 2020 by John Wiley & Sons, Inc.

- *Online 3D environment.* This may simulate the real world, or it may be wildly creative …
- *Avatars.* Avatars are the in-world representations of real people who control them …
- *Real-time interactivity.* VWs include the possibility of interacting with other avatars in the environment in real time (synchronous communication), and usually with a range of objects in that VW.
- 24-hour accessibility….
- *Persistence.* When a user logs out of a VW, their avatar, and the actions taken by that avatar, are not deleted.
- *Social space.* Although VWs may vary in look and theme, all VWs are primarily social spaces that exist for the purpose of humans interacting via their avatars.
- *Numbers.* In most VWs there are many players (sometimes in the hundreds of thousands) online in the world at the same time …
- In many—though not all—VWs, users can also control their own appearance (e.g., height, facial features, eye color), gender, clothing, and even their species. In addition, many VWs allow users some control over their environment … (Sadler 2012, 24–25).

If this VW definition is modified to have a somewhat reduced focus on "social space" with the element of "gaming" added as being of primary importance, this might also function as a definition of MMORPGs. While MMORPGs can be used for educational purposes (see Thorne 2008), the strong social environments existing in VWs such as Second Life, OpenSim, Active Worlds, Club Penguin, and so on, make using them for educational purposes to be quite natural.

As seen in Figure 13.1, this virtual chateau in Second Life (located in a holodeck above the educational sim *EduNation*) provides a 3D space where avatars (ranging from 2 to over 100) can engage in real-time interactivity. In this chateau, this interaction might include a seating area for class discussions, a conference room with a PowerPoint screen, a site for a medieval role-play activity, or simply a ballroom with an integrated dance system.

**Figure 13.1**   Chateau Renoir in Second Life.

This chapter will begin with a discussion of the evolution of VWs from their early text-based incarnations up to those we use today, followed by an overview and categorization of a number of current VWs, utilizing three criteria: their appropriate age level, their level of *gaminess*, their relative emphasis on socialization, their explicit focus on education, and their technical requirements. Next, a synthesis of investigations so far accomplished in the area will be provided, followed by a discussion of the future of VWs.

## A brief history of VWs

Behold! Human beings living in an underground den, which has a mouth open towards the light and reaching all along the den; here they have been from their childhood, and have their legs and necks chained so that they cannot move, and can only see before them, being prevented by the chains from turning round their heads. Above and behind them a fire is blazing at a distance, and between the fire and the prisoners there is a raised way; and you will see, if you look, a low wall built along the way, like the screen which marionette players have in front of them, over which they show the puppets.
I see.
…
Like ourselves, I replied; and they see only their own shadows, or the shadows of one another, which the fire throws on the opposite wall of the cave? (Plato, *The Republic*, 514–520 AD)

The quotation that began this chapter from Vernor Vinge illustrated what many claim is the first modern depiction of a virtual world. However, it could easily be argued that the concept of a world that deceives the eye, and that exists as a reality for the viewers, can be traced back approximately 1,500 years to Plato's "allegory of the cave" in *The Republic*. In this philosophical discussion, the shadows (*virtual* images of a sort) on the cave wall—the only visual input allowed for these hypothetical life-long prisoners—are their reality. A more recent fictional representation of something that hints at the possibility of a technologically constructed VW (or perhaps even virtual reality (VR) as it includes multiple senses) may be seen as early as 1935 in the story *Pygmalion's Spectacles*. Written only 12 years after the first "talkie" arrived in theaters; the main character describes his new invention:

'Listen! I'm Albert Ludwig—Professor Ludwig.' As Dan was silent, he continued, 'It means nothing to you, eh? But listen—a movie that gives one sight and sound. Suppose now that I add taste, smell, even touch, if your interest is taken by the story. Suppose I make it so that you are in the story, you speak to the shadows, and the shadows reply, and instead of being on a screen, the story is all about you, and you are in it. Would that be to make real a dream? (Weinbaum 1935)

Later works by authors such as Vernor Vinge (that began this chapter), William Gibson's *Neuromancer* in 1984, and Neal Stephenson's *Snow Crash* from 1992 took the computer technology that was beginning to develop and ran with it fictionally. That work, in turn, inspired many of the virtual environments that exist online today.
    The history of virtual worlds as they exist on computers and online may be traced back to the creation of the first text-based computer games, beginning with Colossal Cave Adventure (CCA) by Will Crowther in 1975–1976 (for a more thorough history see Sadler, 2012). This virtual text-based environment was based on the real life Mammoth Cave system in Kentucky but included a number of fantasy-inspired components. As seen in Figure 13.2, CCA required

```
WELCOME TO ADVENTURE! ! WOULD YOU LIKE INSTRUCTIONS?


YES
SOMEWHERE NEARBY IS COLOSSAL CAVE, WHERE OTHERS HAVE FOUND
FORTUNES IN TREASURE AND GOLD, THOUGH IT IS RUMORED THAT SOME WHO
ENTER ARE NEVER SEEN AGAIN.  MAGIC IS SAID TO WORK IN THE CAVE.  I WILL
BE YOUR EYES AND HANDS.  DIRECT ME WITH COMMANDS OF 1 OR 2 WORDS.
(ERRORS, SUGGESTIONS, COMPLAINTS TO CROWTHER)
(IF STUCK TYPE HELP FOR SOME HINTS)

YOU ARE STANDING AT THE END OF A ROAD BEFORE A SMALL BRICK BUILDING.
AROUND YOU IS A FOREST. A SMALL
STREAM FLOWS OUT OF THE BUILDING AND DOWN A GULLY.
GO IN

YOU ARE INSIDE A BUILDING, A WELL HOUSE FOR A LARGE SPRING.
THERE IS A SHINY BRASS LAMP NEARBY.
THERE ARE SOME KEYS ON THE GROUND HERE.
THERE IS FOOD HERE.
THERE IS A BOTTLE OF WATER HERE.
```

**Figure 13.2**   Opening scene in Colossal Cave Adventure.

players to find and make use of a number of items in order to both survive and successfully accomplish their adventure.

Unlike modern VWs or MMORPGs, games like CCA were not (initially) available online or as multiplayer environments and so cannot quite be identified as either. CCA was followed by a number of similar adventures, perhaps most notably Zork in 1979 (where this author was slain by a dragon numerous times), but the true birth of online *multi-user* environments began with the creation of multi-user dungeons (MUDs):

> A MUD is a multiplayer computer game that typically combines text instant message chat rooms and role-playing games. Typically, players read descriptions of their environment, objects, events, and characters in a virtual world. Users interact with other players and their surrounding by typing text commands. Many MUDs involve a fantasy world populated by mythical beings. In order to complete quests or adventures, users must complete tasks, while exploring the virtual world. (Childress and Braswell 2006, 188)

In 1978 Roy Trubshaw created a new game which was patterned on one of the variations of Zork that he called MUD. It first ran on the network of Essex University only, but in 1987 it became available on ARPANET (an ancestor of today's Internet), therefore becoming the first true multi-user online role-play environment. This game, which can still be found on the British Legends website http://www.british-legends.com, included the game elements that made its predecessors popular, but added human-to-human text-based communication and competition in the online environment. This meant that players no longer played solely against a computer, but against (or in support of) each other as well.

The evolution of MUDs led to the creation of MOOs (MUDs, Object-Oriented), with the first created by Stephen White in 1990. While these often looked almost identical to MUDs at first glance—still text-based environments that allowed for multiple users—they also integrated a new feature called *object-oriented programming*. This allowed for the owner of the MOO, typically called the wizard, to add elements such a new room or items within a room (again, still text-based) without custom programming a new environment from scratch (a feature that may seem familiar to users of modern VWs like Second Life). Educators soon discovered that these spaces had potential for virtual classroom space, and the use of MOOs flourished in that area. A number of universities, including the University of Arizona (the *Old Pueblo MOO*) had MOOs that instructors were able to use for virtual office hours or other educational activities. This author had his own text-based office in the MOO where he held office hours and engaged in group conferences with his ESL and native English-speaking writing students. The students gave each other text-based feedback on papers, with complete transcripts available for them to examine as they worked on revisions. While almost all MOOs have disappeared since that time, at the time of this printing the SchMOOze University MOO is still available for use by anyone: http://schmooze.hunter.cuny.edu/.

While MOOs did have a number of uses, their lack of a true graphical interface is what likely led to their demise as more visually-oriented gaming and computing platforms continued to evolve. Perhaps the first commercial experiment that addressed this deficit was created by Lucasfilm (of *Star Wars* fame) and was Habitat (1986), made available by *Quantum Link* for the Commodore 64 computer.

As seen in Figure 13.3, Habitat had a graphical (color) interface that is recognizable to users of today's VWs. While voice chat was still something for the future, Habitat users could text chat with other avatars representing their real life users within the 3D spaces and explore the environment which, at its peak, contained 20,000 regions (each screen as seen in the figure was a region). Users of Habitat governed themselves, a philosophy that continues in many VWs like Second Life today, and were responsible for creating their own rules and regulations for virtual living. Randall Farmer, one of the co-creators of this VW, later identified five different types of users: "The Passives, The Actives, The Motivators, The Caretakers, The Geek Gods" (Farmer 1992, 89). While the technology may have advanced considerably since the days of Habitat, the nature of the users still seems quite familiar. As mentioned by Morningstar (his co-creator of Habitat) and Farmer (2001):

**Figure 13.3**   Avatars communicating via text chat in a Habitat region.

At the core of our vision is the idea that cyberspace is necessarily a multiple-participant environment. It seems to us that the things that are important to the inhabitants of such an environment are the capabilities available to them, the characteristics of the other people they encounter there, and the ways these various participants can affect each other. (2001, 173–174)

The creators of moderns VWs would certainly agree. It is this "multiple participant environment" that is essentially social in nature that provides the strong potential for learning. These virtual environments have the potential to provide an environment in which learners may work within a Vygotskian *Zone of Proximal Development* where "the distance between the actual developmental level as determined by independent problem solving and the level of potential development as determined through problem solving under adult guidance or in collaboration with more capable peers" (Vygotsky 1978, 86). By providing access to "more capable peers" and a variety of settings in which to engage in "problem solving" VWs can be ideal language learning/practice environments.

## Overview and categorization of virtual worlds today

One of the key questions that is surprisingly difficult to answer is exactly how many virtual worlds exist. One reason for this difficulty lies in the nebulous division between VWs and MMORPGs, as discussed earlier in this chapter. Sadler (2012) reviewed two popular sites (see below) focusing on both MMORPGs and VWs. As seen in Figure 13.4, in May, 2011, mmorpg.com listed 414 MMORPGS, while mmohut.com listed 290. In the several years since that data were collected, these numbers increased to 757 and 1,215 respectively. Given that there are a number of platforms listed on one but not both of these sites, and that there are a large number of environments that exist solely in languages other than English that are not considered in these counts, the actual number is significantly higher.

Determining how many individuals are making use of VWs is also quite difficult. One reason for this difficulty is that VWs that actually publish user data (which are rare indeed) typically only make available the number of registered accounts. As might be imagined, this number does not actually indicate how many active users are currently engaged in the platform, so this may include players who have not logged in for years. It is also often the case that an individual may have multiple accounts in a single VW (this author has four accounts in *Second Life* used for different machinima characters) or accounts with many different VW platforms (this author has accounts in SL, Active Worlds, There, and many

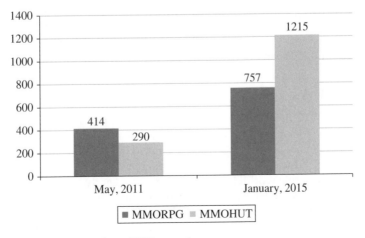

Figure 13.4 Increase in MMORPGs and VWs over four years.

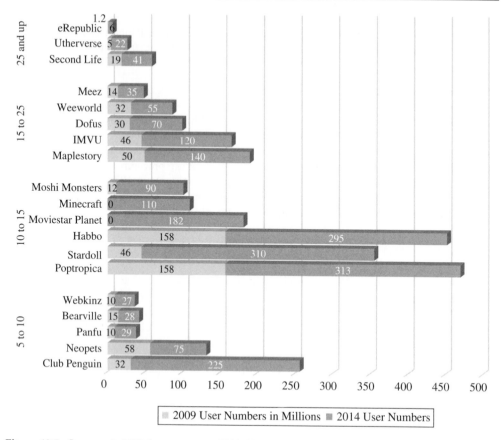

**Figure 13.5**   Increase in VWs by age group: 2009–2014.

other VWs). Therefore, while the number of registered accounts is now most certainly well over 1 billion, the number of active users is doubtless considerably fewer.

Regardless of the true number of active users at any single time, the increasing number of registered VW users is both impressive and rapidly increasing. Figure 13.5 illustrates some of the most popular VWs for four different age ranges, with two numbers included for each. First is the number of registered users in 2009, with the number on the right representing the 2014 user numbers (data modified from KZERO). As can be seen, some of these worlds did not exist in the earlier year (Minecraft's alpha version came out in 2009, but the full version was not released until 2011) and in all cases there was significant growth across the worlds.

## Categories of VWs

In the early days of VW development, the choices were quite limited, especially for those interested in their use for education. One of the first widely available VWs with a significant education component was *Active Worlds* (AWs), created in 1995 and still available today. AW included a significant Educational Universe component that, sadly, has largely faded away, as has the popularity of this world. However, there has recently been significant redevelopment in AW that may signal new development in this environment. More recently, as discussed above, the number of VWs has risen dramatically, which means that educators can choose from environments aimed at young children, teens, or adults, with multiple options at each level. Similar options exist for VWs ranging from those almost entirely focused on social interaction to those that blend into the universe of MMORPGs. Each of the VWs discussed below begins with details (based on an analysis of the VW and materials from supporting websites) in five key areas:

- *Age level*. The specific age ranges recommended for the VW based on the information provided by the company. This may be in grade levels or age.
- *Game level (low, mid, or high)*. A "pure" social environment would rarely be strongly game-like[1] in nature. A MMORPG like World of Warcraft, on the other hand, may include social elements, but the primary goal of WoW is to gain talents, skills, and tools in order to complete quests.
- *Socialization level (low, mid, or high)*. VWs are social spaces, but some are more social than others.
- *Education focus (low, mid, or high)*. Nearly all VWs have potential use for education. The key is in the *way* that they are used. VWs are a tool for teachers in the same way that PowerPoint can be a tool. The education focus discussed below, however, refers to whether the VW was specifically designed by the creators to be used *for* education.
- *Technical requirements (low, mid, or high)*. Some VWs are more graphics intensive than others. Some require more bandwidth, or are more difficult to navigate.

As will be seen below, VWs vary greatly across all of these areas.

*Woogi World*

Age level: Grades K-6
Game level: mid
Socialization level: high
Education focus: high
Technical requirements: low

Woogi World is specifically designed as an education virtual world for children in grades K-6, with no players allowed over the age of 13. The materials available to children in this VW have been carefully designed to meet a number of educational standards both in the United States and internationally. This environment includes the Woogi Academy, which they maintain is "... the only educational platform that seamlessly combines a cutting edge game-based learning model and a social learning community, with world-class academic programs" (Woogi World 2015). The academy (some areas under construction as of the printing of this book) uses a combination of videos, social areas, and online games to provide lessons in music, math, science, reading, and ESL/ESL and is designed to be used by teachers in the classroom and also for independent learning. As seen in Figure 13.6, public areas in the world include (amongst many others) an *English club* and *Woogi Nations*.

In Woogi World avatars may not begin to chat until they have completed a *chat mission* which educates them regarding cyber safety. Chat is monitored and the system automatically filters out a number of words deemed to be inappropriate. Parents can also review the chat logs of their children at any time. Woogi World is an excellent example of a virtual learning environment that integrates a wide variety of games, while also encouraging both socialization and strong educational practices. This is reflected in their connection to educational partners such as *Smithsonian Education*, *Discovery Education*, and the *National Education Association*. Woogi World is browser-based, so it requires no download, and movement is accomplished by simply clicking on a location to advance the avatar. Since this VW is specifically designed for use in education, this world should be considered as a strong option for language teachers working with younger students.

**Figure 13.6**   Woogi World.

*Club Penguin*

Age level: 6–14
Game level: low
Socialization level: high
Education focus: low
Technical requirements: low

Club Penguin is designed for children ranging in age from 6 to 14. However, unlike in the case of Woogi World, there is no officially mandated upper age range for players. This VW has been owned by Disney since 2007, though it was first open to the public in 2005. While Club Penguin does have over 20 games available in the environment, socializing is the primary focus. The primary activities include playing games, adopting pets, customizing avatars (all in the form of penguins) and home (igloos, of course), chatting, engaging in themed events (e.g., seasonal parties), and becoming ninjas or secret agents (Club Penguin 2015). As in the case of almost all VWs, children may get a Club Penguin account for free, but a paid account and/or buying credit in the VW pertinent game currency allows for a wider range of access and *cooler* toys.

One of the pertinent design features of this VW is a strong attention to player safety. As with Woogi World, Club Penguin has standards and tools in place to protect users from inappropriate language. In this VWs parents can choose between their children using either *Standard Safe Chat* or *ultimate safe chat*. *Standard safe chat* is designed to disallow inappropriate words and phrases. It also is designed to prevent the communication of phone numbers and other identifying information. This site also includes live moderators who can be contacted in-world by players clicking the shield icon at the top-right of the screen as seen in Figure 13.7. This figure also illustrates the *Ultimate safe chat* option that parents may select for their children's penguin. Ultimate safe chat does not allow for any user-typed communication. Instead, when a child clicks on the chat feature in this option (the speech bubble in the lower

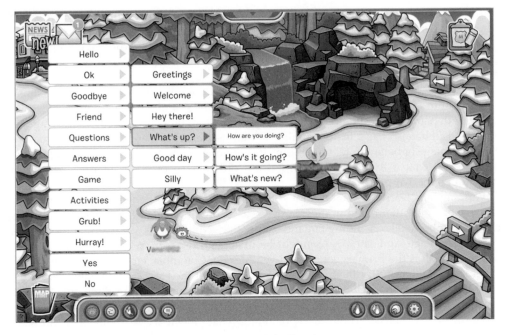

**Figure 13.7** Club Penguin illustrating the Ultimate Safe Chat feature.

menu bar) they are presented with the left-column chat options seen on the game screen (Hello, OK, Goodbye, etc.). Clicking on one of those options (Hello), results in the second column of choices. Selecting *What's up* then results in the choices for the player. Another player wishing to respond may then find potential choices by selecting *Answers*. Club Penguin has no option for voice chat, likely due to the difficulty in moderating voice communication. As with the previous VW, this one is browser-based, with click-to-move travel. For language learners, Club Penguin may be played in six different languages (English, French, German, Portuguese, Russian, and Spanish) via a simple drop-down menu during the login process. This change results in both the ultimate safe chat communication and the user interface showing in that language. Students learning any of those languages can easily find native speakers of those languages with whom to practice. Although it does not have a strong educational focus, teachers looking for a safe place for their students to interact may find Club Penguin to be a strong option.

*Habbo*

Ages: 13+
Gaminess: low
Socialization: high
Education focus: low
Technical requirements: low

Habbo is designed for users 13 or older, with younger individuals not allowed to register. Habbo was founded by the Finnish Sulake Corporation in 2000, where it is the largest social network. Habbo members are given a free basic room in the hotel (which can either be kept private or opened up to other avatars) and paid subscribers receive 35 Habbo coins and a "rare" piece of furniture a month. Habbo actually has three types of currency (coins, duckets, and diamonds), each with its own function. Coins may be used to buy additional furniture for rooms, clothing, and so on. The hotel itself includes a variety of other spaces, such as the lobby, gardens, restaurants, other social areas, and a marketplace where users can buy items for their rooms or avatar. While Habbo did have a significant gaming component in the form of *game rooms* with titles such as World of Zombie, this portion closed in 2014.

As with the previous VWs, movement in Habbo is accomplished by clicking on the square on the floor to which the user wishes to travel. Habbo has a similar policy for users regarding safety, with patrols by adult moderators employed by the company and automatic language filtering. Habbo also has a feature similar to that used in Club Penguin to report inappropriate language or behavior to moderators. It is not unusual to see the term bobba sprinkled through text chat in Habbo since this is the word utilized by their filtering software in substitution for inappropriate terms.

For language learners, Habbo (in a similar manner to Club Penguin) is divided into a number of individual communities, largely based on language. There are currently nine Habbo country hotels, including Finland, Spain, Italy, Netherlands, Germany, France, Brazil, English-language, and Turkey. As might be imagined, users from a number of countries where Spanish is the primary language (e.g., Mexico, Colombia, etc.) also make use of the "Spain" hotel. Figure 13.8 illustrates the waiting room of the Habbo Spain hotel. As shown, all of the avatars in the waiting room at the time of this picture were speaking only Spanish. This environment does not offer the potential for voice chat, but it still is an excellent resource for finding native speakers of a variety of languages for live text chat. While there are some

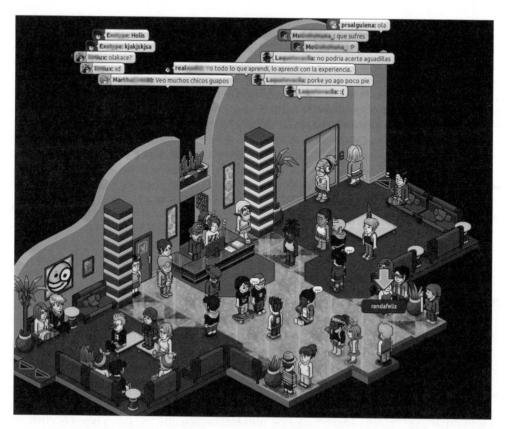

**Figure 13.8**   Habbo Spain waiting lounge.

risks for educators in using Habbo with their students due to user creativity in circumventing the *bobba* function, having access to large number of speakers of a variety of languages makes this VW a powerful tool.

*Second Life*

Age level: 13 and up (restrictions)
Game level: varies
Socialization level: high
Education focus: varies
Technical requirements: mid to high

Second Life (see Figure 13.1), created in 2003 by Linden Lab, is primarily designed for users 18 years and older, but two other age ranges are allowed in-world. Players between 16–17 years old may access regions in SL with a *general maturity rating*, but are not allowed into *moderate* or *adult* rated regions. Individuals between the ages of 13–15 may be allowed into a specific estate owned by an affiliated organization (such as a school). In this case, their avatar will not have the capability to travel off that estate and other avatars are not allowed onto the estate without approval by the organization. This allows for a school to have one or more islands in SL while also providing a safe environment for their students. From its inception, the creators of SL have taken a "hands off" philosophy toward policing the content of this world. This means that some islands are perfectly suited for a wide variety of purposes, ranging from socializing, to gaming, to education, while other islands are most definitely adult in nature. This is not to say that this VW should be avoided for education—some teachers equate using this VW to taking students on a trip to New York. Some areas of that city (museums, Broadway, etc.) are wonderful resources, while other venues (e.g., adult clubs) or neighborhoods may not be appropriate for students. This means that any educator using SL should be educated on the appropriate settings.

Communication in SL is accomplished via text or audio chat. Text chat may be either public or private (via an in-world instant messaging system) with voice chat also having public and private options. Unlike the previous VWs mentioned in this chapter, SL has no restrictions on the language used in-world, though individual islands may have restrictions as determined by the estate owner. Movement in SL may be accomplished either via keyboard arrows or a click to teleport function, but language is used for communication with others in the VW. This VW requires a program download and Linden Labs provides suggestions for minimum graphics requirements for the best user experience (for a more detailed examination of these elements see Sadler 2012).

Second Life consists of several "continents" in addition to many thousands of privately owned (but largely publicly accessible) islands, with the vast majority of the content in those settings created by users of SL. This gives users access to a large variety of venues, as seen in Figure 13.9. The upper-left of the figure shows the Eiffel Tower in the Paris, 1900 sim. This island also includes recreations of Notre Dame Cathedral, the Arc de Triomphe, and a number of Paris street scenes. There are a great number of similar islands scattered across SL either representing famous landmarks (as in the case of Mont Saint-Michel seen in the upper right of the figure) or simply populated by many speakers of a single language. Indeed, over half of the users of SL do not speak English as their first language, and there are registered users of SL from over 250 countries, territories, and regions. While it is likely easier to find speakers of a few languages in some of the other VWs mentioned in this chapter, the number of languages represented in SL make it a valuable tool for language learners. There are also many art venues in SL, as seen in the lower-right side of the figure with the *Inevitability of Fate* exhibit. Virtual environments like SL give skilled users the ability to create almost any environment imaginable, whether it be sculpture or a cathedral. The figure also shows

**Figure 13.9**    Four Second Life venues: Paris, Mont Saint-Michel, Inevitability of Fate, and Virtlantis.

(lower-left) the Virtlantis sim, which has provided a venue for free language learning activities since 2006. This sim, and many other like it, are part of a very strong community of educators in SL in fields ranging from genetics to language learning. Second Life is the VW where the largest amount of educational research has so far taken place.

## Research on virtual worlds

In comparison to other forms of computer-mediated communication (CMC) such as email, message boards, and so on, research into the effect of VWs on language learning and teaching is relatively recent. With the exception of research on Habitat, studies examining VWs have almost entirely been published after 2000. Several books examining the related issue in-depth include *Education in Virtual Worlds: Teaching and Learning in Second Life* (Molka-Danielsen and Deutschmann 2009), *Learning and Teaching in the Virtual World of Second Life* (Wankel and Kingsley 2009), *Learning Online with Games, Simulations, and Virtual Worlds* (Aldrich 2009), *Multi-User Virtual Environments for the Classroom: Practical Approaches to Teaching in Virtual Worlds* (Vincenti and Braman 2011) and *Virtual Worlds for Language Learning: From Theory to Practice* (Sadler 2012). For those interested in exploring the topic in-depth, all of those books are worth a close examination.

Given the social nature of VW environments, it is not surprising that one theme shared by a number of VW studies is their ability to enhance collaboration amongst learners. Sadler (2009) discusses the potential for task-based language teaching virtual construction tasks in Second Life to enhance language learning. This focus on tasks is echoed by Lin et al. (2014), who used both information-gap and reasoning-gap activities in Second Life, finding that it was able "… to provide an environment that simulated real world conditions and to enable the use of the spatial nature of that environment to facilitate student interaction with native speakers of Mandarin on the other side of the world, thus adding authenticity to the communicative aspects of the CFL course in Australia" (20). Studies by Bystrom and Barfield (1999) and Steinkuehler (2004), in keeping with the theorized benefit of working in one's *Zone of Proximal Development*, found that students were able to successfully accomplish tasks better when working with partners. Other studies commenting on the collaborative natures of these environments include work by Churchill and Snowdon 1998; Dillenbourg, Schneider, and Syntenta 2002; Brown and Bell 2004; Price and Rogers 2004; Roussou 2004; Shaffer, Squire, Halverson, and Gee 2004; Gronstedt 2007; Skiba 2007; Ball and Pearce 2009; Bani, Genovesi, Ciregia, Piscioneri, Rapisarda, Salvatori, and Simi, 2009; Sadler and Dooly, 2012; and others.

A second major set of findings regarding VWs and language learning connects to the issue of anxiety. Some of this research found that the use of an avatar (essentially a *masked persona* for the user) helped learners to "loosen…up a bit…" (Love, Ross, and Wilhelm 2009, 68) while they were able to experiment with new and powerful identities" (Shaffer, Squire, Halverson, and Gee 2004, 6). In their study, Grant, Huang, and Pasfield-Neofitou found that college-age students studying Chinese who made use of a virtual environment had a significantly lower level of foreign language anxiety compared to students studying in a real life classroom. In that study they also looked at the issue of computer or technology-related anxiety and how this might affect students making use of the VW. While this is a common issue discussed as a potential weakness of VWs in education, they found that while some students found using a virtual environment to be challenging, "It would also appear that there was not a significant inherent level of technical related anxiety, nor did the technical aspects of interacting in the virtual environment present significant additional levels of technical anxiety" (Grant, Huang, and Pasfield-Neofitou 2013, 7). One possible explanation for this lowered anxiety mentioned in this study, and in research from Childress and Braswell (2006) is that text-based communication in particular "allows them time to more completely formulate their thoughts as they respond to the class discussion" (2006, 188). At the same time, the *play* component that is an integral part of a VW world experience, as demonstrated in research that examined the VW *Quest Atlantis* not only aids in decreasing anxiety but can also lead to "a positive attitude toward English language learning" since students may find it "fun and interesting in comparison to learning English in the classroom" (Zheng et al. 2009, 218).

A number of researchers also discuss the power of VWs to expose learners to the *real world* via the virtual environment. While this may seem counterintuitive, it appears that students can become so immersed in the environment that the virtual and the real can become blurred in a positive manner. As one participant studying Chinese in a VW setting discussed, "As someone who doesn't really have anyone to practice Chinese I feel that the lab classes allow me to use what I have learnt in a real life setting" (Grant et al. 2014, 30). Interestingly, the student makes clear mention of the "lab classes," but the only reference to the virtual environment is as "a real life setting." It appears that students are able to suspend disbelief in the *artificial nature* of these settings since they can give them the opportunity to visit locations and/or engage in educational activities that would not otherwise be possible. While not all participants saw the VW as being *real* in their study, they still found potential real world benefits: "I find these tasks helpful for practicing using the language and they will prepare me to use Chinese in practical situations. Practicing these situations in a 3D environment can make me less nervous if I come across these situations in real life" (30). This real world (RW) connection can include cases such as visiting historical locations or the workshop of a historical feature like the ancient Greek sculptor Phedias (Roussou 2004), creating historical buildings like the Leaning Tower of Pisa (Bani et al. 2009), or creating modern works of architecture (Gu et al. 2009). From the teacher perspective, a VW can make it "…relatively easy to adapt and modify the environment to suit a particular lesson design and to create teaching/learning opportunities that might otherwise not be available in the RW classroom (e.g., shops, restaurants, the mazes, etc.)" (Lin et al. 2014, 20).

From a teacher's perspective, Varli's (2013) research nicely sums up both the benefits of using VWs in the classroom and also where there are still areas in need of improvement. Overall, the teachers in his research (1) are excited and passionate about the opportunities 3D VWs offer for their students, their course content, and their teaching; (2) are curious and impatient about the innovations in VWs' technologies; (3) have positive expectations about the educational practices in VWs; (4) are aware of that face that teaching in VWs is a different phenomenon than teaching in RL; (5) are in favour of social and collaborative learning activities and; (6) are hopeful about the future potential of these online worlds (73).

## The future of VWs

If predictions of future technologies were accurate, humans today would be traveling via personal air cars, with our work being done by groups of robots—made safe, of course, by Isaac Asimov's three laws of robotics as introduced in the short story *Runaround* in 1942. Sadly, this is not the case, but near-future predictions about upcoming advances in VWs may be made with (somewhat) greater accuracy based on products currently under development.

At the time of this book's printing, Second Life will be more than 13 years old and Active Worlds will be more than 20. Over that time, VWs have continued to advance, with massive changes in the quality of the graphics, user interfaces, and possibilities for communication. However, there are a number of upcoming changes in these environments that will begin to shift them from being VWs to more fully developed artificial reality simulators (ARS). This begins the shift from a 3D environment on a computer screen to "the idea of immersion— using stereoscopy, gaze-tracking, and other technologies to create the illusion of being inside a computer-generated scene...." (Rheingold 1991, 112–113). Second Life is currently offering a 2.0 version of a project (experimental) viewer that allows for the use of the Oculus Rift headset (see Figure 13.10) with that VW. The commercial version of Oculus Rift became available in 2015. Oculus Rift headsets (and other similar products) provide a stereoscopic view of 3D online environments that are meant to provide a fully immersive 3D visual connection for users. One very simple benefit of this technology for language learners is that this has the potential to allow them to take a fully immersive 3D walk through the streets of Paris so that they can experience the city from their own classroom.

This technology includes the tracking of head movements and orientation. Therefore, while logged into a VW, the movements made by your real life head are duplicated by the avatar.

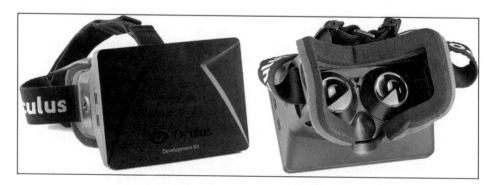

**Figure 13.10**   Oculus Rift headset.[2]

A user looking over her shoulder in real life would see whatever is over the shoulder of her avatar in the virtual environment. Having tried this technology, I found the experience immersive indeed, though my tendency to motion sickness in real life did, sadly, translate into my VW Oculus Rift experience as well.

An even greater leap currently under development by Philip Rosedale (the original creator of Second Life) and a team of researchers is the high fidelity VW. The developers intend to integrate a number of artificial reality tools into this platform to more fully integrate the user experience. While most of these technologies are still in the development phase, in addition to Oculus Rift, Leap Motion, PrioVR, Sixense, and Depthsense cameras are currently being researched as part of the user interface. Leap Motion would give VW users the ability to interact with the environment, and objects in the environment, without the use of a keypad, mouse, or touch display. In essence, users would have the ability to reach toward their screen to grasp a book or other object in the VW and interact with it—opening the book or turning a page. PrioVR will offer a selection of "sensor suits" (ranging from 8–17 sensors depending on need for precision) that will translate not just head and hand but full body motion to the VW. This offers the possibility of having an avatar walk through a house as his user performing a walking motion in the real world, having the avatar sit in a chair, as his user does the same, or having the avatar explore an enormous strand of DNA in the VW by "climbing" it—all of this controlled by RL user motion. Sixense takes this idea a step further by eliminating the sensor suit and using wireless controllers to track movement in a similar way to PrioVR. Finally, Depthsense cameras by SoftKinetic are designed to eliminate all sensors and track body movement, including detailed hand and finger movement.

In addition to the advances in interface described above, the increasing accuracy (though they do still leave much to be desired) of online simultaneous translation programs, both for text- and audio-based communication, continues to make communication with speakers of other languages easier. In 2015, Skype began a preview of their new (near) simultaneous translation feature. While at that time it was only available for English and Spanish, more languages were expected to be added. In addition to the verbal translation, the program will also provide a written transcript of that communication including the utterance by the communicator in their language and the translation into the desired language. The translation will also be applied to any text chat in the conversation. Second Life already provides simultaneous translation of text chat (making use of either Bing or Google translations), although the quality of these translations is not of the highest quality, and voice translation in that and other VWs seems likely in the future as well.

As shown in this chapter, virtual worlds have grown from their text-based infancy of the 1970s to the 3D immersive environments of today. Educators and students now have a wide array of VWs available to them that can grant instant access to native speakers of a huge variety of languages who are located around the world. As these environments and their associated technologies continue to advance, they promise to change the ways that we understand both human-to-human interaction and what it means to be a student of language.

# NOTES

1   Game-like is defined as an environment that is competitive in nature, often including the goal of "winning" by either accumulating experience, points, or kills numbers.
2   Image courtesy of Wikipedia: http://en.wikipedia.org/wiki/Oculus_Rift

# REFERENCES

Aldrich, Clark. 2009. *Learning Online with Games, Simulations, and Virtual Worlds: Strategies for Online Instruction.*
San Francisco, CA: Jossey-Bass.

Ball, Simon, and Rob Pearce. 2009. "Inclusion Benefits and Barriers of 'Once Removed' Participation." In *Higher Education in Virtual Worlds: Teaching and Learning in Second Life,* edited by Charles Wankel, and Jan Kingsley, 47–63. Bingley: Emerald.

Bani, Marco, Francesco Genovesi, Elisa Ciregia, Flavia Piscioneri, Beatrice Rapisarda, Enrica Salvatori, and Maria Simi. 2009. "Learning by Creating Historical Buildings." In *Learning and Teaching in the Virtual World of Second Life,* edited by Judith Molka-Danielsen and Mats Deutschmann, 125–144. Trondheim: Tapir Academic Press.

Brown, Barry, and Marek Bell. 2004. "CSCW at play: 'There' as a collaborative virtual environment." *2004 ACM Conference on Computer Supported Cooperative Work.* Chicago. Accessed January 31, 2017. http://dx.doi.org/10.1145/1031607.1031666

Bystrom, Karl-Erik, and Woodrow Barfield. 1999. "Collaborative Task Performance for Learning Using a Virtual World." *Presence,* 8, no. 4: 435–448.

Club Penguin. 2015. "Parents." Accessed January 3, 2015. http://www.clubpenguin.com/parents?country=US

Childress, Marcus, and Ray Braswell. 2006. "Using Massively Multiplayer Online Role-playing Games for Online Learning." *Distance Education,* 27, no. 2: 187–196.

Churchill, Elizabeth. F., and David Snowdon. 1998. "Collaborative Virtual Environments: An Introductory Review of Issues and Systems." *Virtual Reality,* 3: 3–15.

Dillenbourg, Pierre, Daniel Schneider, and Paraskevi Synteta. 2002. "Virtual Learning Environments." Paper presented at the 3rd Hellenic Conference: Information & Communication Technologies in Education.

Farmer, F. Randall. 1992. "Social Dimensions of Habitat's Citizenry." In *Virtual Reality Casebook,* edited by Carl Eugene Loeffler and Tim Anderson. New York: Van Nostrand Reinhold. Accessed January 8, 2017. http://www.crockford.com/ec/citizenry.html

Gibson, William. 1982. "Burning Chrome." *Omni Magazine,* July.

Grant, Scott John, Hui Huang, and Sarah Pasfield-Neofitou. 2013. "Language Learning in Virtual Worlds: The Role of Foreign Language and Technical Anxiety." *Journal of Virtual Worlds Research,* 6: 1–9. Accessed January 31, 2017. http://dx.doi.org/10.4101/jvwr.v6i1.7027

Grant, Scott John, Hui Huang, and Sarah Pasfield-Neofitou. 2014. "The Authenticity-anxiety Paradox: The Quest for Authentic Second Language Communication and Reduced Foreign Language Anxiety in Virtual Environments." *Procedia Technology,* 13: 23–32. DOI:10.1016/j.protcy.2014.02.005

Gronstedt, Anders. 2007. "Second Life Produces Real Training Results: The 3-D Web World is Slowly Becoming Part of the Training Industry." *Training and Development,* 44–49.

Gu, Ning, Leman Figen Gul, Antony Williams, and Walaiporn Nakapan. (2009). "Second Life—A Context for Design Learning." In *Higher Education in Virtual worlds: Teaching and Learning in Second Life,* edited by Charles Wankel and Jan Kingsley, 159–180. Bingley: Emerald.

KZERO. 2015. "Latest Insight." Accessed January 8, 2017. http://www.kzero.co.uk/

Lin, Tsun-Ju, Szu-Yun Wang, Scott Grant, Ching-Ling Chien, and Yu-Ju Lan. 2014. "Task-based Teaching Approaches of Chinese as a Foreign language in Second Life Through Teachers' Perspectices." *Procedia Technology,* 13: 16–22. DOI:10.1016/j.protcy.2014.02.004

Linden Lab. 2014. "Linden Lab is Developing the Next-generation Virtual World." Accessed January 8, 2017. http://www.lindenlab.com/releases/linden-lab-is-developing-the-next-generation-virtual-world

Love, Edwin, Steven Ross, and Wendy Wilhelm. 2009. "Opportunities and Challenges for Business Education in Second Life." In *Higher Education in Virtual Worlds: Teaching and Learning in Second Life,* edited by Charles Wankel and Jan Kingsley, 65–82. Bingley: Emerald. Accessed January 31, 2017. http:/doi:10.1080/08923641003704002

Molka-Danielsen, Judith, and Mats Deutschmann, eds. 2009. *Higher Education in Virtual Worlds: Learning and Teaching in the Virtual World of Second Life.* Trondheim: Tapir Academic Press. Accessed January 31, 2017. http:/doi:10.1080/08923641003704002

MMOHUT.com. 2015. "Game List." Accessed January 8, 2017. http://mmohuts.com/games

MMORPG.com. 2015. "MMORPG Gamelist." Accessed January 8, 2017. http://www.mmorpg.com/gamelist.cfm

Morningstar, Chip, and F. Randall Farmer. 2001. "Habitat: Reports from an Online Community." In *True Names and the Opening of the Cyberspace Frontier*, edited by James Frenkel, 239–330. New York: TOE.

Plato. *The Republic*, trans. Benjamin Jowett. Project Gutenberg, 2012. Accessed January 31, 2017. http://www.gutenberg.org/files/1497/1497-h/1497-h.htm

Price, Sara, and Yvonne Rogers. 2004. "Let's Get Physical: The Learning Benefits of Interacting in Digitally Augmented Physical Spaces." *Computers and Education*, 43: 137–151.

Rheingold, Howard. 1991. *Virtual Reality*. New York: Simon & Schuster.

Roussou, Maria. 2004. "Learning by Doing and Learning through Play: An Exploration of Interactivity in Virtual Environments for Children." *AMC Computers in Entertainment*, 2, 1: 1–23.

Sadler, Randall. 2009. "Can You Build This? Virtual Construction for Language Learning in Second Life." In *Task-Based III: Expanding the Range of Tasks with Online Resources*, edited LeeAnn Stone and Carol Wilson-Duffy, 212–226. IALT.

Sadler, Randall. 2012. *Virtual Worlds, Telecollaboration, and Language Learning: From Theory to Practice*, Bern: Peter Lang.

Sadler, Randall. 2012. "Virtual Worlds: An Overview and Pedagogical Examination." *Bellaterra Journal of Teaching & Learning Language & Literature*, 5, no. 1: 1–22.

Sadler, Randall, and Melinda Dooly. 2012. "Language Learning in Virtual Worlds: Research and Practice." In *Contemporary Computer-Assisted Language Learning*, edited by Michael Thomas, Hayo Reinders, and Mark Warschauer, 159–182. London: Continuum.

Shaffer, David, Kurt Squire, Richard Halverson, and James Gee. 2004. *Video Games and the Future of Learning*. Madison, WI: University of Wisconsin-Madison and Academic Advanced Distributed Learning Co-Laboratory.

Steinkuehler, Constance. 2004. "Learning in Massively Multiplayer Online Games." Paper presented at the International Conference on Learning Sciences, Santa Monica, California.

Steinkuehler, Constance, and Dimitri Williams. 2006. "Where Everybody Knows Your (Screen) Name: Online Games as 'Third Places'," *Journal of Computer-Mediated Communication*, 11, no. 4: 885–909.

Skiba, Diane. J. 2007. "Nursing Education 2.0: Second Life." *Nursing Education Perspectives*, 28, 3: 156–157.

Thorne, Steven. 2008. "Transcultural Communication in Open Internet Environments and Massively Multiplayer Online Games." In *Mediating Discourse Online*, edited by Sally Sieloff, 305–327. Amsterdam: John Benjamins. Accessed January 31, 2017. http://dx.doi.org/10.1075/aals.3

Varli, Ozan. 2013. "An Exploration of 3D Virtual Worlds through ESL/EFL Teachers' Perspectives in Second Life." In *Online Teaching and Learning: Sociocultural Perspectives*, edited by Carla Meskill, 61–76. London: Bloomsbury.

Vincenti, Giovanni, and James Braman, eds. 2011. *Multi-user Virtual Environments for the Classroom: Practical Approaches to Teaching in Virtual Worlds*. Hershey, PA: IGI Global. DOI:10.4018/978-1-60960-545-2

Vinge, Vernor. 2001. "True Names." In *True Names and the Opening of the Cyberspace Frontier*, edited by James Frenkel, 239–330. New York: TOR.

Virtlantis. 2015. "Virtlantis." Accessed January 8, 2017. http://www.virtlantis.com/

Vygotsky, Lev. 1978. *Mind in Society: The Development of Higher Mental Processes*. Cambridge, MA: Harvard University Press.

Wankel, Charles, and Jan Kingsley, eds. 2009. *Higher Education in Virtual Worlds: Teaching and Learning in Second Life*. Bingley: Emerald Group Publishing Limited. Accessed January 31, 2017. http:/doi:10.1080/08923641003704002

Woogi World. 2015. "The Woogi Academy Mission." Accessed January 8, 2017, http://www.woogiacademy.com/mission.php

Weinbaum, Stanley Grauman. *Pygmalion's Spectacles*, Project Gutenberg, (1935) 2007, Accessed January 8, 2017. http://www.gutenberg.org/etext/22893

Zheng, Dongping, Michael Young, Robert Brewer, and Manuela Wagner. 2009. "Attitude and Self-efficacy Change: English Language Learning in Virtual Worlds." *CALICO Journal*, 27, no. 1: 205–231.

Zheng, Dongping. 2012. "Caring in the Dynamics of Design and Languaging: Exploring Second Language Learning in 3D Virtual Spaces." *Language Sciences*, 34: 543–558. Accessed January 31, 2017. http://dx.doi.org/10.1016/j.langsci.2012.03.010

# 14 Digital Gaming in L2 Teaching and Learning

## JONATHON REINHARDT

## Introduction: A rekindled interest

Every day around the globe, millions of people play digital games (computer or video games—sometimes referred to as games in this chapter for brevity) in a growing variety of genres and titles in dozens of languages. Taking note of this trend, computer-assisted language learning (CALL) researchers and L2 instructors have recently begun examining games as potential second or foreign language (L2) teaching and learning (L2TL) resources, as evidenced by a recent wave of journal special issues (Cornillie, Thorne, and Desmet 2012; Reinhardt and Sykes 2014; Thomas 2011), edited volumes (Reinders 2012), and monographs (Peterson 2013; Sykes and Reinhardt 2012). More accurately, it is a re-examination—CALL experts have been discussing the potentials of digital games as resources for L2TL since the 1980s (e.g., Hubbard 1991; Jones 1982; Meskill 1990; Phillips 1987).

Reasons for this rekindled interest could be that some early negative findings were based on research that was anecdotal, or suffered from limited duration, low numbers, and lack of second language acquisition (SLA) theoretical grounding (Peterson 2013). It is more likely, however, that changes in technology, society, and pedagogy over the past few decades have led to something of a revival. Games used to be considered impractical because they were implementable only in computer labs (e.g., Jordan 1992), but today, the Internet, broadband, and mobile-based technologies (e.g., Holden and Sykes 2011) have increasingly afforded access, portability, and configurability. It was also argued that curricular integration of games was overly difficult because they were self-contained, inauthentic fantasy worlds that used only limited registers (e.g., Phillips 1987). Over the past few decades, however, thanks to the Internet, gaming culture and communities have grown to include a large variety of attendant discourses and paratextual practices (Apperley and Beavis 2011), the nature of which has become linguistically richer and more varied in genre and register (e.g., Thorne, Fischer, and Lu 2012). While curricular integration may still be difficult, it cannot be argued that it is because gaming is an isolated, self-contained practice.

It was once also argued that games appealed only to subsets of learners who are not part of mainstream culture. More recently, however, non-violent, social, and casual games have grown in number and players, appealing to broader, more non-traditional, and more global audiences than ever before. Interacting with, through, and about digital games has become an everyday, language-mediated activity, and for millions of players around the world has become a means to learn languages informally (e.g., Chik 2014). While some students still do

*The Handbook of Technology and Second Language Teaching and Learning*, First Edition.
Edited by Carol A. Chapelle and Shannon Sauro.
© 2017 John Wiley & Sons, Inc. Published 2020 by John Wiley & Sons, Inc.

not like games, it can be counterargued that the fact that some students do not like reading novels or watching films does not preclude their potential as effective L2 resources, if they are implemented appropriately. A final argument against games was that game-mediated interactions do not focus on form in quantities necessary for L2 learning. However, with the social turn in SLA (Block 2003) and growing interest in social-informed pedagogies like multiliteracies (e.g., Kern 2014; Lotherington and Ronda 2014), attention has shifted towards the situated qualities of game-mediated literacy practices, and how gameplay ecologically affords focus on both form and meaning. From a literacies-informed perspective, games are understood as multilingual cultural products as authentic as any other (Reinhardt 2013), and gaming is seen as a socioliteracy practice as real as any other everyday semiotic activity (Thorne 2008).

# A survey of digital games in CALL

This section introduces games in CALL through a discussion of educational gaming and their benefits, digital games in L2TL, games designed specifically for L2TL, game-based CALL applications and research findings on the affordances of games.

## Educational gaming and the purported learning benefits of games

Digital gaming was one of the first uses of computer technology in the 1960s, with the game industry for entertainment beginning in the 1970s and most all familiar game genres having prototypes by the 1980s (Malliet and de Meyer 2005). Educational applications, like the simulation games Lemonade Stand and Oregon Trail, developed by the Minnesota Educational Computing Consortium in 1973, were some of the earliest videogame innovations. Game developers and educators observed that games motivated players to learn often highly complex rules and detailed narratives with seemingly little effort and high levels of engagement. As early as 1981, Malone (1981 as cited in Baltra 1990) observed that digital games built intrinsic motivation by promoting curiosity, evoking fantasy, and offering challenges with clear goals and constant feedback. He added the caveats that games needed to provide for both success and failure, and on occasion seem unpredictable and random to the player.

These observations have been reiterated in work by educational gaming scholars like Marc Prensky, James Gee, and others. Although aspects of Prensky's (2001) digital natives argument have been refuted (Bennett, Maton, and Kervin, 2008), there is some concord with his notion that most young people today, having been raised playing digital games, may be attuned to the experiential, discovery-based pedagogy designed into games. He contrasts this approach with the top-down didacticism found in traditional pedagogy, and argues that schools will fail unless the differences are rectified. Gee (2003, 2004, 2007) also maintains that well-designed games incorporate learning principles that make them highly effective learning spaces. He maintains that games are designed as situated learning spaces, where players learn through embodied, simulated experiences that scaffold opportunities for practice and mastery. Squire (2006, 2008) and Steinkuehler (2008) have built the conceptualization of gaming as a socioliteracy practice and show that social gameplay can develop considerable negotiation and interpersonal skills, multimodal and genre literacies, and computational and critical abilities.

While some early educational games were highly successful, like the adventure-quiz game Where in the World is Carmen Sandiego, others failed, perhaps because they were what has been deemed "chocolate-covered broccoli" (Habgood and Ainsworth 2011). Early designers may have failed because in trying to make digital games that were logistically convenient for schools, authentic in content, aligned with curricular needs, and appealing to everyone, they lost focus on the idea that players play games in order to play, and not necessarily to learn (see Arnseth 2006). While the term "serious game" has been invented in response to this criticism, reflecting the perspective that the learning content and outcomes of educational games should be taken seriously by both teachers and students, the truth remains that games are by definition playful. As Hubbard noted early on (1991), player disposition towards a game, or whether he or she sees it as a game, is fundamental to whether a game retains its motivational capacity. This maxim is still key to the successful design and implementation of any game for learning.

## Digital games in L2 teaching and learning

Early CALL authors were quick to recognize the L2TL potential of games, and many of their observations are still valid today. Baltra (1990) noted that adventure and simulation games in particular could promote language learning for several reasons: (1) they integrated all four skills (2) their goal was not to teach vocabulary or grammar but rather promote goal-oriented activity that required meaningful language use, and (3) they incorporated discovery-based pedagogical techniques, which could promote student-to-student cooperation and interaction. Perhaps because of the absence of games designed specifically for CALL, early instructors chose to work with commercial, off-the-shelf games, supplementing them with teacher-developed wraparound materials, a game-enhanced approach still practiced today (Reinhardt and Sykes 2012). For example, Meskill (1990) outlined a communicative approach to game-enhanced pedagogy that preceded gameplay with vocabulary, schema and strategy building, and discussion activities, and followed it with awareness building and writing activities. She noted that simulation games allowed the instructor to act as a language resource "standing on the sidelines." while learners make "meaning in the new language for a very specific, engaging purpose" (458). In short, using games in CALL is not necessarily new.

Meskill's statement reflects the "guide-on-the-side" constructivist pedagogy of the time, and since then, many have continued to argue for the consideration of games, going deeper into SLA and pedagogical theory for rationale. The use of games can align quite well with task, project, and discovery-based curricula (García-Carbonell et al. 2001; Purushotma, Thorne, and Wheatley 2008; Thorne and Reinhardt 2008), as well as multiliteracies and genre-based approaches (Reinhardt, Warner, and Lange 2014). Sykes and Reinhardt (2012) argue that several key principles of good game design, like goal orientation, interactivity, contextualized language use, and feedback systems have parallels in L2 teaching and learning. For example, goal or objective-oriented activity is fundamental in the design of both a game and of an L2 learning task. Interaction is understood as the sine qua non of L2 learning, just as interactivity is central to the experience of gameplay. Games teach and contextualize the rules and actions of play in narratives and integrated experiences, just as authentic L2 learning activities contextualize meaningful language use. Feedback systems in games are instructional and formative, and provide guidance to players just when, and in the amounts needed. Similarly, feedback in L2TL contexts is most effective when it is targeted, scaffolded, and noticed. Recognizing and leveraging these parallels is key to the design and successful implementation of games for CALL, both those that adapt commercial off-the-shelf games not originally intended for L2 learning, and those designed specifically for that purpose.

## Game-based CALL applications

The earliest uses of games for CALL were game-enhanced, that is, they involved adaptation of existing games not specifically intended for L2 learning. While there are many reasons for research of game-enhanced pedagogy and learning both in and outside of the classroom (Reinhardt and Sykes 2012), much interest and investment has also been directed at game-based applications, or games designed specifically for the purpose of L2TL. Since the 1970s there have been many educational games for learning history, math, geography, and science, but there have been few digital games designed specifically for L2TL, except for a few, relatively new simulated immersion environments (SIEs) (Sykes 2008). These new SIEs are being developed by teams of game developers, publishers, language pedagogy specialists, financiers, government agencies, and universities. For example, the game developer Muzzy Lane worked with Middlebury College to develop MIDDWorld Online, and with McGraw-Hill to develop Practice Spanish: Study Abroad. In both games, players create avatars and engage in a variety of gamified role-play tasks similar to what they might experience in a study abroad situation, in realistic looking but non-specific European or Latin American villages. Game mechanics include quest-like storylines and point systems for health, knowledge, and achievements. A similar SIE for Chinese, Zon was developed by Michigan State University and the Confucius Institute, and an SIE for learning Iraqi Arabic for military purpose, Tactical Iraqi Arabic, was developed by Alelo for the U.S. Department of Defense. The purpose of SIEs is to simulate real-world experiences an L2 user might actually encounter with the purported motivational and learning benefits of game elements like goal orientation and targeted feedback. As "immersive" experiences, SIEs are designed with clear underpinnings in L2 pedagogical approaches compatible with game-based learning principles, for example, the design of MIDDWorld is advertised as mirroring "MIL's unique formula of using engaging and authentic cultural experiences to reinforce language learning in real-world context, rather than by simple memorization drills" (Muzzy Lane 2014).

Most recently, inexpensive online language learning applications, like DuoLingo, Babbel, Busuu, LingQ, and Livemocha, have marketed themselves as game-based, incorporating gamification mechanics like leveling, point, and badge systems into their designs, often combined with social networking mechanics. These applications often reflect a range of sometimes questionable L2 pedagogical approaches, including grammar-translation and memorization drills, and may not necessarily leverage principles of game-based learning beyond the motivational capabilities of gamified feedback and assessment. While they may be effective as memorization tools for highly motivated users, most have yet to be adequately evaluated by the CALL community.

Peterson (2013) and others argue that research on all games in CALL, and development of game-based L2 learning applications, should proceed from a theoretical base of SLA theory. While there are advantages to this deductive approach, as findings can thus serve to support or challenge the theory, in practice it is difficult because of the definition of "game" and how games are produced. It is difficult to create a game that remains a game in implementation when starting from an SLA theory or L2 pedagogical approach, especially if its outcomes are used directly for high stakes assessment, because of learner-player perception and the "broccoli" problem. Moreover, game development usually takes a design-based approach, where design iterations are tested and used to inform redesigns in a rapid deductive-inductive cycle of development and testing. This is not without implication for CALL and SLA theory research, however. Luis Van Ahn, the founder of DuoLingo, claims that he can use algorithms and user data from its 15 million users in one day to determine the best time and order in which to introduce particular linguistic elements in a syllabus, whereas the "offline education system would have taken 15 years to figure (it) out" (Gannes 2014). These sorts of statements, and the flooding of the market with games sometimes based on discredited SLA and L2 pedagogical theories, makes it clear that there is a need for more collaboration between developers, CALL and SLA researchers, and L2 instructors.

## Findings: Affordances for L2TL

The new research wave on games in CALL has led to several notable, common findings on the affordances, or potentials (van Lier 2004), of games for L2TL. First, games offer sheltered contexts for controlled exposure to, and practice with, input that may be repetitive and redundant. For example, deHaan (2005) followed a young adult L2 Japanese learner playing a sports game and documented how the learner-player manipulated the game in order to control and repeat the audio and visual input for learning purposes. Piiranen-Marsh and Tainio (2009) showed how two adolescent players of an adventure role-play game, through multiple play sessions, developed repertoires and fluencies in L2 English by anticipating, repeating, and playing with the language used by non-player characters. This same sheltered quality can also contribute to increased confidence and willingness to communicate and take risks. To illustrate, Reinders and Wattana (2012) found that ten young adult EFL learners who found face-to-face interaction difficult, especially with native speakers, were far more comfortable trying new language in task-based game contexts with fellow learners.

Another common finding is that games of certain designs can serve as environments for peer and expert collaboration that lead to increased linguistic and cultural competence. For example, massively-multiplayer online roleplaying games (MMORPGs) are designed to promote player-player collaboration and interaction through role specialization, so that a warrior player, who can give and take damage but cannot heal, and a priest player, who can heal but cannot take much damage, are encouraged to combine forces to defeat enemies. Noting this jigsaw-like design, Rama et al. (2012) showed how a college age player with high game expertise and low language proficiency leveraged his expertise in World of Warcraft (WoW) group play to develop language skills, while another player with high language proficiency but lower game expertise had a harder time learning to play. Thorne (2008) showed that the massively multiplayer aspect of the design of WoW, which allows strangers to team up, can lead to interpersonal linguistic interactions that are polylingual and transcultural.

Research has also found that the kinds of player-to-player interactions afforded by games can involve negotiation, languaging, and alignment, both in and outside of gameplay. For example, Zheng et al. (2009) showed that two Americans and two Chinese players, in an educational MMORPG, negotiated meanings and understandings by embodying joint actions and aligning activity of their in-game avatars. In her qualitative study of ten college age Chinese college students, Chik (2014) found that many use games for foreign language practice informally, developing both autonomy and social collaboration skills by researching and discussing in-game language online, outside of the game.

Finally, it has been found that because non-educational games have didactic qualities, they may function as informal or implicit learning environments. As a caveat, however, research shows that pedagogical mediation, built either around or into a game, is key to its explicit use for L2TL, and that mediated game environments can afford development of lexical, genre, pragmatic, and narrative competences. To illustrate, Coleman (2002) showed that simulation games can serve as resources for development of register awareness among low proficiency ESL learners. Working with 18 adult ESL learners, Miller and Hegelheimer (2006; see also Ranalli, 2008) showed that life simulation games can be used effectively as resources for vocabulary learning activities, when supplemented with well-designed supporting materials. Sykes (2009) showed how pragmatic competence could be developed in an SIE for college-age Spanish learning, and Reinhardt, Warner, and Lange (2014) showed how 12 advanced college-age German learners developed genre and game literacies through critical and reflective play of casual strategy games.

To summarize this survey section of the chapter, the study of games in CALL has origins in educational gaming research, which has claimed that well-designed games incorporate sound learning principles, although many educational games have not been particularly popular or successful. CALL educators, developers, and researchers have long noted the potential of games for CALL, and that the design of games has parallels in SLA principles and L2 pedagogical design. While many have adapted commercially available games for L2TL, there are a growing number of games intended for L2 learning which tend to simulate language immersion experiences or gamify social networking dynamics, although they may or may not be grounded in current SLA and L2 pedagogical theory. Research on games in CALL has found that they can offer sheltered context for input, afford player collaboration, promote interactions involving negotiation and languaging, and be pedagogically mediated to develop a variety of competences and literacies.

# Interpreting research on games in CALL

The second section of this chapter steps back from common findings to consider how the research might be interpreted, an important undertaking for researchers, instructors, and developers alike. Research to date has been highly diverse in research parameters like theoretical framework, object of investigation, and researcher stance or perspective. This diversity may be due to the vernacular origins of game-enhanced L2TL practices or the non-academic origins of game-based L2TL application development. It may also be that research is still in a descriptive (Blyth 2008) or "false dawn" stage (Peterson 2013), and so publishers are still accepting "bandwagon" pieces that are not rigorously empirical.

Interpreting research requires the employment of heuristics, or cognitive frameworks that help one make sense of theoretical and methodological diversity. One such heuristic associated with SLA theory and used in CALL from its disciplinary beginnings, is constructing a metaphor—a figure of speech applied to a concept that it is not by literal definition—for the sake of comprehension. In CALL, metaphors have been used to make an analogy between a computer and another entity for the purpose of making sense of the computer's function in a particular type of activity. Like computers, games can be understood metaphorically as tutors, tools, or ecologies. A second useful heuristic is identifying a research focus or object of investigation, that is, clarifying whether the research focuses on a genre, a title, or specific game mechanics or behaviors. From this perspective, research can examine genres, like MMORPGs, certain titles, like WoW, or mechanics, like feedback systems, quest structures, or time pressures, that lead to particular behaviors. Finally, another heuristic foregrounding research orientation is important to consider in surveying research on games for CALL, because of the variety of stakeholders who design, sell, teach with, and learn from them. Research has taken player-oriented, pedagogy-oriented, and game-oriented perspectives, informing learning research, curriculum development, and game design respectively.

## *Metaphor: Games as tutors, tools, and ecologies*

Responding to calls to do so (Chapelle 1997), most syntheses of CALL research have focused on SLA theoretical approach (e.g., Bax 2003; Kern and Warschauer 2000; Warschauer and Grimes 2007), and games in CALL syntheses have followed suit. For example, using parameters from psycholinguistic and sociocultural SLA approaches, Peterson (2010) categorized research on L2TL in-game and proto-game technologies, namely multi-user object oriented (MOO) environments, simulation games, virtual worlds, MMORPGs, and educational games. He shows that the principles of both approaches are met in the designs of a variety of game genres and types. Similarly, Filsecker and Bündgens-Kosten (2012) show how three educational games reflect associativist-behaviorist (Mingoville), cognitivist-constructivist (TILTS), and situated-legitimate peripheral participation (Quest Atlantis) principles. These categorizations illustrate that game designs can reflect a particular approach to SLA, especially if they are designed purposefully as SIEs.

Categorizing research on L2TL in gaming according to metaphorical perspective on the function of the game taken by the researcher can add to our comprehensive understanding of the phenomenon. In broad terms, games can be understood as metaphorical tutors, tools, and ecologies. The computer-as-tutor metaphor arose out of the earliest identified benefit of computers, that because of their superhuman information storage and processing capacities they could assume tutor roles and provide constant and consistent input and feedback (Taylor 1990). Research taking the metaphorical perspective of game-as-tutor includes studies that have used the popular life simulation game series The Sims, where gameplay involves the contextualized use of hundreds of everyday vocabulary items. For example, Purushotma (2005) discusses the game as a resource for incidental vocabulary acquisition and its modification potential for more explicit focus on learning. While he focused only on his own use of the game for learning L2 German, his work illustrates how adaptation of a commercial off-the-shelf game can serve a tutorial role for L2 learning. In a similar way, Miller and Hegelheimer (2006) and Ranalli (2008) created supplemental materials for class-room use of the Sims with adult ESL learners, drawing explicit learner attention to vocabu-lary and thereby making the game serve as a vocabulary tutor. DeHaan, Reed, and Kuwada (2010) had 40 pairs of Japanese undergraduate EFL learners play the dance game Parappa the Rapper, one playing the game and one watching the other play, and found that the players scored more poorly on vocabulary retention tests than the watchers. The researchers speculate that the watchers were able to focus on the tutorial nature of the game, while the players had higher cognitive load from having to focus on game rules.

The tool metaphor emerged with socioconstructivist understandings that even as a tutor, technology could be a magister who controls learning or a pedagogue who facilitates learning (Higgins 1983), in both cases functioning as a tool from the learner's perspective. Many studies have examined games as tools for interaction, and the MMORPG genre in particular has been recognized for its potential (Lai, Ni, and Zhao 2012) as a space for inter-action and negotiation. As might be expected, theoretical frameworks focused on interac-tion, discourse, and collaboration are employed in these studies. Peterson (2012), for example, illustrated how four college-age intermediate EFL learners were able to practice a variety of discourse functions in the MMORPG Wonderland. Zheng et al. (2009) showed how four adolescent learners of English and Chinese aligned and negotiated understandings while playing an educational MMORPG, Quest Atlantis. Reinders, and Wattana (2012) found that the quantity of interactions among ten intermediate university age EFL learners in a modi-fied version of the MMORPG Ragnarok Online was considerable, although much like find-ings on regular chat, that fluency was favored over accuracy and complexity.

More recent conceptualizations of technology as environment, microworlds, or ecol-ogies (Lam and Kramsch 2003, van Lier 2004) align with new understandings of media convergence and social or Web 2.0 uses (Warschauer and Grimes 2007), as well as with multiliteracies-informed L2 pedagogies (Kern 2014). From this perspective, technology-mediated L2TL activity is interconnected, dynamic, multinode, and highly contingent on context. A game-as-ecology view considers how games are part of larger, dynamic sys-tems of game-related texts and practices, where people play games, and thus potentially learn from them, at any time, at any place, and with anyone. From this perspective, game playing may be fundamentally incompatible with traditional notions of learning in school, from teachers and textbooks, as knowledge transmission. For example, Thorne, Fischer, and Lu (2012) found that the practices and texts surrounding WoW, that is, the in-game quests, online discussion boards, and online strategy guides, illustrated a much greater variety of linguistic register, genre, complexity, reading level, and function than many believe. Chik (2012) showed that gamers in Hong Kong were self-directed, socially engaged, and highly motivated in learning English and Japanese to play new game releases, but that their language teachers were dismissive, or entirely unaware, of any benefits the activities might provide. Reinhardt and Zander (2011) found that some college-age, intermediate ESL students rejected social game-enhanced learning activities, because they were neither serious nor focused on TOEFL preparation. Holden and Sykes (2011) found that college age advanced Spanish learners' awareness of the language ecologies in local neighborhoods was transformed by playing a mobile game that had the learners solve a local mystery in Spanish. Because the game situated language use outside traditional educational boundaries, learners developed new perspectives on the purpose of learning Spanish and their local linguistic landscape.

An ecological metaphor is congruent with the concept of digital multiliteracies (Knobel and Lankshear 2007; New London Group 1996; Thorne 2013), which recognizes that the development of socioliteracies is multifarious, dynamic, and complex. From this perspective, game playing affords "game literacy" (Gee 2007; Squire 2008), or the critical awareness that game systems, dynamics, and discourses are representative of reality (Bogost 2007), and that even non-playful human activity like learning and working can be game-like, or non-hierarchical and counter-hegemonic. Game literacy involves the capacity to participate in gameful practices (McGonigal 2011). Reinhardt, Warner, and Lange (2014) argue that the development of game literacy may afford the metacognitive awareness that language is systemic, playful, and socially constructed or designed.

## Research object: Game titles, genres, and behaviors

Another useful heuristic for interpretation of research on games in CALL is to identify the object of investigation as not necessarily the game, but rather specific qualities of it, like its genre, its specific title, or the game mechanics that lead to player behaviors that entail language use. Game "genre" is an industry term referring to games that share similar game features, like levels or feedback types, and are associated with certain game mechanics. A game "title" is a specific game, like World of Warcraft, The Sims, or Uncharted, that falls into a certain genre, which for these three titles would be MMORPG, simulation, and action-adventure, respectively. Associated "mechanics" for these three titles and their genres would be questing, building, and killing, respectively.

Not all research is careful to make the distinction between genre, title, and mechanic, and some may assume generalizability of a finding from a behavior derived from a mechanic, to a certain title, to a specific game genre, or the other way around. Most single titles incorporate mechanics that are found in several genres, and so unless a study isolates a mechanic effectively, it may not be clear with which particular behavior it is associated. Some researchers have responded to this problem by adapting or building their own games that test one particular mechanic, at the risk of sacrificing authenticity and making the game less engaging for players, since it is the emergent combination of features and mechanics that make titles uniquely fun and challenging. Ultimately, it is this combination of mechanics in a particular title that should be associated with affordances for language use and learning behaviors, more so than an ill-defined genre to which that title belongs.

Traditional game genres include action, adventure, role play, strategy, and simulation, each of which is traditionally associated with mechanics that may afford, to certain degrees, language use behavior like comprehension, production, and interaction, for example, in order to learn game rules, follow narratives, or collaborate with other players. Action game behaviors usually entail quick reaction time, physical dexterity, and eye-hand coordination, and traditionally involve mechanics like shooting, driving, and parcours-like acrobatics. While action game mechanics may not necessarily involve language use, they may allow players to physically embody game activity, thus affording agency and engagement perhaps more directly than other behaviors do, and the real time nature of action mechanics may drive fluent production by forcing players to act within time limits. Adventure game mechanics include following progressive storylines, finding clues, and solving puzzles, often enshrouded in narratives of mystery and discovery. Adventure behaviors, because they are built around narrative mechanics, most obviously afford language use, particularly comprehension, and clues and puzzles can sometimes be linguistic in nature. Role-play games (RPGs) are typified by character customizability and completion of goal-oriented quests for rewards and experience points. RPGs, because they involve developing a character, may afford identity play of sorts, and completing quests usually demands language comprehension. Strategy game mechanics include planning, exploration, and resource management, and combat that does not require physical dexterity. Simulation mechanics are similar to strategy, but do not usually involve combat, and may instead involve management of a city, farm, business, or life. Strategy and simulation games may afford language use behaviors for comprehending game rules, which tend to be relatively complex and scaffolded for players, and turn-based or timed turn strategy behaviors may afford learners extra time for comprehension, unlike action mechanics.

Researchers have taken several approaches to examining specific game qualities as their objects of investigation. Most researchers start with a particular game title and design and implement a pedagogical or experimental study around it. For example, in their experiment around the music genre game Parappa the Rapper, deHaan, Reed, and Kuwada (2010) found that player attention was divided between game rules and the vocabulary of the game narrative, and associated the resulting behavior with the time pressure game mechanics that typify the music genre. Hitosugi, Schmidt, and Hayashi (2014) looked at vocabulary retention of Japanese-as-an-FL after students played the game Food Force, scaffolded with a series of supporting materials. They found students retained vocabulary from the game better than from their textbook, a finding they attributed to the deep learning afforded by the game. However, while they identified the game as action-adventure, they did not specify how their behavioral outcomes were associated with particular game mechanics or other features of their intervention.

The simulation genre has traditionally received attention as an L2 learning resource (Coleman 2002; Miller and Hegelheimer 2006; Ranalli 2008), perhaps because the mechanics of game object manipulation align language comprehension and production with contextualized meaning, and game progression involves task completion (Purushotma 2005). As mentioned earlier, the MMORPG genre has also received considerable attention (Peterson 2012; Rama et al. 2012; Thorne 2008), probably because typical MMORPG mechanics like grouping and questing align with social interaction and goal orientation behaviors. However, because simulations and MMORPGs are highly complex game ecologies, it is difficult to associate particular features and mechanics to specific outcomes without isolating those mechanics and destroying the functional coherence and authenticity of the game. One solution to this dilemma is to modify the game, as Reinders and Wattana (2012, 2014) did with the MMORPG Ragnarok Online, so that its quests aligned with tasks in their business English curriculum. While this allowed for more research validity, it was only possible because all the players were in one class, and it required sacrificing the affordances that authentic massively multiplayer contexts allow for spontaneous interaction with others.

A third approach researchers take is to design a game that directly tests one or more game behaviors by manipulating the game mechanic with which it is associated. For example, in her own SIE, Sykes (2008) examined how students learned Spanish pragmatics through perception of failure states, and how motivation and learning were affected when a player had a negative experience with an in-game character. Cornillie, Clarebout, and Desmet (2012) designed and implemented a game experiment that measured players' responses to and attitudes towards various sorts of in-game corrective feedback. They found that explicit, immediate feedback was preferred, especially by players with higher game game proficiency levels.

While a mechanics-focused approach is perhaps the most promising with regards to implications for design, it is difficult to carry out because of the amount of effort and investment game development entails. And again, games created primarily to test designs may suffer the educational game "broccoli" problem if they are not authentic and geared towards play, especially with younger learners.

## Research orientation: From the perspective of the game, player-learner, or pedagogy

L2TL researchers traditionally approach a research problem from the perspective of pedagogy, if its answer is to inform instruction and curriculum, or from the perspective of the learner or learning, if it is to inform understandings of SLA more directly. Research on games in CALL can also originate in the perspective of the player-learner or pedagogy, but in addition, may also start from the perspective of the game or game designer. While a study may ultimately incorporate multiple orientations, its initially situated approach is important because it implicates choice of theoretical and methodological frameworks as well as the study's primary purpose—for example, to inform learning research, curriculum development, and/or game design. Interpreting games in CALL research requires recognizing the strengths and weaknesses inherent to each perspective.

Game-oriented research is the primary approach taken by SIE and game-based L2TL application developers, and it aligns with approaches that manipulate specific mechanics through design. As an example of this orientation, Neville (2010) used a game design-based approach to explore how narrative structures share characteristics with SLA and game design theories, and then offers a design rubric that aligns game structures with L2 learning objectives. While his piece is conceptual, it offers a methodical approach to aligning mechanics with outcomes. A strength of this perspective is that it allows for game designs clearly aligned with learning objectives, but a weakness is that a game designed initially with an educational purpose may not function as intended if it is not played and received as a game by its players.

When playing a game for L2 learning, a learner is in effect both a player and a learner whose experience is impacted by variables like gender, age, L2 proficiency, and game literacy. Research from a player-learner-oriented perspective examines how these variables effect individual and sociocollaborative learning in and through game-mediated interactions. Work in this vein includes Sylven and Sundqvist's (2012) examination of the positive correlations between age, gender, game proficiency, and L2 English proficiency among Swedish adolescent game players, and Thorne and Fischer's (2012) exploration of the accounts given by WoW players in online forums regarding their use of the game for informal L2 learning. Ideally, learner-oriented research should inform the development of game-based SIEs and applications as well as game-enhanced pedagogy, and ultimately SLA theory and L2 pedagogy more broadly. One strength of research from this perspective is that it can be highly authentic and ecologically valid, especially when using vernacular games and focused on learning, while a weakness is in specifying which behaviors and outcomes are associated with which mechanics, titles, or genres.

A third orientation to games in CALL research is from the perspective of L2 pedagogy or instruction. Pedagogy-oriented research may focus on how instruction is integrated into a game, how a game is integrated into a curriculum, or the role of the instructor. For example, Lacasa, Martínez, and Mendez (2008) explored the design and implementation of a pedagogical unit meant to develop critical awareness of games as social practices in Spanish primary classrooms. Reinders (2009) offers a series of game wraparound learning activities that develop writing, discussion, and multimedia authoring skills. DeHaan (2011) described two

EFL classroom projects to develop media literacy skills that had learners design games and produce game magazines. Pedagogy-oriented research has the potential to inform L2 pedagogical practice more broadly, and it should inform the work of game developers, although considering the challenges of integrating even L2TL purposed games into curricula, it is not clear that it has. One strength of this sort of research is that it attempts to integrate learning with teaching and thus inform practice, but a weakness is that it may not be rigorously empirical or generalizable beyond its context.

In sum, interpreting research on games in CALL entails consideration of traditional research parameters as well as the use of familiar CALL heuristics adapted to the unique qualities of games. Any interpretation should consider how games in CALL research treats games metaphorically—as tutor, tool, or ecology, how the research approaches its analytic object—as title, genre, or mechanic, and the primary perspective that orients the research problem—a game design, player-learner, or pedagogy-oriented perspective. It is also important that interpretation recognizes the potential strengths and weaknesses inherent to each research approach.

## Implications for future research and practice

The growth and popularity of digital games worldwide has led to a rekindling of research on their use in L2TL that is diverse in perspective, parameters, and purpose—a healthy diversity as long as it is empirical and informed by SLA and L2 pedagogical theory. Considering the differences in their goals, researchers, instructors, and developers should acknowledge the potential for both tension and synergy in future research. Researchers might ask how player-learner variables—motivation, gender, age, proficiency, gaming experience, and gaming preferences—can be examined in an ecologically valid way, without players losing agency and a playful disposition. They might inquire how the social aspect of gameplay impacts learning, and what designs afford what kinds and qualities of social interaction. Instructors might examine the relationship between gaming literacies and other L2 literacies, both traditional and new, and inquire how gaming literacies develop through informal and pedagogically-mediated gameplay. Game developers might ask which game designs, rules, and narratives afford which sorts of L2 learning, and how, and question the role and nature of pedagogical mediation. Researchers, instructors, and developers alike might inquire as to the nature of the tensions between learning and playing, and how well games retain their motivational and educational capacities if not received as games.

While the questions lead in differing directions, if answers are not put in terms that speak to all stakeholders, the field will not move forward. The fact that both the digital game and educational publishing industries have identified L2TL as a potential growth area should be a clarion call for researchers to offer direction, consultation, and guidance, and become full partners in development whenever possible. For their part, L2 educators should develop the critical facilities to evaluate game-based L2 applications, and to enhance their L2 instruction with non-educational games and integrate them effectively into curricula. As practitioners, their experiences developing and implementing instruction and assessing L2 learning are valuable to researchers as well as developers. Researchers and instructors should ground their practices in playing games themselves, observing how L2 learners play games, how and what the games teach, and how people learn them—activities that will foster game literacies. Digital games have great potential to be among the main concerns of CALL and L2TL research into the future—a realization by CALL pioneers being recognized once again as people around the world increasingly discover, create, socialize, and make meaning through digital gaming.

# REFERENCES

Apperley, Tom, and Catherine Beavis. 2011. "Literacy into Action: Digital Games as Action and Text in the English and Literacy Classroom." *Pedagogies*, 5, no. 2: 130–143.

Arnseth, Hans Christian. 2006. "Learning to Play or Playing to Learn – A Critical Account of the Models of Communication Informing Educational Research on Computer Gameplay." *Game Studies*, 6, no. 1. Accessed January 9, 2017. http://gamestudies. org/0601/articles/arnseth

Baltra, Armando. 1990. "Language Learning through Computer Adventure Games." *Simulation and Gaming*, 21, no. 4: 445–452.

Bax, Stephen. 2003. "CALL – Past, Present and Future." *System*, 31: 13–28.

Bennett, Sue, Karl Maton, and Lisa Kervin. 2008. "The Digital Natives Debate: A Critical Review of the Evidence." *British Journal of Educational Technology*, 38, no. 5: 775–786.

Block, David. 2003. *The Social Turn in Second Language Acquisition*. Washington, DC: Georgetown University Press.

Blyth, Carl. 2008. "Research Perspectives on Online Discourse and Foreign Language Learning." In *Mediating Discourse Online*, edited by Sally Magnan, 47–70. Amsterdam: John Benjamins.

Bogost, Ian. 2007. *Persuasive Games: The Expressive Power of Videogames*. Cambridge, MA: MIT Press.

Chapelle, Carol. 1997. "CALL in the Year 2000: Still in Search of Research Paradigms?" *Language Learning & Technology*, 1, no. 1: 19–43.

Chik, Alice. 2012. "Digital Gameplay for Autonomous Language Learning." In *Digital Games in Language Learning*, edited by Hayo Reinders, 95–114. New York: Palgrave Macmillan.

Chik, Alice. 2014. "Digital Gaming and Language Learning: Autonomy and Community." *Language Learning & Technology*, 18, no. 2: 85–100.

Coleman, Douglas. 2002. "On Foot in SIM City: Using SIM Copter as the Basis for an ESL Writing Assignment." *Simulation and Gaming*, 33, no. 2: 217–230.

Cornillie, Fredrik, Geraldine Clarebout, and Piet Desmet. 2012. "Between Learning and Playing? Exploring Learners' Perceptions of Corrective Feedback in an Immersive Game for English Pragmatics." *ReCALL*, 24, no. 3: 257–278.

Cornillie, Fredrik, Steven Thorne, and Piet Desmet. 2012. "Digital Games for Language Learning: Challenges and Opportunities." *ReCALL*, 24, no. 3: 243–256.

deHaan, Jonathan. 2005. "Acquisition of Japanese as a Foreign Language through a Baseball Video Game." *Foreign Language Annals*, 38, no. 2: 282–286.

deHaan, Jonathan W. 2011. "Teaching and Learning English through Digital Game Projects." *Digital Culture and Education*, 3, no. 1: 46–55.

deHaan, Jonathan W., Michael Reed, and Katsuko Kuwada. 2010. "The Effect of Interactivity with a Music Video Game on Second Language Vocabulary Recall." *Language Learning and Technology*, 14, no. 2: 74–94.

Filsecker, Michael, and Judith Bündgens-Kosten. 2012. "Behaviorism, Constructivism, and Communities of Practice: How Pedagogic Theories Help us Understand Game-based Language Learning." In *Digital Games in Language Teaching and Learning*, edited by Hayo Reinders, 50–69. New York: Palgrave Macmillan.

Gannes, Liz. 2014. "Why a Computer is Often the Best Teacher, According to Duolingo's Luis Von Ahn." Accessed January 9, 2017. https://recode. net/2014/11/03/why-a-computer-is-often-the-best-teacher-according-to-duolingos-luis-von-ahn-full-video/

García-Carbonell, Amparo, Beverly Rising, Begoña Montero, and Frances Watts, F. 2001. "Simulation/Gaming and the Acquisition of Communicative Competence in Another Language." *Simulation and Gaming*, 32, no. 4: 481–491.

Gee, James P. 2003. *What Video Games Have to Teach Us about Learning and Literacy*. New York: Palgrave/Macmillan.

Gee, James P. 2004. *Situated Language and Learning: A Critique of Traditional Schooling*. London: Routledge.

Gee, James P. 2007. *Good Video Games and Good Learning*. New York: Peter Lang.

Habgood, M., P. Jacob, and Shaaron Ainsworth. 2011. "Motivating Children to Learn Effectively: Exploring the Value of Intrinsic Integration in Educational Games." *Journal of the Learning Sciences*, 20, no. 2: 169–206.

Higgins, John. 1983. "Computer Assisted Language Learning." *Language Teaching*, 16: 102–114.

Hitosugi, Claire, Matthew Schmidt, and Kentaro Hayashi. 2014. "Digital Game-Based Learning (DGBL) in the L2 Classroom: The Impact of the UN's Off-The-Shelf Videogame, Food Force, on Learner Affect and Vocabulary Retention." *CALICO Journal*, 31, no. 1: 19–39.

Holden, Christopher L., and Julie M. Sykes. 2011. Leveraging Mobile Games for Place-based Language Learning. *International Journal of Game-based Learning*, 1, no. 2: 1–18.

Hubbard, Philip. 1991. "Evaluating Computer Games for Language Learning." *Simulation and Gaming*, 22, no. 2: 220–223.

Jones, Keith. 1982. *Simulations in Language Teaching*. New York: Cambridge University Press.

Jordan, Geoff. 1992. "Exploiting Computer-Based Simulations for Language-Learning Purposes." *Simulation and Gaming*, 23, no. 1: 88–98.

Kern, Richard. 2014. "Technology as Pharmakon: The Promise and Perils of the Internet for Foreign Language Education." *The Modern Language Journal*, 98, no. 1: 340–357.

Kern, Richard, and Mark M. Warschauer. 2000. "Theory and Practice of Network-based Language Teaching." In *Network-based Language Teaching: Concepts and Practice*, edited by Mark Warschauer and Richard Kern, 1–19. New York: Cambridge University Press.

Knobel, Michele, and Colin Lankshear. 2007. *A New Literacies Sampler*. New York: Peter Lang.

Lacasa, Pilar, Rut Martínez, and Laura Méndez. 2008. "Developing New Literacies Using Commercial Videogames as Educational Tools." *Linguistics and Education*, 19, no. 2: 85–106.

Lai, Chun, Ruhui Ni, and Yong Zhao. 2012. "Digital Games and Language Learning." In *Contemporary Computer-Assisted Language Learning*, edited by Michael Thomas, Hayo Reinders, and Mark Warschauer, 183–200. London: Bloomsbury.

Lam, W. S. Eva, and Claire Kramsch. 2003. "The Ecology of an SLA Community in Computer-Mediated Environments." In *Ecology of Language Acquisition*, edited by Jonathan Leather and Jet van Dam, 141–158. Dordrecht: Kluwer Publishers.

Lotherington, Heather, and Natalia Ronda. 2014. "2B or Not 2B? From Pencil to Multimodal Programming: New Frontiers in Communicative Competencies." In *Digital Literacies in Foreign and Second Language Education*, edited by Janel Pettes Guikema and Lawrence Williams, 9–28. San Marcos, TX: CALICO.

Malliet, Steven, and Gust de Meyer. 2005. "The History of the Video Game." In *Handbook of Computer Game Studies*, edited by Joost Raessens and Jeffrey Goldstein, 23–45. Cambridge, MA: MIT Press.

McGonigal, Jane. 2011. *Reality is Broken: Why Games Make Us Better and How They Can Change the World*. New York: Penguin.

Meskill, Carla. 1990. "Where in the World of English is Carmen Sandiego?" *Simulation and Gaming*, 21, no. 4: 457–460.

Miller, Megan, and Volker Hegelheimer. 2006. "The SIMS meet ESL: Incorporating Authentic Computer Simulation Games into the Language Classroom." *Interactive Technology and Smart Education*, 3, no. 4: 311–328.

Muzzy Lane Software. 2014. MiddWorld Online. Accessed January 9, 2017. http://muzzylane.com/project/mil

Neville, David. 2010. "Structuring Narrative in 3D Digital Game-Based Learning Environments to Support Second Language Acquisition." *Foreign Language Annals*, 43, no. 3: 446–469.

New London Group. 1996. "A Pedagogy of Multiliteracies: Designing Social Futures." *Harvard Educational Review*, 66: 60–92.

Peterson, Mark. 2010. "Computerized Games and Simulations in Computer-Assisted Language Learning: A Meta-Analysis of Research." *Simulation and Gaming*, 41, no. 1: 72–93.

Peterson, Mark. 2012. "Learner Interaction in a Massively Multiplayer Online Role Playing Game (MMORPG): A Sociocultural Discourse Analysis." *ReCALL*, 24, no. 3: 361–380.

Peterson, Mark. 2013. *Computer Games and Language Learning*. New York: Palgrave Macmillan.

Phillips, Martin. 1987. "Potential Paradigms and Possible Problems for CALL." *System*, 15: 275–287.

Piiranen-Marsh, Arja, and Liisa Tainio. 2009. "Other-repetition as a Resource for Participation in the Activity of Playing a Video Game." *Modern Language Journal*, 93, no. 2: 153–169.

Prensky, Mark. 2001. *Digital Game-based Learning*. St. Paul: Paragon House.

Purushotma, Ravi. 2005. "You're Not Studying, You're Just ..." *Language Learning and Technology*, 9, no. 1: 80–96.

Purushotma, Ravi, Steven L. Thorne, and Julian Wheatley. 2008. *Ten Key Principles for Designing Video*

*Games for Foreign Language Learning*. Accessed January 9, 2017. http://lingualgames.wordpress.com/article/10-key-principles-for-designing-video-27mkxqba7b13d-2/

Rama, Paul, Rebecca Black, Elizabeth van Es, and Mark Warschauer. 2012. "Affordances for Second Language Learning in World of Warcraft." *ReCALL*, 24, no. 3: 322–338.

Ranalli, Jim. 2008. "Learning English with the Sims: Exploiting Authentic Computer Simulation Games for L2 Learning." *Computer Assisted Language Learning*, 21, no. 5: 441–455.

Reinders, Hayo. 2009. "Using Computer Games to Teach Writing." *English Teaching Professional*, 63: 6–58.

Reinders, Hayo, ed. 2012. *Digital Games in Language Teaching and Learning*. New York: Palgrave Macmillan.

Reinders, Hayo, and Sorada Wattana. 2012. "Talk to me! Games and Students' Willingness to Communicate." In *Digital Games in Language Learning and Teaching*, edited by Hayo Reinders, 156–188. Basingstoke: Palgrave Macmillan.

Reinders, Hayo, and Sorada Wattana. 2014. "Can I Say Something? The Effects Of Digital Game Play On Willingness To Communicate." *Language Learning and Technology*, 18, no. 2: 101–123.

Reinhardt, Jonathon. 2013. "Digital Game-mediated Foreign Language Teaching and Learning: Myths, Realities, and Opportunities". In *Apprendre les langues à l'université au 21ème siècle*, edited by Martine Derivry-Plard, Pascaline Faure, and Cédric Brudermann, 161–178. Marseille: Riveneuve.

Reinhardt, Jonathon, and Julie M. Sykes. 2012. "Conceptualizing Digital Game-mediated L2 Learning and Pedagogy: Game-Enhanced and Game-Based Research and Practice." In *Digital Games in Language Learning and Teaching*, edited by Hayo Reinders, 32–49. Basingstoke: Palgrave Macmillan.

Reinhardt, Jonathon, and Julie M. Sykes. 2014. "Special Issue Commentary: Digital Game and Play Activity in L2 Teaching and Learning." *Language Learning and Technology*, 18, no. 2: 2–8.

Reinhardt, Jonathon, and Victoria Zander. 2011. "Social Networking in an Intensive English Program Classroom: A Language Socialization Perspective." *CALICO Journal*, 28, no. 2: 326–344.

Reinhardt, Jonathon, Chantelle Warner, and Kristin Lange. 2014. "Digital Gaming as Practice and Text: New Literacies and Genres in an L2 German Classroom." In *Digital Literacies in Foreign and Second Language Education*, edited by

Janel Pettes Guikema and Lawrence Williams, 159–177. San Marcos, TX: CALICO.

Squire, Kurt. 2006. "Video Game Literacy: A Literacy of Expertise." In *Handbook of Research on New Media Literacies*, edited by Julie Coiro, Michele Knobel, Donald Leu, and Colin Lankshear, 639–673. New York: Macmillan.

Squire, Kurt. 2008. "Open-Ended Video Games: A Model for Developing Learning for the Interactive Age." In *The Ecology of Games: Connecting Youth, Games, and Learning*, edited by Katie Salen, 167–198. Cambridge, MA: MIT Press.

Steinkuehler, Constance. 2008. "Massively Multiplayer Online Games as an Educational Technology: An Outline for Research." *Educational Technology*, 48, no. 1: 10–21.

Sykes, Julie M. 2008. *A Dynamic Approach to Social Interaction: Synthetic Immersive Environments and Spanish Pragmatics*. Unpublished Doctoral Dissertation, University of Minnesota.

Sykes, Julie M. 2009. "Learner Requests in Spanish: Examining the Potential of Multiuser Virtual Environments for L2 Pragmatic Acquisition." In *The Second Generation: Online Collaboration and Social Networking in CALL*, edited by Lara Lomicka and Gillian Lord, 199–234. San Marcos, TX: CALICO.

Sykes, Julie M., and Jonathon Reinhardt. 2012. *Language at Play: Digital Games in Second and Foreign Language Teaching and Learning*. New York: Pearson.

Sylven, Liss, and Pia Sundqvist. 2012. "Gaming as Extramural English L2 Learning and L2 Proficiency among Young Learners." *ReCALL*, 24, no. 3: 302–321.

Taylor, Macey. 1990. "Simulations and Adventure Games in CALL." *Simulation and Gaming*, 21, no. 4: 461–466.

Thomas, Michael. 2011. "Editorial: Digital Games and Second Language Acquisition in Asia." *Digital Culture and Education*, 3, no. 1: 1–3.

Thorne, Steven L. 2008. "Transcultural Communication in Open Internet Environments and Massively Multiplayer Online Games." In *Mediating Discourse Online*, edited by Sally Magnan, 305–327. Amsterdam: John Benjamins.

Thorne, Steven L. 2013. "Digital Literacies." In *Framing Languages and Literacies: Socially Situated Views and Perspectives*, edited by Margaret Hawkins, 192–218. New York: Routledge.

Thorne, Steven L., and Ingrid Fischer. 2012. "Online Gaming as Sociable Media." *ALSIC*, 15, no. 1. Accessed January 31, 2017. http://alsic.revues.org/2450

Thorne, Steven L., and Jonathon Reinhardt. 2008. "'Bridging Activities,' New Media Literacies and Advanced Foreign Language Proficiency. *CALICO Journal*, 25, no. 3: 558–572.

Thorne, Steven L., Ingrid Fischer, and Xiaofei Lu. 2012. "The Semiotic Ecology and Linguistic Complexity of an Online Game World." *ReCALL*, 24, no. 3: 279–301.

van Lier, Leo. 2004. *The Ecology and Semiotics of Language Learning: A Sociocultural Perspective.* Dordrecht: Kluwer.

Warschauer, Mark, and Douglas Grimes. 2007. "Audience, Authorship, and Artifact: The Emergent Semiotics of Web 2.0." *Annual Review of Applied Linguistics*, 27: 1–23.

Zheng, Dongping, Michael Young, Manuela Wagner, and Robert Brewer. 2009. "Negotiation for Action: English Language Learning in Game-based Virtual Worlds." *Modern Language Journal*, 93, no. 4: 489–511.

# 15 Mobile Learning Revolution: Implications for Language Pedagogy

## AGNES KUKULSKA-HULME, HELEN LEE, AND LUCY NORRIS

## Introduction

In a globalized 21st century, competence in other languages contributes to effective communication and collaboration with people from diverse cultural backgrounds in all areas of life, education, and work (Boix Mansilla and Jackson 2011; Partnership for 21st century Skills 2007; Skills CFA 2013). Logically therefore, language learning should be an important life-long pursuit, carried out in a variety of ways according to changing social, educational, and working life imperatives, as well as personal interests and needs. New technologies make a lifelong commitment to language learning much more feasible and attractive than was the case in the past. In particular, mobile technologies are uniquely suited to supporting language learning on an ongoing basis, in a range of settings, according to a person's ability and adapted to their needs (Gu, Gu, and Laffey 2011; Hsu, Hwang and Chang, 2013; Ng, Lui, and Wong 2015). They are uniquely personal tools with the potential to promote exposure to target languages, capture communication difficulties as they occur, prompt ongoing reflection, and enable selection of affordable learning resources to suit an individual's preferences and situation-specific needs.

Although mobile learning offers certain benefits in the classroom, the use of mobile devices also potentially extends learning beyond the classroom setting. In fact, as noted by Brown (2010), "the distinguishing aspect of mobile learning is the assumption that learners are continuously on the move" (7), perhaps in outdoor settings or in places where everyday life and leisure activities merge with learning. This poses new challenges, since classroom pedagogy implies careful planning, while mobility outside of class exposes language learners to the unexpected: linguistically challenging situations that could not be predicted, chance encounters with online resources and apps, offers of informal connections to target language speakers all over the world. A thoughtful pedagogical response to this reality involves new conceptualizations of what needs to be learned and new activity designs to promote learning. Such a considered response also recognizes that learners may act in more self-determined ways beyond classroom walls, where online interactions and mobile encounters influence their language *communication* interests and needs (see Díaz-Vera 2012). Beyond the classroom, mobile technologies have become integrated into the fabric of people's everyday lives, enabling learning opportunities to take place in a multiplicity of real-world settings. Many

*The Handbook of Technology and Second Language Teaching and Learning*, First Edition.
Edited by Carol A. Chapelle and Shannon Sauro.
© 2017 John Wiley & Sons, Inc. Published 2020 by John Wiley & Sons, Inc.

learners today will instinctively curate and communicate their everyday lives through social media platforms and the capturing functions of their devices. Yet mobile applications have failed to reflect these everyday curation and communication practices and also communicative language teaching models (Kukulska-Hulme and Shield 2008). Burston (2015, 16) bemoans "the lack of pedagogical innovation and failure of even the most recent MALL (mobile-assisted language learning) projects to exploit the communicative affordances of mobile devices."

Dichotomies between formal and informal learning may also require reconsideration for a new pedagogic age of more fluid transitions between these spheres. Due to the near-ubiquity of mobile devices (although access is not universal), language learning now increasingly traverses the classroom and learning takes place "in virtual spaces and out in the world" (Kukulska-Hulme 2013, 2). At the same time, learners must not be left unguided and unsupported (Laurillard 2007). Therefore, in this chapter we address questions as to how teachers can exploit mobile technology to adapt and transform their practice by enabling authentically communicative learning opportunities for their students both in the classroom and beyond the classroom out in the world. First, we consider how teachers need to rethink and adapt their teaching and what models have been elaborated to help them conceptualize changes they can make to their pedagogical practices with technology.

Next, we review relevant published overviews and research studies in mobile language learning, and available guidance for teachers. We suggest a contemporary pedagogic skills-set designed for teachers and educators interested in implementing mobile devices in their current practice and programs. Multimodal mobile interaction is highlighted as a new frontier of language learning research and practice. We go on to propose our perspective on mobile language learning beyond the classroom: the Mobile Pedagogy framework (Kukulska-Hulme, Norris, and Donohue 2015) developed for English language teachers is described, and through it, transformational language learning task designs integrated with mobile approaches are exemplified and considered in detail. Finally, we present examples of tasks employing MALL, and highlight components with reference to the framework suggested here in order to draw out the essential elements comprising a mobile pedagogy for language learning. We conclude by identifying challenges for the successful implementation of MALL approaches and guiding principles for teacher education.

# Adapting language teaching to mobile learning

## *Adaptation in language teaching*

Widdowson (1990, 2) recognized the need for language teaching constantly to adapt in response to changes happening in the world, when he wrote:

> The contexts of language teaching, like the more social contexts within which they are located, are continually changing, continually challenging habitual ways of thinking … Unless there is a corresponding process of critical appraisal, there can be no adaptation, no adjustment to change.

Adaptation means being cognizant of social discourse that takes place in the real world where language items such as demonstratives and deictic adverbs "are focussed on the sociocultural conception of the spaces we live in" (Scollon and Scollon 2003, 36). Balancing in-class and out-of-class learning may be challenging but can be achieved by teachers regularly scheduling reflective scenarios to engineer "noticing" of language (Schmidt 2001) from captured mobile data being brought back into the classroom. Kukulska-Hulme and Bull

(2009) highlight the importance for learners to fully exploit the functions of their devices in order to observe and record language in use as a way to support language acquisition.

While course books based on the communicative approach have continuously striven to replicate the real world and to script authenticated language, teachers' engagement with mobile learning offers an important departure from this relative artificiality. As a result, teachers face the challenge of identifying and creating synchronous real-world learning tasks that are skillfully woven into the everyday. The approach involves teachers drawing on existing training but also developing new knowledge as to how to integrate both virtual and physical settings in innovative ways in order to focus on target structures, grammatical forms, communicative skills, and to explore recycled and newly-emergent vocabulary. Therefore, teachers need to carefully evaluate how learners are already using their mobiles, assess what is communicatively possible for a particular group of learners, and then gradually grade tasks accordingly, as they would in the classroom. A sense of community building through online and face-to-face peer support is even more vital for learners in their autonomous endeavours, in that when they inevitably meet problems there is a fellow learner and teacher behind them to support them.

To help teachers conceptualize changes they can make to their pedagogical practices with technology, a number of models have been elaborated. Cardullo et al. (2015) suggest that the alignment of emerging technologies with Puentedura's (2010) Substitution – Augmentation – Modification – Redefinition (SAMR) model could help teachers to see their potential when used in tandem with Bloom's revised taxonomy of the cognitive domain (Anderson, Krathwohl, and Bloom 2001). Puentedura's SAMR model, similarly to the three technology functions proposed by Hughes (2005) (replacement, amplification, transformation), aims to enhance technology integration by aiding the analysis of technology use proposed by teachers to achieve the learning outcomes of a task. The SAMR model asks if technology functions as a substitute for, or augmentation of, existing tools commonly employed for the same purpose, with some functional enhancement. At "transformational" levels, the SAMR model goes on to prompt an examination of how technology use might allow for modification, significant redesign of tasks or even prompt a radical redefinition of "previously inconceivable" tasks. A different framework designed for teachers constantly required to shift and evolve their understanding and knowledge with regard to the intersecting domains of technology, pedagogy and content, is the Technological Pedagogical and Content Knowledge (TPACK) framework (Koehler and Mishra 2009, 61). While both provide useful insights, neither the SAMR nor the TPACK were designed with language teaching in mind. Thornbury and Meddings point out that language is not a subject; it is a medium (2001). Therefore a framework for language teachers should ideally take the medium, or more broadly, communication modes and media, into account.

## Mobile language-learning: Guidance for teachers

Published literature on mobile learning is extensive and includes publications specifically aimed at educators and trainers (e.g., Bannister and Wilden 2013; Kukulska-Hulme and Traxler 2005; Traxler and Wishart 2011). In mobile language learning, Pegrum (2014) provides both a broad perspective and specific guidance on how to teach language with mobile devices, what aspects of language can be taught, and what kinds of new literacies are needed. Research articles cover a wide range of issues including implications for policy makers, employers and the workforce (Beatty 2013), designing mobile-based classroom learning experiences (Hockly 2013a), and moving from computer assisted language learning (CALL) to task-based language learning with mobile assisted language use (MALU) (Jarvis 2015).

While mobile language learning may not yet be currently reflected in the curricula of English language teacher qualifications or professional development frameworks, there is evidence of interest in mobile language learning from educational technology developers, publishers, and teachers. Discussions around mobile language learning practices are well represented in English language teaching conferences, including 15 presentations at the IATEFL 2015 conference, and 17 in Canada at the TESOL 2015 conference. Practical guides to mobile learning for English language teaching include *Going Mobile* (Hockly and Dudeney 2014) and *Apptivities for Business English* (Sharma and Barrett 2013). Teacher interest in, and sharing ideas about mobile language learning can be seen in social media, blogs, webinars and online teacher resources, with inspiration taken from peers and influential others working in modern foreign language teaching and secondary contexts internationally (e.g., Byrne 2015; Dale 2015; Peachey 2015).

Difficulties may arise when mobile learners are empowered to act in more self-determined ways that may be at odds with current teaching practices, and more guidance on this aspect is needed. Kukulska-Hulme (2013) argues that language learners need to be re-skilled for a mobile world in which learner autonomy will be valued and needs to be supported. The concept of language learner autonomy (Benson 2013; Little 2007) has been put forward as a desirable aim in the context of educating learners who will be able to assume an active role in their learning process and continue learning beyond the classroom. It is not synonymous with individuals working in isolation, without any peer or teacher support. Little (2007) highlights how autonomy within language learning was not found to be directly linked to self-access materials and self-instruction but instead required the careful implementation of pedagogic principles relating to issues such as *learner empowerment, reflection, and target language use*. There are key strategies that teachers can adopt to foster autonomy in learners, such as providing opportunities to negotiate tasks, allowing them to select resources of interest and encouraging groups to make learning decisions. Learners must also be made aware of their language achievements but encouraged to critically assess themselves and, importantly, understand how to develop strategies to enable them to achieve future goals.

Online mobile spaces can be effectively utilized to become regular private or public learning journals. For example, mobile blogs provide the tools for learners to store their reflections in text and other modes, such as video, as they move about their lives. Within mobile pedagogy and learning beyond the classroom, there is a strong need to support learners by incorporating regular dialogic exchanges between teacher and class as to how autonomous collaborations can best be structured, shared, and harnessed by learners as meaningful resources from which to motivate and learn (Laurillard 2007). Some teachers may feel ill-equipped to conduct such conversations with their learners; however, without pedagogic structuring, follow-up classroom work, and clear explanations of identifiable aims and outcomes, many learners will struggle to develop autonomy.

Purushotma argues that while classroom environments and learning have evolved considerably, "the guidance students receive on how to continue learning a language outside of class has remained relatively the same" (2005, 81). Pegrum suggests that pedagogy associated with mobile learning depends on teachers, and their learners, seeing the benefits of both knowledge construction and collaborative networking, which "may require both teacher and learner training in the developing and developed world alike" (2014, 109). Professionally trained classroom educators will have strong existing skills and want to hone and build on these to reflect technological shifts in learners' communication practices for the 21st century (as demonstrated in Figure 15.1).

Despite the growing body of publications offering guidance to teachers, there is, as yet, relatively little advice that would help teachers understand informal learner practices using multiple modes of communication, making use of mobile and social technologies across a range of physical settings ("digital and multimodal literacies" in Figure 15.1). We give a brief overview of this emerging research area in the next section before addressing wider issues of mobile language learning beyond the classroom.

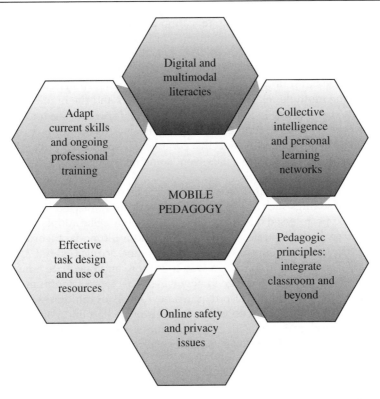

**Figure 15.1** Pedagogic skills and competencies implied by mobile assisted language learning and teaching. 2016 (original artwork designed by Helen Lee).

## Multimodal mobile interaction: New frontiers of language learning

Mobile devices are multifunctional tools that subvert definitions of communication exclusively derived from traditional notions of speech and written text. Their functionality permits learners to exploit a range of modal affordances: to orchestrate ensembles of speech and gesture in their captured videos or to juxtapose visual representations of the world side-by-side with their thoughts expressed in language. A multimodal stance on learners' interpersonal communication in the 21st century includes helping them to understand the dynamic interplay of modes such as gesture, image, sound, proxemics and space, and how they can be brought together to form coherent meanings within a range of communicative and interactional scenarios (see Jewitt 2014 for an overview of multimodal research). Conversely, Kukulska-Hulme, Norris and Donohue (2015, 5) highlight the current "disconnect" between the world of language learning and the reality of multimodal processing; citing the notable contrast in terms of how learners engage with video consumption and creation beyond the classroom. Even basic digital skills, as highlighted by the UK Digital Skills Charter (2014) aiming to prevent digital exclusion, involve individuals and organizations being able to make successful video calls, engage with live chat, exploit social media, understand basic analytics, and crucially to communicate effectively through combinations of graphics, visuals, and text.

The communicative landscape is constantly evolving and pedagogical paradigms need to reflect these economic and societal shifts. As a result, learners' experiences with new technologies represent the spaces where new literacies are created and shaped (Kress and Van Leeuwen 2001). There is increasing interest in the relationships between digital technologies and literacy, multimodal forms of communication and learning, and multimodal research methodologies to investigate learners' interactive practices and experiences (Domingo 2011; Eisenlauer 2014; Flewitt et al. 2014; Jewitt 2006; Lee 2015). Domingo (2011) adopts a multimodal framework to interpret issues of culture, language and identity in terms of how design features are embedded in young people's informal, collaboratively-shared videos. Eisenlauer (2014) discusses the multiple relationships between modes and the implications for mobile learning in that text and image in interplay can serve as effective means for acquiring a new language. However, the multimodal research focus also reveals incongruity of meaning between the modes of language and visuals in a commercial vocabulary app, with one-fifth of the images "in conflict" (335): the visuals were sometimes unclear, decontextualized, and potentially confusing for users.

Lee (2015) explores gesture within second language learners' interactions from a range of dispersed informal settings such as a local café. Learners are connected via the video conferencing program Skype accessed on mobile tablets and phones. She adopts an analytic framework that draws on gesture studies (Kendon 2004) and multimodal theories of interaction (Norris 2004) to explore meaning-making practices around acquisition in L2. Language and gestures operate in ensemble and act as a way to explore and negotiate a range of settings where virtual and material space merge in new ways. This type of communicative scenario can be motivating for learners but also requires new levels of multitasking skills; besides, communication can involve distractions due to levels of background noise present in some public settings. In the research, reflective opportunities via video playback are introduced to encourage critical noticing of language use and gesture in terms of coherency of meaning and effectiveness of multimodal communication.

## Mobile language learning beyond the classroom

Benson and Reinders (2011) have argued that studies of language learning and teaching in settings beyond the classroom are valuable because they provide alternative perspectives on social and cognitive perspectives involved in these processes. The powerful combination of out-of-class and mobile learning certainly calls for a re-examination of the aims and processes of language learning. We view language learning as the development of interpersonal communication resources, emphasizing the importance of fostering learners' personal interests through harnessing their self-directed and everyday interactions out in the world. This is congruent with the Common European Framework of Reference for Languages (CEFR) (Council of Europe 2001) which adopts an action-oriented approach to learning in order to develop communicative competence. The framework highlights issues for learners such as autonomy, communication, fluency, and interactive speaking and listening skills. As we argue in this chapter, mobile devices provide new opportunities for teachers working with a range of learners to help them achieve some of the CEFR assessment goals via mobile resources and settings out in the world.

One very pertinent example is the Fón project reported by Keogh and Ní Mhurchú (2009) who highlight the considerable challenge faced in fostering communicative competence in the Irish language. Factors such as the unpopularity and perceived difficulty of the language, combined with requirements to create spoken production opportunities that could be assessed, were met through the introduction of mobile technologies. The Fón project involved 16 teachers and 368 learners; the students were able to phone "anytime and anywhere" to orally answer a set of questions which were recorded for access and subsequent assessment by teachers. Results demonstrated that teachers felt that the system enabled Irish language learning to travel beyond the classroom and found it effective for monitoring progress. Learners reported very positive benefits with 78% remarking that they were speaking and using more Irish than before the project. This project also illustrates how mobiles may prove essential in preserving cultural heritage and in motivating future generations to engage with old languages in new ways. Jones (2015) supports this view, arguing that digital resources, particularly when mobile, "have the potential to at least partly overcome the particular challenges of learning a language with a limited number of dispersed speakers" (6). In contrast to the Fón project involving teachers and their learners, Jones' case studies of informal Welsh learning reveal that mobile learning in this environment makes use of spare time, multitasking, and "supported a pattern of learning that was often both spontaneous and planned" (2015, 11).

## Language learning and cultural learning for work

Nowadays, learners may study a language in ways that fit around their work and life routines. They could be aiming to achieve personal goals that include building cross-cultural relationships to join social communities, or to overcome cultural and linguistic barriers to manage international teams of people and to articulate their ideas within a workplace setting. Ros i Solé, Calić, and Neijmann note that:

> [L]anguage learning involves not only acquiring information but also forming social relationships and engaging with new cultural backgrounds and emotional selves. Learners, then, are increasingly seen as part of a system that not only involves them in interaction with the social environment, but also engages their personal goals, desires, and day-to-day practices. (2010, 40)

Mobile pedagogy carries implications for a range of targeted language-learning scenarios, ranging from language for specific purposes through to English for international management and workplace learning. Teachers currently operating within these fields will be familiar with the specialized language training and pedagogy these learners require. For example, within successful business language training scenarios the learner's specific job description and workplace setting should ideally drive the syllabus, the focus of tasks, and the exploitation of a range of authentic materials as a way to reflect language as a contextualized part of their everyday work practice. It is the role of the trained teacher to synthesize theoretical language knowledge with the learner's business expertise and practical experience. Today, this involves a balanced pedagogic approach that exploits conceptual and experiential knowledge, and combines these with the integration of communication technologies to improve L2 in order to do a specific job.

Language needs and pedagogic solutions of global organizations frequently include language development through meetings, company presentations, negotiation skills, and building effective social relationships. Lee (2012) demonstrates how authentic communicative tasks on *Skype,* combined with online capturing tools, can be pedagogically harnessed to help workplace learners improve their L2 spoken skills for their global videoconferencing meetings. Mobile devices now support several videoconferencing platforms for such meetings. Teachers can exploit these spaces to implement real-life problem-based scenarios for learners to help them develop key skills for their jobs such as chairing, clarifying information, and developing cross-cultural competence. Today's workplace learners and organizations have already integrated mobile technologies into the workplace as part of their communicative networks and knowledge sharing practices, although business language pedagogy has sometimes lagged behind and failed to reflect these changes.

Mobile technologies can be successfully exploited by teachers and learners to enable communicative skills in L2 to be developed on the job. For example, aspects such as the portability, connectivity, and the ability of devices to capture language use and communication are ideally suited to the flexibility required for workplace learning and learners. Instead of teachers recreating workplace tasks that perhaps inaccurately reflect the workplace, learners themselves can autonomously use mobile video and audio functions on devices to illustrate and represent to their teachers the type of L2 tasks their jobs really require. From this point of view, task-based learning can be more effectively targeted and pedagogically scaffolded to address specific and emerging needs, and to more accurately reflect workplace culture and settings than is possible through generic business language teaching materials.

Dyson (2014) utilized mobile devices to encourage university students to share knowledge, to learn about the information technology sector via a vodcast project. The multimedia and collaborative aspects of devices provided the motivation to enable the students to represent their evolving knowledge in multiple ways in order to become increasingly familiar with the IT profession and the workplace setting they were aiming to enter in their future careers. Mobile technologies have also been exploited in the Qatar oil and gas industry to develop communication skills while people worked on the job. Workers demonstrated improved performance and expressed a wish to engage in further learning opportunities with mobile technologies (Alley et al. 2014). On the other hand, it can be argued that mobile devices on their own do not necessarily provide solutions to the type of complex tasks workplace learners have to perform in their L2. The technology should instead be seen as an enabler which will be most effective when combined with carefully-crafted communicative language teaching and a language teacher's expertise.

Eraut (2004) explains, within an informal workplace paradigm, that professional, managerial and technical performance are complex processes that entail simultaneous use of different types of knowledge that are acquired holistically. Workplace learning that involves experiential learning in isolation may affect the extent to which business people are able to think while performing their jobs in an L2 and, consequently, the quality of the knowledge available to them may be insufficient. Communicating in an L2, while learners are engaged in a series of demanding work-based tasks, can frequently result in *just in time* and *just get by* learning. Therefore, immediate communicative needs in workplace situations will often result in unconscious performances that require engineered reflection to transform them into more explicit sources of knowledge that learners can use to achieve improved task goals. Business learners should be encouraged by teachers working in and with organizations to regularly capture their communicative interactions on the job (within industry confidentiality boundaries). If these authentic scenarios are to be of long-term value it is essential that structured reflection highlights language and discourse skills but also important pragmatic issues; therefore reflection must be introduced at strategic points by an experienced teacher who interacts with learners as part of a democratic workplace team. Figure 15.2 illustrates the implementation of the teaching skills-set from Figure 15.1. Figure 15.2 consists of a framework integrating classroom work with language usage in the world of work beyond the classroom. The teacher uses identified resources including learners' jobs and the work setting to design authentic tasks and encourages learners to exploit video/capturing tools for post-task reflection in the classroom, developing digital literacies as well as language skills.

Following the tasks in Figure 15.2, the teacher will have also developed the digital pedagogic skills to understand the potential of social media for knowledge construction. Sites are pre-identified and harnessed to create networking opportunities, bearing in mind sensitive privacy issues such as opting for a closed access group (see Figure 15.1 again). Students require careful guidance, combined with successful task design and reflective cycles based around social media and video, in order to transform their everyday social practice into effective language learning:

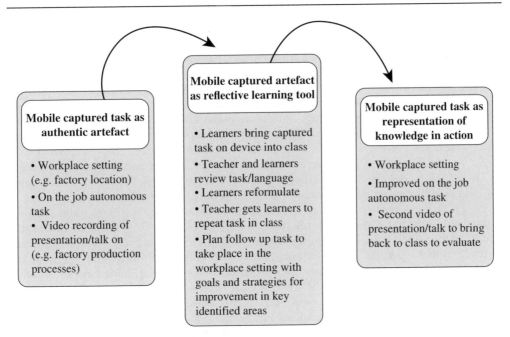

**Figure 15.2**   Mobile task-based framework for workplace language learning: an iterative cycle illustrating autonomous 'on the job' learning integrated with pedagogical input and opportunities for reflection. 2016 (original artwork designed by Helen Lee).

## *Connecting in-class and out-of-class environments*

As described earlier, mobile learning implies an understanding of "how to utilize our everyday life-worlds as learning spaces" (Pachler, Bachmair, and Cook 2010, 6). This is particularly resonant in out-of-class language learning, where teachers, and mobile tools and apps designed specifically for language learning often fail to exploit the connections between life and language learning. This may result from exclusive engagement with institutionally prescribed globally produced core materials and internationally homogenized assessment and testing systems. Enhanced communication between in and out-of-class environments taking learner and learning mobilities into account is key to effective mobile pedagogy, as is a view of language as dynamic, an emergent phenomenon across environments, where learning is a "jointly constructed and socially motivated process, contingent on the concerns, interests, desires, and needs of the user(s)" (Thornbury and Meddings, 2001). Unfolding learning and teaching processes across settings requires new teacher roles (e.g., scaffolding out of classroom language), as discussed in the previous section.

Emerging studies of language in a mobile world, for example, English as an international language (EIL) or English as a lingua franca (ELF), the international rise of English as a medium of instruction (EMI) and content and language integrated learning (CLIL) all provide evidence for "effective global cross-cultural communication as a strong driving force for language learning" (Kukulska-Hulme 2013, 11). Pennycook (2010) expands on this, claiming that

New technologies and communications are enabling immense and complex flows of people, signs, sounds, (and) images across multiple borders in multiple directions. (2010, 593)

As a consequence of this convergence, language teachers need to be able to work with more than language content, and become "(co-) designers of effective learning experiences for their learners" regardless of whether any technology is involved (Laurillard 2012 quoted in Hockly, 2013b, 2).

In this section we consider opportunities for out-of-class language learning to complement in-class teaching by harnessing teacher wisdom and mobile technologies within a framework for Mobile Language Pedagogy. Furthermore, we consider the roles in this for native versus mobile tools and apps and present some examples of mobile language learning activity designs. We begin by considering how a traditional out-of-class homework task might be reconfigured using mobile technologies to assist and enhance language learning.

The SAMR model referred to earlier (Puentedura 2010) informs the design of language-learning activity by facilitating teacher examination of the role proposed for technology to carry out tasks. A written homework task, familiar to language teachers, often used for assessment, is examined here with reference to each layer of the SAMR framework. At the bottom of the SAMR ladder, technology may act as direct tool substitute, "with no functional change" so that a pen and paper are substituted by processing software and a printer. The handwritten essay therefore becomes the word-processed essay, but handed in to the teacher in the same way. This is the S in SAMR, substitution. If, however, learner attention is directed by a task to use word-processing tools such as the speech to text function, or to combine graphics into the text then there is added functionality to the tools being substituted (augmentation). The resulting work might be turned in to the teacher either in print form or digitally. Mobile devices may be used to research handwritten or word-processed work, photograph the results, make notes, or voice record the process for later reflection. Language and the environments in which it is produced or reproduced, may be mobile, and devices support and capture learning between and across contexts and settings.

Moving up the SAMR ladder from substitution, through augmentation, to the modification layer, Puentedura views technology as allowing for "significant task redesign" (2010, 3). In our example this could mean asking students to write their essay as a blog post, so the teacher as sole reader, editor, and critic is replaced by a wider audience of commentators with the potential for expert and peer language and content feedback, joint reflection, and discussion. The environments in which the blog can be added to, commented on, and read in transit are mobile, enabled by learners' and teachers' devices. In the top R layer, Redefinition is when the creation of new previously inconceivable tasks is enabled by technology. Our chapter, for instance, might become a multimedia, multimodal text, combining words (written and spoken), images (moving and still), and published rather than handed in, like the blog post. In this redefinition of a homework task, learner choice is valued, and cross-environment engagement is encouraged and enabled in tandem with those features of mobile devices that allow the recording, broadcasting, and sharing of communication for subsequent study, reflection, and improvement.

## Native mobile device features, generic and specific language learning apps

Mobile devices can be seen to play various roles in the out-of-class language-learning tasks described in the previous section. They can support both multimodal language production and reflection, a learner mobility central to bridging learning made across contexts of use. Additionally, mobile technologies provide potential opportunities for promoting reciprocal communication and facilitate engagement in reading and viewing activities. The activities described are enabled by the native features of mobile devices such as the camera, voice recorder, or video functions, in combination with mobile Internet tools that allow sharing and posting: "mobile assisted" learning. A mobile or technology enhanced learning experience might, in our example, be the use of a generic app such as Evernote to collaborate in the production of a group multimodal text. This app would enable collaboration via shared digital notebooks combining text with images, video, hyperlinks, bookmarking functions, alerts, and calendars. Evernote is not designed for the purpose of language learning, so is an authentic resource, but one that can be usefully incorporated into the arena of second language learning, with a free version. An account of one teacher's experience of using this app originally described in her blog was reposted to ELT Jam on October 5, 2015. In this blog post Lana Haze (2015) provides valuable insights of planning teaching while on the move in a city. She describes bookmarking, tagging ideas, setting alerts, taking, editing and annotating photographs, making audio notes and capturing ideas "that would normally vanish after the third metro stop" as well as keeping notes on learners. In her view, this app enables the creation of "great speaking activities on the go with nothing but your phone" using geolocation and the Evernote atlas features. Comments on this post by other teachers describe how Evernote works to capture their professional development.

As mobile applications proliferate, it becomes more difficult for teachers and learners to understand how they differ from one another, what their most desirable features are, and what the pedagogical benefits to be derived from their use might encompass. The Mobile Pedagogy for ELT research project (2014), carried out by the Open University as part of a British Council research partnership, investigated these areas. Resulting insights gained from a study involving teachers and their learners resulted in a pedagogical framework to guide mobile assisted language teaching and learning (Kukulska-Hulme, Norris, and Donohue 2015).

# A pedagogical framework for mobile assisted language teaching and learning

The Pedagogical Framework (Figure 15.3) was developed to assist teachers in a process of reflection upon the adaptation of their teaching practice to mobile learning. It represents how teacher wisdom, learner mobilities, language dynamics, and device features figure in language-learning activities to be carried out in the range of contexts and cultural settings they occupy. Teacher wisdom utilizes teacher experience, teaching strategies, and effective task designs, which are all highly relevant in mobile learning. Central to enacting a mobile pedagogy is considering pedagogy in relation to the other three spheres of the framework. *Learner mobilities* include the places and times where learning might take place, as well as the personal goals that motivate learners to keep on learning beyond the confines of the classroom. Echoing the mobility of learning and learners across contexts, the sphere of *language dynamics* recognizes the mobility of language in a constant state of flux, partly due to the rapid evolution of communications technology with new channels and media available for language teaching and learning (e.g., social media). The sphere of *device features* and descriptions of the roles they might play in accessing and connecting to language learning opportunities is woven throughout the fabric of this chapter.

Working outward from the four key spheres just described, we have four connecting concepts: learning outcomes, inquiry, rehearsal and reflection. There is no specified starting point for considering these concepts and how they will be enacted, although instructional design approaches often begin with the specification of outcomes. Examples of possible mobile language learning outcomes include, but are not confined to:

- identifying gaps in linguistic (and other) knowledge
- developing the habit of reflection on language learned and processes involved

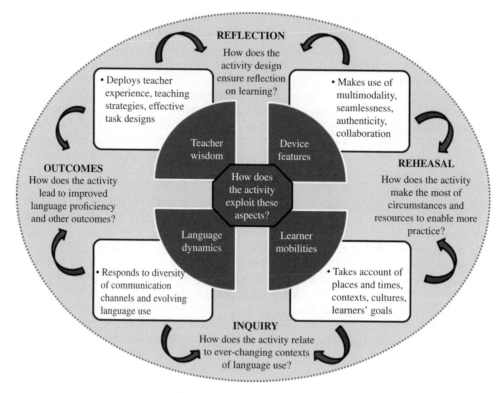

**Figure 15.3**    A pedagogical framework for mobile assisted language teaching and learning. 2015. Source: Agnes Kukulska-Hulme, Lucy Norris, and Jim Donohue, *Mobile Pedagogy for English Language Teaching* (2015, 8).

- learning to notice how language is used
- rehearsing
- experimenting
- developing digital (mobile) literacies
- learning to learn
- developing autonomy

The framework might help to evaluate how an activity leads to improved language proficiency and other outcomes. For instance, assessment is enabled by this facet of the framework, so, for example, analysis of spoken communication might be used to inform teacher evaluation, using learner or teacher recordings, and aiding reflection and repair or correction. The second connecting concept, inquiry (conducted by learners) into changes within disciplinary knowledge and language data (e.g., expressions encountered) positions mobile devices as instruments for posing questions and seeking answers. Next, the territory where language might be rehearsed and practiced by learners is extended by mobile technologies. As Van Lier (1996) points out, learners who only engaged with language during lessons would find themselves in the situation where "progress will either not occur or be exceedingly slow. The students' minds must occupy themselves with the language between lessons as well as in lessons, if improvements are to happen" (1996, 42). Mobile learning can support a greater variety of language forms such as tweets (as summaries) and comments on multimedia posts. In Dr. Diana Hicks' (2014) review of a draft of *Mobile Pedagogy for English Language Teaching* sent to the authors of the guide (Kukulska-Hulme, Norris, and Donohue 2015), the final concept of the framework, namely reflection, was noted to be potentially "as new to language teachers as the concept of mobile learning." This concept includes the teacher helping learners reflect on their learning and what has and has not been learned or understood, for subsequent fine-tuning, repair, and repetition. Reflection also involves thinking about how to apply and progress learning, and setting (new) goals. These things, while prompted by teachers and their learners, are assisted by mobile devices, as in the example given earlier of a learner taking photographs and using a "think aloud" protocol while writing an essay. Wearable devices can promote reflection by monitoring behavior or emotional states and triggering recommendations and reminders (Santos et al. 2015). The *Mobile Pedagogy for English Language Teaching* guide contains examples of learning activities designed to bridge in-class with out-of-class learning and exploit the features of mobile pedagogy (Kukulska-Hulme, Norris, and Donohue 2015). Table 15.1 provides two examples.

**Table 15.1**   Example MALL activities, CEFR descriptors and digital technologies required.

| SAMR | Example MALL activities Teacher wisdom (effective task design and teaching strategies) | CEFR example descriptors Language and learning outcomes, language dynamics | Digital technologies required Device features, Learner mobilities |
|---|---|---|---|
| Modification | A learner makes a voice/video recording of a speaking task done in class to share with partner for reflection and repair beyond class.<br><br>Rehearsal and rerecording of task carried out and shared with the teacher for assessment in or out of a subsequent class. Reflections on learning and language posted on shared LMS/online space. | Can outline an issue or a problem clearly, speculating about causes or consequences, and weighing advantages and disadvantages of different approaches.<br>Can help along the progress of the work by inviting others to join in, say what they think, etc. Can make a note of 'favorite mistakes' and consciously monitor speech for them. | • voice or video recording<br>• connectivity<br>• access to Internet e.g., LMS/virtual platform<br>• curation/sharing/editing note-taking apps or tools<br>• reference apps (dictionary or grammar reference, etc.)<br>• *learners and learning are mobile*<br>• *in or beyond class; seamless*<br>• *multimodal*<br>• *authentic*<br>• *collaborative* |

*(Continued)*

**Table 15.1**   (Continued)

| SAMR | Example MALL activities Teacher wisdom (effective task design and teaching strategies) | CEFR example descriptors Language and learning outcomes, language dynamics | Digital technologies required Device features, Learner mobilities |
|---|---|---|---|
| Redefinition | A learner photographs and maps the places s/he studies in and the things used (e.g., apps, writing implements, favorite chair, etc.) to make an online multimedia interactive image. Thinglink is used to share with the class (or teacher), as homework, or for assessment. | Can write straightforward connected texts on a range of familiar subjects by linking a series of shorter discrete elements into a linear sequence. Can convey degrees of emotion and highlight the personal significance of events and experiences. | • camera<br>• video or voice recording<br>• connectivity (online sharing)<br>• geolocation<br>• access to LMS/ virtual space<br>• reference apps (google maps, dictionary/ phrase book, etc.)<br>• *learners and learning are mobile*<br>• *in or beyond class; seamless*<br>• *multimodal*<br>• *authentic*<br>• *can be collaborative* |

# Conclusions

In this chapter we have argued that mobile phones and other portable devices should enable new ways of learning that embrace learning beyond the classroom. A language learner can use these tools to face daily language challenges, as well as for longer-term development of personal communication resources that will continue to be revisited and enriched over a lifetime. Increasingly, formal learning takes place in informal settings, and informal learning in formal settings, therefore it makes little sense to keep these two spheres separate. Professionally trained classroom educators are well-placed to help lead the mobile revolution and now face the task of spreading the message and implementing innovation in language schools and institutions that may currently have little understanding of what it is to teach and learn a language communicatively with mobile technology. Moreover, teacher training courses must update their syllabus and training focus to begin to reflect the complex ways in which use of mobile technologies are impacting and transforming issues surrounding pedagogy, learning, and modern-day literacy practices.

We must also remember that new learning skills and competencies will continue to be required as technologies and social behaviors continue to change and evolve. Some social exchanges in online and mobile environments are now polylingual rather than being confined to one language (Jørgensen 2008). In the near future, learners will begin to engage with the next generation of wearable devices and technology-rich surroundings where personal devices are part of a repertoire of tools, resources, and social networks that will offer new opportunities for language learning and expansion of cultural knowledge. These opportunities will need to be fully understood by educators, policy makers, and learners, to make sure that the opportunities are not lost.

# REFERENCES

Alley, Mohamed, Mohammed Samaka, John Impagliazzo, Abdulahi Mohamed, and Martha Robinson. 2014. "Workplace Learning Using Mobile Technology: A Case Study in the Oil and Gas Industry." In *Communications in Computer and Information Science, Vol. 479*, edited by Yasmin Bayyurt, Marco Kalz, and Marcus Specht, 250–257. Berlin: Springer.

Anderson, Lorin W., David R. Krathwohl, and Benjamin Samuel Bloom. 2001. *A Taxonomy for Learning, Teaching, and Assessing: A Revision of Bloom's Taxonomy of Educational Objectives*. New York: Longman.

Bannister, Diana, and Shaun Wilden. 2013. *Tablets and Apps in Your School: The Route to Successful Implementation*. White Paper. Oxford: Oxford University Press. Accessed June 19, 2016. https://elt.oup.com/feature/global/mlearning/?cc=gr&selLanguage=en&mode=hub

Beatty, Ken. 2013. *Beyond the Classroom: Mobile Learning – the Wider World*. Monterey, CA: The International Research Foundation for English Language Education. Accessed June 19, 2016. http://www.tirfonline.org/english-in-the-workforce/mobile-assisted-language-learning/beyond-the-classroom-mobile-learning-the-wider-world/

Benson, Phil. 2011. *Teaching and Researching: Autonomy in Language Learning*, 2nd ed. London: Routledge.

Benson, Phil and Hayo Reinders (Eds.) 2011. *Beyond the Language Classroom*. Basingstoke: Palgrave Macmillan.

Boix Mansilla, Veronica, and Anthony Jackson. 2011. "Educating for Global Competence: Preparing our Youth to Engage the World." *Council of Chief State School Officers' EdSteps Initiative and Asia Society Partnership for Global Learning*. Accessed June 19. 2016. http://asiasociety.org/globalcompetence

Brown, Elizabeth J. 2010. *Education in the wild: contextual and location-based mobile learning in action*. A report from the STELLAR Alpine Rendez-Vous workshop series, edited by Elizabeth Brown. Nottingham, UK: University of Nottingham, Learning Sciences Research Institute (LSRI). Accessed June 19. 2016. http://oro.open.ac.uk/29882/1/ARV_Education_in_the_wild.pdf

Burston, Jack. 2015. "Twenty years of MALL project implementation: A meta-analysis of learning outcomes." *ReCALL, 27*, no. 1: 4–20.

Byrne, Richard. 2015. "Free Technology for Teachers." Website. Accessed June 19, 2016. http://www.freetech4teachers.com/

Cardullo, Victoria M., Nance S. Wilson, and Vassiliki I. Zygouris-Coe. 2015. "Enhanced Student Engagement through Active Learning and Emerging Technologies." In *Handbook of Research on Educational Technology Integration and Active Learning*, edited by Jared Keengwe, 1–18. Hershey, PA: IGI Global. DOI:10.4018/978-1-4666-8363-1

Council of Europe. 2001. "Common European Framework of Reference for Languages: Learning, Teaching, Assessment." Accessed June 19, 2016. http://www.coe.int/t/dg4/linguistic/cadre1_en.asp

Dale, Joe. 2015. Twitter feed. @joedale

Díaz-Vera, J., ed. 2012. *Left to My Own Devices: Learner Autonomy and Mobile-assisted Language Learning Innovation and Leadership in English Language Teaching*, 197–212. Bingley: Emerald Group.

Digital Skills Charter. 2014. Accessed June 19, 2016. https://doteveryone.org.uk/digital-skills/digital-skills-charter/

Domingo, Myrrh. 2011. "Analyzing Layering in Textual Design: A Multimodal Approach for Examining Cultural, Linguistic, and Social Migrations in Digital Video." *International Journal of Social Research Methodology, 14*, no. 3: 219–230. DOI:10.1080/13645579.2011.563619

Dyson, Laura E. 2014. "A Vodcast Project in the Workplace: Understanding Students' Learning Processes Outside the Classroom." In *Communications in Computer and Information Science, Vol. 479*, edited by Yasmin Bayyurt, Marco Kalz, and Marcus Specht, 258–271. Berlin, Germany: Springer.

Eisenlauer, Volker. 2014. "Multimodality in Mobile-Assisted Language Learning." In *Communications in Computer and Information Science, Vol. 479*, edited by Yasmin Bayyurt, Marco Kalz, and Marcus Specht, 328–338. Berlin, Germany: Springer.

Eraut, Michael. 2004. "Informal Learning in the Workplace." *Studies in Continuing Education, 26*, no. 2: 247–273. DOI:10.1080/158037042000225245

Flewitt, Rosie, Regine Hampel, Mirjam Hauck, and Lesley Lancaster. 2014 "What Are Multimodal Data and Transcription?" In *The Routledge Handbook of Multimodal Analysis*,

2nd ed., edited by Carey Jewitt, 44–59. London: Routledge.

Gu, Xiaoqing, Fengjia Gu, and James M. Laffey 2011. "Designing a Mobile System for Lifelong Learning on the Move." *Journal of Computer Assisted Learning*, 27, no. 3: 204–215. DOI:10.1111/j.1365-2729. 2010.00391.x

Haze, Lana. 2015. "ELT and Evernote: A Match Made in Heaven." Blog post on *ELT Jam*. Accessed June 19, 2016. http://eltjam.com/ elt-and-evernote-a-match-made-in-heaven/

Hicks, Diana. 2014. Report on draft of *Mobile Pedagogy for English Language Teaching: A Guide for Teachers*. Personal correspondence.

Hockly, Nicky. 2013a. "Mobile Learning." *ELT Journal*, 67, no. 1: 80–84. DOI:10.1093/elt/ ccs064

Hockly, Nicky. 2013b. *Designer Learning: The Teacher as Designer of Mobile-based Classroom Learning Experiences*. Monterey, CA: The International Research Foundation for English. Accessed June 19, 2016. http://www. tirfonline.org/english-in-the-workforce/ mobile-assisted-language-learning/

Hockly, Nicky, and Gavin Dudeney. 2014. *Going Mobile: Teaching with Hand-held Devices*. Peaslake, UK: Delta Publishing.

Hsu, Chih-Kai, Gwo-Jen Hwang, and Carl K. Chang, 2013. "A Personalized Recommendation-based Mobile Learning Approach to Improving the Reading Performance of EFL Students." *Computers & Education*, 63: 327–336. DOI:10.1016/j. compedu.2012.12.004

Hughes, Joan. 2005. "The Role of Teacher Knowledge and Learning Experiences in Forming Technology-integrated Pedagogy." *Journal of Technology and Teacher Education*, 13, no. 2: 277–302. Accessed June 19, 2016. https://www.learntechlib.org/p/26105

Jarvis, Huw. 2015. "From PPP and CALL/MALL to a Praxis of Task-based Teaching and Mobile Assisted Language Use." *Teaching English as a Second or Foreign Language*, 19, no. 1: 1–9. Accessed June 19, 2016. http://www.tesl-ej. org/wordpress/issues/volume19/ej73/ej73a1/

Jewitt, Carey. 2006. *Technology, Literacy, Learning: A Multimodal Approach*. London: Routledge.

Jewitt, Carey. 2014. *The Routledge Handbook of Multimodal Analysis*, 2nd ed. London: Routledge.

Jørgensen, Normann J. 2008. "Polylingual Languaging around and among Children and Adolescents." *International Journal of Multilingualism, 5*, no. 3: 161–176.

Jones, Ann. 2015. "Mobile Informal Language Learning: Exploring Welsh Learners' Practices." *eLearning Papers 45*. Accessed June 19, 2016. http://openeducationeuropa.eu/en/ paper/language-learning-and-technology

Kendon, Adam. 2004. *Gesture: Visible Action as Utterance*. Cambridge: Cambridge University Press.

Keogh, Katrina. A. and Judith Ní Mhurchú. 2009. "Changing Policy and an Innovative Response: Teaching, Learning and Assessing Irish Using Mobile Phones." In *Many Voices: Language Policy and Practice in Europe. CIDREE Yearbook*, edited by Katrina A. Keogh, Judith Ní Mhurchú, Hal O'Neill, and Marie Riney, 127–139. Brussels: CIDREE. Accessed June 19, 2016. http://www. cidree.org/fileadmin/files/pdf/publications/ YB_9_Many_Voices_-_Language_Policy_and_ Practice_in_Europe_.pdf

Koehler, Matthew, and Punya Mishra. 2009. "What is Technological Pedagogical Content Knowledge (TPACK)?" *Contemporary Issues in Technology and Teacher Education*, 9, no. 1: 60–70.

Kress, Gunther, and Theo Van Leeuwen. 2001. *Multimodal Discourse: The Modes and Media of Contemporary Communication*. London: Arnold.

Kukulska-Hulme, Agnes. 2013. *Re-skilling Language Learners for a Mobile World*. Monterey, CA: The International Research Foundation for English Language Education. Accessed June 19, 2016. http://www.tirfonline.org/english-in-the-workforce/mobile-assisted-language-learning/

Kukulska-Hulme, Agnes, and Susan Bull. 2009. "An Overview of Mobile Assisted Learning: Noticing and Recording." *International Journal of Interactive Mobile Technologies*, 3, no. 2: 12–18.

Kukulska-Hulme, Agnes, and Lesley Shield. 2008. "An Overview of Mobile Assisted Language Learning: From Content Delivery to Supported Collaboration and Interaction." *ReCALL*, 20, no. 3: 271–289. DOI:10.1017/ S0958344008000335

Kukulska-Hulme, Agnes, and John Traxler, eds. 2005. *Mobile Learning: A Handbook for Educators and Trainers*. London: Routledge.

Kukulska-Hulme, Agnes, Lucy Norris, and Jim Donohue. 2015. "Mobile Pedagogy for English Language Teaching: A Guide for Teachers." The British Council. Accessed June 19, 2016. http://englishagenda.britishcouncil.org/ research-papers/mobile-pedagogy-english-language-teaching-guide-teachers

Laurillard, Diana. 2007. "Pedagogical Forms for Mobile Learning: Framing Research

Questions." In *Mobile Learning: Towards a Research genda*, edited by Norbert Pachler, 153–175. London: WLE Centre, IOE.

Laurillard, Diana. 2012. *Teaching as a Design Science: Building Pedagogical Patterns for Learning and Technology*. New York: Routledge.

Lee, Helen. 2012. "Developing Communicative Competence on Skype." Paper presented at the International Association of Teachers of English as a Foreign Language Business English Special Interest Group (IATEFL BESIG), Stuttgart Conference, November, 16–18.

Lee, Helen 2015. "Language Learners and Multimodal Interaction via Mobile Devices: An Exploration of Online Gesture." Paper presented at the Conference on Multimodality and Cultural Change, University of Agder, Kristiansand, Norway, June 10–12.

Little, David. 2007. "Language Learner Autonomy: Some Fundamental Considerations Revisited." *Innovation in Language Learning and Teaching*, 1, no. 1: 14–29. DOI:10.2167/illt040.0

Ng, SinChun., Lui Kwok-Fai, and Yuk-Shan Wong. 2015. "An Adaptive Mobile Learning Application for Beginners to Learn Fundamental Japanese Language." In *Technology in Education: Transforming Educational Practices with Technology*, edited by Kam Cheong Li et al., 20–32. Berlin: Springer. DOI:10.1007/978-3-662-46158-7_3

Norris, Sigrid. 2004. *Analysing Multimodal Interaction: A Methodological Framework*. London: Routledge Falmer.

Pachler, Norbert, Ben Bachmair, and John Cook. 2010. *Mobile Learning: Structures, Agency, Practices*. London: Springer.

Partnership for 21st Century Skills. 2007. "Framework for 21st Century Learning." Accessed June 19 2016. http://www.p21.org/our-work/p21-framework

Peachey, Nik. 2015. "Learning Technology Blog for English Language Teachers" (Blog). Accessed June 19, 2016. http://nikpeachey.blogspot.co.uk/

Pegrum, Mark. 2014. *Mobile Learning: Languages, Literacies and Cultures*. Basingstoke: Palgrave Macmillan.

Pennycook, Alastair. 2010. "Popular Cultures, Popular Languages, and Global Identities." In *The Handbook of Language and Globalization*, edited by Nikolas Coupland, 592–607. Chichester: John Wiley & Sons, Ltd.

Puentedura, Ruben. 2010. "SAMR and TPCK Intro to Advanced Practice." Accessed June 19, 2016.

http://hippasus.com/resources/sweden2010/SAMR_TPCK_IntroToAdvancedPractice.pdf

Puroshotma, Ravi. 2005. "Commentary: You're Not Studying You're Just…" *Language Learning & Technology*, 9, no. 2: 80–96.

Ros i Solé, Christina, Jelena Calić, and Daisey D. Neijmann. 2010. "A Social and Self-reflective Approach to MALL." *ReCALL*, 22, no. 1: 39–52.

Santos, Olga C., Mar Saneiro, Jesús G. Boticario, and María Cristina Rodríguez-Sánchez. 2015. "Toward Interactive Context-aware Affective Educational Recommendations in Computer-assisted Language Learning." *New Review of Hypermedia and Multimedia*, 22, no. 1–2: 27–57. DOI:10.1080/13614568.2015.1058428

Schimdt, Richard. 2001. "Attention." In *Cognition and Second Language Instruction*, edited by Peter Robinson, 3–32. New York: Cambridge University Press.

Scollon, Ron, and Suzie, B. K. Scollon. 2003. *Discourses in Place: Language in the Material World*. New York: Continuum.

Sharma, Pete, and Barney Barrett. 2013. "Apptivities for Business English." E-book available from *The Round* website. Accessed June 12, 2016. http://the-round.com/resource/apptivities-for-business-english/

Skills CFA. 2013. "Languages and Intercultural Working – National Occupational Standards." Accessed June 19, 2016. http://www.skillscfa.org/standards-qualifications/language-intercultural.html

TESOL International Association of Teachers of English to Speakers of Other Languages. Accessed June 19, 2016. http://www.tesol.org/

Traxler, John, and Jocelyn Wishart. 2011. "Making Mobile Learning Work: Case Studies of Practice." *ESCalate HEA Subject Centre*. Accessed June 19, 2016. http://www.cumbria.ac.uk/Public/Education/Documents/Research/ESCalateDocuments/MakingMobileLearningWork.pdf

Thornbury, Scott, and Luke Meddings. 2001. "The Roaring in the Chimney." *Modern English Teacher*, 10, no. 3. http://www.hltmag.co.uk/sep01/sart8.htm

UK Digital Skills Charter. 2014. Accessed June 19, 2016. http://www.go-on.co.uk/get-involved/digital-skills-charter/

van Lier, Leo. 1996. *Interaction in the Language Curriculum: Awareness, Autonomy, and Authenticity*: Harlow: Longman.

Widdowson, Henry G. 1990. *Aspects of Language Teaching*. Oxford: Oxford University Press.

# 16 Technology for Task-based Language Teaching

## MARTA GONZÁLEZ-LLORET

## Introduction

The interest in technologies and innovations for language learning is certainly not an isolated phenomenon in today's education arena. Students in affluent parts of the world have grown up surrounded by computers and laptops and by an array of increasingly sophisticated communication devices that support personal, portable, wirelessly networked communication. Many students now consider tablets, e-books, and smartphones essential to their daily existence. They are known as the Generation Z/iGeneration/Net Generation and were born in the early 2000s or later, not knowing anything other than life with the full extent of the Internet and the gadgets and technologies that support its use. This generation is what Prensky (2001) termed "digital natives." The multimodal and interconnected technological life shaped this generation's literacies, the ways of being in and with the world, and their cognitive and learning processes (Rosen 2010; Thorne 2013). The technologization of our society and youth requires teachers to integrate (more or less willingly) digital technologies into their expertise (Nussbaum-Beach and Hall, 2012). Administrators, in turn, are welcoming technology into their institutions to exhibit their up-to-date programs (Chapelle, 2014). Foreign language education is no exception to this trend (Grgurović, Chapelle, and Shelley 2013; Sauro 2011; Zhao 2003), and among current technologies, Web 2.0[1] technologies are gaining growing attention.

In contrast to earlier forms of innovation, Web 2.0 technologies (chats, blogs, wikis, gaming environments, synthetic immersive environments, virtual worlds, etc.) are interactive and dynamic in nature, allowing users not only to harvest information but to transform it, becoming part of a collective intelligence. The excitement and initial motivation to integrate new technologies in the classroom are not sufficient to make them effective tools for language learning, however. It is essential that they be guided by curricular principles based on research on education and language development in their design, use, and evaluation. Among all the existing methodologies for language teaching, I will argue here that the approach to curriculum design known as task-based language teaching (TBLT) is ideal for informing and fully realizing the potential of technological innovations for language learning. The chapter will first outline main principles of TBLT. It will then present the concept of technology-mediated tasks and propose Web 2.0 technologies as a natural match for TBLT. Three strands of previous research on technology and tasks will then be reviewed. The first one presents studies of the effect of computer-mediated communication technologies on L2 interaction through tasks; the second strand presents CMC studies that focused

*The Handbook of Technology and Second Language Teaching and Learning*, First Edition.
Edited by Carol A. Chapelle and Shannon Sauro.
© 2017 John Wiley & Sons, Inc. Published 2020 by John Wiley & Sons, Inc.

on the effect of the tasks at producing interactions that were believed to promote language learning; and the third strand reviews studies that incorporate Web 2.0 technologies and tasks. To conclude, challenges for technology-mediated TBLT are discussed and new lines of future research proposed.

## Task-based language teaching/learning (TBLT/TBLL)

Although differences exist in the conceptualization of tasks and TBLT among scholars in the field, most agree on a set of essential characteristics for what constitutes a task. First, tasks are meaning-oriented, communicative in nature, and focus on the content of the message and not on the language (although pre-tasks and post-tasks or pedagogic tasks, depending on the model of TBLT, can focus on language per se). Tasks are goal-oriented and should be as authentic as possible, incorporating real contextualized language with application outside of the activity itself. Second, the learner is considered to have succeeded on a task if he or she succeeds in doing the task and achieving something with the language rather than by mastering a particular linguistic piece. This idea of doing something with the language, rather than simply knowing something about the language, is an essential principle of TBLT. Learning by doing or experiential learning (Dewey 1938/1997) is at the core of the TBLT methodology, which proposes that a language can be learned by engaging the learners in its use. Finally, in TBLT, language acquisition and not just communicative effectiveness is the main goal. Proponents of TBLT distinguish between learners' development of communicative skills in language use and their acquisition of the language. TBLT's main concern is how tasks, and more comprehensively a task-based syllabus, can promote language acquisition. The goal of TBLT is to promote language acquisition along the three dimensions of fluency, accuracy, and complexity. These three dimensions serve as targets for evaluating success with respect to language acquisition, which would extend beyond success on any single task.

## Technology-mediated tasks

Building on the basic principles of TBLT, technology-mediated tasks are meaning and goal-oriented, communicative, authentic, and oriented to learning by doing. The first technology-mediated tasks that appeared in SLA and computer-assisted language learning (CALL) research were understood more as generic types of tasks, closer to their definition in the weaker version of TBLT,[2] They were tasks such as jigsaw, dictogloss, information-gap activities, decision-making (close-ended) or discussion tasks (open-ended). These were borrowed from researchers investigating learning in face-to-face interaction who had proposed certain types of tasks as optimal activities for language learning (Doughty and Pica 1986; Pica, Kang, and Sauro 2006). However, as González-Lloret and Ortega (2014) suggest, for a full effective integration of technology and TBLT the first condition required is a clear definition of technology-mediated tasks to avoid mistaking the translation of exercises and activities from face-to-face contexts into a computer platform. In 2001, Carol Chapelle had laid out a task framework in which she proposed that tasks in CALL should be authentic, practical, focused on meaning, and appropriate to the students' level and learning goals. CALL tasks, according to Chapelle (2001), should provide opportunities for focus on form (an integral characteristic of TBLT instruction) and have added benefits beyond the learning of language (i.e., developing skills to use technology outside of class, increase their interest in the L2 culture, etc.).

Similar to Chapelle's (2001) framework, González-Lloret and Ortega (2014) propose characteristics for tasks in the context of technology. According to the authors, technology-mediated tasks should primarily focus on meaning, rather than on grammatical forms. They should be learner-centered, considering students' needs and wants for language, their technological applications, and digital skills. Tasks should also be holistic and authentic, drawing on real-world processes of language use. And finally, tasks should bring reflection to the learning process; they should provide opportunities for higher-order learning as part of principles of experiential learning (Dewey 1938/1997). According to González-Lloret and Ortega (2014) such a task definition is central to the investigation of technology-assisted TBLT. In addition, two other conditions are necessary for the integration of technology and tasks: the first is an awareness of the non-neutrality of technology-mediated tasks, and the second is a clear articulation of the technology-mediated tasks within a full TBLT curriculum.

The incorporation of technology is never neutral. Adding technology in a curriculum brings about a whole new set of real-world tasks which in and of themselves should become target tasks and part of the curriculum. For example, incorporating email in a task such as "requesting a letter of recommendation" will entail learning the pragmatics of such a medium for that task, different from a paper letter. Similarly, using a smartphone to look at an interactive map, may transform the common task-based lesson "asking for directions" by adding to the language tasks pedagogic technology tasks on the use of such a tool, how to identify the location, where to enter the target address, how to view the target address in a street view, drop a pin to mark a location, and so on.

Second, the relationships of technology and tasks to a full curriculum must be articulated clearly. Technology must become part of the full programmatic cycle that shapes a TBLT curriculum, from needs analysis all the way to explicit learning outcomes for assessment and evaluation. For example, in a needs analysis for a technology-mediated TBLT it is not enough to find out what students will need to do with language and what language exactly they will need to use to accomplish it, we need to know what technologies will mediate their actions, what affordances they have, and what digital literacies (Shetzer and Warschauer 2000) the students need and already possess in order to use those technologies and accomplish the task. Although we have still not seen many fully developed technology-mediated TBLT curriculums, recent research has started to define the different components for such a curriculum, from illustration of a needs analysis incorporating technology and tasks (González-Lloret 2014), to pedagogical principles and examples of technology-mediated tasks (Gánem-Gutiérrez 2014; Sauro 2014; Solares 2014), issues of task selection and sequencing (Adams and Nik 2014), task implementation (Cantó, de Graff, and Jauregui 2014; Oskoz and Elola 2014), student assessment (Winke 2014), and course evaluation (Nielson 2014).

As for the technologies that best fit principles of TBLT, Web 2.0 technologies are ideal because they allow users to create digital content and communicate with other users. Using Web 2.0 functionalities students can engage in doing things with language and with other speakers rather than just listening, viewing, and reading about language and culture in text-books or on Web pages that others have created. Web 2.0 tools can therefore promote active student engagement in learning, following a "learning by doing" (Dewey 1938/1997) philosophy of education. Web 2.0 technologies can be integrated into language learning instruction as a *medium* for interaction among participants. In this role, "technology provides sites for interpersonal communication, multimedia publication, distance learning, community participation, and identity formation" (Kern 2006, 162). Students can interact with other speakers of the language via computer-mediated communication (video, audio, or text), through their avatars in synthetic/virtual environments (Second Life, Quest Atlantis, etc.) or can collectively embark on quests in multiplayer online games, which provide opportunities for realistic, goal-oriented tasks, as well as authentic input and authentic interaction with other speakers of the language that are required for TBLT. They can work collaboratively and/or share written artifacts through wikis, blogs, collaborative documents, fanfiction sites, and so on, actively contributing to the creation and distribution of knowledge, with a meaning-oriented communicative purpose and for an authentic audience, both of which are essential in TBLT. If task-and-technology integrations are properly motivated by TBLT theory, language-learning tasks which are mediated by these new technologies could potentially help minimize students' fear of failure, embarrassment, or losing face; they could raise students' motivation to take risks and be creative while using language to make meaning, and they could enable students to meet other speakers of the language in remote locations, opening up transformative exposure to authentic language environments and cultural representations, along with immense additional sources of authentic input, all important characteristics of language-learning. Through these tools, language learning opportunities are extended in ways that would be difficult (if not impossible) to orchestrate in traditional classroom settings (Sykes, Oskoz, and Thorne 2008; Thorne and Black 2008).

# Research on tasks and technology

Recent volumes on TBLT and technology (Al-Bulushi 2010; González-Lloret and Ortega 2014; Thomas and Reinders 2010), as well as review studies by Lai and Li (2011) and Thomas (2013), illustrate how the interest on technology and tasks is growing rapidly. However, the body of research on technology-mediated TBLT is still young and accumulated results are still limited. Many concepts still need to be operationalized and a research agenda articulated.

Studies of technology and tasks have focused mainly on the interaction produced by students, following SLA research proposing L2 interaction as a locus for learning and mostly within computer-mediated communication (CMC) as the technology of choice. These studies could be grouped in three main trends: (1) studies that examined the effect that the technology had on interaction produced through tasks borrowed from research on face-to-face communication tasks; (2) studies on the effect that the task, mediated by technology, had on the interaction; and (3) research on tasks developed through new Web 2.0 technologies.

## *L2 interaction in technology-based tasks*

First studies on technology and tasks, mainly on CMC, tried to discover whether the interaction mediated by the computer while engaged in completing a task was similar to face-to-face interactions. Some of these studies employed tasks that were borrowed directly from SLA face-to-face studies and that had been proposed as affective for promoting the types of interactions believed to be productive for language learning such as negotiation of meaning and opportunities for intake. The tasks used were closed-ended tasks such as jigsaws, information-gap tasks, and spot the differences (i.e., de la Fuente 2003; Lee 2002; Monteiro 2014; Smith 2004, 2005; Yilmaz 2012) as well as more open-ended tasks which consisted mainly of a discussion of a topic or artifact (i.e., Abrams 2003; Sauro 2009). Some of these tasks fit within the framework of TBLT, including tasks as part of larger projects (project-based) with a clear focused on meaning and oriented towards a concrete goal (i.e., Freiermuth 2002; Freiermuth and Jarrell 2006; Kitade 2000; Levy and Kennedy 2004). Other tasks were used in studies of telecollaborative (teletandem) projects, with a strong cultural component and a variety of tasks, mainly discussion tasks based on literary pieces, survey data, and media (i.e., Belz 2003; Belz and Kinginger 2002; Furstenberg et al. 2001; Müller-Hartman 2000).

Results about the amount and quality of interaction (modifications, feedback, uptake, etc.) vary across studies. While some of these studies found CMC task-based interaction to be productive and conductive to language learning (e.g., Monteiro 2014; Shekary and Tahririan 2006; Smith 2004; Yilmaz and Yuksel 2011) others found negotiation not as abundant as in face-to-face interaction (e.g., Blake 2000; Jepson, 2005). For a research synthesis of synchronous CMC for SLA see Sauro (2011), and Ortega (2009) for an in depth evaluation of negotiation in CMC research. For a few examples of studies using tasks and technologies other than CMC see Collentine (2013), González-Lloret (2003), Sauro (2014), and Thomas (2013). All these studies have in common their focus on the type of interaction rather than on the task per se. The tasks were borrowed from SLA face-to-face research and transferred into the computer-mediated environment. Clear examples of this transfer are for example, Loewen and Erlam's (2006) replication of a face-to-face study to a CMC environment, and Yanguas' (2010) study comparing the same jigsaw task in video CMC, audio CMC, and face-to-face modalities.

## *Focus on task design in the study of technology-mediated L2 interaction*

In contrast with the research above, the studies presented in this section focus mainly on the task, following the idea from SLA research that the task in itself greatly affects the interaction. Ortega in 1997 pointed out the importance of researching tasks, their conditions, and processes in order to make claims about the effectiveness of CMC for learning, and Blake (2008b) proposed that any technological tool is inherently neutral and its success to be effective for SLA will depend on careful planning, including task design. Lee's (2007) results confirmed that well designed and motivating tasks, with carefully selected linguistic context, are essential for L2 learning to take place. In addition, since CMC is a different form of communication, one that incorporates aspects of both spoken and written language with features of the digital context (Herring 1996), it is essential to study CMC tasks as entities of their own rather than assuming that tasks that are effective at eliciting quality L2 interaction in face-to-face exchanges will also do so in CMC.

Although research is still new, we have a handful of studies which have investigated which types of tasks (in the traditional face-to-face definition), with which characteristics (e.g., level of complexity) and under which conditions (e.g., through which media) could be more effective at producing interactions believed to be conductive to language learning (Blake 2000; Jeong 2011; Keller-Lally 2006; Sauro 2011; Smith 2001, 2003; Yilmaz 2011). The results are quite inconclusive and even contradictory. While Keller-Lally (2006) found no effect on task type (jigsaw, decision-making, or opinion-exchange), Blake (2000), and Jeong (2011) found jigsaw tasks to produce more negotiation than information-gap and decision-making tasks, and Smith (2001, 2003) found decision-making tasks, seeded with unknown lexical items, to elicit more negotiation that jigsaw tasks (which he attributes to lexical items in the jigsaw task viewed as less important than those in the decision-making task). Also Yilmaz (2011) found dictogloss tasks to elicit a higher number of negotiation routines than jigsaw tasks while jigsaw tasks had more unresolved negotiations.

As for task characteristics, one of the most fruitful areas of research in traditional TBLT is task complexity, which examines how manipulation of certain task characteristics renders a task more or less complex and how this affects the fluency, complexity, and accuracy of the learners' production. A few pioneer studies (Adams and Nik 2014; Appel and Gilabert 2002; Baralt, 2014; Collentine, 2010; Nik 2010; Nik, Adams, and Newton 2012) are establishing coding strategies and operationalizing complexity, accuracy and fluency in text chat data. Most of this research has explored the validity of face-to-face task complexity theories, in particular Robinson's (2005) Cognition Hypothesis. Robinson (2005) predicts that any increases in complexity along resource-dispersing dimensions of cognitive complexity (e.g., task structure, planning time, prior knowledge) should result in decreases of complexity, accuracy, and fluency in both monologic and interactive contexts, and increases in amount of negotiation in interactive contexts, while an increase in complexity in resource-directing dimensions (e.g., number of elements, here and now, perspective) should result in an increase of complexity, fluency, accuracy, and amount of negotiation. Knowing whether a task is more or less difficult than another is of great importance for task development and sequencing, both for traditional face-to-face (or pen and pencil) and technology-mediated tasks.

The results of studies of technology-mediated task complexity to date suggest that the Cognition Hypothesis does not necessarily transfer to technology-mediated environments. Adams and Nik (2014) have suggested that this may be due to the unique characteristics of medium (text-based CMC) where opportunities to process output may be more frequent (compared to face-to-face interaction) and where the separation that exists between production and transmission may affect the cognitive burden imposed by the production, making it different from models of speech production. This explanation seems to be supported by Baralt's (2013) study comparing reasoning demands (as a task complexity variable) in a traditional face-to-face and a CMC environment. Her results show that the prediction was true in the face-to-face environment but not in the CMC environment where more learning happened in less complex conditions. So far, these studies suggest that the distinct nature of CMC affects the complexity variables as we know them for face-to-face research, highlighting the importance of studying tasks developed for and embedded in the technology.

## Research on tasks developed through Web 2.0 technologies

Web 2.0 technologies offer ideal interactive spaces for collaborative and intercultural communication in which tasks are an essential component. First, virtual spaces such as gaming environments and social synthetic/virtual environments (VEs) (e.g., Second Life) allow for greater freedom of communication allowing also for real interaction with a variety of speakers (native and non-native). Results of research in virtual environments using tasks suggest that students find tasks in these spaces useful and highly motivating when tasks are well designed and collaborative in nature (Cantó, de Graff, and Jauregi 2014; Gánem-Gutiérrez 2014; Thomas 2013), and include meaningful content and meaningful interactions (Sykes 2012). Tasks in VEs promote negotiation of meaning, including intercultural communication routines (Cantó, de Graff, and Jauregi 2014), and the possibility of a "physical simulation of real-life tasks" (Deutschmann and Panichi 2009, 34). They encourage learner's agency and confidence in L2 use (Thomas 2013; Zheng et al. 2009) and generate opportunities for social discourse and casual conversation (Peña and Hancock 2006; Thorne 2008, 2010) essential components on the repertoire of a language learner.

Furthermore, Web 2.0 tools are useful for helping learners explore intersections between technologies and tasks focused on written communication and exchange of ideas. This research investigates the potential of tasks using blogs (e.g., Solares 2014), wikis (e.g., Oskoz and Elola 2014), and fanfiction sites[3] (e.g., Sauro 2014) to develop writing skills. Both Solares (2014) and Oskoz and Elola (2014) use pedagogic tasks in blogs and wikis to redraw the boundaries of what language instruction can be to teach students process writing, collaborative writing, and genre development, through authentic tasks in an academic setting. Solares (2014) created a storytelling context for which students created narratives using digital posters. Students then uploaded their narratives to a free Web application called *Web Poster Wizard* and voted on the best story by using a class blog. Oskoz and Elola (2014) used chats and wikis to teach the process model of writing with argumentative and expository essays. They developed a series of pedagogic tasks to help the learners through the writing stages of planning, drafting, getting feedback, revising, and publishing. Sauro (2014) proposes fanfiction as a collaborative space in which students can engage in writing tasks with linguistic and technological continuity into the students' online activities outside of classroom. This idea of bridging in and outside of classroom tasks brings authenticity in the classroom, provides learners with a realistic venue, a real audience for their writing, and connects them with other speakers with the same interest, all important tenets of TBLT.

Considering how incorporating tasks in these new technologies can advance task theory and research is an essential question that was posited by Chapelle in 2003 but has still not been fully addressed. As technology-mediated TBLT grows as a field, it is essential to reflect on the implications that the integration of technology has for TBLT as a language-learning methodology. As acknowledged by Van den Branden, Bygate, and Norris (2009), changes in education are often "responses to new technologies" (495), and it may well be that technology is changing TBLT. It may be changing towards a more comprehensive approach to language; one that views language and learning more holistically than has often been the case in the field of TBLT (following the field of SLA); one that includes different language learning perspectives, as for example Sociocultural Theory (e.g., Collentine 2011; Gánem-Gutiérrez 2014; Müller-Hartmann and Schocker-von Ditfurth 2010; Oskoz and Eloloa 2014); one in which learning language and learning culture are fundamental and inseparable parts of communication (e.g., Cantó, de Graff, and Jauregi 2014; Furstenberg et al. 2001) all within a framework that gives priority to activities with the goal of doing something with a language, communicating meaning with a clear objective, in an environment authentic for the learners and their context, all according to their needs.

## Challenges for technology-mediated TBLT

The advancement of technology-mediated TBLT (both theoretically and for its application) is not without challenges. First of all, technology moves incredibly fast, with new technologies becoming obsolete in a blink of an eye. Therefore, researching the potential of some technologies for TBLT may seem an unwise investment. Here, technology-mediated TBLT could learn from CALL research that faces this challenge every day. To avoid investigating tools with expiration dates in recent years, CALL is moving its research focus from individual tools to investigating more general characteristics and affordances of a certain medium, characteristics that most likely will stay constant in spite of improvements and upgrades. More of a challenge is to be able to anticipate the needs of students for technologies that may not even exist yet (Chapelle 2014).

Second, from a programmatic point of view, the incorporation of technology in TBLT poses a challenge for evaluation and assessment. If technology is to be an integral part of the curriculum, it should also be part of the assessment. If we envision student assessment in TBLT as performance-based in nature, then the evaluation of the technology performance should be part of the evaluation of the task (together with language performance). For example, a case in which the use of technology is essential to accomplish language tasks is that of online language courses. In these environments every interaction among students, between student and teacher, and between student and content is mediated by technology. Nielson (2014) presents probably the first effort to describe in detail an example of a technology-mediated TBLT assessment of students' performance in an online language course, highlighting how the technology is not an add-on but rather a strong effect on the entire curriculum that "must therefore be considered at all stages of the design, implementation, and assessment of a program" (316).

Lastly, for a technology-mediated TBLT curriculum to be successful, it is important to incorporate technology as a target of instruction (Chapelle 2014; González-Lloret 2014). This adds value to technology-mediated TBLT since students would be developing their *digital, multimodal, and informational literacies* (Warschauer, 2007) at the same time that they are developing their language competence; two essential life skills for the citizens of tomorrow. This requires teachers to be knowledgeable in the use of multiple technologies as well as experienced in the development of tasks (Hauck 2010). However, in many contexts, this is not the case and we are finding that the lack of experience in the use of technology presents one of the most serious barriers to its successful integration into the language curriculum (Blake 2008a). So, how can we solve this challenge? According to Winke (2013), teacher training, optimal institutional conditions, and the support needed to include technology in their language classes are essential components for success at incorporating technology in the language classroom or conducting online language teaching. Without a doubt, institutional support in the form of workshops and tutorials, and even teachers enrolling on online courses themselves, would be ways of providing the needed education for teachers. However, this remains a clear challenge for most language practitioners (and their institutions) today.

# Research agenda

In a new area of study, such as technology for TBLT, the research agenda is wide open. We need new research on the affordances of emerging new technologies (see for example research on smart spaces with sensory devices that understand participants' movements at Newcastle University, UK (Seedhouse 2017 http://openlab.ncl.ac.uk/ilablearn/?page_id=26), as well as research that revises language-learning theory and methodological choices that integrate the more transparent, everyday tools that now mediate our communication and learning (e.g., Chapelle 2001, 2003, 2014; Doughty and Long 2003; Skehan 2003).

Unresolved issues in task research, as for example the task complexity debate between the Cognition Hypothesis (Robinson 2001) and the Trade-off Hypothesis (Skehan 1998) are also relevant to technology-mediated TBLT, with the technological aspects as added layers of intricacy. Believing that we have one single limited cognitive capacity and that increasing task complexity will lead to competition between accuracy, complexity, and fluency (Trade-off Hypothesis) or that we have different attentional resources and that increasing particular task demands can focus attention and lead to more control of production (Cognition Hypothesis) should influence how we develop and sequence tasks. It may well be that the technology context has a strong effect on the cognitive factors that affect task complexity (which has not been investigated in depth yet), or that other factors such as task condition and task difficulty (Robinson 2007) have more weight in technology-mediated tasks than in face-to-face tasks. Tasks conditions which, according to Robinson (2007) include: (1) task difficulty which refers to learner factors such as ability (i.e., working memory, aptitude, filed independence, etc.) and affective variables (i.e., task motivation, willingness to communicate, self-efficacy, openness to experience, etc.); and (2) interactive factors (i.e., number of participants, amount of contribution and negotiation needed, whether the task requires a convergent or open solution) and characteristics of the participants (i.e., proficiency level, gender, familiarity, shared content and cultural knowledge, status and role). These interactive factors have been explored outside of SLA research in sociology, computer and information science, communication studies and CALL. We have by now ample evidence that factors such as number of participants (i.e., Böhlke 2003), their gender (i.e., Baron 2008; Herring 2000; Savicki, Kelley, and Lingenfelter 1996; Zhan et al. 2015), their attitude towards the technology (i.e., Lou, Abrami and d'Apollonia's 2001 meta-analysis; Reinders and Wattana 2014), and so on, greatly affect the interaction. Therefore more research on task complexity that includes these factors is needed.

Another important area to explore is that of multimodality in technology-enhanced TBLT. With easier access to broadband connectivity, multimedia platforms, and mobile devices, it will be important to investigate the role of multimodality in TBLT, on language development through tasks, and on the efforts at blending technology and tasks (Hampel 2006; Sauro 2009). In particular, it will be crucial to know how multimodality at the task level (one task involving more than one mode) affects language learning and digital development, how it compares with multimodality at a curricular level (different modes for different tasks across the curriculum), and what is the impact that it has on real-life tasks, which more often than not are also multimodal.

Finally, we know that the teacher's role in the success of technology-mediated tasks is essential. Even with the best developed, most interesting, technology-mediated TBLT curriculum, if teachers are not willing and educated to implement it, the curriculum will most likely fail (González-Lloret and Nielson 2014). Therefore, we need more studies on the role that teachers (and teacher education) play in technology-mediated tasks (e.g., Müller-Hartmann 2007; O'Dowd and Ware 2009), from willingness and disposition to incorporate tasks and technology to the actual use of the technology, planning, intervention, and evaluation.

In summary, research in technology and TBLT is in a growing stage and an array of fields and topics are open to investigation. From theoretical and fundamental issues dealing with the nature of tasks, their sequencing, implementation, evaluation, and so on, when mediated by technologies to the rapidly changing world of innovations and their affordances to incorporate effective language-learning tasks.

## NOTES

1   Web 2.0 technologies are defined here as those that allow users to transform information and "harness collective intelligence" (O'Reilly 2005, 2).
2   Skehan (1996) makes the distinction between weak and strong forms of TBLT. The strong form of TBLT emphasizes the importance real-life tasks with a goal outside of the classroom while the weak form understand tasks in a more traditional classroom sense, as facilitative of communication and language work.
3   Fanfiction is the narrative product of fans of a particular text, movie, celebrity, and so on, whose "goal is to expressively rearticulate the source material in such a way as to create something meaningful, minimally for the author/artist, and usually with a broader audience in mind" (Thorne 2010, 145).

## REFERENCES

Abrams, Zsuzsanna Ittzes. 2003. "The Effect of Synchronous and Asynchronous CMC on Oral Performance in German." *Modern Language Journal*, 87, no. 2: 157–167.

Adams, Rebecca, and Nik Aloesnita Nik Mohd Nik. 2014. "Prior Knowledge and Second Language Task Production in Text Chat." In *Technology-Mediated TBLT: Researching Technology and Tasks*, edited by Marta González-Lloret and Lourdes Ortega, 51–78. Amsterdam/Philadelphia: John Benjamins.

Al-Bulushi, Ali. 2010. *Task-Based Computer-Mediated Negotiation in an EFL Context: The Ins and Outs of Online Negotiation of Meaning Using Language Learning Tasks*. Saarbrucken: VDM Verlag Dr. Muller.

Appel, Christine, and Roger Gilabert. 2002. "Motivation and Task Performance in a Task-Based Web-Based Tandem Project." *ReCALL*, 14, no. 1: 16–31. Doi:10.1017/S0958344002000319

Baralt, Melissa. 2013. "The Impact of Cognitive Complexity on Feedback Efficacy during Online versus Face- to-Face Interactive Tasks." *Studies in Second Language Acquisition*, 35: 689–725.

Baralt, Melissa. 2014. "Task Complexity and Task Sequencing in Traditional versus Online Language Classes." In *Task Sequencing and Instructed Second Language Learning*, edited by Melissa Baralt, Roger Gilabert, and Peter Jake Robinson, 59–122. London/New York: Bloomsbury Academic.

Baron, Naomi S. 2008. *Always On: Language in an Online and Mobile World*. Oxford/Oxford University Press.

Belz, Julie A. 2003. "Linguistic Perspectives on the Development of Intercultural Competence in Telecollaboration." *Language Learning & Technology*, 7, no. 2: 68–117.

Belz, Julie A., and Celeste Kinginer. 2002. "The Cross-Linguistic Development of Address Form Use in Telecollaborative Language Learning: Two Case Studies." *The Canadian Modern Language Review*, 59, no. 2: 189–214.

Blake, Robert J. 2000. "Computer-Mediated Communication: A Window on L2 Spanish Interlanguage." *Language Learning and Technology*, 4, no. 1: 120–136.

Blake, Robert J. 2008a. "New Trends in Using Technology in the Language Curriculum." *Annual Review of Applied Linguistics*, 27, no. 1: 76–97.

Blake, Robert J. 2008b. *Brave New Digital Classroom: Technology and Language Learning*. Washington, DC: Georgetown University Press.

Böhlke, Olaf. 2003. "A Comparison of Student Participation Levels by Group Size and Language Stages during Chatroom and Face-to-Face Discussions in German." *CALICO Journal*, 21, no.1: 67–87.

Cantó, Silvia, Rick de Graff, and Kristi Jauregi. 2014. "Collaborative Tasks for Negotiation of Intercultural Meaning in Virtual Worlds and Video-Web Communication." In *Technology-Mediated TBLT: Researching Technology and Tasks*, edited by Marta González-Lloret and Lourdes Ortega, 183–212. Amsterdam: John Benjamins Publishing Company.

Chapelle, Carol. 2001. *Computer Applications in Second Language Acquisition: Foundations for Teaching, Testing, and Research*. Cambridge: Cambridge University Press.

Chapelle, Carol. 2003. *English Language Learning and Technology: Lectures on Applied Linguistics in the Age of Information and Communication Technology*. Amsterdam: John Benjamins.

Chapelle, Carol.2014. "Afterword: Technology-Mediated TBLT and the Evolving Role of the Innovator." In *Technology-Mediated TBLT: Researching Technology and Tasks*, edited by Marta González-Lloret and Lourdes Ortega, 323–334. Amsterdam: John Benjamins.

Collentine, Karina. 2010. "Measuring Complexity in Task-Based Synchronous Computer-Mediated Communication." In *Task-Based Language Learning and Teaching with Technology*, edited by Michael Thomas and Hayo Reinders, 105–128. London; New York: Continuum.

Collentine, Karina. 2011. "Learner Autonomy in a Task-Based 3d World and Production." *Language Learning & Technology*, 15, no. 3: 50–67.

Collentine, Karina. 2013. "Using Tracking Technologies to Study the Effects of Linguistic Complexity in CALL Input and SCMC Output." *CALICO Journal*, 30, no. 1: 46–65.

de la Fuente, María J. 2003. "Is SLA Interactionist Theory Relevant to CALL? A Study on the Effects of Computer-Mediated Interaction in L2 Vocabulary Acquisition." *Computer Assisted Language Learning*, 16: 47–82.

Deutschmann, Mats, and Luisa Panichi. 2009. "Instructional Design, Teacher Practice and Learner Autonomy." In *Learning and Teaching in the Virtual World of Second Life*, edited by Judith Molka-Danielsen and Mats Deutschmann, 27–43. Trondheim: Tapir Academic Press.

Dewey, John. 1938. *Experience and Education*. New York: Macmillan/Collier.

Dewey, John. 1997. *Experience and Education*. New York: Simon & Schuster.

Doughty, Catherine, and Mike H. Long. 2003. "Optimal Psycholinguistic Environments for Distance Foreign Language Learning." *Language Learning and Technology*, 7, no. 3: 50–80.

Doughty, Catherine, and Teresa Pica. 1986. "Information Gap Tasks: An Aid to Second Language Acquisition?" *TESOL Quarterly*, 20: 305–325.

Freiermuth, Mark. 2002. "Online Chatting: An Alternative Approach to Simulations." *Simulation & Gaming*, 32, no. 2: 187–195.

Freiermuth, Mark, and Douglas Jarrell. 2006. "Willingness to Communicate: Can Online Chat help?" *International Journal of Applied Linguistics*, 16, no. 2: 189–212. DOI:10.1111/j.1473-4192.2006.00113.x

Furstenberg, Gilberte, Sabine Levet, Kathryn English, and Katherine Maillet. 2001. "Giving a Virtual Voice to the Silent Language of Culture: The CULTURA Project." *Language Learning and Technology*, 5, no. 1: 55–102.

Gánem-Gutiérrez, Gabriela Adela. 2014. "The Third Dimension: A Sociocultural Theory

Approach to Design and Evaluation of 3D Virtual Worlds Tasks." In *Technology-Mediated TBLT: Researching Technology and Tasks*, edited by Marta González-Lloret and Lourdes Ortega, 213–238. Amsterdam: John Benjamins.

González-Lloret, Marta. 2003. "Designing Task-Based CALL to Promote Interaction: En Busca de Esmeraldas." *Language Learning & Technology*, 7, no. 1: 86–104. Accessed January 3, 2017. http://llt.msu.edu/vol7num1/gonzalez/

González-Lloret, Marta. 2014. "The Need for Needs Analysis in Technology-Mediated TBLT." In *Technology-Mediated TBLT: Researching Technology and Tasks*, edited by Marta González-Lloret and Lourdes Ortega, 23–50. Amsterdam: John Benjamins.

González-Lloret, Marta, and Katherine B. Nielson. 2014. "Evaluating TBLT: The Case of a Task-Based Spanish Program." *Language Teaching Research*. DOI:10.1177/1362168814541745

González-Lloret, Marta, and Lourdes Ortega. 2014. "Towards Technology-Mediated TBLT: An Introduction." In *Technology-Mediated TBLT: Researching Technology and Tasks*, edited by Marta González-Lloret and Lourdes Ortega, 1–22. Amsterdam: John Benjamins.

Grgurović, Maja, Carol A. Chapelle, and Mack C. Shelley. 2013. "A Meta-Analysis of Effectiveness Studies on Computer Technology-Supported Language Learning." *ReCALL*, 25, no. 2: 165–198. DOI:10.1017/S0958344013000013

Hampel, Regina. 2006. "Rethinking Task Design for the Digital Age: A Framework for Language Teaching and Learning in a Synchronous Online Environment." *ReCALL*, 18, no. 1: 105–201. DOI:10.1017/S0958344006000711

Hauck, Mirjam. 2010. "The Enactment of Task Design in Telecollaboration 2.0." In *Task-Based Language Learning and Teaching with Technology*, edited by Michael Thomas and Hayo Reinders, 197–217. London; New York: Continuum.

Herring, Susan C. 1996. *Computer-Mediated Communication. Linguistic, Social, and Cross-Cultural Perspectives*. Amsterdam: John Benjamins.

Herring, Susan C. 2000. "Gender Differences in CMC: Findings and Implications." *Computer Professionals for Social Responsibility Journal*, 18, no. 1. Accessed January 31, 2017. http://cpsr.org/issues/womenintech/herring/

Jeong, Nam-Sook. 2011. "The Effects of Task Type and Group Structure on Meaning Negotiation in Synchronous Computer-Mediated

Communication." In *Selected Proceedings of the 2009 Second Language Research Forum*, edited by Luke Plonsky and Maren Schierloh, 51–69. Somerville, MA: Cascadilla Proceedings Project.

Jepson, Kevin. 2005. "Conversations – and Negotiated Interaction – in Text and Voice Chat Rooms." *Language Learning & Technology*, 9, no. 3: 79–98.

Keller-Lally, Ann M. 2006. "Effect of Task-Type and Group Size on Foreign Language Learner Output in Synchronous Computer-Mediated Communication." PhD dissertation, University of Texas at Austin.

Kern, Richard. 2006. "Perspectives on Technology in Learning and Teaching Languages." *TESOL Quarterly*, 40, no. 1: 183–210.

Kitade, Keiko. 2000. "L2 Learners' Discourse and SLA Theories in CMC: Collaborative Interaction in Internet Chat." *Computer Assisted Language Learning*, 13, no. 2: 143–166.

Lai, Chun, and Guofang Li. 2011. "Technology and Task-Based Language Teaching: A Critical Review." *CALICO Journal*, 28, no. 2: 498–521.

Lee, Lina. 2002. "Enhancing Learners' Communication Skills through Synchronous Electronic Interaction and Task-Based Instruction." *Foreign Language Annals*, 35, no. 1: 16–24. DOI:10.1111/j.1944-9720.2002.tb01829.x

Lee, Lina. 2007. "Fostering Second Language Oral Communication through Constructivist Interaction in Desktop Videoconferencing." *Foreign Language Annals* 40, no. 4: 635–649.

Levy, Mike, and Claire Kennedy. 2004. "A Task-Cycling Pedagogy Using Audio-Conferencing and Stimulated Reflection for Foreign Language Learning." *Language Learning & Technology*, 8, no. 2: 50–68.

Loewen, Shawn, and Rosemary Erlam. 2006. "Corrective Feedback in the Chatroom: An Experimental Study." *Computer Assisted Language Learning*, 19, no. 1: 1–14.

Lou, Yiping, Philip C. Abrami, and Sylvia d' Apollonia. 2001. "Small Group and Individual Learning with Technology: A Meta-Analysis." *Review of Educational Research*, 17, no. 3: 449–452.

Monteiro, Kátia. 2014. "An Experimental Study of Corrective Feedback during Video-Conferencing." *Language Learning & Technology*, 18, no. 3: 56–79.

Müller-Hartmann, Andreas. 2000. "The Role of Tasks in Promoting Intercultural Learning in Electronic Learning Networks." *Language Learning & Technology*, 4, no. 2: 129–147.

Müller-Hartman, Andreas. 2007. "Teacher Role in Telecollaboration. Setting up and Managing

Exchanges." In Online Intercultural *Exchange: An Introduction for Foreign Language Teachers*, edited by Robert O'Dowd, 41–61. Clevedon: Multilingual Matters.

Müller-Hartman, Andreas, and Marita Schocker von Ditfurth. 2010. "Research on the Use of Technology in Task-Based Language Teaching." In *Task-Based Language Learning and Teaching with Technology*, edited by Michael Thomas and Hayo Reinders, 17–40. London: Continuum.

Nielson, Katharine B. 2014. "Evaluation of an Online, Task-Based Chinese Course." In *Technology-Mediated TBLT: Researching Technology and Tasks*, edited by Marta González-Lloret and Lourdes Ortega, 295–321. Amsterdam: John Benjamins.

Nik, Nik Aloesnita Nik Mohd. 2010. "Examining the Language Learning Potential of a Task-Based Approach to Synchronous Computer-Mediated Communication." Unpublished PhD dissertation, Victoria University of Wellington.

Nik, Nik Aloesnita Nik Mohd, Rebecca Adams, and Jonathan Newton. 2012. "Writing to Learn via Text Chat: Task Implementation and Focus on Form." *Journal of Second Language Writing*, 21, no. 1: 23–39. DOI:10.1016/j.jslw.2011.12.001

Nussbaum-Beach, Sheryl, and Lani Ritter Hall. 2012. *The Connected Educator: Learning and Leading in a Digital Age*. Bloomington, IN: Solution Tree Press.

O'Dowd, Robert, and Paige Ware. 2009. "Critical Issues in Telecollaborative Task Design." *Computer Assisted Language Learning*, 22, no. 2: 173–188. DOI:10.1080/09588220902778369

O'Reilly, Tim. 2005. "What Is Web 2.0: Design Patterns and Business Models for the Next Generation of Software." Accessed September 30. http://oreilly.com/pub/a/web2/archive/what-is-web-20.html?page=1

Ortega, Lourdes. 1997. "Processes and Outcomes in Network Classroom Interaction: Defining the Research Agenda for L2 Computer-Assisted Classroom Discussion." *Language Learning & Technology*, 1, no. 1: 82–93.

Ortega, Lourdes. 2009. "Interaction and Attention to Form in L2 Text-Based Computer-Mediated Communication." In *Multiple Perspectives on Interaction in SLA: Research in Honor of Susan M. Gass*, edited by Alison Mackey and Charlene Polio. New York: Erlbaum/Routledge/Taylor & Francis.

Oskoz, Ana, and Idoia Elola. 2014. "Promoting Foreign Language Collaborative Writing through the Use of Web 2.0 Tools and Tasks." In *Technology-Mediated TBLT: Researching Technology and Tasks*, edited by Marta

González-Lloret and Lourdes Ortega, 115–148. Amsterdam: John Benjamins.

Peña, Jorge, and Jeffrey T. Hancock. 2006. "An Analysis of Socioemotional and Task Communication in Online Multiplayer Video Games." *Communication Research*, 33, no. 1: 92–109.

Pica, Teresa, Hyun-Sook Kang, and Shannon Sauro. 2006. "Information Gap Tasks: Their Multiple Roles and Contributions to Interaction Research Methodology." *Studies in Second Language Acquisition*, 28, no. 2: 301–338.

Prensky, Marc. 2001. "Digital Natives, Digital Immigrants." *On the Horizon*, 9, no. 5: 1–6. Accessed January 3, 2017. http://dx.doi.org/10.1108/10748120110424816

Reinders, Hayo, and Sorada Wattana. 2014. "Can I Say Something? The Effects of Digital Game Play on Willingness to Communicate." *Language Learning & Technology*, 18, no. 2: 101–123.

Robinson, Peter. 2001. "Task Complexity, Cognition and Second Language Syllabus Design: A Triadic Framework for Examining Task Influences on SLA." In *Cognition and Second Language Instruction*, edited by Peter Robinson, 287–318. New York: Cambridge University Press.

Robinson, Peter. 2005. "Cognitive Complexity and Task Sequencing: Studies in a Componential Framework for Second Language Task Design." *International Review of Applied Linguistics*, 43, no. 1: 1–32.

Robinson, Peter. 2007. "Criteria for Classifying and Sequencing Pedagogic Tasks." In *Investigating Tasks in Formal Language Learning*, edited by María del Pilar García Mayo, 7–27. Clevedon: Multilingual Matters.

Rosen, Larry D. 2010. *Rewired: Understanding the iGeneration and the Way They Learn*,1st ed. New York: Palgrave Macmillan.

Sauro, Shannon. 2009. "Computer-Mediated Corrective Feedback and the Development of l2 Grammar." *Language Learning & Technology*, 13, no. 1: 96–120.

Sauro, Shannon. 2011. "SCMC for SLA: A Research Synthesis." *CALICO Journal*, 28, no. 2: 369–391.

Sauro, Shannon. 2014. "Lessons from the Fandom: Technology-Mediated Tasks for Language Learning." In *Technology-Mediated TBLT: Researching Technology and Tasks*, edited by Marta González-Lloret and Lourdes Ortega, 239–262. Amsterdam: John Benjamins.

Savicki, Victor, Merle Kelley, and Dawn Lingenfelter. 1996. "Gender, Group

Composition, and Task Type in Small Task Groups Using Computer-Mediated Communication." *Computers in Human Behavior*, 12, no. 4: 549–565. DOI:10.1016/ S0747-5632(96)00024-6.

Seedhouse, Paul, ed. 2017. Task-Based Language Learning in a Real-World Digital Environment: The European Digital Kitchen. *Advances in Digital Language Learning and Teaching* 4. London ; New York: Bloomsbury Academic, an imprint of Bloomsbury Publishing Plc.

Shekary, M., and Mohammad Hassan Tahririan. 2006. "Negotiation of Meaning and Noticing in Text-Based Online Chat." *The Modern Language Journal*, 90, no. 4: 557–573. DOI:10.1111/j.1540-4781.2006.00504.x.

Shetzer, Heidi, and Mark Warschauer. 2000. "An Electronic Literacy Approach to Network-Based Language Teaching." In *Network-Based Language Teaching: Concepts and Practice*, edited by Mark Warschauer and Richard Kern, 171–185. Cambridge: Cambridge University Press.

Skehan, Peter. 1996. "A Framework for the Implementation of Task-Based Instruction." *Applied Linguistics*, 17: 38–62.

Skehan, Peter. 1998. *A Cognitive Approach to Language Learning*. Oxford: Oxford University Press.

Skehan, Peter. 2003. "Focus on Form, Tasks, and Technology." *Computer Assisted Language Learning*, 16, no. 5: 391–411. DOI:10.1076/ call.16.5.391.29489

Smith, Bryan. 2001. "Taking Students to Task: Task-Based Computer-Mediated Communication and Negotiated Interaction in the ESL Classroom." PhD dissertation, University of Arizona.

Skehan, Peter. 2003. "Computer-Mediated Negotiated Interaction: An Expanded Model." *The Modern Language Journal*, 87, no. 1: 38–57.

Skehan, Peter. 2004. "Computer-Mediated Negotiated Interaction and Lexical Acquisition." *Studies in Second Language Acquisition*, 26: 365–398.

Skehan, Peter. 2005. "The Relationship between Negotiated Interaction, Learner Uptake, and Lexical Acquisition in Task-Based Computer-Mediated Communication." *TESOL Quarterly*, 39, no. 1: 33–58. DOI:10.2307/3588451

Solares, María Elena. 2014. "Textbooks, Tasks, and Technology: An Action Research Study in Textbook-Bound EFL Context." In *Technology-Mediated TBLT: Researching Technology and Tasks*,

edited by Marta González-Lloret and Lourdes Ortega, 79–114. Amsterdam: John Benjamins.

Sykes, Julie. 2012. "Synthetic Immersive Environments and Second Language Pragmatic Development." In *The Encyclopedia of Applied Linguistics*, edited by Carol A. Chapelle. Oxford: Wiley-Blackwell. Accessed January 3, 2017. http://doi.wiley. com/10.1002/9781405198431.wbeal1136

Sykes, Julie M., Ana Oskoz, and Steven. L. Thorne. 2008. "Web 2.0, Synthetic Immersive Environments, and Mobile Resources for Language Education." *CALICO Journal*, 25, no. 3: 528–546.

Thomas, Michael. 2013. "Task-Based Language Teaching and CALL." In *Contemporary Computer-Assisted Language Learning*, edited by Michael Thomas, Hayo Reinders, and Mark Warschauer, 341–358. New York: Continuum.

Thomas, Michael, and Hayo Reinders, eds. 2010. *Task-Based Language Learning and Teaching with Technology*. London: Continuum.

Thorne, Steven L. 2008. "Transcultural Communication in Open Internet Environments and Massively Multiplayer Online Games." In *Mediating Discourse Online*, edited by Sally Sieloff Magnan, 305–327. Amsterdam: John Benjamins.

Thorne, Steven L. 2010. "The Intercultural Turn and Language Learning in the Crucible of New Media." In *Telecollaboration 2.0: Language, Literacies and Intercultural Learning in the 21st Century*, edited by Sarah Guth and Francesca Helm, 139–164. Telecollaboration in Education, Vol. 1. Bern: Peter Lang.

Thorne, Steven L. 2013. "Digital Literacies." In *Framing Languages and Literacies: Socially Situated Views and Perspectives*, edited by Margaret Hawkins, 193–219. New York: Routledge.

Thorne, Steven L., and Rebecca Black. 2008. "Language and Literacy Development in Computer-Mediated Contexts and Communities." *Annual Review of Applied Linguistics*, 27, no. 1: 133–160.

Van den Branden, Kris, Martin Bygate, and John Norris, eds. 2009. *Task-Based Language Teaching: A Reader*. Vol. 1. Task-Based Language Teaching. Amsterdam: John Benjamins.

Warschauer, Mark. 2007. "The Paradoxical Future of Digital Learning." *Journal Learning Inquiry*, 1, no. 1: 41–49.

Winke, Paula. 2013. "Supporting Teachers' Efforts in Implementing Technology-Mediated Tasks." Paper presented at the Task-based

Language Teaching Conference, Banff, Alberta, Canada, October 3–5.

Winke, Paula. 2014. "Formative, Task-Based Oral Assessment in an Advanced Chinese-Language Class." In *Technology-Mediated TBLT: Researching Technology and Tasks*, edited by Marta González-Lloret and Lourdes Ortega, 263–294. Amsterdam: John Benjamins.

Yanguas, Íñigo. 2010. "Oral Computer-Mediated Interaction between l2 Learners: It's about Time!" *Language Learning & Technology* 14, no. 3: 72–93.

Yilmaz, Yucel. 2011. "Task Effects on Focus on Form in Synchronous Computer-Mediated Communication." *The Modern Language Journal*, 95, no. 1: 115–132. DOI:10.1111/j.1540-4781.2010.01143.x

Yilmaz, Yucel. 2012. "The Relative Effects of Explicit Correction and Recasts on Two Target Structures via Two Communication Modes: Feedback Type, Salience, and Communication Mode." *Language Learning*, 62, no. 4: 1134–69. DOI:10.1111/j.1467-9922.2012.00726.x

Yilmaz, Yucel, and Dogan Yuksel. 2011. "Effects of Communication Mode and Salience on Recasts: A First Exposure Study." *Language Teaching Research*, 15: 457–477.

Zhao, Yong. 2003. "Recent Developments in Technology and Language Learning: A Literature Review and Meta-Analysis." *CALICO Journal*, 21, no. 1: 7–27.

Zhan, Zehui, Patrick S. W. Fong, Hu Mei, and Ting Liang. 2015. "Effects of Gender Grouping on Students' Group Performance, Individual Achievements and Attitudes in Computer-Supported Collaborative Learning." *Computers in Human Behavior*, 48: 587–596.

Zheng, Dongping, Michael F. Young, Robert A. Brewer, and Manuela María Wagner. 2009. "Attitude and Self-Efficacy Change: English Language Learning in Virtual Worlds." *CALICO Journal*, 27: 205–231.

# 17 Language for Specific Purposes and Corpus-based Pedagogy

## ELENA COTOS

Language for specific purposes (LSP) is a well-established domain in applied linguistics. Its mission is two-fold: (1) to provide foundational knowledge about language users' linguistic needs, which vary considerably depending on the context and purpose of their language use, and (2) to inform the teaching and learning of context-specific language that learners need to acquire in order to successfully engage in target social practices. LSP has bourgeoned into various branches. Branches that concentrate on learners in various academic subject areas are nested under Language for Academic Purposes (LAP). Language for Occupational Purposes (LOP) is associated with professional and vocational contexts. The classification of LSP has also expanded to include language for sociocultural purposes, catering to the needs of socially or physically disadvantaged language learners. While LSP encompasses any language, English for specific purposes (ESP) has been at the forefront of the research in the past 50 years. Therefore, this chapter highlights ESP practices and research, which are also illustrative of work in other languages (e.g., Parodi 2015; Vergaro 2004).

LSP as a "specific-learner-centered language instruction" (Belcher 2009, 2) has undergone great transformations over the past 30 years due to the research tools and methodologies offered by Corpus Linguistics (CL), the study of large quantities of authentic language using computer-assisted methods. This chapter maps out corpus-based pedagogies in LSP, reviewing uses of corpora for reference, exploration, and interactive computer assisted language learning (CALL). First, I describe how corpora can serve as reference resources to create LSP materials. Second, I show direct student uses of corpora in data-driven learning (DDL) approaches where students engage in hands-on explorations of texts. I categorize these approaches into three strands, each with its essential concepts and background in CL research. Next, I show how indirect and direct corpus applications have been translated to interactive CALL technologies, including an example of an inclusive corpus-based tool for genre writing pedagogy. The chapter concludes with potential prospects for future developments in LSP.

## LSP corpora for reference

Widespread access to corpora by materials developers and researchers has created a dynamic relationship between LSP and CL, providing insights for needs analysis (see Dudley-Evans and St. John 1998) with rich descriptions of language in specific contexts of use. LSP researchers and materials developers use corpora for decisions regarding the design of

*The Handbook of Technology and Second Language Teaching and Learning*, First Edition.
Edited by Carol A. Chapelle and Shannon Sauro.
© 2017 John Wiley & Sons, Inc. Published 2020 by John Wiley & Sons, Inc.

needs-responsive curricula, course syllabi, teaching materials, classroom tasks, and assessment. Such uses are referred to as indirect because corpora serve as language sources that inform the content of materials and tasks to be used in the classroom, rather than being directly accessed by teachers and students. To provide language descriptions that closely meet specific learning needs, indirect uses require a relevant corpus of texts and software tools.

## Corpora

Corpora are large machine-readable compilations of authentic texts. They can be general or specialized, depending on what kinds of texts are included in the corpus. The former contain large volumes of text, up to hundreds of millions of words, intended for a range of researchers wanting to investigate particular linguistic phenomena or to provide grammatical and lexical descriptions of a language as a whole. The latter, which are typically compiled for a specific project, can be much smaller and are intended to describe language use in specific contexts.

Specialized corpora are of direct relevance to LSP. Practitioners often choose to compile small corpora based on specific instructional needs. Needs-based corpora are more clearly patterned and more feasible for constructing, managing, and interpreting (Aston 1997). For example, several corpora of academic writing were compiled in Hong Kong: the Hong Kong University of Science and Technology (HKUST) Computer Science Corpus, the Hong Kong Financial Services Corpus, and the Hong Kong Engineering Corpus. Other examples include the Jiaotong Daxue English of Science and Technology (JDEST) Corpus and the Guangzhou Petroleum English Corpus (GPEC). Spoken language is represented in the Michigan Corpus of Academic Spoken English (MICASE) and the Cambridge and Nottingham Spoken Business English Corpus (CANBEC). Corpora containing learner language have also gained popularity. A list of learner corpora can be found on the website of the Centre for English Corpus Linguistics (2016).

The advantage of specialized LSP corpora is that they represent language characteristic of the registers and genres of the contexts of interest to the specific purposes of learners. Registers share patterns of lexical and grammatical features of language that are determined by situational factors (e.g., written or spoken, formal or casual, scientific or technical). Genres are grouped into text types according to distinct sociocultural purposes and discourse conventions (e.g., research articles, grant proposals, business reports). In terms of register, corpus texts are viewed as language used in recurring situations in a society; in terms of genre, corpus texts are viewed as types of regularly recurring messages in a community (Ferguson 1994). The understanding of registers and genres is critical for teaching learners the specific language they need in order to successfully engage in communication with their discourse communities. Therefore, LSP practitioners have to carefully consider these concepts in addition to the subject or practice area.

## Corpus tools

The most common tools used in corpus analysis informing LSP pedagogy are concordancing programs, which are text search engines with sorting functions. The first concordancers became available for personal computers in the 1980s (e.g., *MicroConcord* and *Mini-concordancer*), and later Internet access enabled broad use of web-based concordancers such as *WordSmith* (Scott 1996), *MonoConc Pro* (Barlow 2000), *ConcGram* (Greaves 2009), *AntConc* (Anthony 2014), *WordSearch* (Cortes 2007), and *TextSTAT* (Benini 2010). When queried, these concordancers extract a "collection of the occurrences of a word-form, each in its textual environment" (Sinclair 1991, 32), which is displayed as lists of key words in context (KWICs) called concordance lines. Figure 17.1 shows sample concordance lines from the Corpus of Contemporary American English (COCA), which can be re-sorted to see patterns in the use of the word "develop." The concordancer also shows the word's synonyms, definitions, and its relative frequency in different academic domains. Co-occurring words like "develop" and "understanding," known as collocates, are also displayed. The search was done with a wildcard (*) that replaced the end of the word. In this way, all the different forms of "devel*"—"develop," "developed," "developing" were extracted. Concordancers can also help identify the grammatical and syntactic patterns of search words, their shades of meaning, meaningfully associated collocates, and positional and constituency variation. Some concordancers allow for both phraseological and paradigmatic searches for categories like subject, predicate, and direct object (Flowerdew 2015).

## Corpus-based materials

Considering that "materials should be based on analyses of representative samples of the target discourse" (Hyland 2002, 113), practitioners generally use concordancers to identify frequencies and patterns of certain linguistic features in relevant corpora and then apply the results of their queries to teaching. As corpora lend themselves to the detection of lexis, concordancers have been used to produce frequency and range-based lists of academic vocabulary and collocation lists (Ackermann and Chen, 2013; Durrant 2009; Gardner and Davies 2014). Field-specific vocabulary and collocations have been included in instructional materials for business (Popescu 2007; Walker 2011), engineering (Mudraya 2006), nursing (Yang 2015), and agriculture (Martínez, Beck, and Panza 2009). Additionally, teachers use concordancers to create materials for classroom exercises that prompt students to test linguistic hypotheses, notice contextual meanings, examine collocations, and so on. Corpus-based exercises can range from fill-in-the-blanks and matching of split concordance lines to demonstrating different forms of a particular lexical item.

Because learner corpora capture learners' difficulties in producing specific target language, they have entered the LSP arena with the same pace of pursuit as the corpora produced by native speakers (Granger and Paquot, 2013). Rankin and Schiftner (2011) recommend running comparative searches in a corpus compiled "in-house" from current students and in a relevant native-speaker corpus, and then developing teaching materials taking into account the linguistic differences identified. Similarly, contrastive analyses of native-speaker, learner, and first-language texts as well as of parallel corpora that contain the same texts in different languages are great sources for materials design (Teubert 2004).

Corpora are excellent resources for grammarians and lexicographers who produce reference books, grammars, and dictionaries. One of the most representative pedagogical volumes is the *Longman Grammar of Spoken and Written English* (Biber et al. 1999). It records an exhaustive frequency-based description of lexico-grammatical features of written prose, conversation, fiction, and news in terms of structural characteristics and patterns of use. The textbook *Exploring Academic English* (Thurstun and Candlin 1997) integrates exercises based on concordances for lexical items indicative of sets of rhetorical functions. Recently, the *Professional English Online* and the *Business and Professional English* series by Cambridge University Press have entered the market. Basturkmen's (2010) *Developing Courses for English for Specific Purposes* is an important resource for teachers, showcasing how descriptions of specialist discourse can be used to determine the curriculum.

## LSP corpora for data-driven exploration

Exploiting corpora and concordancing tools with students in the classroom is known as direct corpus application in teaching. A key paradigm in direct corpus application in teaching is data-driven learning (DDL) (Johns 1986, 2002), which is an approach that engages students

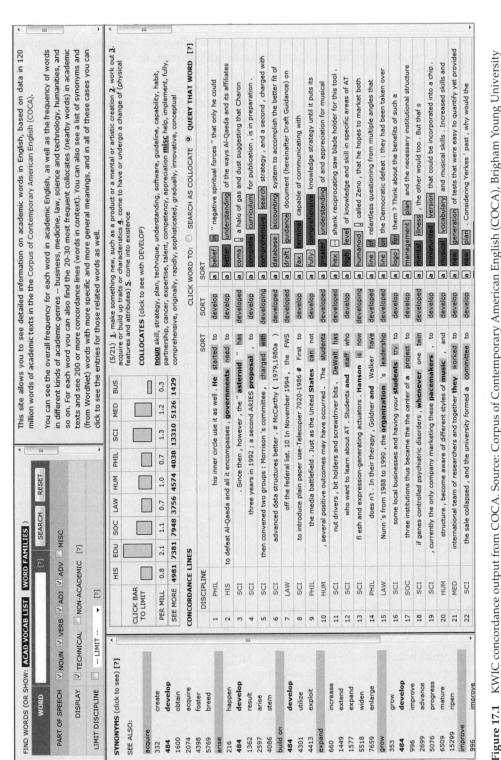

**Figure 17.1** KWIC concordance output from COCA. Source: Corpus of Contemporary American English (COCA), Brigham Young University http://corpus.byu.edu/coca/

as independent analysts—detectives who explore authentic language use captured in a corpus. Corpora are thus used as enhancers of students' linguistic intuition (Gavioli 2005). The teachers are mediators; they carefully designate the linguistic aspects to be analyzed by their students and determine the corpora, tools, and progression of corpus consultation activities.

Lead advocates of DDL in LSP emphasize the pedagogical strengths of this approach, arguing that it is "fully compatible with communicative language teaching; discovery learning and learning by doing; autonomisation and learning to learn; learner-centeredness and individualization; collaborative learning and creativity; task-based as process as well as product orientations; form and meaning in constructivism; with an emphasis on the authentic language of discourse by register/genre" (Boulton 2011, 575). In DDL, students adopt tools and techniques used by corpus linguists; however, they do not carry out the same kinds of analyses as those conducted by linguists. In what follows, I focus on three approaches from CL that have influenced DDL used in the classroom—bottom-up, top-down, and paired.

## Bottom-up approach

The bottom-up approach to corpus-based pedagogy builds upon register analysis in CL research, which focuses on pervasive lexico-grammatical features that "occur frequently in the target text variety because they are well-suited functionally to the [...] situational context of the variety" (Biber 2010, 242). The starting point for CL is bottom-up automatic segmentation of all the texts in a corpus to identify different types of lexico-grammatical features and examine their patterns. Table 17.1 lists some examples of register analysis studies using this approach. Many researchers examined written and spoken LOP workplace registers, although corpus studies of linguistic features especially abound in LAP.

Teachers have particularly favored DDL activities designed using techniques from bottom-up research methods, largely because of the availability and practicality of concordancers. They often encourage students to interpret concordance output vertically by examining frequency lists and concordance lines to identify patterns of language use. Alternatively, students can interpret concordances horizontally by reading the surrounding context and noting specific language choices that express functional or cultural meaning (Braun 2005, 54). Gavioli (2005) provides helpful guidelines for ESP teachers along with a series of activities

**Table 17.1**   Examples of bottom-up register analysis studies.

| *Research focus* | | *Studies* |
| --- | --- | --- |
| Salient linguistic features | Verb types, conditionals, personal pronouns | Ferguson (2001), Kuo (1999), Thomas and Hawes (1994) |
| Semantic prosody | Stance, modality, hedging | Charles (2006), Hyland (2002), Vihla (1999) |
| Co-occurrences of multi-word units | N-grams/lexical bundles/phrases/ clusters, collocations | Cortes (2004), Grabowski (2013), Gledhill (2000) |
| Co-occurrences of words irrespective of constituent/ positional variation | Concgrams, semantic shift units | Cheng et al. (2009), Nelson (2006) |

that engage students with specialized and bilingual corpora. Concordance-based tasks may include students' inductive study of technical vocabulary, searching the corpus and examining KWICs to better understand appropriate use of language in context, conducting different types of searches for comparative purposes, identifying language misuse in learner language, and so on. Similarly, Mudraya (2006) illustrates activities that prompt engineering students to:

1. distinguish between general meaning and meaning as sub-technical vocabulary (*solution of problems* vs *solution from the absorbe*r),
2. supply adjective collocates for general and sub-technical meaning (*possible solution* vs *concentrated solution*),
3. supply verb collocates for general and sub-technical meaning (*attempt a solution* vs *immerse in solution*),
4. exemplify specific syntactic patterns, e.g. *solve + solution method* (*solve/solves/solving/ solved + with* (a vector approach)/*by* (drawing)/*using* (work-energy principle).

Such analysis of technical language is ideal for the study of advanced academic writing, which is placed high on the LSP/ESP agenda. A wealth of publications, including some studies reviewed above, present uses of corpora of research articles in graduate-level writing courses. A classic example of a course for doctoral students is described by Lee and Swales (2006). Their tasks involved queries of lexico-grammatical and discourse patterns in different types of specialized corpora. For example, the students used web- and PC-based concordancers to:

1. generate word lists (e.g., reporting verbs),
2. concordance for errors (e.g., *at the end* v. *in the end*),
3. examine grammatical structures (e.g., *suggest that*),
4. guess/scrutinize word meanings (e.g., *continually* vs *continuously*),
5. generate examples of puzzling pairs (e.g., *seek* vs *search*),
6. guess and verify frequencies,
7. rank word classes most likely to trigger certain structures (e.g., ADJ/N/V + V-ing, *appropriate for modeling*),
8. analyze rare patterns (e.g., V (NP) + V-ing, *led into admitting*).

## Top-down approach

The top-down approach, which builds upon genre research, entails analyses of the internal structure of texts. It is referred to as top-down because the starting point is identifying patterns of text organization using analytic frameworks of possible discourse units (Biber, Connor, and Upton 2007). One of the most productive genre frameworks was developed by John Swales (1981, 1990). He describes discourse in terms of two kinds of discourse units—"moves" (or communicative goals) and constituent "steps" (or rhetorical strategies that accomplish communicative goals). In top-down CL research, the focus is on discursive patterns, constraints, variation, and language choices, which conventionalize the rhetorical identity of texts and establish conformity with the expectations of the target discourse community. Table 17.2 exemplifies works that describe academic and professional genres.

In top-down genre-based teaching, move frameworks developed by researchers have become essential guidelines for students' corpus explorations of the macro-structure of texts. The directions listed below, which are drawn from Swales and Feak (2004, 2012), Robinson et al. (2008), and Cotos (2014), illustrate how teachers introduce the moves and steps before

**Table 17.2**    Examples of top-down genre analysis studies.

| Genre group | Genre investigated | Studies |
|---|---|---|
| Academic genres | Research articles | Cotos, Huffman, and Link (2015), Ozturk (2007), Kanoksilapatham (2007), Stoller and Robinson (2013), Williams (1999) |
| | Doctoral theses | Bunton (2002), Kwan (2006), Thompson (2000) |
| | Conference papers | Rowley-Jolivet (2002) |
| | Grant proposals | Connor (2000), Connor and Upton (2004) |
| | Graduate program applications | Samraj and Monk (2008) |
| Professional genres | Medical consensus statements | Mungra (2007) |
| | Law, management, economics cases | Lung (2008, 2011) |
| | Corporate press releases, earnings calls | Catenaccio (2008), Cho and Yoon (2013), Crawford Camiciottoli (2006) |
| | Negotiation letters | Pinto dos Santos (2002) |

referring their students to the texts in the corpus. Prior to that, they may also work through a text sample requiring students to do the following:

1. identify major purposes of paragraphs and propose a move structure,
2. divide a sample text into moves,
3. identify and discuss move boundaries,
4. identify the step components of moves,
5. re-construct sentences in teacher-modified texts into their original order.

When directed to corpora, students are asked to:

1. examine texts for their organization into sections and subsections, noting the naming conventions and noticeable transitions,
2. examine corpus texts for moves that are present or absent,
3. identify patterns in rhetorical organization,
4. discuss similarities and differences among texts (e.g., from the same and from different journals),
5. reflect and explain reasons for alternative move structures.

Students also focus on the language choices made by authors, but in a deductive rather than inductive way. Commonly, they are asked to identify words or expressions that they think convey the functional meaning of moves or steps (e.g., *has been extensively studied* used to claim topic centrality). Or, they may try to deduct some general trends about the use of verb tenses and their relation to a particular communicative intent (e.g., *this study reports* vs. *the purpose of this study was* when announcing present research).

Rhetorically annotated corpora are particularly helpful for successful completion of such tasks. Cotos, Link, and Huffman (2016) describe how students conduct a rhetorical composition analysis task, accessing a corpus of research articles annotated for moves and steps via the Callisto workbench. Because this tool uses colors to differentiate between tagged moves, it visualizes the move anatomy of each text enabling students to observe and notice:

1.  the distribution of moves,
2.  the sequence of moves,
3.  the occurrence of steps within each move,
4.  the moves and steps that appear more often than others,
5.  the moves and steps that are uncommon in their discipline,
6.  rhetorical overlap (i.e., segments that represent more than one move or step),
7.  similarities and differences in the function of a given step in different texts,
8.  content used to realize steps.

## *Paired approach*

While the bottom-up and top-down approaches have a value of their own, integrating the two can be "the best of both worlds" (Charles 2007, 299). Therefore, CL researchers have combined them into a paired approach, establishing links between the lexico-grammatical features and the generic moves of specialized discourse. Table 17.3 lists several studies that reveal both micro-textual and macro-textual distinctiveness.

Some DDL practitioners exhibit a similar tendency in the classroom, implementing both the analysis of concordance queries and the analysis of text structure. For example, Weber (2001) developed activities for the teaching of legal essays. The students first read entire texts to identify prototypical rhetorical principles inherent to legal cases and selected vocabulary used to convey respective communicative intent. They then consulted the corpus to verify whether the selected expressions displayed patterns of regularity. In their courses on research writing, Charles (2007), Cortes (2007), and Flowerdew (2015) began by raising students'

**Table 17.3**   Examples of combined bottom-up and top-down corpus studies.

| Research focus | Genre | Studies |
| --- | --- | --- |
| Linguistic characteristics of moves | Research articles | Kanoksilapatham (2007), Durrant and Mathews-Aydınlı (2011) |
| Vocabulary-based discourse units | Research articles | Biber, Connor, and Upton (2007) |
| Collocations in moves | Application statements, research articles | Ding (2007), Marco (1999) |
| Interpersonal features in moves | Editorial letters | Flowerdew and Dudley-Evans (2002) |
| Rhetorical structure and pragmatic use of mood, modality, reference system | Sales promotion letters | Vergaro (2004) |
| Lexical bundles and discourse functions | Student and published academic writing | Chen and Baker (2010) |
| Rhetorical unity defined by moves and linguistic features denoting temporal and special aspects | Cover letters | Crossley (2007) |

awareness of the patterns of macro discourse with top-down text analysis tasks, which drew their attention to rhetorical functions, communicative purposes, and various linguistic realizations. Transitioning to bottom-up analysis, they then taught students to conduct concordance searches of specific lexico-grammatical items.

The symbiosis between top-down and bottom-up corpus inquiry can further be augmented with ethnographic insights. For instance, in Hafner and Candlin's (2007) study, students in a professional legal training course were offered online corpus tools as an optional DDL affordance to facilitate their writing of legal documents for their needs outside the classroom. Finding that "students who construct themselves as apprentice lawyers bring this identity to the corpus consultation task," Hafner and Candlin urge LSP teachers to "draw on professional practices when perceiving affordances in corpus tools and resources" (316).

## LSP corpora for interactive computer-assisted language learning

Interaction is an important process in language learning, but conditions for interaction may be limited or unavailable, especially for LSP students. Corpus-based technologies can create enhanced learning conditions if designed as semi-intelligent or intelligent CALL (computer-assisted language learning) systems. Such systems are powered by natural language processing (NLP), a domain of artificial intelligence, which relies on training the computer to recognize spoken or written language. NLP methods somewhat mirror the paired register-genre approach to corpus analysis. Specifically, NLP is concerned with automatically detecting lexico-grammatical features in native speaker and learner corpora. Those features are then used to train computer models to automatically analyze genres and genre components (Stamatatos, Fakotakis, and Kokkinakis 2000). In this section, I briefly review NLP-based tools for reference, DDL, and automated feedback. Then, I describe an example of a pedagogical system that integrates these three types of CALL tools in three respective modules to help students learn how to write research articles in English.

### Interactive reference tools

Several technology-savvy teacher-researchers created novel interactive reference tools for academic English, which illustrate different ways in which corpora can be exploited to create more engaging materials. For example, Williams (2012) developed *DicSci*, a pattern dictionary of science verbs helpful for vocabulary learning. *DicSci* was built bottom-up from a corpus using collocational networks (i.e., chains of collocations extracted from a corpus by means of analyzing proximity and statistical procedures). Williams (2012) refers to it as "organic" because it groups words and presents word uses as growing naturally from the corpus data, as opposed to being determined by someone's intuition. The word "control," for instance, can be the node of a collocation network that contains several words most frequently co-occurring in a given corpus. One of its most frequent collocates is "group" that, in turn, most frequently co-occurs with "subjects." Subsequently, "subjects" collocates with certain verbs (e.g., "recruit," "instruct") and adjectives (e.g., "obese," "sick-listed"). This growing chain of collocates renders the semantic environment of the node word and represents natural language use as captured in the corpus. Kuo (2008) describes a somewhat similar collocation builder system that draws on parallel corpora in English and Chinese to provide collocation examples in both languages.

A few other tools were developed for more specific needs. Pinkwart et al. (2006) designed *Legal Argument Graph Observer (LARGO)*, a tool for teaching law students how to make arguments and formulate warrants for deciding a case. *LARGO* enables students to graphically represent examples of legal interpretations with the hypotheticals they observe while reading texts. Nehm, Minsu, and Mayfield's (2011) *Summarization Integrated Development Environment* (*SIDE*) system assesses the accuracy of students' written explanations of science topics. *Internet Writing Resource for the Innovative Teaching of English* (*iWRITE*), a database-driven online tool for grammar and academic writing, makes use of a learner corpus that was collected "in-house" from students enrolled in L2 writing courses at a North American university (Hegelheimer and Fisher 2006). Bloch (2010) applied research results to the development of a web-based database for academic writing, which contains sentences with reporting verbs functioning as rhetorical devices. In a like manner, Henry and Rosenberry (2001) created a hyperlinked website for teaching application letters relying both on frequencies and on linguistic, discourse, and syntactic features characteristic of the steps that accomplish the moves of this genre.

## Interactive DDL tools

Interactive DDL tools use NLP to enhance students' data-driven explorations of native-speaker and learner corpora, particularly fostering deduction from automatically analyzed texts. Using a science and engineering corpus, Anthony and Lashkia (2003) developed the *Mover*, software that automatically identifies the moves in the abstracts of research articles. Students can collect a small corpus of abstracts and upload it to the *Mover*, which then labels each sentence in each text with a move. This software thus enables the students to analyze move sequences and draw conclusions about the rhetorical organization of abstracts. Also employing a genre-analytic approach, Chang and Kuo (2011) created *Moves And Keywords Engine* (*MAKE*). This tool can be queried for keywords and re-current word combinations such as "the degree to which" and "in the context of," known as lexical bundles, within single and multiple moves identified in a corpus of research articles in computer science. The open-source *Type Your Own Script* (*TYOS*) allows students to exploit learner corpora of initial drafts and revised drafts with mark-up and corrections by the teacher, which highlight rhetorical strategies and language choices (Birch-Bécaas and Cooke 2012).

## Interactive feedback tools

NLP-powered tools that scaffold learners with just-in-time feedback as they are producing language create conditions for a higher degree of interaction. Various interactive feedback tools have been developed for specific domains such as journalism (*Journalism*), navy (*CRES*), biology (*SAGrader*), business (*EPISTLE*), sociology (*APEX Assessor*), education (*ETIPS*), and psychology (*RMT*). A number of such tools are available for academic writing (e.g., *Criterion, MyAccess!, WriteToLearn, Folio, Writer's Workbench, SkillWriter, Writing Roadmap*, etc.). Some writing systems are specific to scientific writing. For example, the *Intelligent Academic Discourse Evaluator* (*IADE*) analyzes students' Introduction section drafts and provides color-coded move-level feedback. *IADE* also presents percent ranges for each move, comparing it with a corpus of Introductions from articles published in students' disciplines. *Scaffolded Writing and Rewriting in the Disciplines* (*SWoRD*) is a web-based tool that implements reciprocal peer review to simulate the journal publication process (Cho and Schunn 2007). To improve peer feedback, Xiong, Litman, and Schunn (2012) developed a tool that instantaneously processes students' peer reviews, detects the presence or absence of features important for quality feedback, and prompts the students to revise their reviews. A tool for writing strategy training, *Writing Pal*, generates feedback using sophisticated algorithms that assess lexical, syntactic, cohesion, and rhetorical features (McNamara, Crossley, and Roscoe 2013).

# An example of "all-in-one" corpus-based tool for genre writing pedagogy

Pedagogical needs for reference materials, DDL practices for exposure to authentic language, and intelligent CALL for feedback-scaffolded language practice—all converge in a recently developed system for scientific writing called *Research Writing Tutor* (*RWT*) (Cotos, 2016). It was created using move analysis results derived from a corpus of 900 journal articles published in the top journals of 30 disciplines (Cotos, et al. 2015). The researchers manually annotated this multidisciplinary corpus for moves and steps, and *RWT* uses the annotations to retrieve and present the corpus data in three interrelated modules.

*RWT for reference.* A learning module, called "Understand Writing Goals," contains web-based pedagogic enrichment materials (Braun 2005). The materials include definitions, explanations, and examples of all the moves and steps pertaining to Introduction, Methods, Results, and Discussion/Conclusion (IMRD/C) sections to be used by teachers when introducing the key rhetorical concepts of the research article genre. The students, in turn, can use these materials for knowledge consolidation. Or, in the case of autonomous learning, this module can serve as a study guide because it also includes a series of video mini-lectures explaining genre-specific content.

*RWT for DDL.* A demonstration module, called "Explore Published Writing," gives students direct access to the corpus (both in its original and annotated form) in a way that allows for paired DDL explorations. It contains a function-based concordancer, which displays excerpts representing a particular step of a particular move, at the same time exhibiting a variety of language choices used to express different shades of functional meaning. From there, students' corpus exploration can shift to top-down macro-level analysis by clicking on any of the concordance lines. That brings up the entire text color-coded for moves and glossed with steps. Such enhancement of corpus data fosters the exploration of co-texts beyond individual concordance lines and the identification of structural patterns in the discipline. Alternatively, teachers may first direct their students to the annotated corpus with tasks that encourage horizontal reading of a given IMRD/C section, and then assign DDL tasks focused on linguistic means of expression in relation to their communicative purposes.

*RWT for interactive feedback.* The third, "Analyze My Writing" module, offers students the opportunity to apply their corpus observations to their own writing and creates conditions for iterative revisions of their drafts. This module operates with the help of an engine that automatically analyzes students' IMRD/C drafts and returns multi-level rhetorical feedback. The feedback provided at macro level is operationalized through color codes, each indicative of a particular move (similar to *IADE*). *RWT* affords navigation flexibility, so the students can open the "Explore Published Writing" module in another window or tab and compare the distribution of colors in their draft with that of the texts in the annotated corpus. Another type of macro-level feedback displays an actual comparison of each move in the student's draft with published disciplinary texts based on median numerical values. This numerical feedback shows range bars with percentages indicating that the draft may have "too much" or "not enough" of a given move, or that the percentage of that move falls within the "goal" range of the discipline. In addition to ranges, the comparison is visualized as summary pie charts. As the purpose of each move is expected to be accomplished with certain steps, the move feedback is accompanied by hints specifying which steps are used to an extent similar to the target discipline, and which steps are lacking or may need to be improved.

The feedback provided at micro level is generated for individual sentences in students' drafts. This type of feedback takes the form of interactive comments or clarifying questions about the functional meaning of the sentence. For example, *RWT* suggests, "*You are likely introducing present research descriptively*" for the sentence "In this paper, we address individual, maternal, and family stressors experienced by low-income adolescents." Or, it may elicit a confirmation of the function of "Only one study to date has addressed how stress may moderate the relationship between food insecurity and adolescents' probability of being overweight or obese" by asking *"Are you indicating a gap?"* Such comments are aimed at encouraging the students to think about intended meaning and to revise their writing where necessary. When revising with *RWT*, the students may need help with interpreting the feedback. To support them in these instances, the analysis module embeds on-demand glosses with brief explanations of the moves and steps next to the macro-level feedback. Students are also encouraged to *"Learn More"* or *"See Examples"* through hyperlinks to relevant content in the learning and demonstration modules, respectively. A note-taking feature added to the draft analysis interface also supports the revision process.

In sum, *RWT* amalgamates core requisites of corpus-based LAP/LSP instruction. Drawing on corpus analysis, the tool provides teachers with attested examples of specialized language use and with a platform for developing tasks responsive to student needs. *RWT* also accounts for the fact that teachers may lack familiarity with the writing conventions of specific disciplines. The tool's corpus-based components and output are learner-centered and easy to interpret, at the same time presenting complex linguistic evidence. Moreover, *RWT*'s automated analysis and feedback on student writing adds an important learner-driven data dimension, which is beneficial for it draws learners' attention to problematic areas in their own production (Nesselhauf 2004) and can enhance motivation (Seidlhofer 2002).

# Future expectations

Saying that CL has a role to play in the advancement of LSP would be an understatement. Corpus methodologies provide versatile approaches and tools for the study of naturally occurring texts at linguistic, functional, rhetorical, and pragmatic levels. To date, LSP has greatly benefited from corpus-based frameworks of analysis, descriptions of authentic language use, and interactive technologies. As the field moves forward, new directions will be charted for corpus-based and computer-assisted LSP.

Given that novel web-applications and computational models for text analysis offer exceptional techniques for utilizing CL findings, LSP is positioned to embrace innovative technologies for the design of instructional materials and principled curricula. Williams (2012), for instance, projects that mind mapping technology, which can display information in a relational way (as in the *DicSci* organic dictionary), will give users access not only to individual entries and phraseological descriptions, but also to super entries linking quasi-synonyms and writing assistance. Coding each word in a corpus with part-of-speech, case, number, and gender tags (known as morpho-syntactic tagging) will be overtaken by pedagogically motivated corpus annotations of both native-speaker and learner corpora (see Pérez-Paredes and Álcaraz-Calero, 2009). This will, in turn, enable new multi-modally human and computer-annotated corpora (Knight et al. 2009) as well as corpora annotated by learners to interfuse with applied NLP (McCarthy and Boonthum-Denecke, 2012) in systems capacitated for powerful language data export features tailored for specific learning goals.

Much like CALL, LSP will continue to evolve in terms of applications that will be both authentic and research-supported. This requires expansive CL study of specialized discourses as well as copious research on language teaching and learning supported by corpus-based materials and tasks. I anticipate that corpus data will be well aligned with pedagogic constructs. Arguably, future research will need to fully exploit the potential of corpus and computer-networking technologies to construct language-learning environments in the light of learning theories and to guide effective implementation of technology-enhanced LSP.

# REFERENCES

Ackermann, Kirsten, and Yu-Hua Chen. 2013. "Developing the Academic Collocation List (ACL)– A Corpus-Driven and Expert-judged Approach." *Journal of English for Academic Purposes*, 12, no. 4: 235–247.

Anthony, Laurence. 2014. "*AntConc* (Version 3.4.3)." Tokyo, Japan: Waseda University. Accessed January 3, 2017. http://www.laurenceanthony.net/software.html

Anthony, Laurence, and George V. Lashkia. 2003. "Mover: A Machine Learning Tool to Assist in the Reading and Writing of Technical Papers." *IEEE Transactions on Professional Communication*, 46, no. 3: 185–193.

Aston, Guy. 1997. "Small and Large Corpora in Language Learning." In *Practical Applications in Language Corpora*, edited by Barbara Lewandowska-Tomaszczyk, and James Patrik Melia, 51–62. Lodz: Lodz University Press.

Barlow, Michael. 2000. *MonoConc Pro*. Houston, TX: Athelstan. Accessed January 3, 2017. http://www.athel.com/mono.html

Basturkmen, Helen. 2010. *Developing Courses in English for Specific Purposes*. New York: Palgrave Macmillan.

Belcher, Diane, ed. 2009. *English for Specific Purposes in Theory and Practice*. Ann Arbor, MI: University of Michigan Press.

Benini, Aldo. 2010. *Text Analysis under Time Pressure Tools for Humanitarian and Development Workers*. Washington, DC. Accessed July 13, 2015. http://aldo-benini.org/Level2/HumanitData/Benini_TextAnalysis_100301.pdf

Biber, Douglas. 2010. "What Can a Corpus Tell us about Registers and Genres?" In *The Routledge Handbook of Corpus Linguistics*, edited by Anne O'Keefe, and Michael McCarthy, 241–254. Oxford: Routledge.

Biber, Douglas, Ulla Connor, and Thomas Upton. 2007. *Discourse on the Move: Using Corpus Analysis to Describe Discourse Structure*. Amsterdam: John Benjamins.

Biber, Douglas, Stig Johansson, Geoffrey Leech, Susan Conrad, and Edward Finegan. 1999. *Longman Grammar of Spoken and Written English*. New York: Pearson Education.

Birch-Bécaas, Susan, and Ray Cooke. 2012. "Raising Collective Awareness of Rhetorical Strategies." In *Corpus-Informed Research and Learning in ESP: Issues and Applications*, edited by Alex Boulton, Shirley Carter-Thomas, and Elizabeth Rowley-Jolivet, 239–260. Amsterdam: John Benjamins.

Bloch, Joel. 2010. "A Concordance-based Study of the Use of Reporting Verbs as Rhetorical Devices in Academic Papers." *Journal of Writing Research*, 2, no. 2: 219–244.

Boulton, Alex. 2011. Data-driven Learning: The Perpetual Enigma. In *Explorations across Languages and Corpora*, edited by Stanislaw Gozdz-Roszkowski, 563–580. Frankfurt: Peter Lang.

Braun, Sabine. 2005. "From Pedagogically Relevant Corpora to Authentic Language Learning Contents." *ReCALL*, 17, no. 1: 47–64.

Bunton, David. 2002. "Generic Moves in PhD Thesis Introductions." In *Academic discourse*, edited by John Flowerdew, 57–75. London: Longman.

Catenaccio, Paola. 2008. "Press Releases as a Hybrid Genre: Addressing the Informative/promotional Conundrum." *Pragmatics*, 18, no. 1: 9–31.

Centre for English Corpus Linguistics. (2016). "Learner Corpora around the World." Accessed January 3, 2017. http://www.uclouvain.be/en-cecl-lcworld.html

Chang, Ching-Fen, and Chih-Hua Kuo. 2011. "A Corpus-based Approach to Online Materials Development for Writing research Articles." *English for Specific Purposes*, 30, no. 3: 222–234.

Charles, Maggie. 2006. "The Construction of Stance in Reporting Clauses: A Cross-Disciplinary Study of Theses." *Applied Linguistics*, 27, no. 3: 492–518.

Charles, Maggie. 2007. "Reconciling Top-down and Bottom-up Approaches to Graduate Writing: Using a Corpus to Teach Rhetorical Functions." *Journal of English for Academic Purposes*, 6, no. 4: 289–302. DOI:10.1016/j.jeap.2007.09.009

Chen, Yu-Hua, and Paul Baker. 2010. "Lexical Bundles in l1 and l2 Academic Writing." *Language Learning & Technology*, 14, no. 2: 30–49.

Cheng, Winnie, Chris Greaves, John Sinclair, and Martin Warren. 2009. "Uncovering the Extent of the Phraseological Tendency: Towards a Systematic Analysis of concgrams." *Applied Linguistics*, 30, no. 2: 236–252.

Cho, Kwangsu, and Christian D. Schunn. 2007. "Scaffolded Writing and Rewriting in the

Discipline: A Web-based Reciprocal Peer Review System." *Computers & Education*, 48, no. 3: 409–426.

Cho, Hyeyoung, and Hyunsook Yoon. 2013. "A Corpus-assisted Comparative Genre Analysis of Corporate Earnings Calls between Korean and Native-English Speakers." *English for Specific Purposes*, 32: 170–185.

Connor, Ulla. 2000. "Variation in Rhetorical Moves in Grant Proposals of US Humanists and Scientists." *Text*, 20, no. 1: 1–28.

Connor, Ulla, and Thomas A. Upton. 2004. "The Genre of Grant Proposals: A Corpus Linguistic Analysis." In *Discourse in the Professions: Perspectives from Corpus Linguistics*, edited by Ulla Connor, and Thomas A. Upton, 235–256. Amsterdam: John Benjamins.

Cortes, Viviana. 2004. "Lexical Bundles in Published and Student Disciplinary Writing: Examples from History and Biology." *English for Specific Purposes*, 23: 397–423.

Cortes, Viviana. 2007. "Genre and Corpora in the English for Academic Writing Class." *ORTESOL Journal*, 25: 9–16.

Cotos, Elena. 2014. *Genre-based Automated Writing Evaluation for L2 Research Writing: From Design to Evaluation and Enhancement*. Basingstoke: Palgrave Macmillan.

Cotos, Elena. 2016. "Computer-Assisted Research Writing in the Disciplines." In *Adaptive educational technologies for literacy instruction*, Scott A. Crossley, and Danielle S. McNamara, 225–242. Routledge, Taylor & Francis Group: New York and London.

Cotos, Elena, Sarah Huffman, and Stephanie Link. 2015. "Move Analysis of the Research Article Genre: Furthering and Applying Analytic Constructs." *Journal of English for Academic Purposes*, 19: 52–72.

Cotos, Elena, Stephanie Link, and Sarah Huffman. 2016. "Studying Disciplinary Corpora to Teach the Craft of Discussion." *Writing & Pedagogy*, 8, no. 1: 33–64.

Crawford Camiciottoli, Belinda. 2006. "Rhetorical Strategies of Company Executives and Investment Analysts: Textual Metadiscourse in Corporate Earnings Calls." In *Explorations in specialized genres*, Vijay K. Bhatia, and Maurizio Gotti, 115–133. Bern: Peter Lang.

Crossley, Scott. A. 2007. "A Chronotopic Approach to Genre Analysis: An Exploratory Study." *English for Specific Purposes*, 26, no. 1: 4–24.

Ding, Huiling. 2007. "Genre Analysis of Personal Statements: Analysis of Moves in Application Essays to Medical and Dental Schools." *English for Specific Purposes*, 26, no. 3: 368–392.

Dudley-Evans, Tony, and Maggie J. St. John. 1998. *Developments in English for Specific Purposes: A Multidisciplinary Approach*. Cambridge, England: Cambridge University Press.

Durrant, Philip. 2009. "Investigating the Viability of a Collocation List for Students of English for Academic Purposes." *English for specific purposes*, 28, no. 3: 157–169.

Durrant, Philip, and Julie Mathews-Aydınlı. 2011. "A Function-first Approach to Identifying Formulaic Language in Academic Writing." *English for Specific Purposes*, 30: 58–72.

Ferguson, Charles. 1994. "Dialect, Register and Genre: Working Assumptions about Conventionalization." In *Sociolinguistic perspectives on register*, edited by Douglas Biber and Edward Finegan, 15–30. New York: Oxford University Press.

Ferguson, Gibson. 2001. "If You Pop Over There: A Corpus-based Study of Conditionals in Medical Discourse." *English for Specific Purposes*, 20: 61–82.

Flowerdew, Lynne. 2015. "Using Corpus-based Research and Online Academic Corpora to Inform Writing of the Discussion Section of a Thesis." *Journal of English for Academic Purposes*, 20: 58–68. DOI:10.1016/j.jeap.2015.06.001

Flowerdew, John, and Tony Dudley-Evans. 2002. "Genre Analysis of Editorial Letters to International Journal Contributors." *Applied Linguistics*, 23, no. 4: 463–89. DOI:10.1093/applin/23.4.463

Gardner, Dee, and Mark Davies. 2014. "A New Academic Vocabulary List." *Applied Linguistics*. 35, no. 3: 305–327. DOI:10.1093/applin/amt015

Gavioli, Laura. 2005. *Exploring Corpora for ESP Learning*. Amsterdam, Netherlands: John Benjamins.

Gledhill, Chris. 2000. "The Discourse Function of Collocation in Research Article Introductions." *English for Specific Purposes*, 19, no. 2: 115–135. DOI:10.1016/S0889-4906(98)00015-5

Grabowski, Łukasz. 2013. "Register Variation across English Pharmaceutical Texts: A Corpus-driven Study of Keywords, Lexical Bundles and Phrase Frames in Patient Information Leaflets and Summaries of Product Characteristics." *Procedia—Social and Behavioral Sciences*, 95: 391–401. DOI:10.1016/j.sbspro.2013.10.661

Granger, Sylviane, and Magali Paquot. 2013. "Language for Specific Purposes Learner

Corpora." In *The Encyclopedia of Applied Linguistics*, edited by Carol A. Chapelle, 3142–46. Oxford: Wiley-Blackwell.

Greaves, Chris. 2009. *ConcGram 1.0: A Phraseological Search Engine*. Amsterdam: John Benjamins.

Hafner, Christoph A., and Christopher N. Candlin. 2007. "Corpus Tools as an Affordance to Learning in Professional Legal Education." *Journal of English for Academic Purposes*, 6, no. 4: 303–18. DOI:10.1016/j.jeap.2007.09.005

Hegelheimer, Volker, and David Fisher. 2006. "Grammar, Writing, and Technology: A Sample Technology-supported Approach to Teaching Grammar and Improving Writing for ESL Learners." *CALICO Journal*, 23, no. 2: 257–279.

Henry, Alex, and Robert. L. Rosenberry. 2001. "A Narrow-angled Corpus Analysis of Moves and Strategies of the Genre: 'Letter of Application.'" *English for Specific Purposes*, 20, no. 2: 153–167.

Hyland, Ken. 2002. *Teaching and Researching Writing*. New York: Longman.

Johns, Tim. 1986. "Microconcord: A Language-learner's Research Tool." *System*, 14, no. 2: 151–162. DOI:10.1016/0346-251X(86)90004-7.

Johns, Tim. 2002. "Data-driven Learning: The Perpetual Challenge." In *Teaching and Learning by Doing Corpus Analysis*, edited by Bernhard Kettemann and Georg Marko, 107–117. Amsterdam: Rodopi.

Kanoksilapatham, Budsaba. 2007. "Rhetorical Moves in Biochemistry Research Articles." In *Discourse on the Move: Using Corpus Analysis to Describe Discourse Structure*, edited by Douglas Biber, Ulla Connor, and Thomas A. Upton, 73–119. Amsterdam: John Benjamins.

Knight, Dawn, David Evans, Ronald Carter, and Svenja Adolphs. 2009. "HeadTalk, HandTalk and the Corpus: Towards a Framework for Multimodal, Multimedia Corpus Development." *Corpora*, 4, no. 1: 1–32. DOI://dx.doi.org/10.3366/E1749503209000203

Kuo, Chih-Hua. 1999. "The Use of Personal Pronouns: Role Relationships in Scientific Journal Articles." *English for Specific Purposes*, 18, no. 2: 121–138.

Kuo, Chih-Hua.2008. "Designing an Online Writing System: Learning with Support." *RELC Journal*, 39, no. 3: 285–299. DOI:10.1177/0033688208096842

Kwan, Becky. S. C. 2006. "The Schematic Structure of Literature Reviews in Doctoral Theses of Applied Linguistics." *English for Specific Purposes*, 25, no. 1: 30–55. DOI:10.1016/j.esp.2005.06.001

Lee, David, and John Swales. 2006. "A Corpus-based EAP Course for NNS Doctoral Students: Moving from Available Specialized Corpora to Self-compiled Corpora." *English for Specific Purposes*, 25, no. 1: 56–75. DOI:10.1016/j.esp.2005.02.010

Lung, Jane. 2008. "Discursive Hierarchical Patterning in Law and Management Cases." *English for Specific Purposes*, 27: 424–441. DOI:10.1016/j.esp.2007.11.001

Lung, Jane. 2011. "Discursive Hierarchical Patterning in Economics Cases." *English for Specific Purposes*, 30: 138–49. DOI:10.1016/j.esp.2010.09.004

Marco, Maria José Luzón. 1999. "Collocational Frameworks in Medical Research Papers: a Genre-based Study." *English for Specific Purposes*, 19, no. 1: 63–86. DOI:10.1016/S0889-4906(98)00013-1

Martínez, Iliana A, Silvia C. Beck, and Carolina B. Panza. 2009. "Academic Vocabulary in Agriculture Research Articles: A Corpus-based Study." *English for Specific Purposes*, 28: 183–198.

McCarthy, Philip M., and Chutima Boonthum-Denecke, ed. 2012. *Applied Natural Language Processing and Content Analysis: Identification, Investigation, and Resolution*. Hershey, PA: IGI Global.

McNamara, Danielle S., Scott A. Crossley, and Rod Roscoe. 2013. "Natural Language Processing in an Intelligent Writing Strategy Tutoring System." *Behavior Research*, 45: 499–515. DOI:10.3758/s13428-012-0258-1

Mudraya, Olga. 2006. "Engineering English: A Lexical Frequency Instructional Model." *English for Specific Purposes*, 25: 235–256. DOI:10.1016/j.esp.2005.05.002

Mungra, Philippa. 2007. "A Research and Discussion note: The Macrostructure of Consensus Statements." *English for Specific Purposes*, 26: 79–89. DOI:10.1016/j.esp.2005.05.005

Nehm, Ross H., Minsu Ha, and Elijah Mayfield. 2011. "Transforming Biology Assessment With Machine Learning: Automated Scoring of Written Evolutionary Explanations." *Journal of Science Education and Technology*, 21, no. 1: 183–196. DOI:10.1007/s10956-011-9300-9

Nelson, Mike. 2006. "Semantic Associations in Business English: A Corpus-based Analysis." *English for Specific Purposes*, 25, no. 2: 217–234. DOI:10.1016/j.esp.2005.02.008

Nesselhauf, Nadja. 2004. "Learner Corpora and their Potential for Language Teaching." In *How to Use Corpora in Language Teaching*, John Sinclair, 125–152. Amsterdam: John Benjamins.

Ozturk, Ismet. 2007. "The Textual Organisation of Research Article Introductions in Applied Linguistics: Variability within a Single Discipline." *English for Specific Purposes*, 26, no. 1: 25–38. DOI:10.1016/j.esp.2005.12.003

Parodi, Giovanni. 2015. "Variation Across University Genres in Seven Disciplines: A Corpus-based Study on Academic Written Spanish." *International Journal of Corpus Linguistics*, 23, no. 2: 469 –99. DOI:10.1075/ijcl.20.4.03par DOI:10.1075/ijcl.20.4.03par#_blank

Pérez-Paredes, Pascual, and José Álcaraz-Calero. 2009. "Developing Annotation Solutions for Online Data Driven Learning." *ReCALL*, 21, no. 1: 55–75. DOI:10.1017/S0958344009000093

Pinkwart, Niels, Vincent Aleven, Kevin Ashley, and Collin Lynch. 2006. "Toward Legal Argument Instruction with Graph Grammars and Collaborative Filtering Techniques." In *Proceedings of the 8th International Conference on Intelligent Tutoring Systems*, edited by Mitsuru Ikeda, Kevin D. Ashley, and Tak-Wai Chan, 227–236. Berlin: Springer.

Pinto dos Santos, Valeria B. M. 2002. "Genre Analysis of Business Letters of Negotiation." *English for Specific Purposes*, 21, no. 2: 167–199.

Popescu, Teodora. 2007. "Teaching Business Collocations." In *Languages for specific purposes: Searching for Common Solutions*, edited by Dita Galova, 164–179. Newcastle-upon-Tyne: Cambridge Scholars Press.

Rankin, Tom, and Barbara Schiftner. 2011. "Marginal Prepositions in Learner English: Applying Local Corpus Data." *International Journal of Corpus Linguistics*, 16, no. 3: 412–434. DOI:10.1075/ijcl.16.3.07ran.

Robinson, Marin S., Fredricka L. Stoller, Molly S. Constanza-Robinson, and James K. Jones. 2008. *Write like a Chemist*. Oxford: Oxford University Press.

Rowley-Jolivet, Elizabeth. 2002. "Visual Discourse in Scientific Conference Papers: A Genre-based Study." *English for Specific Purposes*, 21, no. 1: 19–40.

Samraj, Betty, and Leonore Monk. 2008. "The Statement of Purpose in Graduate Program Applications: Genre Structure and Disciplinary Variation." *English for Specific Purposes*, 27: 193–211. DOI:10.1016/j.esp.2007.07.001

Scott, Mike. 1996. *Wordsmith Tools*. Oxford: Oxford University Press.

Seidlhofer, Barbara. 2002. "Pedagogy and Local Learner Corpora: Working with Learning-Driven Data." In *Computer Learner Corpora, Second Language Acquisition and Foreign Language Teaching*, edited by Sylviane Granger, Joseph Hung, and Stephanie Petch-Tyson, 213–233. Amsterdam: John Benjamins.

Sinclair, John. 1991. *Corpus, Concordance, Collocation*. Oxford: Oxford University Press.

Stamatatos, Efstathios, Nikos Fakotakis, and George Kokkinakis. 2000. "Automatic Text Categorization in Terms of Genre and Author." *Computational Linguistics*, 26, no. 4: 471–495.

Stoller, Fredricka L., and Marin S. Robinson. 2013. "Chemistry Journal Articles: An Interdisciplinary Approach to Move Analysis with Pedagogical Aims." *English for Specific Purposes*, 32: 45–57. DOI:10.1016/j.esp.2012.09.001

Swales, John M. 1981. *Aspects of Article Introductions*. Birmingham: University of Aston, Language Studies Unit.

Swales, John M. 1990. *Genre Analysis*. Cambridge: Cambridge University Press.

Swales, John M., and Christine B. Feak. 2004. *Academic Writing for Graduate Students: Essential Tasks and Skills*, 2nd ed. Michigan: University of Michigan Press.

Swales, John M., and Christine B. Feak. 2012. *Academic Writing for Graduate Students: Essential Tasks and Skills*, 3rd ed. Michigan: University of Michigan Press.

Teubert, Wolfgang. 2004. "Units of Meaning, Parallel Corpora, and Their Implications for Language Teaching." In *Applied Corpus Linguistics: A Multidimensional Perspective*, edited by Ulla Connor, and Thomas A. Upton, 172–189. Amsterdam: Rodopi.

Thomas, Sarah, and Tomas P. Hawes. 1994. "Reporting Verbs in Medical Journals." *English for Specific Purposes*, 13: 129–148. DOI:10.1016/0889-4906(94)90012-4

Thompson, Paul. 2000. "Citation Practices in PhD Theses." In *Rethinking Language Pedagogy from a Corpus Perspective*, Lou Burnard, and Tony McEnery, 91–101. Frankfurt: Peter Lang.

Thurstun, Jennifer, and Christopher Candlin. 1997. *Exploring Academic English: A Workbook for Student Essay Writing*. Sydney: NCELTR.

Vergaro, Carla. 2004. "Discourse Strategies of Italian and English Sales Promotion Letters." *English for Specific Purposes*, 23: 181–207. DOI:10.1016/S0889-4906(03)00003-6

Vihla, Minna. 1999. *Medical Writing: Modality in Focus*. Amsterdam: Rodopi.

Walker, Crayton. 2011. "How a Corpus-based Study of the Factors which Influence Collocation Can Help in the Teaching of Business English." *English for Specific Purposes*, 30, no. 2: 101–112. 10.1016/j. esp.2010.12.003

Weber, Jean-Jacques. 2001. "A Concordance- and Genre-informed Approach to ESP Essay Writing." *ELT Journal*, 55, no. 1: 14–20. DOI:10.1093/elt/55.1.14

Williams, Geoffrey. 2012. "Bringing Data and Dictionary Together: Real Science in Real Dictionaries." In *Corpus-informed Research and Learning in ESP: Issues and Applications*, edited by Alex Boulton, Shirley Carter-Thomas, and Elizabeth Rowley-Jolivet, 217–238. Amsterdam: John Benjamins.

Williams, Ian A. 1999. "Results Sections of Medical Research Articles: Analysis of Rhetorical Categories for Pedagogical Purposes." *English for Specific Purposes*, 18, no. 4: 347–366. DOI:10.1016/ S0889-4906(98)00003-9

Xiong, Wenting, Diane Litman, and Christian Schunn. 2012. "Natural Language Processing Techniques for Researching and Improving Feedback." *Journal of Writing Research*, 4, no. 2: 155–176.

Yang, Ming-Nuan. 2015. "A Nursing Academic Word List." *English for Specific Purposes*, 37: 27–38. DOI:10.1016/j.esp.2014.05.003

# 18 Technology, New Literacies, and Language Learners

## PAIGE WARE

## Introduction

The concept of *new literacies* is no longer all that new. Since its introduction by David Buckingham (1993) over 20 years ago, the term has been adapted by scores of scholars during a time of rapid technological innovation. A brief historical foray into the term shows that it was first defined by directly juxtaposing new literacies against what they were not: not conventional, not print-centric, not decontextualized, not discrete, and not innocuous (New London Group 1996; Street 1995). Soon after this phase of defining new literacies through non-examples, however, researchers across a number of disciplines worked to refine what we might mean by new literacies in particular contexts as they unfold with different types of groups and their unique learning goals. This chapter begins with a conceptual grounding of the term *new literacies* by tracing both its origins and its theoretical bases and by outlining the demands and affordances created by new technologies. It then focuses on several contemporary domains that inform language learning research, including the study of multimodality, identities, and contexts in which new literacies have emerged, both in classrooms and across social networking spaces. It concludes with a discussion of the challenges of the new literacies landscape and future directions for research.

## Origins and theoretical bases of new literacies

New literacies, as they pertain to second language learning, have been explored in two primary disciplines: applied linguistics and literacy studies. In the field of applied linguistics, Mark Warschauer (1999) introduced the term electronic literacies in his ethnography that traced how writing instructors made use of new technologies in starkly different ways depending on their pedagogical beliefs and training, their instructional contexts, and their familiarity with technology. In the subsequent decade, Warschauer (2003) articulated a more nuanced view of electronic literacies as being composed of four types of literacies. The first of these, computer literacy, was concerned with basic terminology and functionality of computers. The second, information literacy, focused on the research, retrieval, and filtering skills needed to participate as critical consumers of the vast resources available on the Internet. Multimedia literacy focused on the ability to create and consume digital texts that combine textual, graphic, auditory, and video modes. Finally, computer-mediated communication literacy described the ability to initiate and sustain contact with distally located others to accomplish a variety of interactional tasks. For many language researchers, these four

*The Handbook of Technology and Second Language Teaching and Learning*, First Edition.
Edited by Carol A. Chapelle and Shannon Sauro.
© 2017 John Wiley & Sons, Inc. Published 2020 by John Wiley & Sons, Inc.

categories have served as useful ways to frame a research agenda, and the two areas that have generated the most language research are those of multimedia literacy and computer-mediated communication (for extended discussions, see Kern 2006; Ware, Kern, and Warschauer forthcoming).

In the tradition of literacy studies, scholars who conduct work on new literacies often situate their work in a field that has become known as New Literacy Studies. Although this work has historically focused less on second language learning and more on first language literacy practices, some of the pioneering work in in this area has also been influential in language education research. This early work includes a seminal article by the New London Group (1996), the moniker used by a group of literacy scholars who articulated a pedagogical framework for *multi* literacies. In this framework, new literacies are the result of a three-part iterative cycle that works in ways to extend the repertoire of literacy. In this cycle, new literacies do not simply emerge as the result of new technological tools or new contexts of textual production and reception. Rather, the resources of human communication—linguistic, material, symbolic, and situational—exist as a set of what the New London Group call *available designs* from which individuals draw when *designing* new texts, which then emerge as *the redesigned*, or texts and products that can function either to reproduce the status quo or to extend, often in novel ways, the repertoire of resources that then feed back into the resources of available designs.

Even as these frameworks have guided inquiry into new literacies in the fields of applied linguistics and literacy studies over the last 20 years, contemporary research on new literacies is, as Mark Pegrum has aptly pointed out, still "unsettled terrain" (2013, 157). The demands imposed by a rapidly expanding view of literacy have led to a splintering into different focal points, which take root in unique ways according to differences in core disciplinary traditions. For example, in new media studies, the notion of participatory learning (Jenkins 2006) has emerged to help explore the social and collaborative environments in which literacy practices take place. For critical literacy theorists, new literacies bring in a multilingual and multicultural lens that was more peripheral in a print-centric view of literacy. In composition studies, Stuart Selber (2004) has suggested a conceptual framework for new literacies that examines the subject positions that individuals inhabit vis-à-vis technology. In his view, the computer can be seen as a tool (functional literacy), as a cultural artifact (critical literacy), and as a hypertextual medium (rhetorical literacy). Many of these different frameworks for thinking about new literacies are reflected in the work of language researchers, whose linguistic lenses can complement these various lines of inquiry.

## Affordances of new literacies

Various frameworks for studying new literacies highlight certain affordances, a notion in applied linguistics that was introduced by Leo van Lier (2000) from the field of psychology to describe properties in the environment that are purposefully made relevant and meaningful by users only through their conscious choices to take up a resource—to use it, discard it, change it, or repurpose it. Affordances reflect not just the availability of different properties in the environment, but are also new forms of literate *practices*. These practices involve many options: creating new types of texts from a wider range of semiotic resources including graphics, sound, and video; communicating with multiple audiences across geographic, linguistic, and cultural lines; establishing new identities, relationships, and social affiliations in online communities; generating new discourse structures and norms through new technologies such as wikis, blogs, and social networking sites; and engaging with and critically reviewing a wider range of informational content on the web.

Turning to the field of literacy studies, literacy scholar Jay Lemke (1998) shows how affordances can be comprised of wide-ranging practices as well as the contexts in which they take place. He emphasizes how language is always situated within other available semiotic systems and other contextualized social influences. Therefore, he argues that choices of how to make use of these symbols cannot be disentangled from understanding their contexts of use. New literacies allow for the co-presence and intermingling of different semiotic resources of graphics, sound, movement, video, and text (Kress 2010) that can be widely and easily shared, borrowed, and adapted on web platforms in ever-novel ways. They are always socially situated, plural, and multimodal and refer to an ever-flourishing array of practices, products, skills, and dispositions made possible by faster, more affordable, more connected, and more elaborated resources for making and sharing meaning (Gee 2000; New London Group 1996; Street 1995). New literacies have multiplied in the last 20 years to such a great number that scholars are now dividing their attention into special areas of literacy study. Disciplinary differences across conceptions of new literacies notwithstanding, most language scholars share a few common entry points, not the least of which is an optimistic view that new literacies are displacing notions of a singular, print-dominant view of literacy. Additionally, language researchers emphasize a combination of one or more elements of digital, multimodal, communicative, and multilingual practices. A new literacies lens in language research thus invites a contextualized perspective and sees textual production and reception as always situated within local and global contexts.

# Contemporary domains of research on new literacies

Synthesizing the main areas of research conducted on new literacies, technology, and language learning can be tackled in a number of ways. A decade ago, the intersection of technology and new literacy practices was divided into *waves* that emphasized first the tools, then the social interactions enabled by the technology (Kern, Ware, and Warschauer 2004). Later, emphasis turned to the *contexts* in which literacy practices took place: formal educational contexts, out-of-school contexts, and online social network spaces (Ware and Warschauer 2012). At other times, research was clustered according to different conceptual *frameworks* of learning, change, and power (Warschauer and Ware 2008). For this synthesis, I will approach the review of research on new literacies, technology, and language learning by spiraling outward across four different *foci*: (1) texts themselves as the primary focus; (2) individuals as the unit of analysis; (3) classrooms as case studies; and (4) connected contexts that link classrooms and communities.

## *New texts and multimodal analysis*

A dominant area of interest to new literacies scholars is that of multimodal texts. At first glance, multimodal genres are easily described as texts that make use of various semiotic resources in some combination of text, language, speech, sound, graphics, or animation. Several scholars have helped expand how we might conceptualize multimodal texts as more than just additive layers of meaning. In Kress's (2003) definition, for example, multimodal texts are created by using "elements of modes which are based on different logics" (46). This notion of the underlying *logics* of modalities was taken up by Hull and Nelson (2005) in their rich semiotic analysis of a digital story, in which they demonstrated that the combined impact of new and old textual forms function synergistically in multimodal texts—in short, the whole text becomes more than the mere sum of its parts. Nelson (2006) extended this work by examining how multimedia authoring was taken up by post-secondary second language writers. He used Kress's (2003) lens of *synaesthesia* which describes two processes by which writers can create new meanings: transformation, the process of repurposing resources within modes in their compositions, and transduction, the process of shifting resources across modes. He documented the importance of cultivating an awareness of these processes among multimedia authors to build their understanding of how authorial choices among textual elements can change meanings in ways that a single, linguistic-centric mode might not.

Researchers examining how multimodal texts are used in classroom contexts often view multimodality as a set of tools that learners can leverage to achieve their communicative purposes more creatively. For example, Castañeda (2013) integrated digital storytelling, a specialized narrative focus within multimodality, into her fourth-year Spanish language classroom. By analyzing students' engagement and writing processes over the course of the project, she uncovered several shifts, including heightened student engagement, greater focus on meaning, and a better understanding of the overall writing process. My own early work (Ware 2006) reflects a process-oriented analysis similar to Castañeda's, in that I examined the ways that two focal 9-year-old language learners engaged with multimodal genres in the context of technology-rich literacy instruction. In that context, the particular focus on digital storytelling was more closely aligned with more traditional U.S. storytelling practices that privilege the single authorial voice and a linear plot-driven narrative. I argued that educators need to consider pedagogical approaches that also invite different, more co-constructed and impressionistic narrative style when engaging with multimodal genres.

In current and future studies of multimodal genres, the focus will likely be less on the tools for generating texts and more on the *relationships between modes* that multimedia authoring demands. Nelson and Kern (2012), for example, recently forwarded the idea of a *relational pedagogy*, which requires the meta-communicative ability to understand how the relationships between forms and contexts generates different meanings that extend beyond a narrower focus on the linguistic aspects and conventions of literacy. In composition studies, too, Sorapure (2006) has promoted the view that these newer forms of multimedia authoring must account for each modality as well as for the relationships among them in the creation of coherent, meaningful texts. Their views resonate with second and foreign language scholars who have recently urged more attention be given to the study of multimodality (Block 2013; Blommaert and Rampton 2011). This shift in focus—from a language-centric view of multimodal genres to one that sees language as just one of many semiotic resources— reflects a parallel in the shift from viewing literacy as a singular, text-centric practice to literacy as plural, multimodal, and socially situated.

## Individuals and identities: Ethnographic studies

Many of the identity studies within the new literacies framework offer descriptive inventories of how individuals can leverage the multiple semiotic resources available to them through new media. Much of this research has taken place outside of formal school settings and has been conducted through ethnographic studies that document how learners engage in multilingual online communities (Lam 2000, 2004, 2009; Skerrett 2012), how they contribute as authors and editors in online fanfiction sites (Black 2008), how they create and exchange multimedia texts (Leander and Boldt 2013; Stornaiuolo, Hull, and Sahni 2011), and how they participate in multilingual gaming communities (Thorne, Black, and Sykes 2009). Primary emphasis is often placed on the constructs of agency, self-representations, and social affiliation. Case studies of small numbers of individuals are common, as their intense online engagement helps scholars better understand the range of what is possible with new literacies by highly engaged individuals who participate in new practices on their own terms in naturalistic (albeit a new kind of "naturalistic"—online) settings.

In identity studies that take a discourse analytic lens, Lam's pioneering work over the last 15 years has contributed in-depth linguistic and semiotic analyses of how immigrant youth engage in online communities. In her earlier pieces, she documented how transnational youth constructed identities in online spaces that served as a third positioning that contrasted with their physical lives. In 2000, for example, she demonstrated how Almon, a transnational youth who had immigrated from China to the United States, developed a strong multilingual presence through his homepage and online communication practices to create a textual presence that, through its complex multilingual presence, established a contrasting identity to the marginalized one he experienced as a language learner within the traditional school context. Lam's later study (2004) of two immigrant adolescents showed how both established a third positioning in the context of a Hong Kong chat room. One of the main conceptual contributions of Lam's early work has been her rigor in providing linguistic evidence of how individuals participate in multiple discourses that "may exist in various relationships of complementarity, contradiction, or conflict with one another" (2000, 459). Lam has shown that immigrant youth who use digital media in multilingual and multimodal ways to interact locally and across borders globally have a particular skill set consisting of the abilities to create, sustain, and challenge conventional and multilingual language practices, and of seeking and critiquing information from a variety of international sources.

Some of the most recent research on identity does not come directly out of the new literacies framework, but rather out of work in migration studies, in which scholars examine communicative practices across borders. In a recent review of research on youth and digital media within this migration studies literature, Lam and Warriner (2012) argue that digital texts demonstrate how youth "are orienting to different sets of cultural norms and practices coming from both local and translocal contexts, across their countries of origin and settlement, as these norms and practices are dynamically brought together and brought to view in new media platforms" (2012, 209). Several studies highlighted in their review underscore this new wave of literacy practices. McGinnis, Goodstein-Stolzenberg, and Saliani (2007), for example, showed how three different U.S. youth used their digital profiles and communication to identify with having ties to their family roots and to their local culture. McLean (2010) examined the case study of an adolescent from Trinidad and Tobago who used her online presence to project a variety of roles of being a student, a teenager, and a person identifying with her homes of Trinidad, the Caribbean, and the United States. Brouwer (2006) examined youth whose parents had immigrated to the Netherlands from Morocco and documented how the youth used social networking to communicate about sensitive topics that helped them understand their local and transnational experiences.

## Classroom-based studies of new literacies

From this early research base on out-of-school literacies, it became clear that learners gained a great deal in these contexts: an expanded network of audiences, a larger variety of participation structures, and a wider range of symbolic resources. These findings showed that language learners could then develop a more positive relationship with the target language and associated communities. For researchers interested in formal school settings, then, the hope was to leverage these positive relationships developed in out-of-school settings for stronger learner roles within classrooms.

Taking up these questions has required a new look at what "counts" as school-based literacy. How might school-based literacy be enhanced and amplified, or possibly diminished and replaced, by newer literacy practices such as those taking place outside of formal settings? Researchers inside formal educational contexts with an interest in new literacies seek ways to understand the relationship among "old" literacies and "new" literacies. Some researchers began by introducing the idea of hybrid genres. Such hybrid genres might, in some cases, serve to reinforce conventional literacy practices, while also having the positive effect of giving language learners a firmer foothold in developing formal literacy skills. Hybrid genres themselves could arguably also become legitimized as new school-based literacies in their own right. Mark Warschauer and I explored hybrid texts in technology-rich public schools and documented how creative teachers encouraged students to demonstrate their knowledge and skills through hybrid textual products (Ware and Warschauer 2006). In one seventh-grade classroom, students created hybrid texts in response to transformation activities; one student displayed her knowledge of the central nervous system through the creation of an illustrated romance story, and another displayed his academic summary of Beowulf as a graphic comic. In a lower-grades classroom, third-grade students completed projects that involved Internet research, the development of a math skills board game, and the creation of a digital movie as the game guide. These types of hybrid texts and practices have flourished in the last decade, becoming more commonplace as educators expand the repertoire of what counts as literacy.

Many classroom-based studies have shown that creative instructors draw on new literacies to enhance classroom learning processes and to expand the repertoire of new literacy practices. An archive of such innovative hybrid texts and practices is publicly available in an online library through the New Media Literacies Project (www.newmedialiteracies.org) developed by Henry Jenkins and his colleagues, whose work on the participatory learning framework (Jenkins 2006) invites creative, collaborative innovation using media literacy. Another large-scale study of innovative new literacies in schools is documented in Warschauer's (2006) monograph showing how adolescent students whose teachers integrated laptops into classroom instruction learned through a more student-centered pedagogy, in which they could hone their writing skills while engaging in the active creation and exchange of texts.

In language learning research, many classroom-based literacy studies have explored writing instruction using blogs and wikis. Unlike early versions of asynchronous discussion boards, blogs can house hyperlinks, images, sound, and multimedia. Although technically blogs can be made private to function as a personal online diary, the studies reviewed above indicate that, at least in the context of language learning research, much of what we are learning stems from shared blogs that are motivated by different audiences. Sykes, Oskoz, and Thorne (2008) showed how blog writing supported second language writers in sharing ideas and expanding their audience. Other research has demonstrated the potential for collaborative writing in blogs to promote confidence and motivation (Storch 2012). In the K-12 educational contexts, the collaborative context of writing in blogs has helped young language learners link their social and academic writing and their in- and out-of-school writing (Gebhard, Shin, and Seger 2011).

Wikis are viewed as more formal than blogs. In language research, wikis have been studied as spaces for students to collaborate on the creation of academic texts. Wiki writing is often viewed as a jointly produced text, rather than as a single-authored essay. Several researchers have examined how language learners offer feedback on one another's accurate production of language forms in wiki writing, though the results are mixed. In some studies, students tended to focus on information exchange rather than corrective feedback (Kessler 2009); however, in their study in which students were explicitly guided toward error correction and provided with instruction in how to do so in small groups, Arnold, Ducate, and Kost (2012) found evidence for constructive peer feedback on form. In yet another study, Elola and Oskoz (2010) found that students were more interested in correcting their own errors in wiki writing, rather than those of their peers.

## Connected contexts: Classrooms and communities

A focus on connections between classrooms and language learners across institutional and geographical lines is more deeply explored in a later chapter of this volume (see Chapter 16, Telecollaboration). In this section, however, I draw attention to the work of a few scholars who have organized English-dominant online exchanges to grapple with intercultural literacy practices. An interesting recent project by Hull and her colleagues (Hull, Stornaiuolo, and Sahni 2010) examined how youth participated in a private social networking site that was created purposefully to serve as an online space in which large numbers of international youth could share multimodal texts and interact with one another. Hull and her colleagues developed a unique site, Space2Cre8, to invite youth in India, Norway, South Africa, and the United States to participate. Within the parameters available at each local context, some of which were out-of-school while others were housed within formal schooling structures, local educators served as offline facilitators for youth who engaged with distally located peers online in a process of sharing their self-created digital arts and of engaging in dialogue with one another. A central tenet in their work is the notion that international online literacy spaces are intimately linked with the goal of literacy as a site for "cultural citizenship" (2010, 331). In these spaces, youth could cultivate what Hull and her colleagues define as "cosmopolitan habits of mind: a respect for legitimate difference, along with communicative dispositions and a repertoire of literate arts that make dialogue across difference possible and productive in its consequences" (2010, 333).

Several other projects have unfolded in which English is the primary language of communication. One large-scale project involving internationally linked youth took place across 139 countries with over 3,000 youth as part of the Junior Summit '98. Cassell and Tversky (2005) analyzed the transcripts from three months of these interactions and found that, despite participants' cultural, linguistic, and social differences, they tended to use English in ways that displayed a collective voice, convergence on topics, and greater understanding of diversity. Keranen and Bayyurt (2006) found that in-service and pre-service teachers in Spain and Turkey, while communicating about culture through English-language discussion boards, reported positive views of their partners. In my own work with Greg Kessler (Ware and Kessler 2014), we examined how youth from Spain and the United States used small-group, English-dominant blogs to communicate using text-based and multimedia messages across a 15-week period. Based on interviews, a classroom assessment of students' discursive language choices, and an analysis of the online transcripts, we found that the adolescent students demonstrated an awareness of the linguistic options by which they could actively maintain online relationships with distally located peers.

## Challenges of the new literacies landscape

Language research, in the context of a new literacies framework, portrays a hopeful outlook. The multiplicity of voices, languages, contexts, resources, and interactions that unfold inside this view of literacy acknowledges the complexity of human communication and connection. However, this landscape carries several challenges, many of which are uniquely tied to the access and amplification effects of new technologies (Warschauer 1999), and others of which are more broadly shared concerns about assessment.

First, differential access to technology and unevenness in the complexity of engagement with new literacies both remain key concerns. The term *digital divide* captures concerns researchers raised years ago that availability of adequate technological infrastructure would be unevenly divided in the population and would exacerbate existing social inequalities (for a discussion see Warschauer 2003). These concerns were exacerbated by what Hargittai (2002) coined a second-level digital divide that showed this split occurring less around access to technology *tools* themselves, but rather around access to more complex *uses* of technology for educational purposes. Comparative case studies have helped to reveal the effects of differences in engagement with technology. Warschauer (2006), for example, examined how a promising district-wide initiative to give all middle-grades students a laptop for use at home and at school was quite successful in high socioeconomic status (SES) schools, but less successful in low SES schools. Attewell and Battle (1999) tackled the question of whether having home computers helped students perform better academically and found, again, that students from high SES homes reaped more benefits than their lower SES peers. In a later study, Attewell and Winston (2003) examined how such differences might be made manifest by examining, this time qualitatively, how students in low and high SES communities used computers at home. They found repeated instances of vast discrepancies. At one end of the continuum, lower SES students tended to use computers for personal entertainment, while at the other end, higher SES students leveraged computers to do academic and project-based work such as writing reports, creating websites, and following the news. Such differences along socioeconomic lines in usage patterns continue to be documented both at an international scale as well as within individual countries and are affected by income status, ethnicity, and home computer access (Erumban and Jong 2006; Kuhlemeier and Hemker 2007; van Deursen and van Dijk 2009).

Part of the tension brought to light in this work surrounding the digital divide is the question of whether technology helps exacerbate pre-existing differences, or whether it merely amplifies them, and thus draws our attention to them. The likely answer is a combination of the two, and in the context of new literacies studies, attention to such amplification is often directed toward literacy practices that cross linguistic, geographic, and cultural boundaries. A set of concerns, as pointed out by Helm, Guth, and Farrah (2012) in their case study of an intercultural exchange between Palestinian and Italian students, is the potential for hegemonic practices to come into play in establishing power dynamics during international online literacy and culture exchanges. They describe, for example, the possible linguistic hegemony involved when online communication relies on English as the default language, rather than on linguistic plurality. To illustrate this possibility, it is worth noting that, in 2010, about 27% of all Internet usage was in English, even though only about 6% of the world population claim English as their first language (Miniwatts Marketing Group 2010). Helm and her colleagues borrowed the term *soft power* to examine how the combined forces of technology, education, and the media can be used as vehicles for exporting particular cultural views and values under the guise of value-free advancements. Language researchers whose work examines such online literacy practices as they cross international lines have strived to leverage these exchanges in ways that address such power issues, but many studies have nonetheless documented unanticipated effects such as the reification of stereotypes and the breakdown of communication (Belz 2002; O'Dowd and Ritter 2006; Ware 2005).

A third concern is that of assessment. For many scholars in the K-12 education sector, new literacies are often seen as one part of the larger umbrella of 21st century skills (Leu et al. 2004). A commonly referenced source for understanding how these skills are defined is the Partnership for 21st Century Skills (2011), a coalition of stakeholders across education, business, community, and governmental organizations. Their framework encompasses the core subject areas in education, along with an array of skills such as creativity, collaboration, problem solving, critical thinking, and communication. A number of literacies are folded in, including information literacy, ICT literacy, and media literacy. With the target audience focused on the educational community, they integrate a framework for assessment, professional development, standards, and curricular ideas.

Even with these frameworks outlining 21st-century skills, however, several scholars have recently suggested that there is little convergence, either on what these core competencies and skills actually entail, or on how to feasibly measure them (Towndrow, Nelson, and Yusuf 2013; Ware and Kessler 2014). Studies on new literacies, even those that purport to document the *development* of skills, tend to focus on highly localized and descriptive inventories of individuals who take up new literacies in particular contexts. Attempts to operationalize any measures of new literacies skills are still in the early years. Questions arise that are not easily resolvable when considering assessment at a large scale. The sheer number of constructs that emerge from any agreed-upon framework for new literacies is just one challenge. Are new literacies to be anchored in core linguistic competencies? Or in the participatory competencies they invoke when involving intercultural and global communication? Or in the symbolic competencies associated with understanding the new types of aesthetics associated with multimodal design?

To illustrate these difficulties through just one example, Towndrow, Nelson, and Yusuf (2013) presented a case study that tackles this thorny issue of how to assess multimodal texts. Their study took place in Singapore, where the official school curriculum has officially added the two new literacies skills of *viewing* and *representing* to the traditional literacy core skills. And yet, even in this progressive educational context, the competencies demonstrated by their focal student's production of a multimodal text go largely unnoticed by the assessment procedures in place. Towndrow, Nelson, and Yusuf use this example to show how the educational culture of assessment still privileges the linguistic elements of texts over other semiotic layering. Their analysis extends further to argue that educators must themselves develop what Mark Nelson and Rick Kern have referred to as *semiotic awareness* (Nelson and Kern 2012), an awareness that distinguishes between the ability to merely *compose* digital multimodal texts, on the one hand, and to purposefully *design* them on the other. In their view, absent of a deep understanding of this distinction, educators are not in a position to assess what is involved in student production of multimodal texts.

Other challenges associated with the idea of new literacies are worth mentioning. First, the primacy of conventional academic literacies over new creative, aesthetic, and communicative literacies creates tension in some educational contexts. In more conventional educational contexts, a hierarchy is assumed, in which the creative or communicative aspects of new literacies serve as handmaidens or as embellishments in the higher goal of strengthening print-dominant literacy skills that tend to focus on developing formal accuracy with commonly taught genres (exposition, persuasion, description, narration) and on fostering appropriate usage of standard grammatical conventions. Also, not all new literacies have proven to be constructive. In my own work (Ware 2008), for example, I documented how some early attempts to weave new literacies into school-based contexts resulted in an overuse of, and in some cases a counter-productive reliance on, the appearance of skill development, rather than active learning. Though the new literacies lens was well intentioned by teachers as supports for academic learning, the multimedia slideshow presentations instead served as a crutch for language learners to complete tasks without engaging directly or meaningfully with the linguistic or cognitive demands. Overwhelmed by the amount of text on the Internet, the adolescent students resorted to cutting and pasting dense text and colorful pictures into their final product with no display of understanding their own work. This example does not reflect a problem with new literacies per se, but it does urge caution in not overestimating what youth can and cannot do within the context of new literacies. Without strong pedagogical support, as Warschauer (1999) found over a decade ago, many technologies can serve to reinforce or amplify the impact of whatever pedagogical orientation teachers—and their students—bring to the learning environment.

# Future directions

To understand where the threads of new literacies, technology, and language learners intersect requires interdisciplinary thinking. Many language and literacy scholars agree that the notion of literacy as a singular construct—one focused primarily on the ability to read and write print-based texts—has been unequivocally displaced in favor of a pluralized view of multiple, or new, literacies that can encompass the many forms of literate expression and participation made possible by technological changes. New literacies, within this interdisciplinary perspective, are situated within particular contexts of reception and production, draw upon multiple symbolic forms of expression, and require a differentiated set of knowledge, skills, and practices. To help understand this expanding array of new literacies, scholars often focus on a subset of these new literacies, such as *multimodal* literacy, *information* literacy, *code* literacy, *computer-mediated communication* literacy, *computer* literacy, or *functional* literacy. Writing in a blog or sustaining intercultural dialogue online, both of which are possible examples of computer-mediated communication literacy, do not necessarily draw on the same set of skills as designing a multimodal digital story or creating a mash-up out of multiple online sources, which might better align with the skills associated with multimodal literacy. Some properties of new literacies may well be shared at the global level—such as their plurality and their engagement with new forms of texts—but not always at the local level. In short, it is very possible to be literate in some ways, but not in others.

One approach to cataloging and tracking this rapid expansion of new literacies is to classify them by their core functionality. Dudeney, Hockly, and Pegrum (2013), for example, recently took such a functionalist approach to group an array of new literacies around four main activity foci: language, information, connections, and re-design. They then further subdivided these four categories in ways that reflect specific core skills that aggregate into each of those larger umbrella terms. In their view, for example, literacies with a *language* focus would include print literacy, texting literacy, hypertext literacy, multimedia literacy, code literacy, mobile literacy, and gaming literacy. *Information* literacies, on the other hand, involve skills of tagging, searching, and filtering information from the Internet. A focus on *connections* would involve personal literacy, network literacy, participatory literacy, and intercultural literacy, while the fourth category of re-design involves what they call *remix* literacy—the skills associated with creatively leveraging a wide range of symbolic resources to create new texts and experiences. In the near future, such strategic descriptions as these will likely lead to greater convergence on which skills and practices align within each of these new literacies practices. Such common footing will help sharpen the growing knowledge base around new literacies.

A second possible direction that future research could take is one that a colleague and I recently described in a review of computer-assisted language learning in the K-12 context in which research turns toward one of two different orientations, toward learning outcomes on the one hand, and learning opportunities, on the other (Ware and Hellmich 2014). Both orientations, we argue, serve key functions for helping ensure that researchers develop a road map in our joint exploration of new literacies. As certain technology-rich literacy practices become more commonplace, and perhaps conventionalized, it behooves researchers and educators to find answers to questions about practicality, scalability, and efficacy. In these cases, a methodological orientation toward learning outcomes using quantifiable measures can help educators and learners maximize learner engagement, language development, and sustainable practices. However, because so many of the literacy practices and the technologies that support them emerge at a rapid pace, we also need continued research on the learning opportunities that new literacies embrace. This work will likely be driven by the qualitative case study research that has supported early inquiry into new literacies.

Each of these possible future directions for research on new literacies will be useful for tracking and understanding the rapid proliferation of new literacies. In looking toward the future, researchers will need to work across both disciplinary and methodological lines to refine our definitions of new literacies and to conceptualize them in ways that allow for more nuanced understandings that can serve different purposes within particular contexts for a number of language learners, educators, and researchers.

# REFERENCES

Arnold, Nike, Lara Ducate, and Claudia Kost. 2012. "Collaboration or Cooperation? Analyzing Group Dynamics and Revision Processes in Wikis." *CALICO Journal*, 29, no. 3: 431–448.

Attewell, Paul, and Hella Winston. 2003. "Children of the Digital Divide." In *Disadvantaged Teens and Computer Technologies*, edited by Paul Attewell and Norbert M. Seel, 117–136. Münster: Waxmann.

Attewell, Paul, and John Battle. 1999. "Home Computers and School Performance." *The Information Society*, 15, no. 1: 1–10.

Belz, Julie A. 2002. "Social Dimensions of Telecollaborative Foreign Language Study." *Language Learning & Technology*, 6, no. 1: 60–81.

Black, Rebecca W. 2008. *Adolescents and Online Fan Fiction*. New York: Peter Lang.

Block, Deborah. 2013. "Moving Beyond 'Lingualism': Multilingual Embodiment and Multimodality in SLA." In *The Multilingual Turn: Implications for SLA, TESOL, and Bilingual Education*, edited by Stephen May, 54–77. New York: Routledge.

Blommaert, Jan, and Ben Rampton. 2011. "Language and Superdiversity." *Diversities*, 13, no.2: 1–21.

Brouwer, Lenie. 2006. "Dutch Moroccan Websites: A Transnational Imagery?" *Journal of Ethnic and Migration Studies*, 32, no. 7: 1153–1168. DOI:10.1080/13691830600821869

Buckingham, David. 1993. "Towards New Literacies, Information Technology, English and Media Education." *The English and Media Magazine*: 20–25.

Cassell, Justine, and Dona Tversky. 2005. "The Language of Online Intercultural Community Formation." *Journal of Computer-Mediated Communication*, 10, no. 2: 00–00. DOI:10.1111/j.1083-6101.2005.tb00239.x

Castañeda, Martha E. 2013. "'I am proud that I did it and it's a piece of me': Digital Storytelling in the Foreign." *CALICO Journal*, 30, no. 1: 44–62. DOI:10.11139/cj.30.1.44–62.

Dudeney, Gavin, Nicky Hockly, and Mark Pegrum. 2013. *Digital Literacies*. Upper Saddle River, NJ: Pearson.

Elola, Idoia, and Ana Oskoz. 2010. "Collaborative Writing: Fostering Foreign Language and Writing Conventions Development." *Language Learning & Technology*, 14, no. 3: 51–71.

Erumban, Abdul A., and Simon B. De Jong. 2006. "Cross-Country Differences in ICT Adoption: A Consequence of Culture?" *Journal of World Business*, 41: 302–314. DOI: 10.1016/j.jwb.2006.08.005

Gebhard, Meg, Dong-Shin Shin, and Wendy Seger. 2011. "Blogging and Emergent L2 Literacy Development in an Urban Elementary School?: A Functional Perspective." *CALICO Journal*, 28, no. 2: 278–307.

Gee, James P. 2000. "Teenagers in New Times: A New Literacy Studies Perspective." *Journal of Adolescent & Adult Literacy*, 43, no. 5: 412–420.

Hargittai, Eszter. 2002. "Second-Level Digital Divide: Differences in People's Online Skills." *First Monday*, 7, no. 4. Accessed February 22, 2016: http://firstmonday.org/article/view/942/864

Helm, Francesca, Sarah Guth, and Mohammed Farrah. 2012. "Promoting Dialogue or Hegemonic Practice? Power Issues in Telecollaboration." *Language Learning & Technology*, 16, no. 2: 103–127.

Hull, Glynda. A., Amy Stornaiuolo, and Urvashi Sahni. 2010. "Cultural Citizenship and Cosmopolitan Practice?: Global Youth Communicate." *English Education*, 42, no. 4: 331–367.

Hull, Glynda, and Mark E. Nelson. 2005. "Locating the Semiotic Power of Multimodality." *Written Communication*, 22, no. 2: 224–261.

Jenkins, Henry. 2006. *Convergence Culture: Where Old and New Media Collide*. New York: New York University Press.

Keranen, Nancy, and Yasemin Bayyurt. 2006. "International Telecollaboration: In-Service EFL Teachers in Mexico and Pre-Service EFL Teachers in Turkey." *TESL-EJ*, 10, no. 3: 1–50.

Kern, Rick. 2006. "Perspectives on Technology in Learning and Teaching Languages." *TESOL Quarterly*, 40, no. 1: 183–210.

Kern, Rick, Paige Ware, and Mark Warschauer. 2004. "Crossing Frontiers: New Directions in Online Pedagogy and Research." *Annual Review of Applied Linguistics*, 24: 243–260.

Kessler, Greg. 2009. "Student-Initiated Attention to Form in Wiki-Based Collaborative Writing." *Language Learning & Technology*, 13, no. 1: 79–95.

Kress, Gunther. 2003. *Literacy in the New Media Age*. New York: Routledge.

Kress, Gunther. 2010. *Multimodality: A Social Semiotic Approach to Contemporary Communication*. New York: Routledge.

Kuhlemeier, Hans, and Bas Hemker. 2007. "The Impact of Computer Use at Home on Students' Internet Skills." *Computers & Education*, 49, no. 2: 460–480. DOI:10.1016/j.compedu.2005.10.004

Lam, Wan Shun Eva. 2000. "Second Language Literacy and the Design of the Self: A Case Study of a Teenager Writing on the Internet." *TESOL Quarterly*, 34, no. 3: 457–483.

Lam, Wan Shun Eva. 2004. "Second Language Socialization in a Bilingual Chat Room: Global and Local Considerations." *Language Learning & Technology*, 8, no. 3: 44–65.

Lam, Wan Shun Eva.2009. "Multiliteracies on Instant Messaging in Negotiating Local, Translocal, and Transnational Affiliations?: A Case of an Adolescent Immigrant." *Reading Research Quarterly*, 44, no. 4: 377–397.

Lam, Wan Shun Eva, and Doris S. Warriner. 2012. "Transnationalism and Literacy: Investigating the Mobility of People, Languages, Texts, and Practices in Contexts of Migration." *Reading Research Quarterly*, 47, no. 2: 195–215. DOI:10.1002/RRQ.016

Leander, Kevin, and Gail Boldt. 2013. "Rereading 'A Pedagogy of Multiliteracies': Bodies, Texts, and Emergence." *Journal of Literacy Research*, 45, no. 1: 22–46. DOI:10.1177/10862 96X12468587

Lemke, Jay L. 1998. "Metamedia Literacy: Transforming Meanings and Media." In *Handbook of Literacy and Technology: Transformations in a Post-Typographic World*, edited by David Reinking, Michael C. McKenna, Lindo Labbo and Ronald D. Kieffer, 283–301. Hillsdale, NJ: Erlbaum.

Leu, Donald J. Jr., Charles K. Kinzer, Julie L. Coiro, and Dana W. Cammack. 2004. "Toward a Theory of New Literacies Emerging from the Internet and Other Information and Communication Technologies." In *Theoretical Models and Processes of Reading*, edited by Robert Ruddell and Norman J. Unrau, 5th ed,, 1568–1611. Newark, DE: International Reading Association.

McGinnis, Theresa, Andrea Goodstein-Stolzenberg, and Elisabeth C Saliani. 2007. "'Indnpride': Online Spaces of Transnational Youth as Sites of Creative and Sophisticated Literacy and Identity Work." *Linguistics and Education*, 18, no. 3/4: 283–304. DOI:10.1016/j.linged.2007.07.006

McLean, Cheryl A. 2010. "A Space Called Home: An Immigrant Adolescent's Digital Literacy Practices." *Journal of Adolescent & Adult Literacy*, 54, no. 1: 13–22. DOI:10.1598/JAAL.54.1.2

Miniwatts Marketing Group. 2010. "Internet World Stats: Internet World Users by Language." [Statistical report]. Accessed December 12, 2015. http://www.internetworldstats.com/stats7.htm

Nelson, Mark E. 2006. "Mode, Meaning, and Synaesthesia in Multimedia L2 Writing." *Language Learning & Technology*, 10, no. 2: 56–76.

Nelson, Mark E., and Rick Kern. 2012. "Language Teaching and Learning in the Postlinguistic Condition?" In *Principles and Practices for Teaching English as an International Language*, edited by Lubna Alsagoff, Sandra L., Guangwei Mckay, G. Hu, and Willy A. Renandya, 47–66. New York: Routledge.

New London Group. 1996. "A Pedagogy of Multiliteracies: Designing Social Futures." *Harvard Educational Review*, 66, no. 1: 60–92.

O'Dowd, Robert, and Markus Ritter. 2006. "Understanding and Working with 'Failed Communication' in Tellecollaborative Exchanges." *CALICO Journal*, 23: 623–642.

Partnership for 21st Century Skills. 2011. "Framework for 21st Century Learning." Accessed February 10, 2016. http://www.p21.org/our-work/p21-framework

Pegrum, Mark. (2013). *Mobile Learning: Languages, Literacies, and Cultures*. Melbourne: Palgrave Macmillan.

Selber, Stuart. (2004). *Multiliteracies for a Digital Age*. Carbondale, IL: Southern Illinois University Press.

Skerrett, Allison. 2012. "Languages and Literacies in Translocation: Experiences and Perspectives of a Transnational Youth." *Journal of Literacy Research*, 44, no. 4: 364–395. DOI:10.1177/10862 96X12459511

Sorapure, Madeleine. 2006. "Between Modes: Assessing Students' New Media Compositions." *Kairos*,10, no. 2: 1–15. Accessed November 23, 2016. http://kairos.technorhetoric.net/10.2/coverweb/sorapure

Storch, Neomy. 2012. "Collaborative Writing as a Site for L2 Learning in Face-to-Face and Online Modes." In *Technology Across Writing Contexts and Tasks*, edited by Greg Kessler, Ana Oskoz, and Idoia Elola, 113–130. San Marcos, TX: CALICO.

Stornaiuolo, Amy, Glynda A. Hull, and Urvashi Sahni. 2011. "Cosmopolitan Imaginings of Self and Other: Youth and Social Networking in a

Global World." In *International Perspectives on Youth Media: Cultures of Production and Education*, edited by JoEllen Fisherkeller, 263–282. New York: Peter Lang.

Street, Brian. 1995. *Social Literacies: Critical Approaches to Literacy in Development, Ethnography, and Education*. London: Longman.

Sykes, Julie, Ana Oskoz, and Steven L. Thorne. 2008. "Web 2.0 Synthetic Immersive Environments and Mobile Resources for Language Education." *CALICO Journal*, 25, no. 3: 528–546.

Thorne, Steven L., Rebecca W. Black, and Julie Sykes. 2009. "Second Language Use, Socialization, and Learning in Internet Interest Communities and Online Gaming." *The Modern Language Journal*, 93: 802–821.

Towndrow, Phillip A., Mark E. Nelson, and Wan Fareed B. M. Yusuf. 2013. "Squaring Literacy Assessment with Multimodal Design: An Analytic Case for Semiotic Awareness." *Journal of Literacy Research*, 45, no. 4: 327–355. DOI:10.1177/1086296X13504155

van Deursen, Alexander J. A. M., and Jan A. G. M. van Dijk, J. 2009. "Using the Internet: Skill-Related Problems in Users' Online Behavior." *Interacting with Computers*, 21, no. 5/6: 393–402. DOI:10.1016/j.intcom.2009.06.005

van Lier, Leo. 2000. "From Input to Affordance: Social-Interactive Learning from an Ecological Perspective." In *Sociocultural Theory and Second Language Learning*, edited by James Lantolf, 245–259. Oxford: Oxford University Press.

Ware, Paige. 2005. "'Missed' Communication in Online Communication: Tensions in a German-American Telecollaboration." *Language Learning & Technology*, 9, no. 2: 64–89.

Ware, Paige. 2006. "From Sharing Time to Showtime?! Valuing Diverse Venues for Storytelling in Technology-Rich Classrooms." *Language Arts*, 84, no. 1: 45–54.

Ware, Paige. 2008. "Language Learners and Multimedia Literacy In and After School."

*Pedagogies: An International Journal*, 3, no. 1: 37–51.

Ware, Paige, and Emily A. Hellmich. 2014. "CALL in the K-12 Context: Language Learning Outcomes and Opportunities." *CALICO Journal*, 31, no. 2: 1–18.

Ware, Paige, and Greg Kessler. 2014. "Telecollaboration in the Secondary Language Classroom: Case Study of Adolescent Interaction and Pedagogical Integration." *Computer-Assisted Language Learning*. DOI:10.1080/09588221.2014.961481

Ware, Paige, and Mark Warschauer. 2006. "Hybrid Literacy Texts and Practices in Technology-Intensive Environments." *International Journal of Educational Research*, 43: 432–445. DOI:10.1016/j.ijer.2006.07.008.

Ware, Paige, and Mark Warschauer. 2012. "Qualitative Research on Information and Communication Technology." In *The Encyclopedia of Applied Linguistics*, edited by Carol Chapelle and Linda Harklau, 4787–4792. Oxford: Wiley-Blackwell.

Ware, Paige, Rick Kern, and Mark Warschauer. Forthcoming. "The Development of Digital Literacy." In *Handbook of Second and Foreign Language Writing*, edited by Paul. K. Matsuda and Rosa Manchon. The Hague: Mouton de Gruyter.

Warschauer, Mark. 1999. *Electronic Literacies: Language, Culture, and Power in Online Education*. Mahwah, NJ: Lawrence Erlbaum Associates.

Warschauer, Mark. 2003. *Technology and Social Inclusion: Rethinking the Digital Divide*. Cambridge, MA: MIT Press.

Warschauer, Mark. 2006. *Laptops and Literacy*. New York: Teachers College Press.

Warschauer, Mark, and Paige Ware. 2008. "Learning, Change and Power: Competing Frames of Technology and Literacy. In *Handbook of Research on New Literacies*, edited by Julie Coiro, Michelle Knobel, Colin Lankshear, and Don J. Leu, 21–240. New York: Lawrence Erlbaum.

# 19 Language Teacher Education and Technology

## GREG KESSLER AND PHILIP HUBBARD

The ubiquitous nature of technology throughout our lives today has ushered in new opportunities and expectations among students and teachers alike. An earlier generation of language teachers using technology often had to introduce the technology itself to students, and options for incorporating that technology were limited. With the routine use of technologies for contemporary social practices many teachers and students are users of at least some of the plethora of new tools, resources, and practices that may be beneficial in the language teaching. Yet taking advantage of this situation is not automatic: simple transfer of practices from personal and social use to the language learning domain cannot be assumed (Winke and Goertler 2008). More than ever, teachers need knowledge of computer-assisted language learning (CALL) principles and practices and skill in adapting them to their own classroom settings. Although that can take place informally for some through individual experimentation or participation in a community of practice (Hanson-Smith 2006; Lave and Wenger 1991), for most teachers a more efficient and effective way is through the formal education process.

As a consequence, interest in preparing language teachers to use technology in their classrooms has continuously grown over the past years. However, the interest and need exceeds the actual practices in language-teacher education programs (Kessler 2006; Oxford and Jung 2007). In this chapter, we examine the current state of the art in CALL teacher education. The chapter begins with a look back at the evolution of teacher education, including the types of pre-service and in-service classes and programs that have been developed over the last couple of decades, as well as touching on frameworks developed to describe this CALL teacher education. It then discusses studies that have yielded insights into promising avenues for conducting such education for teachers, in particular noting an emerging sociocultural turn that mirrors that in SLA. The next section considers current challenges, including the need to prepare candidates not only for teaching today and in the near future, but for an educational culture embracing constant technological change. The following section then explores how this goal might be realized by establishing clear expectations through initiatives such as the TESOL Technology Standards. The final section looks to the future of technology in teacher education considering, a future where language learners exiting our classes will likely be interacting in the target language digitally and where teachers will be expected to integrate disruptive technologies, such as machine translation applications, into the language learning ecology.

*The Handbook of Technology and Second Language Teaching and Learning*, First Edition.
Edited by Carol A. Chapelle and Shannon Sauro.
© 2017 John Wiley & Sons, Inc. Published 2020 by John Wiley & Sons, Inc.

# The emergence of CALL in teacher education

Before the 1980s, it would have been difficult to find any formal education in CALL for teachers. CALL was the province of a small number dedicated enthusiasts, mostly working in relative isolation constructing programs for their own students or for their own experimentation and amusement. However, as interest and numbers grew, they began sharing their experiences and expertise with like-minded others, forming computer user groups within the structure of existing professional organizations and starting new ones. Typical of these groups was Micro Users in ESL Institutions (MUESLI), founded by a group of teachers in England in December 1983 (IATEFL, 1984) and focused on promoting the classroom use of microcomputers for English as a foreign language (EFL).

By the early 1980s, CALL courses and workshops had begun to pop up, albeit sporadically, in language-teacher education programs, typically due to the interest of a specific faculty member or small group in this then arcane and exotic enterprise. For example, Marmo Soemarmo began teaching a computational linguistics class at Ohio University in the late 1970s that by 1983 had formally shifted into Computational Linguistics: Applications of Computers to Linguistic Research and Teaching (Ohio University 1983). An important part of the course focused on teaching MA English as a second language (ESL) teacher candidates how to program interactive language exercises for their students in BASIC. Delcloque's (2000) History of CALL Web Exhibition notes that Alistair Campbell ran a course in BASIC programming for CALL at University of Aberdeen (1981–1985). Delcloque also reports there were important workshops in 1982 at Jordanhill College of Education led by CALL pioneers John Higgins and Tim Johns, among others The emergence of these courses and workshops coincided with the general development of the field as a nascent academic discipline with its own journals and professional organizations and conferences. Computer Assisted Language Instruction Consortium (CALICO) was founded in 1982, and the TESOL CALL Interest Section and MUESLI (later the IATEFL Learning Technologies SIG) were organized the following year. In addition to individual courses and workshops, a few dedicated postgraduate degree programs were developed. Two were launched in 1993, one at the University of Stirling integrating CALL and TESOL (Delcloque 2000) and another at the University of Kent integrating CALL and applied linguistics (Partridge 2006).

Although CALL classes and workshops were being taught in the 1980s and 1990s, little in the way of research or even descriptions of methodology were published to support teacher educators in designing their curricula. Among the few examples are Curtin and Shinall (1985), who offered both a rationale and guidelines for conducting computer-assisted instruction (CAI) workshops for language teachers, Koet (1999), who described a course for teachers integrating Information and Communications Technology (ICT) and language study along with the teacher candidates' evaluation of it, and Daud (1992), who presented case studies of teachers in Malaysia attempting to use CALL, identified challenges, and provided guidance for integrating technology training into teacher education.

In 2002 teacher education became more visible in the field of CALL with the publication of a special issue of *Language Teaching & Technology (LLT)* on the topic. Of the five articles in the issue exploring the theme, two dealt primarily with student needs. However, the three others specifically described the impact of CALL courses more from the perspective of the teacher educator. In a study comparing expert and novice language teachers, Meskill et al. (2002, 54) found that "those novice teachers who had received 'state of the art' training in classroom technologies use were far less comfortable in their implementations than the more experienced teacher who had no formal training with computers but a great deal of classroom experience." Egbert, Paulus, and Nakamichi (2002) surveyed and interviewed 20 ESL teachers who had taken a CALL course to see the degree to which they integrated technology into their subsequent teaching, determining that those who had prior experience were much more likely to do so. Doering and Beach (2002) examined pre-service teachers enrolled simultaneously in a methodology and a technology course who engaged in a hypermedia project with middle-school ESL students. They concluded that the teachers were successful at integrating the tools and practices into an authentic educational context, but that they tended to dominate the online interactions by a 4:1 ratio over the students, undermining the purported value of these settings for facilitating peer communication. Lomicka and Cooke-Plagwitz's (2004) edited volume titled *Teaching with Technology* still dealt mainly with the student side, but four chapters were clearly focused on teacher education. Two in particular (Avendaño 2004; Cooke-Plagwitz 2004) explored the approach of using technology to teach technology, placing teachers in the role of learners (see also Hubbard 2008).

Hubbard and Levy (2006a) published the first edited volume devoted fully to language-teacher education and technology, helping to push CALL teacher education from the periphery of language-teacher education toward the mainstream. Its 20 chapters from teacher educators around the world were distributed across five sections covering foundations of the field; CALL degree programs; CALL pre-service courses, CALL in-service projects, courses, and workshops; and alternatives to formal CALL training. The following year, CALICO produced an edited volume for preparing technology-proficient language teachers (Kassen et al. 2007) with 14 chapters in sections on national frameworks, specific contexts, learning communities, toolboxes, and critical reflection. A special issue of *Innovation in Language Learning and Teaching* on CALL teacher education, edited by White and Reinders (2009) had seven articles, including two focusing on preparing online teachers and two on building teacher autonomy. *ReCALL* had a special issue in 2011 on the more focused area of CALL and computer-mediated communication (CMC) teacher education with six articles on that topic. More recently, *LLT* revisited teacher education with a special issue of seven articles in February 2015. Key generalizations from the *ReCALL* and *LLT* issues are discussed below.

In addition to descriptive studies and empirical research in journals and edited volumes, some authors have attempted to take a more comprehensive perspective on the topic. Hubbard and Levy (2006b) offered a framework for CALL teacher education integrating functional roles (practitioner, developer, researcher, and trainer) and institutional roles (pre-service teacher, in-service teacher, CALL specialist, and CALL professional). Hubbard (2008) broadly outlined the issues, approaches, and processes involved in CALL teacher education, emphasizing the importance of training not just for the present but also for an unknown technological future. The issues noted were the role of technology standards, the need to distinguish in-service and pre-service education, and the importance of developing more technologically competent teacher educators. Approaches included breadth first, the traditional survey course; depth first, where the technology is learned by exploring a single topic deeply (e.g., Chao (2006) for WebQuests); integrated, where technology is implemented throughout a teacher education program (Hegelheimer 2006); and fully online (Bauer-Ramazani 2006) or blended (Lord and Lomicka 2004). In addition to the traditional lecture/demonstration, the following processes were identified:

- project-based (Debski 2006)
- situated learning (Egbert 2006)
- reflective learning (Slaouti and Motteram 2006)
- portfolio-based (van Olphen 2007)
- mentor-based (Meskill et al. 2006)
- communities of practice (Hanson-Smith 2006)

Teacher educators were encouraged to draw on one or more of these processes in creating courses to fit the context and objectives of their particular setting.

A few years later, Motteram (2009) proposed an agenda for CALL course development for teacher education based on an integrated view of technology and teacher education theory with a focus on the place of social computing. The TESOL Technology Standards similarly provide guidance—a chapter in Healey et al. (2011) is targeted specifically at teacher educators. Most recently there has been an emphasis on preparing language teachers for teaching in distance learning or hybrid contexts (Meskill 2013; Meskill and Anthony 2010), often focusing upon the reflexive approach of using these online contexts to learn the skills that can support CALL training (Cooke-Plagwitz 2004; Dooly 2011; Slaouti and Motteram 2006). Along these lines, in their editorial introducing the special issue of *ReCALL* mentioned above, Guichon and Hauck (2011) proposed that reflective practice and situated learning are common to much of current teacher education, and that these should be complemented with a blend of experiential modeling and exploratory practice to support teacher research leading to deeper understanding of the complex processes involved in technology and language teaching. Similarly, in their introductory commentary to the aforementioned *Language Learning & Technology* special issue (Arnold and Ducate 2015) identified three themes in the seven articles: the impact of different types of CALL teacher education, the development of teacher cognition, and the value of reflective and collaborative formats. They concluded that those articles collectively reconfirmed previous findings that

a) both formal and informal training can be beneficial but have unique limitations and constraints, b) teacher development in the area of CALL is not a linear, uniform process and depends heavily on teacher predispositions and teaching contexts, and c) pre-service and in-service teachers benefit greatly from collaborative and reflective forms of CALL training. (Arnold and Ducate 2015, 6)

During this period, both CALICO and EUROCALL launched active Teacher Education SIGS, and the latter has organized international workshops and conferences in the past few years. Moreover, technology is regularly integrated into general language-teacher education textbooks. Arnold (2013) reviewed 11 contemporary methodology texts to determine the degree to which they incorporated eight criteria derived from the TESOL Technology Standards for Teachers (TESOL 2008). She concluded that "Most provide a broad, balanced view of different functions of technology, CALL applications, their potential benefits, and sample tasks" (241). What has emerged from this work collectively is a range of options and resources for meeting the needs and aspirations of both pre-service and in-service teachers as well as those who seek to become experts or CALL professionals (Hubbard and Levy 2006b).

This evolution toward professionalism has resulted in professional organizations establishing benchmarks, or standardized expectations representing the minimal technology skills, knowledge and abilities necessary for language teachers. Broadly across education these include the ISTE and UNESCO standards. (For details, including a concordance across standards, see Healey et al. (2011).) Within language education these include the brief acknowledgment in the front matter of the ACTFL standards and the extensive TESOL Technology Standards. We anticipate that other projects will emerge soon for other language contexts and locales. For instance, Arnold (2013) utilized the TESOL Technology Standards as an evaluative tool in the assessment of foreign language textbooks. This observation helps to explain that while there previously had been a significant interest as to the extent of teacher preparation for CALL, it appears that these topics are being integrated into general language methodology.

# Research into CALL teacher education

For the past two decades research has indicated a need to better understand the process and outcomes of CALL teacher education. Some studies tackle the issue by relying on survey and interview data gathered from teachers, administrators, and other stakeholders. Findings indicate the need to address shortcomings such as a general lack of preparation (Kessler 2006), inadequate breadth (Peters 2006), and lack of contextualization (Egbert 2006) as well as a lack of use following training (Egbert, Paulus, and Nakamichi 2002), and reliance upon informal preparation (Kessler 2007). Other studies have examined teachers' experience from a larger ecological and sociocultural perspective (Motteram 2009; Warschauer 2005). Such investigation takes into account the complex and shifting nature of today's language learning contexts in an attempt to inform future teacher training in a more comprehensive manner. Ecological approaches can be useful for examining models for optimizing informal training as an alternative to no training whatsoever. These alternatives to formal degree programs, including peer mentoring, Communities of Practice (CoPs), conference and in-service workshops, may still account for much of the CALL teacher preparation that occurs today.

This research has helped to identify the considerations, skills, and strategies necessary for CALL practitioners, including contextualizing learning and maintaining authenticity (Egbert 2006), aligning tasks and tools (Levy and Stockwell 2006), and assessing student performance using tools such as portfolios (van Olphen 2007). An example of skills derived from various CALL teacher preparation studies is in Table 19.1.

Given an adequate foundation, teachers can leverage such skills across technologies and, even, generations of technologies, allowing teacher preparation to focus upon appropriateness and creative implementation rather than technical abilities (Hegelheimer 2006).

**Table 19.1**   Basic and Advanced CALL skills for classroom teachers.

| Skill | Example teacher action |
| --- | --- |
| **Basic** | |
| Locate | Use Internet search engine to find relevant movie files |
| Evaluate | Watch videos to determine if the language level is appropriate, if the content is accurate, if the quality of the video is acceptable, etc. |
| Select | Select the file that best meets pedagogical needs |
| Distribute | Determine the best means for distributing a video file to students, including Web links, CDs, local files, etc. |
| Integrate | Construct a language lesson around the content of the video file that utilizes the images, audio, and text in meaningful pedagogical ways. |
| **Advanced** | |
| Create | Create a video using a combination of personally created images, texts and voice recordings. |
| Customize | Edit the movie file expanding the narration with a more challenging version for a higher-level class. |
| Convert | Edit the movie file deleting the audio to utilize as a reading activity. |
| Repurpose | Use instructional materials, media, or technology in multiple contexts with relatively minor alterations. |

*Source*: Adapted from Greg Kessler (2012). "Language teacher training in technology." In *The Encyclopedia of Applied Linguistics*, edited by Carol A. Chapelle, 4. Oxford,: Wiley-Blackwell.

These kinds of guidelines are expanded upon in the *TESOL Technology Standards*. It is important to note that these standards are intended for use in varied language contexts across the globe, particularly as there are no comparable standards yet established specifically for other languages and/or locations.

Even though such standards appear to assume globally applicable knowledge and strategies for teachers, experience and learning occurs in the specific circumstances within a teacher preparation programs (Dellicarpini 2012; Egbert 2006; Kessler and Plakans 2008). Part of the learning experience can include activities in which future teachers assume the perspective of learners to gain insight into learning through technology (Cooke-Plagwitz 2004) as well as experiences as language learners (Kolaitis et al. 2006). Kessler (2010) conducted a discourse analysis of class discussions over the course of a term to gain insight into the emerging perspectives of CALL teachers in training. The analysis revealed that without guidance there is a general trend for future teachers to overlook much of the potential that emerging tools and practices present. There is also a tendency to rely upon the tools and practices that teachers used as language learners themselves. In addition, future teachers have difficulty in relinquishing control over all aspects of the learning environment. Such realizations have contributed to new perspectives on CALL teacher preparation such as teaching how to promote collaboration, work toward learner autonomy and repurpose commonly available technologies (Kessler 2012).

# Evolving technologies and practice

Varied approaches to CALL preparation are being taken, leading to discussions about their merits, including those mentioned above (e.g., depth first breadth first, project-based, and communities of practice). These directions in CALL teacher education take inspiration from research suggesting that technology integration can contribute to increases in student engagement, motivation (Meunier 1997; Warschauer 1996) by providing them with assessment of their learning, feedback, and access to authentic language (González 2008). Teacher education also needs to communicate to prospective teachers the ways that technology integration can also accommodate enhancements in tracking student behavior, individualizing instruction, and training learners to be more autonomous (Hubbard 2013).

## *Assessment*

Technology offers new opportunities for performing both formative and summative assessment of learners. This area of research, computer-assisted language testing (CALT) is situated primarily within language testing (Chapelle and Douglas 2006). It includes research and practice on the use of computers "for eliciting and evaluating test takers' performance in a second language" (Suvorov and Hegelheimer 2013, 1). The two areas pertaining most directly to classroom assessment are perhaps automated writing evaluation (AWE) and automated speaking evaluation (ASE). Both of these areas have benefited from extensive research and development in recent years and there is much they can offer language educators. For example, Link et al. (2014) examined ESL teachers' strategies for implementing AWE in addition to their overall perceptions of the experience with the intention of informing future CALL teacher education. Other research will inform teacher education in the future such as findings by Cotos (2011) that an AWE tool (the Intelligent Academic Discourse Evaluator or IADE) could provide students with feedback on introduction sections for research papers that contributed to significant improvements to their writing. With the increase of computer generated feedback and automated assessment, it is becoming increasingly important that teachers be able to interpret automated feedback and help students make sense of it when necessary.

## Feedback for students

Feedback covers a broad and diverse set of practices in the second language learning literature and there is much debate about the ideal conditions and circumstances that make feedback most salient. This ongoing discussion should be familiar to language teachers. Despite the position one holds, there are numerous enhancements (see, e.g., Chapelle 2001) related to feedback available through technological intervention. These can be divided into delivery mode, feedback focus, and feedback strategies (Ware and Kessler 2012). Feedback for error correction has been recognized as critical for ongoing language learning development (Ferris, 2004, 2006). This kind of feedback can be delivered or exchanged with students through a variety of modes, including face-to-face, human generated digital delivery, and computer generated. Digital feedback can be presented in varied forms to increase salience (Ducate and Arnold 2012). Some recent studies have observed that electronic feedback benefits from greater legibility and permanence (Ferris 2012), and can help students focus more when delivered interactively (Ferris 2010). Others have observed that students benefit when they have the ability to select the mode of delivery (Matsumura and Hann 2004). Computer generated feedback is becoming more common in language instruction and is often linked to the area of assessment. Thus, it is becoming increasingly important that language teachers be prepared to recognize the changing nature of feedback and assessment.

## Observation and monitoring

The ability to observe or monitor student behavior and progress through digital means has brought many benefits to language instructors. Some researchers have explored the potentials for teachers who can observe, track and remotely manage students as they engage in learning experiences (Chun 2013; Fischer 2007). This oversight of students' performance can provide instructors with valuable insights into how students actually use technology for learning. Such insights can help teachers identify linguistic and technological challenges students face. These practices can also contribute to the design of more salient feedback, thus these emerging areas are not only important individually, but as integrated components of a complex and dynamic ecosystem of CALL practice. Establishing familiarity with these practices and maintaining currency are likely to play an increasing role in language-teacher preparation. After all, as the tools that students use continue to gather more valuable information about their progress and performance, language teachers should be familiar with the nature of this information. Language teachers should also be able to gather such information in a manner that enhances the educational experience. Language teachers should be exposed to these practices in pre-service education, but ongoing attention to such issues throughout their careers is likely to be beneficial.

## Social networking

CALL teacher preparation also needs to keep abreast of the emergence of educational uses of the social and new media that has had a dramatic influence over all aspects of communication and learning. These changes have created new opportunities for engagement and collaboration in language teaching and learning (Kessler 2013). The ubiquitous nature of these tools and practices makes them compelling and challenging simultaneously. There may be an assumption that anyone can use such tools without difficulty, but previous CALL research has shown that teachers are often overwhelmed by such potential tools (Kessler 2010) or they may simply be uncertain how to implement new technologies in their classroom (Kessler and Plakans 2008). The pedagogical use of social media for language learning is among the challenges that need to be defined for future work in CALL teacher education.

# Challenges facing CALL teacher education

In 2008, Hubbard identified barriers to integrating CALL training into language-teacher education programs. Three of these—lack of standards, lack of established methodology, and insufficient infrastructure—have been largely dealt with in many settings through the efforts of teacher educators in contexts where the importance of technology is recognized at the institutional level. As a consequence, increases have occurred in the numbers of language teachers learning how to use new technologies. Nevertheless, many language teachers are still graduating without having received sufficient formal preparation and there continues to be a general lack of autonomy among teachers when using technology (Dellicarpini, 2012; Kessler 2010). Fundamentally, four challenges face those working in language-teacher education.

## *Preparing teachers for change*

Teachers need to be prepared to engage with changes in teaching. New technologies are responsible for the rapid introduction of new classroom techniques and course configurations. For example, mobile assisted language learning (MALL) has recently begun to present new opportunities for language learning. However, with the potential innovations, MALL increasingly relies on a bring your own model that introduces challenges for teachers in terms of consistency with disseminating material, gathering student responses or language production, and providing feedback. Formatting issues as well as pay-as-you-go features on some mobile devices can further complicate this scenario (Stockwell 2008). Although there has been a growing body of research into the use of mobile devices in specific CALL contexts, the CALL teacher preparation literature does not addresses this topic directly. The many challenges that the emergence of mobile devices presents will undoubtedly be addressed in future CALL teacher education research, but such new technologies appear in the hands of students before appearing in teacher education courses. As a result, such shifts in practice require that teachers be prepared for a culture of constant innovation.

With respect to course configurations, the number of courses taught in an online or hybrid format, is increasing rapidly, requiring teachers who are able to teach language online. In fact, much of the recent research into CALL teacher preparation directly involves preparing teachers for distance or hybrid instruction (Meskill 2013). With the introduction of MOOCs and the global nature of language teaching and learning, such online and hybrid courses are very appealing to many. There are many unique characteristics that preparation for online teaching addresses, but preparing teachers for a variety of changing contexts can inform face-to-face instruction (Healey et al. 2011). In addition to preparing language teachers for online or hybrid teaching, teacher preparation is also increasingly taking place online (e.g., Bauer-Ramazani 2006; Dooly 2011). These practices have resulted in a better understanding of how online training works. As a result, teacher trainers involved in online contexts have learned to modify the environments and their associated behavior (Meskill 2013).

## *Preparing teachers for interactive materials*

One major change in practice that teachers needs to learn about is the potential for a continuing variety of interactive activities for their students. One type of interactivity is evident in online games. The increasing interest in game related practices in language teaching is largely due to the observations that such practices can provide students with authentic experiences that support language learning and promote engagement (Gee and Hayes 2011; Reinders and Wattana, 2014). Situated SLA researchers have recognized authenticity as a beneficial component in the design of language learning materials, experiences, and environments (Egbert, Hanson-Smith, and Chao 2007), but the links between this idea in SLA and gaming needs to be made if teachers are to see it as a value of games. Game related practices can also help to situate learning in meaningful ways (Gee and Hayes 2011).

Positive outcomes from research into gaming for language learning includes findings of positive contributions to autonomy building and community development (Chik 2014; Reinders and Hubbard 2013). Some researchers also see CALL practices improving student motivation when supported by mobile (Ushioda 2013), game-based (Allen et al. 2014) and collaborative opportunities (Kessler, Bikowski, and Boggs 2012). Nevertheless, research is needed on CALL teacher preparation that directly addresses the various issues associated with gaming and game related practices. Even though gaming is becoming more commonplace in language classrooms, work on CALL teacher education has not yet critically engaged with opportunities and challenges of gaming. Such work is needed if language teachers are to learn to realize some of the promise by creating customized games for their specific learners (Sykes and Reinhardt 2013).

Another type of interactive activity for language learners is made possible by the tutors and tools created by new natural language processing (NLP) technologies. Tutoring systems relying on NLP can offer individualized interactions to students to help them work on specific language features such as articles, verb tenses, and relative clauses. Such tutoring systems, referred to as intelligent CALL (iCALL), hold the potential of increasing the individualization and interactivity of instruction relative to what can be accomplished in the language classroom. They often rely upon learner models and sets of previous learner language production in order to predict future learner behavior and therefore provide good feedback and guidance to students (Dickinson, Brew, and Meurers 2013). NLP-based tools make available to students automated text analysis and automated speech recognition to use for analysis of their own linguistics production (Dickinson et al. 2013). Such systems are becoming more commonplace in language instruction; however, they are often considered unfamiliar and complicated by language teachers (Link et al. 2014). Shermis and Burstein (2013) observed that automated essay evaluation generally fails due to inadequate teacher training, not due to problems with the technology. Others have observed that teachers rarely use automated tools even when they view them favorably (Warschauer and Grimes 2008). This appears to be largely due to a lack of adjustment to pedagogical practices and curricular goals to integrate the capabilities of the systems. Others have found that teachers may not trust or value the scores provided by automated analysis due to observed inconsistencies, but that some teachers can identify these instances as opportunities for intervention (Link et al. 2014). Teachers need to be aware of the potential of automated tools as well as the various ways that they can be used for language teaching, but appropriate and effective training in these areas is rare.

## Preparing teachers for a social future

Another challenge is the social nature of communication and learning that is stimulated by the software tools for communication and networking. With the wealth of emerging social tools that motivate so many people to participate in communication practices, language teachers should learn to make use of such tools for learning activities in class and to extend learning opportunities beyond the classroom. Collaborative language learning practices are becoming more common as the tools that support them are better understood and utilized (Kessler 2013). Like other types of interactivity social networking tools have been found to promote opportunities for language learning. Tools such as wikis that allow multiple contributors to share equal responsibility and control over a written product promote increased participation and audience awareness (Lund 2008) which can improve self- and peer-editing abilities (Kessler 2009) across a variety of task types (Aydin and Yildiz 2014). Collaboration has also been associated with promoting individual writer's abilities (Elola and Oskoz 2010). Collaborative dialogues can support students as they reconstruct knowledge when writing academically (Sun and Chang 2012. Collaborative practices can be beneficial across a range of teacher intervention and group sizes and structures, providing teachers take these circumstances into account (Kessler 2012). Beyond language learning benefits, teachers need to recognize that collaborative production of discourse is increasingly common in a variety of professional contexts in which our language students will ultimately find themselves working (Kessler et al. 2012).

The potential of these collaborative activities, tasks and materials rely upon teachers who are willing and able to experiment with their use in educational contexts. But doing so requires new skills and attitudes toward experimentation because many social networking activities threaten conventional power dynamics that exist within teacher-centered classrooms (Kessler 2012). Storch (2005) concludes a study into the significance of collaborative practices in language learning as requiring, "A reconceptualization of classroom teaching" (169). As one can imagine, reconceptualizing classroom teaching is not something that is easily accomplished. In order to do so, CALL teacher preparation must involve thinking about pedagogy in new ways that align with the affordances of these technologies and their associated social practices (Kessler et al. 2012). Even though the potential for these tools is only beginning to be realized, they clearly offer great opportunities for teaching and learning if teacher preparation is flexible and responsive to developments.

## The challenge of "normalization"

The challenges noted above require significant attention and action on the part of teacher education programs. The need for dramatic attention sits uncomfortably alongside the idea that technology is becoming so normal in education that is will soon be invisible. The inevitability of normalization as described by Bax (2003) suggests that CALL will become normalized, or fully integrated and transparent within language pedagogy. The call for action in teacher education seems unlikely to be taken seriously if it is to address pedagogies that are perceived as already being fully integrated into practice.

Some have observed that this notion of normalization, which may seem plausible to those who regularly work in educational technology, is unlikely to become reality in most teaching situations anytime in the near future (Hubbard 2008; Peters 2006). Chambers and Bax (2006) acknowledge some challenges with this ideal and present solutions that include scheduling technology space effectively and integrating technology into curricula. These suggestions do not address the greatest challenge, which is the appropriate teacher preparation. To achieve adequate teacher preparation faculty in a teacher preparation program need to have the necessary CALL knowledge and experience to reach normalization. Recently, Bax (2011) acknowledged that normalization is more complex and would require a "Needs Audit" to determine the desirability, necessity, and practice related aspects of specific technologies within language teaching and teacher preparation (11). Such an audit should be built upon the foundation of the research presented in this chapter since these extant studies have addressed these, and other important, questions.

## Conclusion

Findings from research on teacher preparation include recommendations that teachers be able to evaluate technology for language learning, integrate tutors and tools, recognize relevant emerging technologies and align integration with pedagogical goals. As research continues to be more sophisticated and aware of the increasingly complex nature of language learning and teaching experience, valuable insights will be offered into how to best conduct CALL teacher preparation to address these recommendations. We can also anticipate the emergence of standards projects establishing specific expectations for a variety of linguistic and cultural contexts. All of these developments are likely to contribute to an increased awareness of the value of lifelong learning among language teachers.

Such work at the global level runs in parallel with the insights into CALL teacher preparation locally. The unique characteristics that define any given institution, instructor, or curriculum can greatly influence the experiences and outcomes of a given class or technological intervention. Moreover, teachers rely on situated practice that occurs in their teaching contexts to recognize the full benefits of CALL practices (Egbert et al. 2002; Kessler and Plakans 2008). It is therefore essential to link and align results from contextualized practices with the more general professional discourse that informs teacher education. Researchers should continue to investigate the circumstances that support successful situated learning across an array of potential contexts to inform future CALL teacher preparation. Such research informed by knowledge of an evolving socio/ecological understanding regarding use of technologies throughout our lives is needed to keep teacher preparation programs relevant to teachers' needs.

# REFERENCES

Allen, Laura K., Scott. A. Crossley, Erica L.Snow, and Danielle S. McNamara. 2014. "L2 Writing Practice: Game Enjoyment as a Key to Engagement." Language Learning & Technology, 18, no. 2: 124–150. Accessed 4 January, 2017. http://llt.msu.edu/issues/june2014/varneretal.pdf

Arnold, Nike. 2013. "The Role of Methods Textbooks in Providing Early Training for Teaching with Technology in the Language Classroom." Foreign Language Annals, 46, no. 2: 230–245.

Arnold, Nike, and Lara Ducate. 2015. "Contextualized Views of Practices and Competencies in CALL Teacher Education Research." Language Learning & Technology, 19, no. 1: 1–9.

Avendaño, Silvio. 2004. "Surfing Together: Training EFL Teachers to use the Internet." In Heinle Professional Series in Language Instruction: Teaching with Technology, edited by L. Lomick, and J. Cooke-Plagwitz, 47–49. Boston: Heinle.

Aydin, Zelih, and Senem Yildiz. 2014. "Using Wikis to Promote Collaborative EFL Writing." Language Learning & Technology, 18, no. 1: 160–180.

Bauer-Ramazani, Christine. 2006. "Training CALL Teachers Online." In Teacher Education in CALL, edited by P. Hubbard and M. Levy, 183–200. Amsterdam: John Benjamins.

Bax, Stephen. 2003. "CALL: Past, Present, and Future." System, 31, no. 1: 13–28. DOI:10.1016/S0346-X(02)00071-4

Bax, Stephen. 2011. "Normalisation Revisited: The Effective Use of Technology in Language Education." International Journal of Computer Assisted Language Learning and Teaching, 1, no. 2: 1–15. DOI:4018/ijcallt.2011040101

Chambers, Angela, and Stephen Bax. 2006. "Making CALL Work: Towards Normalisation." System, 34, no. 4: 465–479.

Chao, Chin Chi. 2006. "How WebQuests Send Technology to the Background: Scaffolding EFL Teacher Professional Development in CALL." In Teacher education in CALL, edited by P. Hubbard and M. Levy, 221–234. Philadelphia: John Benjamins.

Chapelle, Carol A. 2001. Computer Applications in Second Language Acquisition. Cambridge,: Cambridge University Press.

Chapelle, Carol A., and Dan Douglas. 2006. Assessing Language through Computer Technology. Cambridge: Cambridge University Press.

Chik, Alice. 2014. "Digital Gaming and Language Learning: Autonomy and Community." Language Learning & Technology 18, no. 2, 85–100. Accessed January 4, 2017. http://llt.msu.edu/issues/june2014/chik.pdf

Chun, Dorothy. 2013. "Contributions of Tracking User Behavior to SLA Research."

*In Learner-Computer Interaction in Language Education: A Festschrift in Honor of Robert Fischer*, edited by Phillip Hubbard, Mathias Schulze, and Bryan Smith, 256–262. San Marcos, TX: CALICO.

Cooke-Plagwitz, Jessamine. 2004. "Using the Internet to Train Language Teachers to Use the Internet: A Special Topics Course for Teachers of German." In *Teaching with Technology*, edited by Lara Lomicka and Jessamine Cooke-Plagwitz, 65–71. Boston: Heinle.

Cotos, Elena. 2011. "Potential of Automated Writing Evaluation Feedback." *CALICO Journal*, 28, no. 2: 420–459.

Curtin, Constance, and Stanley Shinall. 1985. "A CAI Workshop from Expectation to Evaluation." *CALICO Journal*, 3, no. 2: 27–37.

Daud, Nuraihan Mat. 1992. "Issues in CALL Implementation and its Implications on Teacher Training." *CALICO Journal*, 10, no. 1: 69–78.

Debski, Robert. 2006. "Theory and Practice in Teaching Project-oriented CALL." In *Teacher Education in CALL*, edited by P. Hubbard and M. Levy, 99–114. Philadelphia: John Benjamins.

Delcloque, Phillippe. 2000. "History of CALL: The History of Computer Assisted Language Learning Web Exhibition." Accessed December 17, 2015. http://www.ict4lt.org/en/History_of_CALL.pdf

Dellicarpini, Margo. 2012. "Action Research: Building Computer Technology Skills in TESOL Teacher Education." *Language Learning & Technology*, 16, no. 2: 14–23.

Dickinson, Marcu, Chris Brew, and Detmar Meurers. 2013. *Language and Computers*. Oxford: Wiley-Blackwell.

Doering, Aaron, and Richard Beach. 2002. "Preservice Teachers Acquiring Literacy Practices Through Technology Tools." *Language, Learning, and Technology*, 6, no. 3: 135–41.

Dooly, Melinda. 2011. "Divergent Perceptions of Telecollaborative Language Learning Tasks: Task-as-work Plan versus Task-as-process." *Language Learning & Technology*, 15, no. 2: 69–91.

Ducate, Lara, and Nike Arnold. 2012. "Computer-mediated Feedback: Effectiveness and Student Perceptions of Screen-casting Software versus the Comment Function." In *Technology across Writing Contexts and Tasks*, edited by G. Kessler, A. Oskoz, and I. Elola, 31–56. San Marcos, TX: CALICO.

Egbert, Joy. 2006. "Learning in Context." In *Teacher Education in CALL*, edited by

P. Hubbard, and M. Levy, 167–181. Amsterdam: John Benjamins.

Egbert, Joy, Elizabeth Hanson-Smith, and Chin Chi Chao. 2007. "Introduction: Foundations for Teaching and Learning." In *CALL Environments: Research, Practice, and Critical Issues*, 2nd ed., edited by J. Egbert and E. Hanson-Smith, 1–18. Alexandria, VA: TESOL.

Egbert, Joy, Trena Paulus, and Yuko Nakamichi. 2002. "The Impact of CALL Instruction on Classroom Computer Use: A Foundation for Rethinking Technology in Teacher Education." *Language Learning and Technology*, 6, no. 3: 108–126.

Elola, Idoia, and Ana Oskoz. 2010. "Collaborative Writing: Fostering Foreign Language and Writing Conventions Development." *Language Learning & Technology*, 14, no. 3: 51–71. Accessed January 4, 2017. http://llt.msu.edu/issues/october2010/elolaoskoz.pdf

Ferris, Dana. 2004. "The 'Grammar Correction' Debate in L2 writing: Where Are We, and Where Do We Go from Here? (And what do we do in the meantime?)." *Journal of Second Language Writing*, 13, no. 1: 49–62.

Ferris, Dana. 2006. "Does Error Feedback Help Student Writers? New Evidence on the Short- and Long-term Effects of Written Error Correction." In *Feedback in Second Language Writing*, edited by K. Hyland, and F. Hyland, 81–104. Cambridge: Cambridge University Press.

Ferris, Dana. 2010. "Second Language Writing Research and Written Corrective Feedback in SLA." *Studies in Second Language Acquisition*, 32, no. 2: 181–201.

Ferris, Dana. 2012. "Technology and Corrective Feedback for L2 Writers: Principles, Practices, and Problems." In *Technology Across Writing Contexts and Tasks*, edited by G. Kessler, A. Oskoz, and I. Elola, 7–29. San Marcos, TX: CALICO Monograph Series.

Fischer, Robert. 2007. "How do We Know What Learners are Actually Doing? Monitoring Learners' Behavior in CALL." *Computer Assisted Language Learning*, 20, no. 5: 409–442.

Gee, James, Paul and Elisabeth. R. Hayes. 2011. *Language and Learning in the Digital Age*. London: Routledge.

González, Dafne. 2008. "Using Synchronous Communication Collaboratively in ESP." In *Learning Languages Through Technology*, edited by E. Hanson-Smith and S. Rilling, 11–24. Alexandria, VA: TESOL.

Guichon, Nicolas, and Mirjam Hauck. 2011. "Editorial – Teacher Education Research in CALL and CMC: More in Demand than Ever." *ReCALL*, 23, no. 3: 187–199.

Hanson-Smith, Elizabeth. 2006. "Communities of Practice for Pre- and In-service Teacher Education." In *Teacher Education in CALL*, edited by P. Hubbard and M. Levy, 301–315. Amsterdam: John Benjamins.

Healey, Deborah, Elizabeth Hanson-Smith, Phillip Hubbard, Sophie Ioannou-Georgiou, Greg Kessler, Greg, and Paige Ware. 2011. *TESOL Technology Standards: Description, Implementation, Integration*. Alexandria, VA: TESOL Publications.

Hegelheimer, Volker. 2006: "When the Technology Course is Required." In *Teacher Education in CALL*, edited by M. Levy and P. Hubbard, 117–133. Philadelphia: John Benjamins.

Hubbard, Phillip. 2008. "CALL and the Future of Language Teacher Education." *CALICO Journal*, 25, no. 2: 175–188.

Hubbard, Phillip. 2013. "Making a Case for Learner Training in Technology Enhanced Language Learning Environments." *CALICO Journal*, 30, no. 2: 163–178.

Hubbard, Phillip, and Mike Levy, eds. 2006a. *Teacher Education in CALL*. Amsterdam: John Benjamins.

Hubbard, Phillip, and Mike Levy. 2006b. "The Scope of CALL Education." In *Teacher Education in CALL*, edited by P. Hubbard and M. Levy, 3–21. Amsterdam: John Benjamins.

IATEFL. 1984. "MUESLI News, 1" Accessed January 4, 2017. http://ltsig.iatefl.org/wp-content/uploads/mn8410.pdf

Kassen, M. A., R. Z. Lavine, K. Murphy-Judy, and Peters, M. (2007). *Preparing and Developing Technology-proficient L2 Teachers*, 23–48. San Marcos, TX: CALICO.

Kessler, Greg. 2006. "Assessing CALL Teacher Training: What Are We Doing and What Could We Do Better?" In *Teacher Education in CALL*, edited by P. Hubbard and M. Levy, 23–24. Amsterdam: John Benjamins.

Kessler, Greg. 2007. "Formal and Informal CALL Preparation and Teacher Attitude toward Technology." *Computer Assisted Language Learning*, 20, no. 2: 173–188.

Kessler, Greg. 2009. "Student Initiated Attention to Form in Autonomous Wiki Based Collaborative Writing." *Language Learning and Technology*, 13, no. 1, 79–95. Accessed January 9, 2017 from http://llt.msu.edu/vol13num1/kessler.pdf

Kessler, Greg. 2010. "When They Talk About CALL: Discourse in a Required CALL Class." *CALICO Journal*, 27, no. 2: 1–17.

Kessler, Greg. 2012. "Language Teacher Training in Technology." In *The Encyclopedia of Applied Linguistics*, edited by Carol A. Chapelle. Oxford: Wiley-Blackwell.

Kessler, Greg. 2013. "Collaborative Language Learning in Co-constructed Participatory Culture." *CALICO Journal*, 30, no. 3: 307–322.

Kessler, Greg, Dawn Bikowski, and Jordan Boggs. 2012. "Collaborative Writing among Second Language Learners in Academic Web-based Projects." *Language Learning and Technology*, 16, no. 1: 91–109.

Kessler, Greg, and Lia Plakans. 2008. "Does Teachers' Confidence with CALL Equal Innovative and Integrated Use?" *Computer Assisted Language Learning*, 21, no. 3: 269–282.

Koet, Ton. 1999. "ICT and Language Skills: An Integrated Course." *ReCALL*, 11, no. 1: 65–71.

Kolaitis, M., M. A. Mahoney, H. Pomann, and P. Hubbard. 2006. "Training Ourselves to Train our Students for CALL." In *Teacher Education in CALL*, edited by P. Hubbard and M. Levy, 317–332. Philadelphia: John Benjamins Publishing Company.

Lave, Jean, and Etienne Wenger. 1991. Situated learning: Legitimate peripheral participation. New York: Cambridge University Press.

Levy, Mike, and Glen Stockwell. 2006. *CALL Dimensions: Options and Issues in Computer Assisted Language Learning*. Mahwah, NJ: Lawrence Erlbaum.

Link, S., A. Dursun, K. Karakaya, and V. Hegelheimer. 2014. "Towards Better ESL Practices for Implementing Automated Writing Evaluation." *CALICO Journal*, 31, no. 3: 323–344.

Lomicka, Lara, and Jessamine Cooke-Plagwitz. 2004. *Teaching with Technology*. Boston: Heinle.

Lord, G., and L. L. Lomicka. 2004. "Developing Collaborative Cyber Communities to Prepare Tomorrow's Teachers." *Foreign Language Annals*, 37, no. 3: 401–417.

Lund, Andreas. 2008. "Wikis: A Collective Approach to Language Learning." ReCALL 20, no. 1: 35–54.

Matsumura, S., and G. Hann. 2004. "Computer Anxiety and Students' Preferred Feedback Methods in EFL Writing." *The Modern Language Journal*, 88, no. 3: 403–415.

Meskill, Carla., ed. 2013. *Online Teaching and Learning: Sociocultural Perspectives*. New York: Bloomsbury Academic Press.

Meskill, Carla, and Natasha Anthony. 2010. *Teaching Languages Online*. Bristol: Multilingual Matters.

Meskill, Carla, Natasha Anthony, Shannon Hilliker-VanStrander, Chi-Hua Tseng, and Jieun You. 2006. "Expert-novice Teacher Mentoring in Language Learning Technology." In *Teacher Education in CALL*, edited by P. Hubbard and M. Levy, 283–299. Amsterdam: John Benjamins.

Meskill, Carla, Jonathan Mossop, Stephen DiAngelo, and Rosalie K. Pasquale. 2002. "Expert and Novice Teachers Talking Technology: Precepts, Concepts, and Misconcepts." *Language Learning and Technology*, 6, no. 3: 46–57.

Meunier, Lydie. 1997. "Personality and Motivational Factors in Computer-mediated Foreign Language Communication (CMFLC)." Unpublished manuscript, University of Tulsa.

Motteram, Gary. 2009. "Social Computing and Language Teacher Education: An Agenda for Course Development." *Innovation in Language Learning and Teaching*, 3, no. 1: 83–97.

Ohio University. 1983. "Ohio University Bulletin: Graduate Catalog." Accessed December 17, 2015. https://archive.org/stream/ ohiogradbulletin1983ohio#page/105

Oxford, Rebecca, and Sei-Hwa Jung. 2007. "National Guidelines for Technology Integration in TESOL Programs: Factors Affecting (Non)implementation." In *Preparing and Developing Technology-proficient L2 Teachers*, edited by M. Kassen, R. Lavine, K. Murphy-Judy, and M. Peters, 51–66. San Marcos, TX: CALICO.

Partridge, John. 2006. "Matching Language and IT Skills: The Life Cycle of an MA Programme." In *Teacher Education in CALL*, edited by P. Hubbard and M. Levy, 63–79. Amsterdam: John Benjamins.

Peters, Martine. 2006. "Developing Computer Competencies for Pre-service Language Teachers: Is One Course enough?" In *Teacher Education in CALL*, edited by P. Hubbard and M. Levy, 153–165. Amsterdam: John Benjamins.

Reinders, Hayo, and Phillip Hubbard. 2013. "CALL and Learner Autonomy: Affordances and Constraints." In *Contemporary Computer Assisted Language Learning*, edited by M. Thomas, H. Reinders, and M. Warschauer. London: Continuum Books.

Reinders, Hayo., and Sorada Wattana. 2014. "Can I Say Something? The Effects of Digital Game Play on Willingness to Communicate." *Language Learning and Technology*, 18, no. 2: 101–123.

Shermis, Mark D., and Jill Burstein, eds. 2013. *Handbook of Automated Essay Evaluation*. New York: Routledge.

Slaouti, Diane, and Gary Motteram. 2006. "Reconstructing Practice: Language Teacher Education and ICT." In *Teacher education in CALL*, edited by P. Hubbard and M. Levy, 81–97. Amsterdam: John Benjamins.

Stockwell, Glen. 2008. "Investigating Learner Preparedness for and Usage Patterns of Mobile Learning." *ReCALL*, 20, no. 3: 253–270.

Storch, Neomy. 2005. "Collaborative Writing: Product, Process, and Students' Reflections." *Journal of Second Language Writing*. 14, 153–173. DOI:10.1016/j.jslw.2005.05.002

Sun, Yuh Chih, and Yuh Jung Chang. 2012. "Blogging to Learn: Becoming EFL Academic Writers through Collaborative Dialogues." *Language Learning and Technology*, 16, no. 1: 43–61.

Suvorov, Ruslov, and Volker Hegelheimer. 2013. "Computer-Assisted Language Testing." In *The Companion to Language Assessment*, edited by Anthony John Kunnan, 594–613. Hoboken, NJ: John Wiley and Sons, Inc.

Sykes, Julie, and Jonathan Reinhardt. 2013. *Language at Play: Digital Games in Second and Foreign Language Teaching and Learning*. New York: Pearson.

TESOL. 2008. TESOL Technology Standards Framework. Accessed, May 26, 2016. http:// www.tesol.org/docs/books/bk_ technologystandards_framework_721.pdf

Ushioda, Ema. 2013. "Motivation Matters in Mobile Language Learning: A Brief Commentary." Language Learning and Technology, 17, no. 3: 1–5. Accessed January 4, 2017. http://llt.msu.edu/issues/october2013/ commentary.pdf

Van Olphen, Marcela. 2007. "Perspectives of Foreign Language Preservice Teachers on the Use of a Web-based Instructional Environment in a Methods Course." *CALICO Journal*, 25, no. 1: 91–109.

Ware, Paige, and Greg Kessler. 2013. "CALL and Digital Feedback." In *Contemporary Studies in Linguistics: Contemporary Computer-Assisted Language Learning*, edited by M. Thomas, H. Reinders, and M. Warschauer, 323–339. London: Continuum

Warschauer, Mark. 1996. "Motivational Aspects of Using Computers for Writing and Communication." In *Telecommunication in Foreign Language Learning*, edited by Mark Warschauer, 29–46. Honolulu, HI: Lawrence Erlbaum.

Warschauer, Mark. 2005. "Sociocultural Perspectives on CALL." In *CALL Research Perspectives*, edited by Joy Egbert and Gina Marie Petrie, 41–51. Mahwah, NJ: Lawrence.

Warschauer, Mark, and Grimes, Douglas. 2008. "Automated Writing Assessment in the Classroom." *Pedagogies*, 3, no. 1: 52–67.

White, Cynthia, and Hayo Reinders. 2009. *"Editorial [for the special issue]." Innovation in Language Learning and Teaching*, 3, no. 1: 1–2.

Winke, Paula, and Senta Goertler. 2008. "Did We Forget Someone? Students' Computer Access and Literacy for CALL." *CALICO Journal*, 25, no. 3: 482–509.

# 20 Integrating Assessment with Instruction through Technology

## JOAN JAMIESON AND MATTEO MUSUMECI

Technology has expanded the options for assessing students' learning by providing the means for delivering, scoring, reporting, and collecting data. Indeed, technology-based assessments have become an expected component by individual adults using online language programs and by college students using introductory language textbooks with online resources. Learners' understanding of the language that has been explained and practiced is assessed by these low-stakes online assessments. The degree to which they reflect best practices, or more specifically, principles of assessment design, is reviewed in this chapter.

## Low-stakes assessment design

In the context of language assessment, *stakes* refers to the degree to which the test result, or score, affects someone's life. Low-stakes means that there is little, if any, chance that the language test score will have serious or life-changing consequences (Davies et al. 1999; cf., Kunnan 2013). The assessments that accompany online materials are low-stakes. These low-stakes assessments are primarily used to gauge readiness, to inform placement in a sequence of lessons, or to measure achievement. Any decision taken can be changed with relative ease; still, effort should be made to ensure the quality of these assessments.

A fundamental starting place for designing low-stakes assessments is to determine whether the material a learner sees on a test matches the content and outcomes in the language program (Glaser 1963; Miller, Linn, and Gronlund 2012). For low-stakes assessments to be effective in learning, the learner should be given the opportunity to perceive whether a gap exists between his or her present state and a particular learning outcome. Often, a student responds to a question or a learning activity, and the perception of this gap is a result of feedback. Feedback can be any of numerous signals that focus the learner's attention on a target, such as a recast from a teacher or an incorrect response message from a computer program (Colby-Kelly and Turner 2007; Hill and McNamara 2011; Kulik and Kulik 1988). Finally, the learner should be given information to close that gap if misunderstanding exists, or to move on to more challenging material if the content is understood (Assessment Reform Group 2002; Black and Wiliam 1998; Fulcher 2010). Teacher recommendations, score reports, and suggestions for further study are actions that help learners close the gap or move on (Bangert-Drowns et al. 1991; Stiggins and Chappuis 2005; Wall 2013). Taken together, the

*The Handbook of Technology and Second Language Teaching and Learning*, First Edition.
Edited by Carol A. Chapelle and Shannon Sauro.
© 2017 John Wiley & Sons, Inc. Published 2020 by John Wiley & Sons, Inc.

content match, the opportunity to notice a gap, and suggestions for improvement are seen as core principles for low-stakes assessment design.

These three principles framed the description below of two types of online language assessments: those for online language-learning programs and those for popular university language textbooks. The methods used to conduct this review for both types of materials consisted of four steps. First, the content of one introductory unit (usually Unit 3) was examined for linguistic abilities (i.e., phonology, vocabulary, and grammar), language skills (i.e., listening reading, speaking, and writing), and context (i.e., culture and theme) as these features were found in all materials reviewed. A coding sheet was filled in by the reviewer. Second, the associated assessment was also examined (and the coding sheet updated) to determine a degree of match between the content of the learning material and the content of the assessment. We individually and subjectively considered the content match as adequate (about 75% the same), lacking, or missing. Third, to determine whether the types of questions and responses could help learners to notice their gaps, we coded the feedback learners received according to time and type. Time was coded as immediate or delayed. Type was coded as to whether (1) diacritical errors were explained; (2) students were told each answer was correct or incorrect; (3) correct answers were elaborated; (4) incorrect answers were explained; or (5) teacher comments were able to be provided. Fourth, to determine whether the information received in the score reports could be helpful to close these gaps, we coded who received the score report (i.e., student, teacher, or both) and the type of information they received. The type of information was coded as (1) percent correct overall; (2) breakdown of mistakes; (3) percent or number correct by different content areas; (4) teacher comments; and (5) recommendations for students.

In sum, we reviewed the content in online language-learning programs and textbooks, and compared it to the content coverage in their assessments. We reviewed whether the feedback could help learners to perceive their gaps and whether the information both students and teachers received in the form of score reports could be helpful to close these gaps. Because actual outcomes were not examined, feedback and score reports were used as proxies, assuming that information about errors and detailed information about progress could be beneficial to language learning. This review, conducted in 2014–2015 on materials in the U.S. market, illustrates how assessment principles can be used in the evaluation of language-learning materials.

## Language-learning programs' online assessments

Twelve online language-learning programs were selected for review to include a variety of contemporary online language-learning materials. The sample represented both relatively new programs and those that had been available for over 20 years. They had all achieved some national professional recognition by being reviewed in language-learning journals such as *CALICO* and *Language Learning and Technology*, or other venues such as www.languagesoftware.net and www.pcmag.com. They were primarily self-contained, interactive, online programs that were intended to be used alone or with a teacher who acted as facilitator/coach. Both free and paid programs were included in the sample. Re-purposed older audio files such as Berlitz and Pimsleur language programs were not included.

The 12 online language programs reviewed in this chapter are shown in Table 20.1 to indicate the range of languages available in this format. Checks (√) in the cells indicate the languages offered by each program. Most of the programs offered many different languages with the exception of DynEd's *New Dynamic English* and *Pearson English Interactive*[1] (hereafter, *PEI*), each of which covered only one language, English. For all of the other programs, the design, displays, activities, feedback, and score reports are assumed the same for all of the languages

**Table 20.1** Range of languages covered in learning programs.

| Program | Arabic | Chinese | Dari | Dutch | English | Finnish | French | German | Greek | Hebrew | Indonesian | Irish-Gaelic | Italian | Japanese | Korean | Latin | Pashto | Persian | Polish | Portuguese | Russian | Spanish | Swahili | Swedish | Tagalog | Turkish | Urdu | Vietnamese |
|---|---|---|---|---|---|---|---|---|---|---|---|---|---|---|---|---|---|---|---|---|---|---|---|---|---|---|---|---|
| Transparent Language's Byki Express* | √ | √ | √ | √ | √ |  | √ | √ | √ | √ | √ | √ | √ | √ | √ | √ | √ | √ | √ | √ | √ | √ | √ | √ | √ | √ | √ | √ |
| Duolingo* | √ | √ | √ | √ | √ |  |  | √ | √ | √ | √ | √ | √ | √ | √ | √ | √ | √ | √ | √ | √ | √ | √ |  | √ | √ | √ | √ |
| DynEd, New Dynamic English |  |  |  |  | √ |  |  |  |  |  |  |  |  |  |  |  |  |  |  |  |  |  |  |  |  |  |  |  |
| Fluenz |  |  |  |  |  | √ |  |  |  |  |  |  |  |  |  |  |  |  |  |  |  |  |  |  |  |  |  |  |
| Rosetta Stone's Foundations* | √ | √ | √ | √ | √ |  | √ | √ | √ | √ | √ | √ | √ | √ | √ | √ | √ | √ | √ | √ | √ | √ | √ | √ | √ | √ | √ | √ |
| LingQ* | √ | √ |  |  |  |  | √ | √ |  | √ |  |  | √ | √ | √ | √ |  |  |  | √ | √ | √ |  |  |  | √ |  |  |
| Rosetta Stone's Livemocha* | √ | √ |  |  | √ |  | √ | √ |  | √ |  |  | √ | √ | √ |  |  |  |  | √ | √ | √ |  |  |  | √ |  |  |
| Mango | √ | √ | √ | √ | √ | √ | √ | √ | √ | √ | √ | √ | √ | √ | √ |  | √ | √ | √ | √ | √ | √ | √ | √ | √ | √ | √ | √ |
| Memrise* | √ | √ | √ | √ | √ | √ | √ | √ | √ | √ | √ | √ | √ | √ | √ | √ | √ | √ | √ | √ | √ | √ | √ | √ | √ | √ | √ | √ |
| Pearson English Interactive |  | √ |  |  | √ | √ | √ | √ |  |  |  |  | √ | √ | √ |  |  |  |  | √ | √ | √ |  |  |  |  | √ |  |
| Rocket Languages | √ | √ | √ | √ | √ |  | √ | √ | √ | √ | √ | √ | √ | √ | √ |  | √ | √ | √ | √ | √ | √ | √ | √ | √ | √ | √ | √ |
| Transparent Language Online* | √ | √ |  |  | √ | √ | √ | √ | √ |  |  |  | √ | √ | √ | √ |  | √ |  | √ | √ | √ |  |  |  | √ | √ | √ |

*Notes:* Checks (√) indicate the languages offered; *more languages available than listed.

produced by the same company, although images may differ (e.g., Rosetta Stone's *Foundations for Higher Education*; personal communication, J. Marmorstein, September, 2014).

Some of the programs were published in more than one version. Several programs had free versions of their fuller, paid versions. We reviewed free versions of *Byki Express, Duolingo, LingQ, Livemocha, Memrise,* and *Transparent Language Online*. Some programs had different versions for personal use and institutional use. *Fluenz* had programs only for personal use. Generally, the institutional versions had student versions along with administrator/teacher views, which were accessed through learning management systems (LMS); these were used to schedule lessons and assessments for students and to keep track of student performance data. We reviewed the student version of *Foundations* and the personal version of *Rocket Languages*. *PEI* and *New Dynamic English,* including its *Records Manager*, only had institutional versions.

The review of each program was carried out following the four steps described above.

## Content in online language-learning programs

To compare these programs, we selected introductory material usually in the third chapter or unit. Either French or English lessons were examined, based on the reviewer's knowledge. The language content of each program was checked to see if context, language abilities, and skills were included (Table 20.2).

The content differed somewhat across programs. Table 20.2 reveals that *Fluenz, PEI, Rocket Languages,* and *Transparent Language Online* covered the widest range, whereas *Byki Express, LingQ,* and *Memrise* covered the narrowest range. All of the programs had sections on vocabulary and listening, and included reading of directions, words, phrases, and sentences. All of the programs except *Byki Express* and *LingQ* covered grammar. All of the programs presented their lessons thematically, including topics such as introductions, at home and work, and ordering at a restaurant, except for *LingQ* and *Memrise*. *Mango, PEI,* and *Rocket* also explicitly addressed culture (*Memrise* was a collection of lessons made by users; some lessons not reviewed included cultural and thematic topics).

Many of the programs included sections on pronunciation and speaking. We distinguished pronunciation, which focused on segmentals and suprasegmentals, from speaking, which addressed discourse. *Mango* and *PEI* explicitly included pronunciation instruction. *New Dynamic English, PEI, Livemocha, Rocket Languages,* and *Transparent Language Online* had students compare their voices to a model. *Duolingo, New Dynamic English, Fluenz, Foundations,* and *Mango* used speech recognition software to determine the correctness of the students' responses. The majority of the programs included writing through simple activities in translation and dictation, namely *Byki Express, Duolingo, Fluenz, LingQ, Memrise, Rocket Languages,* and *Transparent Language Online*. *Livemocha, LingQ,* and *PEI* provided an option to submit written and spoken responses to either the teacher/tutor or to community members.

## Content coverage in assessments for language-learning programs

The low-stakes assessment components in these online language programs included pre-tests and achievement tests. Placement tests and readiness tests were pre-tests intended to be used by learners before instruction, whereas review quizzes and unit/module tests were achievement tests intended to be used after instruction (Table 20.3).

The scope of placement tests was over a broad range of content, as opposed to readiness tests which covered a more narrow range of content. *New Dynamic English, PEI,* and *Transparent Language Online* had placement tests. These tests covered a wide range of vocabulary and grammatical structures. *New Dynamic English* and *PEI* included listening, whereas the test for *Transparent Language Online* covered reading; all used multiple-choice items.

**Table 20.2** Language content coverage in an introductory lesson of online programs.

| | | Byki Express | Duolingo | New Dynamic English | Fluenz | Foundations | LingQ | Livemocha | Mango | Memrise | Pearson English Interactive (PEI) | Rocket Languages | Transparent Language Online |
|---|---|---|---|---|---|---|---|---|---|---|---|---|---|
| Context | Culture | n/a | n/a | n/a | n/a | n/a | n/a | * | √ | n/a | √ | √ | * |
| | Theme-based | √ | √ | √ | √ | √ | n/a | √ | √ | n/a | √ | √ | √ |
| Abilities | Grammar | n/a | √ | √ | √ | √ | n/a | √ | √ | √ | √ | √ | √ |
| | Pronunciation | n/a | n/a | √ | √ | n/a | n/a | n/a | n/a | n/a | √ | n/a | n/a |
| | Vocabulary | √ | √ | √ | √ | √ | √ | √ | √ | √ | √ | √ | √ |
| Skills | Listening | √ | √ | √ | √ | √ | √ | √ | √ | √ | √ | √ | √ |
| | Reading | √ | √ | √ | √ | √ | √ | √ | √ | √ | √ | √ | √ |
| | Speaking | n/a | √ | √ | √ | √ | n/a | √ | √ | n/a | √ | √ | √ |
| | Writing | √ | √ | n/a | √ | n/a | n/a | √ | n/a | √ | √ | √ | √ |

Notes: Checks (√) indicate the content covered; *cultural awareness activities available in some languages.

**Table 20.3**    Types of assessments in online language programs.

| Online program | Pre-tests | | Achievement tests | |
|---|---|---|---|---|
| | Placement test | Readiness test | Review quizzes | Unit/Module tests |
| Byki Express | | | | |
| Duolingo | | √ | | |
| New Dynamic English | √ | | √ | √ |
| Fluenz | | | √ | |
| Foundations | * | | √ | √ |
| LingQ | | | | |
| Livemocha | | | √ | |
| Pearson English Interactive (PEI) | √ | | √ | √ |
| Mango | | | √ | |
| Memrise | | | | |
| Rocket Language | | | √ | √ |
| Transparent Language Online | √ | | | √ |

*Note:* * placement test under revision; will be re-released in late 2015 (Robin Stevens, email message to author, January 12, 2015).

*Duolingo* offered learners the option to take a readiness test to "test out" of one lesson and another option to test out of a set of five or ten lessons.

The scope of the achievement tests was within a unit or across several units. Review quizzes were generally interspersed in a lesson or covered one part of a unit. Seven of the language programs had various types of review quizzes. The spacing of the quiz within an instructional unit varied somewhat. *Livemocha* included a quiz on usage and vocabulary as the fourth activity in each lesson. *Rocket Languages* had short teaching and testing options available for each part of each lesson. *Fluenz, Mango,* and *Foundations* provided students with review quizzes after several parts of a lesson. *New Dynamic English* and *PEI* had quizzes available on specific parts of the lesson, and were made available (and subsequently locked) to students through the LMS programs.

Unit tests were usually at the end of a unit or a group of units (i.e., a module) and generally gave scores. *New Dynamic English, PEI, Foundations, Rocket Languages,* and *Transparent Language Online* had tests at the end of each unit or a module that covered the material presented in several lessons. The first two programs "locked" the availability to repeat through their LMS programs. *Foundations, Rocket Languages,* and *Transparent Language Online* had tests after several lessons in a unit. Students could take unit tests in these programs as many times as desired. In *Rocket Languages,* once a score of 80% was achieved, students were emailed a certificate.

The placement, readiness, and review quiz assessments generally covered the abilities and skills introduced in the lesson and used items from the lessons. For the end-of-unit types of tests, *New Dynamic English, Rocket Languages,* and *Transparent Language Online* adequately covered the content in the unit. *PEI's* quizzes and tests did not include speaking or writing. *Foundations* had the least overall content coverage, but was perhaps the most innovative of the assessments. In the "Milestone" test at the end of a unit, a role-play dialogue included some of the unit's content. In the assessment depicted in Figure 20.1, pictures of people on a bus were shown, and then the learner read and heard exchanges of "Hello." The girl said, "What is your name?" A man replied, "My name is Paulo Lima." The learner then saw the

**Figure 20.1** Screen shot of Milestone quiz. Source: Rosetta Stone's *Foundations for Higher Education*, November, 2014. © 2016 Rosetta Stone. All rights reserved.

screen below and was expected to say, "What is your name?" This assessment used speech recognition software to judge the correctness of the student's utterance.

Five programs did not include any quizzes or tests, other than the immediate feedback given after answering each item in the lesson. Tests were not available on the free version of *Byki Express*. *Duolingo* and *LingQ* kept track of performance while students were completing activities, but had no quiz functions. For example, *LingQ* did track the user's vocabulary growth over time, which was used to help identify appropriate lessons, but we did not consider this as either a pretest or an achievement test. *Memrise* had quiz-like activities after learners practiced a set of words and again after returning to the program; this function was claimed to be more limited in the free version that was reviewed than in the paid version.

The item types used to assess the content in the quizzes and tests for all language-learning programs were quite similar. Because introductory lessons were chosen for review, almost all of the quizzes and tests focused on language at the word, phrase, or sentence level. The majority of the vocabulary or grammar items were selected-response. In all the programs, besides reading directions, listening was the major skill included. Listening was often tested with multiple-choice items that looked different from the traditional four-option items: one could click on an area of the screen or drag and drop an object to answer an item. For example, in a listening/vocabulary/grammar item from *New Dynamic English*, a student saw a diagram of streets with pictures of buildings and heard, "What is located behind the Art Museum?" The student needed to click on the correct building.

Many assessments included production of written and spoken responses. Frequently, students typed what they heard spoken in the target language, as in a dictation. A student heard an utterance and had to type it correctly. The response was evaluated by matching the student's response with a predetermined correct answer.

In translation items, students either read on the screen or heard an expression in the first language, and then typed the L2 equivalent. For speaking, many programs used student self-comparison to a model to judge correctness of their spoken responses. In addition to self-assessment, *New Dynamic English*, *Fluenz*, and *Foundations* used speech recognition software to judge the correctness of the student's speech. Both *Rocket Languages* and *Foundations* had options in which students could adjust the model. *Rocket Languages* let learners adjust the speech they heard, whereas *Foundations* let learners set the tolerance level, ranging from easiest to native speaker, against which their responses were scored as correct or incorrect. *PEI* provided an option to send spoken and written responses to the teacher.

Overall, there was a very close match between the content in the lessons and the material covered in the pre-tests and the achievement tests; many of the items, though not all, were the same as those in the lessons. The two exceptions were the placement test items for *New Dynamic English* and *PEI*; those tests included some other items as they were used to place students into one of several language-learning programs developed by DynEd and Pearson, respectively.

## Perception of the gap in language-learning programs' assessments

Feedback was considered by time and type. The programs that had placement and readiness tests gave delayed feedback; that is, students answered one question and then moved to the next, without knowing if the answer was correct or incorrect. Knowledge of one's performance came after all questions had been answered. In contrast, most review quizzes gave learners immediate feedback; that is, the student was told after answering each item if the answer was correct or incorrect. This was the case in *Fluenz*, *Foundations*, *Mango*, and *New Dynamic English*. *PEI* and *Rocket Languages* gave delayed feedback after a set of items was answered. In the unit tests, *New Dynamic English* and *Foundations* gave immediate feedback, whereas *PEI* and *Transparent Language Online* had delayed feedback.

The feedback in these assessments gave students the opportunity to notice the gaps in their knowledge. In the programs with delayed feedback, only *PEI* gave students an opportunity to see whether their answers to each item were correct or incorrect. In the programs with immediate feedback, students' wrong answers were indicated by a sound, a voice saying "No," or by having the prompt remain instead of moving to the next item. After one or two wrong answers, the program would go on to the next item. (Scores were automatically adjusted for a correct response on the second attempt in both *New Dynamic English* and *Foundations*.) *New Dynamic English* rephrased or elaborated correct responses. For example, if the question asked, "Who is the teacher?" and the student responded correctly, the student would hear, "That's right. Richard teaches science and math." *Rocket Languages* showed the correct answer, after which learners were asked to rate the difficulty of the item.

## Closing the gap in language-learning programs' assessments

Students were able to see a summary of their performance in over 80% of the programs. However, two programs, *Fluenz* and *Mango*, recorded no scores. Teachers were able to see score reports in only two programs, *New Dynamic English* and *PEI* through the LMS (as these were the only programs reviewed with an LMS, one could assume that other paid programs which had an LMS, such as *Foundations*, also had this functionality).

The information contained in reports varied. The placement tests for *New Dynamic English*, *PEI*, and *Transparent Language Online* provided students with an overall description of their language proficiency and a recommendation for which lessons to begin with. The readiness tests in *Duolingo* reported a passing score for the lesson(s) covered. For the review quizzes and unit tests, *PEI* provided students with scores on objectives and the

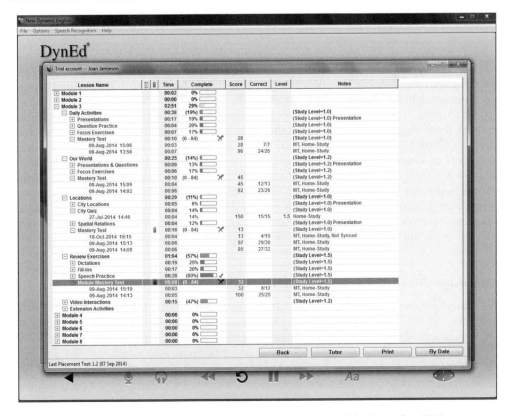

**Figure 20.2**   Performance report. Source: DynEd's *New Dynamic English*, November, 2014.

number of correct items out of the total number of items on each part. *New Dynamic English, PEI, Rocket Languages, Foundations,* and *Transparent Language Online* all provided students with an overall percentage correct score. Figure 20.2 shows a screen shot that a student could see in *New Dynamic English.*

Recommendations to "close the gap" differed across programs. In some programs, students received a score and a message. *Transparent Language Online* set 69% as the passing score. Students were told to congratulate themselves and move on to the next lesson if they passed, but to return to the lesson, practice more, and take the test again if they failed. In *PEI,* students were asked to talk with their teacher or to review the lessons again for those sections of the test on which they did not score well. Students using the review quizzes in *Foundations* were given percentage scores and told that they would be reminded to return to the quiz; reviews were suggested based on students' performance and the time between attempts. There were no recommendations for further study in any program.

Rarely did students receive any other information. One exception was *New Dynamic English,* which offered students feedback and advice on their study behaviors based on individual study habits, frequency of study, length of study, and patterns of mouse clicks (Knowles 2012). Specifically, DynEd provided students with a "study guide" based on past performance when they returned to lessons.

In sum, the assessments for the online language-learning programs contained the same content. However, the information that students received in the form of item-level feedback and summaries of overall performance and recommendations for further study was minimal.

# Thirty-six language textbooks' online assessments

This section describes the low-stakes assessments that accompanied 36 popular academic foreign language texts. To select materials for frequently taught languages, we referred to a Modern Language Association survey (2010) that listed the top ten most studied foreign languages on United States college campuses in order of enrollments: Spanish, French, German, American Sign Language, Italian, Japanese, Chinese, Arabic, Latin, and Russian. We included these languages, but since English was not included in the survey we replaced American Sign Languages with English as a second/foreign language and we added Portuguese as a more modern language (#13 on the list following Ancient Greek and Biblical Hebrew). Eleven languages were examined in total. Six publishers were selected as they distributed textbooks in most of these languages to the foreign language student market: Georgetown University Press, Heinle/Cengage Higher Education, McGraw-Hill Higher Education, Pearson Higher Education, Vista Higher Learning, and Wiley. The textbooks were analyzed using the same four steps as were used with the online materials described above.

## Language textbooks' content coverage

The content analysis of the textbooks for the five most studied languages is shown in Table 20.4. We see that 13 textbooks covered context and all abilities and skills. These language texts were English (*Pathways*), three French (*Espaces, Liaisons, Paroles*), three German (*Kontakte, Sag mal, Treffpunkt*), Italian (*Sentieri*), and five Spanish (*Puntos de partida, ¿Cómo se dice?, Vistas, Unidos, Dicho y hecho*). Eight textbooks covered almost all of the areas but were missing pronunciation, writing, or both. These included two French textbooks, and four Italian and one English (*NorthStar*) and German (*Neue horizonte*). The English text, *Hemispheres*, taught some abilities and skills: themes, grammar, vocabulary, listening, reading, and writing. Finally, one German text, *Lehrbuch der deutschen Grammatik*, was a grammar text.

Table 20.5 displays the content covered for the next six most studied languages in the United States. We see that only two textbooks covered context and all abilities and skills: Arabic (*Al-Kitaab fii taʿallum al-Arabiyaa*, Third Edition, Part 1) and Chinese (*Introductory Chinese Traditional*). Three language titles in Chinese, Japanese, and Russian included only between two and three elements (*Access Chinese, Yookoso!*, and *Nachalo*). The Chinese and Japanese texts covered grammar and vocabulary, while the Russian text included culture, themes, vocabulary, and writing.

In summary, the more frequently studied language textbooks had broader coverage of context, abilities, and skills with the exception of Arabic. The coverage of Chinese, Japanese, and Russian varied by text publisher, with texts from McGraw-Hill (*Access Chinese, Hemispheres, Nachalo*, and *Yookoso*) providing the narrowest coverage.

## Content coverage in comprehensive online assessments

The low-stakes assessments that accompany textbooks came in two types of resources: one type may be considered limited, including webpages that provide abbreviated computer-scored practice; the other type may be considered comprehensive, including online study centers with grade books. The limited resources contained audio and grammar flashcards, web search activities, web link, writing tips, and "ace the test" graded exercises. They did not usually form part of the ongoing cycle of instructional assessment the teacher counted towards the students' course grades. On the other hand, the comprehensive resources provide extensive opportunities for learning. Although both types were identified, only the comprehensive resources are reviewed below.

**Table 20.4** Content coverage by textbooks for 5 most studied U.S. languages.

| Content | | English | | | | French | | | | German | | | | | Italian | | | | | Spanish | | | | |
|---|---|---|---|---|---|---|---|---|---|---|---|---|---|---|---|---|---|---|---|---|---|---|---|---|
| | | Pathways | Hemispheres | North Star | Liaisons | Deux mondes | Points de départ | Espaces | Paroles | Neue horizonte | Kontakte | Treffpunkt | Sag mal | Lehrbuch | Ponti | Prego! | Percorsi | Sentieri | Parliamo italiano | ¿Cómo se dice…? | Puntos de partida | Unidos | Vistas | Dicho y hecho |
| Context | Culture | ✓ | ✓ | n/a | ✓ | ✓ | ✓ | ✓ | ✓ | ✓ | ✓ | ✓ | ✓ | n/a | ✓ | ✓ | ✓ | ✓ | ✓ | ✓ | ✓ | ✓ | ✓ | ✓ |
| | Theme-based | ✓ | ✓ | ✓ | ✓ | ✓ | ✓ | ✓ | ✓ | ✓ | ✓ | ✓ | ✓ | n/a | ✓ | ✓ | ✓ | ✓ | ✓ | ✓ | ✓ | ✓ | ✓ | ✓ |
| Abilities | Grammar | ✓ | ✓ | ✓ | ✓ | ✓ | ✓ | ✓ | ✓ | ✓ | ✓ | ✓ | ✓ | ✓ | ✓ | ✓ | ✓ | ✓ | ✓ | ✓ | ✓ | ✓ | ✓ | ✓ |
| | Pronunciation | ✓ | n/a | n/a | ✓ | n/a | ✓ | ✓ | ✓ | n/a | ✓ | ✓ | ✓ | n/a | ✓ | ✓ | n/a | n/a | n/a | ✓ | ✓ | ✓ | ✓ | ✓ |
| | Vocabulary | ✓ | ✓ | ✓ | ✓ | ✓ | ✓ | ✓ | ✓ | ✓ | ✓ | ✓ | ✓ | n/a | ✓ | ✓ | ✓ | ✓ | ✓ | ✓ | ✓ | ✓ | ✓ | ✓ |
| Skills | Listening | ✓ | ✓ | ✓ | ✓ | ✓ | ✓ | ✓ | ✓ | ✓ | ✓ | ✓ | ✓ | n/a | ✓ | ✓ | ✓ | ✓ | ✓ | ✓ | ✓ | ✓ | ✓ | ✓ |
| | Reading | ✓ | ✓ | ✓ | ✓ | ✓ | ✓ | ✓ | ✓ | ✓ | ✓ | ✓ | ✓ | n/a | ✓ | ✓ | ✓ | ✓ | ✓ | ✓ | ✓ | ✓ | ✓ | ✓ |
| | Speaking | ✓ | n/a | n/a | ✓ | ✓ | n/a | ✓ | ✓ | ✓ | ✓ | ✓ | ✓ | n/a | ✓ | ✓ | ✓ | n/a | ✓ | ✓ | ✓ | ✓ | ✓ | ✓ |
| | Writing | ✓ | ✓ | ✓ | ✓ | ✓ | n/a | ✓ | ✓ | ✓ | ✓ | ✓ | ✓ | n/a | ✓ | ✓ | ✓ | ✓ | ✓ | ✓ | ✓ | ✓ | ✓ | ✓ |

*Note:* Checks (√) indicate the content covered.

**Table 20.5** Content coverage by textbooks for most studied U.S. languages after top 5.

| Skill and ability | | Arabic | Chinese | | | | Japanese | | Latin | Portuguese | | Russian | | |
|---|---|---|---|---|---|---|---|---|---|---|---|---|---|---|
| | | Al-Kitaab fii taʿallum al-ʿArabiyya | Working Mandarin | Introductory Chinese | Access Chinese | Chinese Link | Nakama 1 | Yookoso! | Disce! | Working Portuguese | Ponto de encontro | Nachalo | Golosa | Troika |
| Context | Culture | ✓ | ✓ | ✓ | n/a | n/a | ✓ | n/a | ✓ | ✓ | ✓ | ✓ | ✓ | ✓ |
| | Theme-based | ✓ | ✓ | ✓ | n/a | n/a | ✓ | n/a | ✓ | ✓ | ✓ | ✓ | ✓ | ✓ |
| Abilities | Grammar | ✓ | ✓ | ✓ | ✓ | ✓ | ✓ | ✓ | ✓ | ✓ | ✓ | n/a | ✓ | n/a |
| | Pronunciation | ✓ | ✓ | ✓ | n/a | n/a | n/a | n/a | n/a | n/a | n/a | n/a | ✓ | n/a |
| | Vocabulary | ✓ | ✓ | ✓ | ✓ | ✓ | ✓ | ✓ | ✓ | ✓ | ✓ | ✓ | ✓ | ✓ |
| Skills | Listening | ✓ | ✓ | ✓ | n/a | ✓ | ✓ | n/a | ✓ | n/a | ✓ | n/a | ✓ | n/a |
| | Reading | ✓ | ✓ | ✓ | n/a | ✓ | ✓ | n/a | ✓ | n/a | ✓ | n/a | ✓ | n/a |
| | Speaking | ✓ | ✓ | ✓ | n/a | n/a | ✓ | n/a | ✓ | ✓ | ✓ | n/a | ✓ | ✓ |
| | Writing | n/a | n/a | ✓ | n/a | ✓ | n/a | n/a | ✓ | ✓ | ✓ | ✓ | n/a (until Ch. 5) | n/a |

*Note:* Checks (√) indicate the content covered.

Of the 36 texts examined, 33 had comprehensive online resources. Three of Wiley's titles in *Lehrbuch der deutschen Grammatik*, *Parliamo italiano!*, and *Troika* only included more limited resources. Of the remaining 33 texts, five did not have accompanying online comprehensive assessment options: Pearson's *Points de départ* and McGraw-Hill's *Access Chinese*, *Hemispheres*, *Nachalo*, and *Yookoso*. The different comprehensive resources that publishers used for the remaining 28 titles are shown in Table 20.6, which lists textbook publishers, the names of their technology platform, the languages and their corresponding textbooks, and the web addresses of those resources, where these programs can be browsed.

Our analysis showed that every comprehensive assessment program fully covered the material contained in its corresponding print textbook, which was outlined earlier in Tables 20.4 and 20.5. That said, each did vary somewhat. Vista's *Supersite* (2012) included the largest variety of assessment resources and provided the most instructional resources. Next, *Quia*, *iLrn*, *MyELT*, and *CENTRO* all were able to completely support a course by providing all the essential assessments and in-class ancillary materials. The two programs powered by *Quia*—namely, *CENTRO* and *iLrn*—contained a more developed online learning infrastructure and were easy to navigate. Pearson used *My Language Lab*, a suite of online comprehensive assessment resources. Wiley had its own, in-house online comprehensive assessment option, namely *WileyPlus*.

## Perception of the gap in comprehensive assessments

The comprehensive assessments provided a wide breadth and variety of activities and item types. Each of these assessments was packaged within a learning management system (LMS)-like interface, with multiple internal links. A dashboard, or a program "homepage," directed students to important course resources, due dates, and graded activities.

Delayed feedback was given in virtually all instances when students submitted their work for either computer correction, manual correction by the teacher, or joint computer and manual correction. Some of the item types and feedback used for assessments on different platforms are illustrated in Figures 20.3 and 20.4. As shown in Figure 20.3, CENTRO provided fill-in-the-blank assessment items at the word and phrase level, requiring teacher correction for McGraw-Hill's Italian text, *Prego!*

As shown in Figure 20.4, students provided an audio-recorded, spoken response in Supersite for Vista Higher Learning's German text, *Sag mal*, which was later scored by the instructor.

Each of the major comprehensive assessment programs provided two types of feedback: (1) computer-generated, correct or incorrect response with correct response shown and/or (2) manually-scored, instructor feedback with comments. In these programs, the instructor could leave comments after each individual item and provide overall comments at the end of a particular assessment section. For example, imagine a student misspelled the correct response to an Italian item in *CENTRO*. In the Grading Center, the teacher could provide feedback on a student's response by typing in a comment box. Computer-generated feedback included a red X which indicated an incorrect answer and the teacher's comment directed the student to spell "giorno" with "o" rather than "e." The student received a half point. For items that had multiple points and contained more than one part, the instructor could provide a holistic impression of the student's performance on that item, give a score, and/or leave comments for the student to read. On items where the student recorded a response, the instructor could listen to the recording and provide a general impression of the student's performance.

In *WileyPlus*, the feedback was provided in the form of correct or incorrect answers, usually with a green or red dot to signify a correct and incorrect response, respectively. In *Paroles*, for example, the student could click a button to see the correct answers on the

**Table 20.6** Comprehensive online resources including assessments

| Textbook Publisher | Technology Platform | Languages | Corresponding Textbook(s) Reviewed (n = 28) | Website |
|---|---|---|---|---|
| Georgetown University Press | Quia | Arabic<br><br>Chinese<br>Portuguese | *Al-Kitaab fii taʿallum al-Arabiyaa*, 3$^{rd}$ Edition, Part 1<br>*Working Mandarin for Beginners*<br>*Working Portuguese for Beginners* | Arabic: http://www.alkitaabtextbook.com/books/<br>Chinese and Portuguese: http://books.quia.com/books/students.html |
| Heinle/Cengage Higher Education | iLrn powered by Quia<br>MyELT (for English) | Chinese<br>French<br>German<br>Italian<br>Japanese<br>Spanish<br>English | *Introductory Chinese traditional*<br>*Liaisons*<br>*Neue horizonte*<br>*Ponti*<br>*Nakama 1*<br>*¿Cómo se dice…?*<br>*Pathways, 1* | English: https://myelt.heinle.com/ilrn/authentication/signIn.do?inst=MYELT<br>Other Languages: http://hlc.quia.com/books/ |
| McGraw-Hill Higher Education | CENTRO powered by Quia | French<br>German<br>Italian<br>Spanish | *Deux mondes*<br>*Kontakte*<br>*Prego!*<br>*Puntos de partida* | http://www.mhcentro.com/books/ |
| Pearson Higher Education | My Language Labs | Chinese<br>English<br>German<br>Italian<br>Latin<br>Portuguese<br>Russian<br>Spanish | *Chinese link*<br>*NorthStar*<br>*Treffpunkt Deutsch*<br>*Percorsi*<br>*Disce!*<br>*Ponto de encontro*<br>*Golosa*<br>*Unidos* | MyEnglishLab (English): http://www.myenglishlab.com/courses-northstar.html<br>MyLanguageLabs (Other Languages): http://www.pearsonmylabandmastering.com/northamerica/mylanguagelabs/ |

(Continued)

**Table 20.6** Continued

| Textbook Publisher | Technology Platform | Languages | Corresponding Textbook(s) Reviewed (n = 28) | Website |
|---|---|---|---|---|
| Vista Higher Learning | Supersite | French German Italian Spanish | *Espaces* *Sag mal* *Sentieri* *Vistas* | http://vistahigherlearning.com/students/supersite |
| Wiley | WileyPlus | French Spanish | *Paroles* *Dicho y hecho* | French: https://www.wileyplus.com/WileyCDA/catalog/french.html Spanish: https://www.wileyplus.com/WileyCDA/Section/Spanish.id-402727.html |

## Studiare in Italia

**CAPITOLO 3**

Vocabolario preliminare

**A. Materie di studio...**   Read the following dialogue, then complete the chart with information from the dialogue.

| | |
|---|---|
| VALERIO: | Ciao, sono Valerio, e voi? |
| PRISCILLA: | Priscilla, sono americana. Studio all'Università del Colorado. |
| ALIZA: | Anch'io sono una studentessa dell'Università del Colorado. |
| VALERIO: | Oh, siete del Colorado... Parenti? |
| PRISCILLA: | Sì, Aliza è mia sorella... |
| VALERIO: | Siete qui in Italia per studiare? |
| PRISCILLA: | Sì, studio la storia dell'arte e la lingua italiana. Ma ho un interesse particolare per la storia e la filosofia del Rinascimento (*Renaissance*). |
| ALIZA: | Io invece (*on the other hand*) studio storia moderna e contemporanea. |
| VALERIO: | Che materie interessanti! |
| ALIZA: | Studio anche scienze politiche e economia. |
| VALERIO: | Parlate già bene l'italiano! (*You already speak Italian well!*) E poi siete nel posto giusto (*in the right place*). Firenze è la città del Rinascimento italiano. |
| PRISCILLA: | E tu, Valerio, cosa studi (*are you studying*)? Qual è la tua specializzazione? |
| VALERIO: | Studio letteratura italiana contemporanea, ma ho una passione anche per l'arte. |

Materie di studio di Valerio:

Materie di studio di Priscilla:

Materie di studio di Aliza:

Perché (*Why*) Firenze è la città giusta per Priscilla e Aliza?

Chi sono Aliza e Priscilla?

Submit answers

**Figure 20.3**   Fill-in-the-blank reading assessment item. Source: McGraw Hill's CENTRO for *Prego!* November, 2014.

"Observez" production-type items after the student submitted a constructed, sentence-level response of specific grammatical features. The program also allowed instructors to leave detailed feedback to be delivered to the student via the Gradebook, in written or audio-recorded form, on open-ended, manually-graded WileyPlus questions (Glenn A. Wilson, email message to author, February 17, 2015).

Pearson's *MyLanguageLabs* provided students with correct and incorrect responses, accompanied by the correct answer in all its assessments. The feedback also included some

Figure 20.4 Audio-recorded, speaking assessment item. Source: Vista Higher Learning's Supersite for *Sag mal*, November, 2014.

hint of the correct answer, or wrong-answer feedback in the form of a question or statement that helped students understand their mistake (Bob Hemmer, email message to author, February 8, 2015). This form of analysis was intended to require the student to think more critically about how to reach the correct response, thereby equipping him or her with strategies for learning. For example, in an assessment in MyFrenchLab where the student read through a script and filled in the missing spaces with the correct campus place names, the feedback might include the correct answer and a message: "What is the name of the place where you buy school supplies? It looks like the word 'library' in English." This could push the student to fill the gap in his or her knowledge a little more readily than merely providing the correct answer. Certainly, this was one of the most developed forms of program-generated feedback observed in our review.

In the Vista *Supersite*, feedback was given as a correct or incorrect response. Instructors could also leave feedback for manually-graded assessments and provide students with comments related to the use of diacritics, punctuation, syntax, or grammatical features, in addition to strategies for studying or reviewing material.

**Figure 20.5**    Screenshot of delayed feedback on a student's pronunciation. Source: Heinle/Cengage Higher Education's MyELT for *Pathways*, November, 2014.

Heinle/Cengage's *MyELT* included speaking assessments; the computer automatically compared the student's response to a correct response and measured the student's accurate stress, rhythm, and pronunciation features of words and of the sentence as a whole. As shown in Figure 20.5, the student was provided a "pronunciation check" score, generally out of six points. The feedback associated with this score varied from "needs improvement" to "excellent." Elements of the sentence pronounced correctly were highlighted in green, whereas areas needing practice were shown in red.

## Closing the gap in comprehensive assessments

Each of these low-stakes assessment programs kept track of students' performance by saving the feedback, scores, overall grades, and instructor's comments, so that students could access their grades at any point in time. A student's submission and subsequent attempts on any particular assessment item were also stored so that progress could be tracked in the grade book. In the grade book, therefore, different types of score reporting existed. Quia's *CENTRO* and *iLrn* had almost exactly the same grade book centers, which provided a comprehensive listing of all students' scores on the chapter assessments, as shown in Figure 20.6. In Vista's *Supersite*, each activity was listed according to the section of the lesson (e.g., Lezione 3A, Lezione 3B, and Unità 3 for *Sentieri*), and students saw scores associated with each assessment.

As helpful as these scores might have been, there were very few computer-generated explicit messages to students in any of these systems to direct them to other materials or

**Figure 20.6**   Screenshot of gradebook with names blacked out. Source: Heinle/Cengage Higher Education's iLrn for *Ponti*, November, 2014.

suggest study habits, apart from instructors' comments or computer-generated formative feedback on self-assessments guiding students to reexamine learned material.

## Evaluation and future directions

The following questions have been addressed: Was the content in the text/materials adequately covered? Was the information given for wrong answers helpful to a student? Would the score information help a student and his/her teacher to address strengths and weaknesses?

In general, the assessments that accompanied the language-learning textbooks and online programs covered the same content. In this sense, the response to the question of whether there was a match between learning materials and assessments certainly must be "yes." Many of these low-stakes assessments seemed to require simple recall of information, instead of assessments requiring students to extend their knowledge of a particular language form to the function it fulfilled. As illustrated by Hughes (1989), the view that test content should be based directly on a textbook or an online course is appealing because the test only contains what students have been exposed to. A disadvantage of this approach is related to the scope of transfer: Successful performance on a test that requires students to read aloud sentences containing phonemic contrasts may not indicate successful development of conversational ability.

The low-stakes online assessments that accompanied online language programs and textbooks, then, did include the material covered in the lessons (often exactly), but apart from the Milestone activities in *Foundations*, they did not move beyond the material to include additional situations. We suggest that the positive effects of quizzes and unit assessments could be improved if publishers and web developers added new items used in new situations, in addition to the same items that appeared in the lessons.

The feedback students received in the assessments often let them know if they were right or wrong. This "knowledge of correct response" has long been shown to be an effective tool for learning, with delayed feedback more advantageous than immediate feedback (Kulhavy 1977; Mullett et al. 2014); most of the assessments for textbooks and about half of those for the language-learning programs used delayed feedback, so they were on the right track. Some of the comprehensive assessment programs, such as *MyLanguageLabs*, gave students hints about the right answer, and several provided a means for instructors to type comments to the students. However, unless it was through instructor comments, few of the assessments we reviewed gave students information about why their wrong answers were incorrect. This seems to be an area that publishers and web developers could improve in. Considering the preponderance of multiple-choice items in these assessments, we could envision the possibility of writing helpful feedback messages for wrong answers that students selected. Addressing students' misconceptions could help them identify the gaps in their understanding of the relations between the targeted language forms and functions.

Finally, the last question asked whether the score information would help students and teachers to address strengths and weaknesses, thereby closing the gaps in their understanding. Many assessments provided the means for teachers to add spoken or written comments and to make recommendations. Almost all assessments provided students with percentage correct scores. Percentage correct scores have been used for many years and are certainly helpful as a quick, simple indicator of overall achievement. These are positive attributes of most of the assessments reviewed.

Nevertheless, publishers and web developers could improve the quality of their low-stakes assessments by making a few fundamental adjustments to score reports. Specifically, part scores could be given to help identify content that seems to need more work or has been well learned. *Foundations* does provide this information if the user places the cursor over the circle on the title page which shows the parts of the lesson, but the user may not know that it is available unless a teacher/tutor explains it. *CENTRO*, *iLrn*, *Supersite*, and *PEI* all used part scores. We imagine innovative assessment features would enable students to be responsible for their own learning, to verify that they were closing the gap in their language learning, and to make significant strides in accomplishing learning goals for language development. To further enhance the scores' potential for learning, these scores could be linked to sections of the lessons that students need to review. For students who are doing well, the scores could be linked to future lessons that they might find more challenging.

Fernand Marty (1981) developed computerized French lessons that gave messages to a student like the following: "So far in this course, you have worked with 298 grammar categories. Your general performance score over ALL these categories is 77.7 percent...These scores indicate that you should review some grammar elements" (1981, 38). The student could press a key to see a list of grammar items below a certain score, and could then request a review of the grammar items. This online course that accompanied a text included French lessons that covered two years of instruction at the university and tracked individual performance across different exercises—in 1981! Certainly this type of tracking can still be done, but we did not review any program that recorded students' performances across lessons.

The low-stakes online assessments for the programs and texts reviewed in this chapter are very good, but they could be even better. Thirty-five years after Professor Marty reported on his French lessons, we should expect more from online language assessments intended to help students learn. We should expect more detailed and individualized feedback and score reports that link individual learners to additional, appropriate resources so that these assessments can contribute to improved language learning.

## NOTE

1   The assessments for *PEI* were developed by Joan Jamieson and Carol Chapelle, chapter author and volume editor.

## REFERENCES

Anton, Christine, Tobias Barske, Jane Grabowski, and Megan McKinstry. 2014. *Sag Mal: An Introduction to German Language and Culture.* Boston, MA: Vista Higher Learning, Inc. Accessed June 3, 2016. http://vistahigherlearning.com/educators/highered/german-programs/sag-mal.html

Assessment Reform Group. 2002. *Assessment for Learning.* Accessed June 3, 2016. http://assessmentreformgroup.files.wordpress.com/2012/01/10principles_english.pdf&gt

Bangert-Drowns, Robert, Chen-Lin Kulik, James Kulik, and Mary Morgan. 1991. "The Instructional Effect of Feedback in Test-like Events." *Review of Educational Research*, 61: 213–238.

Black, Paul, and Dylan Wiliam. 1998. "Assessment and Classroom Learning." *Assessment in Education: Principles, Policy & Practice*, 5, no. 1: 7–74.

Blanco, José, and Philip Donley. 2012. *Vistas: Introducción a La Lengua Española*, 4th ed. supersite. Boston, MA: Vista Higher Learning. Accessed June 3, 2016. http://vistahigherlearning.com/students/store/vistas-4th-edition.html

Boyd, Francis, and Carol Numrich. 2014. *NorthStar*, 4th ed. White Plains, NY: Pearson.

Branciforte, Suzanne, and Elvira Di Fabio. 2011. *Parliamo Italiano! A Communicative Approach*, 4th ed. Hoboken, NJ: John Wiley & Sons, Inc.

Accessed June 3, 2016. http://www.wiley.com/WileyCDA/WileyTitle/productCd-EHEP001723.html

Brustad, Kristen, Mahmoud Al-Batal, and Abbas Al-Tonsi. 2014. *Al-Kitaab fii Tacallum al-Arabiyaa, Part 1*, 3rd ed. Al-Kitaab Arabic Language Program. Washington, DC: Georgetown University Press. Accessed June 3, 2016. http://books.quia.com/demo/42475.html

Cameron, Scott, Susan Iannuzzi, and Maryann Maynard. 2009. *Hemispheres.* Columbus, OH: McGraw Hill.

Chase, Becky. 2013. *Pathways 1: Listening, Speaking, and Critical Thinking*, 1st ed. Boston, MA: Cengage Learning and National Geographic Learning. Accessed June 3, 2016. http://ngl.cengage.com/search/productOverview.do?N=200+4294918395&Ntk=P_EPI&Ntt=32280371618433442511903061814194899943

Colby-Kelly, Christian, and Carolyn Turner. 2007. "AFL Research in the L2 Classroom and Evidence of Usefulness: Taking Formative Assessment to the Next Level." *Canadian Modern Language Review*, 64: 9–38.

Cozzarelli, Julia. 2011. *Sentieri: Attraverso l'Italia Contemporanea.* Boston, MA : Vista Higher Learning. Accessed June 3, 2016. http://vistahigherlearning.com/educators/highered/italian-programs/sentieri-1.html

Davies, Allen, Annie Brown, Catherine Elder, Kathryn Hill, Tom Lumley, and Tim McNamara. 1999. *Dictionary of Language Testing*. Studies in Language Testing 7. Cambridge, UK: UCLES.

De Jouet-Pastre, Clemence, Anna Klobucka, Patricia Sobral, Maria de Biaji Moreira, and Amelia Hutchinson. 2013. *Ponto de Encontro: Portuguese as a World Language*, 2nd ed. White Plains, NY: Pearson Higher Education. Accessed. June 3, 2016. http://www. pearsonhighered.com/educator/product/ Ponto-de-Encontro-Portuguese-as-a-World-Language-Plus-MyPortugueseLab-with-eText-multi-semester-Access-Card-Package/9780205981120.page

Dollenmayer, David, and Thomas Hansen, T. 2014. *Neue Horizonte*, 8th ed. Boston, MA: Cengage Learning Higher Education. Accessed June 3, 2016. http://www.cengage.com/ search/productOverview.do?Ntt=13334746035 563924733941248411420500985&N=16& Ntk=P_EPI

Dorwick, Thalia, Ana Maria Pérez-Gironés, Anne Becher, and Cassie Isabelli. 2012. *Puntos de Partida*, 9th ed. New York, NY: McGraw-Hill Higher Education. Accessed June 3, 2016. http://highered.mheducation.com/ sites/0073385417/student_view0/index.html

Duolingo. 2014. Accessed June 3, 2016. https:// www.duolingo.com/

DynEd. 2014. *New dynamic English*. Accessed June 3, 2016. http://www.DynEd.com/us/ products/newdynamicenglish/

Fluenz. 2014. Accessed June 3, 2016. http:// www.fluenz.com/

Fulcher, Glenn. 2010. *Assessment for Learning I: An Introduction*. Accessed June 3, 2016. http://languagetesting.info/features/afl/ formative.html

Glaser, Robert. 1963. "Instructional Technology and the Measurement of Learning Outcomes: Some Questions." *American Psychologist*, 18: 519–521.

Gonglewski, Margaret, Beverly Moser, and Cornelius Partsch. 2013. *Treffpunkt Deutsch: Grundstufe*, 6th ed. White Plains, NY: Pearson Higher Education. Accessed June 3, 2016. http://www.pearsonhighered.com/educator/ product/Treffpunkt-Deutsch-Grundstufe-Plus-MyGermanLab-with-eText-multi-semester-Access-Card-Package/9780205995035.page

Guzmán, Elizabeth, Paloma Lapuerta, and Judith Liskin-Gasparro. 2013. *Unidos*. White Plains, NY: Pearson Higher Education. Accessed June 3, 2016. http://www.pearsonhighered.com/ educator/product/Unidos-includes-multi-semester-access-Code-Access-Card-Package/9780205996667.page

Hatasa, Yukoko, Kazumi Hatasa, and Seiichi Makino. 2015. *Nakama 1: Japanese Communication Culture Context*, 3rd ed. Boston, MA: Cengage Learning Higher Education. Accessed June 3, 2016. http://www.cengage. com/search/productOverview.do?Ntt= nakama||197386229957463895209321816813 47554592&N=16&Ntk=APG%7C%7CP_EPI& Ntx=mode%2Bmatchallpartial

Hill, Kathryn, and Tim McNamara. 2011. "Developing a Comprehensive, Empirically based Research Framework for Classroom-based Assessment." *Language Testing*, 29: 395–420.

Hughes, Arthur. 1989. *Testing for Language Teachers*. Cambridge, UK: Cambridge University Press.

Italiano, Francesca, and Irene Marchegiani. 2015. *Percorsi: L'Italia Attraverso La Lingua e La Cultura*, 3rd ed. White Plains, NY: Pearson Higher Education. Accessed June 3, 2016. http://www.pearsonhighered.com/educator/ product/Percorsi-LItalia-attraverso-la-lingua-e-la-cultura/020599895X.page

Jarvis, Ana, Raquel Lebredo, and Francisco Mena-Ayllón. 2013. *¿Cómo Se Dice…?*, 10th ed. Boston, MA: Cengage Learning Higher Education. Accessed June 3, 2016. http:// www.cengage.com/search/productOverview. do?Ntt=como+se+dice||740129711852276568842737811313512298&N=16&Ntk=APG%7C %7CP_EPI&Ntx=mode%2Bmatchallpartial

Kitchell, Kenneth, and Thomas Sienkewicz. 2011. *Disce! An Introductory Latin Course, Vol. 1*. White Plains, NY: Pearson Higher Education. Accessed June 3, 2016. http://www. pearsonhighered.com/educator/product/ Disce-An-Introductory-Latin-Course-Volume-1-Plus-MyLatinLab-multisemester-access-with-eText-Access-Card-Package/9780205997039.page

Knowles, Lance. 2012. "Testing Reformed." *Language Magazine*. Accessed June 3, 2016. http:// languagemagazine.com/?page_id=119819

Kulhavy, Raymond. 1977. "Feedback in Written Instruction." *Review of Educational Research*, 47, no. 1, 211–232.

Kulik, James, and Chen-Lin Kulik. 1988. "Timing of Feedback and Verbal Learning." *Review of Educational Research*, 58: 79–97.

Kunnan, Antony. 2013. "High-stakes Language Testing." In *Encyclopedia of Applied Linguistics*, edited by Carol Chapelle. Oxford, UK: Wiley-Blackwell. DOI:10.1002/9781405198431. wbeal0504

Lazzarino, Grazianna, and Andrea Dini. 2012. *Prego! An Invitation to Italian, Online Workbook*, 8th ed. New York, NY: McGraw-Hill. Accessed June 3, 2016. http://www.mhcentro.com/demo/36836.html

LingQ. 2014. Accessed June 3, 2016. http://www.lingq.com/

Liu, Jun, Yan Kang, Huiping Wei, and Yifan Chong. 2013. *Access Chinese, Online Workbook*. New York, NY: McGraw-Hill. Accessed June 3, 2016. http://highered.mcgraw-hill.com/sites/0073371882/student_view0/index.html

Lubensky, Sophia, Gerard Ervin, Larry McLellan, and Donald Jarvis. 2002. *Nachalo: Book 1*, 2nd ed. New York, NY: McGraw-Hill Higher Education. Accessed June 3, 2016. http://highered.mcgraw-hill.com/sites/0072433922/student_view0/index.html

Magnan, Sally, Laurie Martin-Berg, and William Berg. 2006. *Paroles*, 3rd ed. Hoboken, NJ: John Wiley & Sons, Inc. Accessed June 3, 2016. https://www.wileyplus.com/WileyCDA/catalog/french.html

Mango. 2014. Accessed June 3, 2016. http://www.mangolanguages.com/

Marty, Fernand. 1981. "Reflections on the Use of Computers in Second-language Acquisition." *Studies in Language Learning*, 3: 25–53.

Memrise. 2014. Accessed June 3, 2016. http://www.memrise.com/courses/

Miller, M. David, Robert Linn, and Norman Gronlund. 2012. *Measurement and Evaluation in Teaching*, 11th ed. New York, NY: Pearson.

Mitchell, James, and Cheryl Tano. 2015. *Espaces: Rendez-vous avec Le Monde Francophone*, 3rd ed. Boston, MA: Vista Higher Learning, Inc. Accessed June 3, 2016. http://vistahigherlearning.com/educators/highered/french-programs/espaces-3rd-edition.html

Modern Language Association. 2010. *New MLA Survey Report Finds that the Study of Languages Other Than English is Growing and Diversifying at US Colleges and Universities*. Accessed June 3, 2016. http://www.mla.org/pdf/2009_enrollment_survey_pr.pdf

Mullett, Hillary, et al. 2014. "Delaying Feedback Promotes Transfer of Knowledge Despite Student Preferences to Receive Feedback Immediately." *Journal of Applied Research in Memory and Cognition*, 3: 222–229.

Nummikoski, Marita. 2012. *Troika: A Communicative Approach to Russian Language, Life, and Culture*, 2nd ed. Hoboken, NJ: John Wiley & Sons, Inc. Accessed June 3, 2016. http://www.wiley.com/WileyCDA/WileyTitle/productCd-EHEP001955.html

Pearson. 2015. *Pearson English Interactive*. Accessed June 3, 2016. http://product.pearsonelt.com/pei/

Potowski, Kim, Sylvia Sobral, and Lailia Dawson. 2012. *Dicho y hecho: Beginning Spanish*, 9th ed. Hoboken, NJ: John Wiley & Sons, Inc. Accessed June 3, 2016. http://www.wiley.com/WileyCDA/WileyTitle/productCd-EHEP001725.html

Rector, Monica, Regina Santos, Marcelo Amorim, and M. Lynne Gerber.2010. *Working Portuguese for Beginners*. Washington, DC: Georgetown University Press Languages. Accessed June 3, 2016. http://press.georgetown.edu/book/languages/working-portuguese-beginners

Robin, Richard, Karen Evans-Romaine, and Galina Shatalina. 2012. *Golosa: A Basic Course in Russian, Book 1*, 5th ed. White Plains, NY: Pearson Higher Education. Accessed June 3, 2016. http://www.pearsonhighered.com/educator/product/Golosa-Basic-Course-Russian-Book-One-Plus-MyRussianLab-Pearson-eText-Access-Card-Package-multisemester-access/9780205980369.page

Rocket Languages. 2014. Accessed June 3, 2016. http://www.rocketlanguages.com/

Rosetta Stone. 2014a. Rosetta Stone's *Foundations for Higher Education*. Accessed June 3, 2016. http://www.rosettastone.com/highereducation/foundations

Rosetta Stone. 2014b. *Livemocha*. Accessed June 21, 2014. http://livemocha.com/Livemocha's website closed on April 22, 2016.

Scullen, Mary Ellen, Cathy Pons, and Albert Valdman. 2013. *Points de Départ*, 2nd ed. White Plains, NY : Pearson Higher Education. Accessed June 3, 2016. http://www.pearsonhighered.com/educator/product/Points-de-dpart-Plus-MyFrenchLab-with-Pearson-eText-multi-semester-Access-Card-Package/9780205990276.page

Sparks, Kimberly, and Van Horn Vail. 2004. *German in Review: Lehrbuch der Deutschen Grammatik*, 4th ed. Hoboken, NJ: John Wiley & Sons, Inc. Accessed June 3, 2016. http://www.wiley.com/WileyCDA/WileyTitle/productCd-047042429X.html

Stiggins, Rick, and Jan Chappuis. 2005. "Using Student-involved Classroom Assessment to Close Achievement Gaps." *Theory into Practice*, 44: 11–18.

Terrell, Tracy, Mary Rogers, Betsy Kerr, and Guy Spielmann. 2009. *Deux mondes: A Communicative Approach*, 6th ed. New York, NY: McGraw-Hill Higher Education. Accessed June 3, 2016. http://highered.mcgraw-hill.com/sites/0073535443/student_view0/

Tognozzi, Elissa, and Giuseppe Cavatorta. 2013. *Ponti: Italiano Terzo Millennio*, 3rd ed. Boston, MA: Cengage Learning Higher Education. Accessed June 3, 2016. http://www.cengage.com/search/productOverview.do?Ntt=150055572177455712514461589531790782997&N=16+4294922390+4294959139&Ntk=P_EPI

Tohsaku, Yasu-Hiko. 2006. *Yookoso!: An Invitation to Contemporary Japanese*, 3rd ed. McGraw-Hill Higher Education. Accessed June 3, 2016. http://highered.mcgraw-hill.com/sites/0072408154/student_view0/

Transparent Language. 2012. *Byki Express, 4, Build 344*. Accessed June 3, 2016. http://www.byki.com/

Transparent Language. 2014. *Transparent Language Online*. Accessed June 3, 2016. http://www.transparent.com/

Tschirner, Erwin, Brigitte Nikolai, and Tracy Terrell. 2009. *Kontakte: Online Arbeitsbuch*, 6th ed. New York, NY: McGraw-Hill. Accessed June 3, 2016. http://www.mhcentro.com/demo/19895.html

Wall, Dianne. 2013. Washback in Language Assessment. In *Encyclopedia of Applied Linguistics*, edited by Carol Chapelle. Oxford, UK: Wiley-Blackwell. DOI:10.1002/9781405198431.wbeal1274

Wong, Wynne, Stacey Weber-Feve, Edouard Ousselin, and Bill VanPatten. 2015. *Liaisons, Enhanced*, 1st ed. Boston, MA: Cengage Learning. Accessed June 3, 2016. http://www.cengage.com/search/productOverview.do?Ntt=9603359442050079752186635404748825187 2&N=16+4294922390+4294966196&Ntk=P_EPI#Overview

Wu, Sue-mei, Yueming Yu, Yanhui Zhang, and Weizhong Tian. 2011. *Chinese Link: Beginning Chinese, Simplified, Character Version, Level 1/Part 1*, 2nd ed. White Plains, NY: Pearson Higher Education. Accessed June 3, 2016. http://www.pearsonhighered.com/educator/product/Chinese-Link-Beginning-Chinese-Simplified-Character-Version-Level-1Part-1/9780205637218.page

Zhang, Phyllis. 2015. *Introductory Chinese Traditional, Volume 1*, 1st ed. Cengage Learning Professional. Accessed June 3, 2016. http://www.cengage.com/search/productOverview.do?Ntt=1813892854662785131583479682560610 024&N=14+4294922390+4294955355&Ntk=P_EPI

Zhou, Yi, and M. Lynne Gerber. 2007. *Working Mandarin for Beginners*. Washington, DC: Georgetown University Press Languages. Accessed June 3, 2016. http://press.georgetown.edu/book/languages/working-mandarin-beginners

# 21 Technology and High-stakes Language Testing

## JONATHAN E. SCHMIDGALL AND DONALD E. POWERS

## Defining technology-mediated high-stakes testing

Tests are typically distinguished as *high-stakes* or *low-stakes* based on the consequences that result from their use (American Educational Research Association, American Psychological Association, and National Council on Measurement in Education 2014). Tests may be deemed "low stakes" to the extent that their use has only indirect or relatively insignificant consequences for stakeholders. Moreover, the consequences that ensue from inappropriate decisions based on low-stakes tests can often be remedied with minimal cost or effort (Fulcher 2010). An example of a low-stakes test use is making incremental decisions about teaching or learning (see the chapter on integrating assessment with instruction through technology in this volume). In contrast, high-stakes testing directly influences a decision that may be life changing for the test-taker (Roever 2001) or extremely costly to remedy if made in error. Examples of high-stakes uses of tests include decisions about admissions into an academic program, professional certification, or immigration authorization. Technology is used in both high- and low-stakes testing, but may be particularly beneficial for high-stakes tests that need to accommodate large test-taker populations with standardized administrations.

Developers of high-stakes tests are expected to provide evidence of (1) the reliability or consistency of test scores, (2) the validity of score interpretations and their intended use, and (3) the adequacy of security procedures that ensure the integrity of the entire testing system (Bartram 2006a). Professional standards call for test developers to describe any test's intended use and to produce evidence about its reliability and validity, but they require the quantity and quality of evidence to be relatively more substantial for high-stakes uses than for low-stakes uses (AERA, APA, and NCME 2014).

Developments in technology have made addressing some of these concerns more feasible while complicating others. Advancements in computer technology have led to innovations in how tests are developed, administered, scored, and monitored, all of which have implications for the previously elaborated concerns. An increase in the availability and quality of mobile devices and internet service has enabled the use of more dynamic test delivery systems, with implications for improving test administration and security. However, the proliferation of mobile devices and small digital recorders has led to ever-evolving threats to test security that can be difficult to detect without invasive surveillance and monitoring procedures.

*The Handbook of Technology and Second Language Teaching and Learning*, First Edition.
Edited by Carol A. Chapelle and Shannon Sauro.
© 2017 John Wiley & Sons, Inc. Published 2020 by John Wiley & Sons, Inc.

In the rest of this chapter, we discuss examples of how technology may be utilized in various stages of high-stakes testing, and we conclude with a brief discussion of the future of high-stakes testing and technology.

# The use of technology across three stages of high-stakes testing

Technological advances have created both opportunities and challenges for the development, administration, scoring, and security of high-stakes language tests. *Test development and administration* refers to activities and procedures that support the design of tests, the production of test items and forms, and the operational administration of the test. *Scoring* refers to activities and procedures that help transform performance on test tasks into an evaluation of that performance, that is, a score. *Security* refers to activities and procedures that help ensure the integrity of the entire testing system, including development, administration, and scoring. A summary of these opportunities and challenges across these stages of testing is provided in Table 21.1.

When compared with traditional paper-based testing, computer-based testing may offer greater conveniences for both test developers and test-takers. Test developers may use technology to support the creation, review, and delivery of test content more efficiently. This can help reduce costs by minimizing production, transmission, and storage costs (Roever 2001). Test-takers may benefit from more flexible and frequent test administrations, and prompter score reporting. However, extending this convenience requires a greater number of testing dates and a need for a larger number of items and forms in order to minimize the likelihood that the same items will be re-administered to test-takers (Dragsow, Luecht, and Bennett 2006). In addition, many language assessments evaluate performance (e.g., examinee-constructed responses for speaking and writing); therefore, the use of automated scoring systems can eliminate some of the inherent subjectivity in human rater scores and thus may improve the reliability or consistency of the scoring process. However, the use of automated scoring has broad implications for the validity argument for test use that needs to be fully considered (Bennett and Bejar 1998; Clauser, Kane, and Swanson 2002). Among them is the possibility that the construct of interest will be significantly underrepresented because of the limitations of automated scoring. Finally, technology has a complex impact on test security. Technological innovation expands not only the tools that test developers may use to ensure

Table 21.1  Opportunities and challenges presented by technology for stages of high-stakes testing.

| | *Test development and administration* | *Scoring* | *Security* |
|---|---|---|---|
| Opportunities | Increased efficiency, flexibility, and standardization | Automated systems providing cheaper, faster, more reliable scoring (at scale) | Monitoring equipment, biometric identification |
| Challenges | Need for more items, test forms | Narrowing construct of measurement | Use of devices that facilitate cheating, infiltration of digital systems |

the integrity of administration and scoring procedures (and those that test-takers may use to legitimately prepare for a test) but also the tools that may facilitate cheating.

This section further explores these three stages in which technology may impact high-stakes language testing, including (1) test design and administration, (2) scoring, and (3) the security of the testing system. The latter impact is particularly critical for high-stakes testing as it may impact validity in a variety of ways, but ultimately determines the integrity and usefulness of the entire system.

## Test development and administration

Developing a language test in a digital environment may facilitate a more efficient development and administration model in which item development, item review, test form assembly, and test administration are managed within a single, coherent system. Such systems can facilitate both the distribution of test items to reviewers and the allocation of approved items to final test forms. If a system is designed to automatically impose quality control checks at each stage of test development, the process may be less vulnerable to lapses that introduce unintended variation across test forms. Since any unintended variation in test forms introduced during the development process undermines claims that test forms are parallel, the benefit of a well-organized digital system may be substantial. Automated test assembly systems can be utilized in conjunction with formal reviews by human test content experts to enhance quality control generally and, specifically, to help minimize expected variation across test forms (Luecht and Sireci 2011).

Using a well-organized digital environment to guide test development may also facilitate the collection of systematic monitoring evidence. In an argument-based approach to validation and test use, the plausibility of claims about reliability and validity are evaluated by examining evidence (Kane 2006). Although the psychometric qualities of test scores provide an important source of evidence for claims about reliability and validity, there are other important sources of evidence. Item and test specifications themselves are critical, foundational sources of evidence for claims that scores are consistent (Bachman and Palmer 2010). However, documentation of item and test specifications and a systematic development procedure is no guarantee that the specifications and procedures are followed absolutely. Collecting evidence to show that specifications were implemented as designed—through item and test form reviews—provides additional evidence to strengthen claims about the integrity of the development process. Examples of this evidence may include documentation showing the outcomes of reviews for each item included in a test form. Documentation of reviews may include the type of review (e.g., alignment with item specifications or construct relevance; potential to discriminate against subgroups or bias), qualifications of the reviewer (e.g., expertise related to what is being tested; familiarity with important subgroups of test-taker population), and outcome of the review (e.g., reviewer comments and evaluations).

High-stakes test developers need to ensure that the test is administered in a standardized, controlled environment. One advantage of computer-based test administration over paper-based or interviewer-mediated test administration is the potential to increase the level of standardization of the test environment across test-takers, particularly when the test procedure involves the use of multimedia (e.g., audio and video recordings). When a test includes multiple components or sections, the sequencing of sections and timing in general is easy to automate in a computer-based administration system. Maintaining standardized administrations helps ensure that all test-takers are evaluated using a comparable test form under the same conditions. Differences between test forms (i.e., items and content that are not interchangeable, or parallel) and test administrations (e.g., in timing, sequencing, or multimedia quality) that impact test-taker performances can reduce the reliability or consistency of test scores, and undermine claims about the validity of test score interpretations (Crocker and Algina 2008).

Incorporating technology into an established high-stakes testing program in order to transform test development and administration procedures may have important implications for score interpretations. Some high-stakes testing programs have moved from paper-based or interviewer-mediated to computer-based administration (e.g., the Test of English as a Foreign Language or TOEFL to the TOEFL Computer-Based Test and internet-Based Test, or TOEFL CBT and iBT; the Oral Proficiency Interview or OPI to the OPI by computer, or OPIc). This shift may alter important features of test tasks (e.g., language input from a tape recorder vs. a video recording; responding to a human interlocutor vs. a computerized prompt). Some researchers have cautioned that performance on a computer-administered test may not reflect the same construct as a paper-based test and that the potential effect of administration mode needs to be carefully examined. In their review of research on this issue, Douglas and Hegelheimer (2007) concluded that studies comparing modes of administration have found mostly small or mixed differences. However, they highlight that computer-administered tests assume some proficiency in using computers. Although the use of technology is increasing, test developers need to ensure that the computer skills required to take a test are minimal and appropriate for the test-taker population. Without careful consideration by the test developer, differences in computer skills among test-takers could become a source of bias by advantaging test-takers with computer skills. Test developers may help minimize this potential bias by making computer-based test preparation materials available, by beginning a testing session with sample practice items, and by providing supportive tools throughout the testing session.

The recent emergence of mobile and touch-screen devices has led to additional ways of inputting test-taker responses, resulting in a need to re-evaluate concerns about digital literacy. The communicative affordances of touch-screen devices differ in some important ways from the keyboard-and-mouse interface of desktop and laptop computers. As a result, the user interface and software design for mobile devices may emphasize haptic input through touch and gesture combinations, and de-emphasize the use of keyboard-driven input. In addition, digital skill sets may differ across types of digital devices, such as the ability to type on (1) a full-size physical keyboard using two hands, (2) a condensed virtual keyboard using two hands or fingers, and (3) a small virtual keyboard using two thumbs. Since some level of digital literacy is required to interact with computer-based tests, test developers need to carefully consider how an inadequate level of such literacy may contribute to systematic error. The detection of differences between scores on a cognitive ability test from mobile and non-mobile devices has led to the suggestion that test-takers avoid taking high-stakes assessments on mobile devices (Arthur et al. 2014).

Besides various modes of input, computers also provide other options. For example, the test administration process can use a fixed or adaptive format, and technology is particularly helpful for implementing adaptive procedures. Fixed formats involve the administration of a pre-specified number and type of items, while adaptive formats utilize prior information gathered during the testing process to make decisions about the number and type of items to administer. Typically, computer-adaptive tests draw upon a pre-tested bank of items that have known or assumed characteristics for the test-taker population (i.e., difficulty and discrimination parameter estimates) and allow more efficient administration by selecting items that better correspond to the test-taker's ability level. Levy, Behrens, and Mislevy (2006) describe different levels of adaptivity that may be introduced into an assessment. They suggest that adaptivity can be introduced in two ways, either independently or simultaneously: with respect to the types of items selected and presented (i.e., item types that measure different constructs), or the number of items presented (i.e., items that measure the same construct, but may vary in difficulty). Typically, in high-stakes computer-adaptive testing, the types of items presented are fixed as variation here can affect the nature of score interpretation and comparisons between test-takers. The nature of adaptivity can be further distinguished by the *locus of control*, or who is given control to make decisions: the test developer (examiner) or the test-taker (examinee). The term *examiner-adaptive* is typically used to refer to a procedure in which the test developer retains the locus of control through an algorithm (computer-adaptive) or decision-making process (examiner-adaptive) that selects items to administer based on the test-taker's performance on previous items. For *examinee-adaptive* tests, the test-taker retains the locus of control and decides or influences which items to take or which constructs to measure. Adaptive tests potentially have the advantage of being able to specify a target level of score reliability in advance, as items can be administered until this target level of reliability is achieved.

Mislevy et al. (2008) explore examples of actual and hypothetical language assessments that incorporate fixed or adaptive procedures, with different loci of control. For example, the administration of China's College English Test (CET-4 WT) is characterized as being fixed with respect to both the number of items and types of items; in other words, all test-takers complete the same test form, or a parallel version of it. The administration of the DIALANG test (diagnostic language assessments) is described as being fully adaptive, although the locus of control is split between the test developer (who controls the number of items presented) and the test-taker (who controls the types of items or constructs targeted). The Oral Proficiency Interview (OPI) is presented as an example of a test whose procedure is fully adaptive, but whose locus of control is completely retained by the test developer. Currently, very few high-stakes language assessments utilize adaptive procedures, and those that do typically use examiner-adaptive (e.g., the International English Language Testing System or IELTS; the OPI) rather than computer-adaptive procedures.

Perhaps in the future more computer-adaptive language tests will take advantage of the benefits to using computer-adaptive or self-adaptive procedures. Typically, in computer-adaptive testing, the test-taker's ability is estimated in real time after each test item is administered. Ability is estimated after each test item is administered and scored, and the next item is selected from the test's item bank that targets a similar ability level. Items can be administered until the error associated with the ability estimate is minimized to a pre-specified level; as a result, test developers can be more confident about the consistency of scores produced by the measurement procedure. Depending on the quality of the test's bank of items and the rules guiding the procedure, this approach can result in a more efficient test that avoids administering items that are either too easy or too difficult for any particular test-taker (Alderson 2000). Self-adaptive testing procedures are designed to incorporate test-taker judgments into the administration process—specifically, a test-taker's initial estimate of his or her proficiency level, or preferences regarding test content. The rationale for self-adaptive tests is driven by claims that giving the test-taker more control produces some tangible benefits such as increased precision for an initial ability estimate, greater relevance of test content to the test-taker, and a reduction of test anxiety.

As Mislevy and his colleagues (2008) observed, high-stakes language tests typically give the locus of control to the test developer, and for good reason. First, attempts to empower test-takers may be misguided as they may leave test-takers "bewildered" instead because they lack knowledge of their own language ability (Mislevy et al. 2008, 22). Another strand of research has identified problems that may occur when test-takers are allowed to choose the difficulty of the questions they are asked. Researchers have documented that such testing yields significantly higher scores than does testing in which the computer objectively selects the sequence of questions, a result attributed to a positive bias (Pitkin and Vispoel 2001). Moreover, self-adapted testing may produce scores that are too low for the most able examinees and too high for the least able, although findings are mixed (Roos, Wise, and Plake 1997). These scores are also less reliable than similar ones from more traditional computer-based tests. And, the average effect of self-adapted testing on test anxiety (a main reason for using them) appears to be "modest at best."

Some researchers have recommended that until problems of test security and item selection can be solved, the use of self-adapted tests should be restricted to low-stakes assessment situations, that is, ones in which test scores carry few, if any, serious consequences (Pitkin and Vispoel 2001). This conclusion is based, in part, on the possibility that test-takers may try to "game" or "outsmart" the system by choosing in ways that they think will give them an advantage (Wise and Kingsbury 2000). For example, a computer-delivered version of the OPI, the OPIc (American Council on the Teaching of Foreign Languages 2012), includes self-adaptive and computer-adaptive components. In their research investigating validity evidence for OPIc test scores, Surface, Poncheri, and Bhavsar (2008) indicate that test-takers may try to manipulate the control afforded them by "underreporting their proficiency because they believe this course of action will lead to an easier test and a higher score." Although this kind of gamesmanship may not necessarily lead to higher scores, claims about the reliability or validity of test score interpretations may be undermined to the extent that this kind of manipulation is an issue.

Even when the locus of control remains with the test developer, the use of computer-adaptive administration procedures may be inappropriate for high-stakes language tests. While the potential benefits of a computer-adaptive approach are substantial, there are challenges associated with it. One particular challenge that is salient for language testing is that item selection in adaptive testing is typically driven by estimated item parameters (i.e., difficulty and discrimination). If item content is not simultaneously considered, then individual tests may not result in appropriate samples of test content (Douglas and Hegelheimer 2007). This issue is compounded when most test-takers are administered a more or less unique test: samples of test content may differ from test specifications for most test-takers, and individual test-takers may receive different samples of content compared to one another. Ultimately, this situation could introduce a potential threat to the validity of score interpretations (Chapelle and Douglas 2006, 41).

In order to address this concern, researchers have developed multi-stage adaptive test models (Luecht and Sireci 2011). Multi-stage adaptive models combine an adaptive approach with a more fixed approach that includes small pre-constructed test forms. These models can help ensure content representativeness and limit the overexposure of the best performing items.

Another well-known challenge associated with computer-adaptive testing is a more practical one. All items must be pre-tested with large samples in order to estimate item parameters, and a large bank of items must be maintained to ensure there are enough items to cover a range of ability levels with a large number of possible items to administer at ability levels expected to frequently occur in the test-taker population. Given these requirements, the cost of building and maintaining an item bank can be extremely expensive (Drasgow and Mattern 2006).

## Scoring constructed linguistic responses

Technology may be used to facilitate the scoring of tests that entail constructed responses (e.g., essays) by providing more efficient, systematic scoring by raters, or through the use of automated scoring systems. The use of technology to facilitate rater scoring is an enhancement to the traditional approach of rater scoring because it can more systematically implement and collect evidence for large-scale rater training, certification, calibration, and for the scoring process itself. Rater calibration or norming is a procedure in which raters score benchmark samples of performances under operational conditions, and are given feedback and monitored to ensure that they are not consistently scoring more severely or leniently than expected. When systematically implemented before each rating period, rater calibration may help mitigate the dangers of individual raters consistently scoring too leniently or severely. This helps ensure a critical quality of test scores: consistency in scoring across different raters.

Using technology to facilitate rater calibration also gives the test developer a platform to monitor rating quality (Jordan, Hughes, and Betts 2011). Avineri et al. (2011) describe the introduction of an online norming system for raters of a high-stakes oral proficiency test. Before each test administration, raters log on to a password-protected training site where they score test-taker performances and produce required supporting annotations, which are automatically submitted to test coordinators. Raters are given immediate automatic feedback that compares their scores and annotations to benchmarks. Subsequently, coordinators review the scores and annotations submitted by raters in order to determine if additional feedback is appropriate. If a rater's scores are substantially discrepant from benchmark scores, the rater is not permitted to rate operationally without additional training or norming.

If test performances are captured digitally, technology can be used to facilitate a more efficient and technically sound rating procedure by minimizing the impact of rater bias. Everson and Hines (2010) describe the architecture and use of the Online Scoring Network (OSN) utilized to score the Test of English for International Communication (TOEIC) Speaking and Writing tests. The OSN system is used to train and calibrate raters, distribute test responses to raters remotely, monitor rater performance in real time, and collect scoring responses efficiently. One of the most powerful features of the system is its ability to ensure independent ratings through a distributed scoring design. During the administration of the test, test-takers complete multiple tasks (e.g., 11 tasks for TOEIC Speaking). During the scoring process, a test-taker's responses are distributed randomly among the rater pool in order to ensure that each response is evaluated by a different rater. This procedure minimizes the potential bias that can be introduced by any single rater (e.g., through severity or leniency), as well as the halo effect, a well-established psychological phenomenon that may occur when a single rater evaluates multiple items by the same test-taker (Everitt and Skrondal 2010).

The application of technology to the automated scoring of speech and writing may improve scoring consistency while providing practical benefits such as reduced cost and scoring time. Bernstein (2013) states that with the use of automated scoring, score consistency or reliability can be maintained across items and over time, provided the scoring system is properly calibrated and maintained. In addition, the use of automated scoring may help minimize delays in score reporting while also minimizing the cost of rating, both tangible benefits for stakeholders.

Automated scoring systems may improve scoring consistency and save time, but these benefits must be weighed against current limitations on what these systems are able to evaluate. In a comprehensive review of the development and current state of automated speech and writing scoring systems, Chapelle and Chung (2010) highlight the benefits and potential of such systems but conclude that there is a need for additional validity research to support their use. Douglas (2013) also focuses on the limitations of automated scoring systems by elaborating the aspects of the speaking and writing constructs targeted by various automated scoring systems. He argues that there are currently important differences between what automated systems and human raters can explicitly evaluate, a point of view shared by other researchers (Chodorow and Burstein 2004; Lee, Gentile, and Kantor 2009; Norris 2001). Concerns about the differences between what automated scoring systems and human raters can measure has led some researchers to emphasize the need to consider how the use of automated scoring may narrow the construct being assessed and threaten particular claims in a validity argument (e.g., Chapelle and Chung 2010). This concern is one of the fundamental objections to automated essay scoring, and the limitations of any automated system should be carefully considered in conjunction with its intended use (Deane 2013).

Researchers have recognized that the use of automated scoring systems may have a substantial impact on the evaluation process, and proposed frameworks that can help ensure valid interpretations of scores (Xi 2010, 2012). Williamson, Xi, and Breyer (2012) describe how automated scoring systems may be implemented using several different scoring paradigms, from a more conservative to more liberal use of automated scoring. They suggest that high-stakes assessments require more evidence to justify the use of automated scoring systems as the sole rater, and that a liberal use of automated scoring should be relegated to low-stakes assessments until a body of supporting evidence is accumulated. Given concerns about the interpretation of scores produced by automated systems, validity evidence may come from a variety of sources: agreement with independent ratings of expert human raters, analyses of scores across subgroups of interest, comparative evaluations of the factors driving automated score production and the construct of interest, and the capacity for the automated system to correctly identify construct-irrelevant "gaming" strategies (Higgins and Heilman 2014).

An important consideration for the use of automated scoring systems is stakeholder acceptance and perceptions of these systems and the scores generated by them (Monaghan and Bridgeman 2005; Powers 2011). Xi, Schmidgall, and Wang (2011) surveyed and interviewed users of the TOEFL Practice Online (TPO), a test that uses the automated scoring system *SpeechRater* to automatically score speaking responses to a simulated TOEFL iBT Speaking test. Xi and colleagues presented study participants with several paradigms in which automated scoring of speech could be used, including (1) in conjunction with a human rater, and (2) in isolation. The researchers found that users indicated that they would have more confidence in the accuracy of scores produced from the "automated scoring in conjunction with human rater" paradigm for a high-stakes assessment. In addition, users indicated that they would be more likely to try to use strategies to "trick" or "game" the automated scoring system in the "automated scoring only" paradigm. The hesitance of stakeholders to place confidence in scores generated from an automated scoring system highlights the need to conduct additional research to support claims about their validity and intended use, particularly for high-stakes decisions.

## Security

One important distinction between high- and low-stakes testing is the level of test-taker motivation that each is likely to generate. With low-stakes tests, often the concern is that examinee performance may be uncharacteristically poor because of a lack of motivation. On the other hand, with high-stakes tests, a greater concern is that examinees will be so motivated that they may resort to inappropriate test taking behavior. Thus, as the perceived stakes of test use increases, the need for a high level of security increases accordingly in order to minimize the possibility of cheating or collusion, which can undermine the integrity of the entire testing system. Research suggests that, when the stakes are comparatively high, the motivation for test-takers to cheat should not be underestimated (e.g., Brennan 2006; Fulcher 2010). The practical implication is that in order to maintain the measurement properties of high-stakes tests, they should be designed for administration within an extremely secure, standardized environment (Roever 2001). Addressing these concerns in a large-scale testing environment requires an active research program and a sophisticated infrastructure.

It is critical for high-stakes language test developers to maintain the integrity of their development, administration, and scoring systems. If the security of any of these systems is compromised, the integrity of score interpretations and the usefulness of test scores may be undermined (Crooks and Kane 1996). The *Standards for Educational and Psychological Testing* (AERA, APA, and NCME 2014) include two standards that explicitly cite the importance of test security:

> Standard 6.6: Reasonable efforts should be made to ensure the integrity of test scores by eliminating opportunities for test takers to attain scores by fraudulent or deceptive means. (116)

Standard 6.7: Test users have the responsibility of protecting the security of test materials at all times. (117)

Test security is emphasized so as to prevent cheating, which can occur in a variety of ways. Cizek (1999) describes three domains in which cheating may be expected to occur: taking, giving, or receiving information from others; using forbidden materials or information; and circumventing the assessment process. Cheating may take the form of test-takers paying for unlawfully obtained and compiled test items, such as those obtained by teams of test-takers that systematically acquire a computer-adaptive test's item bank. Cheating may occur through the use of technology to communicate with a confederate who can provide assistance during the test. Cheating may also occur through blatant deception in which an individual is paid to impersonate someone else during the testing procedure. Although perhaps not cheating per se, other attempts to "subvert" the testing system may be equally detrimental. For instance, test-takers may attempt to exploit known or discovered weaknesses in an automated scoring system—for instance, by "gaming" it to receive a higher score from the system than an expert human rater would have assigned for the same response. Finally, a more sophisticated form of subversion of the measurement procedure involves the memorization of a set of prefabricated responses that may be slightly adapted to a variety of speaking and writing prompts.

Cohen and Wollack (2006) characterize cheating along two dimensions: high versus low tech, and individual versus collaborative. Individual cheating occurs when a test-taker works independently to try to improve his or her score or collect information about the test that can be used for financial gain. Technology can facilitate individual cheating through the use of small electronic devices (e.g., video cameras, cell phones, digital recorders) to help capture item or test information. If individuals gain unauthorized access to the internet during online testing or during unsupervised breaks, cheating can occur through looking up information or sending detailed information to others. In addition, the internet now facilitates widespread international collaborations among test-takers. Cohen and Wollack argue that organized collaborative efforts should be the greatest concern to test developers since they can have the greatest impact; in the case of computer-adaptive testing, collaborative efforts can potentially allow groups to reproduce portions of an item bank relatively quickly.

Technology can be used to facilitate cheating in a variety of ways, but it can also be used to prevent and detect cheating (Cohen and Wollack 2006; Olson and Fremer 2013). Luecht (2006) recommends four areas for test developers to target resources to prevent cheating: identification and authentication, digital security, on-site cheating, and collaborative theft of item banks. A number of steps can be taken to validate the identity of a test-taker before, during, and after the test, including requiring multiple forms of photo identification, on-site digital photos, facial recognition, biometric identification such as retinal scans or fingerprinting, and using access tokens or registration codes provided during the registration process. For computer-administered tests, data security capabilities need to guard against data theft, digital eavesdropping, and denial-of-service attacks that can crash data servers. Thus, the use of computer-delivered tests introduces potential security risks that must be carefully addressed (Alderson 2000). On-site cheating may be prevented or identified through the use of monitoring equipment such as video or audio recording devices, and equipment to prevent or detect the use of digital communication devices such as noise generators, spectrum analyzers, and metal detectors. Even after the test is complete, on-site cheating may still be identified through psychometric analyses and digital security procedures such as voice authentication of test-taker responses and plagiarism detectors (e.g., *Turnitin*). Most high-stakes international English language assessments implement an array of these security procedures, including the TOEFL iBT® (https://www.ets.org/toefl/institutions/about/

security); the IELTS™ (http://www.ielts.org/institutions/security_and_integrity.aspx); and the Pearson Test of English Academic, or PTE Academic™ (http://pearsonpte.com/institutions/about/security/).

Given the variety of threats to security and motivation for some test-takers to cheat for high-stakes tests, test security needs to be a thorough and well-coordinated effort that includes on-site proctors and monitoring systems (Luecht 2006). The use of trained proctors at test sites provides distinct advantages over a system that relies entirely on digital monitoring and analysis (Bartram 2006b). These advantages include having an additional method for authentication, ensuring that instructions regarding the standardized administration procedure are followed, dealing with any problems that may arise unexpectedly during the administration process, and ensuring the security of test materials. In his discussion of web-based testing, Roever (2001) argued that unproctored web-based tests should not be used for high-stakes purposes given their susceptibility to cheating and the challenge associated with establishing the test-taker's identity with certainty. As high-stakes test developers consider moving towards delivery models with more flexibility—such as remotely delivered or mobile assessments—they should consider how unproctored assessments may weaken the test security apparatus and make the testing procedure easier to manipulate (Arthur and Glaze 2011).

Computer-adaptive testing was previously discussed as a test administration condition, but also presents its own security concerns. Some challenges come with any implementation of computer-adaptive testing, but there are additional issues that may make it untenable when test-takers are highly motivated to obtain high scores by any means necessary. Since all items in an item bank must be pre-tested to obtain their parameters in advance, item exposure is a prominent concern (Douglas and Hegelheimer 2007). Large-scale testing requires exposing items to a large number of potential test-takers at least once, and given the significant cost associated with test development, item banks are usually refreshed only periodically. Teams of motivated test-takers may be able to memorize a large number of items that they can later share or sell, even if the item bank is large. The more that items are exposed and shared among potential test-takers, the greater will be the likelihood that subsequent test-takers will have seen and prepared for the items they will encounter, thus undermining the validity of their score interpretations. Many in the testing community have argued that this aspect of computer-adaptive testing is a fundamental flaw that makes it inadvisable for high-stakes testing (e.g., Fulcher 2005; Drasgow and Mattern 2006). Other researchers have suggested that test developers can anticipate potential problems by quantifying the risk of item compromise through careful monitoring of item exposure rates, efficiency of item bank utilization, and average item overlap percentages (Cohen and Wollack 2006). In addition, monitoring programs may be introduced to help identify potential cheaters in real time. However, none of these monitoring activities pre-empt the need for a large item bank, which will always be somewhat vulnerable with any degree of exposure (Cohen and Wollack 2006).

An argument-based approach to validity and test use (e.g., Bachman and Palmer 2010; Kane 2006) can be useful for anticipating and identifying potential threats posed by cheating to claims about the qualities of test scores. In Kane's interpretative use argument (Kane 2013) and Bachman and Palmer's (2010) assessment use argument, one of the implicit assumptions is that a test-taker's performance serves as foundational data upon which to draw inferences about the quality of test scores; for example, that the administration conditions ensure that the obtained performance sample comes from the intended test-taker. Cheating schemes that involve imposters break the link between test-taker and test performance. In this scenario, inferences that link test performances with claims about scores may be supported by statistical analyses but undermined by security violations. Thus, for high-stakes assessments in which test-takers may be motivated to cheat, an additional claim about the quality of the test performance itself needs to be specified, and evidence should be produced to support this claim. This evidence may come from a multi-faceted, technology-assisted security procedure in which identity is verified using multiple tools and procedures.

When cheating is collaborative and allows some test-takers to gain an unfair advantage, it poses a threat to a claim about one of the qualities of score interpretations as identified in Bachman and Palmer's (2010) assessment use argument, that score interpretations are impartial with respect to subgroups of test-takers. To the extent that high-stakes test developers perceive this type of cheating to be a threat, additional evidence should be produced to support the claim that score interpretations are impartial or unbiased. Again, a multi-faceted approach to monitoring test administrations and the quality of test scores is warranted. As an example, unexpectedly or consistently higher test scores obtained at certain test centers may potentially alert test developers to instances in which coordinated cheating may be occurring. Ultimately, the threats to validity posed by cheating can be incorporated as rebuttals to claims in a validity argument so as to allow test developers to take, at least partly with the use of technology, a more proactive approach to identifying potential threats before they compromise the usefulness of the entire testing system.

# Key issues for future research

As technology evolves, some developments have the potential to transform the development, administration, and scoring of high-stakes language assessments. The affordances offered by new digital technology (e.g., touch-screen interfaces, virtual reality, robotics) have the potential to expand the input and output that may be captured and presented during test administration, as well as the nature of the communicative tasks targeted by performance assessments. More immediately, the proliferation and cost of high-speed internet has made the utilization of multimedia (e.g., video) a more feasible option for test developers. Although automated scoring systems are currently limited in many regards, their sophistication has increased dramatically over the last several decades and will probably continue to evolve. The rise of social networks and importance of digital communication has implications for how language use domains are defined, and thus the constructs and tasks in high-stakes language assessments. As high-stakes language assessments and technology evolve, so will the digital tools available to threaten and support test security and the integrity of the testing system. All of these issues are important considerations for stakeholders of high-stakes language assessments.

An initial wave of technological innovation leading to computer-based assessment has already transformed the nature of assessment development, administration, scoring, and security; the emergence of touch screens, virtual reality, and even robotics may further revolutionize the nature of how constructs are measured. The proliferation of mobile and tablet devices has led to interest in developing new task types that utilize multimodal input, and the potential expansion of the construct of measurement. Although the functionality of virtual reality (VR) devices are currently limited, the development of consumer-oriented VR devices such as the Oculus Rift (see Sadler, this volume) suggests that fully-immersive virtual environments may be within reach of test developers who want to create more authentic, interactive tasks. Developing language assessments for administration in these environments will necessitate careful, systematic research to support potentially expanded claims about what language assessments are able to measure.

More immediately, technological change may allow test developers more flexibility regarding the delivery of richer task input such as videos (Douglas 2013). Researchers in language assessment have already begun to examine how replacing audio stimuli with videos may impact the measurement of language skills, particularly for listening comprehension

(Ockey 2007; Suvorov 2013; Wagner 2014). With proper design, the use of multimedia components may help to strengthen the relationship between the stimuli employed during the test and those encountered in real-world tasks. This prospect has led to an increasing interest in multimodal tasks in which, for example, test-takers read a text, listen to interlocutors, and write or speak in response. Since this approach is generally driven by an attempt to more fully represent the rich context of language use in the target language use domain, researchers have been investigating how the use of multimedia (or more "authentic") input may impact the nature of the measurement procedure and subsequent interpretations of test scores. There is some evidence to suggest that the use of technology-enhanced input may increase the authenticity of test tasks (Cohen and Upton 2006; Cumming et al. 2006; Douglas and Hegelheimer 2007).

As real-world communication tasks increasingly rely on digital tools, the use of technology in testing may become necessary in order to support inferences about real-world performance or abilities. The proliferation of digital tools and skills in all areas of communication has led researchers to begin to describe the evolving nature of "21st century skills" (Scalise and Wilson 2011). Communicative tasks themselves increasingly involve technology such as text messaging, podcasting, visual presentations, email, blogging, and word processing (Douglas and Hegelheimer 2007). As communicative tasks increasingly utilize technology, assessment tasks need to incorporate this technology if test performance is expected to extrapolate to real-world performance. Chapelle and Douglas (2006) argue that language ability itself may need to be defined in terms of an interaction between language and technology; for example, a more robust definition of the domain for "reading ability" may include the ability to gather information from the internet as well as traditional print sources.

Test security will continue to be an ever-present concern for high-stakes language assessments. While the proliferation of technology may also facilitate cheating, developers of high-stakes tests may mitigate some of these potential threats to validity by clearly articulating claims in a validity argument and collecting evidence to support these claims. For example, test developers may need to provide evidence that administration conditions help ensure that the obtained performance sample comes from the intended test-taker. This need for evidence may place test developers in a difficult situation, as full disclosure of their test security apparatus could make it easier for highly motivated individual or collaborative efforts to efficiently identify and further exploit any weaknesses in the security apparatus. Thus, one of the challenges for developers of high-stakes assessments moving forward is determining how to respond to stakeholder concerns with documented evidence that does not further compromise the security of the testing system.

When utilized thoughtfully—backed by research and monitoring—the use of technology has shown the potential to have a positive transformative effect on assessment, making tests potentially more affordable, meaningful, and useful.

# REFERENCES

Alderson, Charles J. 2000. "Technology in Testing: The Present and the Future." *System*, 28: 593–603.

American Council on the Teaching of Foreign Languages. 2012. *ACTFL OPIc Familiarization Manual*. White Plains, NY. Accessed January 4, 2017. http://www.languagetesting.com/

wp-content/uploads/2012/07/OPIc-Familiarization-Manual.pdf

American Educational Research Association (AERA), American Psychological Association (APA), National Council on Measurement in Education (NCME)and Joint Committee on Standards for Educational and Psychological

Testing. 2014. *Standards for Educational and Psychological Testing*. Washington, DC: American Educational Research Association.

Arthur Jr., Winfred, Dennis Doverspike, Gonzalo J. Muñoz, Jason E. Taylor, and Alison E. Carr. 2014. "The Use of Mobile Devices in High-stakes Remotely Delivered Assessments and Testing." *International Journal of Selection and Assessment*, 22: 113–123.

Arthur Jr, Winfred, and Ryan M. Glaze. 2011. "Cheating and Response Distortion on Remotely Delivered Assessments." In *Technology-enhanced Assessment of Talent*, edited by Nancy Tippins and Seymour Adler, 99–152. San Francisco: Jossey-Bass.

Avineri, Netta, Zsuzsa Londe, Bahiyyih Hardacre, Lauren Carris, Youngsoon So, and Mostafa Majidpour. 2011. "Language Assessment as a System: Best Practices, Stakeholders, Models, and Testimonials." *Issues in Applied Linguistics*, 18: 251–265.

Bachman, Lyle F., and Adrian S. Palmer. 2010. *Language Assessment in Practice*. New York: Oxford University Press.

Bartram, Dave. 2006a. "Testing on the Internet: Issues, Challenges and Ppportunities in the Field of Occupational Assessment." In *Computer-based Testing and the Internet: Issues and Advances*, edited by Dave Bartram and Ronald K. Hambleton, 13–38. Hoboken, NJ: John Wiley & Sons, Inc.

Bartram, Dave. 2006b. "The Impact of Technology on Test Manufacture, Delivery and Use and on the Test Taker." In *Computer-based Testing and the Internet: Issues and Advances*, edited by Dave Bartram and Ronald K. Hambleton, 135–162. Hoboken, NJ: John Wiley & Sons, Inc.

Bennett, Randy E., and Isaac I. Bejar. 1998. "Validity and Automated Scoring: It's Not Only the Scoring." *Educational Measurement: Issues and Practice*, 17: 9–17.

Bernstein, Jared C. 2013. "Computer Scoring of Spoken Responses." In *The Encyclopedia of Applied Linguistics*, edited by Carol A. Chapelle. Oxford: Wiley-Blackwell.

Brennan, Robert L. 2006. "Perspectives on the Evolution and Future of Educational Measurement." In *Educational Measurement*, edited by Robert L. Brennan. Westport, CT: Praeger: 1–16.

Chapelle, Carol A., and Dan Douglas. 2006. *Assessing Language through Computer Technology*. Cambridge: Cambridge University Press.

Chapelle, Carol A., and Yoo-Ree Chung. 2010. "The Promise of NLP and Speech Processing Technologies in Language Assessment." *Language Testing*, 27: 301–315.

Chodorow, Martin, and Jill Burstein. 2004. "Beyond Essay Rength: Evaluating e-rater®'s Performance on TOEFL® Essays." *ETS Research Report Series*, 2004: i–38.

Cizek, Gregory J. 1999. *Cheating on Tests: How to Do it, Detect it, and Prevent It*. New York: Routledge.

Clauser, Brian E., Michael T. Kane, and David B. Swanson. 2002. "Validity Issues for Performance-based Tests Scored with Computer-automated Scoring Systems." *Applied Measurement in Education*, 15: 413–432.

Cohen, Allan S., and James A. Wollack. 2006. "Test Administration, Security, Scoring, and Reporting." In *Educational Measurement*, edited by Robert L. Brennan, 355–386. Westport, CT: American Council on Education and Praeger.

Cohen, Andrew D., and Thomas A. Upton. 2006. "Strategies in Responding to the New TOEFL Reading Tasks." *ETS Research Report Series* 2006, no. 1: i–162.

Crocker, Linda, and James Algina. 2008. *Introduction to Classical and Modern Test Theory*. Mason, OH: Cengage Learning.

Crooks, Terry J., and Michael T. Kane. 1996. "Threats to the Valid Use of Assessments." *Assessment in Education: Principles, Policy, and Practice*, 3: 265–286.

Cumming, Alister, Robert Kantor, Kyoko Baba, Keanre Eouanzoui, Usman Erdosy, and Mark James. 2006. "Analysis of Discourse Features and Verification of Scoring Levels for Independent and Integrated Prototype Written Tasks for the New TOEFL." *TOEFL Monograph Series, MS-30*: 1–77. Princeton, NJ: ETS.

Deane, Paul. 2013. "On the Relation between Automated Essay Scoring and Modern Views of the Writing Construct." *Assessing Writing*, 18: 7–24.

Douglas, Dan. 2013. "Technology and Language Testing." In *The Encyclopedia of Applied Linguistics*, edited by Carol A. Chapelle. Hoboken, NJ: John Wiley & Sons, Inc. Accessed January 4, 2017. http://dx.doi.org/10.1002/9781405198431.wbeal1182

Douglas, Dan, and Volker Hegelheimer. 2007. "Assessing Language Using Computer Technology." *Annual Review of Applied Linguistics*, 27: 115–132.

Drasgow, Fritz, Richard M. Luecht, and Randy E. Bennett. 2006. "Technology and Testing." In

*Educational Measurement*, edited by Robert L. Brennan: 471–515. Westport, CT: American Council on Education and Praeger.

Drasgow, Fritz, and Krista Mattern. 2006. "New Tests and New Items: Opportunities and Issues." In *Computer-based Testing and the Internet: Issues and Advances*, edited by Dave Bartram and Ronald K. Hambleton, 59–76. Hoboken, NJ: John Wiley & Sons, Inc.

Everitt, Biran S., and Anders Skrondal. 2010. *The Cambridge Dictionary of Statistics*. Cambridge: Cambridge University Press.

Everson, Philip, and Susan Hines. 2010. "How ETS Scores the TOEIC Speaking and Writing Tests Responses." *TOEIC Compendium*: 8.1–8.9. Princeton, NJ: Educational Testing Service.

Fulcher, Glenn. 2005. "Better Communications Test Will Silence Critics." *Guardian Weekly*, February 18, 2005. Accessed July 20. http://education.guardian.co.uk/tefl/story/0,5500,1645011,00.html

Fulcher, Glenn. 2010. *Practical Language Testing*. London: Hodder Education.

Higgins, Derrick, and Michael Heilman. 2014. "Managing What We Can Measure: Quantifying the Susceptibility of Automated Scoring Systems to Gaming Hehavior." *Educational Measurement: Issues and Practice*, 33: 36–46.

Jordan, Sharon, Glyn Hughes, and Cris Betts. 2011. "Technology in Assessment." *Cambridge ESOL Research Notes*, 43: 2–6.

Kane, Michael T. 2006. "Validation." In *Educational Measurement*, edited by Robert L. Brennan: 17–64. Westport, CT: American Council on Education and Praeger.

Kane, Michael T. 2013. "Validating the Interpretations and Uses of Test Scores." *Journal of Educational Measurement*, 50: 1–73.

Lee, Yong-Won, Claudia Gentile, and Robert Kantor. 2009. "Toward Automated Multi-Trait Scoring of Essays: Investigating Links among Holistic, Analytic, and Text Feature Scores." *Applied Linguistics*, 31: 391–417.

Levy, Roy, John T. Behrens, and Robert J. Mislevy. 2006. "Variations in Adaptive Testing and Their Online Leverage Points." In *Online Assessment, Measurement, and Evaluation: Emerging Practices*, edited by David D. Williams, Scott L. Howell, and Mary Hricko, 180–202. Hershey, PA: IDEA Group.

Luecht, Richard M. 2006. "Operational Issues in Computer-based Testing." In *Computer-based Testing and the Internet: Issues and Ddvances*, edited by Dave Bartram and Ronald K.

Hambleton, 91–114. Hoboken, NJ: John Wiley & Sons, Inc.

Luecht, Richard M., and Stephen G. Sireci. 2011. "A Review of Models for Computer-based Testing." *Research Report No. 2011–12*. New York: College Board.

Mislevy, Robert, Carol A. Chapelle, Yoo-Ree Chung, and Jing Xu. 2008. "Options for Adaptivity in Computer-assisted Language Learning and Assessment." In *Towards Adaptive CALL: Natural Language Processing for Diagnostic Language Assessment*, edited by Carol A. Chapelle, Yoo-Ree Chung, and Jing Xu, 9–24. Ames, IA: Iowa State University.

Monaghan, William, and Brent Bridgeman. 2005. "E-rater as a Quality Control on Human Scores." *ETS RD Connections*. Princeton, NJ: Educational Testing Service.

Norris, John. 2001. "Concerns with Adaptive Oral Proficiency Assessment." *Language Learning and Technology*, 5: 99–105.

Ockey, Gary. 2007. "Construct Implications of Including Still Image or Video in Computer-based Listening Tests." *Language Testing*, 24: 517–537.

Olson, John F., and John Fremer. 2013. *TILSA Test Security Guidebook: Preventing, Detecting, and Investigating Test Security Irregularities*. Washington, DC: Council of Chief State School Officers.

Pitkin, Angela K., and Walter P. Vispoel. 2001. "Differences Between Self-adapted and Computerized Adaptive Tests: A Meta-analysis." *Journal of Educational Measurement*, 38: 235–247.

Powers, Donald E. 2011. "Scoring the TOEFL Independent Essay Automatically: Reactions of Test Takers and Test Score Users." *ETS Research Memorandum, RM-11–34*. Princeton, NJ: Educational Testing Service.

Roever, Carsten. 2001. "Web-based Language Testing." *Language Learning and Technology*, 5: 84–94.

Roos, Linda, Steven Wise, and Barbara Plake. 1997. "The Role of Item Feedback in Self-adapted Testing." *Educational and Psychological Measurement*, 57: 85–98.

Scalise, Kathleen, and Mark Wilson. 2011. "The Nature of Assessment Systems to Support Effective Use of Evidence Through Technology." *E-Learning and Digital Media*, 8: 121–132.

Surface, Eric A., Reanna M. Poncheri, and Kartik S. Bhavsar. 2008. *Two Studies Investigating the Reliability and Validity of the English ACTFL*

*OPIc with Korean Test Takers: The ACTFL OPIc Validation Project Technical Report*. Raleigh, NC: SWA Consulting.

Suvorov, Ruslan. 2013. Interacting with Visuals in L2 Listening Tests: An Eye-tracking Study. PhD dissertation, Iowa State University.

Wagner, Elvis. 2014. "Assessing Listening." In *The Companion to Language Assessment*, edited by Antony John Kunnan, 47–63. Hoboken, NJ: John Wiley and Sons, Inc.

Williamson, David M., Xiaoming Xi, and F. Jay Breyer. 2012. "A Framework for Evaluation and Use of Automated Scoring." *Educational Measurement: Issues and Practice, 31*: 2–13.

Wise, Steven, and Gage Kingsbury. 2000. "Practical Issues in Developing and Maintaining a Computerized Adaptive Testing Program." *Psicologica, 21*: 135–155.

Xi, Xiaoming. 2010. "Automated Scoring and Feedback Systems: Where Are We and Where Are We Heading?" *Language Testing, 27*: 291–300.

Xi, Xiaoming. 2012. "Validity and the Automated Scoring of Performance Tests." In *The Routledge Handbook of Language Testing*, edited by Glenn Fulcher and Fred Davidson, 438–451. New York: Routledge.

Xi, Xiaoming, Jonathan E. Schmidgall, and Yuan Wang. June 23–25, 2011 "User Reactions to Using SpeechRater for a Practice Test and Validity Implications." Paper presented at the 33rd Annual Conference of the Language Testing Research Colloquium, Ann Arbor, MI.

# 22 Validation of Technology-assisted Language Tests

## YOO-REE CHUNG

The use of technology in second language assessment has been growing over the past two decades for a variety of assessment purposes in diverse assessment contexts in many parts of the world. Technology is seen as attractive, because it holds potential for language instructors and testing practitioners to assess second language learners' target language skills in more efficient and innovative ways than possible through the use of paper-based tests. Significant affordances include the instant scoring of students' responses and prompt provision of feedback on students' test performance. On the other hand, such efficiencies and innovations in technology-assisted language testing require careful study, because they may lead to language tests that do not necessarily assess the intended language ability or produce the intended effects for test users. Technology affects every aspect of the testing process (see Schmidgall and Powers, this volume). Therefore, research investigating the validity of test score interpretation and use in computer-assisted language testing requires guidance from a systematic yet flexible conceptual framework that embraces every aspect of language testing procedures. Many researchers in language testing use such a framework for validation research. This chapter builds upon current argument-based approaches to validation by highlighting the issues that pertain to technology use in language testing.

## Argument-based approaches to validation in language testing

Validation is the term used in language testing to refer to the process of evaluating the adequacy of the interpretations made on the basis of test scores and the uses of the test scores for a particular purpose (Bachman 1990; Messick 1989). Because validation is concerned with interpretations and uses of test scores, the process of evaluation is necessarily focused on specific tests and specific score interpretations and uses for certain groups of students. This context-specific evaluation process shares many of the same characteristics as the process of evaluation of language learning materials (see Chapelle, this volume). Language testing researchers have developed precise ways of investigating validity to provide a means of constructing validity arguments about test interpretation and use. Methods for argument-based validation originate in educational measurement

*The Handbook of Technology and Second Language Teaching and Learning*, First Edition.
Edited by Carol A. Chapelle and Shannon Sauro.
© 2017 John Wiley & Sons, Inc. Published 2020 by John Wiley & Sons, Inc.

(Kane 2006; Messick 1989) and have been extended, adapted, and further specified for use in language testing (e.g., Bachman 2005; Bachman and Palmer 2010; Chapelle, Enright, and Jamieson 2008, 2010).

The "argument" in argument-based validation refers to the way that the validation studies are planned, carried out, and reported. The argument framework consists of multiple steps, each of which is intended to support test score interpretation and use. Each step in a validity argument consists of five primary elements: grounds and claims, inferences, warrants, assumptions, and rebuttals. Grounds and claims are each statements about one aspect of score interpretation and use. For example, a statement that the test-takers' performance has been elicited in a relevant manner would serve as a conclusion to the step in the argument that claims that the test tasks are sufficiently authentic. The same statement would serve as grounds for a claim about the observations of performance being evaluated appropriately to obtain scores. Grounds are connected to claims by inferences, each of which need to be authorized by a warrant, or a statement indicating that there are good reasons for making the inference. Once an inference is established, the claim comes to serve as grounds for a subsequent claim made in an argument for score interpretation and use. In this way, a validity argument is composed of a chain of inferences, which Kane, Crooks, and Cohen (1999) illustrate using a bridge analogy. A warrant can be conceived in terms of a proposition, or a ticket to the next station, metaphorically speaking (Chapelle et al. 2010).

Validation research is conducted to investigate to what extent each warrant in the argument is supported on the basis of relevant theory and research. Whether a warrant is sustained or not is determined by the extent to which its underlying assumptions are supported with evidence, or backing. Oppositions to warrants are rebuttals, which are statements that, if supported, weaken the argument. Figure 22.1 illustrates this framework of argument-based validation, adapted from Kane (2006), Chapelle et al. (2008, 2010), and Bachman and Palmer (2010), consisting of seven inferences. Chapelle et al. (2008) similarly summarized the practice of making a validity argument for the Test of English as a Foreign Language™ (TOEFL) in a step-wise fashion.

# Technology and validity arguments

Technology-assisted language testing offers many advantages to test users, test-takers, and language instructors, such as facilitation in observation of examinee performance, instant scoring and feedback provision, and assistance in language teachers' preparation of class lessons. Despite these potential advantages, it is imperative to evaluate how the use of technology affects every aspect of score interpretation and use in language assessment. This section raises the considerations for doing so by identifying issues emerging from the incorporation of technology in language assessment, starting at the bottom of the validity argument framework illustrated in Figure 22.1.

## *Domain description inference*

*Domain description* pertains to the relevance of test tasks and characteristics of language produced by test-takers to those observed in the target language use (TLU) domain. The domain description inference in a validity argument requires support for assumptions underlying a warrant that examinee performance on the technology-assisted language test reflects the relevant target language skills used in the target domain. In other words, the argument needs to show that the test tasks are appropriate. In many cases, interactive,

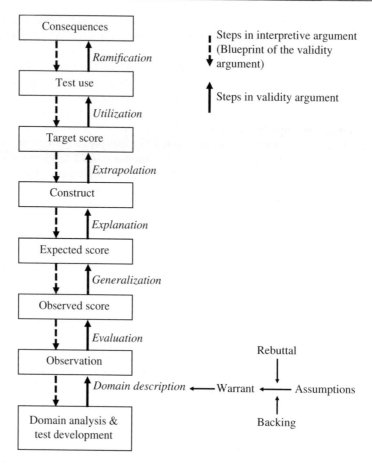

**Figure 22.1**   An argument-based validation framework.

multimedia technologies are used in test tasks in order to construct appropriate, some-times innovative, conditions for eliciting language (Alderson 1990; Brown 1997; Chalhoub-Deville 2001; Jamieson 2005). Such media are often selected because the test designer holds the assumptions that:

- Technology-assisted language testing enhances the authenticity of test tasks.
- Tasks of the technology-assisted language test elicit examinee responses reflective of the characteristics of language used in the target domain.

Both of these assumptions pertain to how well the test tasks reflect the domain of interest to test score users and, therefore, need to be supported by decisions and rationales that are developed during task design.

## Technology for authentic task design

Test designers attempt to create authentic test tasks using multimedia in test prompts. Short video clips or animations are, for instance, intended to help examinees engage with test tasks by providing vivid context or situation visual information including topics, participants, and temporal and spatial settings (Bejar et al. 2000; Ginther 2002). Media also assist in the delivery of complicated content to test-takers using visual aids (e.g., the use of slides or videos for lectures or presentations in a university classroom). Assessing language for specific purposes (LSP) can particularly benefit from the use of technology with multimedia enhancing the contextualization of the target task (Douglas 2000). Virtual worlds, although having rarely been implemented in language testing yet, can also serve as a real-world-like platform for task-based LSP assessment; it allows a designer to "create highly interactive and complex performance simulations … to submerge the examinee in the task environment" (Luecht and Clauser 2002, 72). By incorporating virtual realism, task-oriented LSP tests, such as aviation English tests, could thus elicit test-takers' responses which highly resemble the language produced in the TLU domain.

A question that a test validator needs to pose in this regard is whether the multimedia or the virtual world employed in task design indeed appropriately and effectively enhances the authenticity of the test tasks as intended. The backing for this assumption, therefore, comes from an analysis of the domain of interest using, for example, Bachman and Palmer's (1996) test task characteristics and the relevance of the multimedia in the test task to the topic, setting, participants, and text type (including visual or non-visual input). Such an analysis applied to all the multimedia aspects of the test tasks raises important issues for test design by raising questions about the appropriateness of images. For example, if the topic of the prompt were healthy eating and the test developer had selected an image depicting healthy behavior, the image could be confusing to test-takers if the healthy activity were, for example, of people exercising in a gym. On the other hand, if the image were selected to show what healthy food the people were eating and the answer to the test question could be found in the image, the test question would be ineffective for assessing listening comprehension. In short, the selection of visuals with the appropriate degree of specificity and contextualization is a significant issue for test development.

Several options exist for selecting appropriate specificity and contextualization of visuals as part of prompt design in a listening test. Test developers might decide to use no visuals in order to assess test-takers' listening ability without the benefit of visual information as required for speaking on the telephone, for example. In other cases, visual aids accompanying an audio lecture might contain only a few images relevant to the topic or provide some key terms as well. In an extreme case, the visuals used might contain most pieces of information delivered by the audio lecture in a very detailed way. From an authenticity perspective, all of the above cases are possible and actually occur in the real world. The decision on the question of how detailed information should be included in visual aids should be made based on a clear definition of the construct as well as the analysis of the linguistic and contextual characteristics of the target domain tasks.

## Elicitation of authentic examinee responses

The use of technology in language testing allows for a variety of methods for eliciting test-takers' responses. If the assumption about authenticity of task responses is to be supported in the validity argument, test designers need to take into account the authenticity of the response formats in relation to the mode of language used in the target domain. A domain analysis of test-takers' use of language in academic settings, for example, would find that the use of technology as a mediator for language production is a normal practice. In test design, this has implications for how students' writing and speaking abilities are to be measured. For example, Drag-and-drop response formats adopted for a productive grammatical writing ability test are not a natural mode of output in writing, which can, in turn, lead to inauthentic measurement of the target construct relative to the target domain (Chung 2011). Similarly, multiple-choice and written discourse completion tasks are difficult to support as

elicitation methods for test-takers' productive oral skills to assess their pragmatic competence because of the discrepancy in language mode between the test and the TLU domain,
even though selective or short written responses take little time to score automatically
(Roever 2006). While technical limitations certainly exist to some extent, it is advisable that
test developers consider how germane their response formats are to the mode of target
language use in an attempt to justify their task design in light of the warrant and assumptions of the *Domain description* inference.

# Evaluation inference

The warrant in need of support for *Evaluation* requires the appropriate and fair observation
of test performance across various examinee groups to render scores indicative of their actual
language ability. For a viable validity argument, test designers may posit assumptions that
need support as follows:

- Innovative or multimedia-enhanced tasks create conditions for students to perform in a
  way that is reflective of their ability.
- The automated scoring system produces scores that reflect the intended target language
  abilities.
- The feedback produced by the automated evaluation system accurately and satisfacto-
  rily identifies students' weaknesses in the target language skill.
- The technology-assisted language test is not only accessible to test-takers, but also delivered to them with stability.
- The technology-assisted language testing system is securely protected from infringement.

These assumptions pertain to three aspects of evaluation: observation of test
performance, scoring, and test delivery conditions. Each of these aspects affects the quality
of the observation, which subsequently affects the interpretation and use of test scores.

## Observation of test performance

The issue of observation of test performance concerning *Evaluation* mainly poses a question
of whether examinees' performance on a technology-assisted language test would be appropriately affected by the types of technology used. For example, test developers should ensure
that the technology used in language testing does not work in favor of, or be detrimental to,
particular subgroups of test-takers in ways that are irrelevant to the construct measured by
the test. Test-takers' technology literacy is a potential factor to take into account considering
the fair observation of test performance in technology-assisted language testing. Test-takers'
computer literacy and its impact on test performance have been researched in many studies
(Clariana and Wallace 2002; Kirsch et al. 1998; Lee 1986; Taylor et al. 1999; Wise et al. 1989).
While young language learners in many countries have grown up with technology, test-
takers' computer literacy should not be taken for granted, because test-takers in some parts
of the world still have limited access to computer technology. In addition, as new platforms,
such as tablet PCs or smartphones, continuously evolve along with unceasing technological
advances, test developers should carefully consider the interactivity between test-takers and
the tasks implemented on a variety of platforms to investigate their influences on test
performance. It is also imperative that test designers planning to adopt a new testing
platform make proper efforts to minimize its undesirable effects on test performance, as
demonstrated by Jamieson, Taylor, Kirsch, and Eignor (1998).

## Scoring

If the test developer decides to use an automated scoring system for instant scoring of examinee responses, the performance of the scoring machine should also be evaluated in verification of the quality of the observation of test performance. Normally, human scores serve as a norm against which the performance of the automated scoring system is calibrated and evaluated, provided that human raters are well trained and experienced and produce consistent and reliable scores from both intra-rater and inter-rater perspectives (Williamson, Xi, and Breyer 2012). In their proposition of an argument-based framework for the evaluation of automated essay scoring (AES) systems, Williamson et al. (2012) provide detailed guidelines for test developers and evaluators to refer to with respect to each inference in a validity argument by employing examples of validation practices on *e-rater®*, an AES engine developed by ETS. Concerning the *Evaluation* inference in particular, they offer six different ways to examine the quality of the machine scores as follows:

- general agreement between the human scores and the machine scores,
- degradation of the human-machine score agreement from human-human score agreement,
- standardized mean score difference between human and machine scores,
- degree of tolerance in the human-machine score difference without human adjudication,
- abnormal characteristics requiring human intervention in scoring, and
- relationship between human and machine scores at the task type and reported score level.

The concept of scores can be extended to include learner errors identified, as well as feedback provided by human or machine raters, if one wishes to evaluate the performance of an AES system designed for low-stakes, diagnostic, or formative assessment purposes. As automated feedback systems are intended to evaluate learner output at a micro level of language use, their performance should be investigated in terms of false positives (i.e., identifying correct productions as errors) and false negatives (i.e., failing to identify actual errors) (Weigle 2013). In addition to these criteria, the evaluation of the performance of an automated speech recognition system would require the examination of the system's accuracy in recognizing learner speech and its ability to take into account various characteristics of learner speech affected by learners' first languages.

## Test delivery condition

Test delivery conditions are also a critical dimension to consider in the validation of technology-assisted language testing, in which the observation and the scoring of test performance are heavily influenced by the performance of a test delivery system. From a technical perspective, test delivery conditions, such as accessibility, system stability, and security, should be sustained in order to make a credible evaluation of test performance. Test developers need to consider the technical feasibility and stability of a technology-assisted language test both at the test provider's end and at the test-takers' end. Web-based language tests heavily loaded with multimedia materials, such as Flash-based animations or high-definition video lectures, would require the test provider to be equipped with a high-speed broadband internet connection and one or more high-capacity servers to maintain stable test delivery. The broadband internet access must be available to test-takers as well; otherwise, potential test-takers' access to the testing opportunity may be restricted, or the observation of test performance may be inaccurate. The stability and accessibility of the testing system is therefore a necessary condition for appropriate evaluations of examinee performance on the technology-assisted language test. Lastly, the testing system must be safely secured from any possible infringement for the fair evaluation of examinee performance. The scoring mechanism of the automated scoring system used in testing should also be kept confidential from test-takers to prevent them from attempting to fool the system or use writing strategies that simply satisfy the scoring schemes rather than produce effective writing (Weigle 2013).

## Generalization inference

*Generalization* and *Extrapolation* are related to the consistency of examinees' test performance with their performance which could be observed in the universal domain (of similar test tasks, items, and raters) and in the TLU domain, respectively. The warrant of *Generalization* is that observed scores are stable estimates of expected scores over the parallel versions of tasks. The assumptions to be supported in the validity argument include:

- A technology-assisted language test performs at an acceptable level of reliability.
- The reliability or generalizability of scores produced through technology-assisted language testing is comparable with that of scores produced by paralleled test formats or scoring methods.
- Comparable reliability is maintained across diverse subgroups.

The test is expected to measure test-takers' target language ability consistently across similar test items and assessment settings. Consistency in language assessment is normally evaluated in two ways: reliability and generalizability. While a high reliability is advised, the acceptable level of reliability may vary depending on the level of stakes of the test as long as the decision can be justified. Concerning the *Generalizability* inference in the validation of the AES system, Williamson et al. (2012) particularly raise two empirical issues that guide the investigations in consideration of the inference: (1) the generalizability of machine scores across tasks and test forms compared to human scores and (2) machine scores' predictability of human scores on an alternative test form. The first issue prompts researchers to investigate the extent to which the use of an AES system is attributable to test scores in comparison to human rating; the second issue is, according to the authors, useful for improving the reliability of alternative test forms.

Another way to look into the reliability of a technology-assisted language test and/or an AES system is to examine the consistency of the system performance across diverse subgroups of test-takers. For example, the significance of the difference in the Cronbach's alpha between two examinee subgroups can be examined using a meta-analysis method proposed by Bonett (2010). This method allows us to calculate the confidence interval of the difference between two alpha coefficients obtained from different test administrations. The confidence interval including zero indicates that the difference between the two alpha coefficients is not statistically significant.

## Explanation inference

Apparent credible observations of examinee performance on a reliable test does not necessarily entail that the test measures the target construct as intended. To address this logical gap, the warrant underlying *Explanation* in the validity argument demands that examinees' test performance whose interpretation is to be expanded beyond the scope of testing should correspond to theoretical expectations drawing upon the target construct. Its underlying assumptions include the following:

- Test performance elicited by technology-assisted tasks is relevant to and sufficiently represents the target construct.
- Test-takers' performance on the technology-assisted language test corresponds to the theoretical expectations drawing upon the construct definition.
- Examinees' performance on the technology-assisted language test is consistent with their performance on other tests that measure or tap into the same construct.
- Automated scores relate to the construct.

## Construct relevance and representation

As in the validation of conventional paper-based language tests, the contents and tasks of technology-assisted language tests should prove to be not only relevant to the target construct, but also sufficiently represent it (Bachman 1990). Factor analysis is a useful statistical method to investigate the relevance of the test to the construct as a latent variable in terms of its theoretical dimensions. It, however, does not render enough evidence that the test is sufficiently relevant to the target construct in terms of construct meaning; rather, the pursuit of the backing for the establishment of *Explanation* in the validity argument requires in-depth investigations from multiple perspectives pertaining to how the technology employed affects the construct meaning. A complication that the integration of technology in language testing can bring about is a need for the testing researcher to conceptualize the role of the technology in the construct meaning. For instance, Ockey's (2007) study of performance on a listening comprehension test found that test-takers were rarely engaged with still images in the listening tasks, but the participants had interacted with video input to varying degrees. Drawing upon this finding, he suggested that test developers should clearly define the construct of listening ability in relation to the types of input to be utilized in the computer-based listening test.

If the construct is underrepresented by the technology-integrated design of test tasks, the construct definition should be accordingly narrowed down (Weigle 2013). Take for an example the Versant English Test, a speaking test offered by Pearson. Five out of the six speaking task types of the Versant test are restrictive in eliciting test-takers' speech samples due to the limited performance of its automated scoring system. The test provider accordingly claims that the construct be "a candidate's facility in spoken English—that is, the ability to understand spoken English on everyday topics and to respond appropriately at a native-like conversational pace in intelligible English," in which the facility in spoken English is defined as "the ease and immediacy in understanding and producing appropriate conversational English" (Pearson 2011, 8). This construct definition does not include the discourse-level speaking ability of test-takers, such as the ability to construct extended oral responses in a coherent and cohesive way; nor is it intended to cover the oral English ability required for a specific purpose.

## Correspondence to theoretical expectations

In addition to construct relevance and representation, the evidence that examinees perform on the technology-assisted language test in accordance with the theoretical expectations grounded in the construct definition provides another backing for the establishment of *Explanation*. For example, higher-proficiency examinees are expected to significantly outperform lower-proficiency examinees on the test. If two or more item groups classified by a construct-driven hypothesis are expected to perform distinctively from one another, research results that comply with such an expectation will also add to the support for the warrant of

*Explanation,* as demonstrated in Chapelle, Chung, Hegelheimer, Pender, and Xu (2010) and Chung (2014). The technology can be used to systematically alter the difficulty of items by offering help to test-takers in some cases. For instance, Ginther (2002) reported that content visuals accompanying mini-talks in TOEFL® CBT (Computer-Based Test) facilitated examinees' comprehension of the given aural passages. On the other hand, context visuals accompanying mini-talks were found to make comprehension slightly more difficult, which affected low-proficiency examinees' performance more adversely than that of high-proficiency examinees. A decision regarding the provision of help for test-takers should, therefore, be guided by not only careful considerations about the linguistic, topical, genre-related, and contextual characteristics of the prompt, but also empirical investigations of possible interactions between those characteristics and the nature of the help and their potential impact on examinee performance.

## Convergent and divergent validity evidence

Another backing for *Explanation* in the validity argument can be sought by means of comparing examinees' performance between the technology-assisted language test and another measure of the same or a different construct. If the two tests under comparison measure the same or a similar construct, what is expected are positive, significant correlations at a moderate to strong strength between the scores obtained from those tests. The strength of the correlation would be determined by the extent to which the constructs of the two tests are identical to each other. On the other hand, negative and/or non-significant correlations are expected between two score sets if the compared tests are designed to measure different or unrelated constructs. Evidence that corresponds to these theoretical expectations, hence, fortifies the support of the *Evaluation* inference in validity argument.

## Pertinence of automated scores to the construct

As hinted in the Versant example above, the design of an automated scoring or evaluation system requires special additional attention to its relation to the construct. The scoring rubric originally developed for human rating may not be directly applicable to the design of an automated scoring machine, because machines do not "comprehend" what a human essay or speech intends to mean (Attali 2013). A scoring engine generating human-like scores using advanced statistical approaches may be successful in obtaining reliability, but it should still be put under scrutiny, whether or not the scoring features pertain to the construct. In this way, it is incumbent upon the designer of an automated scoring system to examine the relatedness of proxy features (e.g., speech rate and response length for fluency, accuracy and complexity ratios of grammaticality, etc.) to the target construct in terms of both construct relevance and construct representativeness.

Studies by Quinlan, Higgins, and Wolff (2009) and Ginther, Dimova, and Yang (2010) illustrate well the investigations of construct relevance and coverage issues posed by the validation of the use of an automated scoring system in evaluating language learner output. Quinlan et al. (2009) investigated the construct relevance of the *e-rater®* engine by examining the construct coverage accomplished by its scoring features. Their findings revealed that the system covered low-level aspects of basic writing skills (e.g., vocabulary, grammar, and conventions), while high-level aspects (e.g., ideas and organization) of essay quality were only partially addressed by the system. In regard to the development of an automated speaking scoring system, Ginther et al. (2010) explored the relationships between temporal variables of fluency (e.g., speech rate, speech time ratio, mean length of run, and the number and length of silent pauses) and the examinees' oral English proficiency measured by an institutional semi-direct speaking test called the Oral English Proficiency Test (OEPT). Despite moderate to strong correlations between their fluency measures and the OEPT levels, the measures of interest alone turned out to be unsuccessful in discriminating between adjacent levels. The authors there-fore concluded that the temporal fluency measures underrepresented the construct of the oral English proficiency and that they should be accompanied by other measures in order to achieve scoring with a better construct representation.

Considerations of the relation between the construct and the automated scoring algorithm lead to the refinement or re-conceptualization of the construct as well. Carr and Xi (2010), for instance, illustrated how the attempts to replicate human scores using automated scoring devised for short responses in a reading test allowed them to identify room for refinement in the construct definition. On the other hand, Deane (2013a, 2013b) discussed an approach to develop an automated essay scoring system drawing upon a socio-cognitive conceptual framework of literary skills, called *Cognitively Based Assessment of, for, and as Learning (CBAL)*, which is a research strand initiated by ETS researchers (Bennett 2011; Bennett and Gitomer 2009). Much work remains to be done to improve understanding about the relationship bet-ween automated scoring and construct definition.

## Explanation *in low-stakes testing*

As the scope of the interpretation of low-stakes language test scores is narrower than that of high-stakes test scores, the inference to make in the validity argument for a low-stakes tech-nology-assisted language test is stated in view of course objectives in classroom contexts. Chapelle and Voss (2014) named this inference as *Objectives Reflection*, "to indicate the need to demonstrate that the course objectives have been well reflected by the test tasks and the abilities that the test measures" (9). Following this line of reasoning, the use of a pronunciation software program would be inappropriate for evaluating students' use of organizational cues in a second or foreign language speaking classroom, because the tasks provided by the software are too narrow to demonstrate the students' ability to employ organizational cues in oral communication. However, such software may be appropriate for providing feedback on the aspects of pronunciation targeted by learning outcomes.

## *Extrapolation inference*

*Extrapolation*, the final inference in the validation of test score interpretation for an intended purpose, can be made if support is found for the warrant that test-takers' performance on the technology-assisted language test be consistent with their performance observed in the target domain. In order to have this warrant established, we should support a general assumption that scores obtained from the technology-assisted language testing (whichever scoring method is used) are commensurate with the test-takers' performance in the use of target language skills normally observed in non-testing target contexts. This issue can be explored in terms of predictive validity evidence—that is, by investigating the extent to which test scores successfully predict individual test-takers' performance in real life. The real-world criteria to which such an investigation refers include test-takers' final grades in relevant courses, instructors' observations of test-takers' performance in the classrooms, portfolio evaluation results, and test-takers' self-evaluations. If an automated scoring system is employed, the predictability of the machine scores should also be examined in comparison to the predictability of human scores, as conducted in the prior validation stages.

## *Utilization inference*

Once it is attested that test scores can be adequately interpreted in relation to the construct in the target domain of interest through a series of investigations, the next inference to be made requires evidence that scores are properly used for their intended purpose. The warrant for this *Utilization* inference states that the use of test scores leads to the appropriate decision-making or feedback to students. Below are a few underlying assumptions that may require backing for the establishment of the *Utilization* inference:

- Scores of the technology-assisted language test are used in decision-making for their intended purpose.
- Test users make appropriate decisions based on the scores or feedback generated by the technology-assisted language test.
- The automated feedback is properly utilized in practice by language learners as well as instructors.

## Appropriate decision-making

Mid/high-stakes decisions made with test scores include admissions, placement, certification, or promotion, whereas low-stakes test scores might be used to help instructors understand students' ability, identify the level of achievement, enhance learning by providing instant feedback on specific language areas, or develop students as autonomous learners through interaction with automated feedback. Whether the use of technology-assisted language test scores is appropriate depends on whether the scores work for their intended purpose. When language tests are used to make criterion-referenced decisions in mid/high-stakes contexts, the appropriateness of the use of test scores can be judged in terms of false positives and false negatives checked against another criterion. For example, if a group of students is placed in an ESL listening class through a computerized English placement test, the appropriateness of the placements can be determined by comparing individual students' performance in the placement test with that observed on a second test tailored to the relevant class content. A comparability found in the comparison between the examinee performance across the two measures will serve as a backing for this assumption. If the discrepancy of the examinee performance between the two measures is beyond an acceptable level, it will fail to provide evidence in the validity argument of the use of test scores.

## Usability of automated feedback

Unlike in mid/high-stakes assessment contexts, technology-assisted language assessment offered for low-stakes purposes, as is *Criterion®*, are normally utilized to identify language learners' strengths and weaknesses in the target language skill and, thus, to provide learners with opportunities to correct their errors using the automated feedback. A fundamental goal of grammatical error detection in formative assessment is, for example, to help language learners improve the quality of their writing in the target language by diagnosing common error types and making useful suggestions that can lead to learning (Gamon et al. 2013). The achievement of this goal requires not only the provision of feedback but the actual use of automated feedback by its users.

The usefulness of feedback should be evaluated in view of both the instructors' and students' needs. Language instructors, as one of the stakeholders, may use the feedback to diagnose specifics of their students' language ability and plan their lessons based on the diagnosis. All issues pertaining to a question of whether the provision of automated feedback leads to useable information for the instructors and students are then subject to the investigation. For example, Choi (2010 quoted in Gamon et al. 2013) compared the accuracy of English learning students' essays written in three conditions, which differed in the instructors' use of *Criterion®*, and their essay scores. The results revealed that, in two of three writing assignments, the essays written under the *Criterion*-integrated instruction condition achieved higher scores with higher accuracy through the revision process than the essays written in the other two conditions where *Criterion*® was either never used in instruction or only served as an optional resource for students.

In a similar vein, test validators should examine whether students practically use automated feedback to improve the quality of their target language use. Even if instructors require their students to use automated feedback in revising drafts of a writing assignment, for example, the quality of the drafts may not improve if the students distrust automated feedback or seldom refer to it. Students' use of automated feedback at varying degrees has been witnessed (Chapelle, Cotos, and Lee 2015). In their study, an analysis of the patterns of ESL college students' use of feedback from *Criterion*® in the revision of their writing drafts uncovered that 51 percent of the automated feedback was neglected by students. This relatively high rate of unused feedback calls for educating students in the value of automated feedback as well as the effective use of automated feedback in their learning, especially considering that 70 percent of all revision attempts students made by referring to the automated feedback were reportedly successful in the same study.

## Ramification inference

The final facet to consider in validating the use of technology-assisted language test scores concerns how diverse groups of stakeholders are affected by the use of test scores and what short- and long-term consequences will result. The warrant of the *Ramification* inference accordingly dictates that the decisions made by the use of test scores bring about consequences beneficial to stakeholders. While the appraisal of the consequences of test use should consider "not only individual and institutional effects but societal and systemic effects as well" (Messick 1989, 85), due to limited space, the assumptions below pertain only to the impact on students and language instructors, those most immediately affected within the educational domain:

- Students placed in a second or foreign language class based on their test scores benefit from the language instruction.
- Potential negative impact of score use on students is as minimal as possible.
- Automated feedback promotes students' learning.
- Instructors benefit from the use of automated feedback in their teaching.
- Unintended consequences of score use do not adversely affect stakeholders.

### Intended consequences on students and language instructors

When a test is used for a specific purpose, the test users have in mind certain intended consequences that the test use will bring about. The first step would be to ensure that such intended consequences indeed derive from the test use and that test-takers benefit from the assessment outcomes. For example, those who meet a certain criterion in a mid- or high-stakes language proficiency test will encounter less difficulty in pursuing their academic or career goals. Relevant backing evidence could be found by investigating the impact of the use of test scores on examinees in their near and distant future as well as their perceptions about the consequences of the score use.

Evidence that the use of test results is beneficial to test-takers can also be found in low-stakes assessments. For example, automated feedback may result in a face-saving process of error correction, and the instant provision of feedback on their language use also may support the assumption that students benefit from the use of an AES system in low-stakes assessment contexts (Weigle 2013). Other examples of the benefits of AES in language assessment can also be found in Gamon et al. (2013).

Another aspect worth noting in the validation of the use of a technology-assisted language test for low-stakes assessment is the consequences it brings about for language instructors. An AES system deployed in L2 instruction would allow teachers to have sufficient time to review the automated feedback and tailor their lessons to accommodate students' needs in a timely manner, thereby affecting the overall quality of their teaching. Detailed automated feedback on students' grammar and vocabulary use in writing could also enable the instructors to dedicate more time and effort to discourse-level concerns such as argumentation (Weigle 2013).

## Unintended consequences

The appraisal of the intended consequences of the use of technology-assisted language test scores provides necessary evidence for the *Ramification* inference. However, it does "not provide sufficient justification" (Messick 1989, 85), which can be investigated by taking into account unintended consequences of the test use. One possible unintended consequence of the use of an automated evaluation system is that students may change their writing strategies simply to meet the machine's expectations (Attali 2013; Chapelle et al. 2015). Similarly, students who have learned the scoring algorithm of the evaluation system may study how to fool the system or change their ways to prepare for the test rather than studying how to write well (Weigle 2013). Since such incidences would provide data in support of a rebuttal for the *Ramification* inference, signaling the need for test developers and users should seek ways to mitigate unintended consequences.

# Conclusion

Validation demands extensive effort to investigate aspects of testing from the test design to the consequences of the test use. In addition, the validation process should be iterative as the test undergoes change in design, implementation, or test score use (Williamson et al. 2012). In fact, every attempt to revise the test (e.g., task revisions or construct re-definition) or use it to different ends (e.g., using *Criterion*® for an ESL placement purpose at a university) requires another series of investigations based on any new inferences, warrants, and assumptions that are to be included in the validity argument for the new interpretations and uses.

The assumptions identified in this chapter suggest areas of investigation for the validation of technology-assisted language testing in particular based on the little previous research in this area. Additional potential research issues in the validation of technology-assisted language testing may also include questions such as the following (with the related inference(s) in parentheses):

1. How and to what extent does the adoption of a new testing platform (such as smartphones or tablet PCs) affect test performance and score interpretations? How can language testing on a new technological platform be justified in relation to the language mode used in the TLU domain? (*Domain description*)
2. How do various aspects of technology used in language assessment interact with examinees' cognition pertinent to the use of the target language skill? To what extent are examinees' cognitive activities engaged in technology-assisted language testing consistent with those taking place in TLU contexts? (*Explanation* and *Extrapolation*)
3. To what extent does the virtual-world-based LSP assessment enhance the authenticity of testing? What factors, if any, make the test performance deviate from normal language use, and how could it be amended to better support extrapolation? (*Extrapolation*)

4. In what ways does the adoption of new technology in language testing affect the fairness of testing on a variety of test-taker groups? What measures can be taken to guarantee the fairness in the technology-assisted language testing? (*Evaluation, Explanation,* and *Ramification*)

5. To what extent can the technology-assisted language testing at diverse levels of stakes contribute to learning-oriented assessment? What consequences does the adoption of the technology-assisted language testing in language instruction bring about in relation to language learning, pedagogy, and teacher training? (*Ramification*)

Until recently, most discussions and research efforts made in the validation of technology-assisted language testing have centered on the use of technology in large-scale, high-stakes language tests, partly due to an enormous financial demand the development of such a tool requires, a cost which only corporate entities could afford to invest. Continued advances in technology have, however, begun to make technology-assisted language assessment also available in smaller-scale, low-stakes educational contexts as witnessed in the use of Criterion® in ESL writing classrooms (Chapelle et al. 2015). As a consequence, the future of technology-assisted language testing will become more heavily tied to language learning than it currently is. Therefore, more examples of validation research for technology-assisted language tests should help to expand the field's understanding of such assessments.

# REFERENCES

Alderson, J. Charles. 1990. "Learner-centered Testing through Computer: Institutional Issues in Individual Assessment." In *Individualizing the Assessment of Language Abilities*, edited by John de Jong and Douglas K. Stevenson, 20–27. Clevedon: Multilingual Matters.

Attali, Yigal. 2013. "Validity and Reliability of Automated Essay Scoring." In *Handbook of Automated Essay Evaluation: Current Applications and New Directions*, edited by Mark D. Shermis, and Jill Burstein, 181–198. New York: Routledge.

Bachman, Lyle F. 1990. *Fundamental Considerations in Language Testing*. Oxford: Oxford University Press.

Bachman, Lyle F. 2005. "Building and Supporting a Case for Test Use." *Language Assessment Quarterly*, 2, no. 1: 1–34. DOI:10.1207/s15434311laq0201_1

Bachman, Lyle F., and Adrian S. Palmer. 1996. *Language Testing in Practice: Designing and Developing Useful Language Tests*. Oxford: Oxford University Press.

Bachman, Lyle F., and Adrian S. Palmer. 2010. *Language Assessment in Practice*. Oxford: Oxford University Press.

Bejar, Isaac, Dan Douglas, Joan Jamieson, Susan Nissan, and Jean Turner. 2000. *TOEFL 2000 Listening Framework: A Working Paper*. Princeton, NJ: Educational Testing Service.

Bennett, Randy E. 2011. *CBAL: Results from Piloting Innovative K-12 Assessments* (Research Report No. RR-11-23). Princeton, NJ: Educational Testing Service.

Bennett, Randy E., and Drew H. Gitomer. 2009. "Transforming K-12 Assessment; Integrating Accountability Testing, Formative Assessment and Professional Support." In *Educational Assessment in the 21st Century: Connecting theory and practice*, edited by Claire Wyatt-Smith and Joy Cumming, 43–62. Dordrecht: Springer.

Bonett, Douglas G. 2010. "Varying Coefficient Meta-analytic Methods for Alpha Reliability." *Psychological Methods*, 15: 368–385. DOI:10.1037/a0020142

Brown, James D. 1997. "Computerized in Language Testing: Present Research and Some Future Directions." *Language Learning & Technology*, 1, no. 1: 44–59. Accessed June 15, 2014. http://llt.msu.edu/vol1num1/brown/default.html

Carr, Nathan T., and Xiaoming Xi. 2010. "Automated Scoring of Short-answered Reading Items: Implications for Constructs." *Language Assessment Quarterly*, 7: 205–218. DOI:10.1080/15434300903443958

Chalhoub-Deville, Michelle. 2001. "Language Testing and Technology: Past and Future." *Language Learning & Technology*, 5, no. 2: 95–98. Accessed June 15, 2014. http://llt.msu.edu/vol5num2/deville/default.html

Chapelle, Carol A., Yoo-Ree Chung, Volker Hegelheimer, Nick Pendar, and Jing Xu. 2010. "Towards a Computer-delivered Test of Productive Grammatical Ability." *Language Testing*, 27, no. 4: 443–469. DOI:10.1177/0265532210367633

Chapelle, Carol A., Elena Cotos, and Jooyoung Lee. 2015. "Validity Arguments for Diagnostic Assessment Using Automated Writing Evaluation." *Language Testing*, 32, no. 3: 385–405. DOI:10.1177/0265532214565386

Chapelle, Carol A., Mary K. Enright, and Joan M. Jamieson, eds. 2008. *Building a Validity Argument for the Test of English as a Foreign Language™*. New York: Routledge.

Chapelle, Carol A., Mary K Enright, and Joan M. Jamieson, eds. 2010. "Does an Argument-Based Approach to Validity Make a Difference?" *Educational Measurement: Issues and Practice*, 29, no. 1: 3–13. DOI:10.1111/j.1745-3992.2009.00165.x

Chapelle, Carol A., and Erik Voss. 2014. "Evaluation of Language Tests through Validation Research." In *The Companion to Language Assessment*, edited by Antony J. Kunnan: 1081–1097. Chichester: John Wiley & Sons, Inc.

Choi, Jaeho. 2010. The Impact of Automated Essay Scoring (AEES) for Improving English Language Learners' Essay Writing. Unpublished PhD dissertation, University of Virginia, Charlottesville, VA. Quoted in Michael Gamon, Martin Chodorow, Claudia Leacock, and Joel Tetreault. 2013. "Grammatical Error Detection in Automated Essay Scoring and Feedback." In *Handbook of Automated Essay Evaluation: Current applications and new directions*, edited by Mark D. Shermis, and Jill Burstein, 251–266. New York: Routledge.

Chung, Yoo-Ree. 2011. "Task Effects on Learner Performance in a Computer-delivered Test of Productive Grammatical Ability." Paper presented at the Colloquium on *Interfaces between Second Language Acquisition and Language Assessment: The Next Generation*. Second Language Research Forum 2011, Ames, IA.

Chung, Yoo-Ree. 2014. A Test of Productive English Grammatical Ability in Academic Writing: Development and Validation. Unpublished PhD dissertation, Iowa State University, Ames, IA.

Clariana, Roy, and Patricia Wallace. 2002. "Paper-based versus Computer-based Assessment: Key factors Associated with the Test Mode Effect." *British Journal of Educational Technology*, 33, no. 5: 593–602. DOI:10.1111/1467-8535.00294

Deane, Paul. 2013a. "Covering the Construct: An Approach to Automated Essay Scoring Motivated by a Socio-cognitive Framework for defining Literacy Skills." In *Handbook of Automated Essay Evaluation: Current Applications and New Directions*, edited by Mark D. Shermis, and Jill Burstein, 298–312. New York: Routledge.

Deane, Paul. 2013b. "On the Relation between Automated Essay Scoring and Modern Views of the Writing Construct." *Assessing Writing*, 18: 7–24. DOI:10.1016/j.asw.2012.10.002

Douglas, Dan. 2000. *Assessing Language for Specific Purposes*. Cambridge: Cambridge University Press.

Gamon, Michael, Martin Chodorow, Claudia Leacock, and Joel Tetreault. 2013. "Grammatical Error Detection in Automated Essay Scoring and Feedback." In *Handbook of Automated Essay Evaluation: Current Applications and New Directions*, edited by Mark D. Shermis, and Jill Burstein, 251–266. New York: Routledge.

Ginther, April. 2002. "Context and Content Visuals and Performance on Listening Comprehension Stimuli." *Language Testing*, 19, no. 2: 133–167. DOI:10.1191/0265532202lt225oa

Ginther, April, Slobodanka Dimova, and Rui Yang. 2010. "Conceptual and Empirical Relationships between Temporal Measures of Fluency and Oral English Proficiency with Implications for Automated Scoring." *Language Testing*, 27, no. 3: 379–399. DOI:10.1177/0265532210364407

Jamieson, Joan. 2005. "Trends in Computer-based Second Language Assessment." *Annual Review of Applied Linguistics*, 25: 228–242. DOI:10.1017/S0267190505000127

Jamieson, Joan, Carol Taylor, Irwin Kirsch, and Daniel Eignor. 1998. "Design and Evaluation of a Computer-based TOEFL Tutorial." *System*, 26, no. 4: 285–513. DOI:10.1016/S0346-251X(98)00034-7

Kane, Michael. 2006. "Validation." In *Educational Measurement*, 4th ed., edited by Robert L. Brennan, 17–64. Westport, CT: American Council of Education and Praeger.

Kane, Michael, Terence Crooks, and Allan Cohen. 1999. "Validating Measures of Performance." *Educational Measurement: Issues and Practices*, 18, no. 2: 5–17. DOI:10.1111/j.1745-3992.1999. tb00010.x

Kirsch, Irwin, Joan Jamieson, Carol Taylor, and Daniel Eignor. 1998. *Computer Familiarity Among TOEFL Examinees*. Princeton, NJ: Educational Testing Service.

Lee, Jo A. 1986. "The Effects of Past Computer Experience on Computer Aptitude Test Performance." *Educational and Psychological Measurement*, 46: 727–733. DOI:10.1177/0013164486463030

Luecht, Richard M., and Brian E. Clauser. 2002. "Test Models for Complex CBT." *Computer-Based Testing: Building the Foundation for Future Assessments*, edited by Craig N. Mills, Maria T. Potenza, John J. Fremer, and William C. Ward, 67–88. Mahwah, NJ: Lawrence Erlbaum.

Messick, Samuel. 1989. "Validity." In *Educational Measurement*, 3rd ed., edited by Robert L. Linn, 13–103. New York: American Council on Education/Macmillan.

Ockey, Gary J. 2007. "Construct Implications of Including Still Image or Video in Computer-based Listening Tests." *Language Testing*, 24, no. 4: 517–537. DOI:0.1177/0265532207080771

Pearson. 2011. "Versant™ English Test: Test Description and Validation Summary." Accessed November 1, 2014. http://www.versanttest.com/technology/VersantEnglishTestValidation.pdf

Quinlan, Thomas, Derrick Higgins, and Susanne Wolff. 2009. *Evaluating the Construct Coverage of the e-rater® Scoring Engine* (Research Report No. RR-09-01). Princeton, NJ: Educational Testing Service.

Roever, Carsten. 2006. "Validation of a Web-based Test of ESL Pragmalinguistics." *Language Testing*, 23, no. 2: 229–256. DOI:10.1191/0265532206lt329oa

Taylor, Carol, Irwin Kirsch, Daniel R.Eignor, and Joan Jamieson. 1999. "Examining the Relationship between Computer Familiarity and Performance on Computer-based Language Tasks." *Language Learning*, 49: 219–274. DOI:10.1111/0023-8333.00088

Weigle, Sara C. 2013. "English as a Second Language Writing and Automated Essay Evaluation." In *Handbook of Automated Essay Evaluation: Current Applications and New Directions*, edited by Mark D. Shermis, and Jill Burstein, 36–54. New York: Routledge.

Williamson, David M., Xiaoming Xi, and F. Jay Breyer. 2012. "A Framework for Evaluation and Use of Automated Scoring." *Educational Measurement: Issues and Practice*, 31, no. 1: 2–13. DOI:10.1111/j.1745-3992.2011.00223.x

Wise, Steven L., Laura B. Barnes, Anne L. Harvey, and Barbara S. Plake. 1989. "Effects of Computer Anxiety and Computer-based Achievement Test Performance of College Students." *Applied Measurement in Education*, 2, no. 3: 235–241. DOI:10.1207/s15324818ame0203_4

# 23 Authoring Language-Learning Courseware

## What is language courseware?

Language courseware is generally understood to refer to software applications designed for language learning. Here language courseware will be interpreted broadly to include language-learning programs used for individual self-study or integrated into a teacher-led course of study, and running the gamut from simple single-skill activities to comprehensive online courses. With the rise of peer-to-peer interactions and social learning affordances through the internet, the function of courseware has evolved from the role it played in the early days of computer-assisted language learning (CALL). Rather than being presented as a set of standalone, discrete exercises for enhancing a particular language skill, courseware today is typically integrated into an online learning environment. That is likely to be through a course website, using materials developed in house or provided by a publisher. Increasingly, structured language-learning materials will be available to students online, whether the course is completely online, delivered in a hybrid/blended format, or taught face-to-face. With the rise of artificial intelligence (AI), have come sophisticated "intelligent language tutors" (ILT) which offer personally customized interactions between learner and computer. Today, language-learning software, including ILTs, are increasingly incorporated into a rich communicative environment delivered over the Web or through mobile apps.

## Courseware at the core of early CALL

Language courseware goes back to the earliest days of CALL in the 1960s. The early experiments in developing computer-based language-learning software used workstations connected to a mainframe over a phone line. A considerable number of language-learning programs were developed and delivered by way of this set-up through the Programmed Logic for Automatic Teaching Operations (PLATO) system at the University of Illinois, which began in 1960. PLATO programs were created with the TUTOR programming language, specifically designed for education. It was developed so that actual language teachers would be able to create their own exercises: "The notion was that instructors would wish to make their own PLATO lessons somewhat in the same way that they produced lecture notes, class handouts, and textbooks; hence, much emphasis was put on making TUTOR easy for the nonprogrammer" (Hart 1995, 19). In fact, PLATO was one of the first systems to be usable by non-experts. This has continued

*The Handbook of Technology and Second Language Teaching and Learning*, First Edition.
Edited by Carol A. Chapelle and Shannon Sauro.

to be an important goal in CALL, to enable real teachers to create their own language courseware, tailoring it to the needs of their students and their curriculum.

Authoring in TUTOR for PLATO was relatively simple and intuitive, with a very basic instructional format, that came to be used predominantly in language courseware, namely question—response—feedback. PLATO exercises were largely text-based and focused on one particular skill, with assessment through multiple-choice or short answer format questions. The interactions focused on grammar and vocabulary development, although PLATO did have capabilities to display graphics (through a pneumatic tool to access a microfiche) and play audio (on mounted disks). The monitors used were surprisingly sophisticated, as they were touch sensitive, thereby allowing creation of exercises such as touching the screen to identify a designated vocabulary item in a picture or playing a concentration-style matching game. Many innovations came out of PLATO, including hierarchical menus, an organized help system, spelling/grammar checkers, and programmed review options (Hart 1995).

Much of the pioneering work in developing software for language learning was done in the BASIC programming language, provided for free with most early microcomputers. Graham Davies used BASIC to create a variety of CALL programs such as GDTEST, which featured functionality similar to PLATO (Davies and Steele 1981). There was a widespread view at the time that serious and effective computer-based language learning needed to be developed by teacher-programmers with a background in both language pedagogy and computer programming. This was in part driven by the desire to move beyond the kind of drill and practice exercises typically seen in early CALL, as expressed by Underwood in 1984: "It is ironic that at the same time our profession was discovering communicative methodology, which discouraged piecemeal morphological drill in favor of global practice, the CALL people were busy cutting language up into largely meaningless little pieces (46)." Written under the influence of Krashen's (1982) advocacy of language acquisition over language learning, Underwood laid out an alternative direction for CALL, namely "communicative CALL," in a view remarkably prescient. The notion that language courseware was best developed by individual teacher-programmers is demonstrated by Higgins and Johns' book in 1984 on CALL, nearly half of which is taken up with sample computer code for creating and combining subroutines in BASIC.

As it turned out, relatively few language instructors learned to program in BASIC or in other programming languages. For those who are able and willing to do so, the advantage is the full control over the design and functionality of the software created, as well as the ability to update and customize at will. The challenge in using BASIC or any other general programming language is that everything must be programmed by the developer, not just the content and logic, but also screen layout, file organization, and user guidance. In contrast, an authoring language specifically geared towards education, such as TUTOR, provides built-in help for courseware development, so that not everything need be created from scratch. Another education-oriented authoring language used widely in the 1960s and 1970s was Programmed Instruction, Learning, or Teaching (PILOT). PILOT's syntax is fairly simple, with code consisting of a one- or two-letter command followed optionally by a condition, then some text (Underwood 1984). Also used were SNOBOL and Logo (Sanders 1985). These languages can be quite useful for creating typical exercises with defined correct answers, and they are powerful enough to do much more, although that requires more elaborate coding.

One of the early authoring languages dedicated to CALL was Computer-Assisted Language Instruction System (CALIS, 1979), available for MS-DOS (Borchardt 1995). The creation and evolution of this authoring tool is similar to that followed by other systems of this era. CALIS started out as a text-only program, with no graphics or multimedia. To create CALIS exercises, instructors used a text editor to create a script, which was run by the student in the CALIS program. Writing the scripts involved using the procedure employed in early word processors for entering formatting instructions, namely inserting words or symbols before and/or after a text string to indicate its programmatic role. This is familiar to anyone having written HTML code for the Web, as it uses the same convention. As is the case with other exercise creation tools, the author types in possible correct answers, entered on a new line starting with the plus sign, with other acceptable responses separated by a vertical bar. Anticipated wrong answers can be entered, by writing a new line starting with the minus sign. Following each line of correct or incorrect answers, the author could provide feedback. Wildcard symbols and abbreviations can be used to describe particular patterns such as any sequence of text followed by a particular word. Student responses are parsed to check if they match any of the exact text or patterns which the author had included. The software then displays the preprogrammed feedback to the user. Also available, if the author had incorporated it into the script, was a tutorial window, available by pressing a special key, as well as a help screen.

An authoring tool such as CALIS, or similar tools such as Dasher or MacLang, allowed instructors to create their own computer-based exercises with only minimal technical expertise (Otto and Pusack 2009). This enabled instructors to create learning materials tailored specifically to their needs, that is, using vocabulary, cultural information, or grammar structures that align with textbooks or with other curricular considerations. The fact that the CALIS script is in plain text enabled easy sharing as well as potential portability to other systems (through a global find and replace). Such considerations are important in decision-making about authoring options. Scripting is easier to learn and use than programming code. It is also more readable and portable in that programming code is tied closely to the syntax of the language used and is less easily imported into a new environment. Using a tool such as CALIS eliminates the need to write substantial computer code, but it also limits the functionality to what is enabled by the program creators. While not having to learn general programming is a major time saver, using such a system could be quite cumbersome in that teachers need to enter correct and anticipated incorrect responses and, optimally, supply customized feedback for each.

The use of authoring languages still requires some coding on the part of the instructor. That is eliminated in template systems, which began to appear in the 1960s. These require the teacher to enter only the content of the item, (i.e., question, correct answer, feedback), not any sequencing or formatting code (see Otto and Pusack 2009). Davies developed *GapKit* and *Fun with Texts*, featuring language-learning activities familiar today, known as text manipulation or gap filling, in which a student must reconstruct a text that has been manipulated in some way, such as filling in the blank (cloze exercises) or re-ordering jumbled words or sentences (Davies and Steel 1981). To use these systems authors simply follow the prompts to enter the appropriate content. Versions of the template evolved to incorporate audio playback, enabling text construction based on listening activities. The *ClozeWrite* tool from *Fun with Texts*, as did other similar programs, allowed free-form text entry, which was evaluated using pattern matching, that is comparing the user's answer to a pre-determined set of correct answers. In a technique used by a number of authoring systems, students were given feedback on their input through representation of errors with symbols replacing letters, indicating the locations of errors or misspellings. While this kind of automatic pattern markup can be quite helpful in reducing the time and effort needed to generate feedback, there are several shortcomings to this approach (Pusack 1983). While the software flags where the error is located in the student's answer, it does not explain the error or provide specific guidance for its correction. It also fails to distinguish trivial from significant errors. Finally, this approach is good at finding morphological errors, but is less useful in identifying other problems such as word order.

The "Computer-assisted LEssons for French" (CLEF) program from the 1970s, used similar pattern matching and introduced as well the use of animations to illustrate grammar rules (Davies 2006). For a drill on adjective placement in French, for example, an adjective could be sent drifting across the computer screen to be dropped into its correct position before or after a noun. The software, as is often the case in grammar or vocabulary drills, also made extensive use of colors to draw attention to transformations of words such as the addition of endings to adjectives or changes in verb forms. Such modifications of text remain an important component in language courseware and are consistent with research findings from second language acquisition (SLA) that point to the importance of making salient distinct patterns of form-meaning connections (Chapelle 2009). One of the issues the CLEF developers faced is shared by other courseware creators, namely how to decide on the vocabulary used in the program, in order to have the resulting program be as widely adaptable as possible. They opted to include a large number of French-English cognates, making it easier for beginners (at least those with English as their L1) and allowing the software to be used with a variety of textbooks.

The emphasis in early learning-language courseware was on development of discrete language skills. Some software targeted as well cultural knowledge, most commonly through text-based simulation programs which immerse the user in the target culture in some way, such as a simulated survival scenario in *London Adventure*. *Granville: The Prize Holiday Package* places students in the situation of visiting a French town, going through typical tourist activities such as registering at a hotel, ordering lunch, or making phone calls (Davies 1989). Such simulations were precursors to much more sophisticated programs developed with the media capabilities and artificial intelligence not available when these programs were created. The Tactical Language and Culture Training System, for example, designed for use by U.S. military personnel, offers a highly interactive immersion experience which combines cultural information with practical language training (Johnson et al. 2004).

## Personal computers and authoring tools

Much of the early work in courseware development of the 1960s and 1970s was designed along similar lines to how drill exercises worked in language labs at the time, with heavy emphasis on repetitive exercises focused on grammar and vocabulary, inspired by behavioral learning theories. There was also courseware developed for reading, featuring text annotations and comprehension questions. Listening comprehension and pronunciation exercises were limited due to lack of hardware support. In fact, limitations in the capabilities of the computing environment at the time inhibited widespread use of language-learning software. Computer terminals, such as those used in PLATO, were quite expensive and, because they shared processing with other users of the connected mainframe computers, could at times be slow and unresponsive. The advent of personal computers in the 1980s brought about tremendous change in the computing environment and new opportunities for the development and use of language-learning software. Personal computers were relatively inexpensive and could be used without any network or mainframe connection. This changed significantly the development environment, with the prospect of language teachers having their own office computers for teaching and research. In this decade teachers began to develop their own courseware on PCs through the availability of authoring tools, such as HyperCard (1987).

Authoring tools provide more control than templates over aspects of an exercise such as formatting, feedback, and inclusion of optional items such as help screens. In contrast to authoring languages, authoring tools provide simplified methods for creating exercises with easy-to-use code and procedures for entering questions and feedback. Of course, in the process, they also sacrifice the greater control over presentation and program logic available through the use of an authoring language. Earlier authoring programs written originally for use on mainframe or minicomputers were ported over to the PC environment. From the multitude of computer platforms and operating systems through the 1980s, there was eventually industry consolidation around just two, MS-DOS/Windows from Microsoft and the Apple Macintosh. In the process, some programmers who had developed for other platforms were forced to either abandon their projects or to re-create their work, which often meant learning a new programming language. This issue remains current, as developers—professional or casual—need to make decisions based on anticipated longevity of hardware and software.

Just as word processors eventually did away with the necessity of entering formatting codes, (special codes around items to designate print formatting) that development was paralleled in authoring tools. CALIS, for example, was ported to Microsoft Windows, becoming WinCALIS, and featuring a script editor, which eliminated the need to learn and write CALIS commands. WinCALIS also supported Unicode, a major factor in allowing courseware to be created for multiple writing systems. Much of the early work in CALL involved efforts to be able to display text written in non-Roman alphabets on computer displays (see Borchardt 1995; Higgins and Johns 1984; Underwood 1984). Another major addition with WinCALIS was the option to incorporate multimedia. The ability to incorporate sound and be able, with some confidence, to enable its playback on student computers, was a major development for language-learning courseware. Audio is important of course for developing listening comprehension, but it can also be used in multiple other ways, such as providing accompaniment to readings, audio feedback for computer drills, or pronunciation practice. The growing popularity of the Macintosh during the 1980s, at least in North America, was due in part to its built-in support for multimedia.

Also supplied at this time free with every Macintosh computer was a general authoring tool used widely for creation of language courseware, HyperCard. Authors of HyperCard programs created individual "pages" which could then be combined into "stacks," using a hypertext linking system familiar today from its use on the World Wide Web. It was possible to create HyperCard stacks without any scripting at all, through using icons and pull-down menus to incorporate buttons or other such elements, to add sound and other media, or to create links to other pages or elements on the screen. Text could be entered directly into a text box or copied and pasted from a text file. Advanced users could take advantage of the scripting language built into HyperCard, HyperTalk, to customize layout and functionality and to add more sophisticated interactions. The basic authoring requirements of HyperCard were at a low enough level that technically unsophisticated language teachers were able to create useful courseware. Some instructors who put time and effort into creating extensive HyperCard learning materials were able to make that work available commercially. George Metevski's *Russian HyperTutor*, for example, featured extensive grammar tutorials and drills and was used widely in teaching Russian (Metrevski 1995). Metrevski tied the vocabulary and grammar sequencing of *Russian HyperTutor* closely to the most widely used textbook for beginning Russian at the time. One of the issues he and other developers of language-learning software faced was distribution. The most common delivery system was on floppy disks, which had limited capacity, restricting therefore the inclusion of large graphics or multimedia resources.

HyperCard stacks ran only on Macintosh computers. Another limitation was the initial lack of support for color. A similar authoring tool for PCs, ToolBook (1989), supported color but worked only on Microsoft operating systems. A considerable number of language-learning programs were developed using ToolBook. James Pusack described his experience in using ToolBook to create *Kontakte*, a software accompaniment to a German textbook (Pusack 1999). ToolBook uses the metaphor of the book as the basic structure for created materials. Another popular tool used for courseware development, Macromedia Director (1987), was based on the concepts of cast and score. While HyperCard and ToolBook could be used by regular language instructors to create courseware, Director required a higher level of technical expertise. Jones and Frommer (1999) have described the long development process (six years) of a Director based French project, *Portes Ouvertes*, which created 20 different templates, including some innovative interactions such as coin dragging and telephone dialing. Another powerful tool for creating courseware, Authorware (1987), was also created by Macromedia. Authorware uses an icon-based approach, linking the icons representing different project assets, such as text, multimedia files, or graphics to provide the flow and structure of the program. Authorware is particularly well adapted to providing branching, the capability of sending the user to different screens depending on choices or responses to assessments. In contrast to the fairly simple process of creating courseware with HyperCard or ToolBook, using a tool such as Authorware is complex enough to need considerable planning and advanced preparation before beginning a project. Projects are typically storyboarded before the start of any development. This involves setting down on paper the flow and logic of the program in as much detail as possible. The choice of an authoring environment for courseware depends not only on the technical expertise of the developer and the scope of the program but also on the intended use and audience. Using Authorware for a series of grammar exercises designed to be used locally would be overkill, as a template system would be more appropriate. Use of a sophisticated authoring tool is mandated for projects that require a more complex structure or use a model not available through a template or an authoring language.

Creating sophisticated learner adaptive programs in Authorware requires extensive use of the scripting functionality. This is true as well with another development tool used widely in the development of language courseware, namely Flash (1996). Flash, also from Macromedia, uses a timeline for authoring. It requires knowledge of the scripting language (ActionScript) for most projects. Flash is used extensively for encoding video for internet streaming, although YouTube in 2015 changed the default video delivery format from Flash to HTML5. Flash has been used for language-learning software, most notably with the *SMILE* exercise generator (Server-Managed Interactive Learning Exercises), which allows creation of a variety of exercises (Godwin-Jones 2007). As is the case with other Flash-based projects, SMILE exercises have been rewritten in HTML and JavaScript, so as to be more compatible with contemporary web browsers and mobile devices.

# Multimedia courseware

Most early language-learning software targeted a specific skill area, such as reading comprehension or grammar knowledge. With the ability to incorporate audio and video, new opportunities emerged for multimodal courseware. In the early days of CALL, the ability to create courseware incorporating audio was problematic, let alone using video. However, there were early courseware projects which incorporated video. Some of the first uses were developed at Brigham Young University. Through development of courseware under the Time-shared Interactive Computer Controlled Information Television (TICCIT) project, which created an extensive set of language courseware, there was interest developed in the use of video for language learning (Hendricks, Bennion, and Larson 1983). This led to experimentation with the use of laserdiscs in the 1970s. *Macario* was an adaption of a feature film for practicing Spanish listening comprehension. Each scene of the movie was richly annotated, with notes and comprehension questions. A quite innovative program for Spanish, *Montevidisco*, featured learners interacting with local citizens. A clip from the laserdisc was shown to students, who answered a multiple-choice question to determine the next scene to be shown.

Laserdiscs were also used in several quite sophisticated language-learning projects developed at the Massachusetts Institute of Technology as part of the Athena project (Murray, Morgenstern, and Furstenberg 1989). The programs developed at MIT are notable, not only for the high production values, but also in the theoretical considerations used in their development. The creators were intent on moving away from programmed learning and incorporating instead accepted principles of second language acquisition such as the importance of users negotiating meaning in social contexts and carrying out communicative tasks, with the aim being "not so much mastery of the grammatical and syntactic code as the ability to use this code to perform or have others perform certain actions" (Murray, Morgenstern, and Furstenberg 1989, 98). The developers sought to provide intrinsic motivation, that is, interest in the progression of the story, rather than the extrinsic motivation of completing an assignment by answering a set of questions. In *No recuerdo* students' task is to help an amnesiac scientist recall important information vital to saving lives. *À la rencontre de Philippe* involved helping a young Frenchman find a place to live after a break-up with his girlfriend.

*Philippe* used scripted video shot on location in Paris with professional actors speaking at a normal rate of speech in natural, colloquial language. However, in order to enable the program to be used by students at a lower level of French proficiency, an alternative soundtrack was supplied, with the same dialogue, but spoken more deliberately. The program supplies in fact multiple ways to help students understand the video and provides a variety of pathways through the story with different endings, depending on student choices. The principle of learner control, already used in the TICCIT project, is an important consideration in program design, as it is crucial for student motivation and flexibility in usage. Providing some degree of learner control is consistent with SLA findings that support for modified interactions between learner and computer by providing control over program elements such as help requests, modification of responses, and access to review, all can help the learner draw connections between form and meaning (Chapelle 2009). Unfortunately, in many multimedia programs a confusing and cluttered user interface often interfered with the learner's ability to find and use available resources (see Trinder 2003).

One of the elements included in *Philippe* to enhance students' intrinsic motivation was what the developers described as "whimsy," episodes or interactions providing fun or humor (Murray, Morgenstern, and Furstenberg 1989). The MIT programs were designed to be integrated into classroom instruction, as the basis for class discussions, rather than as standalone programs. Having a variety of options for the progression of the story, including lighter sides to Philippe's dilemma, provides a rich vein of conversation possibilities in class. Many courseware projects are designed to be used autonomously, mostly in individual settings. That need not be the case. In fact, integrating courseware use into social settings, such as classroom pair work, can be beneficial (Hubbard and Siskin 2004). Increasingly today, language-learning software is part of a more global approach to communicative language learning, in which work on language mechanics is integrated into a richly social learning environment. This has changed the nature of courseware as well in that greater emphasis today is placed on holistic evaluation of student output, rather than on identifying discrete errors. Often courseware today is implemented in the context of communicative language learning through serving as an impetus for student-to-student interactions.

Laserdiscs were displaced by CD-ROMs, then by DVDs, and eventually by digital video. In the 1980s and 1990s a number of multimedia CD-ROMs were developed. A good number were created to accompany textbooks. The scope and sophistication of the multimedia programs varies considerably. One of the better-known products was the *Triple Play Plus* series (1994), available for multiple languages. It was one of the first language-learning programs to incorporate automatic speech recognition (ASR), the ability to recognize and evaluate users' spoken input. It included as well a number of games, a common feature to many multimedia titles. The *Who is Oscar Lake* (1996) series, also available in multiple languages, was built around a mystery which the user is invited to solve through clues and viewing clips. Integrating a game element into language courseware is recognized today as an important factor in creating student engagement (Kessler 2013). Because of the expense, video used in multimedia courseware was rarely created specifically for the project, and not normally with the same professionalism evident in *Philippe*. In fact, the video quality of *Oscar Lake*, rendered in QuickTime, the digital video format from Apple, was small and jerky compared to the video playback of laserdiscs. Digital video improved dramatically in time and clearly has major advantages in terms of production, portability, and integration. Many multimedia projects re-purposed existing video. The *Kontakte* project (1996), for example, used newscasts from German TV (Pusack 1999). *Nuevos Destinos* (1997) was created as a software companion to a Spanish-language telenovela, with the user being placed in the role of a legal assistant at a law office (Blake 1999). One of the advantages of scripted video is greater control over vocabulary, language level, and cultural content. On the other hand, video such as that used in *Philippe* can be faulted with a lack of authenticity (see Kramsch and Andersen 1999). At the same time, using television broadcasts from the target culture could be seen as lacking in authenticity as well, in that the clips are not being used in the manner for which they were intended. The integration of video can be particularly useful from a cultural perspective. However, assuming that video is an objective representation of a target culture is problematic. Video clips always provide a particular perspective, and, typically in their use in courseware, show only a selection from a larger video, sometimes provided with minimal cultural context (Kramsch and Andersen 1999).

To allow non-technical instructors to build their own multimedia applications incorporating authentic language materials, several template-based authoring systems for use of video were developed, including IconAuthor, MaxAuthor, and MALTED. One free tool for video annotation is ANVILL, which allows importation of data from a variety of sources, including from phonetics tools, such as the widely used PRAAT. This enables features such as accurate speech transcription. An important component of L2 video is the possibility of including transcriptions as well as L1 or L2 subtitles. Particularly useful is the ability for the viewer to switch at will among the different options. The *Libra* video authoring template was used to create a number of language-learning programs including *Drehort Neubrandenburg Interaktiv* (1994) and *La Marée et ses secrets* (1994). The latter program was used by French beginners after just two weeks of instruction, with the program being adaptable to higher levels as well (Fischer and Farris 1999). That flexibility in usage can be valuable in assuring a return on investment for the effort and expense of creating multimedia courseware. One of the design choices made for that project was to provide an initial lockstep introduction to the program, which was intended to make sure users were familiar with all the features and functions of the program (Blake 1999). This is a recurring issue in language courseware design, namely to ensure that users take advantage of the features included for assistance and further exploration, such as help screens, grammar references, dictionaries, or richer feedback options. It seems evident that learners taking the active steps to consult available help mechanisms may lead to deeper processing and therefore more likely language acquisition. That process can also be helpful in building metacognitive awareness in the learners of mechanics and strategies for language learning.

Most multimedia projects necessitate a development team, not a single individual. Needed are not just content experts, but also instructional designers, graphic artists, multimedia specialists, and programmers. The experience, time, and effort involved in such projects make them quite different from earlier projects which often involved work by a single teacher-programmer. In practice, most language-learning projects necessitate funding of some kind, whether that be provided by a grant agency, a university fund, or a commercial entity.

# Intelligent language tutors

The need for funding applies as well, and perhaps even more, to projects for the development of intelligent language tutors (ILTs), which need the expertise of specialists in computational linguistics and artificial intelligence. ILTs use artificial intelligence to provide a more personal and individualized learning experience. Rather than general feedback or pattern responses, ILTs are able to provide more tailored feedback, often based not just on what the user has typed, but also drawn from a user profile. That profile may include information on the individual's previous work with the program as well as other data about the user, such as language background, field of study, or principal area of interest in learning the target language. Such programs are "intelligent" because they are able to analyze and evaluate text input by using built-in knowledge about the language to parse, or take apart, the utterance and analyze its form and meaning to determine its appropriateness, comprehensibility, and/or grammatical correctness (Heift and Schulze 2007). The program does this based on a language model or "expert system" as well as a language corpus, i.e., a large collection of texts in the target language. Advances in the field of artificial intelligence in recent years have resulted in much more successful natural language processing (NLP). Consumers today often encounter NLP, for example, in automated voice exchanges, where NLP is paired with automatic speech recognition, which has likewise improved tremendously.

The effort and resources required to build an ILT are such that it would be advantageous for these projects to be built cooperatively or to share resources or code. Most programs are built with computer languages commonly used in computational linguistics, namely Lisp and Prolog, along with those used on web servers, Java and Python, but they are normally built from scratch, resulting in quite different approaches and code bases. Designing the architecture of the ILT to be modular is a step towards interoperability and flexibility, allowing parts of the system to be turned off or on and to be updated individually. That makes it easier as well to add additional modules in the future. What would increase even more the versatility of ILTs would be the ability for non-programmers to modify the content. The *Tutor Assistant* is an authoring tool for ILTs which enables that functionality (Toole and Heift 2002). Flexibility is important as well in providing options to accommodate as wide a range of learners as possible. That could mean providing different pathways for analytical learners who prefer a deductive approach (rules first) and for global learners, who learn better from an inductive method (examples first). When possible, providing different language choices for feedback and other help functions also makes the system more universally usable.

One of the better-known and successful ILTs is *E-Tutor* for German. Its structure is typical of an ILT in that it incorporates a language knowledge module which parses sentences to provide phrase descriptors and detailed error information, an analysis module, which generates possible responses and updates the student module, which dynamically evolves based on student performance. The nature, amount, and ordering of feedback is one of the most difficult issues that ILT developers face. Language learners will often make more than one error in a sentence, so that the system must decide which errors to flag, in which order, and how much feedback to provide for each. Some errors may result from typos, and others may be grammatically incorrect but not critical to comprehensibility. Some systems will provide more detailed feedback to beginners while advanced leaners get only a hint at the error. One approach to user feedback is to have the system place errors into categories and automatically provide feedback on those judged most critical, while giving the student the option to see or not feedback on others. Such decisions can be built into the system or be determined by the teacher or by the individual student, by setting defaults in the student module. *E-Tutor* features an "error priority queue" which ranks errors and is instructor adjustable (Heift 2004). Another factor for authors to take into consideration in determining user feedback is how much metalinguistic information to provide, that is grammatical or linguistic explanations. Studies have shown that providing such feedback can be more effective than simple flagging of errors (Nagata 1993) and that learner uptake from feedback is increased if the error is both explained and highlighted (Heift 2004). That is likely to depend on the individual learner, so that best practices in this area would seem to point to the importance of flexible feedback, which is at least in part under the user's control.

*E-tutor* uses in its design the metaphor of the electronic textbook, as do other ILTs such as *Robo-Sensei* (for Japanese) or *Tagarella* (for Portuguese). These and other ILTs have evolved from focusing almost exclusively on grammar and vocabulary to include other areas such as reading or listening comprehension. One of the benefits of an ILT is the ability to collect samples of student L2 to build a learner corpus. The detailed information that can be collected is important in being able to provide individualized feedback, but it also provides linguistic data on common errors and problems. This can be useful in improving the functionality of the ILT and in determining where additional feedback or help materials might be warranted. It is relatively easy to analyze learner input for grammatical and lexical errors. It is more difficult to evaluate and measure other aspects of the user's L2 such as complexity, fluency, and creativity. It is possible to compare an individual learner's input with similar utterances from a learner corpus, comparing sentence length or examining syntactical complexity. One of the other areas that could be examined is the use of collocations or idiomatic expressions, important indicators of lexical sophistication, so crucial for fluency and natural sounding language output (Tschichold 2003). An area of importance in second language acquisition is pragmatics, the use of language which is not just grammatically and lexically correct, but also situationally and culturally appropriate. Assessing user input from this perspective is quite difficult, as there are likely to be many different utterances that could be acceptable, and which would likely range from possible but improbable to highly idiomatic (see Tschichold 2003). Providing in the feedback to the user examples of pragmatically appropriate responses—even if the user's utterance is acceptable—may be advisable.

In contrast to the proliferation of multimedia CD-ROMs for language learning, there have been relatively few publicly released ILTs. A good number of projects received preliminary funding to support a proof-of-concept prototype but were not able to fund final development to enable production versions. This is not surprising, given how difficult a task ILTs face, dealing with the complexity of human language and of second language acquisition. ILTs often are designed as research demonstration projects, rather than shareable or commercial products. There are relatively few reviews or studies of ILTs with the exception of those by the developers themselves. Developers of ILT tend to focus, as one would expect, on the functionality and effectiveness of the software, rather than on the user interface design. The user experience can be quite different from that provided by commercial software. In particular, graphics and multimedia do not display the same high production values.

## Commercial courseware and open educational resources (OER)

In recent years, language-learning software such as *Rosetta Stone* or *Tell Me More* have gained prominence (Nelson 2011). Although such products are sometimes used to provide the primary delivery system for language courses, they are more often used as supplements to classroom instruction or independently by learners in self-instructional contexts. Integrating such commercial software into instructed language learning can be problematic in terms of vocabulary, grammar sequencing, and cultural content. A commercial alternative to standalone software such as *Rosetta Stone* are the quite widely used electronic workbooks which many publishers are now supplying with basic language textbooks. Such products as Pearson's *Mylanguagelab* or Cengage's *Centro* feature multimedia resources, grammar references, cultural activities, and interactive exercises. Students have access to these websites typically only as long as their course of study. Often the sites do not integrate into other systems a language teacher may be using, such as an electronic gradebook or a learning management system. Unfortunately, there have been few studies on the effectiveness of publishers' electronic workbooks. The use of such resources, given the expense and comprehensiveness, is likely to mean that local resources are not developed in support of language instruction. That may not be an issue in some educational settings, but it is possible that curricular requirements or standardized testing may make it imperative to be able to modify materials to meet local needs.

Given the expense, limited access, and inflexibility of much commercial software, one of the recent developments in the creation of language courseware is the rise of shareable teaching and learning materials, often referred to as open educational resources (OER). These can range from quite simple and basic, such as vocabulary grammar drills created with tools such as *Quia* (a web-based exercise creator) to full-fledged courseware incorporating grammar tutorials, exercises, readings, dialogue, and multimedia. Several projects out of the University of Texas' Center for Open Educational Resources and Language Learning (COERLL) fall into this latter category, including *Français interactif*, an open first-year French curriculum, and *Brazilpod*, a collection of Portuguese language-learning resources. The Open Learning Initiative from Carnegie Mellon University features online resources for a variety of languages, including Arabic, English, and Spanish. The well-regarded language courses available from the BBC also are in this category, as are the variety of courseware from the Open Courseware Initiative. There are sites such as Merlot or LORO which act as OER aggregators and feature peer reviews of linked content. While smaller units of OER content, sometimes called "learning objects," can provide useful learning content for teachers and students, they can sometimes be difficult to integrate into a specific course or curriculum (Friesen 2004). Some learning objects have rich metadata which provide information on provenance, targeted proficiency level/skill, and typical completion time (Meskill and Anthony 2007). One method that has been used to link learning objects together or integrate them into a web delivery system is to use SCORM, a standard which allows results and assessment scores to be sent to supported systems (Godwin-Jones 2007).

## Web delivered courseware

Most of what today is produced as OER is available as web-based resources. In fact, today, language courseware is overwhelmingly designed to be delivered over the internet. In the 1990s, most of that development was done in programming environments that were not native to web browsers namely Java and Flash and which necessitated the use of special browser plug-ins to run. Plug-ins are software components added to web browsers that enable special features or functionality. Several ILTs, including *E-Tutor*, are written in Java and designed to run in the Java plug-in as applets in a web browser. Flash has also been used extensively, for example, for the rich internet applications from the Center for Language Education and Research (CLEAR, Michigan State University). The use of Java and Flash enabled the kind of interactivity and media integration that at that time were not possible in the native web environment using HTML. Plug-ins, however, were not an ideal solution, as they tended to cause performance issues and also could not be fully integrated into webpages. Another early option to move beyond static webpages was server-based interactivity through CGI scripts, or common gateway interface, written in Java or Perl. This method however could be slow, as a new page had to be received from the Web server, and since the entire page was replaced, did not work well for designing interactive courseware.

The arrival of JavaScript in the mid-1990s changed dramatically the nature of Web inter-activity. JavaScript (officially ECMAScript) is a scripting language which is incorporated into the source of the webpage, along with HTML and CSS (cascading style sheets). JavaScript is client-side code and is natively supported by Web browsers, which means that it runs efficiently and can be integrated into the Web page structure. What that means in practice is that a script can manipulate objects on the page, for example, showing a checkmark for the correct answer to a question and providing appropriate feedback. JavaScript syntax and logic will seem familiar to anyone acquainted with earlier scripting languages such as those used in HyperCard or ToolBook. Since JavaScript is embedded into HTML, the source code used for a Web page can be viewed. This makes learning and borrowing much easier than in other development environments. Web browsers incorporate JavaScript debuggers, which enables code errors to be identified and rectified. As both HTML and JavaScript can be created with a basic text editor, this makes development of interactive web pages more universally feasible than in environments requiring special-ized authoring software.

JavaScript has evolved considerably since its origins, to the point at which web applica-tions using JavaScript can be quite complex and sophisticated. One of the JavaScript tech-niques used frequently is to pull data from a server in the background, then use CSS to update on the fly information on the page, as requested by the user or in response to an action, such as answering a question. This technique, called AJAX for asynchronous JavaScript plus XML, enables the kind of transparent interactivity familiar from authoring tools such as *Director*. For language-learning software, this allows queries for information housed on a server, such as from a language corpus. That data will most likely be encoded in XML, extensible markup language, a more flexible and generic markup language than HTML. Maintaining program data in a standard, well-structured, open format such as XML is desirable so as to separate content from formatting. XML offers as well a significant chance to future-proof data, as its structure makes it easy to translate the data into different formats, such as JSON (JavaScript object notation), a lightweight data-exchange format of increasing popularity.

Authoring tools have been created which allow instructors to create exercises which take advantage of the power and flexibility of JavaScript. A tool frequently used by language teachers is *Hot Potatoes*, which features a wide variety of exercise types. Another template tool for creating online learning materials is *COMET*, out of Yale University, which consists of a series of web-based applications for annotating readings or video and for creating differ-ent kinds of online exercises. One of the first and most complete tools for creating online courseware is InGenio, from the CAMILLE research group, created by a consortium of European universities. InGenio is a dedicated CALL authoring shell as well as a content manager, so that it is both a creation tool and a content repository. It provides 14 different exercise templates and features a student assessment facility that allows instructors and stu-dents to monitor the learning process.

Many language instructors in higher education are likely to be using a web-based course management system, usually called a learning management system (LMS) or virtual learning environment (VLE). These are server-based software tools that are quite useful for course management, including grade recording, assignment distribution and submission, and document archiving. They also provide a consistent and familiar inter-face to students, as they tend to be used widely across institutions where they have been adopted. As they are generic teaching tools, they do not offer specific language-learning activities. They do include options for creating a variety of exercises, although formats and feedback options are limited. Content or exercise creation in most LMS can mean that the content resides in a proprietary system, with limited options for export and reus-ability. Moreover, by virtue of the extensive features and functions built into an LMS, the implicit message to instructors may be that this is the sum total of how the web can be used in teaching and learning, definitely a far cry from the real power and potential of that medium. Most LMS now allow plug-ins or integration of third-party applications, which are able to supply tools and functions important for language learning such as voice tools. The LMS which is most easily customizable for language learning is *Moodle*, which also has the advantage of being open source. Many of the external tools and services are increasingly integrated into an LMS through use of an interoperability standard and application program interface (API) called learning tools interoperability (LTI). The LTI-based integration of third-party tools, services, and repositories of learning objects or assessments supplements the built-in functionality of the LMS. This allows as well assessment data from the use of those resources to be sent to the LMS gradebook. A variety of potential online language-learning activities, including multiplayer games are LTI enabled (Martínez-Ortíz et al. 2013).

An LMS is generic and standardized. At the opposite end of the spectrum in terms of flexibility and creativity are "mashups." These are Internet-based resources or applications which combine content or functionality from more than one source. That might mean adding an alternative soundtrack to an online video, customizing a mapping service to reflect personal travel, or writing new captions or dialogues for cartoons or comic strips. Typically, publicly available and free resources are used and combined into a single, web-based presentation. A popular use of mashups is the integration into a Web page of data feeds, such as news sources or blog posts. This is typically done through syndicated (subscribed) content in rich site summary (RSS) format. The set of rich internet applications from CLEAR (Michigan State University) enable creation of a variety of mashups by instructors or students. Thorne and Reinhardt (2008) describe a variety of mashup options for language learning. Designated "bridging activities," they involve student remixing of internet content from a variety of sources including blogs, wikis, chat, and gaming. Such personalized learning content can be effective in engaging student motivation.

The most recent version of the web authoring language, HTML 5, includes features which are important in language-learning applications including native playback for audio and video, enhanced graphics, and robust language support (Godwin-Jones 2014). The video format allows playback without the need for a plug-in and therefore better integration into the other elements of the page. It also makes it easier, through WebVTT (video text tracks) to include a variety of subtitles and turn them off and on programmatically or at the request of the learner. One of the new elements associated with HTML5 is Canvas, a graphics rendering standard which uses scripting to draw and manipulate images. Form elements on the page (for user input such as text entry fields or radio buttons) can be easily tied to graphic representations using Canvas. Among other additions to HTML5 are a speech input field in forms and advanced text manipulations, such as Ruby annotations, important for some Asian languages. There are other features of HTML5 which make it a good candidate for the development of courseware. The stateless nature of Web pages (i.e., no data kept upon leaving a page) has traditionally been overcome through the use of browser "cookies," which, however, have limited storage capacity and raise security and privacy issues. The new "Web storage" is more robust and reliable. In terms of interactivity, HTML5 allows any element of the page to be "draggable." It also includes support for parsing text with patterns (i.e., "regular expressions"). Since not all features are implemented at the same time in all browsers, it is advisable to use progressive enhancement in designing web apps, that is, assuring basic functionality in all browsers, while enabling more advanced features for supported browsers. This can be done automatically by using available JavaScript libraries. A JavaScript library, such as the popular jQuery, is a set of pre-written JavaScript which allows for easier development of JavaScript-based applications. These libraries have become very popular with developers, as they make it easier and faster to create rich internet applications.

Using HTML5 allows content also to be packaged as an e-book in the EPUB format. EPUB 3, the most recent version of the standard, includes support for interactivity through scripting, making it possible to create courseware for delivery through e-readers. This format has the advantage of being available off-line, once the e-book has been downloaded. Using an open standard such as EPUB makes the content usable on a variety of platforms. It also offers some specific features of potential use in language learning. It supports the use of media overlays for creating synchronized audio, which matches up spoken and written texts. This is used heavily in e-books for children, but it clearly could be valuable in second-language learning as well. Media overlays also allow switching from one modality to another, for example, by starting to read at home and then switching to audio mode in the car. EPUB 3 also offers robust support for non-Latin writing systems, including vertical writing and right to left page progression. Using HTML5 to deliver a web app makes content usable on mobile devices, through the built-in web browsers on smart phones and tablets. Many projects designed for mobile delivery use a proprietary development environment to produce native apps for the targeted platforms. This makes it easier to integrate with the device hardware, but it also means that separate code (using different programming languages) must be written for each platform. Increasingly, authoring tools are taking into consideration mobile users, making the content at last partially usable on phones and tablets.

One of the directions holding a good deal of potential for language learning in the mobile space is the development of games. Projects such as *Mentira*, for example, leverage the capability of mobile devices to enable place-based interactions between students and native speakers. *Mentira* was created with the game authoring took Augmented Reality and Interactive Storytelling (ARIS), an open source platform from the University of Wisconsin. One of the challenges with games and other forms of informal language learning available today is integrating those experiences and the second-language development they enable into formal learning settings. We seem likely to see in the future more courseware development along the lines of *Mentira*. The program has a focus on a particular area of linguistic competence of cultural significance—in this case, the use of pragmatics in Spanish—within a rich social-collaborative environment, here students working together to carry out tasks, taking them into a Spanish-speaking neighborhood to engage with native speakers. This takes place in a local context with mobile devices, engaging students in an environment that is both competitive and collaborative. This corresponds to current language pedagogy emphasizing shared knowledge construction through task-oriented interactions in a real-world setting.

A collaborative learning environment is today the normal context for the delivery of language courseware. The process of creating and delivering language-learning software has changed significantly since its beginnings in the 1960s. Today, developers are unlikely to be working independently creating discrete language-learning exercises for particular skills. Instead, most developers will be part of a team that includes subject experts, media specialists, and instructional designers. They will be taking advantage, to the extent possible, of pre-built frameworks for creating applications. The delivery system will inevitably be internet-based, using either the open web, a proprietary delivery system such as an LMS, or mobile-friendly apps. Delivery and record keeping are likely to be cloud-based. Courseware will continue to be integrated into a social learning environment with rich peer-to-peer collaborative functionality. The majority of language teachers are likely to continue to rely on commercial courseware, developed and marketed in conjunction with textbooks.

# REFERENCES

Blake, Robert. 1999. "Nuevos Destinos: A CD-ROM for Advanced Beginning Spanish." *CALICO Journal*, 17, no. 1: 9–24.

Borchardt, Frank L. 1995. "Language and Computing at Duke University; Or, Virtue Triumphant, for the Time Being." *Calico Journal*, 12: 57–83.

Chapelle, Carol. 2009. "The Relationship Between Second Language Acquisition Theory and Computer-Assisted Language Learning." *Modern Language Journal*, 93: 741–753.

Davies, Graham. 1989. "CALL and NCCALL in the United Kingdom: Past, Present, and Future." In *Modern Technology in Foreign Language Education*, edited by William Flint Smith, 161–180. Lincolnwood, IL: National Textbook.

Davies, Graham, ed. 2006. "Information and Communications Technology for Language Teachers (ICT4LT)." *Slough: Thames Valley University*. Accessed July 12, 2015. http://www.ict4lt.org/en/index.htm

Davies, Graham, and David Steel. 1981. "First Steps in Computer-Assisted Language Learning at Ealing College of Higher Education." Accessed February 14, 2015. http://www.ict4lt.org/en/Davies_Steel_1981.doc

Fischer, Robert, and Michael Farris. 1999. "The Libra Multimedia Authoring Environment and CALL Multimedia Courseware." *CALICO Journal*, 17, no. 1: 59–81.

Friesen, Norm. 2004. "Three Objections to Learning Objects and E-learning Standards." In *Online Education Using Learning Objects*, edited by Rory McGreal, 59–70. London: Routledge.

Godwin-Jones, Robert. 2007. "Tools and Trends in Self-paced Language Instruction." *Language Learning & Technology*, 11, no. 2: 10–17.

Godwin-Jones, Robert. 2014. "Towards Transparent Computing: Content Authoring Using Open Standards." *Language Learning & Technology*, 18, no. 1: 1–10.

Hart, Robert. 1995. "The Illinois PLATO Foreign Languages Project." *CALICO Journal*, 12, no. 4: 15–37.

Heift, Trude. 2004. "Corrective Feedback and Learner Uptake in CALL." *ReCALL*, 16: 416–431.

Heift, Trude and Matthew Schulze. 2007. *Errors and Intelligence in Computer-Assisted Language Learning: Parsers and Pedagogues*. New York: Routledge.

Hendricks, Harold, Junius Bennion, and Jerry Larson. 1983. "Technology and Language Learning at BYU." *CALICO Review*, 1, no. 3: 23–46.

Higgins, John, and Tim Johns. 1984. *Computers in Language Learning*. London: Collins ELT.

Hubbard, Philip, and Claire Bradin Siskin. 2004. "Another Look at Tutorial CALL." *ReCALL*, 16: 448–461.

Johnson, W. Lewis, Carole Beal, Anna Fowles-Winkler, Ursula Lauper, Stacy Marsella, Shrikanth Narayanan, Dimitra Papachristou, and Hannes Vilhjálmsson. 2004. "Tactical Language Training System: An Interim Report." In *Intelligent Tutoring Systems*, 336–345. Berlin: Springer.

Jones, Chris, and Judith Frommer. 1999. "Building the Portes Ouvertes CD-ROM." *CALICO Journal*, 17, no. 1: 83–100.

Kessler, Greg. 2013. "Collaborative Language Learning in Co-constructed Participatory Culture." *CALICO Journal*, 30, no. 3: 307–322.

Kramsch, Claire, and Roger Andersen. 1999. "Teaching Text and Context through Multimedia." *Language Learning & Technology*, 2, no. 2: 31–42.

Krashen, Stephen. 1982. *Principles and Practice in Second Language Acquisition*. Oxford: Pergamon.

Martínez-Ortíz, Itziar, Ángel del Blanco, Javier Torrente, Ángel Serrano, Pablo Moreno-Ger, Baltasar Fernández-Manjón, and Eugenio Marchiori. 2013. "Addressing Serious Games Interoperability: The E-adventure Journey." *JADLET Journal of Advanced Distributed Learning Technology*, 1, no. 1: 60–76.

Meskill, Carla, and Natasha Anthony. 2007. "The Language of Teaching Well with Learning Objects." *MERLOT Journal of Online Learning and Teaching*, 3, no. 1: 79–93.

Metrevski, George. 1995. "Russian HyperTutor: Designing Interactive Multimedia for the Macintosh." *Journal of Computing in Higher Education*, 6, no. 2: 120–137.

Murray, Janet, Douglas Morgenstern, and Gilberte Furstenberg. 1989. "The Athena Language Learning Project: Design Issues for the Next Generation of Computer-based Language Learning Tools." In *Modern Technology in Foreign Language Education*, edited by William Flint Smith, 97–118. Lincolnwood, IL: National Textbook.

Nagata, Noriko. 1993. "Intelligent Computer Feedback for Second Language Instruction." *Modern Language Journal*, 77: 330–339.

Nelson, Katharine. 2011. "Self-study with Language Learning Software in the Workplace: What Happens?" *Language Learning & Technology*, 15, no. 3: 110–129.

Otto, Sue, and James Pusack. 2009. "Computer-Assisted Language Learning Authoring Issues." *The Modern Language Journal*, 93: 784–801.

Pusack, James. 1983. "Answer-Processing and Error Correction in Foreign Language CAI." *System*, 11, no. 1: 53–64.

Pusack, James. 1999. "The Kontakte Multimedia Project at The University of Iowa." *CALICO Journal*, 17, no. 1: 25–42.

Sanders, Ruth. 1985. "Pilot, Snobol, and Logo as Computing Tools for Foreign-Language Instruction." *CALICO Journal*, 3, no. 2: 41–47.

Thorne, Steven, and Jonathon Reinhardt. 2008. "Bridging Activities, New Media Literacies, and Advanced Foreign Language Proficiency." *CALICO Journal*, 25, no. 3: 558–572.

Toole, Janine, and Trude Heift. 2002. "The Tutor Assistant: An Authoring System for a Web-based Intelligent Language Tutor." *Computer Assisted Language Learning*, 15, no. 4: 373–386.

Trinder, Ruth. 2003. "Conceptualisation and Development of Multimedia Courseware in a Tertiary Educational Context: Juxtaposing Approach, Content and Technology Considerations." *ReCALL*, 15: 79–93.

Tschichold, Cornelia. 2003. "Lexically Driven Error Detection and Correction." *CALICO Journal*, 20, no. 3: 549–559.

Underwood, John. 1984. *Linguistics, Computers and the Language Teacher*. Rowley, MA: Newbury House.

# 24 Design-based Research

## JULIO C. RODRÍGUEZ

Design-based research (DBR) is a type of participatory research in which researchers and practitioners collaborate toward a common goal, namely creating new understanding of an educational intervention or issue through the progressive refinement or improvement of a design. DBR emerged in the early 1990s as an approach to research that blurred the distinction between basic and applied research and that focused on promoting and understanding innovation in learning through technology. This chapter provides an overview of the emergence and development of the DBR paradigm based on seminal contributions in the literature that have helped define and refine the goals and main characteristics of this type of inquiry. Connections between DBR and computer-assisted language learning (CALL) are established through both this seminal work and DBR research in CALL. The chapter concludes by examining challenges presented by the implementation of DBR, including issues pertaining to validity and reliability.

## Origins of DBR

One of the first descriptive accounts of DBR appears in a 1990 technical report by Allan Collins sponsored by the Office of Educational Research and Improvement. This report lays out a proposal to construct a "systematic science of how to design educational environments so that new technologies can be introduced successfully" (Collins 1990, 4). Together with Collins' (1990, 1992), Anne Brown's (1992) research on Fostering a Community of Learners (FCL) also stands out in the literature as seminal work in DBR. Her piece has had noticeable impact on much subsequent work in DBR since it constitutes one of the first operationalizations of the principles specified in Collins' (1990) report in an empirical study. Twenty years after these seminal publications, Anderson and Shattuck (2012) reported an exponential increase in DBR studies as well as a marked increase in international contributions. The researchers selected and analyzed a small group of 47 studies among the most cited DBR articles published between 2002 and 2011 and reported that a high proportion of the interventions described in their sample (68%) involved the use of digital technologies (23).

Although McKenney and Reeves (2013) report that Anderson and Shattuck's (2012) meta-analysis of work in DBR includes only two articles about language education, a growing body of research in CALL within the last decade can clearly be seen as associated with the DBR paradigm. This increase in DBR studies in CALL can be attributed to a natural alignment between what researchers perceive as needs in CALL research and some of the features of DBR. For example, both DBR and CALL research are methodologically diverse and multidisciplinary by nature (Egbert and Petrie 2005) and intrinsically interventionist. Moreover, much CALL research, like DBR entails testing particular

*The Handbook of Technology and Second Language Teaching and Learning,* First Edition.
Edited by Carol A. Chapelle and Shannon Sauro.
© 2017 John Wiley & Sons, Inc. Published 2020 by John Wiley & Sons, Inc.

learning designs against how well they promote the ultimate goal of the interventions. A research paradigm such as DBR, which is sensitive to the messiness and complexity typical of technology-rich language-learning contexts, provides the necessary guiding principles to enhance the connections between CALL research and practice. At the same time it also expands and further defines the researchers' theoretical understanding of the many factors that come into play in the development of the language learners' communicative competence, which is typically considered the ultimate goal of a CALL intervention (Chapelle, 1997, 1999).

The growing body of DBR research in instructional technology and CALL has helped further define and conceptualize DBR. Within the first decade of work in DBR, three special issues in major journals have helped define DBR and shape the conversation. The special issue of *Educational Researcher* in 2003 started this thread followed by a special issue in the *Journal of the Learning Sciences* in 2004 and a subsequent special issue in the *Educational Psychologist* in 2004. Collectively, these special issues provide a body of knowledge about DBR that highlights its various strengths and identifies aspects in this type of inquiry that are in need of further consideration or refinement and has fueled discussions across disciplines in the use of technology for teaching and learning. In the field of CALL, a *CALICO Monograph* published in 2013 (Rodríguez and Pardo-Ballester 2013) constitutes one such field specific exploration.

## *Defining DBR*

In the first 25 years of DBR, researchers made explicit efforts to further refine and specify the nature of DBR inquiry. As result of those efforts, the following main desirable elements of DBR have been identified: dual goal, synergy between design and research processes, iteration, methodological pluralism, intervention, exploration, and collaboration. Although it is difficult to find representative samples of research that can be held as models of incorporation of all these qualities, the studies presented in Table 24.1 collectively illustrate the features.

One main distinguishing feature of DBR is the duality of its goal, which entails both the design of learning environments and the development of theory that is relevant to design. Brown (1992) originally referred to this relationship as the "tension" between the goals of concurrently contributing to theory and practice. The dual goals of DBR can then be summarized as the product of two concurrent activities: the activity of designing something and the activity of generating new theoretical understanding. The latter arises from observation of what was designed during its enactment and the identification of emergent phenomena of interest. As Table 24.1 illustrates, DBR studies in CALL always connect the activity of designing with the activity of theorizing.

The synergies between the activities of design and research afford opportunities to generate new understanding in various ways. In his analysis of the potential of DBR in educational research, Edelson (2002) explored this concept in depth and argued that decisions that need to be made to determine a design outcome fall into three categories: design procedure decisions, problem analysis decisions, and design solution decisions. The processes that involve these decisions create opportunities to develop three types of theory: domain theories (e.g., a theory that describes the general principles to design learning experiences for heritage language learners of less-commonly taught languages), design frameworks (e.g., a collection of design guidelines to achieve particular goals), and design methodologies (specifications to create types of designs). Also from the perspective of educational research, McKenney and Reeves (2014) further refine the idea of theoretical understanding by specifying types of knowledge generated by DBR, which they classify into declarative (for example, descriptions of products, concepts, or theories); procedural (for example, specification of design or implementation protocols); or observable (empirical findings).

**Table 24.1** A synopsis of empirical DBR studies in CALL (in chronological then alphabetical order)

| Study | Research context and Technology | What was designed and why | Theory, methods and data |
|---|---|---|---|
| Lund (2008) | EFL, high school *Wikis* | Wiki-based language-learning activities to investigate emergent activity types in collective language production. | Interaction analysis; corpus of videotaped interactions, learner responses to questionnaires. |
| Pardo-Ballester and Rodríguez (2009) | Intermediate Spanish, university level *Online glosses* | Elaborated readings and multimedia glosses to scaffold domain-specific materials (engineering and business). | SLA (elaborated input); learner perceptions questionnaires, video screen captures. |
| Wang, Song, Stone, and Yan (2009) | EFL *Virtual Worlds (Second Life)* | To investigate learner perceptions and readiness to use SL for language learning and how the affordances of the environment might mediate EFL learning. | Social constructivism; evaluation research approach; mixed methods; pre- and post-program surveys, interviews, learner blog postings. |
| Pardo-Ballester and Rodríguez (2010) | Intermediate Spanish, university level *Reading and gloss interfaces* | Reading interface featuring multimedia glosses to scaffold comprehension of domain-specific materials (engineering and business). | Agile interface development, SLA (elaborated input); learner perceptions questionnaires. |
| Hung (2011) | EFL, university level *Video* | A pedagogical design with a focus on tailoring digital video technology to enhance reflective tasks in multimedia environments. | Cognitive theory of multimedia learning and multimedia learning principles drawn from SLA theory; data triangulation using field notes, audio and video recordings, learner reflections in the TL, course evaluations and teacher/researcher field notes. |
| Wong, Boticki, Sun, and Looi (2011) | Chinese, elementary school *Mobile game* | Mobile Computer-supported Collaborative Learning (mCSCL) application to learn Chinese characters in a collaborative game environment. | Mobile Computer-supported Collaborative Learning (mCSCL) design and SLA; video and audio recordings while learners played game, software logs of learner interactions, and focus group interviews. |
| Zheng (2012) | Chinese *Virtual Worlds* | Vitual Quest that provides problem-solving spaces to apply knowledge gained in the classroom. | Ecological and dialogical perspectives to language education; multimodal analysis of video screen captures, video transcription, audio and text chat recordings. |

| Study | Context / Tool | Focus | Methodology / Data |
|---|---|---|---|
| Bush and Sorensen (2013) | ESL<br>*Social networking tool* | Social media platform to explore student perceptions toward CALL materials. | Analysis of learner and instructor survey and instructor interviews. |
| Caws (2013) | French as second language, higher education<br>*Web-based library of videos and transcripts (FrancoToile)* | A web-based library of videos and transcripts and tasks associated with the library aimed at developing learners' critical and electronic literacies and improving the web interface. | Educational ergonomics; pre- and post-task questionnaires, activity sheets, video screen captures, recordings of focus group interviews. |
| Johnson, Khoo, and Campbell (2013) | Teacher education course on CALL<br>*Moodle, Google Docs and Sites, Panopto* | Curricular redesign to improve the use of ICT within CALL teacher education. | Case study; constant comparison approach using evaluative (quantitative and qualitative) data, including student interviews, teacher interviews, instructor's reflective journal, notes from the regular teacher-researcher team project meetings, and group reflections; interpretations within and across findings in each iteration. |
| Martínez-Álvarez and Bannan (2013) | Bilingual education (English/Spanish) in elementary schools in U.S. and Peru<br>*Web-based CALL system (GoInquire)* | An instructional sequence (Instruction in Science Reading: INSCIREAD) combined with a web-based system (GoInquire) to support emergent bilinguals and their teachers in the acquisition of domain knowledge (water erosion) and language. | Integrated Learning Design Framework (ILDF) model; Pre/post instruction elicitation, field notes, learner work on computers (text and drawings), final group discussion and interviews with learners, meetings notes with practitioners. |
| Pardo-Ballester and Rodríguez (2013) | Intermediate Spanish, university level<br>*Virtual Worlds* | Instructional activities for synthetic environments to formulate design principles to guide language learning activity design in virtual worlds. | Sociocultural theory and SLA; screenshots and researcher notes, synchronous chat transcripts with NSs, learner perception questionnaire, pre/post oral proficiency test (Versant test), virtual world notecards, instructor notes, and video screen capture of in-world meetings. |
| Sumi and Takeuchi (2013) | EFL in Japan | Implementation and further refinement of an instructional model (Cyclic Model of Learning) to improve language teaching and learning. | Ecological perspective; interviews, quizzes, blogs, video recordings, questionnaires, classroom observation notes. |

Iteration is also an essential feature of DBR since it is through recursiveness that knowledge is generated and refined (Barab and Squire 2004; Cobb 2001). The distinctive presence of iteration in DBR further gives the research process both a longitudinal and cyclical quality. DBR undertakings typically involve more than one instantiation of a (re)design and subsequent analysis and revision, often extending for prolonged periods of time and encompassing the analysis and report of the same variable under different conditions.

This type of embedded longitudinality in DBR is difficult to find in CALL research. Arguably, much of the research in CALL appears to follow Cobb's (2001) model for theory testing: (1) theory is developed; (2) principles or models for design are drawn from theory; (3) principles are incorporated in the design, and (4) the design is enacted and evaluated. In a CALL research context. This sequence can be illustrated with the following example: (1) interactionist SLA theory emerges; (2) Doughty and Long (2003) draw principles from interactionist SLA theory for optimal less-commonly taught language (LCTL) psycholinguistic environments for distance foreign language learning; (3) Freiermuth and Jarrell (2006) incorporate Doughty and Long's principles to the design of LCTL tasks; and (4) Freiermuth and Jarrell (2006) implement the design and evaluate it. In this model, as Edelson (2002) points out, the research and design processes are distinct, often performed by different people, and occur in sequential fashion. Further, the design processes are not expected to generate or refine theory but rather apply it. In contrast, DBR is deeply integrated with practice and such integration occurs through cyclical rather than sequential processes.

The methodological stance of DBR, which can be described as methodological pluralism or mixed methods, also constitutes one of its salient features. The application of mixed methods of enquiry can be associated with American pragmatism, which recognizes the need for multiple perspectives to solve educational problems and is reflected in the writings of philosophers such as John Dewey and Richard Rorty. The DBR approach to research is pragmatic in nature, so the pervasive use of mixed methods in DBR is not coincidental (Anderson and Shattuck 2012; Confrey 2006). Table 24.1 illustrates the range of methods and approaches used in DBR research in CALL. They include case studies, focus groups, surveys, interviews, and corpus analyses, to name a few.

DBR is interventionist by nature (Cobb et al. 2003). Because DBR seeks to generate knowledge by looking into the processes and outcomes produced by the enactment of a design, research tends to occur in authentic, naturalistic learning settings, which are typically dynamic, messy, and extremely challenging to capture and replicate. The naturalistic quality of DBR results in least two concrete methodological consequences: heightened awareness of contextual factors and responsiveness to the local dynamics of the context. DBR researchers strive to account for the interplay of multiple factors in the interventions they report as well as to provide rich descriptions of the context (DBR Collective 2003). With regard to the latter consequence, DBR is concerned with the local impact of interventions and is expected to inform local practice (see Barab and Squire, 2004, for further discussion of this topic).

DBR was originally conceived as a type of research that could effectively explore innovative learning designs. In order to do this, DBR was engineered to facilitate the identification of emergent properties in the designs it explores. This feature can then be associated with DBR's methodological plasticity and responsiveness to context. When emergent properties are identified, adjustments are made to procedures and measurements. This type of principled adjustment allows the researchers to fine tune aspects of the intervention that are likely to confirm a hypothesis or generate further insights. This quality of DBR is illustrated in Lund's (2008) study, which uses DBR to identify emergent language practices across cultures and contexts using technology tools for collective language production (Wikis). The practitioner and researcher realized that understanding how learners perceived a transition from a local and private activity to a distributed and collective one was important to explain the learners' experience the process that is the focus of the research. An open-ended response instrument is created and used to gather additional data points which are incorporated into the ongoing analysis. Although principled adjustments in DBR provide flexibility to adjust processes, researchers have warned it should be applied with caution. O'Donnell (2004), for example, has pointed out that this flexibility can lead to "reactive adjustments to local events that are not central to the overall implementation" (258), which may result in a loss of focus.

DBR inquiry is also characterized by collaboration. DBR projects often become a collaborative endeavor in which the researcher and implementer both seek to make meaning out of the experience and fulfill complementary roles. The researcher becomes a participant observer and the implementer provides insights that inform the processes of research and design. This type of participatory enquiry does not occur in paradigms where practitioners and, by extension, their knowledge, are not part of the design process and are simply expected to be consumers of the research upon its completion. The role of the researcher in DBR is also distinct since DBR scholars assume the role of both the researcher and designer and draw from methods in those two fields when they engage in DBR.

## The expected outputs of DBR

The expected outputs from DBR result from processes including the following four activities in relation to what is designed and researched: (1) analysis, (2) prototyping or development, (3) enactment or implementation, and (4) evaluation and (further) refinement (Plomp and Nieven 2010; Reeves and McKenney 2013). Figure 24.1 presents a schematic view of DBR activities highlighting the two foci of the process: inquiry and design. The activities associated with each and both lead to the expected outputs, namely refinement of theory or generation

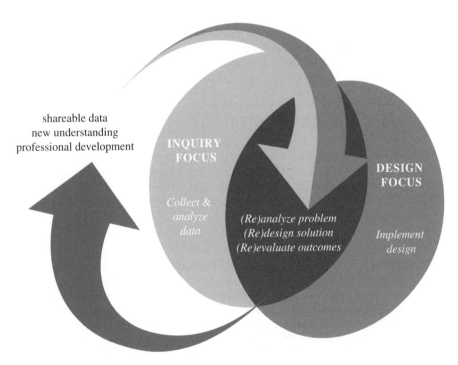

**Figure 24.1**   A schematic view of design-based research.

of prototheories (new understanding), documented processes connected with outcomes of interest (shareable data), and professional development of the practitioners involved.

An important aspect of DBR is to produce research that yields those tangible outputs. According to Amiel and Reeves (2008), DBR radically changes the focus of research from that of research asking "what works?" to such questions as "how can we make a particular design work and why?" In order to be able to answer the latter, researchers must carefully document processes, connect them with outcomes of interest, and make them available to researchers. The idea of documenting processes in DBR extends beyond reporting on particular data and methods of analysis. DBR studies often include rich descriptions that also document the rational for changes in the designs or adjustments in the conjectures that are being tested. Wang and Hannafin (2005) described this feature of DBR as *contextual*, in reference to the deep connections that DBR studies elucidate between the design processes and the locus of research. Akin to this characteristic is the idea that DBR processes are expected to lead to the production of contextually relevant and usable knowledge. DBR studies often document contexts in ways that allow other designers to create parallel contextual conditions (Wang and Hannafin, 2005).

Another expected output of DBR is the creation or further refinement of theory. The concept of theory-building has been discussed extensively in the DBR literature and remains one of the areas that enjoys the most diversity of opinions. Researchers have interpreted this concept in two distinct ways, namely as the refinement of existing theory and the creation of new theoretical understanding. The latter notion has been described as the generation of "prototheory" (DBR Collective 2004), "design guidelines" (Amiel and Reeves 2008) or as "local theory" (Ormel et al. 2012).

Finally, professional development of the practitioners involved is also considered an important output of DBR. As DBR has evolved, the need for professional development to be part of the process has been acknowledged by many researchers. In contexts where practitioners work with researchers seeking solutions to complex problems, it becomes necessary to infuse professional development in order to ensure the designs are implemented and understood as they were meant to be. For example, in a large-scale DBR study in sheltered language instruction, teachers involved in the research of an innovative model (Sheltered Instruction Observation Protocol) spent one or two years learning about the model and participating in three-day professional development summer institutes every year of the research program (see Echevarria, Powers, and Short 2006).

# The potential of DBR in CALL

DBR promises enormous potential to advance research in CALL, especially with regard to cyclical design processes that could potentially inform theory and practice. A growing number of CALL studies to date have been framed as DBR endeavors. Table 24.1 presents the empirical work in CALL marking the nascent efforts to use DBR research in this field. These studies were identified through searches in main language and instructional technology publications, such as *CALICO Journal and Monograph Series*, *Computers in Human Behavior Journal*, *Language Learning & Technology*, *Language Sciences Journal*, *ReCALL Journal*, and so on. Only studies that are explicitly identified as DBR studies by their authors were included. Collectively, these studies illustrate the breadth in research contexts, technologies, and the types of designs involved. Although all of them are framed around improving a design through an iterative processes of refinement with the purpose of solving a problem and further advancing theoretical understanding, they are markedly different in terms of the theoretical and methodological approaches they embrace. In a way, they represent the multiplicity of ways of knowing about language teaching and learning without necessarily limiting theoretical options to those that are prevalent in second language acquisition (SLA).

In fact, many of these studies tend to bring in multidisciplinary perspectives that enrich the profession's understanding of CALL by borrowing relevant knowledge from a range of fields such as Computer Science, Educational Technology, Educational Psychology, Instructional Design, and so on.

Two CALL research areas that are particularly well positioned to take advantage of DBR are materials development and professional development. DBR provides a valuable conceptual foundation to develop not just research-informed but also evidence-based instructional materials, tools, or practices. The necessity to anchor designs to relevant, existing theory (O'Donnell 2004) (research-informed development) and to provide evidence of the impact of such designs in naturalistic contexts (DBR Collective 2003), creates unique opportunities to test, refine, or generate new theoretical understanding grounded on actual practice. In other words, DBR makes it possible to generate situated theoretical knowledge of learning and teaching through the principled design and development of materials and language-learning experiences. Utilizing DBR in this area could help generate design principles for materials development that are anchored to research on practice rather than "creative intuition" (Tomlinson 2013), so that rather than developing materials by anticipating what learners might do and what might be desirable learning outcomes, materials can be designed and revised based on what learners actually did and how well learning outcomes were met. Furthermore, DBR could be used to create, refine, and formalize frameworks for materials development that are informed by such design principles.

DBR also holds promise for contributing to the field through the perspective of making CALL materials development the locus rather than the object of research. Typically, when materials are addressed in language-learning research, they are often perceived as something to evaluate. Tomlinson and Masuhara (2010) affirm that the "aspect of materials development which has received the most attention in the literature is evaluation" (7). Although this is a useful perspective, the impact of materials is better understood when the processes that created them are also taken into account when they are studied. A DBR approach in CALL can help reveal how the design decisions underlying instructional materials, tools, or processes impact learning experiences. By focusing on the design decisions involved and their impact on language learning, researchers may also be able to elucidate new theoretical understanding in relation to language learning, thus creating a much stronger tie between materials development, research and theory.

One way to bridge research with materials development in CALL has been the formulation of CALL design principles based on inferences drawn from theory and empirical research. For example, Plass (1998) put forward a hybrid model for the design and evaluation of multimedia software interfaces derived from cognitive and educational psychology. Following a similar approach, Hoven (1999) proposed a model for listening and viewing comprehension for self-access CALL environments drawing from research in listening and viewing framed within sociocultural theories of language learning. Doughty and Long's (2003) methodological principles for distance foreign language task design provide a further example of deriving CALL design principles from theory. Drawing extensively from empirical research, they propose "universally desirable instructional design features" (51) informed by cognitive and interactionist SLA theory.

DBR embraces the concept of designing from existing theory but offers an alternative approach to the one described above to establish a link between research and practice. This alternative approach can be described as having more depth and less breadth than the studies mentioned above and differs from more traditional ones in four main ways. First, although DBR designs and interventions are also expected to be grounded in the existing relevant research, the resulting theoretical understandings are drawn from evidence of how well actual designs that are operationalized in authentic instructional environments perform. In other words, claims drawn from the existing research need to be substantiated with appropriate evidence, and evidence becomes the foundation of the new understanding.

Second, DBR researchers participate in the whole process, that is, they create a design by drawing from theory, implement it, measure its outcomes, and synthesize principles derived from the evidence. According to Hoadley (2004), a higher degree of methodological alignment can be achieved by having the same people engage in the entire process, which may provide DBR a strength lacking in other research paradigms. Hoadley (2004) asserts that "forcing individuals to carry ideas all the way from explanation to prediction to falsification to application seems like the missing link in educational research that will ensure our theories have practical implications" (205). Several DBR studies illustrate this process applied to the development of tasks (e.g., Caws 2013), instructional tools (e.g., Pardo-Ballester and Rodríguez 2010; Wong et al. 2011), instructional methods (e.g., Hung 2013; Sumi and Takeushi 2013), and curriculum redesign (e.g., Johnson, Khoo, and Campbell 2013).

Third, designs for learning are expected to be put through iterative cycles of evaluation and refinement, which presents opportunities to revisit theoretical claims or conjectures based on evidence gathered during implementation. As a consequence, it is common for DBR studies to report on multiple iterations. Although not all DBR studies necessarily report multiple iterations, many of them do (e.g., see Bush and Sorensen 2013; Caws 2013; Pardo-Ballester and Rodríguez 2010; Wong et al. 2011).

Finally, although one of the dual goals of DBR is to generate or refine theory, there is no claim of universality in the principles or models that emerge. In other words, knowledge generated through DBR is not intended to prescribe but rather guide practice, and theoretical knowledge is not understood as a universal truth but rather a conceptual understanding that can be constantly revised as new knowledge is generated.

As mentioned earlier, in addition to the area of CALL materials development, research on CALL professional development is also well positioned to take advantage of DBR. The way the field has typically construed professional development as *teacher training* betrays the assumptions implied in the role of the teacher as a passive agent to be instructed in the *finite right ways* of using technologies to support instruction. DBR departs from this notion and involves instructors in in two meaningful ways: in an externally referenced and in a self-generating fashion. The former arises from the need to provide the instructor with the relevant background so that the instructional processes are aligned with theoretical assumptions. For example, a DBR study that focuses on project-based learning (PBL) would provide the instructor professional development that would include referential information on PBL. Several DBR studies point to this need (e.g., Bush and Sorensen, 2013; Echevarria et al. 2006; Reeves and McKenney 2013). The latter arises out of the DBR expectation that the instructors will be involved in the creation and evaluation of what is designed. This process itself creates professional development opportunities through the discussions and decisions that instructors and researchers are bound to have. This type of self-generating professional development can become an enriching experience for both instructors and researchers adding a necessary reflective quality not just to teaching but to research.

## Some challenges of DBR

DBR researchers strive to make their findings meaningful and useful and in doing so, are confronted with a number of challenges. Some of the challenges that have surfaced in the early DBR literature include (1) the difficulties in comparing across designs (Collins et al. 2004); (2) the consequent call for standards (e.g., Bell 2004; Collins et al. 2004; Dede 2004; O'Donnell 2004); (3) the call for specification in the reporting of DBR, especially in terms of the strategies used to generate new theoretical understandings through design (Ormel et al. 2012); and (4) the lack of guidelines to identify minimum criteria to begin an intervention (O'Donnell 2004) or at which point an intervention should be abandoned or considered to merit further exploration (Dede 2004). Despite the eclecticism of the challenges presented in the literature, many of them fall into four main areas of concern: data availability, validity, rigor, and reliability.

As mentioned earlier, Brown's (1992) vision was to create repositories of DBR data that researchers can share and reuse. Collins et al. (2004) called for the creation of common DBR data repositories to enable sharing and collaborative analyses. Although large-scale data repositories are now common in other disciplines, such as in the natural sciences, and the technology necessary to enable such data banks is available, DBR research has not lived up to its promise to provide this type of resource. Anderson and Shattuck (2012) reported they found no evidence of this type of undertaking in their analysis of a decade of research in DBR.

Validity is always a concern in any kind of research enterprise. Four main types of validity are frequently mentioned in the DBR literature: (1) ecological validity, (2) treatment validity, (3) systemic validity, and (4) consequential validity. Because DBR research is bound to occur in naturalistic settings, researchers often claim that DBR studies have strong ecological validity (Barab and Squire 2004; Bell 2004). Treatment validity refers to the extent to which interventions align with the theories they embody and has been proposed as a way to assess and describe the validity DBR studies (Hoadley 2004). Systemic validity has been defined as the extent to which DBR research informs theory and practice (Hoadley 2004). That is, it refers to the extent to which DBR research produces what Lagemann (2002) described as *usable knowledge* or the Design-Based Research Collective described as *outcomes of interest*. Finally, consequential validity refers to the extent to which the intervention results in a benefit to those involved in the experience. Barab and Squire (2004) affirm that DBR "offers a model of inquiry that embraces this notion of consequential validity, but design-based researchers need to be clear about the kinds of claims they make from design experiments and the limitations of their findings" (8).

Related to the notion of validity in research is the idea of rigor. DBR researchers have explored ways to augment rigor in DBR. One of the concepts that has been proposed is the notion of defining "embodied conjectures" (Sandoval 2004). This concept is related to the idea that learning or teaching designs are influenced by preconceptions of how people learn that emerge from existing theoretical knowledge. Sandoval (2004) argues that it is possible to increase the rigor of DBR by purposefully mapping conjectures to the design and then design studies that test them. In her critique of Sandoval's (2004) study, O'Donnell (2004) agrees and adds that it is of key importance that the original conjecture be grounded on an understanding of the relevant research literature.

DBR researchers are also concerned with issues related to reliability, which is defined here as the extent to which the implementation of a particular design solution repeatedly yields anticipated outcomes. One strategy proposed is the use of *micro phases* or prototyping phases in design-based research to ensure reliability of the design before the final field work study. As DBR aims to establish how and why a particular intervention works in a certain context, micro research phases provide researchers with an opportunity to refine the design and to gain a more informed understanding of why an invention may (or may not) work in that context (Plomp and Nieven 2010). Micro phases involve a series of small-scale design studies that result in the subsequent reevaluation of the materials before the final product is used in a school-based study. The use of micro phases is part of what Plomp and Nieven (2010) refer to as the prototyping stage: "each cycle in the study is a piece of research in itself (i.e., having its research or evaluation question to be addressed with a proper research design)" (25). Each phase should be presented as a separate study as there may be different research questions, population groups, data samples, and methods of data analysis. This approach was used by Mafumiko (2006), who undertook a micro-scale investigation to improve the chemistry curriculum in Tanzania, and Squire (2005), who conducted three cases in the use of the computer game *Civilization III* with different student groups in different settings in order to refine his design.

# Conclusion

The growing body of DBR research in CALL presented in this chapter demonstrates how the qualities of DBR can enrich CALL research and provide a principled approach to integrating research and practice. DBR also has yet unrealized potential in connection with the integration of technology into complex language-learning experiences, that is, prolonged and sustained learning sequences such as those arising out of project-based, service learning, or study abroad learning experiences. At a macro level of technology integration, DBR offers a framework to analyze and improve technology integration at the program level. For example, in the field of foreign language education, there are numerous yet untapped opportunities to look into technology integration within language programs with specific, unexplored needs, such as full and dual-immersion language programs. Similarly, curricular implementation of pedagogical approaches such as project-based learning, whose success often relies on the successful integration of technology, provide rich opportunities for DBR endeavors. At a micro level of technology integration, the design of innovative learning experiences also presents opportunities for DBR. Learning experiences designed for contexts that incorporate emerging technologies or innovative pedagogical processes that are not yet well understood are often built upon theoretical knowledge that needs to be refined or expanded upon. These are fertile grounds for DBR. More specifically, mobile language learning (Hoven and Palalas 2011) and digital game-based language learning (Sykes and Reinhardt 2013) are areas that have emerged in the last decade that might benefit from further development of theoretical understanding. These are just a few examples of the potential for DBR in CALL today, where its potential still remains largely untapped.

# REFERENCES

Amiel, Tel, and Thomas C. Reeves. 2008. "Design-Based Research and Educational Technology: Rethinking Technology and the Research Agenda." *Educational Technology & Society*, 11, no. 4: 29–40.

Anderson, Terry, and Julie Shattuck. 2012. "Design-Based Research: A Decade of Progress in Education Research?" *Educational Researcher*, 41, no. 1: 16–25.

Barab, Sasha, and Kurt Squire. 2004. "Design-Based Research: Putting a Stake in the Ground." *The Journal of the Learning Sciences*, 13, no. 1: 1–14.

Bell, Philip. 2004. "On the Theoretical Breadth of Design-Based Research in Education." *Educational Psychologist*, 39, no. 4: 243–253. DOI:10.1207/s15326985ep3904_6

Brown, Ann L. 1992. "Design Experiments: Theoretical and Methodological Challenges in Creating Complex Interventions in Classroom Settings." *Journal of the Learning Sciences*, 2, no. 2: 141–178.

Bush, Michael, and Meg Sorensen. 2013. "An Alternate Reality Experience for Language Learning: A Design-Based Evaluation." In *Design-Based Research in CALL*, edited by Julio C. Rodríguez and Cristina Pardo-Ballester, 11: 81–108. San Marcos, TX: CALICO.

Caws, Catherine G. 2013. "Evaluating a Web-Based Video Corpus through an Analysis of User Interactions." *Recall*, 25, no. 1: 85–104. DOI:10.1017/S0958344012000262

Chapelle, Carol A. 1997. "CALL in the Year 2000: Still in Search of Research Paradigms?" *Language Learning & Technology*, 1, no. 1: 19–43.

Chapelle, Carol A. 1999. "Research Questions for a CALL Research Agenda: A Reply to Rafael Salaberry." *Language Learning & Technology*, 3, no. 1: 108–113.

Cobb, Paul. 2001. "Supporting the Improvement of Learning and Teaching in Social and Institutional Context." In *Cognition and Instruction: 25 Years of Progress*, edited by S. Sharon Carver and David Klahr, 455–478. Mahwah, NJ: Lawrence Erlbaum.

Cobb, Paul, Jere Confrey, Andrea diSessa, Richard Lehrer, and Leona Schauble. 2003. "Design Experiments in Educational Research." *Educational Researcher*, 32, no. 1: 9–13.

Collins, Allan. 1990. Toward a Design Science of Education. Report No. 1. New York,: Center for Technology in Education. Accessed June 3, 2016. http://files.eric.ed.gov/fulltext/ED326179.pdf

Collins, Allan. 1992. "Toward a Design Science of Education." In *New Directions in Educational Technology*, edited by E. Scanlon and O'Shea. New York: Springer-Verlag.

Collins, Allan, Diana Joseph, and Katerine Bielaczyc. 2004. "Design Research: Theoretical and Methodological Issues." *The Journal of the Learning Sciences*, 13, no. 1: 15–42.

Confrey, Jere. 2006. "The Evolution of Design Studies as Methodology." In *The Cambridge Handbook of the Learning Sciences*, edited by Keith R. Sawyer, 135–152. New York: Cambridge University Press.

Dede, Chris. 2004. "If Design-Based Research Is the Answer, What Is the Question? A Commentary on Collins, Joseph, and Bielaczyc; diSessa and Cobb; and Fishman, Marx, Blumenthal, Krajcik, and Soloway in the JLS Special Issue on Design-Based Research." *The Journal of the Learning Sciences*, 13, no. 1: 105–114.

Dede, Chris. 2005. "Commentary: The Growing Utilization of Design-based Research." *Contemporary Issues in Technology and Teacher Education*, 5, no. 3/4: 345–348.

Design-Based Research (DBR) Collective. 2003. "Design-Based Research: An Emerging Paradigm for Educational Inquiry." *Educational Researcher*, 32, no. 1: 5–8.

Doughty, Catherine J., and Michael H. Long. 2003. "Optimal Psycholinguistic Environments for Distance Foreign Language Learning." *Language Learning & Technology*, 7, no. 3: 50–80.

Echevarria, Jana, Kristin Powers, and Deborah Short. 2006 "School Reform and Standards-Based Education: A Model for English-Language Learners." *The Journal of Educational Research*, 99, no. 4: 195–208.

Edelson, Daniel C. 2002. "Design Research: What We Learn When We Engage in Design." *The Journal of the Learning Sciences*, 11, no. 1: 105–121.

Egbert, Joy, and Gina Mikel Petrie. 2005. *CALL Research Perspectives (ESL & Applied Linguistics Professional Series)*. Mahwah, NJ: Lawrence Erlbaum Associates, Inc.

Freiermuth, Mark, and Douglas Jarrell. 2006. "Willingness to Communicate: Can Online Chat help?" *International Journal of Applied Linguistics*, 16, no. 2: 189–212. DOI:10.1111/j.1473-4192.2006.00113.x

Hoadley, Christopher M. 2004. "Methodological Alignment in Design-Based Research." *Educational Psychologist*, 39, no. 4: 203–212.

Hoven, Debra. 1999. "A Model for Listening and Viewing Comprehension in Multimedia Environments." *Language Learning & Technology*, 3, no. 1: 88–103.

Hoven, Debra, and Agnieszka Palalas. 2011. "(Re)-Conceptualizing Design Approaches for Mobile Language Learning." *CALICO Journal*, 28, no. 3: 699–720.

Hung, Hsiu-Ting. 2011. "Design-Based Research: Designing a Multimedia Environment to Support Language Learning." *Innovations in Education & Teaching International*, 48, no. 2: 159–169.

Hung, Hsiu-Ting. 2013. "Capitalizing on the Dual Goals of Design-Based Research in Computer-Assisted Language Learning Contexts." In *Design-Based Research in CALL*, edited by Julio C. Rodríguez and Cristina Pardo-Ballester, 11: 67–80. CALICO Monograph Series. San Marcos, TX: CALICO.

Johnson, Marcia E., Elaine Khoo, and Lucy Campbell. 2013. "Cycles of Teacher Reflection: Using Course-Cast Software to Enhance Fully Online Language Teacher Education." In *Design-Based Research in CALL*, edited by Julio C. Rodríguez and Cristina Pardo-Ballester, 11: 109–25. CALICO Monograph Series. San Marcos, TX: CALICO.

Lagemann, Ellen C. 2002. *Usable Knowledge in Education: A Memorandum for the Spencer Foundation Board of Directors*. Chicago, IL: Spencer Foundation.

Lund, Andreas. 2008. "Wikis: A Collective Approach to Language Production." *ReCALL*, 20, no. 1: 35–54.

Mafumiko, Fidelice S. M. 2006. Micro-Scale Experimentation as a Catalyst for Improving the Chemistry Curriculum in Tanzania. Ph.D. dissertation, University of Twente.

Martínez-Álvarez, Patricia, and Brenda Bannan. 2013. "Blending Practices: DBR and CALL to Enrich Emergent Bilingual Learners' Concept and Language Development." In *Design-Based Research in CALL*, edited by Julio C. Rodríguez and Cristina Pardo-Ballester, 11: 127–156. San Marcos, TX: CALICO.

McKenney, Susan, and Thomas C. Reeves. 2013. "Systematic Review of Design-Based Research Progress: Is a Little Knowledge a Dangerous Thing?" *Educational Researcher*, 42, no. 2: 97–100.

McKenney, Susan, and Thomas Reeves. 2014. "Educational Design Research." In *Handbook of Research on Educational Communications and Technology*, 4th ed., edited by J. Michael Spector, M. David Merril, Jan Elen, and M.J. Bishop, XXXV: 131–139. New York: Springer.

O'Donnell, Angela M. 2004. "A Commentary on Design Research." *Educational Psychologist*, 39, no. 4: 255–260. DOI:10.1207/ s15326985ep3904_7

Ormel, Bart J. B., Natalie N. Pareja Roblin, Susan McKenney, Joke M. Voogt, and Jules M. Pieters. 2012. "Research–practice Interactions as Reported in Recent Design Studies: Still Promising, Still Hazy." *Educational Technology Research and Development*, 60, no. 6: 967–986. DOI:10.1007/s11423-012-9261-6

Pardo-Ballester, C., and Julio C. Rodríguez. 2009. "Using Design-Based Research to Guide the Development of Online Instructional Materials." In *Developing and Evaluating Language Learning Materials*, edited by Carol A. Chapelle, Heesung G. Jun, and Ivon Katz, 86–102. Ames, IA: Iowa State University.

Pardo-Ballester, C., and Julio C. Rodríguez.2010. "Developing Spanish Online Readings Using Design-Based Research." *CALICO Journal*, 27, no. 3: 540–553.

Pardo-Ballester, C., and Julio C. Rodríguez. 2013. "Design Principles for Language Learning Activities in Synthetic Environments." In *Design-Based Research in CALL*, edited by Julio C. Rodríguez and Cristina Pardo-Ballester, 11: 183–209. CALICO Monograph Series. San Marcos, TX: CALICO.

Plass, Jan. 1998. "Design and Evaluation of the User Interface of Foreign Language Multimedia Software: A Cognitive Approach." *Language Learning & Technology* 2, no. 1: 35–45.

Plomp, Tjeerd, and Nienke Nieven, eds. 2010. *An Introduction to Educational Design Research*, 3rd ed.

The Hague: SLO Netherlands Institute for Curriculum Development.

Reeves, Thomas C., and Susan McKenney. 2013. "Computer-Assisted Language Learning and Design-Based Research: Increased Complexity for Sure, Enhanced Impact Perhaps." In *Design-Based Research in CALL*, edited by Julio C. Rodríguez and Cristina Pardo-Ballester, 11: 9–21. CALICO Monograph Series. San Marcos, TX: CALICO.

Rodríguez, Julio C., and Cristina Pardo-Ballester, eds. 2013. *Design-Based Research in CALL*. Vol. 11. San Marcos, TX: CALICO.

Sandoval, William A. 2004. "Developing Learning Theory by Refining Conjectures Embodied in Educational Designs." *Educational Psychologist*, 39, no. 4: 213–23. Doi:10.1207/s15326985ep3904_3.

Squire, Kurt D. 2005. "Resuscitating Research in Educational Technology: Using Game-Based Learning Research as a Lens for Looking at Design-Based Research." *Educational Technology*, 45 no. 1: 8–14.

Sumi, Sejiro, and Osamu Takeushi. 2013. "The Cyclic Model of Learning: An Attempt Based on the DBR in an EFL Context." In *Design-Based Research in CALL*, edited by Julio C. Rodríguez and Cristina Pardo-Ballester,157–182. San Marcos, TX: CALICO.

Sykes, Julie M., and Jonathon Reinhardt. 2013. *Language at Play: Digital Games in Second and Foreign Language Teaching and Learning (Theory and Practice in Second Language Classroom Instruction)*. Boston: Pearson Education, Inc.

Tomlinson, Brian. 2013. *Developing Materials for Language Teaching*, 2nd ed. London: Bloomsbury Publishing.

Tomlinson, Brian, and Hitomi Masuhara, eds. 2010. *Research for Materials Development Evidence for Best Practice*. London: Continuum.

Wang, Feng, and Michael J. Hannafin. 2005. "Design-Based Research and Technology Enhanced Learning Environments." *Educational Technology Research and Development*, 53, no. 4: 5–23.

Wang, Charles Xiaoxue, Hongbo Song, David E. Stone, and Qiaoqiao Yan. 2009. "Integrating Second Life into an EFL Program in China: Research Collaboration across the Continents." *TechTrends*, 53, no. 6: 14–19. DOI:10.1007/ s11528-009-0337-z

Wong, Lung-Hsiang, Ivica Boticki, Jizhen Sun, and Chee-Kit Looi. 2011. "Improving the

Scaffolds of a Mobile-Assisted Chinese Character Forming Game via a Design-Based Research Cycle." *Computers in Human Behavior,* 27, no. 5: 1783–1793.

Zheng, Dongping. 2012. "Caring in the Dynamics of Design and Language: Exploring Second Language Learning in 3D Virtual Spaces," *Language Sciences,* 34: 543–558.

# RESOURCES

ThinkerTools Research Group
http://thinkertools.org/Pages/research.html
A PEER Tutorial for Design-based research
http://dbr.coe.uga.edu/explain05.htm

Interviews with Design-based Research Experts
http://dbr.coe.uga.edu/expertinterview.htm

# 25 Evaluation of Technology and Language Learning

## CAROL A. CHAPELLE

Evaluation is so integral to much of our scholarship and practice in technology and language learning that it may be difficult to pinpoint exactly what it consists of. In 2006, Hubbard defined evaluation of computer-assisted language learning (CALL) as "the process of (a) investigating a piece of CALL software to judge its appropriateness for a given language-learning setting, (b) identifying ways it may be effectively implemented in that setting, and (c) assessing its degree of success and determining whether to continue use or to make adjustments in implementation for future use" (313). He laid out a procedure to help direct evaluators' attention to important aspects of the software in a way that would produce systematic judgments about their value. In the same year, Levy and Stockwell (2006) defined CALL evaluation more generally in part by distinguishing it from research. Evaluation, they suggested, should be seen as being driven by pragmatic decision-making questions about whether or not something worked in a particular context. Research, in contrast, is concerned with explanation of why things work. The distinction they make between evaluation and research contrasts with the approach to evaluation of technology for language learning presented by Chapelle (2001), which draws upon empirical results of research as one source of support for an evaluation argument, which refers to multiple types of support for claims about the value of specific aspects of technology for language learning. This latter approach has been developed in evaluation studies examining a variety of aspects of materials and their use in classrooms (Gruba et al. 2016; Leakey 2011).

In this chapter, I examine the types of arguments that have been used in the evaluation of technology for language learning. Evaluation arguments are made at a variety of levels from individual tasks to entire courses in a range of contexts (Chapelle 2007). In this chapter, I have not distinguished among the various levels, but instead concentrated on the evaluation arguments that have appeared in in the professional literature, for example, in journals such as *ReCALL* and *Language Learning & Technology*. Their appearance in peer-reviewed journals indicates a level of acceptability of the arguments on the part of professionals in the field. I suggest that understanding the types of arguments considered acceptable by the field about the quality of language-learning materials and activities is useful for understanding evaluation practices in the field. I conclude by suggesting that the perspective of evaluation as argument holds the potential for improving the profession's capacity for designing and critiquing evaluations of technology for language learning, which play an important role in building knowledge in the field.

*The Handbook of Technology and Second Language Teaching and Learning*, First Edition.
Edited by Carol A. Chapelle and Shannon Sauro.
© 2017 John Wiley & Sons, Inc. Published 2020 by John Wiley & Sons, Inc.

# Evaluation as argument

Professionals in technology and language learning recognize the complexity of evaluating the materials, activities, courses, and programs created using new technologies. In view of the nature and range of the objects of evaluation, they have not been able to simply adopt evaluation methods from colleagues who work in materials evaluation (Tomlinson 2003) or program evaluation (Alderson and Beretta 1992; Norris et al. 2009). Technology is different. The complexity of materials development and use is greater when technology is involved. The teachers' roles are different. The audiences for evaluation findings are more varied, demanding and in some cases more political. Materials and program evaluation typically evaluates the quality of business as usual; technology evaluators often find themselves evaluating the quality of innovation. In doing so, technology evaluators cannot rely solely on comparing the innovation with the status quo. Innovation is intended to change the status quo, not to replicate it (Garrison and Anderson 2003). At the core of the issue is the fact that technology affords opportunities for communication, interaction, and learning that are out of reach in face-to-face learning without technology. But how does one evaluate the quality of new affordances for learning?

Principles of evaluation were outlined in in Alderson and Beretta's *Evaluating Second Language Education*, where Alderson (1992) presented a framework describing the factors involved in designing an evaluation including the purpose, audience, evaluator(s), content, method, and timing. The framework and other treatments of evaluation in applied linguistics (e.g., Lynch, 1996) build on the classic work in social science, most fundamentally, Cronbach's *Designing Evaluations of Educational and Social Programs* (1982). Cronbach defined program evaluation as

> inquiries that represent serious attempts to improve a program or a kind of service by developing a clear picture of its operations and the fate of its clients. The investigation may be a pilot study of an early version of the program; or it may be a review of a long-established operation, made with an eye to change or even termination. (Cronbach 1982, 2)

If Cronbach's "clients" are second language learners, and the "program" a language program, course, plan for the day, or even CALL program, the relevance of the basic principles is evident. Patton (2008) added the audience for the evaluation results: evaluation should be "done for and with specific intended primary users for specific, intended uses" (37).

In planning and interpreting evaluations of technology for language learning, evaluators need a means of moving from the general parameters to useful heuristics for deciding how evaluations should be planned, carried out, interpreted, and reported in view of the intended uses and audiences. Ruhe and Zumbo's (2009) book entitled *Evaluation in Distance Education and e-Learning* presents such heuristics for e-learning in general. As an introduction to their perspective on evaluation, they define professional program evaluation as "a rigorous, evidence-based argument in support of evaluative claims" (11). The use of the terms "argument" and "claim" are important because they highlight the need for evaluators to make explicit the claims that they are evaluating and to plan an investigation that will determine the extent to which the claims can be supported. The results of the investigations are then used in support of an argument about the credibility of the claims.

Like e-learning in general, CALL evaluation is conducted to support claims, which are value statements about technologies for language learning. Claims can refer to value statements about CALL materials, technology-assisted activities, online courses, or distance and mobile learning. They can refer to a various aspects of the technologies that are intended to provide value and therefore are important targets for investigation. Some examples of the claims made by authors are the following:

> The tasks fostered interaction among students and between students and the tutor and thus promoted the negotiation of meaning needed for language acquisition. The focus of tutorials was generally on meaning, and communication was the most important overall outcome. (Hampel 2006, 117)

> ...strong support for the claim that technology made a measurable impact in FL learning came from studies on computer-assisted pronunciation training, in particular, automatic speech recognition (ASR). These studies demonstrated that ASR can facilitate the improvement of pronunciation and can provide feedback effectively. (Golonka et al. 2014, 70)

> The positive effect of RWL on reading rate and vocabulary recognition gains was statistically significant, which supports the claims that extensive RWL outside of class can help students improve various facets of their English ability. (Gobel and Kano 2014, 290)

The second two of these statements use the term "claim" to make it easy to find an explicit claim, but the first statement serves as a claim, too. In our field, evaluators attempt to develop credible arguments in support of claims made about technology and language learning, but what counts as a credible argument? What kind of arguments do professionals make and accept as support for value-based claims about language learning and technology?

# Five types of argument

Evaluations of technology for language learning today are developed to support a variety of claims about effectiveness of instruction, appropriateness of materials, and other specific positive features of learning activities. In support of the different types of claims authors make, a variety of types of arguments are put forth in the journal articles and evaluation reports. Such arguments are constructed on the basis of a combination of theoretical rationales, judgmental analyses of materials, activities or courses, and empirical research. In many of the studies reported in technology journals, multiple lines of support are intertwined implicitly in such a way that it is difficult for readers who are not in the field to detect the rationales guiding the evaluation. Moreover, because evaluations are designed and reported in view of their intended audiences, certain aspects of evaluations are more likely to be reported in the professional journals. However, the implicit assumptions underlying many evaluations and the selection process that takes place in writing a journal article are seldom evident to readers. To reveal the types of arguments that appear in the professional literature, I analyzed the types of arguments that are put forth to support claims about technology and language learning in the professional literature. These five types of arguments are not the only ones that might be found for technology and language learning; nor are they mutually exclusive. In contrast, authors frequently combine and mix arguments depending on the claims they are trying to support. Even through these arguments appear intertwined in individual evaluation studies, it is informative to examine them one by one.

## Comparative argument

Comparative arguments to support claims about the value of technology for language learning are made based on quantitative research comparing students' learning outcomes from computer-assisted language learning to those from classroom instruction that is not enhanced with computer technology. Such evaluations are carried out using well-established research methods from education consisting of investigations of two groups of students who participate in the same process of instruction except for the technology-assisted intervention provided to the experimental group. Such research yields statistical results quantifying the measurable differences in achievement between the experimental group and a control group on multiple types of learning outcomes such as grammar, writing, speaking, reading and listening (e.g., Chenoweth and Murday 2003). If experimental procedures have been followed according to guidelines, the results can be used to support or refute a claim about the superiority of the technology condition for learning. Additional data may be gathered as well about, for example, students' learning styles, satisfaction, and time spent on the course (Chenoweth and Murday 2003). However, the argument for (or against) the effectiveness of the technology interventions rests primarily on the quantitative results attained from the comparisons of test scores from two groups.

The strongest support for general comparative claims about technology and language learning comes from research that statistically summarizes across multiple comparison studies. Such a meta-analysis study (Norris and Ortega 2006) became possible to do after the turn of the century, when technology comparison studies had been carried out over the previous 30 years. Zhao (2003) conducted one such meta-analysis, which summarized the results of nine comparison studies appearing from 1997 through 2001. The findings indicated that overall the technology using groups across studies tended to outperform the students in the no-technology condition. Expanding on the scope of Zhao's meta-analysis, a second meta-analysis was conducted on studies published in the period from 1970 through 2006 (Grgurovic, Chapelle, and Shelley 2013). The researchers searched for studies comparing technology for language learning with no-technology conditions published in six journals in addition to dissertations. The overall number of studies found over the 36 years was over 200, but only 42 of these met the criteria for inclusion, because of methodological shortcomings in the research or inadequate reporting of results. Most of the 42 studies included more than one outcome assessment (for example, assessing outcomes in both reading and vocabulary in one study). The findings of this meta-analysis indicated that when comparisons between CALL and non-CALL groups were made in rigorous research designs, the CALL groups performed better than the non-CALL groups, as indicated by a small, but positive and statistically significant weighted mean effect size of 0.257. Overall, results did not indicate that CALL was inferior to no-technology conditions.

In short, the meta-analysis results provide moderate support for claims that technology using language learners' benefited relative to those who did not learn in the technology condition. Despite the commonsense appeal of such a scientific-looking method, professionals in CALL have been critical of research that supports the use of technology for language learning by comparing outcomes. The methodological issues have been described in the literature for some time (Chapelle and Jamieson 1991; Dunkel 1991; Pederson 1987). In addition, researchers and developers in the field note that this type of quantitative summary lacks the detail needed to use research results to improve instruction by developing better learning materials and tasks (Chapelle 2003). Many teachers and researchers in applied linguistics want to learn how students and teachers work with language learning through technology, what they think of particular types of tasks, and what kind of challenges they face when undertaking innovation. Above all, however, today the design of the comparison study which assumes that the no-technology condition is the normal classroom does not comport with the reality of language teaching in many programs throughout the world. In other words, in many settings the experiment is over. Without waiting for results of comparison studies, technology tends to be adopted for various other reasons by program administrators, departments, universities, and perhaps most important, by students.

## *Authenticity argument*

The authenticity argument is used to support claims that language-learning tasks are valuable because they require students to use the same types of technologies that they are comfortable with for their everyday practices. Such arguments bypass questions about whether or not technology-based tasks are superior to a no-technology condition for learning. Instead, these arguments rest on the assumption that language instruction should be delivered in a manner that is authentic to the ways in which students access information and entertainment as well as communicate outside the language classroom. Today, authenticity arguments are made for the use of mobile devices including cell phones for language learning because "the students currently possess their cell phones" (Bibby 2011, 52) and they are accustomed to using them regularly. Similar arguments have been made for other technologies in the past, such as pod-casts, which O'Bryan and Hegelheimer (2007) argued could be used to provide students with academic lectures to accompany their ESL classes because of the popularity of MP3 players among students outside the classroom. Kukulska-Hulme and Shield (2008) begin their review of mobile-assisted language learning with the observation that mobile technologies are regularly used outside the classroom by students and teachers. Such arguments draw upon research and informal observation about the communication practices of the current generation of students.

The use of such claims in evaluation has been criticized for the way that they implicitly assume that communication practices outside the classroom should serve as the model for instructional practices. "By using authenticity claims to support our didactic designs, we might embrace tacit assumptions tied in with these, to which, in isolation, we might not subscribe. Ideally, these assumptions, which may otherwise 'sneak in' with authenticity claims, should be made explicit and subjected to scrutiny" (Buendgens-Kosten 2013, 283). However, the argument that pedagogical tasks should be developed through consideration of language practices outside the language classroom is not new in language teaching. A central goal of language teaching is to prepare students for language practices that they will need outside the classroom. The authenticity argument for technology simply adds to this general goal by recognizing the importance of the way language is mediated through technology outside the classroom. What is needed then is not to abandon the authenticity argument, but to use it with a better understanding of the scope and limitations of the claims it supports.

A more refined concept of authenticity in applied linguistics has been developed in task-based language learning (e.g., Long 2005) and extended to technology-mediated task-based language learning (González-Lloret, 2014). Researchers in task-based language learning lay out a process for conducting needs analysis that examines the linguistic tasks that the learning materials are intended to prepare students for. Concepts from Task-based language teaching (TBLT) have been proposed for making stronger authenticity arguments about the students' needs for technology use.

> In a technology-mediated TBLT program, the NA [needs analysis] should address not just the language necessities (linguistic and pragmatic) to complete the tasks, but also the informational and multimodal digital skills needed to effectively engage with the technology. In addition, a NA should help us gather information about what innovations and technological tools are most appropriate for the curriculum, as well as inform us about the necessary training for students and teachers to be able to use them successfully. (González-Lloret 2014, 23)

In addition to these methods, consideration needs to be given to how much weight should be placed on authenticity arguments in view of the nature of the technology use learners engage in outside the classroom and the intended role of school in increasing learners' literacy levels and their language use across various contexts. For example, the claim that Lund makes for the use of wiki activities, entails that assumption that normal communication practices are to be challenged rather than modeled: "The central claim in the article is that wiki activities challenge established language production practices in school, and involve an epistemological shift for those involved" (Lund 2008, 36). This is obviously an area in need of additional careful analysis and evaluation.

## *Corpus linguistic argument*

A corpus linguistic argument underlies claims that use of technology can provide students with access to the linguistic data they need for language learning. The corpus linguistic argument is that language learning—like legitimate linguistic research—requires those studying the language to examine large samples of language from relevant contexts. Based on such examinations, learners are claimed to be able to solve their learning problems independently, raise their consciousness about linguistic generalizations, find models, and test hypotheses (Chen 2011). These claims requiring corpus linguistic arguments were inspired by the pedagogical approach called data-driven learning, which was introduced to refer to the idea that learners, like corpus linguists, could benefit from examining the language directly, that is, searching a corpus of texts seeking, words, phrases, and grammatical constructions to gain information about the instances occurring in actual examples of language (Higgins and Johns 1984).

The impetus for such claims comes from corpus linguistics but can be bolstered by a variety of qualitative and quantitative empirical studies. A special issue of *ReCALL Journal* provided a collection of empirical studies investigating the extent to which claims made about manifestations of data-driven learning could be supported. In each evaluation study, the particulars of what is being taught and learned vary as do the methodologies used to support claims about learning. The editors summarize the methodologies as consisting of

> rigorous experimental/laboratory studies lasting just a few minutes (including one semi-replication study), generally on a specific (lexicogrammar) language point, while others are more ecological and cover an entire semester with a much more open language focus; these are generally backed up by questionnaires and other instruments to gather feedback from participants. (Boulton and Pascual Pérez-Paredes 2014, 123)

The claims are about students' learning of specific aspects of language (e.g., passive voice or formulaic sequences) or more generally for advances made in gaining independence, for example. Quantitative research often adopts the comparative methodology described above, but the comparisons are often made between two pedagogical variations of data-driven learning. For example, in a study investigating the teaching of linking adverbials, Cotos (2014) provided each of the ESL students of advanced academic writing with a corpus of research articles relevant to their own field of study and some of the students were given a learner corpus as well. For the learner corpus group, the pedagogy started with an identification of common problems in the use of linking adverbials. Both groups then worked with the research article corpus and the improvement in participants' written production and their knowledge of linking adverbials was assessed by analyzing data collected before and after instruction. Cotos interpreted these findings as supportive of the claim that "supplementing corpus materials with learner output promises to be effective practice that can be readily integrated in DDL instruction with positive impact" (Cotos 2014, 218).

Investigating claims about the utility of corpora of field specific language for students of English for Academic Purposes, Chang (2014) conducted a qualitative case study to compare ten graduate students' use of and attitudes toward two corpora. One corpus contained academic English with samples from across a range of fields and the other contained samples of texts from each student's own discipline. Each of the students participated in weekly interviews and a final survey to assess their opinions about the utility of each of the corpora for the students' writing needs over a 22-week period. The findings serve in an argument that the field specific corpora were more useful than the other two. Students' comments about the general academic corpus such as, "but it seems hard to search for English in the field I need" (249) are an important part of the argument. Other comments about students' reasons for using the field specific corpus also serve as part of the argument: "Although a word is frequently used, if it is not used in my field, I feel that I don't need to use it" (250).

These two examples reveal some specific variations on corpus linguistic arguments in support of claims about the value of corpora for language learning. They provide a good example of the evolution of arguments which begin as pedagogical hypotheses about connections between linguistics and language teaching. What began as innovative approaches to teaching have evolved into specific claims which are being investigated and, in some cases, supported by empirical research.

## *Theory-based argument*

Theory-based arguments are used to provide support for claims about learning outcomes and the value of particular types of learning processes that students engage in through technology use. Theoretical perspectives in second language acquisition are useful in evaluation arguments because they hypothesize ideal conditions for second language learning that can be constructed through the use of technology (Chapelle 2003). Such conditions result in students, for example, receiving optimal input, engaging in interaction, being given opportunities to notice gaps between their performance and the target language, and participating in collaborative goal completion (Chapelle 1998; Doughty and Long 2003). Based on theory-driven expectations about the effects of certain conditions on outcomes, learning processes, or both, evaluators make relevant observations as learners work with the pedagogical materials. The findings then are used in support of claims about the success of the conditions. As shown in Figure 25.1, even though the claims are supported by interpreting observations, it is the theoretical hypotheses about conditions that make the interpretations meaningful. In Figure 25.1, the arrows refer to the various ways interpretations are made when evaluators use theory to guide evaluation studies. The schematic diagram is a much simplified outline of a complex, iterative process that evaluators may go through as they assess the potential observations they might be able to make. Such interpretations, which are possible because second language acquisition researchers have developed explanations about how learning occurs as a result of students' exposure to linguistic input, interaction, mental processing, mediated actions and social collaborations, are an essential part of an argument that uses learning process data. The researcher can describe the learning conditions created in a computer-mediated chat task, for example, with reference to these explanations for learning (e.g., Pellettieri 2000).

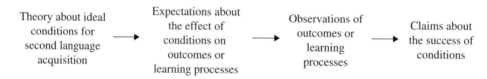

**Figure 25.1**   Schematic diagram of the logic behind the use of second language acquisition theory to guide research for supporting claims about the success of technology for language learning.

Theory-based claims about the success of the conditions provided by the technology-mediated learning (e.g., appropriate input, feedback or collaboration) for learning outcomes can be supported by the type of comparisons described above as comparative arguments. The difference between the comparative arguments and theory-based arguments is that the latter type of evaluation research is designed based on a theory-based explanation about why learning outcomes are better in one condition than in another. Theory-based claims about learning processes require a theory that posits valuable behavior for learners to engage in, thought processes, or even exposure to certain types of input while they are working on technology-mediated tasks. Such theorized aspects of the teaching and learning process provide a basis for evaluators to plan the types of observations of learning processes that they make in the evaluation study and to interpret the observations.

Plenty of examples of theory-based arguments in evaluation studies can be found in the professional literature today. They use second language theory to interpret the value of the learning processes that students engage in as they use technology for language learning (Chapelle 2009). For example, Suzuki (2013) used sociocultural theory to direct her observation of private turns, or the inner speech, that students of Japanese engaged in during the learning process. Data were gathered using video recordings of students' behavior in front of the screen in addition to synchronized recordings of the on-screen activity. The data were interpreted with respect to the value of private turns as posited by sociocultural theory.

A second example comes from a study that used dynamic systems theory (DST), which theorizes in broad strokes the complexity of language development through a number of general processes that work together allowing learning to occur from language experience (Larsen-Freeman and Cameron 2008). Sockett (2013) summarized the main tenets of DST in his study of advanced learners of English in informal online communication activities. Students who were considered experienced in second language acquisition research reported their language-learning experiences on blogs. Sockett (2013) interpreted their reports through the lens of DST to identify reported behaviors supportive of language development from a DST perspective. Evidence of these processes was what Sockett sought in his study, where he wanted to identify processes indicative of informal learning. Outside of formal English language classes, students become involved in "informal target language practices such as chatting or social networking online, downloading or streaming original version television series, and choosing music in English via on-demand services" (Sockett 2013, 48). Sockett describes learning in these settings as incidental, occurring while students are communicating for enjoyment.

In CALL evaluation studies, it is not unusual to see the mixing of theoretical perspectives, constructs, data collection methods, and frames of interpretation because of the pragmatist's stance that underlies much of the evaluation of technology for language learning. The pragmatist wants to gain an understanding of how things work in order to be able to make recommendations for use and improvement. For example, Lee (2008) introduced the theoretical basis for her study with Skehan's cognitive perspective on the value of feedback for learning (Skehan 2003) and a sociocultural point of view, which theorizes the value of corrective feedback embedded within a social context where learners work collaboratively to solve linguistic problems (Nassaji and Swain 2000). Each of these perspectives provides a useful level of hypotheses about learning processes for the data that were collected, the instances of feedback that the learners receive, and the nature of the collaborations among participants. This type of theory-mixing might be seen as problematic by some researchers in applied linguistics, but in the CALL professional journals, the pragmatic orientation tends to welcome both mixed-methods research and theory-mixing.

## *Pedagogy-based argument*

Pedagogy-based arguments support claims about the value of technology-mediated learning for meeting pedagogical requirements. Such requirements are proposed by materials developers or teachers based on their interpretations of generally accepted teaching principles in the field or innovations intended to improve teaching practice. Such pedagogical principles are not necessarily based on the types of theories noted above; instead, they typically come from insights gained from previous research and practice as well as the impetus to improve practice in view of the affordances made possible through technology. These arguments are particularly valuable in pushing forward evaluation of the specific pedagogical affordances for learning that are beyond the scope of second language theories, such as those for collaboration on the internet (e.g., Belz, and Thorne 2006). Figure 25.2 shows the role of pedagogical principles in the processes of conceptualizing and conducting and interpreting evaluation research. The process is the same as the one outlined for theory-based arguments except for the initial motivation being a pedagogical one.

Pedagogically-based arguments have been constructed for many different aspects of language learning because computer technologies provide multifaceted ways of improving learning. The argument in support of data-driven learning described above is one type of pedagogical argument because it begins with the pedagogical notion that learners need to have access to data consisting of lots of examples of language use as they are creating their own novel texts. I distinguished the data-driven learning argument from other pedagogical arguments because of its basis in corpus linguistics which has been so rich in generating specific language-based claims about learning.

One can similarly identify arguments used to support other pedagogically-motivated claims about the value of learning vocabulary or intercultural communicative competence, for example. For example, a pedagogically-motivated argument for vocabulary teaching is evident in the design and research of vocabulary strategy training (Ranalli 2013). The pedagogy was developed to take advantage of technology affordances including web-based dictionary skills and self-paced instruction, which were based on Ranalli's teaching and learning experience. The pedagogical principles, then, guided the evaluation, which examined the extent to which learners developed their dictionary skills and took advantage of the individualized practice.

Pedagogically-based arguments support claims about the value of the use of telecollaboration for developing learners' intercultural communicative competence through cross-cultural exchanges. The definition of the pedagogical goal, the construct of intercultural communicative competence, is critical for the way that the evaluation is conducted and presented. For that reason, Byram's (1997) definition of intercultural communicative competence—which consists of the components of attitudes, knowledge, skills of interpreting and relating, skills of discovery and interaction, and critical cultural awareness—has been important in evaluation studies using technology for developing learners' intercultural communicative competence. For example, in the classic project for culture learning in foreign language teaching, Cultura (Furstenberg, Levet, English, and Maillet 2001), the researchers showed

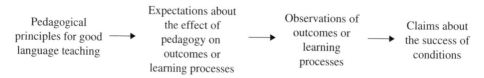

**Figure 25.2**   Schematic diagram of the logic behind the use of pedagogical principles to guide research for supporting claims about the success of technology for language learning.

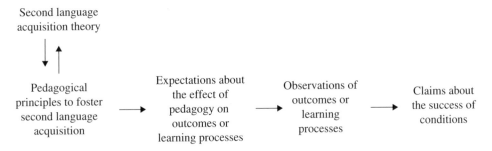

**Figure 25.3**   Schematic diagram of the logic behind the use of second language acquisition theory connected with pedagogical principles to guide research for supporting claims about the success of technology for language learning.

data such as this comment from an American student, whose cultural knowledge had been expanded by the experience of participating in a task designed to raise awareness of value differences among American and French students: "Hi everyone! When I first read the words all of you used associating to 'individualism,' I felt completely shocked. The ideal that Americans hold so closely to themselves is scorned by another country!" Such data are used in the evaluation argument in support of the claim that the carefully planned internet collaborations fostered conversations in which the cultural differences were recognized, thereby achieving the pedagogical goals.

Such pedagogically-based arguments are valuable in their own right for the way that they support new pedagogical claims. At the same time, both the design and evaluation of learning tasks can benefit from an integrated theory-pedagogy perspective. An integrated approach expresses pedagogical principles that are consistent with or derived from certain theoretical perspectives of second language acquisition. In constructing principles that are useful in design and evaluation, this process also holds the potential for making demands on the development of theory. Figure 25.3 illustrates the theory-pedagogy integration that can form the basis for evaluation research.

An example of this approach appears in frameworks of qualities for evaluation of CALL materials which include characteristics such as language-learning potential, meaning focus, and positive impact (Chapelle 2001). These qualities are defined based primarily on interactionist second language acquisition theory (e.g., Gass 1997), and therefore serve as a step toward planning an evaluation study with an integrated theory-pedagogy basis. However, such a framework also reveals the many important characteristics of pedagogy that such a theory does not include, such as development of intercultural competence. The framework allows for inclusion of cultural dimensions of language learning within impact but the evaluator has to specify the pedagogical goals. For all evaluation studies, the evaluator needs to formulate the specific claims that provide the basis for their evaluation.

# Improving evaluation

The many approaches to evaluation arguments outlined above reveal the centrality of evaluation to the process of innovation that lies at the heart of technology use for language learning. Making explicit the types of arguments that appear in evaluations creates the opportunity to better understand and improve evaluation practices. The perspective of evaluation as argument has implications for how evaluation can be planned, communicated to others and interpreted.

Each evaluation study is different and therefore each one needs to be planned by formulating the claims that the evaluation is intended to investigate. How does an evaluator decide upon appropriate claims for a particular evaluation? The view of the evaluation as a situation-specific argument is useful for conceptualizing the planning phase because it prompts evaluators to think about the audience for the results of the evaluation and its context (Patton 2008). Depending on the purpose of the evaluation study, the audience can be other developers and researchers of technology for language learning, teachers and students, administrators of educational programs, or program officers at a funding agency. When one or multiple audiences have been identified and their interest in the evaluation is understood, the type of claims that are appropriate for guiding the evaluation will become easier to formulate. The professional journals in CALL are full of studies that present arguments sufficiently convincing to professionals in technology and language learning, but such arguments are not necessarily appropriate for other audiences. The process of formulating claims can be informed by the arguments that have been developed by others as well as through the use of advice or guidelines such as those outlined by Hubbard (2006) or Chapelle (2001). Regardless of the source of ideas, the claims are specific to the context for each of the evaluations.

In the planning stage, evaluators also need to consider the feasibility of investigating the claims. In other words, claims need to be made that can actually be investigated and, with the methods that are feasible, possibly supported. If the evaluation is to determine that data-driven learning activities, for example, are beneficial for language development, will the data needed for investigating such a claim be possible to obtain? Conducting the evaluation requires the expertise to organize data collection, conduct appropriate analyses, and make plausible interpretations. Research methods in education and in applied linguistics provide guidance on basic methodologies, but the research and arguments developed in CALL add to these methodologies by providing details and examples of studies that investigate the unique interactions that occur in computer-mediated learning (e.g., Smith, this volume). The comparison studies require knowledge from the domain of quantitative research design and language assessment. The authenticity arguments require grounding in needs analysis particularly as it pertains to technology-mediated task-based language learning. The linguistic analysis requires a foundation in corpus linguistics and usage-based approaches to language development. The interpretations of processes and strategies are based on knowledge of theoretical approaches to second language acquisition and qualitative research. And the arguments based on pedagogical principles require a convergence of knowledge from second language pedagogy, theory and multiple forms of research methods, including discourse analysis.

The concepts of argument and claim are useful for evaluators as they communicate what their studies are and are not intended to do. Clear communication is needed if results are to be synthesized. The growing number of syntheses of research on technology and language learning need to identify the intended claims made in the studies. One such summary found that in the majority of the studies no claims were made about measureable outcomes (Golonka et al. 2014). Instead, the review found many other claims about, for example, frequency of dictionary look ups, vocabulary acquisition, improvement of accuracy of production, and effectiveness of intelligent feedback, and learners' preference for technology over other modes of learning. Golonka et al. (2014) defined what they would consider to constitute strong, moderate and weak empirical evidence in arguments supporting each of the claims. Most claims were found to be supported only weakly, meaning that claims had been made on the basis of a single well-designed study or expert opinion based on theory or practice; or a study with a questionable methodology. The goal of this summary was to assess the strength of the support for such claims about genres of technology use for language learning within the field.

This important goal is more likely to be realized if authors introduce their evaluation studies and draw interpretations that recognize the interconnectedness of any individual study to a particular type of technologies and pedagogies, as Cotos and Huffman (2013) did in their study of the feedback provided by their automated writing evaluation system: "our results are very informative for the intended purpose of [Research Writing Tutor] RWT, being the first building block for its effectiveness evaluation argument. We also hope that this work not only helps build the growing body of knowledge about L2 writers' interactions with AWE systems, but also motivates the emergence of more principled approaches to AWE design, evaluation, and implementation" (Cotos and Huffman 2013, 94). This statement illustrates the evaluators' intended link between their context-specific evaluation study and knowledge that generalizes to genres of technology use. Both of these studies appear in the special issue of *ReCALL* edited by Boulton and Pérez-Paredes (2014), which gathers together research whose results can be used to support claims about the value of data-driven learning, a genre of technology use for language learning. It would be productive to have more evaluation studies that systematically address the generalizability of the results (Jamieson and Chapelle 2010).

## Conclusion

The perspective of evaluation as argument and the five types of argument help to reconcile the apparent disparities in discussion of evaluation in the literature. Hubbard's (2006) definition of evaluation is focused on decision-making about a particular piece of software for a given setting. Evaluation arguments in this context need to be useful for the teachers in a particular program making decisions about materials selection and adaptation for use. Similarly, other discussions of evaluation (Leakey 2011; Levy and Stockwell 2006) focus on arguments with a decision-making function. In this chapter, I have examined more closely the nature of the arguments that appear in the evaluation studies in the professional literature. This perspective of evaluation as argument maintains the core idea of the context-specificity of evaluation arguments, but takes into consideration the broader audience for the evaluation, as well, that is, the profession. Specific contexts with real teachers and learners are necessarily the sites where evaluations are carried out, but where professionals in CALL are engaged in such evaluations, teachers and learners seldom represent the complete scope of the audience for the results.

A more revealing perspective on evaluation needs to encompass more than the decisions to be made in a particular context to examine the claims that the authors attempt to support through their studies and the arguments used to do so. It is the claims and arguments that are critical to developing knowledge about genres of technology use for language learning in the field. It is therefore important for authors to make clear their claims and arguments in published evaluation studies, and some guidance for doing so can be found in argument-based validation in language testing (Chapelle, Cotos, and Lee 2015; Chung, this volume; Norris, 2008). Whether evaluation arguments are about language tests or pedagogy, claims and arguments are central in selecting research methods and reporting results.

## Acknowledgments

I am grateful to James Ranalli and Ruslan Suvorov for their insightful comments on an earlier version of this chapter.

# REFERENCES

Alderson, Charles J. 1992. Guidelines for the Evaluation of Language Education. *Evaluating Second Language Education*, edited by Charles J. Alderson and Alan Beretta, 274–304. Cambridge: Cambridge University Press.

Alderson, Charles J., and Alan Beretta, eds.1992. *Evaluating Second Language Education*. Cambridge: Cambridge University Press.

Belz, Julia A., and Steven L. Thorne. 2006. "Introduction: Internet-mediated Intercultural Foreign Language Education and the Intercultural Speaker." In *Internet-mediated Intercultural Foreign Language Education*, edited by Julia A. Belz, and Steven L. Thorn. Boston: Thomson Heinle.

Bibby, Simon. 2011. "Do Students Wish to 'Go Mobile'? An Investigation into Student Use of PCs and Cell Phones." *International Journal of Computer-Assisted Language Learning and Teaching*, 1, no. 2: 43–54.

Boulton, Alex, and Pascual Pérez-Paredes. 2014. "ReCALL Special Issue: Researching uses of Corpora for Language Teaching and Learning Editorial Researching Uses of Corpora for Language Teaching and Learning." *ReCALL*, 26, no. 2: 121–127. DOI:10.1017/S0958344014000068

Buendgens-Kosten, Judith. 2013. "Authenticity in CALL: Three Domains of 'Realness'." *ReCALL*, 25, no. 2: 272–285. DOI:10.1017/S0958344013000037

Byram, Michael. 1997. *Teaching and Assessing Intercultural Communicative Competence*. Clevedon: Multilingual Matters.

Chang, Ji-Yeon. 2014. "The Use of General and Specialized Corpora as Reference Sources for Academic English Writing: A Case Study." *ReCALL*, 26, no. 2: 243–259.

Chapelle, Carol A. 1998. "Multimedia CALL: Lessons to be Learned from Research on Instructed SLA." *Language Learning & Technology*, 2, no. 1: 22–34.

Chapelle, Carol A. 2001. *Computer Applications in Second Language Acquisition*. Cambridge: Cambridge University Press.

Chapelle, Carol A. 2003. *English Language Learning and Technology: Lectures on Applied Linguistics in the Age of Information and Communication Technology*. Amsterdam: John Benjamins Publishing.

Chapelle, Carol A. 2007. "Challenges in Evaluation of Innovation: Observations from Technology Research." *Innovation in Language Learning and Teaching*, 1, no. 1: 30–45.

Chapelle, Carol A. 2009. "The Relationship Between SLA Theory and CALL." *Modern Language Journal*, 93, no. 4: 742–754.

Chapelle, Carol A., Elena Cotos, and Jooyoung Lee. 2015. "Diagnostic Assessment with Automated Writing Evaluation: A look at Validity Arguments for New Classroom Assessments." *Language Testing*, 32, no. 3: 385–405.

Chapelle, Carol A., and Joan Jamieson. 1991. "Internal and External Validity Issues in Research on CALL Effectiveness." In *Computer-assisted Language Learning and Testing: Research Issues and Practice*, edited by Patricia Dunkel, 37–59. New York: Harper & Row, Newbury House.

Chen, Hao-Jan H. 2011. "Developing and Evaluating a Web-based Collocation Retrieval Tool for EFL Students and Teachers." *Computer Assisted Language Learning*, 24, no. 1: 59–76. DOI:10.1080/09588221.2010.526945

Chenoweth, Ann N., and Kimmaree Murday. 2003. "Measuring Student Learning in an Online French Course." *CALICO*, 20, no. 2: 285–314.

Cotos, Elena. 2014. "Enhancing Writing Pedagogy with Learner Corpus Data." *ReCALL*, 26, no. 2: 202–224.

Cotos, Elena, and Sarah Huffman. 2013. "Learner Fit in Scaling up Automated Writing Evaluation." *International Journal of Computer-Assisted Language Learning and Teaching*, 3, no. 3: 77–98.

Cronbach, Lee J. 1982. *Designing Evaluations of Educational and Social Programs*. San Fransisco, CA: Jossey-Bass.

Doughty, Catherine J., and Michael H. Long. 2003. "Optimal Psycholinguistic Environments for Distance Foreign Language Learning." *Language Learning & Technology*, 7, no. 3: 50–80.

Dunkel, Patricia, 1991. "The Effectiveness Research on Computer-assisted Instruction and Computer-assisted Language Learning." In *Computer-assisted Language Learning and Testing – Research Issues and Practice*, edited by P. Dunkel 5–36. New York: Harper & Row, Newbury House.

Furstenberg, Gilberte, Sabine Levet, Kathryn English, and Katherine Maillet. 2001. "Giving a Virtual Voice to the Silent Language of Culture:

The CULTURA Project." *Language Learning & Technology 5, no.* 1 (2001): 55–102.

Garrison, Randy D., and Terry Anderson. 2003. *E-learning in the 21st Century: A Framework for Research and Practice*. London: RoutledgeFalmer.

Gass, Susan M. 1997. *Input, Interaction, and the Second Language Learner*. Mahwah, NJ: Lawrence Erlbaum Associates Publishers.

Gobel, Peter, and Makimi Kano. 2014. "Implementing a Year-long Reading while Listening Program for Japanese University EFL Students." *Computer-Assisted Language Learning*, 27, no. 4: 279–293.

Golonka, Ewa M., Anita R. Bowles, Victor M. Frank, Dorna L. Richardson, and Suzanne Freynik. 2014. "Technologies for Foreign Language Learning: A Review of Technology Types and their Effectiveness." *Computer Assisted Language Learning*, 27, no. 1: 70–105.

González-Lloret, Marta. 2014. "The Need for Needs Analysis in Technology-mediated TBLT." In *Technology-mediated TBLT: Researching Technology and Tasks*, edited by Marta González-Lloret and Lourdes Ortega, 23–50. Amsterdam: John Benjamins.

Grgurović, Maja, Carol A. Chapelle, and Mack C. Shelley. 2013. "A Meta-analysis of Effectiveness Studies on Computer Technology-supported Language Learning." *ReCALL Journal*, 25, no. 2: 165–198.

Gruba, Paul, Mónica S. Cárdenas-Claros, Ruslan Suvorov, and Katherine Rick. 2016. *Blended Language Program Evaluation*. London: Palgrave Macmillan.

Hampel, Regina. 2006. "Rethinking Task Design for the Digital Age: A Framework for Language Teaching and Learning in a Synchronous Online Environment." *ReCALL,*18, no. 1: 105–121 DOI:10.1017/S0958344006000711

Higgins, John, and Tim Johns. 1984. *Computers in Language Learning*. London: Collins.

Hubbard, Philip. 2006. "Evaluating CALL Software." In *Calling on CALL: From Theory and Research to New Directions in Foreign Language Teaching*, edited by Laura Ducate and Nike Arnold, 313–338. San Marcos, TX: CALICO.

Jamieson, Joan, and Carol A. Chapelle. 2010. "Evaluating CALL Use Across Multiple Contexts." *System*, 38, no. 3: 357–369.

Kukulska-Hulme, Agnes, and Lesley Shield. 2008. An Overview of Mobile Assisted Language Learning: From Content Delivery to Supported Collaboration and Interaction. *ReCALL*, 20: 271–289

Larsen-Freeman, Diane, and Lynne Cameron. 2008. *Complex Systems and Applied Linguistics*. Cambridge: Cambridge University Press.

Leakey, Jonathan. 2011. *Evaluating Computer-assisted Language Learning: An Integrated Approach to Effectiveness Research in CALL*. Oxford: Peter Lang.

Lee, Lina. 2008. "Focus-on-form through Collaborative Scaffolding in Expert-to-novice Online Interaction." *Language Learning & Technology*, 12, no. 3: 53–72.

Levy, Mike, and Glenn Stockwell. 2006. *CALL Dimensions: Options and Issues in Computer Assisted Language Learning*. Mahwah, NJ: Lawrence Erlbaum.

Long, Michael H., ed. 2005. *Second Language Needs Analysis*. Cambridge: Cambridge University Press.

Lund, Andreas. 2008. "Wikis: A Collective Approach to Language Production." *ReCALL*, 20, no. 1: 35–54. DOI:10.1017/S0958344008000414

Lynch, Brian K. 1996. *Language Program Evaluation: Theory and Practice*. Cambridge: Cambridge University Press.

Nassaji, Hossein, and Merrill Swain. 2000. "A Vygotskian Perspective on Corrective Feedback in L2: The Effect of Random versus Negotiated Help on the Learning of English articles." *Language Awareness*, 1, no. 1: 34–52.

Norris, John M. 2008. *Validity Evaluation in Foreign Language Assessment*. New York: Peter Lang.

Norris, John M., and Lourdes Ortega, eds. 2006. *Synthesizing Research on Language learning and Teaching*. Amsterdam: John Benjamins.

Norris, John M., John McE. Davis, Castle Sinicrope, and Yukiko Watanabe, eds. 2009. *Toward Useful Program Evaluation in College Foreign Language Education*. Honolulu, HI: University of Hawai'i, National Foreign Language Resource Center.

O'Bryan, Ann, and Volker Hegelheimer. 2007. "Integrating CALL into the Classroom: The Role of Podcasting in an ESL Listening Strategies Course." *ReCALL*, 19, no. 2: 162–180.

Patton, Michael Q. 2008. *Utilization-focused Evaluation: The New Century Text*, 4th ed. Thousand Oaks, CA: Sage.

Pederson, Kathleen M. 1987. "Research on CALL." In *Modern Media in Foreign Language Education: Theory and Implementation*, edited by William F. Smith, 99–132. Lincolnwood, IL: National Textbook Company.

Pellettieri, Jill. 2000. "Negotiation in Cyberspace: The Role of *chatting* in the Development of

Grammatical Competence in the Virtual Foreign Language Classroom." In *Network-based Language Teaching: Concepts and Practice*, edited by Mark Warschauer and Richard Kern, 59–86. Cambridge: Cambridge University Press.

Ranalli, Jim. 2013. "Online Strategy Instruction for Integrating Dictionary Skills and Language Awareness." *Language Learning & Technology*, 17, no. 2: 75–99.

Ruhe, Valerie, and Bruno D. Zumbo. 2009. *Evaluation in Distance Education and E-learning: The Unfolding Model*. New York: The Guilford Press.

Skehan, Peter. 2003. "Focus on Form, Task and Technology." *Computer Assisted Language Learning*, 16, no. 5: 391–411.

Sockett, Geoffrey. 2013. "Understanding the Online Informal Learning of English as a Complex Dynamic System: An Emic Approach." *ReCALL*, 25, no.1: 48–62. DOI:10.1017/S095834401200033X

Suzuki, Satomi. 2013. "Private Turns: A Student's Off-screen Behaviors during Synchronous Online Japanese Instruction." *CALICO Journal*, 30, no. 3: 371–392. DOI:10.11139/cj.30.3.371-392

Tomlinson, Brian. 2003. "Materials Evaluation." In *Developing Materials for Langauge Teaching*, edited by Brian Tomlison, 16–36. London: Continuum.

Zhao, Yong. 2003. "Recent Developments in Technology and Language Learning: A Literature Review and Meta-analysis." *CALICO Journal*, 21, no. 1: 7–27.

# 26 Research Methods for Investigating Technology for Language and Culture Learning

## DOROTHY M. CHUN

## Introduction

Although it is difficult to pinpoint exactly when the field of computer-assisted language learning (CALL) began producing a body of research, the oldest journal exclusively devoted to CALL, the *CALICO Journal*, published its first article in 1983 and celebrated its twenty-fifth anniversary in 2008. The homepage of its website contains lists of "seminal" and "highly-cited and influential" articles. In 2009, Hubbard published a four-volume collection of seminal CALL studies published between 1988–2007, and in 2016, the journal *Language Learning & Technology* reached the twenty-year mark and in a special issue featured commentaries from the authors of the most highly-cited articles. In addition, meta-analyses and meta-syntheses of particular aspects of CALL research (e.g., multimedia vocabulary annotations, computer-mediated communication (CMC), telecollaboration, gaming) are increasing in number. On the basis of the aforementioned lists and collections of excellent research, the methodologies of selected studies will be used to highlight how appropriately chosen methods can contribute to our knowledge of the extent to which technology-based pedagogies are effective for language and culture learning, or *languaculture* learning, to adopt Agar's (1994) term. I use the term *languaculture* in part to retain the same acronym *CALL* and in part because many teachers and applied linguists recognize language and culture as inseparable constructs (e.g., Byrnes 2009; Kramsch 1993).

There are various ways that this chapter could be organized. One could categorize studies into quantitative, qualitative, or mixed methods and discuss how these different methods have been used in the seminal studies. One could examine the different aspects of languaculture (e.g., speaking, reading, grammar, vocabulary, culture, identity), how they have been taught, learned, and researched using technology, and the methods used to conduct the research. One could use the underlying theory of second language acquisition or learning in general (e.g., interactionist, cognitive/psycholinguistic, sociocultural, ecological) as the starting point for organizing a discussion of methodology. Or one could begin with the technologies themselves, investigating how they have been employed for teaching a particular facet of language (e.g., speech recognition, CMC, blogs, mobile apps, video chat), or how

*The Handbook of Technology and Second Language Teaching and Learning*, First Edition.
Edited by Carol A. Chapelle and Shannon Sauro.
© 2017 John Wiley & Sons, Inc. Published 2020 by John Wiley & Sons, Inc.

they actually facilitate research (e.g., tracking user behavior, screen capture, eye tracking), and review the different methodologies that have been used in the research. Finally, one could take a historical perspective and attempt to trace the trends in the type of methodologies used over the years.

I have chosen the perhaps ambitious path of integrating the components above to reflect the complexity of the research endeavor. By focusing on seminal studies, I hope to show how all of the variables come into play in selecting an appropriate methodology, and how the reporting of the results of a given study will depend on the methodology chosen. However, I will generally follow the topics presented in this volume, beginning with the more "traditional" aspects of vocabulary and grammar, reading and writing, listening and speaking, and pragmatics and intercultural competence. Then I turn to learning language and culture in "newer" technological environments, for example, mobile assisted language learning, telecollaboration, digital gaming, and virtual environments, and to emerging goals for the 21st century, for example, development of learner identity and digital literacies.

## Brief overview of research methods

In early research on technology for learning in general, it was common to conduct controlled studies of whether using technology resulted in similar (or better) learning outcomes as compared to not using technology, for example, a control group would be taught in a traditional manner without technology and an experimental group would receive instruction/treatment using technology. But the field of educational technology in general and CALL in particular have moved away from this type of research and instead are investigating the affordances that particular technologies provide to learn particular aspects of language and culture, with particular types or groups of learners.

One of the leading figures in the field of CALL, Chapelle (1997), stressed early on the need for empirical research methods for CALL, suggesting applying research on instructed SLA to CALL. She favored interactionist theories of SLA but also acknowledged that other effective research methods from cognitive psychology, constructivism, psycholinguistics and discourse analyses could be used. In particular, Chapelle (1998) suggested that research methods for evaluation of CALL learning outcomes include process-oriented observations of learners working on L2 tasks and introspective methods to gain evidence about learners' strategies while working on L2 tasks. In an update to her 1997 article, Chapelle (2010) stated "The need was clear at that time, as it is now, for research designs to move beyond quantitative, outcomes-oriented studies comparing learning through technology to learning in a classroom — a paradigm inherited from education" (27).

In line with the social turn in second language acquisition (SLA) (Block 2003), other CALL pioneers Warschauer and Kern (2000) viewed network-based language teaching from socio-cognitive perspectives, and suggested a shift from primarily quantitative research methods to principally qualitative methods that considered classroom cultures as well as language use. A few years later, Kern, Ware, and Warschauer (2004) wrote of a second wave of papers about online language learning research, proposing that early research on networked language learning focused on linguistic interaction and development, followed by intercultural awareness and learning, and was moving in the direction of new multiliteracies and their relation to learner identity.

Levy (2000) reported on a corpus of 177 journal articles and book chapters on CALL, noting a multiplicity of methods and techniques and that "many studies show a mixture of quantitative and qualitative approaches to answer a wide variety of research questions" (180). Similarly, Felix (2008) in an overview of two decades of CALL effectiveness studies, discussed successful research design models, finding almost equal numbers of experimental and non-experimental studies. Important observations she made were the emerging trend toward investigating both learning *outcomes* and learning *processes,* and that a combination of various data collection methods within a single study would help to strengthen confidence levels about the results. "Because there is such a large scope for research in this area, there cannot be a single best design model" (148); researchers need to match their design to their research questions.

In a retrospective on "Twenty-Five Years of Theory in the *CALICO Journal,*" Hubbard (2008) reported that there is no single "theory of CALL" (387), noting that the most commonly cited theories were either general learning theories or SLA theories but there was nothing akin to "native CALL" theories (394). This would imply that there are also no research methodologies based on CALL theories. In introducing his four-volume series, Hubbard (2009) reiterated that most of the research and development in CALL has been driven by external theories, and he cited two of the more influential views as those of Chapelle (2001), who links the design and evaluation of CALL tasks to principles derived from interactionist SLA research studies, and Bax (2003), who views "normalization" as the defining direction for the field (3). Normalization refers to a state where technology is fully integrated into language teaching and is no longer special or unusual, in the way that books, pencils and blackboards were in traditional classrooms. Interestingly, Bax called for more in-depth ethnographic studies of individual environments and action research methods for investigating CALL. Bax (2011) revisits the issue of the normalization of technology in language education, adopting a neo-Vygotskian conceptual framework and reiterates the call for qualitative, ethnographic approaches to study the social, cultural, and contextual factors of technology use in educational settings. He suggests an action research mode, "in which the change agent seeks to implement a new technology by one mechanism, using one approach, and then carefully observes the impact of the change, inviting contributions from the stakeholders, and then attempting a further step in response" (12). This is typical of the reiterative nature of much action research, which can be defined broadly as a method that seeks first to understand the causes of a certain (pedagogical) situation and then to produce change in it. In the case of SLA, language teachers would start with their own classroom practice, develop some kind of action or intervention, make a change, and analyze and reflect on the results.

I conclude this overview with a discussion of two meta-analyses of CALL research, each reviewing a different body of research. Grgurović, Chapelle, and Shelley (2013) compiled empirical research on language outcomes and included studies which (1) measured performance on language tests, (2) used an experimental or quasi-experimental design, (3) employed a pre-test/post-test design or post-test design only. One of their concluding recommendations was that future quantitative research designs that use control-treatment comparisons should employ random placement of subjects into conditions, and when that is not possible as is often the case, to verify the comparability of groups with a pre-test at the outset of the study (192).

Sauro's (2011) meta-synthesis of the role of synchronous computer-mediated communication (SCMC) for SLA operationalized SLA as the development of Canale and Swain's (1980) framework for communicative language teaching based on Hymes' (1972) notion of communicative competence. Her qualitative research synthesis revealed that almost half of the 97 studies explored grammatical competence, using cognitive or cognitive-interactionist approaches. Thirty-one studies explored strategic competence (e.g., negotiating breakdowns taking cognitive-interactionist approaches or facilitating communicative effectiveness as analyzed with sociocultural approaches and discourse analysis). An additional 22 studies investigated sociocultural competence (again from sociocultural and discourse analytic perspectives), and 11 studies focused on discourse competence. The studies incorporated and built on research in face-to-face contexts and also utilized technological tools and strategies unique to CMC contexts. A wide variety of methods were used, depending on the learning outcomes that were targeted.

In summary, the work discussed in this section, in particular, the two meta-analyses/syntheses, can be seen as a sign that CALL is a maturing area of research. The fact that CALL research has extensively been conducted through the lens of different SLA theories using different methodologies, for example, quantitative methods to study aspects of language ranging from grammatical competence to strategic competence, or qualitative methods to explore questions ranging from linguistic interaction to intercultural competence, reflects the reality that such a complex set of languaculture learning outcomes requires an equally nuanced understanding of appropriate methodologies to study them.

# Research methods for teaching and learning different aspects of languaculture

This section discusses representative studies for the different aspects of second language and culture learning, with the caveat that it is not possible in this chapter to include every type of study in each of the categories that has been investigated.

## *L2 grammar and vocabulary*

Many early studies of L2 grammar learning investigated the role of computer feedback, for example, Brandl (1995), who investigated learners' behavior and preferences for different kinds of feedback in a German CALL program. He performed quantitative analyses of learners' selection of four kinds of feedback and qualitative analyses of interviews with the learners. Heift (2002) studied the impact of learner control on the students' error correction process in an intelligent language tutoring system, which provided detailed error-specific and individualized feedback. The system recorded all of the students' interactions with the program, and percentages of the different types of interactions were calculated. Based on 4,456 server requests, she ascertained that students tended overwhelmingly to correct their errors, and that they showed distinct interaction patterns depending on their language skill. A similar type of quantitative investigation of learner behavior was also employed by Heift (2010) in a longitudinal study of learner uptake. Program logs of learner behavior were compiled over the course of three semesters, and results showed significant differences in learner uptake at the advanced level depending on the degree of specificity of the feedback.

For the investigation of L2 vocabulary acquisition with CALL, a number of studies compared the effects of different types of multimedia annotations on learning. For example, Chun and Plass (1996) reported on a classroom learning situation, using a within-subjects design (but not an experimental study with random assignment of learners to different treatment groups). A key component of the study was the lookup behavior recorded by the multimedia program that was compared to the students' vocabulary learning with text, picture, and video annotations. Similarly, in the study by Plass et al. (1998), learners had the freedom to look up whichever types of annotations they wished, and results of questionnaires about their learning preferences divided them into visualizers and verbalizers. Al-Seghayer (2001) also used a within-subject design, three conditions (different types of multimedia annotations), and two types of tests (recognition and production vocabulary tests). He supplemented the quantitative data with qualitative data from interviews and questionnaires. The above studies found that different multimedia annotations were effective for vocabulary learning (picture glosses were most effective in Chun and Plass 1996 and video glosses were most effective in Al-Seghayer 2001). In addition, the behavior logs analyzed by Chun and Plass showed that when learners looked up both text and picture annotations, they performed better on the vocabulary tests, and Al-Seghayer' interviews with learners confirmed that the students believed that the video annotations showed the meaning of the word more clearly than the text or picture annotations.

In contrast, Laufer and Hill (2000) used an experimental methodology to study what kind of information L2 learners select when using a CALL dictionary. Their study included a pre-test, a tutorial showing students the variety of lookup options at their disposal, and a retention post-test. Log files in their program tracked user behavior. They found that different students exhibited different lookup preferences and that the use of multiple types of dictionary information seemed to reinforce retention.

The meta-analysis by Yun (2011) on the effect of hypertext glosses on L2 vocabulary acquisition during the period 1990–2009 identified approximately 200 articles, reports, and papers. However, based on a set of criteria, including that the study had to have either an experimental or a quasi-experimental design, that is, had to have a control group and a treatment group (with or without random assignment) as well as a pre- and post-test of vocabulary, only ten studies were eligible for the meta-analysis. This is one indication that a great majority of CALL studies on hypertext glosses have not used quantitative experimental (or quasi-experimental) designs. Among the eligible studies, text glosses in combination with visual glosses were found to be moderately effective for L2 vocabulary acquisition, and studies with large samples provided a bigger effect size.

## L2 reading and writing

Similar to the research on L2 vocabulary learning, studies of L2 reading also explored the effect of multimedia and hypertext glosses on overall reading comprehension. In suggesting a research agenda for studying text comprehension in multimedia environments, Chun and Plass (1997) combined interactive theories of reading comprehension with theories of multimedia learning and suggested that research methodologies of empirical studies should seek to strike a balance between authentic learning situations and rigorous experimental conditions. They suggested using a combination of methods to assess specific elements of the reading process, for example, tests, grades, written essays, observations of learner behavior, self-reports and think-aloud protocols, eye movement, and for affective factors, questionnaires, and interviews.

Contrary to the above suggestion, Abraham's (2008) meta-analysis of the effect of computer-mediated glosses for reading comprehension (and incidental vocabulary learning) restricted the included studies to only those employing an experimental design, that is, those with a treatment group vs. a control group. Out of 125 books, articles, book chapters, and refereed conference papers published up to 2007, only 11 fulfilled the criterion of using an experimental design. He found an overall medium effect for learners who had access to glosses performing consistently better on measures of reading comprehension and vocabulary learning than those without access.

Yanguas (2009) investigated the effects that different types of multimedia glosses have on text comprehension (and vocabulary acquisition) when the goal is exclusively comprehension of a computerized text. Using both quantitative and qualitative analyses, his experimental method utilized a pre-post test design and also a treatment and a control group, which was supplemented by think-aloud protocols that were analyzed qualitatively. The results of both types of analyses showed that with regard to reading comprehension, the combination gloss group (those who saw both textual and pictorial glosses) significantly outperformed all other groups. The combination of quantitative and qualitative analyses lent greater confidence to his conclusions.

Seminal research on L2 writing using CALL tools often investigated different forms of CMC. For example, Sotillo (2000) compared the types of discourse functions and syntactic complexity produced by learners in two modes of CMC, namely SCMC and asynchronous (ACMC). Syntactic complexity was measured using T-unit analyses, for example, the total number of units, the error-free T-units, and the number of subordinate clauses were counted and reported quantitatively. Discourse functions were categorized qualitatively, and the research method used was not experimental, that is, there was no random assignment of learners to a control or experimental group. Stockwell and Harrington (2003) also investigated syntactic development in native-speaker non-native speaker email interactions by quantitatively recording the number of linguistic text features (T-units) and calculating lexical mastery (type/token ratios). They measured overall language proficiency based on proficiency ratings, basing their work theoretically on the Interaction Hypothesis and on the psycholinguistic conditions that facilitate language learning.

A study by Strobl (2014) on computer-supported collaborative writing was based on constructivist learning principles and investigated the effect of online collaboration on academic writing in a foreign language. Individual and collaborative writing processes were compared by applying a mixed-methods approach: quantitative instruments measured quantity, complexity, accuracy, fluency, and coherence/cohesion, while qualitative analyses were employed for content selection, organization, and planning discussions. Results indicated that although no statistically relevant difference was found between the individual and collaborative writing tasks in terms of complexity, accuracy, and fluency, raters scored collaboratively constructed texts significantly higher on appropriate content selection and organization.

## *The relationship between L2 writing and speaking*

CMC, both asynchronous and synchronous, has been studied by CALL researchers as a possible bridge between writing and speaking. Indeed, online "chatting" often displays characteristics closer to oral conversation than to traditional written genres. Early research compared text-based electronic discussion with oral face-to-face discussion, for example, Kern (1995) and Warschauer (1995). Warschauer (1995) performed a controlled experiment comparing face-to-face and electronic discussion in an L2 classroom. Using a counterbalanced, repeated measures study of the amount and equality of participation, he quantified student participation as well as lexical and syntactic complexity. An added qualitative component analyzed differences in turn-taking and formality and students' attitudes. Kern's (1995) seminal work likewise compared transcripts of classroom interaction with networked computers with face-to-face interactions, quantitatively reporting on turns, T-units, and morphosyntactic features, while qualitatively analyzing characteristics of discourse, specifically discourse functions, and questionnaire results of learners' impressions.

Using a psycholinguistic model of speech production and working memory theory, Payne and Whitney (2002) used a quasi-experimental design with pre- and post-tests and an experimental and a control group (but no random assignment to groups). Their results showed that SCMC can directly improve L2 oral proficiency. Similarly, Abrams (2003) also used an experimental design employing a control group to study the effect of SCMC and ACMC on oral performance. She measured lexical richness and diversity, syntactic complexity, and the number of idea units and words produced by L2 learners.

By using the methodology of analyzing both chat transcripts and video-enhanced chatscripts, Sauro (2012) examined L2 performance in text-chat and spoken discourse and found no significant differences in either lexical or syntactic complexity of the narratives in the two modalities. Her study was not experimental in that she did not employ pre- and post-tests or control and experimental groups, but rather the two conditions were "controlled" by the use of a single consistent interlocutor for both modalities and the same narrative tasks.

In a meta-analysis of text-based SCMC and its effect on SLA, Lin, Huang, and Liou (2013) investigated how SCMC contributes to oral skills. Their methodological criterion for whether to include studies reported on between 1990–2012 was that an experimental or quasi-experimental design had been employed. Only ten studies matched their criteria, and most of the studies took an interactionist perspective. They concluded that both data collection and analysis needed to be expanded, for examples, by new methodologies such as screen capture and recording non-verbal behaviors. Their findings included a small but positive overall effect of text-based SCMC tasks on SLA and suggested that intermediate learners may benefit more from SCMC tasks if they are grouped into pairs or small groups.

## L2 *listening and speaking*

Studies using technology for L2 listening comprehension include those that controlled the rate of speech and the effect of multimedia annotations to support listening. Zhao (1997) conducted his experiment on an individual basis whereby each subject was able to try four different listening conditions with varying degrees of learner control on the speech rate. McBride's (2011) experiment, on the other hand, had a pre-test—treatment—post-test design and subjects were assigned in a semi-random fashion to one of the four experimental groups. The results of Zhao's study were that students' listening comprehension improved when they were given control over the speech rate in their listening tasks. McBride concluded that the group that was trained on slow materials fared the best in comprehension, apparently because their bottom-up processing improved.

Jones (2003) grounded her study in a generative theory of multimedia learning and conducted a study of vocabulary acquisition with multimedia annotations during a listening activity. She used an experimental between-subject design, with learners randomly assigned to one of four groups (a control group and three experimental groups) and pre- and post-tests. Her quantitative results showing that students learned vocabulary best when they selected both verbal and visual annotations while listening were complemented with qualitative interview data indicating that learners believed that the availability and choice of multimedia annotations were helpful for vocabulary learning.

Due to research (e.g., by Anderson-Hsieh, Johnson, and Koehler 1992) suggesting that suprasegmentals (prosody, intonation) have a greater impact on global pronunciation ratings than segmentals (vowels and consonants), CALL studies have investigated the effect of prosody training on L2 speaking. Hardison (2004) conducted two experiments, the first using a pre-test-post-test design to determine whether computer-based training that permits visual displays of pitch contours in real time would help in the acquisition of French prosody by American speakers. The quantitative results were supplemented by qualitative results of anonymous learner questionnaires, with both indicating the usefulness of computer-assisted speech training.

Levis and Pickering (2004) also used speech visualizations to develop materials for teaching discourse-level uses of intonation. And Chun et al. (2015) reported on a study of L2 learners of Mandarin Chinese who created their own visualizations of the four Mandarin tones (and the neutral tone) and were able to improve their pronunciation, as measured both auditorily and acoustically. They studied an authentic learning environment in which learners received training during their normal class hours, deciding against an experimental design with random assignment to a control and a treatment group. Native-speaker ratings of the learners' tones revealed an improvement between pre-test and post-test, and acoustic analyses indicated that the students' pronunciation of some tones improved in the post-test.

## How CMC promotes SLA in general

Depending on the underlying theoretical approach taken to study SLA, different learning goals are targeted. The sub-sections above discussed the traditional aspects and skills in second language learning, namely vocabulary and grammar, reading and writing, and speaking and listening, with the observation that digital media have changed communication and have blurred the lines between writing and speaking. This sub-section presents studies that do not fit into the traditional categories. For example, if SLA is operationalized as the development of Canale and Swain's (1980) four types of communicative competence (see discussion of Sauro's 2011 research synthesis in section 2 above), then different aspects of SLA are studied.

An early longitudinal study of computer-assisted classroom discussion examined an intra-class networked discussion and found that second-semester L2 German learners developed interactive competence over the course of two semesters (Chun 1994). Transcripts of the discussions were analyzed with regard to the number and length of turns, syntactic complexity, and different discourse structures. Blake (2000) in a highly-cited study of CMC based on the Interaction Hypothesis analyzed the chatscripts from dyads who had carried out online tasks. He sought to determine what promotes negotiations, based on Varonis and Gass' (1985) schema (trigger, indicator, response, reaction). His quantitative data on the number of negotiations and the statistical analyses comparing tasks and types of negotiations were complemented by qualitative data on student attitudes and reflections.

Like Blake (2000), Smith (2003) also saw negotiation patterns in his CMC study that were similar to those observed in face-to-face communication (the Varonis and Gass 1985 model). But he proposed that the model be expanded in order to be able to allow for a delay, sometimes a long delay, between the initial trigger and the indicator. This is due to the nature of CMC, that turns are not always adjacent to each other as they are in face-to-face conversation. Analyses of chatscripts included calculations of total turns for each dyad as well as ratios of negotiated turns to total turns.

Two studies that were both concerned with interactional features of synchronous CMC chat used different underlying theories and thus reported on different types of learning outcomes. Fernández-García and Martínez-Arbelaiz (2002) took an interactionist perspective in analyzing chat data of native speakers of English learning Spanish and found that instances of negotiation, critical for SLA, did occur in the online conversations. By comparison, although Darhower (2002) also studied CMC data from English-speaking learners of Spanish, in applying a sociocultural lens to his analyses, he described the most salient features of the interactions, attributing learning to the social interaction between learners and more knowledgeable partners. While both studies used discourse analysis as their methodology for data analysis and both concluded that online chat can support language learning, each delineated specific areas of competence that are improved by CMC by working from different theoretical perspectives.

In a meta-analysis of CMC and SLA studies between 2000–2012, Lin (2014, 2015) restricted the studies to those that were experimental or quasi-experimental. Her aim was to determine whether there was a link between the use of CMC and SLA, operationalizing SLA as "the acquisition of tools language learners need to rely on in order to successfully carry out communication with target language users" (2014, 123) and the tools included speaking, reading, writing, listening, as well as grammar, vocabulary, and pronunciation. With such a broad scope, 59 studies were identified and drew on interactionist and sociocultural theories of SLA, and they were highly diverse with respect to a number of features, including research design. Findings discussed in the 2014 article showed a positive and medium effect of CMC interventions, but that communication taking place asynchronously or synchronously did not seem to have a differential effect on SLA. The 2015 article delineated how among the four language skills which CMC was intended to facilitate, writing skills produced the largest effect size, and that studies using smaller groups produced a larger effect size than those using larger groups or no grouping.

# Research methodologies for teaching and learning L2 pragmatics and intercultural competence

Pioneering work in using technology for teaching culture was reported in Furstenberg et al. (2001). Their groundbreaking *Cultura* model has been used for two decades with great pedagogical success and has been researched extensively (e.g., Chun 2014). Research on online intercultural exchanges or telecollaboration began with more quantitative analyses of email, forum discussions and text chats, and has moved to more qualitative, contextualized, discourse-based analyses of the processes of such exchanges and how cultural understandings are expressed by participants over time (Chun 2015).

Seminal studies on telecollaboration include those of Belz (2002, 2003), O'Dowd (2003), Thorne (2003), Thorne and Payne (2005), which employed a variety of research methods. Belz (2002) investigated the socio-institutional dimensions of telecollaborative foreign language study within the theoretical framework of social realism using an exploratory multi-strategy approach. In contrast, Belz (2003) employed a case-study approach to study linguistic perspectives on the development of intercultural competence in telecollaboration. Like many others, she based her analyses on Byram's (1997) model of intercultural communicative competence (ICC), examining the key moments in a seven-week email correspondence between German and American learners. She also employed appraisal theory, an extension and refinement of systemic functional linguistics, and provided quantitative analyses of different types of modalities and linguistic features of the learners' language, as well as of attitudinal appraisal. Her data revealed the German speakers' tendency toward negative appraisal and categorical assertions in contrast to the American student's communication patterns of indirectness and implicitness.

Thorne (2003) also used a case-study approach to investigate internet tools and their meditational affordances as cultural tools for intercultural communication and language learning. Taking a cultural-historical approach, he reported on three different case studies, providing excerpts from emails and synchronous chats, demonstrating that internet communication tools are not neutral media.

In reporting on a year-long email exchange between Spanish and English university language learners, O'Dowd (2003) used qualitative methods to identify key characteristics of the exchanges which helped to develop learners' ICC. A variety of ethnographic techniques were used, for example, participant observation, reviewing the actual email data as well as emails from students containing feedback on the exchange, questionnaires, and interviews with students, a researcher's reflexive journal, and feedback from a partner teacher. In addition, he suggested action research as a method for this type of research, a recommendation echoed by Müller-Hartmann (2012) and Chun (2015).

Edited volumes and special issues on intercultural competence include Thorne and Payne (2005), O'Dowd (2007), and Dooly and O'Dowd (2012). Thorne and Payne (2005) suggested that a substantial strand of CMC research prior to 2005 investigated negotiation of meaning with an interactionist approach, but that using CMC tools for intercultural communication was emerging as critical for teaching L2 pragmatics and that language and culture are inseparable. Based on the individual articles in all of these collections, it is evident that when the focus is intercultural communication qualitative methods of analysis are often employed. A reasonable alternative to choosing either a quantitative or qualitative method is to use multiple methods, as all research methods have inherent strengths and limitations, and triangulation of different methods can compensate to some extent for the weaknesses. The current trend of having ICC as one of the primary goals of telecollaboration and of second language/languaculture learning in general has motivated many researchers to take sociocultural approaches and utilize multiple methodologies, including action research, which is intended to inform teaching practices in the immediate context.

## Research methodologies for teaching and learning languaculture in other contexts

Some of the emerging areas of interest in technology-based learning include digital literacies/multiliteracies/21st century literacies, development of learner autonomy and learner identity, games and virtual worlds. Guikema and Williams's (2014) volume *Digital Literacies in Foreign and Second Language Education* includes a wide range of topics and research methods, from conceptual pieces to survey studies to classroom-based studies using digital storytelling and digital games. Primarily qualitative methods, including case studies, were used. One study by Jiménez-Caicedo, Lozano, and Gómez (2014) on learner agency and the use of blogs for developing L2 literacy employed Q Methodology, which provides a framework for the study of human subjectivity and according to Brown (1993) allows researchers to investigate viewpoints (e.g., perspectives, attitudes, beliefs, and motivations) in a systematic way. It is based on the premises that subjectivity is communicable and that when asked to rank statements about a particular topic, participants will always do so from their own (subjective) point of view. Jiménez-Caicedo and his colleagues (2014) used QM to analyze their students' subjectivities about the use of blogs for developing their Spanish academic literacy and cultural awareness, concluding that students' agency played an important role in the three different ways they used blogs: one group saw blogs as primarily a tool for practicing grammar and vocabulary, while another believed that blogs were an important tool for motivating real language use, and a third group felt that blogs were a space where they could explore and experiment with the L2 rather than a space where instructors would make grammatical corrections.

A study by Zheng et al. (2009) explored affective factors in learning English as a foreign language in a 3D game-like virtual world. Using mixed methods, a post-test only quasi-experimental design was employed to study patterns of language and media use and to determine self-efficacy toward advanced use of English, attitude toward English, and self-efficacy toward e-communication. Exploratory factor analysis was performed on questionnaire items, producing a solution in which the three factors were empirically identified, and multivariate analyses were conducted to determine the differences in self-efficacy and attitude between the experimental and control groups.

A highly-cited paper by Lam (2000) on L2 literacy and development of learner identity presented a case study of a teenager writing on the internet, using ethnographic and discourse analytic methods. The examination of the Chinese immigrant teenager's written correspondence in English with a transnational group of peers on the internet showed how the correspondence related to his developing identity in the use of English and how texts were composed and used to represent identity online.

The use of games and simulations is a growing sub-field of CALL. Although technically not a meta-analysis in the quantitative sense, Peterson (2010) described seven studies of computerized games and simulations for language learning that appeared between 2001–2008. These were based on psycholinguistic or sociocultural theories of SLA and were generally qualitative, descriptive studies (e.g., case studies) that analyzed transcripts of learners' interactions in multiuser object-oriented (MOO) domains, in three-dimensional web-based simulated virtual worlds, in commercial simulation games, in massively multi-player online role-playing games (MMORPGs), and in a game- and simulation-based training system. Discourse analysis of the transcripts was frequently used to determine the types of negotiation of meaning, interactions, and collaborations used by the players. Observations by the researchers revealed the presence of autonomous and exploratory learning. One study used mixed methods to investigate the use of a stand-alone commercial simulation game combined with supplementary web-based materials for vocabulary learning. Pre- and post-vocabulary tests revealed significant gains in vocabulary knowledge, and pre- and post-project surveys were conducted to assess the students' perceptions of the game and their vocabulary learning.

In their overview of research in games and social networking, Sykes and Holden (2011) reported similar methodologies, including ethnographic observations of language learners playing MMORPGs and analyses of the attendant discourses (discussion forums, machinima groups, and modding communities), along with interviews with the learners.

In Reinhardt and Sykes's (2014) special issue of *Language Learning & Technology* on game-informed L2 teaching and learning, all of the articles report on non-linguistic gains: autonomy and community, willingness to communicate, daily self-reports of engagement, motivation, attitudes, and perceptions of performance. One was a qualitative case study of the use of language play while microblogging (with Twitter). Discourse analysis of the students' tweets and retrospective interviews indicated that they took ownership of the task and engaged in ludic language play.

## Methods for triangulating data collection

In the field of CALL, a very influential and innovative study that introduced a new methodology for studying CMC was reported by Smith (2008), who showed convincingly that by simply using the finished "product" of chat log files, much information on the "process" of chatting is being neglected or ignored. In his particular study of self-repair in task-based activities, he first evaluated the chat data by using only the chat log file; he then examined the video file of the screen capture of the entire interaction. His results are persuasive that fundamental differences in interpretation and conclusions are reached about the chat interaction, depending on the type of data that is collected and the evaluation methods that are employed.

Related or follow-up studies to Smith (2008) include ones by Smith and Sauro (2009), Sauro and Smith (2010), and Sauro (2012). These articles provided details of how to code the additional information provided by the screen capture and utilize quantitative methods for comparing the different learner actions, for example, preemptive or self-initiated deletions as opposed to reactive deletions, as well as the more traditional measures of syntactic complexity, grammar, and lexical diversity. Sauro (2012) used controlled conditions and screen capture software to compare the complexity of adult ESL learners' output in text-chat as compared to spoken discourse. She suggested that additional methods, such as stimulated recall sessions in which learners can view the videos of their text-chat sessions might prompt participants to articulate what they were thinking as they composed and edited their chat turns.

Another novel methodology being used in SLA and CMC research is the use of eye-tracking technology. Smith (2012) attempted to study the construct of noticing, which is key in cognitively-oriented approaches to SLA, by recording participants' eye gaze while they were engaged in a short chat interaction task. Specifically, the question was whether eye tracking could be employed as a measure of noticing of corrective feedback when non-native learners performed a task with a native speaker in a synchronous CMC setting. Noticing events, that is, increased visual attention as shown in "heat maps" of the eye gaze, to the recasts provided by the native speaker, were tracked by the software. The heat map data was compared with the data from stimulated recall and both were highly and positively correlated with one another. Smith concluded that the two methodological techniques used in conjunction with each other may help SLA researchers better understanding the construct of noticing.

# Summary and conclusions

The foregoing discussions of the multiplicity of both areas for CALL research and methodologies to study them suggest that the choice of a research methodology for CALL studies depends primarily on four considerations: (1) which aspect of language or culture is being taught/learned; (2) which theory of learning is considered most appropriate for teaching/learning that aspect of language or culture; (3) which technologies are being employed for teaching that particular facet of language or culture; (4) which technologies are available for conducting and analyzing the study.

The general trend in terms of research methods seems to be continuing to employ quantitative and/or qualitative methods as appropriate to the theoretical perspective taken. Traditional quantitative studies that use experimental and quasi-experimental methods are still needed to continue to research the effects of various applications or integrations of technology with languaculture learning. But it is also common for studies to be conducted in authentic learning situations, for example, as part of regularly scheduled language courses, and increasingly, the lines between in-class or course-related learning and learning outside of the classroom or non-course-related learning are becoming blurred. Qualitative studies using ethnographic methods and action research, often described as cyclical and participatory, can be used appropriately in real-world learning environments. This also aligns with sociocultural and ecological theories of language and culture learning. Developing ICC, for example, cannot be measured with the same types of quantitative instruments as mastery of linguistic elements.

The foregoing sections illustrate how the underlying learning theories in combination with the chosen methodology not only influence the research questions posed but can also result in very different conclusions. Ideally, mixed or multiple methods employed in a given study will yield the most comprehensive and persuasive results. That is, in addition to assessing particular components or skills of languaculture learning, querying learners' attitudes and perceptions about their learning can also contribute to our understanding of the ecology of the learning environment.

For the future, as technology and learning become increasingly integrated and we approach Bax's (2003, 2011) concept of "normalization," and as the goal of developing digital and multiliteracies transcends language and culture learning, we must be open to whatever new technologies emerge. As with using video-enhanced screen capture and eye-tracking technologies to research SLA, CALL researchers have access to new technologies for teaching and for research: Web 2.0 blogs, wikis, and social networks; games, virtual worlds; mobile apps that can be used untethered and ubiquitously; Web 3.0 tools to connected intelligence and augmented reality; Web 4.0 tools that are predicted to be ultra-intelligent electronic agents for personalized learning, for example, learner analytics tools that not only track learner behavior but adapt to the learner's proficiency level. These technologies, when used with pedagogical approaches that focus, for example, on task-based teaching and learning, on the five Cs, or on recording and analyzing non-verbal learner behavior, open new possibilities for teaching and research. It will be up to us to think of new ways to use technology to aid and inform our research endeavors.

# REFERENCES

Abraham, Lee B. 2008. "Computer-Mediated Glosses in Second Language Reading Comprehension and Vocabulary Learning: A Meta-Analysis." *Computer Assisted Language Learning*, 21, no. 3: 199–226. DOI:10.1080/09588220802090246

Abrams, Zsuzsanna Ittzes. 2003. "The Effect of Synchronous and Asynchronous CMC on Oral Performance in German." *The Modern Language Journal*, 87, no. 2: 157–167.

Agar, Michael. 1994. *Language Shock: Understanding the Culture of Conversation.* New York: William Morrow and Company.

Al-Seghayer, Khalid. 2001. "The Effect of Multimedia Annotation Modes on L2 Vocabulary Acquisition: A Comparative Study." *Language Learning & Technology* 5, no. 1: 202–232.

Anderson-Hsieh, Janet, Ruth Johnson, and Kenneth Koehler. 1992. "The Relationship between Native Speaker Judgments of Nonnative Pronunciation and Deviance in Segmentals, Prosody, and Syllable Structure." *Language Learning*, 42, no. 4: 529–555.

Bax, Stephen. 2003. "CALL—Past, Present and Future." *System*, 31, no. 1: 13–28.

Bax, Stephan. (2011). Normalisation Revisited: The Effective Use of Technology in Language Education. *International Journal of Computer-Assisted Language Learning and Teaching*, 1, no. 2: 1–15.

Belz, Julie A. 2002. "Social Dimensions of Telecollaborative Foreign Language Study." *Language Learning & Technology*, 6, no. 1: 60–81.

Belz, Julie A. 2003. "Linguistic Perspectives on the Development of Intercultural Competence in Telecollaboration." *Language Learning & Technology*, 7, no. 2: 68–117.

Blake, Robert. 2000. "Computer Mediated Communication: A Window on L2 Spanish Interlanguage." *Language Learning & Technology*, 4, no. 1: 120–136.

Block, David. 2003. *The Social Turn in Second Language Acquisition.* Edinburgh: Edinburgh University Press.

Brandl, Klaus K. 1995. "Strong and Weak Students' Preferences for Error Feedback Options and Responses." *The Modern Language Journal*, 79, no. 2: 194–211.

Brown, Steven R. (1993). "A Primer on Q-Methodology." *Operant Subjectivity*, 16: 91–138.

Byram, Michael. 1997. *Teaching and Assessing Intercultural Communicative Competence.* Clevedon: Multilingual Matters.

Byrnes, Heidi. 2009. "Revisiting the Role of Culture in the Foreign Language Curriculum." *The Modern Language Journal*, 94, no. 2: 315–317. Doi:10.1111/j.1540-4781.2010.01023.x

Canale, Michael, and Merrill Swain. 1980. "Theoretical Bases of Communicative Approaches to Second Language Teaching and Testing." *Applied Linguistics*, 1, no. 1: 1–47.

Chapelle, Carol A. 1997. "CALL in the Year 2000: Still in Search of Research Paradigms?" *Language Learning & Technology*, 1, no. 1: 19–43.

Chapelle, Carol A. 1998. "Multimedia CALL: Lessons to Be Learned from Research on Instructed SLA." *Language Learning & Technology*, 2, no. 1: 22–34.

Chapelle, Carol A. 2001. *Computer Applications in Second Language Acquisition.* Cambridge: Cambridge University Press.

Chapelle, Carol A. 2010. "Research for Practice: A Look at Issues in Technology for Second Language Learning." *Language Learning & Technology*, 14, no. 3: 27–30.

Chun, Dorothy M. 1994. "Using Computer Networking to Facilitate the Acquisition of Interactive Competence." *System*, 22, no. 1: 17–31.

Chun, Dorothy M., ed. 2014. *Cultura-Inspired Intercultural Exchanges: Focus on Asian and Pacific Languages.* Honolulu, HI: National Foreign Language Resource Center.

Chun, Dorothy M. 2015. "Language and Culture Learning in Higher Education via Telecollaboration." *Pedagogies: An International Journal*, 10, no. 1: 1–17. DOI:10.1080/15544 80X.2014.999775

Chun, Dorothy M., and Jan L. Plass. 1996. "Effects of Multimedia Annotations on Vocabulary Acquisition." *The Modern Language Journal*, 80, no. 2: 183–198. DOI:10.2307/328635

Chun, Dorothy M., and Jan L. Plass. 1997. "Research on Text Comprehension in Multimedia Environments." *Language Learning & Technology*, 1, no. 1: 60–81.

Chun, Dorothy M., Yan Jiang, Justine Meyr, and Rong Yang. 2015. "Acquisition of L2 Mandarin Chinese Tones with Learner-Created Tone Visualizations." *Journal of Second Language Pronunciation*, 1, no. 1: 86–114.

Darhower, Mark. 2002. "Interactional Features of Synchronous Computer-Mediated Communication in the Intermediate L2 Class: A Sociocultural Case Study." *CALICO Journal*, 19, no. 2: 249–277.

Dooly, Melinda, and Robert O'Dowd, eds. 2012. *Researching Online Foreign Language Interaction and Exchange: Theories, Methods and Challenges*, Vol. 3. Telecollaboration in Education. New York: Peter Lang.

Felix, Uschi. 2008. "The Unreasonable Effectiveness of CALL: What Have We Learned in Two Decades of Research?" *ReCALL*, 20, no. 2: 141–161.

Fernández-García, Marisol, and Asunción Martínez-Arbelaiz. 2002. "Negotiation of Meaning in Nonnative Speaker-Nonnative Speaker Synchronous Discussions." *CALICO Journal*, 19, no. 2: 279–294.

Furstenberg, Gilberte, Sabine Levet, Kathryn English, and Katherine Maillet. 2001. "Giving a Virtual Voice to the Silent Language of Culture: The Cultura Project." *Language Learning & Technology*, 5, no. 1: 55–102.

Grgurović, Maja, Carol A. Chapelle, and Mack C. Shelley. 2013. "A Meta-Analysis of Effectiveness Studies on Computer Technology-Supported Language Learning." *ReCALL* 25, no. 2: 165–198. DOI:10.1017/S0958344013000013

Guikema, Janel P., and Lawrence Williams, eds. 2014. *Digital Literacies in Foreign and Second Language Education*. Vol. 12. CALICO Monograph Series. San Marcos, TX: CALICO.

Hardison, Debra M. 2004. "Generalization of Computer-Assisted Prosody Training: Quantitative and Qualitative Findings." *Language Learning & Technology*, 8, no. 1: 34–52.

Heift, Trude. 2002. "Learner Control and Error Correction in ICALL: Browsers, Peekers and Adamants." *CALICO Journal*. 19, no. 3: 295–313.

Heift, Trude. 2010. "Prompting in CALL: A Longitudinal Study of Learner Uptake." *The Modern Language Journal*, 94, no. 2: 198–216.

Hubbard, Philip. 2008. "Twenty-Five Years of Theory in the CALICO Journal." *CALICO Journal*, 25, no. 3: 387–399.

Hubbard, Philip, ed. 2009. *Computer Assisted Language Learning: Critical Concepts in Linguistics*. Vol. 1–4. London and New York: Routledge.

Hymes, Dell. 1972. "On Communicative Competence." In *Sociolinguistics*, edited by J. B. Pride and J. Holmes, 269–293. London: Penguin.

Jiménez-Caicedo, Juan Pablo, María E. Lozano, and Ricardo L. Gómez. 2014. "Agency and Web 2.0 in Language Learning: A Systematic Analysis of Elementary Spanish Learners' Attitudes, Beliefs, and Motivations about the Use of Blogs for the Development of L2 Literacy and Language Ability." In *Digital Literacies in Foreign and Second Language Education*, edited by Janel P. Guikema and Lawrence Williams. Vol. 12. CALICO Monograph Series. San Marcos, TX: CALICO.

Jones, Linda C. 2003. "Supporting Listening Comprehension and Vocabulary Acquisition with Multimedia Annotations: The Students' Voice." *CALICO Journal*, 21, no. 1: 41–65.

Kern, Richard G. 1995. "Restructuring Classroom Interaction with Networked Computers: Effects on Quantity and Characteristics of Language Production." *The Modern Language Journal*, 79, no. 4: 457–476.

Kern, Richard, Paige Ware, and Mark Warschauer. 2004. "Crossing Frontiers: New Directions in Online Pedagogy and Research." *Annual Review of Applied Linguistics*, 24: 243–260. DOI:10.1017/S0267190504000091

Kramsch, Claire. 1993. *Context and Culture in Language Teaching*. Oxford: Oxford University Press.

Lam, Wan Shun Eva. 2000. "L2 Literacy and the Design of the Self: A Case Study of a Teenager Writing on the Internet." *TESOL Quarterly*, 34, no. 3: 457–482. DOI:10.2307/3587739

Laufer, Batia, and Hill, Monica. 2000. "What Lexical Information Do L2 Learners Select in a CALL Dictionary and How Does It Affect Word Retention." *Language Learning & Technology*, 3, no. 2: 58–76.

Levis, John, and Lucy Pickering. 2004. "Teaching Intonation in Discourse Using Speech Visualization Technology." *System* 32, no. 4: 505–524.

Levy, Mike. 2000. "Scope, Goals and Methods in CALL Research: Questions of Coherence and Autonomy." *ReCALL*, 12, no. 2: 170–195.

Lin, Huifen. 2014. "Establishing an Empirical Link between Computer-Mediated Communication (CMC) and SLA: A Meta-Analysis of the Research." *Language Learning & Technology*, 18, no. 3: 120–147.

Lin, Huifen. 2015. "A Meta-Synthesis of Empirical Research on the Effectiveness of Computer-Mediated Communication (CMC) in SLA." *Language Learning & Technology*, 19, no. 2: 85–117.

Lin, Wei-Chen, Hung-Tzu Huang, and Hsien-Chin Liou. 2013. "The Effects of Text-Based SCMC on SLA: A Meta Analysis." *Language Learning & Technology*, 17, no. 2: 123–142.

McBride, Kara. 2011. "The Effect of Rate of Speech and Distributed Practice on the Development of Listening Comprehension." *Computer Assisted Language Learning*, 24, no. 2: 131–154. DOI:10.1080/09588221.2010.528777

Müller-Hartmann, Andreas. 2012. "The Classroom-Based Action Research Paradigm in Telecollaboration." In *Researching Online Foreign Language Interaction and Exchange: Theories, Methods, and Challenges*, edited by Melinda Dooly and Robert O'Dowd, 163–94. Bern: Peter Lang.

O'Dowd, Robert. 2003. "Understanding the 'Other Side': Intercultural Learning in a Spanish-English E-Mail Exchange." *Language Learning & Technology*, 7, no. 2: 118–144.

O'Dowd, Robert, ed. 2007. *Online Intercultural Exchange: An Introduction for Foreign Language Teachers*. Vol. 15. Clevedon: Multilingual Matters.

Payne, Scott J., and Paul J. Whitney. 2002. "Developing L2 Oral Proficiency through Synchronous CMC: Output, Working Memory, and Interlanguage Development." *CALICO Journal*, 20, no. 1: 7–32.

Reinhardt, Jonathon, and Julie M. Sykes. 2014. "Digital Game and Play Activity in L2 Teaching and Learning." *Language Learning & Technology*, 18, no. 2: 2–8.

Peterson, M. 2010. "Computerized Games and Simulations in Computer-Assisted Language Learning: A Meta-Analysis of Research." *Simulation & Gaming* 41, no. 1: 72–93. DOI:10.1177/1046878109355684

Plass, Jan L., Dorothy M. Chun, Richard E. Mayer, and Detlev Leutner. 1998. "Supporting Visual and Verbal Learning Preferences in a Second-Language Multimedia Learning Environment." *Journal of Educational Psychology*, 90, no. 1: 25–36.

Sauro, Shannon. 2011. "SCMC for SLA: A Research Synthesis." *CALICO Journal*, 28, no. 2: 369–391.

Sauro, Shannon. 2012. "L2 Performance in Text-Chat and Spoken Discourse." *System*, 40, no. 3: 335–348. DOI:10.1016/j.system.2012.08.001.

Sauro, Shannon, and Bryan Smith. 2010. "Investigating L2 Performance in Text Chat."

*Applied Linguistics*, 31, no. 4: 554–577. DOI:10.1093/applin/amq007

Smith, Bryan. 2003. "Computer–mediated Negotiated Interaction: An Expanded Model." *The Modern Language Journal*, 87, no. 1: 38–57.

Smith, Bryan. 2008. "Methodological Hurdles in Capturing CMC Data: The Case of the Missing Self-Repair." *Language Learning & Technology*, 12, no. 1: 85–103.

Smith, Bryan. 2012. "Eye Tracking as a Measure of Noticing: A Study of Explicit Recasts in SCMC." *Language Learning & Technology*, 16, no. 3: 53–81.

Smith, Bryan, and Shannon Sauro. 2009. "Interruptions in Chat." *Computer Assisted Language Learning*, 22, no. 3: 229–247. DOI:10.1080/09588220902920219

Sotillo, Susana M. 2000. "Discourse Functions and Syntactic Complexity in Synchronous and Asynchronous Communication." *Language Learning & Technology*, 4, no. 1: 82–119.

Stockwell, Glenn, and Michael Harrington. 2003. "The Incidental Development of L2 Proficiency in NS-NNS Email Interactions." *CALICO Journal*, 20, no. 2: 337–359.

Strobl, Carola. 2014. "Affordances of Web 2.0 Technologies for Collaborative Advanced Writing in a Foreign Language." *CALICO Journal*, 31, no. 1: 1–18. DOI:10.11139/cj.31.1.1–18

Sykes, Julie M., and Christopher L. Holden. 2011. "Communities: Exploring Digital Games and Social Networking." In *Present and Future Promises of CALL: From Theory and Research to New Directions in Language Teaching*, edited by Nike Arnold and Lara Ducate, 311–336. San Marcos, TX: CALICO.

Thorne, Steven L. 2003. "Artifacts and Cultures-of-Use in Intercultural Communication." *Language Learning & Technology*, 7, no. 2: 38–67.

Thorne, Steven L., and Scott J. Payne. 2005. "Evolutionary Trajectories, Internet-Mediated Expression, and Language Education." *CALICO Journal*, 22, no. 3: 371–397.

Varonis, Evangeline M., and Susan M. Gass. 1985. "Non-Native/non-Native Conversations: A Model for Negotiation of Meaning." *Applied Linguistics*, 6: 71–90.

Warschauer, Mark. 1995. "Comparing Face-to-Face and Electronic Discussion in the Second Language Classroom." *CALICO Journal* 13, no. 2/3: 7–26.

Warschauer, Mark, and Richard Kern G., eds. 2000. *Network-Based Language Teaching: Concepts and Practice*. Cambridge: Cambridge University Press.

Yanguas, Iñigo. 2009. "Multimedia Glosses and Their Effect on L2 Text Comprehension and Vocabulary Learning." *Language Learning & Technology*, 13, no. 2: 48–67.

Yun, Jeehwan. 2011. "The Effects of Hypertext Glosses on L2 Vocabulary Acquisition: A Meta-Analysis." *Computer Assisted Language Learning*, 24, no. 1: 39–58. DOI:10.1080/09588221.2010.523285

Zhao, Yong. 1997. "The Effects of Listeners' Control of Speech Rate on Second Language Comprehension." *Applied Linguistics*, 18, no. 1: 49–68.

Zheng, Dongping, Michael F. Young, Robert A. Brewer, and Manuela Wagner. 2009. "Attitude and Self-Efficacy Change: English Language Learning in Virtual Worlds." *CALICO Journal*, 27, no. 1: 205–231.

# 27 CALL Meta-analyses and Transparency Analysis

## HSIEN-CHIN LIOU AND HUI-FEN LIN

## Introduction

The recent publication of meta-analysis papers on technology and second language learning may signal a new level of maturity in the field. In education, Glass (1976) first proposed meta-analysis and coined the term, defining it as "the analysis of analyses ... it ... refer[s] to the statistical analysis of a large collection of results from individual studies for the purpose of integrating the findings. It connotes a rigorous alternative to the casual, narrative discussions of research studies which typify our attempts to make sense of the rapidly expanding research literature" (3). Only when multiple studies have been conducted on a particular question with sufficient rigor is it possible to assess the state of the art through the means of a research synthesis such as meta-analysis. In applied linguistics, Norris and Ortega (2006) define meta-analysis as playing a specific role in the multiple approaches which researchers have for synthesizing research results. Other approaches to research synthesis are narrative reviews and vote-counting, which are chosen when materials to be reviewed do not lend themselves to quantitative analysis, a sufficient number of studies to be reviewed does not exist, or insufficient resources are available to carrying out a meta-analysis.

In second language acquisition (SLA), the numbers of meta-analytic reports are not large, but meta-analysis has evolved to the stage where researchers are examining their methodological rigor (Li, Shintani, and Ellis 2012; Plonsky 2012). Felix (2005), for example, commented on 13 meta-analytic CALL reports which were published after 1991 including those synthesizing L1 studies and suggested that more meta-analyses be conducted with special attention paid to methodological rigor. Indeed, ten years later, a number of meta-analytic studies on technology and second language learning have been conducted, as we will show in this chapter. In reviewing this research, we will devote particular attention to the methodological issues of procedures for conducting meta-analysis as well as the rigor of meta-analytic studies, and we explore possible reasons for differences across meta-analyses by conducting a transparency analysis. To achieve these aims, we first introduce the key components for conducting a meta-analysis. Second, we address methodological rigor by examining how transparently existing CALL meta-analytical reports are documented in L2 context.

*The Handbook of Technology and Second Language Teaching and Learning*, First Edition.
Edited by Carol A. Chapelle and Shannon Sauro.
© 2017 John Wiley & Sons, Inc. Published 2020 by John Wiley & Sons, Inc.

# Procedures for conducting a meta-analysis

Standard procedures for conducting a meta-analysis evolved in several fields such as medical science (Egger, Smith, and Phillips 1997), general education (Lipsey and Wilson 1993), and SLA (Masgoret and Gardner 2003). Very similar to a quantitative experiment, meta-analysis, at a very basic level, included steps such as formulating research questions, collecting data and reporting the outcomes. A few more essential steps were proposed by meta-analysts as it evolved as a systematic review that aggregates the outcomes of studies (e.g., Aytug et al. 2012; Cooper 2010; Egger, Smith, and Phillips, 1997; Oswald and Plonsky 2010) as described in the following five steps.

## *Step 1—formulating the problem*

Like primary research, a meta-analysis starts with posing research questions. At this stage, the researcher contextualizes the entire research problem by justifying why a synthesis is needed. Among CALL meta-analyses, types of research questions can be seen as (1) comparing effects of language learning outcome in CALL versus non-CALL context, (2) comparing effects of one technology and another, and/or (3) discerning differential effects of certain instructional strategies in CALL environment. Additionally, definitions of key terms (both conceptual and operational types) must be provided. In some cases where the relationship of interest is not straightforward, examining or searching for factors that might potentially affect the relationship may be undertaken. The next crucial element is identifying the kinds of primary studies the analyst would include based on a predetermined rationale by the researcher. For CALL, the criteria may include participants (young or adult learners, for instance), language of publication, outcome measure, time frame, research design (to include studies with or without control groups), availability of data for effect size calculation, and source (e.g., being published or not). To illustrate, in the analyses by Lin, Huang, and Liou (2013 on SCMC) and Chiu (2013 on vocabulary), both included the duration of technology use as a variable that may influence the effectiveness of technology use. This allowed them to generalize their conclusions only to those settings where technology is used for language learning for a certain duration. Such definition of variables helps researchers to avoid overgeneralizing the finding beyond the scope of the meta-analysis.

## *Step 2—searching the literature*

Similar to sampling in a primary study, researchers need to specify search terms (key words) and use the best strategy to search for studies to be included in the meta-analysis according to predetermined inclusion and exclusion criteria. They typically begin by using search engines (e.g., Google Scholar) and electronic databases to identify the initial pool of primary studies. Results from the initial search are complemented with manual checks through books or journals on library shelves, tracing references in the primary studies, with consultation of authors or experts in the field. The researchers must decide whether or not to include both published and unpublished studies. Standard sources on meta-analysis recommend inclusion of unpublished sources so as not to obtain results affected by the "publication bias" that may have chosen to publish only those primary studies in which positive results were obtained. In CALL meta-analyses, both published and unpublished studies had been included for comparison. For CALL, researchers may start from common digital databases with examples shown in Table 27.1. The next priority search is CALL journals. Within most of the journal issues online, a keyword search function is usually available to avoid energy

**Table 27.1**   Possible sources to locate potential meta-analysis and their examples.

| Source to locate | Examples |
| --- | --- |
| Digital databases | Education Abstracts Full Text (Wilson), Education Resources Information Center (ERIC), ProQuest Psychology Journals, Springer Online Journal Archives, JSTOR-Arts and Sciences III Collection, EBSCOhost, Linguistics and Language Behavior Abstracts (LLBA), and the Social Science Citation Index (SSCI, Thomson Reuters) |
| CALL journals | *CALICO Journal, Computer-Assisted Language Learning, ReCALL, Language Learning & Technology, System, International Journal of Computer Assisted Language Learning & Teaching,* and the *JALT CALL Journal* |
| SLA journals | *Language Learning, the Modern Language Journal, TESOL Quarterly, Canadian Modern Language Review, Journal of Second Language Writing, Foreign Language Annals, Second Language Research,* and *Studies in Second Language Acquisition* |
| Educational technology journals | *Journal of Computer-Assisted Learning, the British Journal of Educational Technology* (BJET), *Educational Technology Research & Development* (ETR&D), *Australasian Journal of Educational Technology* (AJET), and *Computers and Education* |

spent on manually going through each issue of the journal. Occasionally, journals related to SLA or language learning and teaching may include CALL studies. The last group of journals for searches may be ones which are related to educational technologies but not specifically to language learning and teaching.

## *Step 3—gathering information from and evaluating the quality of studies*

The third step is to set the inclusion and exclusion criteria that define which of the studies identified by the search is appropriate for the meta-analysis. In this stage, researchers need to make decisions on essential characteristics that a study needs to possess in order to be included. For example, a study might need to provide the kind of data from which calculation of effect size is possible. In this stage, researchers also need to determine the data to extract from the study. Types of study features may include: (a) publication information (type of document, publication date), (b) methodological quality information (research design, measurement quality), (c) demographic information (grade level, subject matter), and (d) substantive moderators (instructional method, time-on-task). Moderator variables are to be defined by meta-analysts via some justification. In CALL, examples are synchronicity of CMC (asynchronous or synchronous), treatment length, L2 learners' proficiency, and so on. Regarding publication bias, some statistical methods can be applied: the funnel plot, a trim-and-fill analysis, or a fail-safe N statistic (Li, Shintani, and Ellis 2012). To ensure methodological rigor, it is advised in Li, Shintani, and Ellis (2012) that random assignment be employed in grouping, and pretesting, and reliability and validity of outcome measures are provided by researchers to enhance the reliability of the analysis if more than one coder is involved in assigning study features or even moderator variables. With more than one coder, then it is a good practice to report how coders agree concerning the coding process (Raffle 2006).

## *Step 4—analyzing and integrating the outcomes of research*

To meta-analyze a group of primary studies, Step 4 is to aggregate their results by calculating effect sizes. An effect size is a standardized measure of treatment effect/strength and can be expressed in many forms such as the correlation between two variables, the mean difference between two comparison groups or the ratio with which something occurs. An effect size in meta-analysis is to represent the magnitude of a treatment effect by aggregating findings from studies that have measured different outcomes or used diversity of measurement scales. Moreover, a weighting method needs to be applied to studies with a larger sample size when calculating effect sizes because they carry more precise estimates of the population effect. In order to determine the statistical significance of the mean effect sizes, 95% confidence intervals can be calculated for each weighted mean effect size (Lipsey and Wilson 2001; Norris and Ortega 2000, 449–450). Confidence intervals that contain the value zero indicate that the mean effect sizes are not statistically significant (Norris and Ortega 2000). To determine the variability of effect size distribution, a homogeneity test, that is, a within-group Q test can be conducted. The test is to verify if the studies are similar enough to be combined to calculate a mean effect size that stands for the overall effect. Depending on the results of the test, either a random-effects model or fixed-effects model concerning between-study variance can be selected for further analyses. Generally, if the Q test is found to be significant, a random-effects model can be chosen.

## *Step 5—interpreting the evidence and presenting the results and conclusion*

In Step 5, conclusions and implications from the meta-analysis are drawn. Effect sizes are interpreted based on some established guidelines (e.g., Cohen's *d*) and more importantly according to theory or practice of specific domain (Norris and Ortega 2006). Results drawn from a meta-analysis allow researchers in certain communities to chart where they are in existing knowledge, and to identify common patterns in studying findings and gaps that need to be filled in existing literature. Furthermore, the results of a meta-analysis also generate knowledge that could inform teaching or revisit theories that have been commonly held as true.

# A brief survey of established meta-analysis reporting guidelines

As more meta-analyses have been conducted across subject areas, some researchers are conducting systematic appraisals of meta-analyses to assess their methodological rigor. Conceptually, "rigor" means the quality of a meta-analysis, that is, how well it is conducted. To assess rigor, researchers have operationalized the concept through a set of criteria that can be used to make an evaluation rubric. When the rubric is used by a meta-analysis evaluator, a total score can be calculated that reflects the rigor of the meta-analysis.

   In the following, the meta-analysis reporting criteria that guide a transparency analysis of this study are briefly introduced. The MUTOS framework developed by Ahn, Ames, and Myers (2012) was used to evaluate 56 meta-analyses. It includes components of a study such as **M**ethod (e.g., study design), **U**nits (e.g., grade level), **T**reatments (e.g., type of treatment, treatment duration), **O**bserving operations (e.g., type of measure), and **S**etting (e.g., study location). Among the reports they assessed, they found data evaluation and analysis were more problematic than the other areas. In particular, statistical methods were not explained in a transparent manner, which impedes generating credible and generalizable meta-analytic findings to inform educational practices.

Similarly, Aytug et al. (2012) gauged the transparency and completeness of the reporting of meta-analysis in the field of industrial organizational psychology and organizational behavior, and call for attention given to the consequences of deficiencies in implementing and reporting meta-analyses. They collected views on conducting meta-analyses from different experts in their discipline, while incorporating consideration of various sources of quality measures. Then, they came up with a 42-item checklist based on stages of reporting a meta-analysis: research question, literature search, methods, results, discussion, and conclusion. The 42 items cover similar concerns close to the MUTOS framework (Ahn et al. 2012). To give transparency scoring, 18 items from the original checklist were regarded as "ethically imperative" (Aytug et al. 2012, 110) as they obtained feedback from experts in the field. Addressing 40 years of educational technology research, Tamin et al. (2011) surveyed 25 meta-analyses on educational technology by the use of a second-order analysis to synthesize the findings, which drew the statistics from each meta-analytic report and calculated pooled effect sizes across original meta-analytic reports. Plonsky (2012), a scholar in SLA, addressed meta-analysis and generalizability for the area of language teaching. A 22-item instrument (127) was devised and proposed for journal editors, manuscript reviewers, and readers of meta-analyses to assess the internal validity of a meta-analytic report. Although he advocates making supplementary data online available as a means to increasing the generalizability of findings, he has not yet refined his instrument in view of the results of other SLA meta-analyses. Some items in his instrument were similar to those straightforward (low-inference) ones in the 18-item checklist (Aytug et al. 2012), but others require a researcher's subjective judgment concerning a value assigned. Thus, we adopted the 18-item checklist as our research instrument in gauging how rigorously CALL meta-analyses were conducted in this chapter.

# Transparency of CALL meta-analyses

In view of the emerging consensus about quality characteristics in meta-analyses, we investigated the rigor of CALL meta-analyses by conducting a transparency analysis. Our transparency analysis began with a search of the literature to find the relevant meta-analyses. Then, we coded each CALL meta-analytic report based on an evaluation rubric. We also test if there was a correlation between their publication year and the level of transparency.

## *Literature search*

We searched through major CALL journals to locate meta-analytic reports. The journals we targeted included *CALICO Journal, Computer Assisted Language Learning, ReCALL, Language Learning & Technology, International Journal of Computer Assisted Language Learning & Teaching, CALL-EJ,* or *JALT CALL Journal*. We also searched general educational technology journals, such as *Journal of Computer Assisted Learning, Computers and Education, BJET* or *ETR&D*. For each journal, we conducted an electronic search using keywords such as meta-analysis, research synthesis, quantitative review, meta-analytic, and effect size. The first screening of possibly eligible meta-analysis was carried out by reading both the abstract and method section of each report. When in doubt about the eligibility, we read through the full paper and made our final inclusion/exclusion decision.

# Coding

One item concerning artifact corrections from the 18 items was found irrelevant to the 13 CALL meta-analyses, and was excluded, resulting in 17 items for the final analysis. The 17 items (see Appendix for a full list) examine various aspects of four sections in a meta-analytic report: research questions (three items), literature search (three items), methods (five items), results (two items), and discussion/conclusion (four items).The two authors of the chapter used the checklist to first independently code each of CALL meta-analytical reports found through literature search. After face-to-face discussion on various sources of discrepancy from the initial coding, the two coders formally assigned the rating to the 17 items for all the meta-analytic reports. To ensure reliability of the coding, inter-rater reliability was calculated at three stages of the coding: one at the first independent coding, another after clarifying several high-inference items, and the last one after resolving disagreement between the two coders. The inter-rater reliability was calculated following this formula, where n stands for the number of items agreed upon by two coders and N stands for total number of items:

$n/N$

It has to be noticed that the total number of items takes into account the sub-items of item 4 (literature search) and item 5 (types of studies included in the review), totaling 31 items. The resulted inter-rater reliability is 0.79, 0.94, and 1.00 respectively at three stages of coding.

# Items coded for each component

We described in the following the number of items we coded for each section and what we were looking for in these items (Table 27.2).

## Descriptive information and research question—3 items

Using the 17-item checklist, we coded the effect sizes metrics and averaging and weighting methods used in the meta-analysis. We also examined if there were clear research questions prescribed for the analysis.

## Literature search—3 items

We surveyed almost exclusively possible reference and citation databases that meta-analysts would use to search for potential primary studies and examined if the included reports have used one or more of them. We also coded the types of studies included in the review. It has to be noticed that there were multiple sub-items for both items and each report might use more than one reference/citation database or reviewed more than one type of studies. Furthermore, we looked for evidence that keywords used in the study were reported.

## Method—5 items

We coded if the report specified independent and dependent variables and whether operational definitions are provided for variables. We also recorded the method that coders resolved disagreement and whether inter-coder reliability was reported. Additionally, we also looked for the list of study features that were coded in the report.

## Result—2 items

As for the results section of the report, we coded whether tabular or graphic display of overall estimate and rationale for the selection of moderators were provided.

**Table 27.2** Summary of coding categories (items) and coding processes

| Coding categories | Coding processes |
| --- | --- |
| *Descriptive information and research question* | |
| Effect size metric(s) | Coding the effect sizes metrics |
| Effect size averaging and weighting method(s) | Averaging and weighting methods used in the meta-analysis |
| Clear statement of the research question | Examining if there were clear research questions prescribed for the analysis |
| *Literature search* | |
| Reference and citation databases searched (electronic database, journal hand search, reference list, citation search, conference programs, websites/internet, and other) | Surveying almost exclusively possible reference and citation databases that meta-analysts would use to search for potential primary studies, and examining if the included reports had used one or more of them |
| Types of studies included in the review (journal articles, book chapter, book, dissertations/theses, conference abstracts, government report, company report, unpublished, and other) | Coding the types of studies included in the review |
| Keywords used to enter databases and registries | Looking for evidence that keywords used in the study were reported |
| *Method* | |
| Independent and dependent variables of interest | Coding if the report specified independent and dependent variables Coding if operational definitions are provided for variables |
| Operational definitions of variables | |
| Reporting of intercoder reliability (if more than 1 coder) | Recording the method that coders resolved disagreement |
| Method of resolving disagreements (if more than 1 coder) | Recording if inter-coder reliability was reported |
| Did the study report what study features were coded? | Looking for the list of study features that were coded in the report |
| *Result* | |
| Tabular or graphic display of overall estimate | Coding if tabular or graphic display of overall estimate |
| Rationale for the selection of moderators provided | Coding if rationale for the selection of moderators were provided |
| *Discussion/Conclusion* | |
| Statement of major findings | Looking for availability of major findings |
| General limitations | Looking for study limitations |
| Consideration of alternative explanations for observed results | Looking for alternative explanations for observed results |
| Implications and interpretation for theory, policy, or practice | Looking for implications and interpretation of the findings for theory, policy, or practice |

## Discussion/Conclusion—4 items

This section looked for the availability of major findings, study limitations, alternative explanations for observed results and implications and interpretation of the findings for theory, policy, or practice.

## Data extraction and transparency scoring

Four kinds of marking were designed for these 17 items. "Open-ended" items required the coders to enter the coding depending on the information provided in the study; dichotomous items asked the coder to enter either Y or N, which represented if the specified information is reported (Y) or not (N). A three-level coding (e.g., Y/Searched, but the list of websites is not provided/N) was designed for items in which complete or partial information might be reported. The last type of marking asked the coders to select one from a prescribed list of codes. Each item was then scored 1, 0.5 or 0, with a value of 1 assigned to items for which information was reported and 0.5 for the three-level code items for which only partial information is reported. A zero is assigned to items for which information is not reported. For questions with multiple sub-items (e.g., literature search and types of studies included in the review), we assigned 1 point to that item if they reported at least one of the sub-items because we were interested in whether they did "report" the item rather than what decision they made on that item. For example, a meta-analysis might report that when searching studies, only journal and electronic databases were searched, leaving out conference programs. This item was awarded 1 because it did report how it located primary studies regardless of the fact that conference programs or other possible sources were not tried. The score of each report was then summed and the total averaged to yield an overall transparency score.

# Results

We first presented a summary of the collective 13 CALL studies, followed by a set of tallies we obtained regarding the overall transparency of reporting from these studies, and the transparency score of each individual component and finally the correlation analysis results between publication year and transparency score.

## Sample

The sample consisted of the 13 meta-analytic reports shown in Table 27.3, which includes features such as their citation and journal source, type of technology used, total number of included studies in each and total subjects analyzed among its overall included studies, their effect sizes, major findings, and period of primary studies included. The 13 reports cover general CALL effectiveness of using various technologies, strategy-oriented Web-based learning, vocabulary learning, CMC, synchronous CMC, gaming, concordancing, and online glosses.

Out of the 13, one came from a book chapter (Cobb and Boulton, 2015), three came from general educational technology journals (Chang and Lin 2013; Chiu 2013; Chiu et al. 2012), and nine from four CALL journals (*CALICO, CALL, LLT,* and *ReCALL*). They were mainly published between 2003 and May of 2015. The included studies of analysis ranged from nine to 59 which were published between 1984 and 2012 (with much wider ranges of studies searched understandably), whereas the total subject numbers, from 419 to 3,562. All yielded final positive cumulative effect sizes, which ranged from 0.26 to 1.69. This may suggest that

**Table 27.3** Summary of the 13 CALL meta-analytic reports.

| Study Publication source | Research design | Outcome | No. of studies/ sample size | Effect sizes | Findings | Inclusion Period |
|---|---|---|---|---|---|---|
| Abraham 2008, *CALL* | Computer-mediated glosses vs. non-glosses | Reading and vocabulary | 11/542 | $d = 0.73$ (reading) $d = 1.40$ (vocabulary) | Computer-mediated Glosses > non-glosses | ~2007 |
| Chang and Lin 2013, *AJET* | Web-based strategy instruction vs. non-web based | English achievements | 31/3,414 | $d = 0.67$ | Web-based strategy instruction > non-web based | 1992~2010 |
| Chiu, Kao, and Reynolds 2012, *BJET* | Digital game-based learning (DGBL) vs. non-DGBL | English performance | 14/1,116 | $d = 0.67$ (fixed) $d = 0.53$ (random) | Digital game-based learning (DGBL) > non-DGBL | 2005~2010 |
| Chiu 2013, *BJET* | CALL vs. non-CALL | Vocabulary | 16/1,684 | $d = 0.75$ | CALL > non-CALL | 2005~2011 |
| Cobb and Boulton 2015, book chapter | Corpus vs. non-corpus | Vocabulary, grammar, error correction, lexical retrieval, translation | 21/NA | $d = 1.69$ (within) $d = 1.04$ (between) | Corpus > non-corpus | 1989~2012 |
| Grgurović, Chapelle, and Shelley 2013 *ReCALL* | CALL vs. Non-CALL | Reading, writing, vocabulary, communication, grammar, pronunciation, integrated skills | 37/NA | $d = 0.24$ | CALL > non-CALL | 1970~2006 |
| Lin, Huang, and Liou 2013 *LLT* | Text-based SCMC (text chat) vs. F2F/voice chat | Grammar, oral proficiency | 10/562 | $d = 0.33$ | Text chat > voice chat/ F2F | 1990~2012 |
| Lin 2014 *LLT* | CMC | Overall effect of SLA (RWLS) | 59/3,562 | $g = 0.44$ | CMC > non-CMC | 2000~2012 |

(Continued)

**Table 27.3** (Continued)

| Study Publication source | Research design | Outcome | No. of studies/ sample size | Effect sizes | Findings | Inclusion Period |
|---|---|---|---|---|---|---|
| Taylor 2006 CALICO | Computer-assisted L1 (CALL L1)vs. paper-based L1 glosses | Reading comprehension (no details specified) | 18/875 | $g = 0.53$ | Computer-assisted L1 > paper-based L1 glosses | ~2002 |
| Taylor 2009 CALICO | Computer-assisted L1 (CALL L1)vs. paper-based L1 glosses | Reading comprehension | 32/1,845 | $g = 0.51$ | Computer-assisted L1 > paper-based L1 glosses | ~2006 |
| Taylor 2013 CALICO | Computer-assisted L1 (CALL L1)vs. paper-based L1 glosses | Reading comprehension | 27/1,458 | $g = 0.73$ | Computer-assisted L1 > paper-based L1 glosses | ~2011 |
| Yun 2011 CALL | Multiple hypertext gloss vs. single hypertext | Vocabulary | 10/1,560 | $g = 0.46$ | Multiple hypertext gloss > single hypertext | 1990- 2009 |
| Zhao 2003 CALICO | CALL vs. non-CALL | Language learning | 9/419 | $d = 1.12$ | CALL > non-CALL | 1997 ~ 2001 |

CALL generally performed better than non-CALL contexts or the target technology chosen as the research focus did better than the other technological choices.

## *Overall transparency*

The overall mean transparency score across the 13 CALL meta-analyses, as shown in Table 27.4, is 10.69 (SD=2.93) out of a maximum score of 17.00 (10.69/17.00=62.9%). Compared with the assessment done by Aytug et al. (2012) for the field of management, they obtained 52.83% based on a 42-item checklist from which our 17 items were a sub-set. Our average score is higher, which may not be surprising as we included meta-analyses which were more recently conducted. The average sub-item scores for each of the four sections was 4.85 out of a possible total score of 6.00 (Research questions and literature search); 2.31 out of a possible total score of 5.00 (Methods); 1.08 out of a possible total score of 2.00 (Results) and 2.46 out of possible total score of 4.00 (Discussion and Conclusion). The methods sections obtained the lowest average scores among the four sections (2.31 out of a total of 5.00, similar to the finding in the general education field, Ahn et al. 2012), which alerts future CALL analysts to pay particular attention to transparency of their research methods and procedures.

Of the 13 meta-analyses, Lin, Huang, and Liou (2013) is the most transparent analysis, which reported 16 of the 17 items that we deemed to be critical and ethical for readers to understand the meta-analytic procedures. Four other studies, namely, Lin (2014), Yun (2011), Abraham (2008), and Grgurović, Chapelle, and Shelley (2013) provided at least two-thirds of items that contributed to the report quality of a typical meta-analysis. Three studies, namely, Chiu (2013), Chang and Lin (2013), and Zhao (2003) reported fewer than

**Table 27.4**   Transparency scores for each included meta-analysis (N=13).

| Study | RQ+LS[a] | Methods | Results | Discussion/ conclusion | Total score |
|---|---|---|---|---|---|
| Lin, Huang, and Liou (2013) | 6 | 5 | 2 | 3 | 16 |
| Lin (2014) | 6 | 5 | 1 | 3 | 15 |
| Yun (2011) | 6 | 3 | 1 | 3 | 13 |
| Abraham (2008) | 6 | 3 | 1 | 3 | 13 |
| Grgurović, Chapelle, and Shelley (2013) | 6 | 3 | 1 | 2 | 12 |
| Chiu, Kao, and Reynolds (2012) | 4 | 4 | 1 | 2 | 11 |
| Taylor (2009) | 4 | 2 | 1 | 3 | 10 |
| Cobb and Boulton (2015) | 4 | 1 | 1 | 3 | 9 |
| Taylor (2013) | 4 | 1 | 1 | 3 | 9 |
| Taylor (2006) | 5 | 1 | 1 | 2 | 9 |
| Zhao (2003) | 5 | 0 | 1 | 2 | 8 |
| Chiu (2013) | 4 | 1 | 1 | 1 | 7 |
| Chang and Lin (2013) | 3 | 1 | 1 | 2 | 7 |
| Range | 0–6 | 0–5 | 0–2 | 0–4 | 0–17 |
| Mean | 4.85 (80.83%) | 2.31 (46.20%) | 1.08 (54.00%) | 2.46 (61.50%) | 10.69 (62.88%) |
| SD | 1.07 | 1.65 | 0.28 | 0.66 | 2.93 |

[a] Research questions and literature search

half of the 17 types of information needed for a thorough examination of a meta-analyst's decision-making. Among the scores based on the four sections of the checklist, the CALL meta-analysts obtained the lowest scores in methods compared with the other three sections.

## Reporting at each stage of the meta-analysis

In order to look into the level of transparency for each individual section in the reports beyond what a holistic transparency score can suggest, we conducted further analysis based on the four major sections (i.e., research question/literature search; methods; results and discussion/conclusion). Six items examining transparency of reporting related to research questions and the literature search strategies were analyzed. Table 27.5 shows the percentages of studies that reported such information.

### Research questions

Only approximately 69% of our sample provided a clear statement of the research question(s). About one-third of the studies embedded their questions in the purpose statement of the report. Some even did not specify the questions of interest in the meta-analysis. Grgurović et al. (2013) provided a good example of research questions for a meta-analysis. In their report, the questions are clearly numbered and are formulated to fulfill an overarching purpose of the study, "It sought to respond to the following research questions which aimed to yield an overall result as well as to isolate any factors that may play a role in effectiveness [of computer technology-supported language learning]" (168).

**Table 27.5**   Percentages of meta-analysis papers (n = 13) reporting research question and literature searching.

| Item reported | Yes | Partially | No |
|---|---|---|---|
| 3. Clear statement of the research question | 69.2 | | 30.8 |
| 4. Reference and citation databases searched | | | |
|    Electronic database | 69.2 | | 30.8 |
|    Journal hand search | 46.2 | | 53.8 |
|    Reference list | 38.5 | | 61.5 |
|    Citation search | 7.7 | | 92.3 |
|    Conference programs | 7.7 | 15.3 | 77.0 |
|    Personal contacts | 0.0 | | 100.0 |
|    Websites/Internet | 30.8 | | 69.2 |
| 5. Types of studies included in the review | | | |
|    Journal articles | 100.0 | | 0.0 |
|    Book chapter | 15.4 | | 84.6 |
|    Book | 7.7 | | 92.3 |
|    Dissertations/theses | 61.5 | | 38.5 |
|    Conference abstracts | 23.1 | | 76.9 |
|    Government report | 23.1 | | 76.9 |
|    Company report | 0.0 | | 100.0 |
|    Unpublished—not further specified | 69.2 | | 30.8 |
|    Keywords used to enter databases and Registries | 46.2 | | 53.8 |

## Reference and citation databases searched

All studies in our analysis reported information on how they searched for eligible studies. Notice that we evaluated if the authors reported such information regardless of their decision in terms of what to or not to search. As indicated, electronic databases are the major source to look for potential studies (69.2%) followed by a manual journal search. Reference lists provided by primary studies and websites were also consulted to locate as many studies as possible. A small percentage of studies also relied on citation search to expand the repertoire of the primary studies. Out of the 13 CALL meta-analytic studies, only one searched conference programs and also provided a list of the programs. Two studies searched conference programs but did not list the program (as previously noted, items that reported partial information is awarded 0.5 point). Ten studies did not search conference programs.

## Types of studies included in the review

As expected, journal articles (100%) are the major type of studies included in the meta-analysis. More than 60% of the studies also included dissertations or theses in the review. About 69% of the studies included unpublished studies without further specifying the sources or search strategies of them. Book and book chapters were rarely included in meta-analysis probably due to its variety in the scope and difficulty of conducting an efficient search. As also shown in Table 27.5, less than half of the meta-analyses (46.2%) reported key words used to search potential studies. Failure to do so is a major weakness in the report since key words used to locate primary studies provide readers and consumers of the meta-analysis results sources to evaluate the coverage of the search and the extent to which those key words are able to define the subject area appropriately and thus conduct a valid search. There were also wide varieties in the number of keywords used in the report. The minimum number of keywords used is 1 and the maximum 19. Zhao (2003), for example, used one overachieving key word, "computer assisted language learning" paired with limitation in year, document type, and language to retrieve the first body of potential studies. Abraham (2008), on the other hand, used up to 19 keywords in different combinations to identify primary studies. The number and precision of key words used may vary depending on the scope of the review. Zhao's meta-analysis reviewed recent developments in technology and language learning, the scope of which is much larger compared to Abraham (2008), which focused on a more specific topic area and outcome, that is, computer-mediated glosses in second language reading comprehension and vocabulary learning.

## Methods

Table 27.6 shows the findings of the methods section in our sample. Close to seventy-seven percent of the studies reported the independent and dependent variables in their analyses. However, only about one-third of the studies provided operational definitions of their variables. Chiu, Kao, and Reynolds (2012), for example, provided a very clear operationalization for their independent variable, "Operationalizations of drill and practice games … are adopted from Kiili (2005). In drill and practice games, players simply modify actions until their scores improve. These behaviors are only based on trial and error" (E104). Lin (2014) also provided operational definitions of major constructs based on conceptual definitions in the literature in a separate complete section titled, "definition of terms" (123). In our sample, only 39% of studies used multiple coders and 30.8% of these studies reported on how they resolved disagreement. Unexpected, only less than half of the studies, that is, 46% in our sample reported what study features were coded.

**Table 27.6**   Percentages of meta-analysis papers (n = 13) reporting aspects in methods sections.

| Item reported | Yes |
|---|---|
| 7. Independent and dependent variables of interest | 76.9 |
| 8. Operational definitions of variables | 38.5 |
| 9. Reporting of inter-coder reliability (if more than 1 coder) | 38.5 |
| 10. Method of resolving disagreements (if more than 1 coder) | 30.8 |
| 11. Did the study report what study features were coded? | 46.2 |

**Table 27.7**   Percentages of meta-analysis papers (n = 13) reporting in result section.

| Item reported | Yes | No |
|---|---|---|
| 12. Tabular or graphic display of overall estimate of effect size | 92.3 | 7.7 |
| 13. Rationale for the selection of moderators provided | 15.4 | 84.6 |

## Results

Our findings of reports in the results section are shown in Table 27.7. As indicated, the majority of studies (92.3%) provided tabular or graphic display of the overall estimate of the effect size. Surprisingly, only two of the 13 studies in our sample provided justification for their selection of moderators. Lin (2014), for example, provided rationale for each of her seven moderators in a separate section. Lin, Huang, and Liou (2013) selected their moderators following a prior meta-analysis, that is, Plonsky's meta-analysis (2011) on the effectiveness of traditional L2 strategy instruction.

## Discussion and conclusion

All studies in our sample, as shown in Table 27.8, reported the major findings in a more or less similar way. The majority of meta-analyses also discussed pedagogical implications drawn on the results or suggested advancement in either theory or policy. None of the meta-analyses has attempted alternative explanations for their obtained results and only about half of the meta-analyses addressed the limitation of their reviews.

# Is there a correlation between publication year and transparency score?

To understand if the CALL discipline has changed or even improved the level of transparency as more and more meta-analyses were conducted, we carried out a correlation analysis between publication year and the overall transparency score. We hypothesized that more recent meta-analyses would be more complete and transparent in their reports compared to prior ones because guidelines, resources books, and publshed meta-analyses are becoming more readily available and mature as useful references for meta-analysts. We tested this hypothesis using one-talied Spearman rank-order correlation and the results showed that, contrary to expectations, there is essentially no association between the year of publication and level of transparency ($r_s = .11$). This finding varies only slightly when the transparency score for each of the sections is considered separately: methods ($r_s = .27$), literature search ($r_s = -.12$),

**Table 27.8**  Percentages of meta-analysis papers (n = 13) reporting in discussion and conclusion section.

| Item reported | Yes | No |
|---|---|---|
| 14. Statement of major findings | 100 | 0.0 |
| 15. General limitations | 53.8 | 46.2 |
| 16. Consideration of alternative explanations for observed results | 0.0 | 100 |
| 17. Implications and interpretation for theory, policy, or practice | 92.3 | 7.7 |

results ($r_s$ = .16) and discussion and conclusion ($r_s$ = .19). Perhaps over time as more meta-analyses are conducted a relationship will emerge, but with the limited number of studies conducted within this short timespan, a relationship between time and transparancy is not yet evident.

## Discussion

We have reviewed 13 meta-analyses in CALL and evaulated their methodological rigor of reporting in terms of the extent to which the meta-analysts transparently reported findings and research procedures based on a 17-item evaluation rubric across different meta-analytic procedures that are important for examining methdological rigor and replicability. We also conducted further analysis on possible relationships between the level of transparnecy and publication year that would contribute or are associated with it. However, no clear relationship between publication years and transparency scores was found. In the following, we summarized the results by focusing on areas in which less than 60% of our sampled meta-analyses reported information, as they need more improvement.

In the "research questions and the literature search strategies" section, although a variety of searching strategies were handy, most meta-analysts still relied heavily on electronic databases (69.2%) as the major strategy of seaching for eligible studies. Since the included studies have to form a representative body of the research, diverse search strategies should be attempted to retrieve as many studies as possible (Ahn et al. 2012; Cooper, Hedges, and Valentine 2009). We especially recommend reference list and citation search; the former is readily available in a primary study while the latter provides additional sources of studies (such as those from Google scholar) that might deal with a similar topic and hence the possiblity of locating potential eligible studies. Another weakness that needs to be improved is the keywords used to enter databases and registries. Less than half of the studies provided the keywords. Specified key terms to locate potential studies are important information to judge the rigor and representativess of the retrieved body and for replication purposes.

"Methods" is the section that we found great improvement was needed. Although the majority of studies reported the independent and dependent variables, less than half of the studies provided conceptual/operational definitions for them. An operational definition reflects the construct it defines and measures and can vary from study to study. Operational definitions also delimit the scope the results can be generalized. It is therefore indispensable information to be provided in the report. A lack of transparency in the reporting of inter-coder reliabilty and how coders resolved inconsistency is also observed in the body of meta-analyses that we sampled. Meta-analyses demand consistent and valid coding before the coders go through sophisticated analytic procedures. This is especially true for high-inference items. Inconsistent or invalid codings can render the results questionable.

About two-thirds of our studies failed to report such information, which leaves us to question their results. A very high percent of the meta-analyses sampled provided a table or graph to present the effect size; however, only two studeis provided the rationale for selecting specific moderators. Moderators played an important role in explaining the relationship between two variables, and the choice of moderators has to be justified from either the theoretical or practice perspectives so that the results of the moderator analysis could inform the generalizabilty of the meta-analysis and be used to examine if the evidence suggested is consistent with what is really practiced (Ahn et al. 2012).

"Discussion and conclusion" is the section that demands least improvement. All studies in our sample reported the general findings from which pedagogical and theoretical implications were drawn. A little bit more than half discussed the limitation of their studies. However, none of the studies attempted alternative explanations for observed results. Methdological rigor and generalizability of the results of a meta-analysis, to some extent, were determined or limited by the way a meta-analysis was conducted. When discussing the results, alternative explanations taking into consideration the limitations and inherent bias in the primary studies might help uncover the true picture of certain interventions (Ahn et al. 2012).

# Conclusion

In this chapter, we provide a brief introduction of meta-analysis as a way of systematic research synthesis and examine the transparency, or methodological rigor of 13 CALL meta-analytic reports. Through a 17-item checklist, we found the existing CALL meta-analyses may be slightly better than those reported in Aytug et al. (2012) in the field of industrial organizational psychology and organizational behavior. When we looked into the differences of the CALL reports, their development of rigor did not show a clear relationship as time goes. Several pitfalls are obvious when we look into this body of the literature. Key words for searching in the literature were not provided in some of the CALL reports, whereas others either did not provide the rationale or definitions of their chosen moderator factors, or not specify study features. Others did not mention how they coded the features across the primary studies as to whether more than one coder was involved in the analysis process, naturally no inter-rater reliability available.

These obvious pitfalls should be avoided by future CALL meta-analysts about potential threats to methodological rigor of conducting meta-analyses. Like most empirical studies, there is always the issue of garbage-in-garbage-out: when the included primary studies applied poor research methods and yielded unreliable findings, a meta-analysis has no means to correct those weaknesses while pooling them with other studies together. This leaves researchers a huge challenge when making a judgment on whether to include particular studies or not. When we wrote this chapter, we decided to include them all as long as it was a meta-analysis since there were not many published in the field of CALL. Future researchers can avoid such a limitation in this chapter by figuring out precise inclusion criteria. Furthermore, although meta-analyses pool evidence from various primary studies and sometimes provide new insights different from the original studies, caveats need to be raised as the post hoc nature of meta-analysis does not allow stretching its conclusion too far away from the group of primary studies the meta-analyst has tried to analyze and gauge.

Claiming replication of previous research is a common way in scientific inquiry, Porte (2013) encourages CALL scholars to pursue the line by stating: "Replication provides the cement between the bricks of our research endeavors and ensures that the essential connection between past research and present is made in a way that favors a systematic, coherent integration of existing and new knowledge" (13). Plonsky (2012) links meta-analysis to replication and an increase of generalizability. With higher degrees of transparency in reporting meta-analyses, future researchers may be better able to replicate more CALL meta-analyses when a greater number of empirical studies are available. These encourage CALL researchers to pursue more and better meta-analyses for the field.

# Appendix

**Essential items coded for each CALL meta-analysis (mainly out of Aytug et al. 2012, 107–108)**

| *Item* | *Code* |
|---|---|
| **Descriptive information and research question (RQ)** | |
| 1. Effect size metric(s) used | Open-ended |
| 2. Effect size averaging and weighting method(s) Hunter-Schmidt, Hedges-Olkin, p values, other | |
| 3. Clear statement of the research question | Y/N |
| **Literature search (LS)** | |
| 4. Reference and citation databases searched | |
| Electronic database | Y/Searched, but specific databases are not listed/N |
| Journal hand search | Y/Searched, but specific journals are not listed/N |
| Reference list | Y/N |
| Citation search | Y/N |
| Conference programs | Y/Searched, but the list of conference programs is not |
| provided/N Personal contacts | Y/N |
| Websites/internet | Y/Searched, but the list of websites is not provided/N |
| Other | Open-ended |
| 5. Types of studies included in the review | |
| Journal articles | Y/N |
| Book chapter | Y/N |
| Book | Y/N |
| Dissertations/theses | Y/N |
| Conference abstracts | Y/N |
| Government report | Y/N |
| Company report | Y/N |
| Unpublished—not further specified | Y/N |
| Other | Open-ended |
| 6. Keywords used to enter databases and registries | Y/Some of them are provided/N |
| **Methods** | |
| 7. Independent and dependent variables of interest | Y/N |
| 8. Operational definitions of variables | Y/Some of them are provided/N |
| 9. Reporting of intercoder reliability (if more than 1 coder) | Y/N |
| 10. Method of resolving disagreements (if more than 1 coder) | Y/N |
| 11. Did the study report what study features were coded? | Y/N |
| **Results** | |
| 12. Tabular or graphic display of overall estimate | Y/N |
| 13. Rationale for the selection of moderators provided? | Y/N |

| Item | Code |
|------|------|
| **Discussion/Conclusion** | |
| 14. Statement of major findings | Y/N |
| 15. General limitations | Y/N |
| 16. Consideration of alternative explanations for observed results | Y/N |
| 17. Implications and interpretation for theory, policy, or practice | Y/N |

Note: Y Yes; N No.

# REFERENCES

Ahn, Soyeon, Allison J. Ames, and Nicholas D. Myers. 2012. "A Review of Meta-analyses in Education: Methodological Strengths and Weaknesses." *Review of Educational Research*, 82, no. 4: 436–476.

Aytug, Zeynep G., Hannah R. Rothstein, Wencang Zhou, and Mary C. Kern. 2012. "Revealed or Concealed? Transparency of Procedures, Decisions, and Judgment Calls in Meta-analyses."*Organizational Research Methods*, 15: 103–133.

Cooper, Harris. 2010. *Research Synthesis and Meta-analysis: A Step-by-step Approach*, 4th ed. New York: Sage.

Cooper, Harris, Larry V. Hedges, and Jeffrey C. Valentine. 2009. *The Handbook of Research Synthesis and Meta-Analysis*, 2nd ed. New York: Russell Sage Foundation.

Egger, Mattias, Davey G. Smith, and A. N. Phillips. 1997. "Meta-analysis: Principles and Procedures." *British Medical Journal*, 315, no. 7121: 1533–1537.

Felix, Unix. 2005. "What do Meta-Analyses Tell us about CALL Effectiveness?" *ReCALL*, 17, no. 2: 269–288.

Glass, Gene V. 1976. "Primary, Secondary, and Meta-analysis of Research." *Educational Researcher*, 5: 3–8.

Kiili, Kristian. 2005. "Digital Game-based Learning: Towards an Experiential Gaming Model." *Internet and Higher Education*, 8: 13–24.

Li, Shaofeng, Natsuko Shintani, and Rod Ellis. 2012."Doing Meta-analysis in SLA: Practice, Choices, and Standards." *Contemporary Foreign Language Studies*, 384/12: 1–17.

Lipsey, Mark W., and David B. Wilson. 1993. "The Efficacy of Psychological, Educational, and Behavioral Treatment: Confirmation from Meta-analysis." *American Psychologist*, 48, no. 12: 1181–1209.

Lipsey, Mark W., and David B. Wilson. 2001. *Practical Meta-Analysis*. Thousand Oaks, CA: Sage.

Masgoret, A. M., and R. C. Gardner. 2003. "Attitudes, Motivation, and Second Language Learning: A Meta-analysis of Studies Conducted by Gardner and Associates." *Language learning*, 53, no. 1: 123–163.

Norris, John, and Lourdes Ortega. 2000. "Effectiveness of L2 Instruction: A Research Synthesis and Quantitative Meta-analysis." *Language Learning*, 50: 417–528.

Norris, John, and Lourdes Ortega, eds. 2006. *Synthesizing Research on Language Learning and Teaching*. Philadelphia, PA: John Benjamins.

Oswald, Fredrick L., and Luke Plonsky. 2010. "Meta-Analysis in Second Language Research: Choices and Challenges." *Annual Review of Applied Linguistics*, 30: 85–110.

Plonsky, Luke. 2011. "The Effectiveness of Second Language Strategy Instruction: A Meta-Analysis." *Language Learning*, 61, no. 4: 993–1038.

Plonsky, Luke. 2012. "Replication, Meta-Analysis, and Generalizability." In *Replication Research in Applied Linguistics*, edited by Graeme Porte, 116–132. Cambridge: Cambridge University Press.

Porte, Graeme. 2013. "Who Needs Replication?" *CALICO Journal*, 30, no. 1: 10–15.

Raffle, Holly. 2006. Assessment and Reporting of Intercoder Reliability in Published Meta-analyses Related to Preschool through Grade 12 education. PhD dissertation, Ohio University.

Tamin, Rana M., Robert M. Bernard, Eugene Borokhovski, Philip C. Abrami, and Richard F. Schmid, 2011."What Forty Years of Research Says About the Impact of Technology on Learning: A Second-Order Meta-Analysis and Validation Study." *Review of Educational Research*, 81, no. 1: 4–28.

## CALL meta-analyses coded in the chapter

Abraham, Lee B. 2008. "Computer-mediated Glosses in Second Language Reading Comprehension and Vocabulary Learning: A Meta-analysis." *Computer Assisted Language Learning*, 21, no. 3: 199–226.

Chang, Mei-Mei, and Mei-Chen Lin. 2013. "Strategy-oriented Web-based English Instruction – A Meta-analysis." *Australasian Journal of Educational Technology*, 29, no. 2: 203–216.

Chiu, Yi-Hui. 2013. "Computer-assisted Second Language Vocabulary Instruction: A Meta-analysis." *British Journal of Educational Technology*, 44: E52–E56.

Chiu, Yi-Hui, Wen-Kao Chian, and Reynolds Barry Lee. 2012. "The Relative Effectiveness of Digital Game-based Learning Types in English as a Foreign Language Setting: A Meta-analysis." *British Journal of Educational Technology*, 43: E104–E107.

Cobb, Tom, and Alex Boulton. 2015. "Classroom Applications of Corpus Analysis." In *Cambridge Handbook of Corpus Linguistics*, edited by Douglas Biber and Randi Reppen, 478–497. Cambridge: Cambridge University Press.

Grgurović, Maja, Carol A. Chapelle, and Mack C. Shelley. 2013. "A Meta-analysis of Effectiveness Studies on Computer Technology-supported Language Learning." *ReCALL*, 25, no. 2: 165–198.

Lin, Huifen. 2014. "Establishing an Empirical Link between Computer-mediated Communication (CMC) and SLA: A Meta-Analysis of the Research." *Language Learning & Technology*, 18, no. 3: 120–143.

Lin, Wei-Chen, Hung-Tzu Huang, and Hsien-Chin Liou. 2013. "Effects of Text-based SCMC on SLA: A Meta-analysis."*Language Learning & Technology*, 17, no. 2: 123–142.

Taylor, Alan M. 2006. "The Effects of CALL Versus Traditional L1 Glosses on L2 Reading Comprehension."*CALICO Journal*, 23, no. 2: 309–318.

Taylor, Alan M. 2009. "CALL-based Versus Paper-based Glosses: Is There a Difference in Reading Comprehension?"*CALICO Journal*, 27, no. 1: 147–160.

Taylor, Alan M.2013. "CALL versus Paper: In Which Context are L1 Glosses More Effective?"*CALICO Journal*, 30, no. 1: 63–81.

Yun, Jeehwan. 2011. "The Effects of Hypertext Glosses on L2 Vocabulary Acquisition: A Meta-analysis." *Computer Assisted Language Learning*, 24, no. 1: 39–58.

Zhao, Yong. 2003. "Recent Development in Technology and Language Learning: A Literature Review and Meta-analysis." *CALICO Journal*, 21, no. 1: 7–27.

# 28 Researching Technology-mediated Multimodal Interaction

## THIERRY CHANIER AND MARIE-NOËLLE LAMY

Language learners have access to a wide range of tools for communication and interaction through networks, where multiple options exist for creating meaning. This chapter introduces the study of such multimodal meaning-making for language learning. The study of meaning-making through the use of technology for mediation has been pursued since the technology became widespread. An overview of multimodality in interaction is offered in the introduction to a Special Issue of Semiotica by Stivers and Sidnell (2005); for multimodality in communication, see Kress (2010); for multimodality in classroom-based language learning, see Royce (2007) and Budach (2013); for a discussion of digital mediation see Jones and Hafner (2012), and for a summary about technology-mediated language learning see Hampel (2012). These sources provide a starting point for the investigation of multimodality in language learning, which is relatively recent in computer-assisted language learning (CALL) research. In view of the importance of such meaning-making resources for learning, this chapter introduces the meaning of "mode" and "multimodality" before introducing the research and theoretical issues in the study of multimodality in language learning. It then describes a corpus-based approach for studying multimodality in CALL, drawing attention to important methodological factors such as transcription that come into play in conducting such research.

## Multimodality in online learning

During online communication in a second language (L2), learners orchestrate various resources including language, in its written and spoken forms, as well as images, colors, movements, and sounds. Responding to even a simple written post requires at minimum two such resources: the linguistic mode, that is, the written language, and the visual mode, which involves the choice of fonts and the organization of spaces on the screen. In addition to language and image, online tools such as a floating magnifier facilitates the understanding not only of written communication but also of pictures. In online shops such tools can be used to reveal enlargeable images of the product to allow the shopper to see products in greater detail. The floating magnifier tool in itself has no meaning but the enlarged image or written text probably does. For language learners, the floating magnifier may be used to support a vocabulary or grammatical gloss, and an image may carry a cultural reference. The

*The Handbook of Technology and Second Language Teaching and Learning*, First Edition.
Edited by Carol A. Chapelle and Shannon Sauro.
© 2017 John Wiley & Sons, Inc. Published 2020 by John Wiley & Sons, Inc.

physical material also includes keys to be pressed for text creation, screens to be tapped, pads to be stroked or hotspots to be clicked for opening up video or audio channels. In computer-mediated interactive language learning (henceforth CMILL), learning is affected by the resources that are available to learners and their use. Therefore, the design of learning activities and research on their use needs to take into account of the materiality of the modes available to learners and how they are used to create meaning multimodally (Lamy 2012a).

## *What are modes?*

Mode in linguistics refers to the resources used to express meaning. For example, Kress and van Leeuwen (2001) showed that readers make sense out of a page of a newspaper by combining their understanding of the linguistic content (linguistic mode), with their interpretation of the layout and photos or cartoons (visual mode). In other words, language users combine semiotic resources to convey messages through simultaneous realization of linguistic and non-linguistic modes in printed media. In CMILL, the resources to be co-orchestrated by participants are made up of a greater variety of modes than those in print media or audio-video alone. CMILL is carried out through the use of modes, which are accessed and manipulated with tools to carry out certain learning objectives. The integration of these three aspects of communication makes up modality. The relationships between the three are illustrated in Table 28.1.

**Table 28.1** Modality as a set of relationships among objectives, tools, and modes in CMILL. Adapted from Lamy (2012b).

| *Main CMILL objectives facilitated* | *Tools* | *Modes* |
|---|---|---|
| Information seeking (preliminary to engagement with tasks or people) | Screens | Dual modes: linguistic (written) and visual |
| Accessing and interacting with materials and people | Screens (conventional, tactile), pads, microphones, speakers | Multiple modes: linguistic (written, sometimes spoken), visual, kinetic, aural if music is involved) |
| Reflective activities (revisiting tutorials and conversations), sharing audio-visual material | Recording and screen capture tools | Multiple modes: linguistic (written and spoken) |
| Communication and interaction (e.g., Like button); create tele-presence; help with turn-taking (e.g., raised-hand button) | Hot buttons | Multiple modes: linguistic (written and spoken), visual, kinetic |
| Written exchanges; peer collaboration; feedback; commenting; group bonding | Asynchronous sending/ receiving channels; synchronous messaging channels | Mainly written linguistic mode, with elements of visual mode |
| Oral communication and interaction; collaborative work; feedback; group bonding | Webconferencing | Multiple modes: linguistic (spoken and some written), visual, kinetic |

The objectives refer to the types of communication and learning activities that the students engage in such as information seeking as part of a communication task, reflection on their past work, and peer collaboration to produce a written product. The tools are the software and hardware configured in a way that allows learners to use them to accomplish learning objectives. These tools are socially-shaped and culturally-constructed to provide access to the modes of communication. Kress (2010) explains the connection between tools and modes, by noting, for example, that an image shows the world and a written text tells the world. Therefore modes offer "distinctive ways of representing the world" (96). So while a tool may borrow a representation from the world (a cursor may be materialized on screen as a hand or a pair of scissors) the tool merely indicates by this that its function is to grab or to cut. Its function is not to represent hands or scissors to the user. Materialized through the use of tools, modes combine together to facilitate meaning-making in learning. Thus we can define modality as the relationship between tools and modes.

## What is multimodality?

Multimodality is the complex relationship that develops between multiple tools and modes when they are co-deployed in different combinations, in learning situations to work toward particular objectives. In online audio-visual environments the complex meaning-making (or semiotic) possibilities that open up to language learners are materialized through hardware and software. New meanings emerge in learning situations through learners' physical relationship to tools (sometimes called embodiment), through participants' body language on screen (another form of embodiment), through learners' engagement with still and moving images, with sounds, and with each other's language outputs. All of this is experienced in simultaneous integration or, as some multimodality researchers put it, co-orchestration.

Another way of expressing this integration is by examining the notion of mediation. Mediation is always present in any kind of human interaction, including multimodal ones. The separate meaning-making resources of mediation in online learning are illustrated in Figure 28.1 as three circles, labeled A, B and C. Circle A represents the resources available through the participants' physical bodies. Circle B represents the resources that are available through the technology. Circle C symbolizes the meaning-making resources available through language.

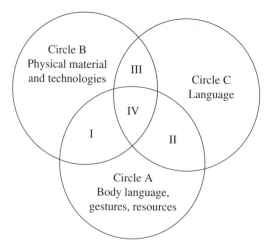

**Figure 28.1**   Schematic diagram showing components Mediation in CMILL.

In any situation of meaning-making, these separate components of mediation form intersecting areas (shown in the figure with Roman numerals). In offline meaning-making, only two types of resources are present: for instance when we hail friends across a coffee-bar, we are making meaning with our smiling face, our waving arm, and our cheerful call of their name (represented by Area II, where Circles C and A intersect, that is, where language and body language meet). Language is often part of meaning-making, but Area I, at the intersection of Circles A and B, represents instances when language is not involved. For example, a piano tuner using auditory senses and hands (Circle A) to tune a piano (Circle B) would create meaning without language. Finally, an example of Area III might be two computers programmed to communicate with each other.

In online multimodality, the three components intersect: for example when we edit our photos and upload them to a social network site, we are working mainly with our hands and eyes (resources in Circle A), with our tablet/phone/laptop (resources in Circle B), with the language of our editing suite's instructions, and with our own language (resources in Circle C) to create captions and label albums. In addition if we interact with others (for example by engaging with them in "commenting" on the photographic network) we again bring in resources from Circle C. Our online interaction is thus mediated through technology, through our own body and through language (a triple overlap represented by Area IV in the middle of the figure). Area IV is therefore the space where phenomena of interest to researchers in multimodality within CMILL reside.

## Research on multimodality in online learning

Research on multimodality examines two questions: "What aspect of the learning is mediated through the technology?" and "How is the learning situation experienced, especially in terms of affect?" Erben (1999) showed participants creating new discursive practices by altering the content of their exchanges (through "reducing" and "amplifying" meanings) as they strove to find workaround responses to what they experienced as an unwieldy communication platform. His findings made it clear that the "what" of communication was affected, as participants adapted to the crudeness of the mediation tools at their disposal at the time. On the other hand, Goodfellow et al. (1996) as well as McAndrew, Foubister, and Mayes (1996) reported on the "how," showing that video-based learning interactions were experienced as stressful, although at the same time video was seen by learners as motivational.

These two lines of investigation have continued to structure much CMILL research in recent years. First, the issue of the "what" needs to be thoroughly understood if communication distortion/breakdown is to be avoided and also, more positively, if the communicative affordances of the multimodal environment are to be maximized. In the decades that followed the pioneering studies above, scholars continued to explore many aspects of mediation as reflected in several of the articles on multimodal learning in *ReCALL 25* (2013) and elsewhere. For example, Codreanu and Celik (2013) found that tool management influenced the content of the learning while Satar (2013) analyzed the mediating effects of gaze, and Wigham and Chanier (2013a, 2013b) studied the mediation of the learning through digital gestures in SecondLife. Dooly and Sadler (2013) looked at how SecondLife mediated the transfer of knowledge from theory to practice, and Monteiro (2014) studied video-mediated corrective feedback. As Wang and Chen pointed out in 2012, "in-depth research is needed to establish the extent to which visual cues mediated through videoconferencing tools are important to collaborative language learning. Such research is more urgently needed now than it was 5 years ago as broadband technology has already made good quality of video transmission a reality" (325). A wider discussion of what tools and affordances best mediate learning in CMILL can be found in Hampel (2014) and in the domain of synthetic worlds, a review of mediational tools appears in Schwienhorst (2002). Finally, Reinhardt and Sykes' (2014) edited issue on game-informed L2 teaching and learning.

The second line of research, centering on "how" the learning situation is experienced, that is, on affect, has produced literature on psychological variables. These range across anxiety, anger, regret, desire and poor self-esteem. An early study of Web use (Yang 2001) identified anxiety as a factor connected to cognitive overload. However, other anxiogenic factors in language interaction on platforms did not come to the fore until the late 2000s, with work by Hurd (2007), de los Arcos (2009), de los Arcos et al. (2009), Coryell and Clark (2009), Develotte, Guichon, and Vincent's (2010) analysis of gaze in desktop conferencing from a socio-affective viewpoint and Tayebinik's and Puteh's (2012) literature review article on self-esteem.

Scholars whose work has included both what and how of learning during the last decade are Wang and to a lesser extent her co-authors Chen and Levy. They studied desktop videoconferencing, which they later called "synchronous cyber face-to-face" from several angles: participants' perceptions of the benefits of tools (Wang 2004), focus on form in task completion (Wang 2006), task design (Wang 2007), teacher training (Wang et al. 2010), collaboration (Wang and Chen 2012) and the question of how principles of instructed language learning can be applied in these environments (Chen and Wang 2008). They found that potential learning benefits could arise in multimodal environments provided tools were used in a way that was balanced and appropriate to pedagogies, to technologies, and to audiences. They also found potential learning losses due to synchrony nerves and anxiety (including among teachers). There are indications that the affect-oriented strand of multi-modality research in CMILL is a continuing concern of scholars.

## Theoretical underpinnings

Few scholars of multimodality in language learning ground their work theoretically except to claim an affiliation to "sociocultural approaches." Among those who identify a theoretical basis for their work, the literature is broadly divided into those using technoliteracy frame-works and those relying on semiotic theories. In the former category, the aim is to investigate obstacles and facilitators in the development of learner competence with the platforms and tools, while the latter are more interested in understanding how learners orchestrate meanings mediated to them through a variety of modes in the online situation.

On the one hand the technoliteracy-oriented CMILL community has long insisted that task design is key and should closely match the communicative affordances of the environments. The practical consequences of this are outlined by Hampel (2014) "Tasks need to be appropriate to the environment, and it is crucial that activities that make use of digital environments take account of their functionalities and affordances" (18). Others have also stressed the centrality of pedagogy and task design, with studies focusing on audiographic conferencing; webcam-assisted conferencing; SecondLife; and processing overload. For an overview on multimodality research and literacy in CMILL, see Ho, Nelson, and Müller-Wittig (2011).

On the other hand, CMILL scholars using social-semiotic theories have responded to a different priority: the need to understand a learner's meaning-making in multimodal situations. One seminal text explaining how social semiotics can account for multimodal communication is Kress (2010). However critics have complained about what they see as the over-prominent role played by language in Systemic Functional Linguistics, a theory that Kress and others (O'Halloran and Smith 2011) consider to be core to the shaping of social-semiotic theories. These critics have argued that for online language-learning settings, it is necessary to further root social-semiotic analysis in notions of place and embodiment. Among these scholars some concentrate on the relationship of the body with the physical environment of the virtual experience (Jones 2004; Lamy 2012a), others on silence and gaze (Stickler et al. 2007; Develotte et al. 2010), and others yet on social presence (Dahlberg and Bagga-Gupta 2011, 2013; Lamy and Flewitt 2011). However an unresolved issue in the social-semiotic analysis of CMILL exchanges remains that of their linguistic component, and of how to transcend language-based methods such as discourse analysis (Sindoni 2013) or conversational analysis, so as to fully recognize their multimodal dynamics.

Given that technology has now opened up possibilities for fully-documented, accurate, and exhaustive capture of multimodal exchanges, both the technoliteracy and the social semiotics research communities should be able to establish a synergistic relationship between their theories and the empirical data that they collect. However the complexity of multimodal environments, and the sophistication of the tools that can capture it, combine to create massive datasets, and not all researchers need all data. So the choice of an appropriate window of observation for each particular project and the selection of relevant categories of data for collection, storage, and analysis are key.

# The need to analyze multimodal data in education

The difficulties of collecting and handling online multimodal data have been problematized in non-educational fields. See for example Smith et al. (2011). Also, for an overview of almost two decades of semiotics-based investigation of multimodal data, see O'Halloran and Smith (2011) and O'Halloran et al. (2012). In contrast, the CMILL literature provides few methodological publications focusing on the treatment of multimodal data in language-learning contexts online. An article entitled "What are multimodal data and transcription?" applied to education more generally (Flewitt et al. 2009) pointed to this gap in the field, and will serve as our introduction the problems of working with multimodal data. "Drawing on findings from across a number of disciplines and research fields including applied linguistics, visual ethnography, symbolic representation and computer-mediated communication" (53), the authors outline issues such as the transcription, description, and analysis of multimodal texts and, before all else, the definition of a unit of analysis for research. They state that in dynamic texts (i.e., conversations) "units of transcription are usually measured as turns of speech, but it is questionable whether this convention is useful for multimodal analysis" (47). Because other modes come into play, Flewitt et al. suggest either linking measurement to the visual mode and using visual frames as units or timeframes can provide definitions for the unit for analysis.

However, kinesics data (how the on-screen moves of the artifacts are understood), proxemics (how distant participants "feel" they are to one another), or postural, gestural, and gaze elements should also be included. The authors conclude that "the representation of the complex simultaneity of different modes and their different structure and materiality— has not been resolved in transcription, nor have satisfactory ways as yet been found to combine the spatial, the visual and the temporal within one system" (47). Researchers can negotiate these difficulties by making pragmatic decisions about priorities for recording/ transcribing, depending on the object of the research, but in any case they need to be aware that fully represented multimodal transcriptions may be "illegible," which outweighs the advantage of their descriptive accuracy. Finally, Flewitt et al. discuss examples from various researchers prioritizing different semiotic components but they again conclude that all of these representations "pose significant disadvantages for research dissemination, where the dominant media are still printed, written or visual formats" (52). This work has important implications for research-oriented corpus-building (see Dooly and Hauck 2012).

# Methodology for developing CMILL research

The need to investigate multimodal interactions in online language learning means that studies should examine situations where participants (learners, teachers, natives, etc.) are involved in activities which span over several weeks, including several hours a week. The coverage of the data collected for analysis is a key factor. This is one of the reasons for adopting a corpus-based approach for systematically gathering, transcribing and coding large amounts of longitudinal multimodal data. Our corpus-based approach is intended to overcome the limitations of the approach to research introduced by Flewitt et al. (2009), which introduces different, incompatible ways of collecting, organizing, and analyzing data. Our corpus-based methodological approach which navigates from transcription to coding and analysis suggests a compatible way to support multiple analyses in addition to sharing data among researchers.

## *Motivations for a corpus-based approach*

This corpus-based approach seeks to address a range of scientific criteria that apply to research on second language acquisition (Mackey and Gass 2005) such as validity (Do the data allow for meaningful interpretations? Is the scope of relevance of the results clear not only to our sample but to other contexts?), and reliability (Is the manner of data collection, organization, and analysis sufficiently consistent to allow for comparable results to be obtained by other researchers?). We developed a corpus-based approach based on our experience initiated in 2005 with the concept of LEarning and TEaching Corpus (LETEC) in online multimodal learning situations. It combines work on speech corpora related to first language acquisition and computer-mediated communication (CMC) corpora and its model, which encompasses multimodal interactions. It addresses issues of meaningfulness and consistency by fitting with the expectations and conceptual frameworks of researchers in applied linguistics in addition to encompassing quality criteria for gathering and analyzing data.

### *The experience of the language acquisition community*

Researchers investigating interaction through spoken language have needs for data that are similar to those of CMILL researchers. For example, Jenks (2011, 71), who specializes in the topic of transcribing speech and interaction, reminds us this overlap:

> In face-to-face another types of multimodal interaction, non-verbal conduct (e.g. gaze, body, posture, pointing and nodding) is equally as important, prevalent, and multifunctional, as stress, intonation, and voice amplitude.

In language acquisition, researchers have to start by defining what kinds of observations and measures will best help capture the development process over time. Generally interactions need to be captured in authentic contexts rather than in laboratory conditions. For example, decisions have to be made, when studying discourse addressed by adults to children (i.e., Child Directed Speech), about the number of subjects to be studied in order to fulfill scientific criteria, about the type of situations in natural settings, the length of every window of observation (What time of the day? What child activity? Should the researcher be present or absent?). Choices need to be made concerning the repetition of the observations. Hoff (2012) provides a good introduction to these issues. Opportunities and pitfalls have been extensively studied over time by the language acquisition community. All these research protocols may illuminate the way we can develop multimodal CALL research in informal settings.

The longstanding tradition of building research on corpora illustrates the benefits CMILL may expect when following a similar route. Large repositories of corpora have been built over time by an international set of researchers following a unique methodology such as CHILDES on first language acquisition (MacWhinney 2000). The research planning is presented as a three-step process (O'Donnell cited in Segouat et al. 2010), which we synthesize as: (1) May I find appropriate data in existing corpora, or when extracting parts of different corpora? (2) What if I recombined and rearranged them with a different perspective in mind? (3) I will consider developing a new corpus if (and only if) answers to the two previous questions are negative. This perception of research as a cumulative process, and of the analysis as a cyclical one, with researchers reconsidering previous data, mixing them with new data, measuring things differently in accordance with new theoretical frameworks, is a reality in language acquisition studies, and more generally in spoken corpora. A good illustration is presented in (Liègeois 2014) around the *Phonologie du Français Contemporain* (PFC) corpus which gathered together a community of international researchers over 15 years to pave the way for fundamental discussions about the nature of language acquisition.

## Quality criteria for CMILL corpora

Since research questions in CMILL are always connected to learning situations, data collection will not only refer to multimodal interactions, listed in the previous section. It will also encompass: (1) the learning situation, (2) the research protocol, and (3) the permissions for access. The learning situation refers to the learning design if it is in a formal situation, and to other elements of the context if it is in an informal situation. It also refers to all the necessary information about the participants (e.g., learners and teachers) biographical and sociological information, level of expertise not only with respect to language but also with the technological environment, and so on. The research protocol refers to questionnaires, participants' interviews, methodology for data collection and coding, and so on. The permissions for access specifies how data have been collected (how the question of ethics and rights have been taken care of? It provides the consent form used, and explains the anonymization process on raw data), and how the corpus contents can be freely used by other researchers.

In order to become a scientific object of investigation a corpus has to meet several quality criteria: systematic collection (Were the data collected systematically in view of the research phenomena at stake? Is the coverage representative?); coherent data organization: coherence for packaging the various parts of the corpus, interlinking them (e.g., video files with transcriptions), coherence when coding and transcribing; data longevity, including a short-term window in order to be able to use several types of analysis tools and collect data in nonproprietary formats; and a middle-term window in order to deposit the data, share them, and store them in an archive; human readability, including information allowing researchers who did not participate in the experiment to work with the corpus; machine readability for data storage and, beforehand, for analysis purposes; the so-called OpenData criteria, related not only to the aforementioned permissions, but also to the guarantee of continuing access to the internet and to efficient identification of the corpus on Web search, as described by Chanier and Wigham (2016).

These criteria aim at the issues of validity and reliability by striving to make clear what the corpus represents and how usable it is for the purpose of analysis. Representativeness relates not only to the systematic way of collecting data, but also to the way its scope has been delineated (Baude et al. 2006). All these kinds of data build up what we called a LETEC corpus (Chanier and Wigham, 2016; Reffay, Betbeder, and Chanier 2012; see the Mulce corpora repository, 2013, from which 50 corpora can be downloaded). The LETEC contains not only data, but also their detailed metadata which describe: conditions of data collection, aggregation, organization, coding, general information about the learning situation, about the technological environment, and so on. These elements of information provide a basis for a meaningful analysis.

## Conceptualization of multimodal acts

A critical aspect of making research interpretable across different projects is to have a scheme for classifying and analyzing the many different types of multimodal data. The analytic scheme needs to capture certain types of relevant actions performed and/or perceived by CMILL participants within a given space. Beißwenger et al. (2014) call the site of interactions the "interaction space" (henceforth IS), which is an abstract concept temporally situated at the point when interactions occur online. The IS is defined by the properties of the set of environments used by the participants. Participants in the same IS can interact (but do not necessarily do so, cf. lurkers). They interact through input devices mainly producing visual or oral signals. Hence when participants cannot hear or see other participants' actions, they are not in the same IS. Within a variety of different ISs, multiple types of multimodal acts have been studied in various research projects, from data collected and organized in LETEC corpora. All such acts can be classified as either verbal or non-verbal acts (cf. figure 28.2).

Verbal acts, such as those studied by corpus linguistics, are based on textual and oral modes. In synthetic worlds such as SecondLife, every participant can choose to use audio and textchat in order to publicly communicate with other participants located close to her/his avatar. S/he can also decide to communicate with people not co-present (Wigham and Chanier 2013a, §2.1). For the sake of simplicity, we will assume that audio and textchat can be heard or read by participants in the same location. When studying interactions between various kinds of acts, it is useful to distinguish between a verbal act which is realized as an en bloc message and an adaptive one. Once a textchat message has been sent to a server, it appears to the other participants as a non-modifiable piece of language (it becomes a chat turn and has lost any indication of the way it had been planned by its author before being sent). On the contrary, a participant's utterance (e.g., in an audio chat act) can be planned, then modified in the heat of the interaction while taking into account other acts occurring in other modalities of communication (Wigham and Chanier 2013b).

As regards non-verbal acts, a great deal of attention is paid in social semiotics and in CALL research to acts related to the body, whether generated by actual human body (mediated through webcams) or by avatars in synthetic worlds. Wigham and Chanier (2013a) presented a classification of such acts (for another viewpoint see Shih 2014): proxemics, kinesics (which includes gaze, posture, and gestures), and appearance. Another type of non-verbal derives from actions in groupware. These share-edited tools, such as word processor, concept map, whiteboard can be integrated within wider environments for example, audiographic, or used besides video conference environments. They have been largely developed and studied by the computer-supported collaborative learning (CSCL) community (Dyke et al. 2011). Within these environments knowledge is collaboratively built and negotiated with interaction switching between non-verbal acts and verbal acts (Ciekanski and Chanier 2008).

Lastly we will consider non-verbal acts based on the use of icons. A first type of iconic tool is specifically oriented toward conversation management: such tools ease the turn-taking (icon raised hand), reduce overlap, restrain talkative participants, so as to encourage the more reserved ones to take the floor; they allow quick decisions and clarifications to be made (voting yes/no); they focus on technical aspects without interrupting the conversation flow (icons talk-louder, talk-more softly) or they mediate social support (clapping icon). The second type of iconic tool displays signs of participants' presence, for example icons show when a participant enters or leaves the interaction space, or is momentarily absent.

## From transcription and coding to analysis

The scheme for classifying multimodal acts in CMILL situations provides a conceptual framework for categorizing multimodal data in CMILL, but to carry out research, the data also need to be transcribed so they can be analyzed. A transcription is a textual version of material originally available in a non-textual (or non-exclusively textual) medium. It is generally considered as a biased, and reduced version of reality (Flewitt et al. 2009; Rowe 2012) that the researcher wants to study, or, more precisely, not of reality but of the data which have been collected. One may wonder whether this weakness primarily arise from the data collection itself. For example, on the one hand, linguistic and paralinguistic features of a spoken interaction can be precisely transcribed. But, on the other, an audio file captures only a limited part of the interaction: who is the exact addressee of a speech turn? What is the surrounding context? A video recording will bring much more information. However, in face-to-face situations, if a single camera is recording, important alternative perspectives may be missed. The "reality" of online multimodal interaction may be easier to capture than the face-to-face one. Actually a video-screen capture with audio-recording will accurately record the online context and participants' actions. It will not render the context and the action of an individual participant, but the shared context of all the participants. What is recorded into the video-screen capture is the common ground on which participants interact.

### The need for shared transcription conventions

If individual studies are to build upon a common knowledge base, researchers need to be able to examine data across studies. For example, Sindoni (2013) studied participants' use of modalities in (non-educational) online environments that integrate audio, video, and text chat. She focused on what she termed "mode-switching," when a participant moves from speech to writing or the other way round. When analyzing transcriptions of video-screen online conversations, she observed that participants could be classified according to their preferred interaction mode (oral or written). She also observed that "[a]s anticipated, both speakers and writers, generally carry the interaction forward without mode-switching. This was observed in the whole video corpus" (Sindoni, 2013, §2.3.5). Hence she concluded that "those who talked did not write, and those who wrote did not talk. Turn-taking adheres to each mode."

In several CMILL situations that we studied, we had similar research questions. When analyzing data assembled in LETEC corpora such as Copéas or Archi21 (Mulce repository 2013), we observed that learners had a preferred mode of expression (oral or written), at least those at beginner level (Vetter and Chanier 2006). In contrast with Sindoni (2013), analyses of audiographic and 3D environments show that learners were mode-switchers (even modality-switchers). Choices of mode/modality depended on the nature of the task, and on the tutor's behavior (see Wigham and Chanier 2013b).

At this stage, one may expect that scientific discussions could take place between researchers studying online interactions, to debate contradictions, fine differentiations of situations, tasks, and so on. In order to allow this, data from the different approaches need to be accessible in standard formats, with publications clearly relating to data and data analyses, and explicit information given about the format of the transcriptions, their code, and transcription alignments with video. However Sindoni's data are not available. The inability to accumulate findings across CMILL studies or to contrast data from one study with other examples, available in open-access formats, is still holding back the scientific advancement of the CALL field. Overcoming these limitations will require researchers' development of common guidelines for transcription, coding, and analysis.

## Transcription, coding, and analysis

Jenks (2011, 5) describes the main functions of transcription as the following: (1) represent; (2) assist; (3) disseminate and (4) verify. Transcription seeks to represent the interaction, that is, a multimodal discourse which it would have been impossible to analyze in its "live" state. Transcription assists the analysis which will be made of the data. Henceforth this research depends on the coding of interaction, whether this code will be compatible with analysis tools. Dissemination refers to the repeated process of analysis, either by the data compiler when s/he plans to publish several articles out of her/his corpus, or by the community. This function is essential to conform to the principle of rigor in scientific investigation (Smith, et al. 2011, 377):

> The fact of being able to store, retrieve, share, interrogate and represent in a variety of ways [...] the results of one's analysis means that a semiotician can conduct a variety of analyses, and then explore the range of such analyses [...]. Different analyses and perspectives upon analysis are encouraged, so that an analyst may produce multiple interpretations of a text.

The last function of transcription refers to the need of the academic community to know, as Jenks (2011, 5) put it, "whether any given claim or observation made is demonstrably relevant to the interactants and interaction represented in the transcript." Checking this claim requires procedures for estimating the level of agreement between transcribers.

The first function, representation, requires deliberation because transcription represents only a partial view of interaction corresponding to phenomena the researcher wants to examine. Obviously, the richness of multimodal acts, as sketched in Figure 28.2, cannot be simultaneously transcribed to represent all of the multimodal perspectives captured through the video.[1] It is therefore important to adopt a methodological approach when transcribing and coding by taking into account the decision steps enumerated in Table 28.2.

The first step (first line of Table 28.2) is to choose appropriate software for integrating video-screen capture and transcription layers of verbal and non-verbal acts for every participant. The aim is to appreciate whether these products and events support L2 language development. Co-occurrence of these modes could be compared to a concert performance, and the transcription task to writing a music score, where all the instruments/modes can be read and interpreted after having been aligned (cf. time priority, step 3 in Table 28.2). Once the layout of

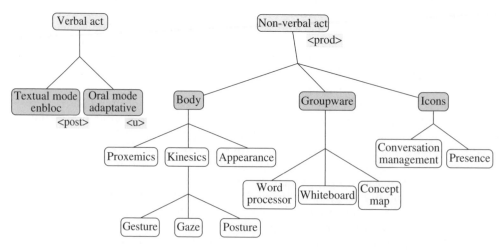

**Figure 28.2**   Multimodal acts as collected and studied within Mulce corpora repository (2013).

**Table 28.2** Decision steps with their respective main features and comments for transcription and coding.

| Decision steps | Main features | Comments |
|---|---|---|
| 1. Choose software: integration of video screen capture and transcription layers | • Corresponding to varying participants and modes<br>• Timeline: ever layer aligned on the video | Avoid page-based transcriptions, Smith (ibid., 360)<br>Numerous open access software |
| 2. Adopt (extend) coding scheme | • Easily learnable<br>• For speech: prefer standard (and extensible) existing codes<br>• For non verbal: detail your code and make it publicly available | Check code reliably applied by coders (Rowe, 2012, 204)<br>e.g., CHAT used in CHILDES<br>Extend it for your specific needs.<br>e.g., (Saddour et al., 2011) |
| 3. Prioritize when coding interactions: time description | • Beginning and ending times of an online session<br>• Beginning and ending times of every interaction<br>• Guarantee timeline continuity: code speech silences (not pauses) as acts | Relationships with other course activities<br>Allows: sequencing of acts, duration of each one, observing simultaneity / overlap of acts<br>Priority to speech verbal acts with silences coding allow study of interplay between verbal and non-verbal modes |
| 4. Select output format | • Standard format for transcription and coding (e.g. XML or TEI compliant) | Guarantee machine readability and automatic processing<br>Use of interoperable software analysis<br>Depends of the features of the transcription software |

the music score is "printed," that is, once the different layers, corresponding to each participant and the various modes have been opened within the transcription software, with the video ready for alignment, the coding process can start. In synchronous multimodal CALL environment, the alignment is preferably made around the speech verbal acts.

The second step concerns speech transcription (cf. coding scheme in Table 28.2), that is by at least typing the words corresponding to the sound signal. Table 28.2, line 2, lists key points to take into consideration and related issues. A large part of them are shared by the community of speech corpora. Out of this transcription (including words in the textchat tools), many software packages are able to automatically calculate word tokens, work types, and mean length utterance. This computation can measure individual participant contribution: numbers of turns; floor occupied in sessions; vocabulary diversity, and so on.

A further step (cf. Output format in Table 28.2), specific to CMILL concerns, is to relate this methodology to a more abstract model, such as the interaction space one. It is as an extension of the Text Encoding Initiative (TEI), well known in corpus linguistics and other fields of Humanities. It encompasses text types such as manuscripts, theater, literature, poem, speech, film and video scripts. The TEI is specifically designed to accept different levels of annotations, each one corresponding to a specific type of analysis (e.g., morpho-syntactic, semantic, discursive). The IS model, under development, is designed for CMC in general, and includes multimodal discourse. It is the product of a European research workgroup, TEI-CMC (Beißwenger, Chanier, and Chiari 2014). The CoMeRe repository (Chanier et al. 2014) provides access to corpora of various CMC genres (SMS, blogs, tweets, textchat, combinations of email-forum-textchat, and multimodal acts coming from 3D, audiographic environments).

## Conclusion

The multimodal corpus-based approach to research on online language learning described in this chapter is not used widely in the study of CALL today. However, there is a need to expand the community of CALL researchers who adopt a corpus-based approach. Learning designs for CMILL need to take full account of the material and multimodal nature of the technical and learning resources involved in order to promote learning mediated through these resources. In order for research to improve CMILL, researchers need to investigate learners' performance in such interaction spaces. Sharing these data and documenting the processes through which they were created is a necessary step for deepening research on multimodal CALL. The LETEC corpus provides an example of how the field might move forward to investigate CMILL by collecting a corpus of CMILL data. It has served as a site for exploration of the various challenges facing the researcher with the transcription of these data, their coding in a standard way, and analysis. As researchers continue to work with this and other multimodal corpora, this area will continue to see advances that will help to improve CMILL.

## NOTE

1   Collecting multimodal data and transcribing them are time-consuming processes. As regards transcriptions, estimated ratios vary from 15:1 for speech (i.e., 10 mn of audio requires 2.5 hours to transcribe it) to 23:1 for both speech and gesture (Rowe 2012).

## REFERENCES

Baude, O, Blanche-Benveniste, C, et al. 2006. "Corpus Oraux, Guide des Bonnes Pratiques 2006." Accessed March 7, 2016. https://hal.archives-ouvertes.fr/hal-00357706

Beißwenger, Michael, Thierry Chanier and Isabella Chiari. 2014. "Special Interest Group on CMC of the Text Encoding Initiative (TEI) Consortium." Tei-c.org. Accessed March 7, 2016. http://wiki.tei-c.org/index.php/SIG:Computer-Mediated_Communication

Budach, Gabriele. 2013. "From Language Choice to Mode Choice: How Artifacts Impact on Language Use and Meaning Making in a Multilingual Classroom."

*Language and Education*, 27: DOI:10.1080/09500782.2013.788188

Chen, Nian-Shing, and Yuping Wang. 2008. "Testing Principles of Language Learning in a Cyber Face-to-Face Environment." *Educational Technology & Society*, 11, no. 3: 97–113.

Chanier, Thierry, Celine Poudat, Benoit Sagot, Georges Antoniadis, Ciara Wigham, Linda Hriba, Julien Longhi, and Djamé Seddah. 2014. "The CoMeRe corpus for French: structuring and annotating heterogeneous CMC genres". *Journal of language Technology and Computational Linguistics*, 29, no.2:1–30.

http://www.jlcl.org/2014_Heft2/1Chanier-et-al.pdf.

Chanier, Thierry, and Ciara Wigham. 2016. "Standardizing Multimodal Teaching and Learning Corpora." In *Language-Learner Computer Interactions: Theory, Methodology and CALL Applications*, edited by Hamel Marie-Jo, and Catherine Caws, 215–240. Amsterdam: John Benjamins. DOI:10.1075/lsse.2.10cha

Ciekanski, Maud, and Thierry Chanier. 2008. "Developing Online Multimodal Verbal Communication to Enhance the Writing Process in an Audio-graphic Conferencing Environment." *ReCall*, 20, no. 2. DOI:10.1017/S0958344008000426

Codreanu, Tatiana, and Christelle Celik. 2013. "Effects of Webcams on Multimodal Interactive Learning." *ReCall*, 25, no. 1. DOI:10.1017/S0958344012000249

Coryell, Joellen E., and M. Carolyn Clark. 2009. "One Right Way, Intercultural Participation, and Language Learning Anxiety: A Qualitative Analysis of Adult Online Heritage and Nonheritage Language Learners." *Foreign Language Annals*, 42, no. 3: 483–504.

Dahlberg, Giulia M., and Sangeeta Bagga-Gupta, S. 2013. "Communication in the Virtual Classroom in Higher Education: Languaging Beyond the Boundaries of Time and Space." *Learning, Culture and Social Interaction*, 2, no. 3: 127–142.

De los Arcos, Bea. 2009. Emotion in Online Distance Language Learning: Learners' Appraisal of Regret and Pride in Synchronous Audiographic Conferencing. PhD diss., The Open University. Accessed March 7. http://oro.open.ac.uk/id/eprint/44076

De los Arcos, Bea, Jim A. Coleman, and Regine Hampel. 2009. "Learners' Anxiety in Audiographic Conferences: A Discursive Psychology Approach to Emotion Talk." *ReCALL*, 21, no. 1: DOI:10.1017/S0958344009000111

Develotte, Christine, Nicolas Guichon, and Caroline Vincent. 2010. "The Use of the Webcam for Teaching a Foreign Language in a Desktop Videoconferencing Environment." *ReCALL*, 22, no. 3: DOI:10.1017/S0958344010000170

Dooly, Melinda, and Mirjam Hauck. 2012. "Researching Multimodal Communicative Competence in Video and Audio Telecollaborative Encounters." In *Researching Online Foreign Language Interaction and Exchange: Theories, Methods and Challenges*, edited by Melinda Dooly

and Robert O'Dowd, 135–161. Bern: Peter Lang.

Dooly, Miranda, and Randall Sadler. 2013. "Filling in the Gaps: Linking Theory and Practice through Telecollaboration in Teacher Education." *ReCALL*, 25, no. 1. DOI: 10.1017/S0958344012000237

Dyke, Gregory, Kristine Lund, Heysawn Jeong, Richard Medina, Daniel Suthers, Jan van Aalst, et al. 2011. "Technological Affordances for Productive Multivocality in Analysis." In *Proceedings of the 9th International Conference on Computer-Supported Collaborative Learning (CSCL)*, Hong-Kong, China, 454–461. Accessed March 7, 2016. https://halshs.archives-ouvertes.fr/halshs-00856537

Erben, Tony. 1999. "Constructing Learning in a Virtual Immersion Bath: LOTE Teacher Education through Audiographics." In *WORLDCALL: Global Perspectives on Computer-assisted Language Learning*, edited by Robert Debski and Mike Levy, 229–248. Lisse: Swets and Zeitlinger.

Flewitt, Rosie S., Regine Hampel, Mirjam Hauck, and Lesley Lancaster. 2009. "What Are Multimodal Data and Transcription?" In *The Routledge Handbook of Multimodal Analysis*, edited by Carey Jewitt, 40–53. London: Routledge.

Goodfellow, Robin, Ingrid Jefferys, Terry Miles, and Tim Shirra. 1996. "Face-to-Face Language Learning at a Distance? A Study of a Videoconference Try-Out." *ReCALL*, 8, no. 2: DOI:10.1017/S0958344000003530

Hampel, Regine. 2012. "Multimodal Computer-Mediated Communication and Distance Language Learning." In *The Encyclopedia of Applied Linguistics*. Hoboken, NJ: John Wiley & Sons, Inc. DOI:10.1002/9781405198431.wbeal0811

Hampel, Regine. 2014. "Making Meaning Online: Computer-mediated Communication for Language Learning" In *Proceedings of the CALS Conference 2012*, edited by Anita Peti-Stantić and Mateusz-Milan Stanojević, 89–106. Frankfurt: Peter Lang.

Ho, Caroline, M. L., Mark Evan Nelson, and Wolfgang K. Müller-Wittig. 2011. "Design and Implementation of a Student-generated Virtual Museum in a Language Curriculum to Enhance Collaborative Multimodal Meaning-making." *Computers and Education*, 57, no. 1: 1083–1097.

Hoff, Erika., ed. 2012. *Research Methods in Child Language: A Practical Guide*. Oxford: Wiley-Blackwell.

Hurd, Stella. 2007. "Anxiety and Non-anxiety in a Distance Language Learning Environment: The Distance Factor as a Modifying Influence." *System*, 35, no. 4: DOI:10.1016/j.system.2007.05.001

Jenks, Christopher J. 2011. *Transcribing Talk and Interaction*. Amsterdam: John Benjamins.

Jones, Rodney H. 2004. "The Problem of Context in Computer-mediated Communication." In *Discourse and Technology: Multimodal Discourse Analysis*, edited by Philip Levine and Ron Scollon, 20–33. Washington, DC: Georgetown University Press.

Jones, Rodney H., and Christoph A. Hafner. 2012. *Understanding Digital Literacies: A Practical Introduction*. New York: Routledge.

Kress, Gunther, and Theo Van Leeuwen. 2001. *Multimodal Discourse: The Modes and Media of Contemporary Communication*. London: Arnold.

Kress, Gunther (2010) *Multimodality A Social Semiotic Approach to Contemporary Communication*. London: Routledge.

Lamy, Marie-Noëlle. 2012a. "Click if You Want to Speak: Reframing CA for Research into Multimodal Conversations in Online Learning." *International Journal of Virtual and Personal Learning Environments*, 3, no. 1: 1–18.

Lamy, Marie-Noëlle. 2012b. "Diversity in Modalities." In *Computer-Assisted Language Learning: Diversity in Research and Practice*, edited by Glenn Stockwell, 109–126. Cambridge: Cambridge University Press.

Lamy, Marie-Noëlle, and Rosie Flewitt. 2011. "Describing Online Conversations: Insights from a Multimodal Approach." In *Décrire La Communication en Ligne: Le Face-à-face Distanciel*, edited by Christine Develotte, Richard Kern, and Marie-Noëlle Lamy, 71–94. Lyon, France: ENS Editions.

Liègeois, Loïc. 2014. Usage des Variables Phonologiques dans un Corpus d'Interactions Naturelles Parents-enfant: Impact du Bain Linguistique et Dispositifs Cognitifs d'Apprentissage. PhD dissertation, Clermont University. Accessed March 7, 2016. https://tel.archives-ouvertes.fr/tel-01108764

Mackey, A., & Gass, S. M. 2005. *Second Language Research: Methodology and Design*. Abingdon: Routledge.

MacWhinney, Brian. 2000. "The CHILDES Project: Tools for Analyzing Talk: Volume I: Transcription Format and Programs, Volume II: The Database." *Computational Linguistics*, 26, no. 4: 657–657.

McAndrew, Patrick, Sandra P. Foubister, and Terry Mayes. 1996. "Videoconferencing in a Language Learning Application." *Interacting with Computers*, 8, no. 2: 207–217.

Monteiro, Kátia. 2014. "An Experimental Study of Corrective Feedback during Video-Conferencing." *Language Learning and Technology*, 18, no. 3: 56–79.

Mulce Repository. 2013. *"Repository of Learning and Teaching (LETEC) Corpora*. Clermont Université: MULCE.org." Accessed March 7, 2016. http://repository.Mulce.org

O'Halloran, Kay L., Alexey Podlasov, Alvin Chua, and K. L. E. Marissa. 2012. "Interactive Software for Multimodal Analysis." *Visual Communication*, 11, no. 3: 352–370.

O'Halloran, Kay L., and Bradley A. Smith, eds. 2011. *Multimodal Studies: Exploring Issues and Domains*. New York: Routledge.

Reffay, Christophe, Marie-Laure Betbeder, and Thierry Chanier. 2012. "Multimodal Learning and Teaching Corpora Exchange: Lessons learned in 5 years by the Mulce project." *International Journal of Technology Enhanced Learning (IJTEL)*, 4, no. 1–2. DOI:10.1504/IJTEL.2012.048310

Reinhardt, Jonathon, and Julie Sykes. 2014. "Special Issue Commentary: Digital Game and Play Activity in L2 Teaching and Learning." *Language Learning & Technology*, 18, no. 2: 2–8.

Royce, T. D. 2007. "Multimodal Communicative Competence in Second Language Contexts." In *New Directions in the Analysis of Multimodal Discourse*, edited by Teddy D. Royce and Wendy Bowcher, 361–390. Mahwah, NJ: Lawrance Erlbaum.

Rowe, Meredith. L. 2012. Recording, Transcribing, and Coding Interaction. In *Research Methods in Child Language: A Practical Guide*, edited by Erika Hoff: Oxford: Wiley-Blackwell. DOI:10.1002/9781444344035.ch13

Saddour, Ines, Ciara Wigham, and Thierry Chanier. 2011. *Manuel de transcription de données multimodales dans Second Life*. Accessed 2016-03-07. http://edutice.archives-ouvertes.fr/edutice-00676230

Satar, Müge H. 2013. "Multimodal Language Learner Interactions via Desktop Conferencing within a Framework of Social Presence: Gaze." *ReCALL*, 25, no. 1: DOI:10.1017/S0958344012000286

Schwienhorst, Klaus. 2002. "The State of VR: A meta-analysis of Virtual Reality Tools in Second Language Acquisition." *Computer Assisted Language Learning*, 15, no. 3: DOI:10.1076/call.15.3.221.8186

Segouat, Jérémie, Ammick Choisier, and Amelies, Braffort. 2010. Corpus de Langue des Signes: Premières Réflexions sur leur Conception et Représentativité. In *L'exemple et Le Corpus Quel Statut? Travaux Linguistiques du CerLiCO*, 23: 77–94. Rennes: Presses Universitaires de Rennes.

Shih, Ya-Chun. 2014. "Communication Strategies in a Multimodal Virtual Communication context." *System*, 42: DOI:10.1016/j.system.2013.10.016

Sindoni, Maria Grazia. 2013. *Spoken and Written Discourse in Online Interactions: A Multimodal Approach*. New York: Routledge.

Smith, Bradley A., Sabine Tan, Alexey Podlasov, and Kay L. O'Halloran. 2011. "Analyzing Multimodality in an Interactive Digital Environment: Software as Metasemiotic Tool." *Social Semiotics*, 21, no. 3: 359–380.

Stickler, Ursula, Caroline Batstone, Annette Duensing, and Barbara Heins. 2007. "Distant Classmates: Speech and Silence in Online and Telephone Language Tutorials." *European Journal of Open, Distance and e-Learning*, 10, no. 2. Accessed January 5, 2017. http://www.eurodl.org/

Stivers, Tanya, and Jack Sidnell. 2005. "Multimodal Interaction." Special Issue of *Semiotica*, 156, no. 1–4: 1–20.

Tayebinik, Maryam, and Marlia Puteh. 2012. "The Significance of Self-esteem in Computer Assisted Language Learning (CALL) Environments." *Procedia – Social and Behavioral Sciences*, 66: DOI:10.1016/j.sbspro.2012.11.294

Vetter, Anna, and Thierry Chanier. 2006. "Supporting Oral Production for Professional Purpose, in Synchronous Communication With heterogeneous Learners." *ReCALL*, 18, no. 1. DOI:10.1017/S0958344006000218

Wang, Yuping. 2004. "Supporting Synchronous Distance Language Learning with Desktop Videoconferencing." *Language Learning & Technology*, 8, no. 3: 90–121.

Wang, Yuping. 2006. "Negotiation of Meaning in Desktop Videoconferencing-Supported Distance Language Learning." *ReCALL*, 18, no. 1: DOI:10.1017/S0958344006000814

Wang, Yuping. 2007. "Task Design in Videoconferencing-Supported Distance Language Learning." *CALICO Journal*, 24, no. 3: 591–630.

Wang, Y., Chen, N-S., and Levy, M. 2010 "Teacher Training in a Synchronous Cyber face-to-face Classroom: Characterizing and Supporting the Online Teachers' Learning Process. " *Computer-Assisted Language Learning*, 23, no. 4: 277–293.

Wang, Yuping, and Nian-Shing Chen. 2012. "The Collaborative Language Learning Attributes of Cyber Face-to-face Interaction: The Perspectives of the Learner." *Interactive Learning Environments*, 20, no. 4: 311–330.

Wigham, Ciara, and Thierry Chanier. 2013a. "A Study of Verbal and Non-verbal Communication in Second Life – the ARCHI121 experience." *ReCall*, 25, no. 1. DOI: 10.1017/S0958344012000250

Wigham, Ciara, and Thierry Chanier. 2013b. "Interactions Between Text Chat and Audio Modalities for L2 Communication and Feedback in the Synthetic World Second Life." *Computer Assisted Language Learning*, 28, no. 3. DOI:10.1080/09588221.2013.851702

Yang, Shu Ching. 2001. "Language Learning on the World Wide Web: An Investigation of EFL Learners' Attitudes and Perceptions." *Journal of Educational Computing Research*, 24, no. 2: 155–181.

# 29 Technology-Enhanced SLA Research

## BRYAN SMITH

## Defining SLA and SLA research

Second language acquisition (SLA) is the study of the human capacity to learn languages other than the first, during late childhood, adolescence, or adulthood, and once the first language or languages have been acquired (Ortega 2009). Within the field of applied linguistics, of which SLA is a part, there is a distinction typically made between second and foreign language acquisition, with the former occurring where the target language (the language being learned) is spoken by the local community and the latter occurring in settings in which the target language is *not* spoken by the local community. In this chapter the terms acquisition and learning will be used interchangeably as will the terms second and foreign language (L2).

SLA is a broad and diverse field, which has been rapidly expanding in scope and methodology ever since it emerged in the 1960s. Today the field remains interdisciplinary as it was in the past, with as many as 60 theories, models, hypotheses, and theoretical frameworks of SLA (Long 2007). According to VanPatten and Benati (2010) some of the (broad) questions that SLA theories are developed to address include the following:

What do learners do when acquiring another language?
What stages of acquisition do they go through?
What does their developing second language (interlanguage) "look like"?
What is the nature of their errors?
What factors affect SLA?
What are the mechanisms that learners use to understand and produce an L2?
How does fluency develop?
How do we explain learner variability in eventual attainment of an L2?

In attempting to answer these and other major questions, a number of competing SLA theories, approaches, and frameworks have emerged, bringing with them their own set of ontological, epistemological, and methodological stances, which largely determine the specific questions as well as what the researchers count as data, and accept as evidence. This fact makes it difficult to talk about SLA as a cohesive entity. Accordingly, we frame our

*The Handbook of Technology and Second Language Teaching and Learning*, First Edition.
Edited by Carol A. Chapelle and Shannon Sauro.
© 2017 John Wiley & Sons, Inc. Published 2020 by John Wiley & Sons, Inc.

discussion of technology-enhanced SLA research in terms of three theoretical frameworks that are widely researched and especially compatible with CALL inquiry: cognitive approaches, the interaction approach, and sociocultural theory.

## Cognitive approaches to SLA

There are a host of cognitive approaches to SLA, which can be broadly classified into traditional information processing and emergentism (Ortega 2009). Cognitivists believe that in order to properly understand the final state of fluent L2 development we need to understand the processes by which this expertise came about. Cognitive science is also concerned with functional and neurobiological descriptions of the learning processes, which, through exposure to representative experience, result in change, development, and the emergence of knowledge (N. C. Ellis 2002). Information processing theories all share the belief that the human cognitive architecture is made up of *representations* and *access*. Mental processing is comprised of automatic (unconscious) operations and voluntary or controlled (conscious) operations. Cognitive resources such as attention and memory are limited, and performance is variable and vulnerable to stressors, such as those factors that make a language learning task more difficult such as time pressure.

In contrast, emergentist SLA scholars argue for a usage-based explanation of language development (including SLA). They argue that fluent language use is exemplar based and is made up of "a huge collection of memories of previously experienced utterances" rather than knowledge of abstract rules (the latter explanation championed by generative linguistics). Emergentists take most language learning to be "the gradual strengthening of associations between co-occurring elements of the language," and they see fluent language performance as "the exploitation of this probabilistic knowledge" (N. C. Ellis 2002, 173). Cognitive theory directs researchers to investigate constructs such as working memory, which can be assessed through the use of technology.

## The interaction approach

The interaction approach (IA) grew out of Long's Interaction Hypothesis, which was first developed in the early 1980s. Since then it has been updated (Long 1996) and rigorously researched. The IA essentially says that through input and interaction with interlocutors, language learners have opportunities to notice (Schmidt 1990) differences between their own formulations of the target language and the language of their conversational partners. They also receive corrective feedback, which both modifies the linguistic input they receive and pushes them to modify their own linguistic output during conversation. This interaction helps draw learners' attention to or lead them to notice a linguistic problem (Long 1996). Attention as a result of interaction may also lead learners to notice linguistic input in the absence of a problem. Interactionally modified input, is that which occurs as needed during goal-oriented conversation and is argued to be more effective (in terms of learning the target word or structure) than pre-modified input, which is modified to be target-like before any learner error occurs (R. Ellis et al. 1999). An example of pre-modified input might appear in a listening passage that provides simplified or glossed language for vocabulary referring to technical concepts. Thus, the major constructs of this approach to SLA include input, interaction, corrective feedback, attention and output (Gass 1997). Some of the most commonly investigated phenomena that inform these constructs include negotiated interaction (Long 1996), whereby learners first have a breakdown in understanding and then regain understanding through a series of communication moves, such as recasts, which are a type of corrective feedback and learner uptake, whereby a learner appropriates the target language forms of their interlocutor in some productive way (Lyster and Ranta 1997). Such constructs have also been investigated in settings where technology is used to mediate the interactions.

## Sociocultural theory

Sociocultural theory (SCT) has its origins in the work of Russian psychologist Lev Vygotsky in the early part of the 20th century. SCT argues that while human neurobiology is a necessary condition for higher mental processes, learning is essentially a social process whereby the most important forms of human cognitive activity develop through participation in cultural, linguistic, and historically formed settings such as family life, peer group interaction, and institutional contexts like schooling, organized social activities, and workplaces. SCT posits that everything is learned on two levels—first on the social level (between people) and only later on the individual level. Human mental functioning is a mediated process. That is, just as humans use material tools such as a hammer to mediate the act of building a table, we also have the capacity to create and use inwardly directed symbolic tools such as language to mediate our own psychological activity, our connection to the world, to one another, and to ourselves. As children (and language learners) develop they move through stages whereby they are controlled first by the objects of their environment (object-regulated), then by others in this environment (other-regulated), and finally they gain control over their own social and cognitive activities (self-regulated).

From the SCT perspective of SLA, language learning is facilitated by social interaction. During interaction, learners and more capable peers engage in collaborative dialogue involving scaffolding. This type of interaction is viewed as central to the learning process, as it facilitates the operation of the zone of proximal development (ZPD). The ZPD is "the distance between the actual developmental level as determined by independent problem solving and the level of potential development as determined through problem solving under adult guidance or in collaboration with more capable peers" (Vygotsky 1978, 86). One of the most compelling aspects of the ZPD is that rather than measuring the level of development a learner has already attained, the ZPD is forward looking in that it suggests that what one can do today with mediation is suggestive of what one will be able to do independently in the future. The notion of dynamic assessment and systemic-theoretical instruction have recently emerged as pedagogical applications of SCT including applications using technology (Lantolf and Poehner 2014).

## Defining SLA-relevant research in computer-assisted language learning (CALL)

The rapid development of computer technology has afforded SLA researchers many possibilities to investigate aspects of SLA theory, which are not available to them in a face-to-face environment. Most times this type of research employs computer technology as a tool in order to control or regulate some aspect of the instructional environment. Such studies, despite their use of computer technology, are not considered CALL studies since the study is not primarily concerned with employing computer technology for teaching and learning foreign languages. An example of this type of research is DeKeyser (2005) who used the computer to execute a speeded grammaticality judgment test. These types of technology-assisted SLA studies have been outlined in detail elsewhere (see, for example, Hulstijn 2000) and will not be discussed here.

What is most interesting for this volume on *Technology in Second Language Teaching and Learning* is the difference between an SLA-relevant question asked in a CALL study and one that does not yield SLA-relevant results. That is to say, just as not all applied linguistics or L2 pedagogy research questions have *direct relevance* to SLA, not all CALL studies ask SLA questions or yield SLA-relevant results. Indeed, SLA-relevant CALL studies are still rather rare even if they are now growing in number and sophistication. CALL has only begun to emerge as a cohesive area of inquiry since the 1980s. During the early years CALL was an avocation, not a vocation for most CALL practitioners (Fischer 2012). Many came to CALL from other academic fields having no formal training in CALL because of the newness of the field. Most early CALL scholars were faculty members in foreign language departments who had primary professional responsibilities in literature or linguistics. Fischer points out that in those days the technology was the focus, but in the 1990s a shift from technical matters to language learning matters occurred. Success in CALL no longer lay in writing software alone, but rather in using this software to help students learn L2 vocabulary and specific language structures, for example. In other words, interest grew in the use of computers for second language acquisition (Fischer 2012).

Today, those interested in the nexus of CALL and SLA critically evaluate the use of a particular tool or app in terms of its potential for facilitating L2 learning. Embracing this challenge sets SLA-relevant CALL inquiry apart from CALL research that is not SLA-relevant. For example, CALL studies that solely explore *learner attitudes* toward using a given application in the L2 classroom or learner *perceptions* of an app's facility for L2 learning, though important and interesting, may not be directly relevant to SLA. In order for CALL research to be SLA-relevant, clear connections need to be made, for example, between student attitudes toward technology X and, say, learner motivation in regard to their present L2 learning context. The researcher would work within an SLA theoretical framework that makes the link among attitudes, motivation, and instructed SLA.

Some of the questions that one needs to consider in determining the degree of SLA-relevance of a CALL study are the following: (1) Is this study a CALL study? As mentioned above a CALL study is defined here as one that is primarily concerned with employing computer technology for teaching and learning foreign languages. Note that computer technology is broadly defined here and includes desktops, laptops, tablets, hand held devices, and smartphones, among other technologies, (2) Is the CALL study firmly grounded in an identifiable SLA theoretical framework? A theoretical framework refers to the theory or approach that researchers select to guide their research. It is the application of a collection of interrelated concepts and coherent explanations of certain phenomena that guides the research and allows researchers to test aspects of the theory and describe the results. The theoretical framework helps determine what the researcher will measure, what variables will be examined, the relationship between these variables, and what research questions will be posed, (3) Does the study examine key assumptions, constructs, hypotheses, and so on, which are relevant to this theoretical framework for SLA? Not only do researchers need to introduce a theoretical framework that informs the study, but the study must also reflect an exploration of specific constructs and hypotheses that emerge from and are relevant to that same theoretical framework, and (4) Does the study explicitly or implicitly investigate some aspect of the argued affordances of CALL environments for SLA? In other words is there some expectation that the affordances of the specific CALL environment in the study, including the specific CALL tasks in question (Chapelle 2001), may impact some aspect of learner processes, interactional patterns or outcomes?

The most compelling SLA-relevant CALL studies are those that have a strong theoretical rationale for hypothesizing that the affordances of a specific CALL environment are likely to impact the results at a process or outcome level (question 4 above). For example, in an examination of explicit recasts in an SCMC environment, Smith (2012) argues that such written corrective recasts are necessarily more explicit (and therefore more noticeable) than those found in oral recasts due to the written nature of the medium itself as well as the message permanence afforded.

## Three SLA-relevant CALL studies

Using the four considerations discussed above, I outline three exemplary SLA-relevant CALL studies from three of the most widely employed theoretical frameworks. Each of these studies focuses on computer-mediated communication in one form or another, reflecting CMC's predominant position in CALL research in recent years.

### Cognitive approach

Payne and Whitney (2002) used Levelt's (1989) model of language production as well as key concepts from Working Memory theory (Baddeley 1986) to explore whether SCMC can help improve learners' L2 oral proficiency by developing the same cognitive mechanisms that underlie spontaneous conversational speech.

Is the study primarily concerned with employing computer technology for teaching and learning foreign languages?
Four sections of a third semester university-level Spanish course were used for this study. These were intact groups with the students in the experimental groups (meeting online in a chat room) engaged in the same activities on the same days as those in the control groups did face to face. All groups engaged in weekly threaded discussion as preparation for synchronous discussions, weekly online drills and practice activities with feedback, weekly online quizzes with feedback, independent viewing of the video accompanying the textbook, and a collaborative research and writing project involving multiple drafts of an essay. One important question when studying text-based chat interaction is whether such interaction can yield cross-modal benefits for spoken proficiency. They asked the following CALL-related research questions: *Can L2 oral proficiency be indirectly developed through chat room interaction in the target language? Can individual differences in working memory capacity effectively predict the rate of L2 oral proficiency development for different types of learners in a chat room setting?*

Is the study firmly grounded in an identifiable SLA theoretical framework?
Though Levelt's model of language production is one of L1 production, many researchers have used and adapted this model to depict L2 language production processes. For example, deBot (1996) combined Levelt's model with Anderson's (1982) notions of declarative and procedural knowledge as he explored Swain's Output Hypothesis (1995, 2005) from a psycholinguistic perspective. Likewise, Payne and Whitney (2002) employed Levelt's model in combination with another psycholinguistic concept, working memory, in order to propose mechanisms that influence L2 acquisition. SLA studies have shown that verbal working memory capacity is an especially important variable in predicting L2 vocabulary development and overall L2 proficiency.

Does the study examine key assumptions, constructs, hypotheses, and so on, which are relevant to this theory of SLA?
Key to many cognitive approaches to SLA are the constructs of controlled and automatic processing. All processing falls into one or the other category. Controlled processing involves "a temporary sequence of nodes activated under control of, and through attention by, the subject" (Schneider and Shiffrin 1977, 2–3). Put another way, controlled processing is that which is under the conscious and intentional control of the individual and these processes

are constrained by the amount of attentional resources available. In contrast, *automatic processes* are the activation of a sequence of nodes that "nearly always becomes active in response to a particular input configuration," and that "is activated automatically without the necessity for active control or attention by the subject" (2). That is to say, automatic processes require comparatively few cognitive resources and can be performed in parallel with other automatic processes. Initial learning requires controlled processes, which require attention and time. With practice the linguistic skill requires less attention and becomes routinized, thus freeing up the controlled processes for application to new linguistic skills. L2 learning, then, is viewed as the process by which linguistic skills become automatic. Cognitively-oriented SLA researchers drawing upon Levelt's (1989) model acknowledge that controlled processing plays a central role in L2 production in terms of lexical access and articulation (at least until a high level of L2 proficiency has been achieved). Indeed, L2 fluency seems to vary as a function of automatic processing ability. In Levelt's (1989) model, working memory is associated with controlled processing. Since controlled processing plays such a central role in L2 lexical access and articulation, then limitations in working memory capacity are likely to have an impact on L2 performance and arguably SLA.

Does the study explicitly or implicitly investigate some aspect of the argued affordances of CALL environments?
Payne and Whitney (2002) argue that the affordances of synchronous chat interaction can help improve some L2 processes. For example, the rate of delivery during (written) SCMC interaction is much slower than that in spoken interaction. This in itself should reduce the processing demand on learners. Also, the message permanence afforded by the chat environment allows learners to refresh memory traces, which is not possible in spoken interaction. All of this suggests that learners with lower WMC will benefit from the SCMC environment where processing demands are reduced but where the task and other features of the interaction are the same. Essentially, then, in terms of the first research question Payne and Whitney predicted (and found) that the participants in the CALL environment (experimental group) would show at least the same degree of oral proficiency development over one semester as those participants in the control group. In terms of research question 2, there was a lower correlation between oral proficiency gain scores and one of the WMC tests in the experimental condition (SCMC) as compared with the control condition (F2F), indicating that learners with a lower WMC benefited from the chat environment.

## Interactionist approach

In a study of teacher-learner (text-based) SCMC interaction during online conferences, Smith and Renaud (2013) used eye-tracking technology to explore the relationship between L2 recasts, noticing, and learning of the recast targets.

Is the study primarily concerned with employing computer technology for teaching and learning foreign languages?
This study examined the effectiveness of teacher-provided corrective feedback during one-on-one online conferences with students. The task was for students to meet virtually with the instructor and discuss (in the target language) a draft of a written assignment due the next week. The teachers were asked to provide full recasts to learners when it seemed natural to do so. Recasts may be defined as discourse moves by an interlocutor that, within the context of communicative activity, correctly restate or rephrase all or part of a learner's utterance to be more target-like by changing one or more sentence components, while still acknowledging and retaining its central meaning. For example, when a learner of German says something like *Ich habe Hunger nicht** (I am not hungry) the teacher may provide the recast

*Ah, Sie haben keinen Hunger* (Oh, you're not hungry). The online conferences were viewed by the instructors as part of the regular curriculum and they typically held either face-to-face or online conferences with students for each of three major writing assignments over the course of the semester. In this way instructors had clearly integrated computer technology as a tool to facilitate the teaching and learning of the target language.

Is the study firmly grounded in an identifiable SLA theoretical framework?
This study espouses a cognitive interactionist theoretical framework. From this theoretical perspective, corrective feedback provided in the form of recasts is thought to be especially beneficial for learners as they provide a focus on formal aspects of the learner's output as problems arise while retaining the overarching focus on meaning and not significantly hindering the flow of communication. That is to say, by using recasts (a form of implicit negative feedback), teachers may deal with many of their students' language problems incidentally while working on their subject matter of choice, with fewer of the interruptions and other unpleasant side effects caused by traditional overt "error correction" practices (Long 2007).

Does the study examine key assumptions, constructs, hypotheses, and so on, which are relevant to this theory of SLA?
Attention to and noticing of formal aspects of the target language are key elements in the interactionist approach to SLA. The assumption is that learners are able to attend to and make use of the positive input and negative feedback that recasts supply, provided that they are able to notice the recast's corrective intent. Smith and Renaud's (2013) study employed eye-tracking technology as a measure of what learners attended to in the corrective feedback. These eye-movement records were compared with learners' performance on individually tailored post-tests that consisted of both target-like and non-target-like learner-generated sentences from the original online conference. In this way the researchers could determine the degree to which learners attended to each recast and, based on the post-test results, they could calculate the effectiveness of the recasts.

Does the study explicitly or implicitly investigate some aspect of the argued affordances of CALL environments?
The potential benefits of text-based SCMC for language learning include an increased participation among students, an increased quantity and heightened quality of learner output, an enhanced attention to linguistic form, and an increased willingness to take risks with their L2. The slower speed of typing as well as a software- and network-induced lag time between turns, coupled with the heightened salience of input and output afforded by the permanence of the written message on the screen means that interlocutors have more time to both process incoming messages and produce and monitor their output. This increased planning time is argued to contribute to L2 performance by freeing up attentional resources. Learners have been shown to make use of this increased planning time to engage in careful production that results in more complex language (Hsu in press; Sauro and Smith 2010). In this study, many of the instructor-provided recasts were complex in nature, whereby one recast targets more than one linguistic item in the participant's previous message. Although partial recasts that target a single linguistic item have been argued to be easier for learners to attend to, we might expect the increased processing time and message permanence afforded by the chat interface to mediate this partial/complex issue by making the multiple targets in complex recasts more salient to learners.

## Sociocultural theory

Most of the current research on gaming in L2 settings espouses some form of sociocultural theory as its theoretical framework. For example, Rama et al. (2012) conducted a qualitative study that examined two college-age Spanish learners' experiences while participating in the Spanish-language version of the wildly popular massively multi-player online game (MMOG) *World of Warcraft (WoW)*.

Is the study primarily concerned with employing computer technology for teaching and learning foreign languages?
This study posed the single research question—*What affordances for second language development and socialization might online gaming environments offer?* As part of the class, participants were each given a Spanish-language versions of *WoW*. They were asked to play the game at their discretion over the course of a seven-week period and were encouraged to play about five hours per week. Data collection included journal entries kept by students reflecting on their gaming experience each week, regular meetings, and semi-structured interviews with the instructor, and chat logs of the text-based interaction that occurred during each gaming session. The gaming sessions occurred outside of the classroom, but were connected to a specific Spanish course and, therefore, can be viewed as extracurricular in nature (Sylvén and Sundquist 2017).

Is the study firmly grounded in an identifiable SLA theoretical framework?
The authors explicitly identify sociocultural theory as the guiding theoretical framework. As mentioned above, SCT views language learning as emerging from the learner's interactions with other people and the environment, which are mediated by symbolic (in this case language) and material (in this case the *WoW* game) tools. Indeed, from this theoretical perspective, any opportunity for authentic and active interaction in the target language is viewed as beneficial for L2 learning. Further, as Vygotsky's Zone of Proximal Development (ZPD) emphasizes the interplay between a learner's capabilities and the learning environment, this study focused specifically on the interactions with Spanish native speakers by an expert gamer with lower Spanish ability. These interactions were contrasted against the interactions of another student, who was a novice gamer but an advanced Spanish speaker.

Does the study examine key assumptions, constructs, hypotheses, and so on, which are relevant to this theory of SLA?
The unit of analysis in this exploratory study was not only the affordances of the learning environment or discrete aspects of the individual learner's linguistic output (or input received), but rather the *affordances for second language development and socialization* that emerge from the learner's interactions within the learning context. Indeed, MMOGs are argued to offer a range of affordances for L2 learning due to the engaging communicative contexts of these environments. Play in these environments requires collaborative interaction, which in turn is mediated by meaningful target language use. From a sociocultural perspective, these interactions, often with more capable others, may provide opportunities for learners to build on their existing competencies in a supportive and engaging context. The data analysis occurred in two steps. First, the researchers employed an inductive process aimed at identifying patterns in the participants' language use identifiable from the chat logs. These included type of utterance, length of pauses between utterances, the role that participants played in the exchanges, and changes over time. This phase also examined participants' journal entries and interview transcripts in order to identify emerging themes. Step 1 revealed the notion of *affordances for language learning and socialization* as an important organizing construct. The second step of the data analysis coded for specific examples of (and references to) affordances for language learning in the data. In addition to confirming affordances found in previous research on gaming in similar contexts, the study identified three new affordances of *WoW*: it allows for and supports the creation of safe learning and languaging spaces; it emphasizes communicative competence, or the ability to communicate meaningfully and effectively within a given context, and it promotes goal-directed collaborative action between experts and novices.

Does the study explicitly or implicitly investigate some aspect of the argued affordances of CALL environments?

Text-based CMC interaction has long been argued to reduce the anxiety felt by many learners as they attempt to communicate in the target language. This is largely due to the mediated nature of the online exchanges as well as the written modality. In a text-based CMC environment learners are not require to speak, just type. This low-anxiety setting has been described in previous game-based research. Additionally, CMC interaction research has identified dyadic or small group interaction as the most likely to yield more linear and cohesive dialogue. Though not explicitly investigated, the creation and use of guilds (rather than the general chat channel) in this study, which afford more private and manageable chat interaction with smaller groups of people, is consistent with this CALL affordance. Further, synchronous CMC environments potentially offer extensive opportunities for purposeful target language use in an authentic and engaging communicative context. Not only can learners take risks with language (with little downside to non-target like utterances in text-based SCMC, at least), they receive a potentially vast amount of linguistic input from a variety of partners across many communicative contexts. They may review their own and others' target language use because of the message permanence and slow motion nature of the interaction (compared to that in F2F). Rama et al. (2012) describe this affordance in terms of the WoW space *"providing opportunities for language learners to interact with native speakers in ways that allow time for reflection on language production"* (335). One of the participants in this study (Silvania) made limited contributions to the group chat, however, these tended to be in complete, grammatically correct utterances. This participant's journal entries suggested that the CMC medium provided her with the opportunity and motivation to improve her writing (and speaking) skills. Though evidence of gains in specific aspects of language proficiency is sparse in this study (nor was such evidence explicitly sought), there is ample evidence of growing familiarity with certain Spanish vocabulary, expressions, and phrases that suggest a strengthening of learners' communicative competence in the MMOG environment. Upon seeing an example of one of the learner's chat transcripts, the learner's professor commented to one of the researchers that the learner had completely formulated a question and expressed himself in Spanish in a manner that exceeded the level of most of the other students in the class. Though anecdotal, this expert comment may be taken as evidence of target language development that can be traced to participation in the MMOG. Indeed, just as CMC research in general has found an increased participation among students, an increased quantity and heightened quality of learner output, an enhanced attention to linguistic form, and an increased willingness to take risks with their L2, among other benefits, results of this study suggest that participation in these spaces can have a positive impact on students' confidence and perceived competence, as well as their willingness to interact in the target language.

## Data in SLA-relevant CALL research

CALL researchers can employ computer technology to gather a variety of types of data that are not available to them in face-to-face learning settings. Generally speaking, CALL researchers collect and analyze SLA-relevant learner data in two environments. The first type is that yielded by Human-Computer interaction (HCI). An example of HCI is a learner independently using a multimedia or a web-based language learning program such as *etutor* for learning German (Heift 2010). The other type of learner data is that yielded by human-human interaction (HHI). In HHI learners use the computer as a vehicle for interacting directly with other language learners, native speaker peers, or teachers. An example of HHI is using a synchronous chat program in order to complete some language learning task with another learner. In both HCI and HHI computer technology can be especially beneficial in helping researchers capture the best possible record of how learners are engaging with computer programs and/or other learners. This can be referred to as learner process data (Chapelle 2003). A distinct, but related affordance is that computers are well suited for simultaneously capturing multiple forms of learner data (allowing for richer interpretations and triangulation), which will potentially strengthen the plausibility of data-driven interpretations they will make.

## Multiple modality methods in data collection

The method of data collection employed has long been acknowledged to affect outcomes in applied linguistics research (Beebe and Cummings 1995; Smith 2012). Computer technology affords researchers with opportunities to simultaneously record visual, audio, and textual data in a way that is easily synchronized for later analysis. For example, relying solely on an audio file of a stretch of learner interaction may lead to a different interpretation of the data from a video record (plus audio) of the same interaction. In a study that illustrates this very point Smith and Gorsuch (2004) explored the nature of task-based learner-learner interaction during SCMC. Findings clearly showed video and audio data merged and re-interpreted with traditional chat scripts can provide a fuller picture of what learners do while engaged in task-based SCMC than chat scripts alone. The visual data captured also showed that other factors such as facial expressions and body language often provided essential information required to sufficiently interpret aspects of SCMC learner interaction. For example, facial expressions (if captured) can show an indication of non-understanding in instances where the chat transcript and audio records do not, something that is very important from an interactionist theoretical perspective.

In an exploration of how task-based language teaching (TBLT) operates in real teaching contexts, Seedhouse and Almutairi (2009) employed Transana3 software to align video, audio, and tabletop computer screen records with the transcripts of the interaction onto a single screen, making several data sources available simultaneously for a multimodal and holistic analysis. This approach allowed them to compare task-as-work plan (what is supposed to happen) with task-in-process (what actually happens). Their findings suggest that during task-based interaction, a significant amount of learners' attention is spent on coordinating verbal elements with non-verbal elements of interaction and with task-related actions in a precisely timed, multi-dimensional manner. It is only through capturing and tracking multiple modalities of learner interaction is such subsequent analysis and conclusions possible. A study by Suzuki (2013) conducted within a sociocultural theoretical framework also provides a clear illustration of the benefits of multimodal data collection.

## Capturing learner process data

Researchers investigate what students do when they use a particular program or tool (Fischer 2007, 2012) or engage in a particular CALL task (Chapelle 2001). Tracking techniques such as computer logs have shown that there is often a mismatch between students' reported and actual use of specific CALL program components. Fischer (2007) found that students were not consistently aware of what they did as they used a particular program, which calls into question the accuracy of their perceptions of the value of the program's components. Fischer (2007) also explained how tracking in CALL can be used to investigate SLA constructs such as input enhancement, negotiation of meaning, corrective feedback, noticing the gap, sociocultural learning, hypothesis testing, and metalinguistic reflections. He argues that through tracking learner behavior many studies have not only confirmed the operation of fundamental SLA principles but have also extended our understanding of these principles. For example, in terms of input enhancement, tracking shows that whereas perceptual saliency (e.g., adding color and/or bold face) has an impact on students' behavior, it is functional saliency (e.g., elaborating word meanings and grammatical features with multi-media annotations) which has an impact on students' learning.

## Tracking learner behavior

Researchers track learners' behavior by recording keystrokes, mouse clicks, scrolling up and down and other actions in relation to a stimulus from the computer program (in HCI) or inter-locutor (in HHI). *When* learners perform these actions is easily identified through timestamps. Moreover, researchers are able to use video screen capture programs in order to visibly inspect how learner navigates a computer program or other online task in real time. More recently, some researchers have been employing eye-tracking technology in SLA-relevant CALL studies. The following illustrate various forms of tracking used in such SLA-relevant studies.

### HCI

Drawing upon the SLA frameworks of strategies (Cohen 1998; O'Malley and Chamot 1990; Oxford 1993), individual differences and learning styles (Reid 1995; Skehan 1989), Pujolà (2002) developed a web-based ESL program, ImPRESSions, focusing on listening and reading comprehension for Spanish-speaking students. The program presented the content of the same news stories in both written and video formats within the software, and students had virtually complete control over their learning in the program. Recording students' actions with ScreenCam as they used the program, Pujolà hypothesized that students with lower decoding abilities in English would make more use of the available transcripts and subtitles for the video clips than students with higher decoding abilities. However, he discovered that students within each group behaved in varied, idiosyncratic ways in how they navigated through the program and accessed its help devices. The tracking data allowed Pujolà to derive two categories of usage patterns: a global approach in which students infrequently sought help of any kind and compulsive consultors in which students repeatedly clicked on various buttons, especially the rewind/replay buttons for the video clips, because they thought they had to understand every detail of the material to be learned.

Drawing on constructs from *processing instruction* (VanPatten 1993, 1997), noticing (Schmidt, 1990), and *consciousness raising tasks* (R. Ellis 1995; Smith 1993), Collentine (2000) tracked the number of times students accessed various components of a Spanish learning program and the amount of time they spent on each. Using regression analysis he estimated the contribution of the amount of time spent on each component to students' post-test scores. On the one hand, his analysis revealed that students' use of the audio component contributed significantly to their post-test performance but that they under-utilized this component as they navigated through the program. On the other hand, stu-dents' use of the video component did not contribute to their post-test performance even though they over-utilized it.

### HHI

In her exploration of the relationship between linguistic complexity in the input in a 3D envi-ronment and subsequent learner output in SCMC, Collentine (2013) used the tracking mech-anism built into the 3D environment to track the nature and amount of computer-generated input, learner responses, and the order in which learners interacted with objects in the virtual world. Results of quantitative and qualitative analyses suggest that for linguistic complexity to be evident in learner SCMC output, the input must have certain linguistic features and contain propositional information to assist learners in completing the task. Her data question the notion that linguistic complexity in input necessarily elicits linguistic complexity in output (Leow et al. 2003).

Writing from a cognitive interactionist theoretical perspective, Sauro and Smith (2010) examined the chat interaction by learners of German engaged in dyadic task-based SCMC. They examined typed and sent L2 output as well as that which is typed but then deleted (unsent) during synchronous written computer-mediated communication. Video screen capture records were used to get at the unsent output, which is normally not available from chat transcripts. The chat interaction was coded and analyzed for syntactic complexity, productive use of grammatical gender, and lexical diversity. Results showed that chat output that exhibited evidence of online planning displayed significantly greater linguistic complexity and lexical diversity than chat output that did not exhibit online planning. They argued that L2 learners appear to make good use of the increased online planning time afforded by chat to engage in careful production and monitoring.

## Eye tracking

CALL researchers have only recently begun employing eye-tracking technology in explorations of instructed SLA in CALL environments. Eye tracking affords researchers the ability to capture aspects of learner process data not available during face-to-face interaction. Eye movements during reading (in this case during text-based SCMC) can be used to infer moment-by-moment cognitive processing of a text by the reader without significantly altering the normal characteristics of either the task or the presentation of the stimuli (Dussias 2010). These eye movements are considered indicators of perceptual and cognitive processes. For example, eye-movement patterns reveal cognitive processes during pronoun resolution and co-reference and resolving lexical and syntactic ambiguity during reading in both L1 and L2 (Rayner 1998). The duration of an eye fixation is interpreted as an indicator of the processing time applied to the object being fixated on. A long fixation duration indicates either difficulty in extracting information, or greater engagement with the object (Just and Carpenter 1976).

Smith (2010, 2012) investigated the use of eye-tracking technology to help pinpoint learners' attention to and noticing of feedback in an L2 SCMC task-based environment. Recasts were chosen as the specific type of corrective feedback (CFB) investigated. Using eye fixation data as a measure of "noticing events" learners were found to attended to about 60% of the intensive recasts they received by a native speaker interlocutor. Lexical recasts were much easier than grammatical recasts for learners to notice, retain, and accurately produce on subsequent chat interaction and delayed written post-tests.

Using heat map records and stimulated recall records, Smith (2012) found that both stimulated recall and eye-tracking records were favorable predictors of learner noticing with the eye-tracking record being slightly more discriminating in its prediction on immediate post-test success. There was no significant relationship between the linguistic category of the recast and noticing in the eye-tracking condition. However, in the stimulated recall condition learners were much more likely to report having noticed recasts targeting semantic features than morphological recasts. This last finding has implications for SLA as it suggests that leaners show evidence of heightened attention to recasts, regardless of the linguistic category of the target. When considered in combination with the results from Smith (2010) these findings suggest that even with heightened attention on morphological recasts, learners were less able to attend to these features at a level that allowed them to make use of the teacher recast on the post-test. For SLA theory this is important as it is consistent with previous research by Mackey, Gass, and McDonough (2000) and Nabei and Swain (2002) who had positive findings for noticing lexical feedback over other types. This evidence is also compatible with an input processing theoretical perspective (VanPatten 1996), which argues that learners prefer to process information lexically over other features in the input and also emergentist notions of *blocking* and *overshadowing* (Ellis and Sagarra 2010).

# Conclusion

One of the major challenges in conducting SLA-relevant CALL research is dealing with the seemingly irreconcilable relationship between fast-paced technological development on the one hand and our need to fully explore in a principled way whether and how these technologies can be employed to facilitate second language acquisition, on the other. It is clear that the effectiveness of CALL for SLA cannot reside in the medium itself. Rather, effectiveness must be judged in how these technologies are put to use in ways that are consistent with theoretical and pedagogical developments in instructed SLA. Indeed, research suggests that L2 courses supported by instructional technology are at least as effective as and perhaps superior to those courses with no technology (Grgurović, Chapelle, and Shelley 2013), though it is difficult to imagine the latter. The current environment is fostering a degree of confluence of instructed SLA research with SLA-relevant CALL research, which has the potential to inform and shape SLA theory. Likewise, assertions, predications, and expectations from SLA theory must "hold up" in CALL environments and F2F environments alike. It is precisely this convergence of SLA and CALL research that may provide the building blocks for a developing CALL theory, which, as Hubbard (2008) describes, reflects a set of claims about the meaningful elements and processes within some domain of CALL, their interrelationships, and the impact that they have on language learning development and outcomes.

# REFERENCES

Anderson, John R. 1982. "Acquisition of Cognitive Skill." *Psychological Review,* 89: 369–406.

Baddeley, Alan. 1986. *Working Memory.* Oxford: Oxford University Press.

Beebe, Leslie, and Martha Clark Cummings. 1995. "Natural Speech Act Data Versus Questionnaire Data: How Data Collection Method Affects Speech Act Performance." In *Speech Acts Across Cultures: Challenges to Communication in a Second Language,* edited by S. M. Gass, and J. Neu, 65–86. Berlin: Mouton de Gruyter.

Chapelle, Carol A. 2001. *Computer Applications in Second Language Acquisition.* Cambridge: Cambridge University Press.

Chapelle, Carol A. 2003. *English Language Learning and Technology: Lectures on Applied Linguistics in the Age of Information and Communication Technology.* Amsterdam: John Benjamins.

Cohen, Andrew D. 1998. *Strategies in Learning and Using a Second Language.* New York: Longman.

Collentine, Joseph G. 2000. "Insights into the Construction of Grammatical Knowledge Provided by User-Behavior Tracking Technologies." *Language Learning & Technology,* 3: 44–57.

Collentine, Karina. 2013. "Using Tracking Technologies to Study the Effects of Linguistic Complexity in CALL Input and SCMC Output." In *Learner-Computer Interaction in Language Education,* edited by Phil Hubbard, Mathias Schulze, and Bryan Smith, 46–65. St. Marcos, TX: CALICO.

deBot, Kees. 1996. "Review Article: The Psycholinguistics of the Output Hypothesis." *Language Learning,* 46, no. 3: 529–255.

DeKeyser, Robert. 2005. "What Makes Learning Second Language Grammar Difficult? A Review of Issues." *Language Learning,* 55, Suppl 1: 1–25.

Dussias, Paola. 2010. "Uses of Eye-Tracking Data in Second Language Sentence Processing Research." *Annual Review of Applied Linguistics,* 30: 149–166.

Ellis, Nick. 1999. "Cognitive Approaches to SLA." *Annual Review of Applied Linguistics,* 19: 22–42.

Ellis, Nick. 2002. "Frequency Effects in Language Acquisition: A Review with Implications for Theories of Implicit and Explicit Language Acquisition." *Studies in Second Language Acquisition,* 24: 143–188.

Ellis, Nick, and Nuria Sagarra. 2010. "The Bounds of Adult Language Acquisition: Blocking and Learned Attention." *Studies in Second Language Acquisition*, 32: 553–580.

Ellis, Rod. 1995. "Interpretation Tasks for Grammar Teaching." *TESOL Quarterly*, 29: 87–106.

Ellis, Rod, Rick Heimbach, Yoshihiro Tanaka, and Atsuko Yamazaki. 1999. "Modified Input and the Acquisition of Word Meaning by Children and Adults." In *Learning a Second Language through Interaction*, edited by Rod Ellis, 63–114. Amsterdam: John Benjamins.

Fischer, Robert. 2007. "How do We Know What Students Are Actually Doing? Monitoring Students' Behavior in CALL." *Computer Assisted Language Learning*, 20, no. 5: 409–442.

Fischer, Robert. 2012. "Diversity in Learner Usage Patterns." In *Computer-assisted Language Learning Diversity in Research and Practice*, edited by Glenn Stockwell, 14–32. Cambridge: Cambridge University Press.

Gass, Susan M. 1997. *Input, Interaction, and the Second Language Learner*. Mahwah, NJ: Lawrence Erlbaum.

Grgurović, Maja, Carol Chapelle, and Mack Shelley. 2013. "A Meta-analysis of Effectiveness Studies on Computer Technology-supported Language Learning." *ReCALL*, 25, no. 2: 165–198.

Heift, Trude. 2010. "Developing an Intelligent Language Tutor." *CALICO Journal*, 27, no. 3: 443–459.

Hsu, Hsiu-chen. In press. "The Effect of Task Planning on L2 Performance and L2 Development in Text-based Synchronous Computer-mediated Communication." *Applied Linguistics*.

Hubbard, Phil. 2008. "25 Years of Theory in the CALICO Journal." *CALICO Journal*, 25, no. 3: 387–399.

Hulstijn, Jan. 2000. "The Use of Computer Technology in Experimental Studies of Second Language Acquisition: A Survey of Some Techniques and Some Ongoing Studies." *Language Learning & Technology*, 3, no. 2: 32–43.

Just, Marcel A., and Patricia A. Carpenter. 1976. "Eye Fixations and Cognitive Processes." *Cognitive Psychology*, 8, no. 4: 441–480.

Lantolf, James P., and Matthew E. Poehner. 2014. *Sociocultural Theory and The Pedagogical Imperative in L2 Education: Vygotskian Praxis and the Theory/practice Divide*. New York: Routledge.

Leow, R., Takako Egi, Ana Maria Nuevo, and Ya-Chin, Tsai. 2003. "The Roles of Textual Enhancement and Type of Linguistic Item in Adult L2 Learners' Comprehension and Intake." *Applied Language Learning*, 13: 93–108.

Levelt, Willem J. M. 1989. *Speaking: From Intention to Articulation*. Cambridge, MA: MIT Press.

Long, Michael H. 1996. "The Role of the Linguistic Environment in Second Language Acquisition." In *Handbook of Second Language Acquisition*, edited by W. Ritchie and T. Bhatia, 413–468. San Diego, CA: Academic Press.

Long, Michael H. 2007. *Problems in SLA*. Mahwah, NJ: Lawrence Erlbaum.

Lyster, Roy, and Leila Ranta. 1997. "Corrective Feedback and Learner Uptake: Negotiation of Form in Communicative Classrooms." *Studies in Second Language Acquisition*, 19: 37–67.

Mackey, Alison, Susan M. Gass, and Kim McDonough. 2000. "How Do Learners Perceive Interactional Feedback?" *Studies in Second Language Acquisition*, 22: 471–497.

Nabei, Toshiyo, and Merrill Swain. 2002. "Learner Awareness of Recasts in Classroom Interaction: A Case Study of an Adult EFL Student's Second Language Learning." *Language Awareness*, 11: 43–62.

O'Malley, J. Michael, and Anna Uhl Chamot. 1990. *Learning Strategies in Second Language Acquisition*. Cambridge: Cambridge University Press.

Ortega, Lourdes. 2009. *Understanding Second Language Acquisition*. New York: Routledge.

Oxford, Rebecca. 1993. "Research on Second Language Learning Strategies." *Annual Review of Applied Linguistics*, 13: 175–187.

Payne, J. Scott, and Paul J. Whitney. 2002. "Developing L2 Oral Proficiency through Synchronous CMC: Output, Working Memory, and Interlanguage Development." *CALICO Journal*, 20, no. 1: 7–32.

Pujolà, Joan-Tomás. 2002. "CALLing for Help: Researching Language Learning Strategies Using Help Facilities in a Web-based Multimedia Program." *ReCALL*, 14: 235–262.

Rama, Paul S., Rebecca W. Black, Elizabeth van Es, and Mark Warschauer. 2012. "Affordances for Second Language Learning in World of Warcraft." *ReCALL*, 24: 322–338.

Rayner, Keith. 1998. "Eye Movements in Reading and Information Processing: 20 Years of Research." *Psychological bulletin*, 124, no. 3: 372–422.

Reid, Joy M. 1995. *Learning Styles in the ESL/EFL Classroom*. Boston: Heinle and Heinle.

Sauro, Shannon, and Bryan Smith. 2010. "Investigating L2 Performance in Text Chat." *Applied Linguistics*, 31: 554–577

Schneider, Walter, and Richard Shiffrin. 1977. "Controlled and Automatic Human Information Processing: Detection, Search, and Attention." *Psychological Review*, 84: 1–66.

Schmidt, Richard. 1990. "The role of Consciousness in Second Language Learning." *Applied Linguistics*, 11: 127–158.

Seedhouse, Paul, and Saad Almutairi. 2009. "A Holistic Approach to Task-based Interaction." *International Journal of Applied Linguistics*, 19, no. 3: 311–338.

Sharwood Smith, Michael. 1993. "Input Enhancement in Instructed SLA: Theoretical Bases." *Studies in Second Language Acquisition*, 15: 165–179.

Skehan, Peter. 1989. *Individual Differences in Second Language Learning*. Sevenoaks: Edward Arnold.

Smith, Bryan. 2010. "Employing Eye Tracking Technology in Researching the Effectiveness of Recasts in CMC. In *Directions and Prospects for Educational Linguistics*, Vol. 11, edited by Francis M. Hult, 79–97. New York: Springer.

Smith, Bryan. 2012. "Eye Tracking as a Measure of Noticing: A Study of Explicit Recasts in SCMC." *Language Learning & Technology*, 16, no. 3: 53–81.

Smith, Bryan, and Greta J. Gorsuch. 2004. "Synchronous Computer Mediated Communication Captured by Usability Lab Technologies: New Interpretations." *System*, 32: 553–575.

Smith, Bryan, and Claire Renaud. 2013. "Eye Tracking as a Measure of Noticing Corrective Feedback in Computer-mediated Instructor-student Foreign Language Conferences." In *Interaction in diverse educational settings*, edited by Kim McDonough, and Alison Mackey, 147–165. Philadelphia: John Benjamins.

Suzuki, Satomi. 2013. "Private Turns: A Student's Off-screen Behaviors during Synchronous Online Japanese Instruction." *CALICO Journal*, 30, no. 3: 371–392.

Swain, Merrill. 1995. "Three Functions of Output in Second Language Learning." In *Principle and Practice in Applied Linguistics: Studies in Honour of H. G. Widdowson*, edited by Guy Cook, and Barbara Seidlhofer, 125–144. Oxford: Oxford University Press.

Swain, Merrill. 2005. "The Output Hypothesis: Theory and Research." In *Handbook of Second Language Teaching and Learning*, edited by Eli Hinkel, 471–483. Mahwah, NJ: Lawrence Erlbaum.

Sylvén, Liss Kerstin, and Pia Sundquist. 2017. "Computer-Assisted Language Learning (CALL) in Extracurricular/Extramural Contexts." *CALICO Journal*, 34, no. 1: i–iv.

VanPatten, Bill. 1993. "Grammar Teaching for the Acquisition Rich Classroom." *Foreign Language Annals*, 26: 435–450.

VanPatten, Bill. 1996. *Input Processing and Grammar Instruction in Second Language Acquisition*. New York: Ablex.

VanPatten, Bill. 1997. "The Relevance of Input Processing to Second Language Theory and Second Language Teaching." In *Contemporary Perspectives on the Acquisition of Spanish: Volume II*, edited by Ana Teresa Pérez-Leroux, and William R. Glass, 93–108. Sommerville, MA: Cascadilla Press.

VanPatten, Bill, and Alessandro G. Benati. 2010. *Key Terms in Second Language Acquisition*. London: Continuum.

Vygotsky, Lev S. 1978. *Mind in Society: The Development of Higher Psychological Processes*. Cambridge, MA: Harvard University Press.

# 30 Toward Langua-technocultural Competence

## SHANNON SAURO
## AND CAROL A. CHAPELLE

The chapters included in the *Handbook* paint a picture of important advances in technologies that have resulted in fundamental changes in language teaching and learning. By focusing up close on the learning activities, their development, and research investigating them, the papers in the *Handbook* depict some of the possibilities and excitement in a new generation of second language teaching. In this final chapter, we synthesize the main messages of the chapters into one that indicates that technology has arrived in the lives of language learners. After examining the implications of the arrival of technology and inspired by themes found in the science-fiction television series Star Trek, we look to the future to speculate on language teaching issues to come with expanded technology use by expanding learner populations.

## Technology has arrived!

The chapters in the *Handbook* present a complex range of new ideas, practices, and needs that suggest important developments in second language teaching. From the many directions, we identified three fundamental themes that seem to be significant as we look forward to second language teaching in the future. The first is the multimodal nature of the language abilities that need to be taught and investigated in language teaching and research in order to engage with the reality of the world in which students learn and use language. The second is the continuous innovative nature of language teaching and learning that teachers need to make part of their conceptions of themselves as teachers. The third is the integral role of research in understanding and using the changing landscape of English language teaching and learning. Each of these themes is explained by culling the perspectives put forth in the previous chapters before looking to the future to speculate on implications for technology and second language learning and teaching.

## Communicative competence is multimodal

The authors of Chapters 3 through 9 provide vivid descriptions of how students can learn the various aspects of a second language in the digital age. In doing so, they present an updated vision of what each of these aspects of communicative competence means. Overall, the picture is a definition of competence that includes contexts in which language is used, taught, and learned. The contexts necessarily include provision of technological affordances,

*The Handbook of Technology and Second Language Teaching and Learning*, First Edition.
Edited by Carol A. Chapelle and Shannon Sauro.
© 2017 John Wiley & Sons, Inc. Published 2020 by John Wiley & Sons, Inc.

not the least of which is the connection made possible to the people, language, and culture that the learner is studying. To capture the significance of this connection, in Chapter 9, Sykes refers to the object of study for second language learners as languaculture. Languaculture is also the term used by Chun in Chapter 26 when she describes the object of research in studies of CALL. The term languaculture, as Sykes explains originated outside of CALL to capture the goals of foreign language study with a term that denotes the inseparability of language and culture as well as the necessary inclusion of culture in the study of language.

Chapters 3 through 9 suggest that language study today would be even better characterized by the term langua-technoculture to denote the technology-mediated nature of so much of learners' second language experience. The impetus for the term langua-technoculture is most vividly depicted in Sykes' discussion of learning intercultural competence and interlanguage pragmatics. She argues that "learners must be equipped to participate in everyday interactions that occur in, through, and around digital discourse spaces" (128), such as those found on Facebook, YouTube, Twitter, and fanfiction sites. In other words, the repertoire of pragmatic competence to be learned needs to cover the competence to act in the range of spaces where students have opportunities for language contact. Sykes' focus on pragmatics which is itself defined with reference to the context of communicative acts is a clear example, but the lingua-technocontext thread runs throughout these chapters: from grammar to speaking, the technology is the mediator not only for learning but also for the emerging competence that students are expected to develop.

For both grammar and vocabulary learning, the authors of Chapter 3 and Chapter 4, respectively depict learners in interaction with technologies which provide access to help. In doing so they present technology-based pedagogies as spanning the divide between options for implicit vs. explicit teaching of language. Tutorial CALL, and especially intelligent tutorial CALL, is good for deductive presentation and interactive practice with pre-selected grammar and vocabulary. Tools such as concordancers and vocabulary tools that respond to the users' input make possible implicit learning with language focus as needed. The authors emphasize the importance of training learners to use these tools if they are to have the desired impact during the course and beyond. In other words, the authors see such training as pertaining to both students' learning and use of the language.

The confluence of strategic technology learning and strategic technology use is most evident in the teaching of writing. Li, Dursun, and Hegelheimer introduce their discussion of technology in second language writing in Chapter 6 with the observation that writing has changed dramatically and that "the same wave of technologies affecting writing practices provides a wealth of tools for the teaching of second or foreign language writing" (77). Writing is a mode of communication that can challenge any language user to create an effective message in a given context, and therefore technological tools are likely to continue to be developed and refined for all writers. In this context, becoming a good writer, in part, means learning to use the technological tools that contribute to writing quality.

The tools for communication are not limited to writing. In Chapters 5, 7, and 8, the authors describe scenarios in which learners use real world communication tools as part of their learning processes. In Chapter 8, Blake describes the use of speaking resources such as Skype that provide opportunities for structured speaking tasks in class and speaking for a range of social and instrumental purposes beyond the classroom. Liaw and English describe the use of the enormous repository of texts available on the internet for engaging in reading-based projects in Chapter 5. They even suggest that mobile devices make practical the vision of ubiquitous learning when it comes to learning to read. In Chapter 7, Hubbard similarly identifies the value of internet sources for developing listening skills, citing in particular "development of content for listening [which] involves the collection of enriched media for the learner in terms of topic, language level, and other features, a process known as content curation" (103) Curation can result in a manageable collection of audio-visual resources from the overwhelming number available on the internet. All such resources and tools that students are taught to use in the classroom represent aspects of potential development for the langua-tecnocultural competence they will need beyond the classroom.

The fact that much of students' language use out of the classroom is mediated through technology is enormously important for language teaching. At the same time, it is critical to recognize the technologies designed specifically to help learners learn and access the language. The tutorials and tools described for learning vocabulary by Ma in Chapter 4 and for learning grammar by Heift and Vyatkina in Chapter 3 play a central role in developing basic knowledge of the language and technology skills. Beyond these, tools such as grammar checkers, pronunciation feedback tools, as well as tools and materials developed to scaffold students' understanding of written, aural, and visually presented messages play a critical role in language learning. That communication is multimodal and that oral language can be captured and replayed are facts for language users today. For language *learners*, in contrast, multimodality and repeatability can provide a degree of redundancy in messages that makes meaning accessible and therefore can aid in learning. Insofar as learners recognize the value of particular technology uses, succeed in learning the relevant strategies, and take responsibility for their own learning, the potential appears to exist for a transformation in second language learning practices.

Technology-integrated conceptions of language knowledge and skills need to be updated to include the technology-mediated contexts in which language learners communicate and learn. Moreover, the need exists for applied linguists to better understand the nature of multimodal communication in these contexts. As Chanier and Lamy demonstrate in Chapter 28, communication is accomplished through a variety of semiotic resources of which language is an important one. Chanier and Lamy therefore explain the significant issues involved in researching such multimodal communication. Findings from multimodal discourse analysis and learning have important implications for both language teaching and assessment. Broadly stated, one implication is that choices made about what to teach and what to test need to be constantly open to revision. Similarly, how to teach and how to test must be open to change. In other words, the idea of langua-technoculture put forward bit-by-bit in Chapters 3 through 9 points to the need for innovation in second language teaching to be an ongoing project.

## *Diffusion of innovation should be normal*

Because contexts of language learning and use are rapidly changing, teachers and materials developers need a mechanism to incorporate innovation into teaching. In other words, the practice of seeking out, creating, and trying innovative approaches to teaching needs to become normal. In the classic work in sociology on the diffusion of innovation, innovation is defined as "an idea, practice, or object that is perceived as new by an individual or other unit of adoption" (Rogers 2003, 12). Based on Rogers' definition (from an earlier edition of the book), which has served in language education (Markee, 1997), software and technology-based pedagogical practices have typically qualified as innovation in language teaching. Diffusion of technology-based pedagogy across a wide range of teachers proves to be a slow, labored process, with teachers often lacking the basic computer skills and motivation for exploring the ever-changing options for students learning.

The situation seems to be slowly changing. *Handbook* authors describe many innovations that are within reach for language teachers today, in part because the majority draw upon technologies and pedagogies that are being used across the curriculum. Distance learning, blended learning, and telecollaboration, for example, are not limited to language learning, and therefore a larger community of educators may be the ones who bring language teachers into discussions of these innovations. Similarly, virtual worlds, digital gaming, and mobile learning are not the exclusive domain of language learning and teaching. As the authors in Chapters 10 through 15 explain, however, technology-based pedagogies offer relevant affordances for language learning.

In Chapter 10, White outlines a long history of distance learning, which encompasses courses across the curriculum. Modern distance learning for language study became much more interesting with the advent of technology, and today White sees the need for pedagogical innovation through strategic use of new tools. In Chapter 11, Grgurović also situates blended language learning within the broader context of blended learning in education, which has been an object of great interest due to the success that has been achieved in classes through blended learning. Grgurović concludes from a review of 26 investigations of blended language learning studies, "The positive findings suggest that blended learning is likely to continue," (164) but as with distance learning, attention is needed to the specific tools and pedagogical tasks that make up the online parts of the curriculum.

Telecollaboration is also introduced within a history of general education where opportunities for cross-cultural contact and learning were valued. Dooly explains in Chapter 12 how the internet has made possible the goal of achieving such contact on a scope unimaginable even 25 years ago. Participation in telecollaborative second language learning keeps growing at a rapid pace, and with this growth teachers and researchers are seeing a growing number of new issues and opportunities. Dooly points to the need for "inquiry into related questions and issues concerning content, materials, assessment, and curriculum when dealing with telecollaboration as an integral part of the language learning process" (177). Not the least of the issues is the need for a better grasp of cultural, social, and political issues, perhaps in part through developing transdisciplinary projects for student learning.

In Chapters 13, 14, and 15, the authors describe technological advances created for amusement, enjoyment, and convenience across many facets of life. Each of the advances, virtual worlds, digital gaming, and mobile technologies, respectively, is described in terms of the way that they have been used as a basis for new second language pedagogies. Sadler's discussion of virtual worlds in Chapter 13 describes software tools and practices used for creating innovative tasks for language use, that "promise to change the ways that we understand both human-to-human interaction and what it means to be a student of language" (199). In Chapter 14, Reinhardt describes the innovative nature of digital gaming in second language learning and stresses the need for research to keep pace with the growth in popularity of games for second language learning. The suggestions raise issues similar to those discussed in Chapter 24 on design-based research, which emphasizes the importance of teachers, researchers, and developers working together to gain insight about learning in these contexts. Mobile language learning is described by Kukulska-Hulme, Lee, and Norris as having transformational implications for language teaching and learning because of its natural capacity for bridging the formal learning of the classroom with the informal learning opportunities outside the classroom.

Three other areas of technology-based pedagogy included in the *Handbook* depict innovations that are unique to second language teaching and were developed on the basis of theory, research, and practice in applied linguistics and language teaching. In Chapter 16, on the use of technology in task-based language teaching, González-Lloret argues that "the approach to [second language] curriculum design known as task-based language teaching (TBLT) is ideal for informing and fully realizing the potential of technological innovations for language learning" (234) because of its basis in theory and research on instructed second language acquisition. Taking a different point of departure from applied linguistics, Cotos describes an approach to corpus-based pedagogy in computer-assisted language teaching for specific purposes. She introduces the ways that corpora can serve as sources of reference to create

LSP materials and how learners can interact directly with corpora. These basic concepts form the basis for sophisticated CALL materials for teaching LSP writing that combine indirect and direct corpus applications to create interactive tools for genre-based writing pedagogy. In Chapter 18, Ware describes the bases for the technology-literacies interface that has been so important in conceptualizing the new forms of multimodal literacies students need for schooling and for work in society. The lens on literacy that she offers is needed to appreciate the fact that "it is very possible to be literate in some ways, but not in others" and to use this fact in developing curriculum, materials, and assessments for language learners.

With respect to low-stakes assessment of learners' language abilities, Jamieson and Musumeci report that technologies are used to accompany beginning-level foreign-language textbooks and online courseware. Their evaluation of the assessments included in 12 online language programs and 36 textbooks examined the degree of the content match between the course and the assessments, the opportunity they provide for learners to notice a gap between their knowledge and correct responses, and provision of suggestions to test-takers on how they can improve their knowledge. Their analysis shows that provision of some form of online assessment has become common for commercially available language materials even if their scope of coverage and quality of feedback is limited. In high-stakes assessment, Schmidgall and Powers report how new technologies have been embraced to provide numerous benefits despite challenges that technology places on the testing process.

The spirit of innovation seems to be alive in practices that have yielded so many new options for learning from technological affordances. However, for diffusion of innovation to take place, teachers and future teachers need to develop an attitude of continual openness. Li, Dursun, and Hegelheimer interpret openness with respect to the use of technological tools for writing instruction: "Openness in this domain means that L2 writing teachers are expected to experience these technologies themselves" (89). Development of such an attitude to complement knowledge of technology is a challenge for teacher education. For teachers to transform their experiential knowledge into opportunities for students to participate and learn from these new affordances, teacher education must play an important role in fostering teachers' enthusiasm for innovation. It is no wonder then that Kessler and Hubbard end their discussion of language teacher education in Chapter 19 with the observation that "Researchers should continue to investigate the circumstances that support successful situated learning across an array of potential contexts to inform future CALL teacher preparation. Such research informed by knowledge of an evolving socio/ecological understanding regarding use of technologies throughout our lives is needed to keep teacher preparation programs relevant to teachers' needs" (288).

## Research must be integral to teaching and learning

The concerns that Kessler and Hubbard express from the vantage point of teacher education are evident in the work of some researchers and developers as well. Perhaps most directly relevant is the type of research-development synergy that Rodríguez portrays in his chapter on design-based research. Design-based research may seem to be the result of what should be a natural synergy between research and language instruction. In the relationship, theory also plays a central role—so central that Rodríguez underscores that an important strand of discussion in the DBR community is about the nature of theory and the role it plays in the process of designing and evaluating learning activities. Today, most experts in the field would find it difficult to approach the many decisions they must make in the development of CALL materials without an integrated research program that works from and contributes to theory. To help clarify the nature and use of theory, Rodríguez outlines four elements that are critical to the synergy: (1) theoretical claims drawn from previous research need to be supported by additional evidence, (2) DBR researchers both use and contribute to theory,

(3) iterative cycles of theorizing and designing materials allow for revision of both theory and designs, and (4) universality of theoretical findings is not the goal.

The congruence between theory and practice in these studies positions them to speak to theory. Moreover, the fact that such studies draw upon a range of research designs opens the possibility for asking a variety of research questions and providing relevant answers to those questions. Chun's review of CALL research in Chapter 26 summarized the existing collection of research as including studies that use experimental or quasi-experimental designs from quantitative traditions, case study, discourse analysis and ethnography from qualitative traditions, as well as mixed methods within a single study to address a range of research questions. Chun connects the choice of research methods to the theory underlying the pedagogy and the languaculture target of the instruction. In other words, research methods depend on what is taught and explanations for how it is taught.

In Chapter 29, Smith expands on the types of explanations, or theories that have been prominent in CALL research as falling within one of three major categories: cognitive approaches, interactionist approaches, and sociocultural theory. Some CALL studies are considered *SLA-relevant* because findings can be interpreted as pertaining to the theoretical perspectives that provided the basis for the CALL activities. In this environment, he argues, "predications and expectations from SLA theory must 'hold up' in CALL environments and F2F environments alike" (456) if they are to be treated as theories with universal relevance. He also suggests that it is the "confluence of SLA and CALL research that may provide the building blocks for a developing CALL theory" (456). Both Smith and Chun note the importance of meta-analysis for advances in theoretical understanding of various types of CALL activities for learning. In Chapter 27, Liou and Lin underscore their importance with a discussion of quality in meta-analytic studies of CALL.

Between the momentum toward SLA-relevant studies that seek to inform universalist SLA theory and the project-specific principles developed in DBR lies a large body of evaluation studies that are more difficult to characterize. Some are motivated by theory or pedagogical beliefs. However, to encompass the range of investigations that are conducted to evaluate of the quality of CALL activities, Chapelle refers to them in Chapter 25 as presenting a range of rationales and evidence to present evaluation *arguments*. This general perspective on evaluation has been used with success in language testing, where the evaluation of the test for its particular purpose is conceptualized by stating a series of claims about the test interpretation and use which are justified by particular types of evidence, as Chung explains in Chapter 22. The research methods required to support claims depend on the nature of the evidence sought and the result is a validity argument.

Applying this perspective to CALL evaluation, research methods are selected in view of the theoretical basis for the learning and what is taught, as Chun noted. An additional consideration, however, is the *use* and *user* of the results. Results need to speak to the type of claims that are relevant and useful to a certain audience. The idea of evaluation as argument that Chapelle presents in Chapter 24 has a scholarly tradition in social science, language education, and language testing. As a first step toward extending the basic principles to CALL evaluation, she provides examples of the types of arguments that have appeared in CALL journals with the aim of helping to clarify the motivations for theoretical and methodological choices made in evaluation studies. The move toward greater clarity in research purposes should be helpful in working toward the goal of developing the situated knowledge that is the goal of DBR and that Hubbard (Chapter 7) points to for increasing understanding of technologies used for teaching listening. His vision is "to continue to expand our research base to understand the conditions under which [particular technological] features are more and less helpful, passing those findings on to developers, teachers, and learners who will in turn help us to refine them" (104).

These chapters can leave little doubt that when technology is involved research becomes integral to teaching and learning. Moreover, the DBR approach to research underscores the importance of designers of materials being at the same time researchers and theorists. All three roles are often filled by teachers, as well. Therefore, authoring tools have long been a central issue in the CALL community. In the *Handbook*, authoring tools figure heavily into the historical introduction to the field presented by Otto in Chapter 2 because a large part of what it meant to be working in CALL for at least the first two decades meant that one was developing CALL materials. Godwin-Jones' discussion in Chapter 23 focusing explicitly on authoring tools demonstrates the range of practices included under the umbrella of authoring. He points out that today's courseware developers tend to work on teams that build authoring tools, create multimodal content, and try out many iterations of designs before courseware is launched. CALL professionals can hope for concepts from DBR to infiltrate the courseware development process in coming years when they have more fully saturated the CALL community.

Regardless of what happens in the CALL community, however, the march of technology continues forward. Language learners already use their mobile, laptop, and desktop devices to mediate their language use. They are already engaging in some forms of langua-technoculture, but what will these practices entail in the future?

Discussion of technology prompts authors to speculate on what might be coming next, and we do so in the final section of this chapter by taking a page from the predictions of science fiction to explore areas of research and development needed to increase knowledge in the area of second language teaching and learning with technology.

## To boldly go: L2 teaching and learning issues for the future

The mid- to late-twentieth century U.S. science-fiction television series Star Trek and its offshoots, set in the 23rd and 24th centuries, both predicted and inspired technologies that, as the chapters in this volume exemplify, have become a part of the daily reality for many in the 21st century. These include portable communication devices that allow for remote (Kukulska-Hulme, Lee, and Norris, Chapter 15, this volume) multimodal communication and interaction (Chanier and Lamy, Chapter 28, this volume), virtual simulation environments that support both immersive learning (Sadler, Chapter 13, this volume) and entertainment opportunities (Reinhardt, Chapter 14, this volume), extensive data storage and intelligent computer applications that assist with information storing, gathering, and sharing (Cotos, Chapter 17, this volume), and translation tools that support interaction between communities with different language systems. Students and teachers in computer-enhanced 21st-century language classrooms might find themselves rather at home on a 24th-century starship.

However, the Star Trek universe was not without its problems, and even 300 years in the future, technology is still unable to resolve all challenges encountered by those exploring new societies and languages on other planets throughout the galaxy. In particular, while technology facilitated interaction, it did not always guarantee effective communication or understanding. In one memorable episode, highly sophisticated translation devices proved almost useless when used to communicate with members of a society that spoke completely in metaphors that were drawn from their own traditions and historical events, all of which were entirely unfamiliar to those outside their society (Menosky and LaZebnik 1991). As a result, in order for communication to succeed, it was necessary for a member of this society to first find a way to teach their histories, myths, and ways of thinking to outsiders. This challenge depicted in science fiction relates directly to challenges echoed in Sykes'

(Chapter 9, this volume) discussion of intercultural communicative competence and Chun's (Chapter 26, this volume) broadening of computer-assisted language learning (CALL) to computer-assisted languaculture learning. Future work in CALL must consider this inextricable link between language and culture and the mediating influence of technology, or langua-technoculture as we suggested in this chapter to account for the 21st-century challenges of teaching and communicating across languages and cultures.

## What learners are served by technology and how?

In her historical retrospective of technology for language teaching and learning, Otto (Chapter 2, this volume) traces the shift in language learner populations who first benefited from computer-assisted language learning in the mid-20th century (primarily university students at a few institutions) to those in the present day (young and old learners both in and outside of formal educational contexts). While university foreign language students still drive a good deal of the research on technology for language teaching and learning as reflected in many of the studies reviewed throughout the *Handbook*, the increasingly ubiquitous nature of digital communication tools means ever-expanding and diverse groups of language learners will push the scope of technology-enhanced language teaching, particularly through the growing options available for study through distance learning (White, Chapter 10, this volume). These expanding learner populations include, for example, autonomous learners engaged in extramural language learning (Sundqvist and Sylvén 2014) such as those identified in Reinhardt's (Chapter 14, this volume) discussion of online gamers, some of whom find their way into formal language-learning contexts.

The reach of technology into daily life also means that previously unexplored learner populations have specific language-learning needs that may be met through computer-assisted language learning. In Europe, for instance, research on the use of digital tools such as Whatsapp, Facebook, and various voiceover internet protocols (VOIP) networks by refugees entering Germany has demonstrated how instrumental social media has been in assisting in their travel to and assimilation into new countries (MiCT 2016). Much like the space explorers of Star Trek, who depended upon hand-held mobile technologies to survive on new planets, for many of these refugees, a local SIM card is as essential for survival as food and shelter. Included among these populations are unaccompanied minors, children under 18 traveling without an adult. For instance, in 2015, 35,000 unaccompanied minors sought asylum in Sweden, a country of 9.8 million, with a large number settling in Malmö, Sweden's third largest city (Sauro 2016). These linguistic and culturally diverse and often digitally savvy youth now face the prospect of receiving instruction in Swedish as a second language in order to be educated in Swedish schools. In what way, therefore, can technology facilitate the learning of a non-global language by digitally-connected youth fleeing war, oppression, and violence without the support of their families? This is just one such example of second language learner populations whose learning needs can hopefully be met by digital tools and which have not been explored in depth by research in CALL. Such learners and their technology also represent a rich area for collaboration between practitioners and researchers hoping to develop tools based on local theories and conduct research on the relevant populations, as described by Rodríguez's (Chapter 24, this volume) discussion of design-based research into CALL.

As has been noted throughout the *Handbook*, future research and practice in technology-mediated language learning must investigate and take into account the technologies and practices that best meet the needs of diverse learning contexts (Li, Dursun, and Hegelehimer, Chapter 6, this volume). The crews of galactic starships chronicled in Star Trek similarly had to assess how to meet a continuing stream of unimagined challenges with new technologies, and therefore our look to the future benefits from their experience.

## What skills and knowledge do L2 learners need?

Much as the imagined technology of the 23rd and 24th centuries required the characters of Star Trek to develop skills and knowledge for negotiating conflict with and strategizing solutions to new societies and contexts, so too must 21st-century learners develop skills and knowledge for dealing with new communities and contexts made available to them through digital communication tools. In education circles, such skills and knowledge are often subsumed under the term of 21st-century skills. In her synthesis of different frameworks for 21st-century skills, Suto (2013) found the following abilities were considered essential: "problem-solving, ICT operations and concepts, communication, collaboration, and information literacy" (22) many of which K-12 CALL practitioners regularly grapple within the framework of "New Literacies" in the context of L2 teaching (Ware, Chapter 18, this volume).

Several of these abilities were highlighted by Chun, Kern, and Smith (2016) in their recent overview of principles for technology and language teaching and learning, including ways of dealing with new texts and genres supported by digital communication technologies. These new text types allow not only for new kinds of communication, story-telling, and textual production, but also require critical approaches to reading. The need for critical reading echoes the concerns raised by Liaw and English (Chapter 5, this volume) in their discussion of the need for language educators to find ways to help learners deal with issues of distraction and information overload that so much new information and text types bring. Relating directly to the 21s-century skills associated with information literacy, they also argue that successful L2 reading in the digital age is far more than the ability to decode but also requires the ability to critically evaluate texts. Within this environment of distracting texts and expanding text types, how then can educators best focus their learners' attention in a manner that is productive for language learning?

With the proliferation of new text types come new ways of teasing, misleading, and even verbally attacking, all of which have ramifications for L2 learners and users and yet which are seldom addressed in studies of language learning (Chun, Kern, and Smith, 2016). A rare example is touched upon in Pasfield-Neofitou's (2011) study of Australian learners of Japanese in online communities, in which one participant's choice of language (English or Japanese) or use of online platform was driven by concerns over hostile or abusive posts directed at non-Japanese or less proficient Japanese speakers. Such choices reveal how one autonomous language learner strategized opportunities for target language practice in an environment in a manner that was conducive to her own socio-affective needs as an L2 speaker. Questions worth further exploration include what other strategies both successful and unsuccessful L2 users employ in online spaces to carve out opportunities for comprehensible input, pushed output, feedback, and attention to form. In other words, the knowledge, skills, and strategies that make up langua-technocultural competence need to be investigated continually across various contexts by addressing questions such as the following:

## What tasks, tests and teachers best serve learners' needs?

The most famous training exercises featured in Star Trek is the no-win scenario known as the Kobayashi Maru, which was designed to test the character and command skills of future starship captains in the face of certain loss. This simulation task required cadets to either rescue or abandon the crew and passengers of a civilian space vessel, the Kobayashi Maru, stranded in enemy territory. As a no-win scenario, whatever choice the cadet makes would result in the certain death of hundreds, possibly the cadet's own crew, and the likelihood of starting a war. The goal of this simulation, therefore, was to offer insight into the cadet's leadership and decision-making skills in the face of extreme stress and a hopeless outcome (Memory Alpha 2016a). While this 23rd-century task is higher stakes than the tasks required of learners in the language classroom, it does serve as an example of the complex skills increasingly required of technology-mediated tasks facing language learners in the 21st century.

The development of 21st-century skills requires that language educators devise technology-mediated tasks which not only draw upon students' abilities and needs with respect to language and digital skills (González-Lloret, Chapter 16, this volume) but which also facilitate communication, collaboration, critical thinking, and problem-solving in linguistically and culturally diverse digital contexts. These are the challenges that Dooly (Chapter 12, this volume) articulates in her discussion of tasks and projects for telecollaboration which prepare language learners for the transdisciplinary demands of both the 21st-century classroom and work space. Crucial to these often transnational digitally-mediated educational and work spaces is intercultural competence, a concept which invokes again Chun's argument for understanding CALL as computer-assisted languaculture learning. The fact that such spaces are created, inhabited, and maintained through the use of technology suggested our evolution of the term to langua-technoculture.

One area with an established history in CALL for supporting both language and culture learning is telecollaboration (O'Dowd 2016). Recent critiques of telecollaboration have argued that tasks found in the telecollaboration literature tend to focus on factual information sharing instead of true intercultural learning or "learners moving between cultures and reflecting on their own cultural positioning" (Liddicoat and Scarino 2013, 117). Addressing this concern, a growing consensus in the telecollaboration literature points to the need for offline activities such as reflective tasks and scaffolded discussions led by teachers who guide students into developing cultural knowledge and intercultural awareness in a more structured fashion (O'Dowd 2016) and from the beginning of their language study (Chapelle 2016).

Another emerging area of task development which integrates langua-technocultural learning is that which looks to the online media practices of language learners outside the classroom as a model for the development of fanfiction and fan tasks inside the classroom (Sauro 2014). Fanfiction, defined as creative writing that reimagines and transforms an existing text, television show, movie, or other piece of media, is perhaps one of the best known fan practices. Among autonomous second language learners, fanfiction has been used to foster both linguistic and identity development (see for example, Black 2006). Building upon these online fan practices, recent work in advanced language classrooms has incorporated the use of fanfiction tasks modeled on digital fanfiction genres found in online fan spaces and social media to support both linguistic and literary competence (Sauro and Sundmark 2016).

What work in telecollaboration, fandom tasks and in areas such as the teaching of grammar (Heift and Vyatkina, Chapter 3, this volume), speaking (Blake, Chapter 8, this volume), and vocabulary (Ma, Chapter 4 this volume) highlight is the significant role of the teacher in developing and implementing effective tasks that support langua-technocultural learning, either through or around digitally-mediated interaction. The role of the teacher speaks to the importance of teacher preparation in training language teachers to work effectively with technology to meet the needs and goals of diverse learner populations. However, the increasingly ubiquitous nature of technology for learning and teaching underlies one of the particular challenges of teacher preparation in the 21st century, that of normalization, in which CALL practices become so fully integrated within language teaching as to be nearly invisible (Kessler and Hubbard, Chapter 19, this volume).

As CALL practices become normalized, the risk is that the impetus for effective teacher preparation in CALL may also disappear, particularly when the majority of language teachers are themselves natives of the so-called digital generation. As the examples from telecollaboration show, effective teaching with technology entails more than the understanding of how to keep up with ever-changing digital tools; it also requires intercultural competence, the ability to adapt to new context and spaces, and the ability to design tasks and interventions around technology that enable L2 learners to develop these same skills. Questions for the future include, for example, what tasks will be most effective to support langua-technoculture learning and assessment (and not just language learning and assessment), and how teacher preparation can help overcome the normalization of technology and foster openness to the normalization of the diffusion of innovation?

## How does technology mediate languaculture learning?

In Star Trek, one of the first technologies introduced to viewers was the transporter, a device that enables almost instantaneous transportation by dematerializing an object (or passenger) into subatomic particles and then rematerializing it elsewhere. Due to safety concerns, initial use of the transporter was often limited to non-biological material, so that most human transportation was mediated by shuttlecraft (Memory Alpha 2016b). As the technology to ensure safety grew, so too did reliance on the transporter until it became the primary tool for human transportation. In conjunction with the refinement of technology, the changing needs of space travelers, and the knowledge and skills these travelers brought with them, the functions of the transporter also grew. Particularly innovative uses included storage of refugees' subatomic particles in a buffer while a starship passed through a warzone (Taylor 1998) or programming a transporter to run in constant diagnostic mode to hold a lone stranded traveler running out of supplies in a form of stasis until he could be rescued 75 years later (Moore 1992).The example of the Star Trek transporter, both how it limited and facilitated transportation and other practices, illustrates the recursive relationship between technology/tool and user, which underlies the concept of affordances and how these might mediate languageculture learning and use.

Affordances is a concept that originated in psychology (Gibson 1977) to explain an animal's behavior in response to its environment based on what the environment provides or affords the animal. More recently, the concept has been expanded to include not only the possibilities and constraints of environments or tools (including digital technologies and new media) but also users' perceptions of these technologies' possibilities and constraints based on their own prior knowledge and experience (Lee 2007).

As the overview of the many areas encompassed by CALL included in this *Handbook* show, language teachers, students, and researchers bring with them increasingly sophisticated and varied experiences with digital technologies. As a result, the affordances and perceived affordances of language-learning technologies represent a crucial direction for researchers and practitioners to consider. Indeed, as Hubbard (Chapter 7, this volume) argues, the constantly evolving pace of technological innovation makes questions asking whether new digital tools are effective for language learning less relevant or useful than questions that account for actual and perceived affordances of the tool; for example, for which types of users in conjunction with which other tools, practices, beliefs, prior experiences, and in what manner do existing and emerging digital technologies mediate langua-technoculture learning and use? Kern's (2014) exploration of the affordances of video-conferencing as part of a telecollaboration project for languaculture learning is an illustration of this type of question. Analysis of language learners' interaction and their understanding of their own practices revealed both how the technology mediated the message being conveyed as well as how managing the affordances of the video-conferencing tool was crucial in the resulting communication and in users' understanding of the learning experience.

Overviews of the extensive body of CALL research and teaching practices included in this *Handbook* provide a starting point for examining how language learning and teaching with technology has changed as a result of the actual and perceived affordances of digital technologies for specific learner populations. Such an examination of changes in learning and teaching with technology can facilitate an understanding of how the use of a particular tool has shifted over time (e.g., the complexity of language users generate in synchronous text-chat environments over the past 20 years), in what ways the normalization of technology may promote or actually hinder L2 learning processes and outcomes (e.g., the influence of automatic correction or character selection on writing and reading abilities), how the integration of specific tools has changed in response to changing social realities (e.g., concerns about cyberbullying, copyright law, and identity theft), how language users negotiate the transnational pragmalinguisic contact zones opened up by social media (Sykes, Chapter 9, this volume), and what all of these mean for both language learning and language teaching with technology.

# Conclusion

Technology-mediated language learning, teaching, assessment and research might often have been driven by the technologies themselves, but the changing global landscape and diverse needs and backgrounds of learners who now have access to technology-mediated language teaching require new venues of exploration. The science-fiction television series Star Trek encapsulates a pop culture allegory for the future of L2 teaching and learning with technology that asks the field to explore diverse learner populations whose familiarity with digital technologies and specific langua-technoculture needs are different from those we regularly investigated, that the langua-technoculture learning tasks and assessments designed for these populations also account for the skills and knowledge required of these 21st-century language learners and users, and that investigations of digital tools consider the actual and perceived affordances of these populations.

## REFERENCES

Black, Rebecca.W. 2006. "Language, Culture, and Identity in Online Fanfiction". *E-learning*, 3, 180–184.

Blake, Robert J. 2017. "Technologies for Teaching and Learning L2 Speaking." In *The Handbook of Technology and Second Language Teaching and Learning*, edited by Carol A. Chapelle and Shannon Sauro, 107–117. Oxford: Wiley-Blackwell.

Chanier, Thierry, and Marie-Noëlle Lamy. 2017. "Researching Technology-Mediated Multimodal Interaction." In *The Handbook of Technology and Second Language Teaching and Learning*, edited by Carol A. Chapelle and Shannon Sauro, 428–443. Oxford: Wiley-Blackwell.

Chapelle, Carol A. 2016. *Teaching Culture in Introductory Foreign Language Textbooks*. London: Palgrave Macmillan.

Chapelle, Carol A. 2017. "Evaluation of Technology and Language Learning." In *The Handbook of Technology and Second Language Teaching and Learning*, edited by Carol A. Chapelle and Shannon Sauro, 378–392. Oxford: Wiley-Blackwell.

Chun, Dorothy M. 2017. "Research Methods for Investigating Technology for Language and Culture Learning." In *The Handbook of Technology and Second Language Teaching and Learning*, edited by Carol A. Chapelle and Shannon Sauro, 393–408. Oxford: Wiley-Blackwell.

Chun, Dorothy M., Richard Kern, and Bryan Smith. 2016. "Technology Use, Language Teaching, and Language Learning." *The Modern Language Journal*, 100 (Supplement 2016): 64–80.

Cotos, Elena. 2017. "Language for Specific Purposes and Corpus-Based Pedagogy." In *The Handbook of Technology and Second Language Teaching and Learning*, edited by Carol A. Chapelle and Shannon Sauro, 248–264. Oxford: Wiley-Blackwell.

Chun, Yoo-Ree. 2017. "Validation of Technology-Assisted Language Tests." In *The Handbook of Technology and Second Language Teaching and Learning*, edited by Carol A. Chapelle and Shannon Sauro, 332–347. Oxford: Wiley-Blackwell.

Dooly, Melinda. 2017. "Telecollaboration." In *The Handbook of Technology and Second Language Teaching and Learning*, edited by Carol A. Chapelle and Shannon Sauro, 169–183. Oxford: Wiley-Blackwell.

Gibson, James, J. 1977. "The Theory of Affordances." In *Perceiving, Acting, and Knowing*, edited by Robert Shaw and John Bransford, 67–82. Hillsdale, NJ: Lawrence Erlbaum.

Godwin-Jones, Robert. 2017. "Authoring Language Learning Courseware." In *The Handbook of Technology and Second Language Teaching and Learning*, edited by Carol A. Chapelle and Shannon Sauro, 348–363. Oxford: Wiley-Blackwell.

González-Lloret, Marta. 2017. "Technology for Task-Based Language Teaching." In *The Handbook of Technology and Second Language Teaching and Learning*, edited by Carol A. Chapelle and Shannon Sauro, 234–247. Oxford: Wiley-Blackwell.

Grgurović, Maja. 2017. "Blended Language Learning: Research and Practice." In *The Handbook of Technology and Second Language Teaching and Learning*, edited by Carol A. Chapelle and Shannon Sauro, 149–168. Oxford: Wiley-Blackwell.

Heift, Trude, and Nina Vyatkina. 2017. "Technologies for Teaching and Learning L2 Grammar." In *The Handbook of Technology and Second Language Teaching and Learning*, edited by Carol A. Chapelle and Shannon Sauro, 26–44. Oxford: Wiley-Blackwell.

Hubbard, Philip. 2017. "Technologies for Teaching and Learning L2 Listening." In *The Handbook of Technology and Second Language Teaching and Learning*, edited by Carol A. Chapelle and Shannon Sauro, 93–106. Oxford: Wiley-Blackwell.

Jamieson, Joan, and Matteo Musumeci. 2017. "Integrating Assessment with Instruction through Technology." In *The Handbook of Technology and Second Language Teaching and Learning*, edited by Carol A. Chapelle and Shannon Sauro, 293–316. Oxford: Wiley-Blackwell.

Kern, Richard. 2014. "Technology as Pharmakon: The Promise and Perils of the Internet for Foreign Language Education". *The Modern Language Journal*, 98, no. 1: 340–357. DOI:10.1111/j.1540-4781.2014.12065.x

Kessler, Greg, and Phillip Hubbard. 2017. "Language Teacher Education and Technology." In *The Handbook of Technology and Second Language Teaching and Learning*, edited by Carol A. Chapelle and Shannon Sauro, 278–292. Oxford: Wiley-Blackwell.

Kukulska-Hulme, Agnes, Helen Lee, and Lucy Norris. 2017. "Mobile Learning Revolution: Implications for Language Pedagogy." In *The Handbook of Technology and Second Language Teaching and Learning*, edited by Carol A. Chapelle and Shannon Sauro, 217–233. Oxford: Wiley-Blackwell.

Lee, Carmen. K.-M. 2007. "Affordances and Text-Making Practices in Online Instant Messaging." *Written Communication*, 24, no. 3: 223–249.

Liaw, Meei-Ling, and Kathryn English. 2017. "Technologies for Teaching and Learning L2 Reading." In *The Handbook of Technology and Second Language Teaching and Learning*, edited by Carol A. Chapelle and Shannon Sauro, 62–76. Oxford: Wiley-Blackwell.

Li, Zhi, Ahmet Dursun, and Volker Hegelheimer. 2017. "Technology and L2 Writing." In *The Handbook of Technology and Second Language Teaching and Learning*, edited by Carol A. Chapelle and Shannon Sauro, 77–92. Oxford: Wiley-Blackwell.

Liddicoat, Anthony J., and Angela Scarino. 2013. *Intercultural Language Teaching and Learning*. Oxford: Wiley-Blackwell.

Liou Hsien-Chin, and Hui-Fen Lin. 2017. "CALL Meta-Analyses and Transparency Analysis." In *The Handbook of Technology and Second Language Teaching and Learning*, edited by Carol A. Chapelle and Shannon Sauro, 409–427. Oxford: Wiley-Blackwell.

Ma, Qing. 2017. "Technologies for Teaching and Learning L2 Vocabulary." In *The Handbook of Technology and Second Language Teaching and Learning*, edited by Carol A. Chapelle and Shannon Sauro, 47–61. Oxford: Wiley-Blackwell.

Memory Alpha. 2016a. "Kobayashi Maru Scenario." Accessed September 9, 2016. http://memory-alpha.wikia.com/wiki/Kobayashi_Maru_scenario

Memory Alpha. 2016b. "Transporter." Accessed July 7, 2016. http://memory-alpha.wikia.com/wiki/Transporter

Markee, Numa. 1997. *Managing Curricular Innovation*. Cambridge: Cambridge University Press.

Menosky, Joe, and Phillip LaZebnik. (Writers) 1991. "Darmok." Gene Roddenberry and Nick Berman (Producers). *Star Trek: The Next Generation*. Los Angeles, CA: Paramount.

MiCT. 2016. "Information to Go: How Do Refugees from Syria and Iraq Find the Right Information Before, During and After Their Journeys to Germany?" Accessed June 29, 2016. http://www.mict-international.org/wp-content/uploads/2016/06/mictbrief_en_20160623.pdf

Moore, Ronald D. (Writer). 1992. "Relics." Rick Berman (Producer). *Star Trek: The Next Generation*. Los Angeles, CA: Paramount.

O'Dowd, Robert. 2016. "Learning from the Past and Looking to the Future of Online Intercultural Exchange." In *Online Intercultural Exchange: Policy, Pedagogy, Practice*, edited by Robert O'Dowd and Tim Lewis, 273–293. New York: Routledge.

Otto, Sue E. K. 2017. "From Past to Present: A Hundred Years of Technology for L2 Learning." In *The Handbook of Technology and Second Language Teaching and Learning*, edited by Carol A. Chapelle and Shannon Sauro, 10–25. Oxford: Wiley-Blackwell.

Pasfield-Neofitou, Sarah. 2011. "Online Domains of Language Use: Second Language Learners' Experiences of Virtual Community and Foreignness." *Language Learning & Technology*, 15, no. 2: 92–108.

Reinhard, Jonathon. 2017. "Digital Gaming in L2 Teaching and Learning." In *The Handbook of Technology and Second Language Teaching and Learning*, edited by Carol A. Chapelle and Shannon Sauro, 202–216. Oxford: Wiley-Blackwell.

Rodríguez, Julio C. 2017. "Design-Based Research." In *The Handbook of Technology and Second Language Teaching and Learning*, edited by Carol A. Chapelle and Shannon Sauro, 364–377. Oxford: Wiley-Blackwell.

Rogers, Everett M. 2003. *Diffusion of Innovations*, 5th ed. New York: Free Press.

Sadler, Randall W. 2017. "The Continuing Evolution of Virtual Worlds for Language Learning." In *The Handbook of Technology and Second Language Teaching and Learning*, edited by Carol A. Chapelle and Shannon Sauro, 184–201. Oxford: Wiley-Blackwell.

Sauro, Shannon. 2016. "Does CALL Have an English Problem?" *Language Learning & Technology*, 20, no. 3: 1–8.

Sauro, Shannon. 2014. "Lessons from the Fandom: Task Models for Technology-Enhanced Language Learning." In *Technology-mediated TBLT: Researching Technology and Tasks*, edited by Marta González-Lloret and Lourdes Ortega, 239–262.. Philadelphia: John Benjamins.

Sauro, Shannon, and Björn Sundmark. 2016. "Report from Middle Earth: Fan Fiction Tasks in the EFL Classroom." *ELT Journal*. DOI: 10.1093/elt/ccv075

Schmidgall, Jonathan E., and Donald E. Powers. 2017. "Technology and High-Stakes Language Testing." In *The Handbook of Technology and Second Language Teaching and Learning*, edited by Carol A. Chapelle and Shannon Sauro, 317–331. Oxford: Wiley-Blackwell.

Smith, Bryan. 2017. "Technology Enhanced SLA Research." In *The Handbook of Technology and Second Language Teaching and Learning*, edited by Carol A. Chapelle and Shannon Sauro, 444–458. Oxford: Wiley-Blackwell.

Sundqvist, Pia., and Liss Kerstin Sylvén. 2014. "Language-Related Computer Use: Focus on Young L2 English Learners in Sweden". *ReCALL*, 26, no. 1: 3–20.

Suto, Irenka. 2013. "21st Century Skills: Ancient, Ubiquitous, Enigmatic?" *Research Matters. A Cambridge Assessment Publication*,15: 2–8.

Sykes, Julie M. 2017. "Technologies for Teaching and Learning Intercultural Competence and Interlanguage Pragmatics." In *The Handbook of Technology and Second Language Teaching and Learning*, edited by Carol A. Chapelle and Shannon Sauro, 119–133. Oxford: Wiley-Blackwell.

Taylor, Michael. (Writer). 1998. "Counterpoint." Brannon Braga (Producer). *Star Trek: Voyager*. Los Angeles, CA: Paramount.

Ware, Paige. 2017. "Technology, New Literacies, and Language Learners." In *The Handbook of Technology and Second Language Teaching and Learning*, edited by Carol A. Chapelle and Shannon Sauro, 265–277. Oxford: Wiley-Blackwell.

White, Cynthia J. 2017. "Distance Language Teaching with Technology." In *The Handbook of Technology and Second Language Teaching and Learning*, edited by Carol A. Chapelle and Shannon Sauro, 135–148. Oxford: Wiley-Blackwell.

# Index

Note: page numbers in *italics* refer to information contained in tables, page numbers in **bold** refer to diagrams.

*The Handbook of Technology and Second Language Teaching and Learning*, First Edition.
Edited by Carol A. Chapelle and Shannon Sauro.
© 2017 John Wiley & Sons, Inc. Published 2020 by John Wiley & Sons, Inc.